The Four Horsemen

The Four Horsemen

Riding to Liberty in Post-Napoleonic Europe

RICHARD STITES

OXFORD
UNIVERSITY PRESS

OXFORD
UNIVERSITY PRESS

Oxford University Press is a department of the University of Oxford.
It furthers the University's objective of excellence in research,
scholarship, and education by publishing worldwide.

Oxford   New York

Auckland   Cape Town   Dar es Salaam   Hong Kong   Karachi
Kuala Lumpur   Madrid   Melbourne   Mexico City   Nairobi
New Delhi   Shanghai   Taipei   Toronto

With offices in

Argentina   Austria   Brazil   Chile   Czech Republic   France   Greece
Guatemala   Hungary   Italy   Japan   Poland   Portugal   Singapore
South Korea   Switzerland   Thailand   Turkey   Ukraine   Vietnam

Oxford is a registered trade mark of Oxford University Press
in the UK and certain other countries.

Published in the United States of America by
Oxford University Press
198 Madison Avenue, New York, NY 10016

Library of Congress Cataloging-in-Publication Data
is available.
ISBN 978-0-19-997808-3

1 3 5 7 9 8 6 4 2

Printed in the United States of America
on acid-free paper

CONTENTS

Editors' Preface   vii
Preface   xi

1. Before the Barricades Went Up   3

2. Rafael del Riego: The Ride Through Andalusia   28

3. Guglielmo Pepe: Marching into Naples   121

4. Alexandros Ypsilanti: Across the River Pruth   186

5. Sergei Muraviev-Apostol: Into the Steppe   240

6. The Torn Cloth of Memory   322

Notes   339
Bibliography   395
Index   419

EDITORS' PREFACE

Richard Stites (1931–2010) began work on this book several years before his death. He completed the manuscript and had worked his way through most of the revisions he planned before his health prevented further work in the last two months of his life. He left versions of his text, in various stages of completion, on different computer hard drives in his office at Georgetown University and in his home away from home, Helsinki.

Some months after Richard's death, his friend, lawyer, and literary executor, Ray Hanna, sought the help of historians to usher Richard's final book into print. We accepted the task for two reasons. First was gratitude to Richard for being the ray of sunshine he was. Second was the conviction that the book, which we had read in an earlier draft, deserved an audience.

Once we had puzzled out which versions of which chapters contained the latest revisions, we found that with the exception of Richard's uniquely idiosyncratic citation format, the text was in excellent shape. We corrected a few typos, corralled some wayward accent marks, and standardized some spellings. With the invaluable help of Christina Petrides, we wrestled Richard's citations into conventional footnotes. Katriona McNeill helped track down, complete, and standardize imperfect entries in the bibliography. But that was all. We made the difficult decision not to include illustrations, only a few of which Richard had had a chance to collect. He oversaw the production of the maps.

Once we had the manuscript in fully presentable shape, we approached Susan Ferber of Oxford University Press. Despite the inherent difficulties of producing a posthumous book, she agreed to inspect it and sent it to two anonymous reviewers. Those reviewers, whom we wish to thank here, recommended no changes to the text beyond correcting the occasional misspelling in proper names. We handled the copy editor's queries and proofreading of the final printed text. In attending to these routine chores we left the meaning of the text just as it was. Fortunately, Richard wrote lucidly, so we were rarely called upon to resolve an ambiguity or clarify a sentence. *The Four Horsemen*, sadly, is a posthumous book, but it is all Richard's book.

The Four Horsemen presents a unified story of four uprisings against monarchical rule in Europe in the 1820s. In the aftermath of the Napoleonic Wars, proponents of autocracy had consolidated their rule throughout most of Europe, dashing the dreams of liberals everywhere. Some of those with broken dreams chose to rise in rebellion. The uprisings in the 1820s in Spain, Naples, Greece, and Russia are familiar stories to those versed in the national histories of those lands.

This book rejects the national frameworks in favor of a more pan-European one. Stites finds that these uprisings had many parallels as well as connections among them. The underlying grievances behind the uprisings, their format and practice, their suppression, and their translation into popular culture all showed common features. The revolutionaries themselves were well aware of their comrades fighting parallel battles in other countries, and on occasion took inspiration from one another. A few individuals, like miners moving from gold rush to gold rush, took part in more than one revolt—transnational insurgents trivial to nationalist accounts of these events but important to a fuller, pan-European understanding.

In the introduction to her influential book *Politics, Culture, and Class in the French Revolution*, Lynn Hunt wrote that the endless debates on the long-term origins and outcomes of the French Revolution had obscured "the character of the experience itself," and that the process of revolution as lived by its participants in all its immediacy merited closer examination.[*] Stites takes a similar approach in his account of the four risings against the Congress of Vienna system. He focuses not on contexts and outcomes but on process. Each individual story reads like a straightforward narrative account. Yet, taken together, the narratives fuse into a new vision, bringing out crucial aspects of each revolution that may not have been evident within a strictly national context. Such, for example, is the critical role of the Spanish political catechisms, which directly inspired one of the most important documents of the Decembrist movement—Muraviev-Apostol's revolutionary catechism.

As a work of Russian history (after all, Richard's lifelong passion), the book makes a remarkable contribution: it shifts the standard assumption of cultural transmission from France and Germany to Russia and moves the focus southward, clearly demonstrating the active and enthusiastic adoption of Spanish, Neapolitan, and Greek models by Russian liberals. Not all revolutionary winds blew from Paris.

One good reason that no one before Stites presented a transnational vision of the uprisings of the 1820s is that to do it properly one has to handle sources in

---

[*] Lynn Hunt, *Politics, Culture and Class in the French Revolution* (Berkeley: University of California Press, 1984), 3.

Spanish, Italian, Greek, Russian, French, and German. Stites also consulted materials in Bulgarian, Romanian, Serbian, Danish, and Swedish. Few people are as prepared to practice transnational European history as was Richard Stites. Argyrios Pisiotis, Maria Antonietta Iannella, Ron Earnest, and Francisco LaRubia-Prado kindly reviewed the Greek, German, Italian, and Spanish spellings and transliterations.

This book occupies a special place in Richard's intellectual evolution. According to Abbott Gleason, Richard and he discussed this project while they were graduate students at Harvard in the 1960s. Before dedicating his career to Russian history, Richard wrote a master's thesis at George Washington University on the French Saint-Simonians, and the extraordinarily complex, and to our consciousness often contradictory, political currents of the European 1820s continued to fascinate him throughout his life. The book brings together many of the interests that animated his earlier writings: liberation, revolution, popular culture, and high culture. Like his other books, it displays a careful attention to personalities and a tactile approach to events. We agree wholeheartedly with one of the manuscript's anonymous readers, who noted, "In all earnestness, I can't remember enjoying reading a history book as much as I have enjoyed reading this one in quite some time."

Catherine Evtuhov and John R. McNeill

PREFACE

This book, a narrative history of revolutions in Spain, Naples, Greece, and Russia and their relationships, has no overarching thesis or theory to bind it together; the analysis changes from one topic to another. In the main, these include constitutional liberalism in early nineteenth-century Europe; the extraordinary migratory history of the Spanish constitution of 1812; secret societies; military uprisings, the transfer of ideas, methods, and people across frontiers; the formation of an international community of revolutionaries; guerrilla warfare; the cultural face of insurgent liberalism (and nationalism) and its appropriation of Christian symbols and language for secular purposes; the role of the church; the well-worn groove of Holy Alliance armed intervention; and the punitive vengefulness of Restoration governments. Aimed at the educated reader, the book may offer some insights to specialists as well.

Since this study deals with events in four societies, the question arises: Is it comparative? Is it cross-national? I agree with the energetic editors of a recent work about the usefulness of these two categories—protean as they may be—and with some of their contributors who rightly assert that all history is in a sense comparative.[1] The revolutions retold in the present book took place in three countries and one homeland of a subjected people: Spain, Naples, Russia, Greece. They shared some common ground, though acute differences disallow any kind of universal applicability, especially of the kind that bleeds into speculative history with alleged predictive power. And of course each country varied greatly within its own borders. As a whole, this study gives more weight to cross-national elements in the revolutions and the regimes they created or tried to create: common intellectual sources, similar practices, outright mimicry, parallel biographies, physical movement of revolutionaries from one struggle to another, and other interconnections. In making comparisons, the topic-by-topic approach can be fruitful, as in the many studies of comparative revolutions in Europe and elsewhere, such as the classic *Anatomy of Revolution* by Crane Brinton, written seventy years ago.[2] I have avoided this method in favor of sequential national experiences for two main reasons. The cases I look at will be for most readers less well known than those Brinton chose: the English, American, French, and Russian Revolutions. More important, such a method would virtually eliminate the drama and the narrative pull required to bring the story to life.

I first discovered the moving epic of Riego in the years before I turned to Russian history. More recently my interest was reignited by the marvelous insights in a pioneering article on Spain and the Decembrists by Professor Isabel de Madariaga. I thank her and Dr. Janet Hartley for bringing it to my attention.

My warm thanks go out to Diego Léon Marquez Alonso, my cicerone in Madrid; María Jesús Franco Durán, of the Archivo General Militar at the Biblioteca Central Militar; Sonia Fernández, of the Museo Municipal; and the marvelous staff of the Biblioteca Nacional. In Naples, Paolo Macry, of the university; Rosa Rossi and the librarians of the Sezione Napoletana of the Biblioteca Nazionale; and Dr. Dorena Caroli made the visit memorable as well as productive. Gaetano and Sandra were my hosts on the Via Tribunale and Leonardo my companion in Nola. I commend the patience of the bibliographers at the Gennadius Library in Athens for helping a non-Greek-speaker find an abundance of sources. To my friends at the Slavonic Library of the National Library of Finland in Helsinki, particularly Irina Lukka, and at the National Library in St. Petersburg, who have seen me through decades of research, I give a resounding thank-you.

Some of the research for this book was conducted at the Library of Congress and facilitated by the helpful staff of the European and Hispanic Reading Rooms, particularly Harry Leich and Georgette Dorn. Georgetown University's Lauinger Library and Interlibrary Loan filled in many a gap in sources, and I thank Christina Petrides for her wonderful assistance in locating and acquiring for me hundreds of titles for fact and footnote checking. I thank James Amelang, of the Universidad Autónoma, for helpful pre-visit advice on research in Madrid; Tommaso Astarita and John Davis for helpful contacts in Naples; John McNeill for the same in Athens; and Ismini Lamb and Polyvia Parara for translating Greek materials. Helpful readers and listeners have been numerous, in seminars at the University of Pennsylvania, the Washington, D.C., workshop on Russian history, the Latin American Studies Program's conference "Cadiz Liberalism: East and West," and the European University of St. Petersburg.

I am indebted to colleagues who have read all or part of a bulky manuscript: Isabel de Madariaga, Abbott Gleason, Theophilus Prousis, Theofanis Stavrou, Patrick O'Meara, Mikhail Dolbilov, and my Georgetown colleagues Tommaso Astarita, Roger Chickering, James Collins, Peter Dunkley, Alison Games, David Goldfrank, Andrzej Kaminski, John McNeill, Aviel Roshwald, James Shedel, and John Tutino. A special thanks to Catherine Evtuhov and Boris Gasparov for unending support. I dedicate this book to Natalia Baschmakoff for her loving friendship and intellectual stimulation.

Funding has come from three generous sources: in 2004–5 a grant from the National Council for East European and Russian Research; in 2007 a summer grant from the Georgetown University Graduate School; and for the years 2007–2009 a professorship awarded by the Board of Visitors of the Georgetown School of Foreign Service. I especially thank its chairman, Paul Pelosi, Deans Robert Gallucci and Peter Dunkley, and Charles King.

I have used mostly anglicized forms for place names, though not for most personal names. In earlier times when almost everything foreign seemed exotic, it was natural for English and other Europeans to domesticate names. Nowadays, when university classrooms from Berkeley to Moscow—to take only one kind of venue—are filled with Pedros, Tanyas, Timos, Johanns, and Luigis, there is no reason not to display the originals for earlier times as well. In a gesture of respect for the real names of the kings of Spain and Naples, they shall be Fernando and Ferdinando, respectively, instead of the usual Ferdinand for both. I use a modified, reader-friendly Library of Congress transliteration from Slavic languages and Greek. The Greek and Russian or Old Style (OS) Orthodox calendar was twelve days behind the Western or New Style (NS) in the nineteenth century. I have used the NS through the chapters on Spain and Italy and provided both in the Greek chapter. Unless otherwise noted, Russian dates are OS.

The Four Horsemen

Before the Barricades Went Up

First menace rocked the Pyrenees
And Naples' Vulcan spewed his flame.
A one-armed prince to the Peloponnese
From Kishinev unveiled his game.
—Alexander Pushkin, *Evgenii Onegin*[1]

A few lines later in this poem, Pushkin added the Russian conspirators later known as the Decembrists as part of a common movement engulfing Europe. In a series of revolts starting in 1820, four officers issued pronunciamentos in obscure European towns: Cabezas de San Juan in southern Spain, Avellino in the Kingdom of Naples, Iaşi (Jassy) in the Ottoman Empire, and Vasilkov in the Russian Empire. From there, they rode forth on horseback to bring political freedom and a constitution for Spain, Naples, and Russia, and national independence for the Greeks. All of the officers who launched these exploits from Andalusia to the snowy fields of Ukraine—Colonel Rafael del Riego, General Guglielmo Pepe, General Alexandros Ypsilanti, and Colonel Sergei Muraviev-Apostol—had served in the Napoleonic wars, and three of the four attempted the "Praetorian option"—the use of "military force to secure political changes that would benefit the army and the wider society of which it formed a part."[2] The cycle of revolt began on New Year's Day 1820 and ended two thousand miles away and six years later on January 1, 1826, with the final act of the Decembrist uprising. The expeditions ended in failure, and the revolutionaries who led them became martyrs. Riego of Spain and Sergei Muraviev-Apostol of Russia were hanged; the Russo-Greek Ypsilanti landed in prison; the Neapolitan Pepe escaped into exile, and two of his compatriots were executed.

Europe in 1815, still recovering from a quarter century of euphoria and mutilation from violent revolution and then from the marauding armies of Napoleon, his allies, and his enemies, longed for stability and peace. Though many of the victors over Napoleon thirsted for vengeance and ached to turn back the clock to 1788, the royal peacemakers and their ministers forged uneasy compromises that came to be known as the Restoration but might better be seen as a "Recu-peration"[3]: putting legitimate dynasties back on their thrones, easing in mod-erate constitutions in some places and tearing up Napoleonic ones in others, hammering out new frontiers, and meeting in congress from time to time to check any major challenges to the world they had re-created. For the next eight years, the Great Powers—Russia, Prussia, Austria, Britain, and, from 1818, a duly vetted France—convened in various European towns and, in a far from monolithic way, discussed, agreed and disagreed, and ruled on what to do about perceived threats to the Vienna peace and the status quo. Among the distur-bances in Spain, Naples, Greece, and Russia, only the last succumbed strictly to domestic repression; the others fell under the stern scrutiny of the Great Powers.

The first wave of insurrection since the Congress of Vienna unfolded before the railway began spreading tentacles across continental Europe. In all but a few places the clangor and smoke of industry had yet to join the sounds of hoofbeats and village bells and the pungent odors of country life and nature. Subsequent revolts dotted the European landscape in the 1830s, 1848–49, 1870, and 1905—to recall only the famous ones. Most took the form of "barricade revolutions," where rebels and government troops shot at each other on city streets. In a sense the 1820s expeditions constituted the last of the horseback-mounted epics where officers led their men from provincial towns in the hopes of reaching the capital and overturning the old order.

In the early twentieth century, during and after World War I, we see armed units riding—though sometimes in trains or armored cars rather than in the saddle—to bring down a regime. But this wave was led by "Whites," counterrev-olutionaries determined to destroy radical forces in the cities of Europe: General Kornilov's march to Petrograd in 1917, General Mannerheim's siege of Tampere and capture of Helsinki in 1918, the Freikorps rolling into Red Munich in 1919, Admiral Horthy's Szeged army smashing the Hungarian Soviet Republic in Budapest in the same year, the Kapp putsch targeting Berlin in 1920, and Mus-solini's vaunted "march" on Rome in 1922. As those rides embodied much of the political atmosphere of their time, so those of the 1820s did for theirs.

In Europe's Peripheral Vision

Surveys of European history usually treat the revolutions of the 1820s as objects of Great Power diplomacy and Holy Alliance intervention, only rarely delving into the inner dynamic of events on the ground.[4] Space limitation always requires choices and the choices generally follow a pattern of favoring the actions of the great courts: Britain, France, Austria, Prussia, Russia. These not only stood as victors (plus a reinvited loser) of the age, but, with Prussia becoming Germany, dominate historical accounting until the Great War. After that, the club members were Britain, France, Germany, Italy, and Russia. In writing European history, the tilt is still toward an unstated Western heartland of Britain, France, and Germany—with Russia as an outlier.

In this scenario, Italy makes guest appearances in a few segments of the great show: the Risorgimento and Fascism. Spain, after helping expel Napoleon, is kept largely in the wings until 1936. Greece gets its moment of fame in the war of 1821—though even there sharing the stage with philhellenism and Great Power diplomacy. Russia, due to its size and periodically perceived menace, forms an exception. It is even allowed plenty of space to perform its domestic history throughout the nineteenth and twentieth centuries—though almost always treated as something alien to Europe. Even countries inside the club are sometimes seen to have experienced a Sonderweg—enjoying or suffering exceptionalism. But the fringe nations are always seen as exceptional.

Exceptionalism implies a norm. To those looking eastward at Europe from England, it all seemed "different." Ditto the view from Paris and Berlin. Russians long claimed to have saved Europe from the Mongol yoke; the Poles held back the barbarous Russians, and the Germans did so to the Slavs; the French tried to curb the "Huns." Most scholars now agree that Edward Said exaggerated in his presentation of orientalism. He also understated the fact that it was really one element in what might be called exoticism—a perception of certain societies and peoples as despotic, cruel, oversexed, stagnating, poverty-stricken, priest-ridden, lacking in individualism—or all of these. Culturally speaking, those realms perched on the edge of Europe became steadily subjected to the mental habit of dividing the heartland of the northwest from the rest. Exoticism was deployed almost everywhere toward the regions south of the Pyrenees and of Rome, east of Berlin, and southeast of Vienna. The Iberian, Apennine, and Balkan peninsulas on the geographical margins of Europe became culturally marginalized as well. The Balkans were said to begin in the back streets of Vienna. "Real" Europeans applied orientalism not only to the Ottoman Empire but also to its Christian Greeks, especially after the glow of philhellenism got dimmed by volunteers' experience fighting on the ground instead of on the page.

For the Mediterranean lands that experienced the upheavals of the 1820s, we may call this attitude "meridionalism"—a way of exoticizing the European south through clichés, including a view of Latin exuberance as turmoil. Spain provided the most vivid examples of meridionalism. At the Congress of Vienna in 1815, that country was labeled a "secondary court" and pretty much remained that way until its civil war of the 1930s captured the world's attention. Cultural insult accompanied political contempt. Literary travelers such as Théophile Gautier and Alexandre Dumas echoed Voltaire's famous "L'Afrique commence aux Pyrénées."[5] The liberal Abbé de Pradt wrote that "Spain is rather a kingdom

of Africa than of Europe," and the Italian liberal Pecchio agreed.[6] The conservative Russian statesman Count S. R. Vorontsov, alarmed at the revolt of 1820,
believed that the Spanish army had usurped unlimited power, causing Spain in
the future to be ruled like Algeria—that is, an untrammeled, criminal tyranny.[7]

The 1820s unleashed a rush of travel writings on Spain. By midcentury it had
become a playground for literary, dramatic, and operatic cliché through "car-
menization" in Prosper Merimée's story and Bizet's opera, which highlighted the
dance, the dagger, and the ardent temper of Spaniards. Dumas, Gautier, Washington Irving, and Hans Christian Andersen presented their readers with pictures of Spain as distinctly "borderland." From the middle of the century to its
end, Mikhail Glinka, Chabrier, Lalo, and Rimsky-Korsakov offered musical portraits of an essentially rhythmic folk. In much darker tones, a deep European
tradition dating from the sixteenth century fashioned what a twentieth-century
Spaniard called a "black legend" of Spain as the land of Inquisition, torture, and
bestial colonial policies. Persistent "myths of Spanish arrogance, cruelty, and
vengefulness" recurred in foreigners' accounts.[8]

Italy remained spared the harshest versions of meridionalism, diluted by the
charm of its classical ruins for those embarked on the Grand Tour. The presence
of bandits evoked romantic tropes—especially for North European painters—
as well as tales of dread. But within the peninsula, the Kingdom of Naples, to the
south, was (and sometimes still is) haughtily called "Africa" or "the Indies"—
imparting images of backwardness, laziness, and violence.[9] At the time of the
1820 revolt in Naples, the Austrian chancellor Prince Metternich referred to the
Neapolitans as "a semi-barbarous people of absolute ignorance and boundless
cruelty, hot-blooded as the Africans, a people who can neither read nor write,
whose last word is the dagger."[10] The Greeks, struggling for independence in the
1820s, for a time basked in the glow of European philhellenism and were seen as
the noble descendants of great Athenian philosophers and stalwart Spartan
fighters. Once the volunteers landed on Greek soil and witnessed the realities of
that war, their high opinion began to shift into the more familiar contours of a
patronizing Balkanism.

The tsarist empire represented a different case in European eyes. Its perceived
backwardness and barbarism, a perception dating to the sixteenth century, faded
for a time as Russian armies ejected Napoleon in 1812 and stormed across Europe
together with allied forces. But with the rise of the Eastern Question in the 1830s,
the land of the tsars became the target of popular as well as diplomatic Russopho-
bia in Britain and France for its forward policies in the Near East. Though one of
the Great Powers, Russia invited clichés in any era and any situation: a remote and
frightening land of snow and bears inhabited by people who were, though clothed
in European apparel, really "Tatars," easily unmasked by scratching their skins
(Napoleon) and ruled by an oriental despot in a slave empire (Custine).[11]

Before getting indignant about the arrogant nineteenth-century Northwest's condescending—if not racist—view of South and East, let us remind ourselves of these still lingering attitudes—extended by colonialism—toward the "developing" reaches of our planet. After all, geographical-cultural elitism and hierarchy existed (and still does) even within the "advanced" countries. Comparison intrudes itself into every attempt to observe the Other, whether in travel accounts, diplomatic discourse, fiction, or simple common speech. How could it be otherwise, when folks who have thriving institutions, relatively high economic and educational levels, political participation, and a dozen other indices of progress or civilization measure their societies against those who lack those advantages?

In fact, the four countries or would-be countries in this study did to varying degrees lag behind on most of those things measurable on a graph of modernization. In this respect they also evinced several similarities noted—if sometimes exaggerated—at the time and still recognized in the historical literature. Even when admitting the primitiveness of and brutal rule over, say, a southern Ireland or a Carpathian Ruthenia, denizens of London and Vienna had a point when they differentiated their realms from the fringes of Europe. And a more crucial point is that certain personages of the Iberian, Italian, and Balkan peninsulas and of the Russian empire shared that feeling of marginality and longed to join the ranks of "Europe." It might also be noted that some of their defining stereotypes were self-imposed. Like the British of not so long ago, Greeks used to speak of going to Europe, and in the period covered by this book, Neapolitans traveled to "Italy." Such geographical self-definitions implied no inferiority of the traveler.[12]

The peculiar multiethnic history of the Mediterranean and Russian lands resulted partly from their common experience on the edge of Christian Europe and thus lying directly in the path of outside incursions by Muslim invaders— Moors, Saracens, Ottomans, and Tatars, to say nothing of other medieval invaders such as Visigoths, Normans, Germans, and French. The Mediterranean Sea, as a watery continent, contained its own "countries": the Balearic Sea, dotted with palmy islands; the Ligurian Sea; the Tyrrhenian Sea, guarded by Elba, Corsica, Sardinia, and Sicily; the Adriatic and Ionian, with their Byzanto-Venetian legacy; and the isle-studded Aegean Sea. Spaniards ruled Naples for centuries; Venetians held sway over the Ionian Islands; Catalonia had had a kingdom in the Morea. And France, Spain, and Naples were ruled by Bourbon kings in 1820. The Mediterranean linkage played an important role in the 1820s revolts.

Though land use and peasant life both differed from one society to another and also shared characteristics with other parts of Europe, it is worth noting that various forms of manorial and seigniorial power on the land lingered long in the southern and eastern spheres of Europe—the Spanish mayorazgo, Neapolitan latifundium, Ottoman çiftlik in Greece, and Russian serf-worked pomestie. The Mesta in Spain and the Dogana of Neapolitan Foggia were systems favoring land routes for sheepherding.[13] Partly because of a combination of topography and grinding poverty and inequality, brigandage thrived throughout the Mediterranean and occasionally surfaced in Russia. At least since the eighteenth century, writers and painters had romanticized bandits, staged them in picturesque woods and craggy defiles, and dressed them in gorgeous clothes. The idealization reached a peak in the canvases of the early nineteenth century and in the poetry of Byron and his imitators.[14] But unlike the mythic prototypes, most real bandits killed, raped, and tormented; they looted everyone and usually kept the spoils. Marauding bands may have controlled the excesses of class exploitation, but they did not abolish it.[15] In art, Francisco Goya deromanticized the bandit and put the blood and terror into his frightful representations.[16]

In the two eastern monarchies, the Osmanli had been ruling since the late Middle Ages and the Romanovs since 1613. Their latest scions, Sultan Mahmud II and the autocratic Tsar Alexander I, held power unchecked by elected bodies. In the West, Bourbon family members had climbed to power as the Borbón dynasty in Spain and the Borbone in Naples. Carlos IV of Spain, the great-grandson of Louis XIV, was brother to Ferdinando I of Naples and father to Fernando VII of Spain. The last two defeated the liberals in 1821 and 1823, respectively. When unencumbered by Jacobin revolution or Napoleonic incursion, they were considered absolute monarchs, and in Spain their supporters were called *absolutistas*.

The term "absolutism" has come under much criticism recently by historians of early modern France[17]—a critique that needs to be extended elsewhere. Just as common sense tells us that "totalitarianism"—a much more all-encompassing term—never brought total control of a realm and everything in it, so the infinitely lighter absolutism was never absolute. European monarchs were believed to be constrained by divine and natural law. More concretely, they were hemmed in by privileged groups, historical liberties, feudal practices, and a wide array of pressures and entrenched customs.

To liberals, absolutism connoted a whole system of privilege and uncurbed authority. The Spanish and Neapolitan kings operated in a web of deference: court and church rituals and practices that raised them to a near godlike level, thus making any challenge tantamount to sacrilege. Indeed, court etiquette seemed to assert the sanctity of the monarch's every move—the levée, the ball, the hunt—choreographed routines so finely tuned that they sometimes excluded any kind of independent expression of thought or emotion. Some of the Restoration courts tried to emulate the past, wearing wigs and mounting portraits of Louis XIV on their palace walls, keeping their dungeons ready for guests, and acting out whimsical gestures for the sake of displaying power. The power of the Russian throne, with its French-speaking court and elaborate ceremonial system emulating those of the West, attracted the parallel term "autocracy." The Ottoman sultan, in the eyes of his Greek subjects, was not only an all-powerful master but also an alien in both ethnicity and religion.

It is not hard to understand the Restoration monarchs' fear of liberals and reformists. Nightmare memories of the French Revolution swirled around them; in their slippery-slope visions, reform meant constitution, constitution led to republic, and republic to terror and to the guillotine blade, under which some of their relatives had fallen. In reaction, those in high places performed according to a rigid script, adopted a posture of icy reserve, and paid obeisance to Talleyrand's famous piece of advice: "Surtout, pas trop de zèle." Though some sovereigns of the age were fairly earthy—George III and Ferdinando of Naples— court culture required the kind of stiff arctic behavior captured so brilliantly in the novels of Stendhal, who only half jokingly laid out the best to way to survive at a conservative court: do not read Voltaire or Rousseau, avoid foreign newspapers even if they bring good tidings such as "fifty Liberals . . . shot in Spain," attend daily mass, and have "two or three fat monks" as friends.[18]

The four realms stricken by uprisings in 1820 had experienced to varying degrees a recent taste of Bonapartism: the Jacobin Republic of 1799 in Naples, its bloody repression, and rule by the puppet king Murat; the French occupation of Spain; the Napoleonic assault on Ottoman Egypt and the Ionian Islands; and the Grande Armée's invasion of Russia in 1812. This legacy in various ways shaped the contours of the post-Napoleonic wave of European revolutions on Europe's perimeter: the Ukrainian steppe, the Romanian provinces of the Ottoman Empire, the tip of the Balkan peninsula, and the Iberian and Apennine peninsulas. That same legacy also molded the response to these revolutions by those in power.

While the term "wave" implies coherence, the details reveal much disparity. Many of the features in common among the four states, however striking the similarity, were shared by other societies. As to the uprisings, the Spanish and Neapolitan cases bore similar features: an officer's pronunciamento in a provincial town, declaring for a constitution to limit the powers of a Bourbon king. But the distinct differences among the four concerned were profound. Without uncovering them, one would be in effect assuming the nearsighted and hard-of-hearing character of the advocates of intervention who saw through a glass very darkly a common plot, a coordinated threat of social destruction, and resulting international disorder. The narratives contained in the following chapters will elaborate the differences. Here only the obvious must be announced. The Greeks, unlike the others, lived under alien rule, that is by people of different language, origins, and faith. And although Ypsilanti's ride ended in disaster, his fellow Greeks, unlike the others, emerged victorious in a national struggle and with the aid of foreign powers. The Russian Decembrists never came to power, not even for a day.

Dreaming of Liberty

The word "liberal," quite aside from the dynamic that has modified its meanings again and again up to our time, already began to gain different connotations soon after the moment of its coinage in Spanish. Derivatives of its root, *libertas*— "liberty," *liberté, libertad, libertà*—and its non-Latin equivalents *Freiheit* and *svoboda* rang out in different pitches depending on time and place. One divider drew a sometimes blurred line between political freedom and national independence; another involved a continuum of degree and pace of change in domestic policy from moderate and incremental to radical and deep. Confusion reigned then and still does about where liberalism stops and radicalism begins. Muddying the semantic waters further, privileged groups of this era spoke of "historical liberties" to buttress conservative or reactionary aims, and the kings of Naples and Spain in the 1820s claimed to be enslaved by constitutions and schemed to regain their own "liberty," free of parliamentary restraints.

Whether working for a constitutional monarchy or a republic, liberals of this era opposed, among other things, whimsical executive power; irrational, confused, and unfair laws; entrenched privilege of church and nobility; and the drain on the economy of unproductive populations such as monks and nuns. Arbitrary rule became a negative totem: when post-Napoleonic liberals spoke of fighting absolutism or "tyranny," they meant all the forces that worked against broad participation, forces atop which rested the monarch. A Piedmontese liberal put it succinctly: "Absolute power, even when wisely and humanely wielded, necessarily deprives mankind of many precious and useful possessions, and renders insecure and transitory those that they enjoy."[19] Against this, the liberals touted political freedom as transparency, reason, balance, compromise, and rule of law—abstractions that translated into civil rights, representation, an independent judiciary offering equal justice for all, and a free press. The last was especially hated by autocrats and their courtiers not only because it could promote criticism, expose injustice, and spread political dissent, but also because the very scope of its "freedom" violated the principle of deference and the royal immunity from any adverse opinion whatsoever.

A constitution, a magic document that would reorder or create the nation and redistribute the power needed to enact change, lay at the heart of all liberal dreams in the 1820s. Liberals sought models already operating and perused current political thought, grounded in Enlightenment ideas and glossed by their own country's semi-fictitious historical "traditions." Joseph de Maistre in 1814 asserted that writing constitutions was a grave error—nay, impossible, since constitution is a "divine work." Drafting laws and charters is like writing with water— they are easily dissolved at whim by new authors. All must emanate from a higher will, that is, from God.[20] But man-made models—written or otherwise, in force or dead—abounded before de Maistre wrote in 1814: England, Corsica, the United States, France, Poland, Spain in 1812, Sicily, and the nearly dozen Napoleonic satellite shams. The French Charte and other instruments sponsored by Tsar Alexander operated from 1815 on.[21]

The Spanish constitution of 1812, adopted by the Cortes in beleaguered Cadiz during the French invasion, stands center stage in this story. Quashed by the returning king, it was put into force once again in 1820 as a result of Riego's revolt. The document inspired insurrections in Naples and Portugal in the same year and in Piedmont in 1821. Lurking backstage, the more conservative 1815 bicameral constitution of Louis XVIII of France, the Charte, became an alternative possibility for some of the liberals themselves and for the more moderate diplomats of the Holy Alliance. The insurgent Greeks, having no king except the sultan, opted for a republic initially and ended up with a European dynasty. Russian Decembrists, though heavily influenced by the Spanish example of revolt, did not choose the 1812 constitution as a model. They did, however, divide into constitutionalists and republicans.

For Spanish liberals, a constitution meant a parliament as a space of mutual recognition, knowing the nation, and a school for cooperative life in justice and freedom. Liberalism, to most of its adherents, with or without the label, implied participation in the "nation," a chance to decide one's own affairs, or something in between. Many pointed to parliamentary life in and of itself as a school for citizenship. In spite of the modulations that liberalism has undergone in the two centuries since, a core of its values remains relevant for our own time. An American political scientist has recently set out to define that core: "As many people as possible should have as much say as is feasible over the direction their lives will take."[22]

Aside from numerous textual and functioning examples, Mediterranean and Russian liberals looked for guidance to contemporary commentators. The study of the genealogy of ideas holds little charm for historians nowadays, who have long been alert to the hazards—and often irrelevance—of tracking "influence," the alleged or even demonstrable impact of a thinker's ideas on another's action. Theorists' notions change over time and are often full of contradictions or dense complexities; actors also change, as do their circumstances, sometimes daily. Yet ideas do not spring from nowhere, and it would be imprudent to ignore the powerful liberal or quasi-liberal intellectual currents of the time, for they illustrate not only the structure of information exchange but also the similarities in the sources of revolutionary and political action across countries and individuals. Even when the effect of certain writers was tenuous, the recurrence of themes and the reputation of their authors often gave weight to the counterrevolutionary belief that a community of ideas signified a conspiracy of evil. Those holding and acting on liberal notions drew on sources from the Enlightenment through the

French Revolution and from their French and English contemporaries. A telling moment came at the trial of the Decembrists in 1826 when the president of the court, a general, addressed the convicted conspirators: "You, sirs, have read everything, Destutt de Tracy, Benjamin Constant and Bentham and look what that got you, and I, in all my life have read nothing but the Holy Scriptures and look what I have gained"—pointing to the orders and medals on his chest.[23]

Benjamin Constant, not exactly a household word, has captured renewed attention in our time, when liberalism is again challenged from right and left—both in theory and practice. Drawing from the Scottish Enlightenment and other intellectual springs, Constant preferred a constitutional monarchy to a republic and looked with some suspicion at the popular masses. He believed that a "free" society required as a minimum liberty of person, press, and expression, as well as limited government, private property, due process, a jury system, and an independent judiciary. Constant loathed arbitrary Restoration governments along with coups against moderate regimes; and he equally abhorred revolutionary despotism and the persecution of religion. After drafting a liberal ruling instrument for Napoleon during the Hundred Days in 1815, he took up the role of permanent critic of the Restoration.[24]

In a recent book, Alan Wolfe has offered a brilliant defense of Benjamin Constant's virtues and locates the essence of his vision of liberty in an 1819 speech given in Paris to the Athénée Royale:

> For each [citizen] it is the right to be subject only to laws, and to be neither arrested, detained, put to death or maltreated in any way by the arbitrary will of one or more individuals. It is the right of everyone to express their opinion, choose a profession and practice it, to dispose of property, and even to abuse it; to come and go without permission, and without having to account for their motives or undertakings. It is everyone's right to associate with other individuals, either to discuss their interests, or to profess the religion which they and their associates prefer, or even simply to occupy their days or hours with their inclinations and whims. Finally, it is everyone's right to exercise some influence on the administration of government, either by electing all or particular officials, or through representations, petitions, demands to which the authorities are more or less paid to pay heed.[25]

A. L. C. Destutt de Tracy's 1806–7 *Commentary on Montesquieu's Spirit of the Laws* outlined his hostility to any kind of hereditary power, defining despotism as a brutal or abusive monarchy. He deemed citizens' rights more important than the actual form of the state, and he posed free inquiry against obscurantist religion. The practical teaching in Destutt de Tracy's work appealed to the sober side of revolutionaries—not to their romantic impulses. The *Commentary* was translated into English (by Thomas Jefferson) in 1811 and into Italian in 1820; the Neapolitan liberal Melchiorre Delfico became his admirer and correspondent. Destutt de Tracy's translated works began to enter Spain around 1817, and about a dozen of them appeared in the years of the liberal regime, some of them made by Cortes members. The Frenchman translated the Spanish constitution and eagerly supported revolts in Greece, Spain, and Naples, lamenting the intervention in the last two.[26] Franco Venturi noted that the *Commentary* "resounded throughout the whole period of the liberal revolutions, from the Spain of 1820 to the Russia of 1825." An American historian wrote that "the Russian Decembrists, along with numerous other liberals, *Carbonari*, and revolutionaries of the 1820s used this *Commentary* as their political Bible."[27] The Decembrist Mikhail Orlov recalled that his circle considered it "the epitome of wisdom."[28]

Jeremy Bentham, the English philosophical radical whose utilitarian doctrine advanced the famous formula "The greatest happiness for the greatest number," became a virtual political guru for insurrectionary leaders who eagerly sought and got his advice. The eccentric thinker was revered in Spain, Naples, and Greece by liberal elements or those who saw themselves as such.[29] In Britain, the welcoming refuge for revolutionary exiles, the slippery term "liberal" could denote free trade, national liberation, a free press, and civil rights, among other things.[30] How much more protean was the word on the continent, where most of these things were absent? Bentham's agents could be found wandering the Mediterranean, preaching the sermons of their master. "Rid yourselves of Ultramaria," he wrote to the Spanish liberals in reference to their Latin American colonies—to no avail.[31] Though Bentham's views were probably more widely dispersed than most others, his sweeping, universal, and coldly rational approach—as well as his impenetrable style—no doubt made more passionate spirits balk at his formulations, however they might publicly shower him with praise.

The liberals who came to power in Spain and Naples faced enemies on many sides: from above, from below, to their left and right, and from abroad. The last proved fatal. The French political thinker Baron Louis Bignon, in a legal and historical treatise, judged the Neapolitan parliament as "admirably courageous in regard to patriotism and dignity." He quoted ironically the letter of the three monarchs of the Holy Alliance to the Neapolitan king, Ferdinando, against its own argument, since that alliance claimed to be "uniquely appointed to insure and protect from any threat to the political independence and territorial integrity of all states." Condemning in effect a despotic international, Bignon noted that "kings, under this system, constitute a nomadic tribe who go from place to place pitching their tents in different countries." He added a charge of paranoia: "A free Naples threatens Vienna, a liberated Madrid offends Berlin, a constitutional Lisbon outrages St. Petersburg."[32]

The shadow of the French Revolution hung over the nineteenth century in almost the same way that the Bolshevik Revolution of 1917 hung over the twentieth. When after the peace of 1815 signs appeared of anything recalling the frightening 1790s, a problem arose for would-be interveners. It might be summarized by two images emanating from the kitchen, aptly a place much revered by the French: the Appetite and the Boiling Pot. If liberalism gains traction anywhere, what to do? Feed the reform process slowly and gradually and risk escalation as the appetite grows with the eating? Or keep the lid on the pot and risk explosion? Unhindered monarchs wished to remain that way; Bentham famously understood the "quantity of pain" that they felt in being disobeyed.[33] Some of the crowned heads known as absolute monarchs in those days possessed a classical view of power and of the right to think independently. They seemed to echo King Creon in Sophocles' *Antigone* (and even more so in Jean Anouhil's 1942 adaptation), who said, "Proud thoughts do not sit well / Upon subordinates."[34]

The international system known as the Holy Alliance supported restored monarchs in the name of European stability. Though the alliance was a product of Tsar Alexander I's mystical conversion, its policy chief, Prince Metternich, had imbibed anti-liberalism as a sixteen-year-old boy when the French Revolution broke out. While a student in Strasbourg, he was disgusted by enthusiastic liberal demonstrations in its favor on the streets of the city.[35] Aside from a general enmity toward any kind of political unrest in their own and other countries, the Great Power leaders and their conservative allies had a tendency sometimes to overreact and overinterpret. The fairly innocuous student festival at Wartburg in 1817 and the more political assassinations of August Kotzebue in 1819 and the Duc de Berry, a French royal, in 1820 all conjured up images of a pan-European conspiracy. The French reactionary press conflated the assassin's knife with the "liberal idea."[36]

This way of reading events, together with the fear that reform could spiral into radicalism within a state and then spread across Europe inhabited the language and the policies of the Holy Alliance decision-makers. While ready to implant constitutions in some countries after 1815, as in the case of the French Charte, they loathed those that were introduced from below. To that loathing was added the fear that, once begun, political change inevitably spreads its tentacles or bacilli, as in the classical metaphor "hydra of revolution" or in the modern one likening revolution to an infectious disease.[37] The fear was well-founded: "Never in European history," wrote Eric Hobsbawm, speaking of the generation after 1815, "and rarely anywhere else, has revolutionism been so endemic, so general, so likely to spread by spontaneous contagion as well as by deliberate propaganda."[38]

One may speak also of liberalism's enemy below. In the twentieth century, we became accustomed to the notion (sometimes mythologized) of "peasant nationalism" and other popular mentalities as fuel for communist and national liberation movements around the world, in Yugoslavia, China, and Vietnam, to mention only a few. Equally dominant is the image of the urban working class manning the barricades, from Lyons in the 1830s to Moscow in 1905. But the "crowds and power" nexus, problematic even in those familiar cases, assumed a very different shape in this revolutionary generation. To the French Vendée, the best-known example, must be added numerous instances of popular coun- terrevolutionary action. The Kingdom of Naples alone produced the peasants and urban slum dwellers of 1799 who drowned the Jacobins in blood; the Cal- derari, formed in the late 1810s to counter the Carbonari; and the guerrillas in the intervening years who fought for their king against Prince Murat. The Span- ish right in 1822–23 registered great success in mobilizing peasant and urban crowds against the liberal constitutional regime.

How does one talk about peasant and other popular mentalities? It is prob- ably wiser to put the term "class consciousness" to the side since it evokes too many inappropriate and anachronistic images and puts a clamp on phenomena that constantly wriggle from beneath its grip. The same holds for terms such as "pre-modern," which is teleological, and "primitive," which is condescending. We may take only half of the formulation by the Russian poet Alexander Push- kin, who called the massive Pugachev Rebellion of the eighteenth century "senseless and merciless," and try to understand how and why crowds—whose members are seldom (except when drunk) unthinking—become merciless. The crowd turns into a mob when it embraces disorder and violence. Bribery, loot- ing, priestly sermons, radical or reactionary propaganda, and genuine grievances play a role at various times. In Greece, anti-Turkish hatred predominated, though sometimes social resentment divided Greeks as well. The Neapolitan revolt of 1820–21 caused virtually no bloodshed and no anti-liberal popular violence. There is no denying that poorly educated people had a less than rigorous grasp of political language at that time. At the onset of the French Revolution, crowds shouted, "Vive le roi! Vive M. Necker."[39] Spanish and Neapolitan ones cried out, "Long live the King! Long live the Constitution!" In the crucial Spanish case, after three years of sporadic cheering the new regime, popular masses welcomed in an army of intervention. The "people" could swing in any direction, driven by ignorance, inexperience, reverence, or hope for or fear of change. The gap between metropolitan revolutionary elites and the masses always yawned dan- gerously.

It would be too simple to argue, as some have, that liberals were their own worst enemies, but their weaknesses cannot be ignored. Revolutionaries, even those endowed with pristine and dreamy ideals, had to bend to practical needs. They realized that their followers sometimes needed motivations that were more concrete. When the last Decembrist leader, Sergei Muraviev-Apostol, failed to rouse his troops around a political program wrapped in a religious ritual, he switched to a totally familiar object of loyalty: a new tsar, Constantine, presented as the legitimate heir. Both the Spanish and Neapolitan rebels offered those who joined their cause material rewards. Less forgivable were the character flaws— boasting and rabble-rousing—that surfaced among some of the liberal leaders once they tasted victory. Examples of corruption, abandonment of liberal values, and outright betrayal of the revolution emerged all too often in Spain and Naples; a clash of ambitions and ideas racked the unity of the Decembrists' cause; and civil war erupted in the midst of the Greek struggle for independence.

Moderate liberals such as Martínez de la Rosa, General Pepe, and the Russian Nikita Muraviev also faced the liberal dilemma that plagued the rise of constitutional states: the tension between their dream of a free and prosperous nation and their mistrust of the masses, who were seen as not yet ready for full political participation. Regular themes in all four countries include the gulf between the masses and the intelligentsia and the question of "timeliness" of major reforms. The great Spanish historical novelist Benito Pérez Galdós highlighted the problem in a dialogue taking place in 1820: a character declares that "the people must be enlightened in order for them to be able to practice liberty." His companion replies: "And it is necessary to practice liberty in order to be enlightened."[40]

A cognate issue involved the Spanish and Neapolitan liberals' reluctance to recognize the aspirations to independence of their affiliated territories: Spanish colonies in Latin America and the Sicilian half of the Neapolitan kingdom. Liberals in Madrid and Naples wished these outliers to share in the new constitutional order within the old structures. The rebels in Palermo and in the South American llanos and mountains thought otherwise, and so the leaders in each European peninsula had to face rebellion while trying to consolidate their own revolutions. The cost in lives and treasure along with missing armies helped debilitate their regimes. In Greece, the fissiparous and highly heterogeneous local forces plunged the revolution into civil strife. What might have happened to a victory of the Russian Southern Society with its restrictive plans on regional autonomy can only be imagined.

The Revolutionary Spirit

In this era, the principal insurrectionary impulse—if one may use such a sweeping term—combined an ideological outlook, liberalism, and a personalized spirit. The chief leaders in question, Riego, Pepe, Ypsilanti, and Muraviev-Apostol, however one may judge their efforts, were emphatically not mentally ill—nor wild sectarians, though certainly possessed of outsized personalities. As men of action, they and their comrades who took a revolutionary path differed from the bookish and legalistic, though no less brave and honorable, colleagues who entered the scene after the banner of freedom was raised. The active rebels the 1820s moved in an aura of self-sacrifice for a noble cause that was couched in the poetic pathos of the Romantic era.[41] Whether survivors or martyrs, they were depicted alongside comrades as equal brothers. Like the Four Sergeants of La Rochelle, executed in France in 1822, the four rebel Spaniards of 1820 and the five Decembrists hanged in 1826 appeared on coins, in bas relief, and in pictures as if welded together. They or their admirers self-consciously dipped into classical history and mythology—the brothers Horatii and the Gracchi—for models of fraternal solidarity and heroism. Ypsilanti addressed his followers as a band of brothers.

The heroic posture, hard to check and easily spread, could readily slide into unwise bravado. When Francis Scott Key in 1812 injected into what became the U.S. national anthem the words "No refuge could save / the hireling and slave," he offered a terse summary of an Enlightenment trope that had wide circulation. In various readings, it proposed that freedom endowed a people not only with its rewards but also with virtue and superior martial force. The exalted fiction that one's foes are "slaves" and thus unable to prevail against a "free people" was intoned by Neapolitan and Spanish parliamentarians facing armies of intervention; and it was implicit in Russian Decembrists' allusions to the possibility of invasion after their assumption of power. The diplomat Capodistria, no revolutionary and indeed hostile to the liberal regime in Naples, still warned that one could not "reform the mind with bayonets."[42] True enough, but they could certainly overthrow revolutionary regimes.

In November 1820, after Spain and Naples had adopted the Spanish constitution of 1812 by means of a popular-military revolt, an American visitor to Italy made a wry observation: "It was once thought that none but sages and statesmen could organize and secure constitutions, but now it requires only a regiment of soldiers to raise their caps in the air on the points of their bayonets, and to cry out a constitution in the fashion of England or a constitution in the fashion of Spain."[43] The four horsemen of this story were all officers whose rides and marches, though lacking the epic scope and subsequent mythologizing of those of Bolívar, Garibaldi, Mao, or Che Guevara, won esteem among European liberals because the daring of a military mutiny was married to a pronunciamento rather than to a triumphant order of the day declaring some battlefield victory or conquest. This neo-praetorian version of armed revolt avoided the palace coups of guardsmen and the peasant jacqueries of the past. Three of the revolts were ignited with little loss of blood. All were led by men who had trooped through Europe fighting for or against Napoleon.

The shade of Bonaparte still hovered over Europe, even before the emergence of the Napoleonic myth. His years had spawned in tens of thousands of young men—and some women—varying experiences of battlefield adventure, heroic resistance, radical activity, and tyrannical realities. The hooves of his armies had torn up the continent in wars that reared the generation of Riego, Pepe, Ypsilanti, Muraviev-Apostol, and thousands like them. The four rebels and their comrades, almost all children of those long European struggles, valued daring action and sacrifice for a noble cause. As agents in the grand scheme of history, they tried to reclaim the theatricality associated with the colorful and tragic landscape of the Napoleonic era. But the revolts they triggered owed little to either the Jacobin extremism of the 1790s or the aggressive domination of the French imperium. Veteran officers had gained not only martial experience but also expectations for the postwar world. Disgruntlement arose among Russian officers who compared the prosperous Europe of their campaigning with the poverty of their homeland, and among their Spanish and Neapolitan confreres who saw Restoration favoritism replacing the Napoleonic merit system in matters of assignment and promotion. And, it must be said, some veterans, stewing in idleness, hoped for a new chance at action and glory.

The Decembrist colonel Pavel Pestel at his interrogation told his captors, "Each age has its own distinctive features. This one is marked by revolutionary ideas. . . . From one end of Europe to the other, everywhere one sees the same thing—from Portugal to Russia, not excluding a single state—even the polar opposites of England and Turkey. All of America displays the same spectacle. The spirit of transformation everywhere set, so to speak, minds seething."[44] Though the rebels of the 1820s held sturdy patriotic loyalties, their attraction to the international dimension of revolution was partly attributable to a kind of pre-nationalist cosmopolitanism that also led such nonradical border crossers as Pozzo di Borgo the Sardinian and the Greeks Capodistria and Ypsilanti to serve in Russia, Metternich the German in Austria, and Lord Acton and General Nugent in Naples—to say nothing of itinerant dynasts.

A mix of motives led many warriors to act out an extraordinary willingness to fight and die for foreign causes. Mercenaries and international armies (and naval crews)—the Grand Armée being only the latest and biggest of them—had long stormed across the land and sailed the seas. Money and forced recruitment did not account for all of this. In the Napoleonic wars, Poles fought from one end of Europe to the other. Seeing the French emperor as their champion, they served in his armies under King Joseph both in Naples and in Spain. Altogether, some one hundred thousand Polish warriors perished during the wars of 1797 to 1815.[45] At other times, they became idealized models for liberals and nationalists. The taste for adventure of the sort that later fed colonialism could move volunteers from one part of the political spectrum to the other. The epithet "turncoat" lost much of its meaning in this panorama of perpetual reinvention of loyalties as fighting men changed sides again and again.[46]

Into this broad stream flowed the rivulet of liberal internationalism in the 1820s. Revolts galvanized constitutionalists across Europe. Ideas, like waves emanating from diverse sources in the depths, broke raggedly on faraway shores. The aquatic metaphor is apt since in this pre-railroad era much of the knowledge traffic was seaborne. Maritime activity—naval and merchant—had ballooned enormously during the Napoleonic wars. The Mediterranean offered a highway for revolutionary ideas and for rebel refugees sailing from one revolution to another, from Naples to Barcelona, via Genoa and Marseilles. The watery road took European philhellenes to the battlegrounds of Greece. Insurgent Hellenic sea captains carried proclamations as well as arms and men as they threaded through the Aegean. In the west, the Spanish port of Cadiz funneled in Latin American patriots and their aspirations, and in the east, the Black Sea port of Odessa spilled out conspirators into the Balkans. These routes together with a burgeoning press allowed notions of revolutionary solidarity to overflow national borders. Many of those who came to be called liberals believed in a pan-European or even world brotherhood of liberty and often addressed each other as such across frontiers. A "circuit of revolutions"[47] that generated liberal legions began and ran all the way up to the Paris Commune of 1871.[48] Their presence hardened conservative belief in an organized international conspiracy directed from some central point.

But it was precisely from the divergence between the moderate and what we might call the dynamic-heroic ends of the liberal spectrum that one of its greatest maladies arose: schism and sectarianism. A pattern emerged, one common to most revolutions and even minor upheavals, of moderates and radicals fighting both reaction and each other. Though the cases are not symmetrical, one can see the pattern in the schism between *moderados* and *exaltados* in Spain, Muratists and Carbonari in Naples, the Northern and Southern Societies of the Russian Decembrists, and even the incoming post-rebellion diaspora Greeks and the Friendly Society, which had triggered the Greek uprising. Many exceptions arose, as when some liberals on horseback veered to the right, or when diffident ones swung into action. Temperament often played as much of a role in the conflicts as ideology.

Though their power has often been exaggerated, secret societies grew and fed into all the uprisings of the 1820s: Spanish Masons, Italian Carbonari, the Greek Friendly Society, and Decembrist societies. They flowered in the early nineteenth century in spite of rigorous regimes of censorship, repression, police spies, informants, and agents provocateurs. Their similarities offer few surprises. Form and ritual easily traveled and, though they were adapted to local cultures, retained a more or less common shape. Initiations might have been vociferous and colorful in one place, dark and solemn in another, festive or rigidly conspiratorial, but they mostly employed an analogous language.[49]

Heaven and Earth

Expressive behavior and artifacts of all kinds—art, popular festivities, propaganda, religion—worked their way to various degrees into all the revolutionary movements and regimes. While the marching columns that triggered them began in provincial places, cultural feeders operated in the port cities of Cadiz, Naples, Odessa, and Petersburg. In Cadiz in 1810 and Madrid in 1820 people watched theatrical representations of liberty and martyrdom. The prestigious San Carlo theater in Naples retained a traditional repertoire, though local houses staged freedom plays. The Greeks of Odessa, Bucharest, and Iași prepared for liberation by mounting antique dramas designed to raise patriotic consciousness. Though the Decembrists never got to organize a public culture, they harnessed poetry to their designs, wrote and attended plays where actors declaimed historical themes of tyrannicide or national resistance, and dreamed of post-revolutionary culture. In historical memory, the names of Goya, Quintana, Martínez de la Rosa, Rossetti, Koraïs, Solomós, and Ryleev still hover like an aura around the liberal explosions of the 1820s.

Spreading secular liberal propaganda to the common people presented a challenge to liberal regimes of the 1820s. Under mostly private auspices, pictures, playing cards, and fans bearing liberal images appeared in Spain during the liberal triennium, and the Spaniards had some success in mounting constitutional plaques and organizing ceremonies that mixed civic, military, and religious ritual forms. Some of these things eventually emerged in Greece as well. The Neapolitans mostly lacked the time and the Decembrists wholly the chance to follow suit. What bound most of the liberal cultural outputs was an undercurrent of Romanticism and a vital if troubled intersection with Christianity.

When Tatiana, a protagonist of Alexander Pushkin's novel in verse, *Eugene Onegin* (1823–31), enters the eponymous hero's study, she finds there a portrait of Lord Byron and an unnamed statuette in the familiar pose and furrowed brow of Napoleon. The literature on how these two figures in real life captured the imagination of the post-1815 generation is stupendous. Though the French emperor was far from a liberal, he stood as the major emblem of dramatic political and social change, as did Byron for European sensibilities. Victor Hugo, in an aphoristic mode, asserted that "Romanticism is liberalism in literature."[50] In our own time, the cliché abides. In the words of a prominent Latin American scholar, "Liberalism and romanticism are two inseparable aspects of the first half of the nineteenth century. Never were politics and art so united." He called the 1812 Spanish constitution and its inspiration perfect illustrations of Romanticism and idealism.[51] Poets and rebel leaders were seen to be subject to enthusiasm or exaltation, and to a psychological posture in direct opposition to the ethos of court and aristocratic milieux or stodgy bourgeois society.

The ambivalent relation of liberalism and religion offers a more concrete historical tapestry. The belief that society needed organized religion was held by conservative figures as diverse as Burke, Napoleon, and Bonald,[52] but also by Marx—in tones of lamentation. The Catholic and Orthodox agents of the 1820s revolts remained devout, as did most other liberals; indeed many tried to create a syncretic nexus between their revolutionary ideas and Christian doctrine as they understood it. Tocqueville attributed the spread of radicalism outward from the French Revolution to its religious flavor. In 1794 Buonarotti, appealing to Jesus of Nazareth, said: "Your doctrine, disfigured by tyrants, is ours." In the same year, a Polish Jacobin declared that "Jesus was the most fervent democrat." Examples are legion. Though the majority of clergy everywhere opposed radicalism, some priests embraced it, and clerics were present in all the Italian revolutions.[53] Like the term "liberation priest" in the Latin America of our time, "revolutionary clergy" was no oxymoron. Abbots, friars, and parish priests took part in the insurgencies, sometimes violently, in Spain, Italy, and Greece, where religion and nationalism meshed easily—to say nothing of the resistance against Napoleon.

On preparing overturns and coming to power, liberal and nationalist leaders, aware of the deep-seated piety of their countrymen, drew upon traditional devotional forms. Churchmen were recruited for inspiring revolt, as in Russia; initiating secret society members, as in Naples and Greece; and organizing liberal processions, festivities, and constitutional swearing ceremonies as in Spain and Naples. From Cadiz to the Balkans, the Te Deum laudamus—We Praise thee, O God—was performed in gratitude for the coming order, just as it had been done for coronations and battlefield victories. Possibly the most effective popular engine of liberal-national communication in this era was religio-political propaganda in the form of sermons and catechisms. A catechism—from the Greek word for proclamation or publication—provides verbal instruction via dialogue and brief phrases, usually in the form of question and answer. Unlike an open or Socratic dialogue, it inculcates doctrine by rote learning: setting up the questions with prescribed answers. From the Reformation onward, the Catholic hierarchy had been trying to intensify its outreach to believers. The scores of catechisms they produced reflected the constant tensions between the desire to teach correct theology and the need to simplify by means of short, cheap, and portable catechisms—especially for school use. In 1765, a French bishop called religious teaching "the science of salvation."[54]

Since the church had regularly shored up authoritarian monarchies, it is no surprise that the master of political masquerade, Napoleon Bonaparte, enlisted the catechism to enhance its majesty. Political passages were added to the standardized catechism of 1807 and dictated by Napoleon himself: "Q: What are the duties of Christians with respect to the princes who govern them, and what are in particular our duties toward Napoleon I, our Emperor? A: . . . love, respect, obedience, fidelity, military service, tributes ordered for the preservation and defense of the Empire and of his throne; we also owe him fervent prayers for his safety and for the spiritual and temporal prosperity of the State." Alluding to the Biblical comment about rendering unto Caesar that which belongs to Caesar, the catechism declared that Napoleon and his successors had been anointed ruler by God and confirmed by the pope. He was credited with re-establishing the holy church. Failure in one's duty to the emperor would insure eternal damnation.[55]

In eighteenth-century France, the *philosophes* had long adapted the catechism to secular purposes, and revolutionaries welcomed its use for radical political ends. Johann Heinrich Füssli, a Zurich-born artist, wrote a 1775 political cate-chism on happiness and patriotism. Ignac Martinovics, a Hungarian freethinker, pantheist, Jacobin, and former Franciscan friar executed in 1795, used cate-chisms in each of his two republican secret societies.[56] Nothing remotely radical can be found in the standard Catholic catechisms, yet the use of one word in the French catechism of 1807 suggested how even sacred documents could be adapted to other purposes. Jesus Christ was stated to have delivered the world from "the tyranny of the devil and hell."[57] For the composers of political cate-chisms, it was a no great difficulty to suggest that liberation from a more worldly tyrant was the natural counterpart to deliverance from the underworld tyrant.

In this context, the Spanish catechisms evolved from pure documents of faith to organs of patriotic propaganda in the war against the tyrant and anti-Christ Napoleon; and then as liberal-Christian texts celebrating a constitutional order. Spanish catechisms of the national struggle were copied or adapted in Germany, Italy, and Russia. In Dresden, Heinrich von Kleist turned a Spanish document of 1808 (see Chapter II) into *Katechismus der Deutschen* in 1809—though it saw the light only later. Ernst Moritz Arndt published anonymously in St. Petersburg a *Kurzer Katechismus für deutsche Soldaten* in 1812 and another one a few years later.[58] Most strikingly, the men who fashioned the revolutions of the 1820s used political catechisms to teach constitutionalism to the masses, as in the Spanish and Neapolitan regimes; or to prepare for a revolt, as with the Greek and Russian revolutionaries. Russia's rebels, the Decembrists, in 1826 used a political cate-chism as the pronunciamento announcing the overthrow of the tsar. In a sense, catechisms became leftist equivalents to the conservative international master document: the Holy Alliance. Though measuring the impact of religious mes-sages can be hard, the power of the word, when handed down from on high, was great. And the question and answer format came to have as much authority as the actual content of the catechism—the possibility for secular adaptation.

In the case of the liberal regimes in Spain and Naples, syncretic propaganda did not suffice to save them. Liberals there again and again asserted their devotion to king and faith and even had a Catholic monopoly included in their constitutions.

Liberals, chastened heirs of 1789, upheld rather than persecuted religion, and they managed to win a segment of clerical support. But confessing to a national faith was one thing; mixing it in with liberal programs, such as dissolution of monasteries, was another. Those conservative churchmen who hated any infringement on traditional ways and institutions never mastered the mature lexicon of compromise and moderation, and they came to see liberals in power as nothing more than Jacobin anti-Christians. In Spain, priests not only turned the power of the pulpit against the liberal government but took up arms as well.

Death and Transfiguration

During the generation or so following the French Revolution, the "romantic agony" of the gothic and the grotesque occupied a prominent place in the European imagination alongside the romance of blissful liberation. It has been argued that during the bruising twenty-year war and the subsequent widely perceived misrule of the Restoration, a Europe-wide sense of catastrophe hovered, a "calamitous rupture" brought on by those events and by the clamor of poets about how industrialization was alienating humanity from nature.[59] Aside from the unthinkable battlefield losses, the expanding public forum increasingly opened up discussion of the silent and not so silent violence carried out in the name of politics. Incarceration and executions in particular captured the imagination in news reports, iconography, and opera, where "the prison came to serve as the principal image of political oppression" and condensed and crystallized a radical critique of the state.[60]

The fortresses, citadels, town prisons, dungeons, and oubliettes that dotted Europe in 1800 were freely used by the Napoleonic forces, yet they seemed to take on a mantle of more hideous cruelty when regained by the Restoration and repopulated by its enemies. And so the motif of the dissident or revolutionary prisoner came to dominate the popular image and the story of imprisonment. That image rose up to haunt readers and onlookers, to say nothing of what the reality did to the inmates. The black terror of gradual live burial within four walls fed the fascination with the fate of the languishing captive. Popular European engravings and book illustrations of the eighteenth and nineteenth centuries abounded in horrific scenes of dungeons, often set in Spain or Italy, and sometimes featuring a rescuing maiden.[61] The popularity of visual representations of the prison, especially its creepy architecture, owed much to the fanciful eighteenth-century graphic horrors of Piranesi's *Carceri*, with their thick walls, ring bolts, and chains.[62]

The reading public could derive much guilty pleasure from novels that featured the prison theme. Eighteenth- and nineteenth-century English and American writers in particular had a thing about Latin fiends: Walpole his Manfred,

Radcliffe her Montoni, Browning his Duke of Ferrara, Poe his Spanish inquisitors, Baron Corvo his Borgias. From an Atlantic Protestant viewpoint, Catholic Europe presented a perfect setting for iniquities in the midst of backwardness. In 1824, in the aftermath of bloody reaction in Spain and Naples, Walter Scott wrote of a region "where tyranny and Catholic superstition still continued to exercise their sway over the slave and the bigot."[63]

Ann Radcliffe filled her gothic tales with "sympathetic terror," "horrid apprehensions," and horrific pleasures through suspense, eerie supernaturalism, and the entrapment of innocent victims. Like Horace Walpole earlier, in *The Castle of Otranto*, she set her villains in Catholic countries.[64] The sixteenth-century Italian setting of *Mysteries of Udolpho* (1794), though remote from the events of the 1820s, featured dungeons, poison, and bandits that fed nicely into the stage melodramas that came of age within a few years of its publication and into the imagery of those who recounted, read about, or experienced the terrors of the political prison. The recollections of the Spanish liberal Juan Van Halen of torture in a Spanish Inquisition dungeon in the 1810s reminded the French radical Armand Carrel of the novels of Anne Radcliffe.[65] The Decembrist Mikhail Lunin framed his incarceration in Russia around his remembrance of reading *Mysteries of Udolpho*.[66]

Stendhal's *The Charterhouse of Parma* puts a prison at the very center of both the political and love plots and almost lovingly describes the young Bonapartist's 120-pound shackle. In "Vanina Vanini," Stendhal turns the victim into a Carbonaro persecuted in the Papal States. Perhaps the best-known prison tale of Italian dungeons and torture chambers, Victorien Sardou's 1887 play *Tosca*, set in Rome in 1800, became world famous when made into Puccini's opera of 1900. William Mudford's story "The Iron Shroud" (1830) featured a cell embedded in rock on the cliff in Sicily that exactly describes the prison of the 1820 Neapolitan liberal Guglielmo Pepe. The story's prisoner is the "victim of vengeance, the dark ferocious and inexorable vengeance of an Italian heart."[67]

Beethoven's opera *Fidelio* (1805) helped advance what became a Romantic trope about prisons and politics. Set in Spain, it twined the love story around a petty tyrant, his political prisoner, a dungeon alive with clanging chains and murder plots, and a chorus singing a hymn of freedom.[68] Three years after *Fidelio*'s opening, Napoleon's armies began the conquest of Spain. Thomas Dick's *Philosophy of Religion* (1825) described how the French general Lassalle entered Toledo in 1808 and opened the torture chambers in the Palace of the Inquisition. Possibly inspired by this work, Edgar Allan Poe in 1842 published "The Pit and the Pendulum," set in the dungeons of the Toledo Inquisition.[69] Primarily a gothic thriller, the tale displayed a political tone in its portraits of the inquisitors and their diabolical death machine, and in the moment when French troops throw open the torture chambers of the Inquisition to free the victim of tyrannical intolerance.

The romantic haze of the nineteenth century, in our time virtually dissipated, allowed people to empathize with characters who were sometimes imagined and sometimes modeled on the real ones who fought for freedom from despotism and ended up behind bars. The liberal narrative was strongly enhanced by literature and the arts, especially in popular versions. They became the lens through which many people of the nineteenth and early twentieth centuries would see the world of revolution, reform, repression, tyranny—and its instruments of incarceration and punishment. Ironically, that mechanism also drove survivors of prison life to set to paper the memories of their days and nights of unfreedom. In adopting, consciously or otherwise, familiar styles from well-known fiction, the rebels of the post-Napoleonic age were neither falsifying or plagiarizing but following the most natural procedures of narrative, where previous stories help structure one's own memories.

The main characters in this chain of historical episodes of the 1820s—along with hundreds of others—all did time in captivity: Riego as a prisoner of war in France and on death row in 1823; Pepe in the wake of the failed 1799 Neapolitan Republic; Ypsilanti in Hungarian and Austrian fortresses; and Muraviev-Apostol in the Peter and Paul Fortress in St. Petersburg. Is there any cause to doubt the veracity of those who described, directly or indirectly, any of these experiences? Skepticism may flow from what we know about exaggerated tales, for instance of the Bastille (a longtime symbol of tyranny), or from the embellishments and inflations inherent in most memoir literature. And perhaps some readers might harbor a relative lack of sympathy for the convicts of that era in light of the much greater terrors of the camps and prisons of the following century. Measuring the relative cruelty of prison systems anywhere presents obstacles. Did those English observers residing in the shadow of a Newgate, Brixton, or Dartmoor believe that their own sites of punishment were somehow more humane than those in the south or east of Europe?[70]

What we can say for certain is that the image of some houses of detention assisted in heroizing their inmates—and mostly for good reason—for contemporaries and for later readers of history. The Caracca Arsenal Fortress of the Four Towers, near Cadiz, was considered "one of the most horrible in Spain," with its numerous dungeons holding hundreds of Spanish liberals and Latin American patriots.[71] One of them, the renowned Francisco de Miranda, betrayed by Bolívar, died there in 1816. Miranda allegedly would lift his heavy chain, riveted to two pillars, and lament that its first link had been forged by his own people.[72] A year later, the liberal Juan Van Halen began his harrowing sojourn in the hands of the Spanish Inquisition.

Stendhal's fictionally constructed Citadel of Parma, darkly lowering over a plain, contained the Farnese Tower, with coffin-like cells where the prisoner lies horizontal, unable to move year after insane year. This was Stendhal's invention.

But the prisons of Italy, especially in the Papal States and the Kingdom of Naples, gained in the early nineteenth century a fearsome notoriety, which, however exaggerated by later Risorgimento historiography, surely deserved the reputation. Forts, arsenals, castles, and island prisons housed thousands of criminals and politicals, often mixed together. For sheer negative propaganda value, the citadels of Austria, home to many an Italian patriot, claimed the most laurels. In the 1790s, Lafayette spent time in a dungeon at Olmütz, where his cell lay below the level of the moat. The Austrian prison regime included *carcere duro*, solitary confinement in shackles, and the "little horse" (*cavaletto*), an eight-foot bench with body vise and manacles, used for flogging.[73] The dreaded Spielberg Fortress in Moravia stood out as the chief emblem of Austrian penal cruelty and Metternich's vindictiveness. For a decade, the Spielberg held Silvio Pellico, convicted in the Milan conspiracy of 1821, who became its most famous resident. His *My Prisons*, though suffused with Christian piety rather than a denunciation of Austria, became a Risorgimento bible.[74] As of the 1960s, the book had averaged six editions per year since its publication, had been translated into twelve languages—including twenty-two different French translations[75]—and is still read in Italian schools.

Prison life sometimes produced, particularly in literature, a positive feeling of inner release and spiritual freedom. The images fit perfectly into the dual revolution in politics and creative romanticism, and sometimes even merged.[76] In real life, many kinds of transformations occurred behind prison walls; most of all, claustrophobic internment sharpened the thirst for total liberation not only from prison cells but from all despotic and personal restraints. The tyrannical state became constructed as a prison from which is subjects must be released, an urge that translated into the revolutionary iconography of shattered chains and half-blind convicts emerging from a dark world.

> And when thy sons to fetters are consign'd—
> To fetter and the damp vault's dayless gloom,
> Their country conquers with their martyrdom.
> And Freedom's fame finds wings on every wind.[77]

The ultimate martyrdom—Romantic or otherwise—of course could only come with the sacrifice of life for a faith. Riego, Pepe, Ypsilanti, and Muraviev-Apostol explicitly stated either in a secret society oath or in a pronunciamento their willingness to die for their ideals. The insurgents of the 1820s held no monopoly on the idea of sacrificing one's life for a higher cause: soldiers had been going into battle for centuries under the banner of ideas—religious, dynastic, or national service—and sometimes for the very honor of the fighting unit itself, such as a tradition-laden regiment or ship. Liberals asked themselves and their followers to lay down their lives for an idea: "freedom." And the leaders—not only Greeks but Spaniards, Italians, and Russians—constantly climbed further into distant meaning when they invoked for themselves or others classical models of sacrifice: Leonidas and the Three Hundred of Thermopylae, Brutus, and Cato. The classical model was amplified by the more recent example of secular martyrdom: the death of Jean-Paul Marat as depicted in the painting by Jacques-Louis David.

The heroic self-chosen death by immolation, by assassination of a tyrant followed by suicide, or by sacrifice in battle or revolt all drew from classical traditions. For the first, the chief model in the eighteenth and early nineteenth century seems to have been the Roman Cato the Younger (d. 46 BCE), who took his own life on the battlefield rather than live in a world ruled by Julius Caesar.[78] The recognition or prediction by others of a violent redemptive death became an attribute of the Romantic hero. At least three Russian Decembrist leaders were said to have been warned by a Parisian palmist of a violent end; two of them were indeed hanged. In fact, the cult of revolutionary martyrdom, like the catechisms and sacred oaths and solemn masses deployed for civic purpose, was part of a huge appropriation of the most affective elements of sacred culture, an appropriation that characterized the late eighteenth- and early nineteenth-century political left—and, for a much longer time, national liberation struggles.

‖ 2 ‖

Rafael del Riego

The Ride Through Andalusia

Take this, take this. I bring you freedom!

—Donizetti, *Elixir of Love*

On January 1, 1820, the thirty-three-year-old Lieutenant Colonel Rafael del Riego, commander of an infantry battalion of the Asturias Regiment, was stationed in a little Spanish town about halfway between Cadiz and Seville, Las Cabezas de San Juan—the Headlands of St. John—so named in medieval times for the hills with watchtowers to guard against Moorish incursions. Riego, on that day in that place, issued a pronunciamento that set off a revolution destined to reverberate from the Mediterranean to the Baltic Sea. He announced his refusal of the king's order to take the men on an overseas expedition to crush the Latin American independence movement and his intention to restore the liberal constitution of 1812. Early on this Sunday morning, as the churches were emptying, Riego emerged from his quarters next to the Iglesia de San Juan Bautista and walked to the plaza, where the battalion stood in formation under a clear sky. Wearing a gray frock coat, with a saber in a steel scabbard and a baton in his right hand, he hung the baton on a coat button, signaled with his saber to the drummer to begin a roll, and had the flag raised. With an expressive look, Riego began his address.

> Soldiers, my love for you is great. Because of this, I as your commander cannot permit you to leave your country aboard some rotten vessels to go off and wage an unjust war in the New World—nor to have you abandon your parents and siblings, leaving them sunk into abject poverty and oppression. You owe them your life, and so are duty bound in gratitude to survive and support them in their old age. Further, if necessary, you must sacrifice your own lives in order to burst the chains that have bound them in oppression since 1814. An absolute king,

FRANCE

SPAIN

★ Madrid

PORTUGAL

Detail
area

Bienvenida • Villagarcía
Berlanga • Fuenteovejuna • Bélmez
Llerena • Azuaga • Espiel

CÓRDOBA

Rio Guadalquivir

Rio Genil

Montilla
Aguilar

SEVILLA •
Marchena

Ultrera
Osuna • Estepa
Gilena
Morón • Villanueva de S. Juan
Las Cabezas • Montellano
Campillos • Antequera
Lebrija • Puerto Serrano • Cañeta
Colmenar
Trebujena • Villamartín • Grazalema
Arcos • Bornos
Jerez
Ronda
El Puerto de Santa María
MÁLAGA
CÁDIZ • Puerto Real
San Fernando • Alcalá de los Gazules
Chiclana • Merdina- • Marbella
Sidonia • Jimena • Estepona • Fuengirola
Conil
Los • MEDITERRANEAN
Vejer • Barrios • SEA
ATLANTIC • San Roque
OCEAN
Algeciras

0   25   50 (kilometers)
0   25   50 (miles)

driven by whim and fancy, imposes on them unbearable duties and taxes. He vexes them, oppresses them, and, finally—the very peak of misfortunes—snatches their beloved sons in order to sacrifice them to his pride and ambition. Yes, they are taking you from the paternal nest to venture to faraway unhealthy climes to continue a senseless war which could easily be ended by returning to the Spanish nation its rights. The Constitution, yes, the Constitution is sufficient to appease our brothers in America.

Riego concluded the harangue by raising his sword to the sky and, with a ringing voice, exclaimed: "Long live the constitution!" The men in the ranks wore the wonderfully operatic military uniforms of the era: tall drum-shaped peaked cap with plume, blanket roll atop square field pack, high collar, and epaulettes, with a saber swinging from the left hip. They repeated his shouts of "Viva!"; at one point the soldiers broke ranks and surrounded Riego's horse.[1]

From the balcony of the mayor's building, Riego addressed his officers and the townspeople: "Spain is living at the mercy of an arbitrary and absolute power, exercised without the slightest respect for the fundamental laws of the Nation. The king, who owes his throne to the multitudes who struggled in the Independence war, has nevertheless not sworn to the Constitution; the Constitution—a pact between monarch and people—is the foundation and embodiment of every modern Nation. . . . For Spain to be saved, it is essential that the king swear to and honor the Constitution of 1812, the legitimate and civil affirmation of the rights and duties of Spaniards—of all Spaniards from the king to the lowest peasant." Riego affirmed that the Spanish people were about to regain the "sacred rights" that the ungrateful King Fernando VII had stolen from them, and he promised to use all his strength to throw off the "shameful bonds of despotism."[2]

Turning to practical matters on the same day, Riego, in order to keep news of the uprising from prematurely spreading, ordered a picket of sentries posted around the town for one day, forbidding anyone to leave on pain of execution. This and later threats of capital punishment contradicted Riego's stated opposition to violence toward adversaries, and he did not enforce the threat. He informed his troops what awaited them. The rebels, he and his co-conspirators, had canceled the expedition to Latin America, declared the constitution in full force, and had their leader Colonel Antonio Quiroga assume the rank of general and commander of the new army—all in defiance of the royal government. This meant revolution and inevitable armed struggle against forces loyal to the king. Urging his men to maintain discipline, he promised that at the end of the glorious battle, they would be discharged and receive their pay and the honors they deserved.[3] Riego told two of his officers that he would endure silently all the torments of the Inquisition in order to insure liberty for his country. In order to regain the ancient rights of Spanish history, he said, "we must use the forces available to us" and show the world that we are not "a band of ambitious [men] or a horde of rebellious traitors."[4]

After his proclamations, Riego organized elections for a new town government. This delayed his departure, and it was not until late afternoon of the same day that he led his men out of town through the unwelcome gift of a severe winter thunderstorm toward their first objective.[5] Thus was launched in a materially modest but symbolically very Spanish way the first of a series of uprisings that would alarm, frighten, and inspire Europeans for the next five years.

Spanish Agonies

"Such be the sons of Spain, and strange the fate! / The fight for freedom, who were never free," wrote Byron in *Childe Harold*. The national agony of Spain that began in 1808 with the French usurpation exacerbated and obscured the layers of unfreedom and social suffering that had been accumulating for centuries. The peasantry, constituting about five-sixths of the population, almost wholly illiterate, toiled under various forms of dependence. In Andalusia especially, peasants had sporadically mounted jacqueries demanding *reparto* or division of the great estates. Periodically blood and terror stalked the countryside in the form of desperately poor smugglers and brigands, long before the horrors of guerrilla war in the French occupation. Foreign observers in words and Francisco Goya on canvas captured them in frightening images. Andalusian *braceros* became bandits and smugglers, sometimes as a result of persistent poverty, unemployment, and irrational customs laws; others were attracted by the flamboyant costumes, songs, bravado, profit, and fellowship. Smugglers often featured as heroes on the stage, singing, "¡Yo! Que soy contrabandista! ¡Yo ho!" Stagecoaches traveling across the country required a mounted guard.[6]

The urban poor—whose humblest stratum, beggars, thronged outside church doors—could turn violent, especially in the *barrios bajos* of southern Madrid. The *populacho*, as the mob was called, could swing in any direction, from liberal to reactionary. Even in tranquil times, festive Spaniards would pour into the streets for almost any occasion—coronation, return of the king, end of a war, constitution, military victory, religious feast, execution, or new water supply system. Church bells tolled and the crowds sang and danced. *Majos* and *majas*, lower-class figures who dressed and acted flamboyantly, mocked upper-class petits-maîtres and gallomanes. The interaction between them became fodder for a Spanish satirical stage genre, the *sainete*.[7] According to the census of 1797, some 30 percent of the active male population were unproductive, mostly clergy and nobles. The latter clung to entail and mortmain, which put a chokehold on the land market,[8] and it held exclusive sway over officer ranks in the military. The educated middle classes in the towns, except for adherents of the Enlightenment, the *ilustrados*, had little use for books but preferred theater and the *tertulia*, gatherings with animated conversations about religion, philosophy, and politics. Out of this milieu political circles eventually emerged.

In a country of about ten million at the dawn of the nineteenth century, tens of thousands of Spaniards served the church. Burgos, a town of nine thousand, had fourteen parish churches and forty-two monasteries. Most clerics were poorly educated, and an unusually large number resided in monasteries and convents, a fact sharply satirized by Goya among others. The parish clergy, however, though celibate, participated closely in the life of their congregations and in this respect somewhat resembled the married priests of many Orthodox countries. The regular rhythms of church festivals, processions with images, street theater, and popular piety mingled together in a web of daily life and ritual that stressed the outward forms of devotion more than cerebral dogma. In a land that harbored very few atheists or deists, commitment to the faith and to church rites as a way of life remained firm and even passionate for the vast majority.[9]

A persistent image of the Spanish clergy in this era portrays them as die-hard obscurantists and conservatives, if not reactionaries. This certainly held true for many and probably most. Inside and outside Spain, popular awe of the Inquisition reinforced the image, later buttressed by the discovery of Goya's visual assaults upon it.[10] Yet, though still active and powerful in opposing the Enlightenment, the Spanish Inquisition no longer functioned as the frightening instrument of legend: its last burning of a victim took place in 1780.[11] Religion certainly intersected with politics. The church was adept at mobilizing believers against the enemy of the moment—Moors, Jews, Amerindians, Protestants, and Napoleon and his alleged disciples: constitutionalists and liberals. But God could be invoked in many different ways. Priests and monks appeared as liberal reformers as well as anti-liberals; and as guerrillas, unafraid to pick up a weapon to capture a bandit or mow down French invaders. A student of Latin America found that "the war for independence could present itself as a religious war because the discourse of legitimation" came from a providential reading of God-chosen leaders, as in the Old Testament.[12] The same held true for the Iberian homeland.

Atop a national collage of misery and splendor sat monarchs from a branch of the Bourbon royal line, the Spanish Borbón dynasty. King Carlos III had transferred from the Neapolitan throne to Madrid in 1759 and presided over a phase of limited reforms inspired by the European Enlightenment.[13] His son Carlos IV (1788–1808)—the last king of "free Spain" before the French incursion, and a cousin of Louis XVI—was indecisive rather than vigorously reformist or reactionary. The crisis of the Old Regime began in his reign with internal scandal and ended with outside intervention. The scandal turned around the figure of Manuel Godoy, a favorite of the queen and one of the most unpopular courtiers in history, though far from unenlightened. More than a decade of policy disasters included losing a war with France in 1793 and two wars with Britain that ushered in the naval defeat at Trafalgar and a hemorrhage of men and treasure. For these and other actions and his suspected intimate relationship with the queen, large segments of the population turned against Godoy, including the poor of Madrid.

With the court hopelessly divided and the leadership beholden to Napoleon, Spain agreed to join the French in the conquest of Portugal, completed late in 1807. The continued influx of French troops into Spain after that war heightened paranoia in Madrid. In March 1808 rumors flew about a Godoy plan to spirit away the royal family—in fact, he wished to protect the king from the French. At Aranjuez, the royal winter home, Prince Fernando, heir to the throne, joined jealous nobles in using the urban mob to set off an anti-Godoy *motín* or tumult. Crowds gathered, sacked Godoy's home, killed some of his friends, and sought to lynch him as well. Though the minister barely managed to save his skin, King Carlos dismissed him from office the next day to appease the violent crowd. Fernando hated Godoy and feared his influence over his mother, and this hatred, publicly voiced, endeared the crown prince to the populace. King Carlos, fearing further mob violence, abdicated on March 19 in favor of his son, who became Fernando VII.[14] The Aranjuez episode proved to be the first example of Spanish crowd violence effecting political change—even though it involved a narrow dynastic issue.[15]

The growing tragicomedy escalated as French commander Joachim Murat occupied Madrid and Carlos IV annulled his abdication. Napoleon cut the Gordian knot in his usual peremptory way: he summoned father and son to Bayonne, in southern France, and there completed the astonishing game of catch-the-crown by forcing Fernando to give it back to his father, who then ceded it to Napoleon. The French emperor in turn granted the kingship of Spain to his brother Joseph Bonaparte. In line with his practices elsewhere in French-dominated Europe, Napoleon ordered up what Karl Marx later called "one of his ready-made constitutions."[16] A week after his appointment as king of Spain, Joseph convened a Cortes at Bayonne made up of some sixty-five renegade Spanish notables, who approved a draft constitution. These and like-minded figures inside Spain came to be called *afrancesados*, whom many considered collaborators or even traitors during the coming war. Fernando, by contrast, always remained absolved of the charge even though he had sought Napoleon's support, had caved in to him, spent the war years in luxurious exile, and was thus the first, along with his father, of the *afrancesados*.[17] But such was the enduring power and charisma of monarchy and dynasty in the Spain of this era that he was known as "The Desired One" (*El Deseado*) in the popular mind.

The Bayonne constitution of April 1808 mirrored the French constitution of the year VIII (1799), the model for other satellite instruments of rule in the burgeoning French imperium. The bicameral legislature, comprising Cortes and Senate, had consultative rather than real power. Some bodies were appointed, others elected. The constitution had no force and the Cortes it created never met. Nevertheless, a French template, now fitted over Spain, introduced the Napoleonic Code, local departments that superseded the old provinces, the abolition of feudalism and the Inquisition, and the closure of two-thirds of the monasteries. Formal equality before the law, freedom of press, and individual security rights completed the standard picture, although a Catholic monopoly over religion constituted a major concession to Spanish tradition.[18]

In Madrid, on what the Spanish still celebrate as Dos de Mayo (May 2), the French commander tried to gather the remaining royal family to take them to France. Seeing this as an abduction of the royals, the city exploded in a violent demonstration at the Puerta del Sol that turned into a battle with the invaders, an event immortalized by Goya. The French troops brutally repressed the rioters there and carried out executions all around Madrid. About two hundred Spaniards fell in front of firing squads. Anti-French violence in the name of Fernando VII then broke out in other parts of Spain. In one notable case, mobs in Valencia, urged on by a Catholic friar, massacred some 330 Frenchmen in one night. Similar outrages—some spontaneous, some planned—were perpetrated through the summer in many parts of Spain; they were driven by varying motives but aimed chiefly at French officials, suspected or real collaborators, landowners, and Godoyists. Some local officials protected the French by jailing them. By the summer of 1808, special committees and juntas had rejected King Joseph in favor of Fernando. Spain was now locked into a national uprising against the "intruder king." At the Battle of Bailén on July 19, 1808, the Spanish regular army defeated the French. Joseph retreated to Vitoria and Napoleon sent additional troops into Spain. In September a Supreme Central Junta assumed leadership of the resistance, and on November 22 it proclaimed Spain as the liberator of Europe from the Napoleonic yoke.[19]

Thus began one of the most devastating of the many local wars embedded in the generation-long revolutionary and Napoleonic hostilities. The literature on the Spanish War of Independence is staggering.[20] On the battlefields, a French army of 110,000 faced a Spanish one of 100,000, plus 30,000 urban militia. Recruits ranged in age from teenagers to men in their forties, including priests. Local units bore banners of their patron saints.[21] The Spanish army was later fortified and even partly superseded by British forces, which were decisive for the eventual victory.

A guerrilla warfare of armed civilians in bands provided the most dramatic, though by no means the most militarily crucial, episodes in this war. The word "guerrilla," long a part of our language, translates as "little war," fought by *guerrilleros*. Some thirty thousand of them joined in bands, ranging from those of eight thousand fighters to tiny ones of a dozen people—men and women, laymen and priests, mostly rural inhabitants, but all ferociously anti-French. Some harbored anti-urban feelings and social gripes. They built cults around daring leaders; usually displayed pride, lack of discipline, and cruelty to collaborators; and sometimes descended into banditry. Starting in 1808, a local priest or landowner, faced with French occupation, would lead armed villagers into the hills, secure the cooperation of the nearby villages, harass the enemy troops, and return after the enemy decamped or was killed. By the years 1811–13, the movement had grown in size and shape, fleshed out by refugees, deserters, and criminal elements. It achieved a certain density in Galicia, Navarre, and Catalonia—longtime haunts of smugglers and brigands. In popular terminology, guerrilla warriors were called "land corsairs."[22]

Irregular combat—nowadays known in military jargon as asymmetrical warfare—did not begin with the Spaniards, but it has long been identified with and defined by their struggle. A few years after it ended, an anonymous Neapolitan veteran of this war who, with thousands of other Italians, had fought on the French side, offered a firsthand description of bands large and small that flooded enemy-occupied territory, mounted improvised assaults and rapid withdrawals, and destroyed lines of supply and communications. The guerrillas knew when to flee and when to fight. Each success drew more of the population into the struggle. Then the bands united, tried to create a proto-state, and expelled the enemy.[23] By demoralizing the enemy, assaulting collaborators, and exacting forced requisitions from the people, guerrilla bands also created an atmosphere of permanent menace, insecurity, and instability. "A war of civilians if not quite a civil war," one historian has called it.[24] In fact, it was that also, since some pro-French elements set their own bands on the patriots.

The presence in the Spanish maelstrom of Napoleonic multinational troops complicated the martial landscape. Italians in particular were flung into battle from one corner of Europe to another: Germany, Switzerland, the Tyrol, Carinthia, Illyria, Dalmatia, the Ionian Islands—and above all Spain and Russia. Some thirty thousand Italians served in the Iberian Peninsula, and only nine thousand returned.[25] Between 1808 and 1812 several waves arrived. About two thousand came from the Kingdom of Naples, among them a few who would return to Spain in 1823 to defend it against a different French invading army. The Italians and the French, shocked by guerrilla warfare, became among the first to describe it in what now sound like clichés. But their remarks gave it wide publicity. Accustomed to conventional battlefield warfare, they registered their amazement at the sadism exhibited on both sides.[26]

A Russian account reported that few guerrillas who entered the regular forces "knew how to subordinate their wild hatred to the discipline of the barracks." They declared it no sin to kill a Frenchman, an act justified for the sake of Spain.[27] Others told of how guerrillas stuffed a dead enemy's genitals in his mouth and of how the Napoleonic invaders sometimes tortured children and forced their parents to watch. One Italian veteran called the struggle "war in miniature one piece at a time."[28] The invaders seemed willfully blind to their own depredations. A Dalmatian officer, Milossevitz (Milošević), spoke of "ignorant and superstitious people," an elusive enemy comprising the entire population, who struck and then disappeared into inhospitable and mountainous land.[29]

Polish units of the Napoleonic army made their way to Spain as well in separate infantry and cavalry units. General Józef Chłopicki headed the Vistula Legion and later became a leader in the 1830 Polish uprising. A light cavalry unit, whom the Spaniards dubbed "los infernos lanceros," won renown for a brilliant mounted charge at Somosierra, opening the road to Madrid. One of the officers, Colonel Andrzej Niegolewski, left an account stressing the honorable service of his compatriots. But to the Spanish resistance, the Poles, like other forces in Spain, had come as conquerors, whatever they thought of their mission.[30] Ludwik Mateusz Dembowski (1768–1812)—Polish patriot, Jacobin, and Napoleonic officer—in 1808 described guerrilla fanaticism, wily traps, scorched earth, and bloody sieges. "The Spanish priests," he related, "with a crucifix in one hand and a dagger in the other have become popular leaders."[31] Some things die hard: in the Spanish Civil War of the 1930s, a Nationalist commander described his soldiers as holding a grenade in one hand and a rosary in the other.[32] Some witnesses thought the Poles to be the most barbarous of the invaders. Vengeance fueled unspeakable levels of cruelty and atrocities. There can be no denying those of the guerrilla forces, but is there any way to measure the relative sadism of either side? Goya's series *The Disasters of War*, though exhibited much later, was the first to capture on canvas the "blood-soaked awfulness of the world" in such horrifying detail.[33]

Then and ever since, a mythic halo, fashioned by Spaniards and foreigners alike, has surrounded the Spanish guerrillas, celebrating them as noble heroes, freedom fighters, popular idols, liberals, Robin Hoods, and most of all victorious underdogs who defeated the French. British historian Charles Esdaile, using archival sources, has demythologized the Spanish guerrillas and nearly obliterated their lingering romantic image. He argues that the behavior of the occupying troops rather than any ideology accounted for the emergence of peasant guerrilla bands, though social and economic grievances and the protection of traditional society got blended in, as in other European resistance movements. Many bands attracted deserters, draft dodgers, brigands, and other criminals. Though some commanders tried to control or punish bandit-like behavior, they had limited success. But Esdaile also rescues the irregulars from demonization by the French enemy. Guerrilla activity offered a mixed picture and one in perpetual flux. Most important, he concludes that, contrary to popular wisdom, Spain witnessed no massive popular support for the war of liberation—whether driven by Catholic faith or by constitutional liberalism. Guerrilla leaders, to the extent that they held any political views, could come from the left, the right, or anywhere else.[34]

Whatever the reality on the ground, many Spaniards looked at a war being waged by Spanish guerrillas and regulars together with the British (whose contribution was decisive) as an emphatically *Spanish* war of liberation from a foreign despot. The experience of this war, as in most others—especially against an enemy foreign occupier—spurred influential Spaniards to reexamine fundamental values, those that divide a people as well as those that unite them.

During the merciless saga unfolding in Spain, an assembly of provincial juntas—committees of notables—formed a Supreme Central Junta in the town at Aranjuez. On request, the junta received from around the country some 150 *cahiers*—position papers—that expressed a range of identifiable political colorings and views on the purpose of the war. All parties saw the enemy as the tyrant Bonaparte, and the war's object as the restoration of Fernando VII. A cautious "legitimist" current was flanked by two others that foreshadowed a polarity that would rend Spain for generations: a die-hard right interested mainly or only in the restoration of deposed King Fernando VII, and an emerging left that wished to harness the national liberation war to a liberal political struggle for freedom within Spain—thus linking the word "liberal" with liberation.[35]

The left, a highly variegated and fluid group, divided during this war over cooperation with the French invaders and King Joseph. *Afrancesados*, either reluctantly or enthusiastically, viewed the Napoleonic presence in Spain as a progressive moment. Their opponents adhered to straightforwardly patriotic and anti-French aims: a kind of national liberalism set against Napoleon's emphatically international and rational but none too liberal imperial ideology. Spanish liberals desired to bring back the king as a constitutional monarch. Fusing Enlightenment ideas and the invented traditions of an imagined past of "historical liberties," they sought major reform as the inspiration to fight on and as the key to victory. Their gradually unfolding project included a unicameral parliament with no separate chamber of corporate power and identity for the privileged noble elite and clergy; a flow of laws to expand the market; a guarantee of personal security, civil rights, and freedom of expression; and a curb on the influence of the papacy, the Inquisition, and the monastic clergy.[36]

Spanish liberals were an eclectic bunch: prominent patriots such as the Count of Toreno and Manuel José Quintana, plus lesser-known figures from a few liberal bases including Cadiz, Corunna, Oviedo, and Valencia.[37] In order to fuse their project with the patriotic liberation and thereby point the anti-French struggle in the proper direction, liberals won support from some leaders of guerrilla units such as Juan Díaz Porlier and Don Luis Lacy. This natural desire to co-opt heroes and appropriate widespread combative emotional capital did not enjoy universal success. Many a liberal smile hid a heart full of ambition. And some converts turned out to be a mixed blessing. One of the most spectacular guerrilla chiefs, Francisco Espoz y Mina, took his time to become an anti-absolutist and thus an ally of the liberals. As with many partisan leaders, he was wreathed in lore. He was said to have initially greeted the constitution of 1812 by nailing a copy to a tree and "executing" it. The political commitment of Mina and many others was secondary to various personal motives.[38] Nevertheless, guerrilla leaders were seen as national heroes at the time; and some became martyrs after Fernando was restored. As the liberal movement began to take shape out of the turbulence of war, it became and remained heterogeneous in social origins and aspirations; and it nursed a healthy fear of the fury of the masses, now unleashed in the war against the French.

Absolutists of all stripes and all classes blasted the liberals as children of 1789. Among the first to become openly hostile as well as secretly intriguing could be found groups with names such as Persians, Immobiles, or Serviles; in some ways, they foreshadowed the Carlists of the nineteenth century and the Fran-coists and post-Franco "Bunker" of the twentieth. A vital ally of the right, the clergy, emerged when the French occupiers closed many monasteries, drasti-cally reduced the number of religious orders, took their property and revenue, abolished the Inquisition, and dissolved the ecclesiastical courts. The Spanish right included those grandees who wanted a king they alone could control; but they interpreted the war as an anti-French "crusade for Church and king."[39] Since some liberals shared the invaders' willingness to weaken some aspects of ecclesi-astical life and property, they were marked as anti-church, especially by the monks who became a major force of anti-liberalism.[40] Many preachers spewed forth hatred of both the French occupiers and the burgeoning Spanish liberals. The vast majority of the clergy had little if any knowledge of Napoleon's utili-tarian, even cynical view of the church as mostly a guarantee of social order— and they would have denied such a perspective. He was to them the Antichrist, the Beast with Seven Heads; and his troops the agents of world atheism. In one sample of guerrilla fighters with known occupations, a fairly large percentage were clergy—137 out of 322.[41] Some of these were foot soldiers of the right. Prominent among them was Jerónimo Merino, known as "El Cura" (The Priest), who became one of the most ferocious of the anti-liberals. Yet Spanish parish priests, friars, and monks exhibited a wide variety of motivations. Neither a uni-fied liberal nor a reactionary clergy held sway during the war with the French.

All the political formations arising at the time emanated from a small elite and not from the ground up. Yet, the bare notion that Spain lacked large-scale popular support for the War of Independence—the title later bestowed on it—needs some qualification. The right and left political currents in this war, the emotional and doctrinal defiance shown by the Catholic Church, and the dramatic exploits of the guerrillas—however criminally and counterproductively some acted—produced an environment that looked like a massive, all-national resistance movement not only in the haze of retrospective mythology but at the time as well. The Spanish resistance, far from being only a battle of kings, generated widespread passions about the enemy invader as an alien force and about the future of a postwar Spain. And so it was seen by sympathizers all over Europe.

Revolutionary Cadiz

The Atlantic port city of Cadiz, appended to a curving peninsula jutting out from southern Spain, fell under threat of occupation from the French military forces in 1810. At this moment, one of the darkest of the war, Spanish deputies gathered in a Cortes to make a constitution. One historian has argued that Cadiz was no hotbed of liberal ideas and that most of the liberal-minded leaders of the 1810 Cortes hailed from other parts of Spain.[42] True, but Cadiz, the country's busiest port, outstripping even Barcelona, had become a refuge for progressive elements from all over the country. A Spanish patriot called the city "the tabernacle of Spanish independence."[43] Liberals all over Europe recognized and hailed the city of Cadiz as the birthplace of Spanish constitutionalism. Indeed, Cadiz and its suburb León entered the bellicose lexicon of rebels in Naples, Greece, and Russia.

Cadiz (the name means "fortified place" in Phoenician), originally an island at the delta of the Guadalete River, developed after 1492 into a natural port for Spain's Atlantic fleet, an emporium for Latin American trade, and a target of vicious raids by English battle fleets and Barbary corsairs. Its thriving merchants and businessmen with international connections fed off the colonial system until liberation wars erupted in the new world. In Cadiz, a beehive of colonials and a haven of foreigners, money counted and relative openness and tolerance prevailed.[44] With the biggest concentration of Latin Americans in all of Spain, Cadiz acquired a reputation not only for cosmopolitanism but also as an underground headquarters and recruiting station for Latin American liberators such as Francisco Miranda, who perished in a Cadiz dungeon. Since Madrid, now ruled by a usurper, had lost its charisma as a sacred center, Cadiz became the unofficial capital of the resistance.

Cadiz, where streets, theaters, and cafés came alive with talk, enjoyed a Mediterranean climate and an air of lightness and energy. Its courtyards and patios flowed into the streets. Sidewalk cafés along fine promenades such as Calle Ancha—Broad Street—hosted society and literary figures and visiting foreigners. A Russian naval officer from one of the frigates that the tsar sold to Spain marveled in 1818 at the crowds and saw the cafés and squares as sites of adventure.[45] Café habitués read newspapers and journals, socialized, mixed gossip with political talk, and sometimes forged friendships and associations. A modern scholar sees the café in this era as a kind of anti-salon, a counter-academy, and to some degree an alternative to the church as a meeting place of sociability— somewhere between aristocratic salon and plebeian wine shop.[46] Inside the homes of the educated elite flourished the *tertulia*, a political and literary salon, the term originating from the section in the theater where learned wits sat and often quoted Tertullian, the Roman Christian.[47] Some *tertulias* played host to enlightened clergymen and to liberal leaders such as Augustín Argüelles, Toreno, Quintana, and Martínez de la Rosa.[48] The number of such liberal spirits increased as refugees from battle-torn Spain poured in.

The exact origin of the Spanish noun *liberal* remains obscure. In its first use in Britain, as "liberales," British statesman Castlereagh in 1816 equated them with Jacobins.[49] But the word enjoyed wide currency in many tongues long before that. Among the various sources and inspirations for Spanish liberal ideals one must count the Spanish Enlightenment, the ideas of the hated French occupiers, and British political traditions.[50] In Cadiz, the exchange and interaction of opinion and information from street, café, *tertulia*, and press (cafés in print) raised the political consciousness of the intelligentsia and widened its discourse into public opinion. From it emerged a still fluid liberalism.[51] Beneath the open forum of public opinion, secret societies emerged from 1808 onward with links to English and French Freemasonry. Not always political in the narrow sense, Spanish Masons for the most part opposed popular superstition and ignorance and blamed the Inquisition for both.[52]

Cadiz, already a forcing house of new ideas and a home to people of broad horizons, in 1810 became the target of a definitive French military conquest and a rallying point for the resistance. In January of that year, King Joseph invaded the southern province of Andalusia, a "Patriot stronghold."[53] The resisting Junta had retreated to Seville, where the liberals Gaspar Melchior de Jovellanos and Manuel José Quintana called for the summoning of a Cortes. Pressed further by the advancing French, the Junta withdrew from Seville to Leon, on the outskirts of Cadiz. Having ruled (or made claim to rule) over unoccupied Spain for sixteen months, the Junta ceded its power to a regency. Bowing to a near universal, if abstract, love for "the Desired One," the liberals emphatically recognized the exiled king as the legitimate monarch. But they also tried to leverage the resistance movement into the summoning of a body that would continue the armed snuggle against the French, expel them, and return Fernando to the throne as a constitutional monarch.

Arriving in Cadiz, the liberal leaders worked furiously for their vision of a nationally elected Cortes that would mount reforms and issue a new constitution. Two years after the independence struggle began, Cadiz and León became the birthplace of that constitution. Rough-and-ready elections took place where feasible; substitutes were appointed to represent those in occupied areas unable to vote and in the Americas. On September 24, 1810, the new deputies marched in a procession through the streets of León along a route lined with troops and cheering crowds shouting vivas and singing patriotic songs from the balconies. At the Church of San Pedro, the archbishop of Toledo officiated at a mass of the Holy Spirit and swore in the deputies. They vowed to uphold the Catholic religion and allow no other faith in Spain, evict the oppressor, and preserve entire the dominions of Fernando VII. From the church, the company marched to the theater that became the first home of the Cortes.[54]

The Cortes deputies sat in the parterre and loges of the theater facing a throne, surrounded by ermine, representing the absent King Fernando VII. Father Diego Múñoz Torrero, former rector of the University of Salamanca and a liberal Catholic priest, delivered a memorable speech on the division of powers and the inviolability of the Cortes deputies.[55] Like most brand-new deliberative bodies, this one suffered from some ego-fed oratory, harsh debates, and public rowdiness. Citizens in the gallery viewed the proceedings as a spectacle and occasionally booed long-winded speakers. The rare angry public protest, exaggerated by historians, dealt with marginal matters. For example, in cold weather the crowd began to resent the banning of their capes and caps—a security measure, since those garments were commonly used in Spain and elsewhere by assassins to conceal weapons (thus the origin of the term "cloak and dagger"). A few months after the Cortes opened, the French, who had arrived on the outskirts of León, laid siege to it. The whizzing cannonballs and the church bells that rang the alarm added an aura of menace to the Cortes for the next two years until the siege was lifted. The martial thunder may have frightened some, but it caused little physical damage and none to the work of the Cortes.[56]

The Cortes had at first 102 deputies, including 46 for the occupied areas and 28 for the American colonies; the total later swelled to 223. Among the nobles, bureaucrats, and clergy (which accounted for about a third, including five bishops) sat many lay children of the Enlightenment and priests who desired a genuine reformist parliamentary monarchy.[57] But against these ranged conservatives or Serviles, both words first used here in Cadiz.[58] The Serviles, apparently happy to bear such a label, held a self-consciously unctuous and deferential loyalty to the absolutist king. Liberals prevailed on the big issue: to modernize the nation by a series of drastic reforms embodied in a constitution. The victors softened the impact of change at the very first session by declaring that while sovereignty resided in the Cortes, Fernando VII remained the sole legitimate monarch, his previous abdication null and void. In the following year, the Cortes issued one of many statements exalting the king, and it inaugurated San Fernando Day as a religious festival to honor "the rising of the Nation in the name of King Fernando VII."[59]

But the lawmakers also made symbolic points by decreeing early on that in every Spanish city a Te Deum was to be sung and artillery salvos fired to demonstrate popular gratitude for the formation of the Cortes.[60] While the drafting of the new constitution was proceeding, the Cortes passed a series of reforms inspired by British practice and by the last fifty years of revolutionary history in Europe and America. It introduced freedom of the press in order to protect the people from the whims of rulers and as "a means of enlightening the nation in general and the only way to raise the consciousness of true public opinion."[61] It passed a law of habeas corpus and an order for speedier judicial procedure in the military. The deputies voted unanimously to "abolish torture forever in all the dominions of the Spanish monarchy" and passed a decree ending evil conditions in the prisons.[62] On the social front, where liberalism always proved weak in practice, the Cortes abolished feudal jurisdictions and special class-based privileges on paper. But it ran out of the time needed to enforce the new dispensation and also incurred the enmity of the large landowners.

The role of two crucial institutions in any state of this period—the army and the church—had to be redefined in Spain with great care. Both had deep roots in the nation's history and mythology; both retained a conservatism natural to their functions and thus a potential resistance to change. The old Spanish army had recruited vagabonds, poor peasants, and even criminals; allowed the privileged to buy their way out of service; and required proof of nobility for entry into cadet schools. The ranks were subjected to blind obedience and atrocious punishments. The Cortes abolished abuse of soldiers and tried to strike a balance between discipline and citizens' rights. It endeavored to curtail buyouts but was forced to continue them for revenue purposes. Recognizing the valorous contribution of all social classes in the struggle against the French, the deputies opened certain military academies and higher ranks to all classes and introduced universal military liability.[63] The army was now meant to be an instrument comprising citizen soldiers for the defense of the nation and not of the king alone. The Cortes took control of the army's size, pay rates, discipline, and promotion schedules. It organized a national militia in each province for local defense and for a role in any larger war in time of need. The king was not permitted to deploy these forces without permission of the Cortes.[64] Predictably, some officers resented political interference with the army. Marshal Laguna praised the old army of "Chosen Spaniards" as a "sacrosanct military profession, the most glorious in society." He called the politicians "a troop of perverse egoists who were endangering public security."[65]

The clergy, though not united in a party, formed the largest single group in the Cortes, and included liberal priests and champions of social underdogs. The liberals—frocked or lay—tried to win the church's support by coining the slogan "religión y Patria." Most of all, the framers of the constitution staunchly supported the church. Article 12 stated that "the religion of the Spanish nation is and will forever be the one and true Catholic, Apostolic, Roman faith. The nation protects it with wise and just laws and forbids the exercise of any other."[66] In the opinion of one scholar, the constitution as a whole "exuded a powerful religious and even clerical and intolerant overtone."[67] The insistence on a Catholic monopoly resulted from a reluctant compromise by the liberals, who feared the reactionary church and believed that liberalism and Catholicism were compatible, though it turned out otherwise.[68]

The Catholic monopoly did not appease dyed-in-the-wool Serviles and conservative clerics. They resented ecclesiastical confiscations and the order for primary schools in the towns to teach the three Rs as well as religion.[69] The chief complaint arose over the fate of the Inquisition. A pamphlet of 1811, *The Incompatibility of Spanish Liberty with the Reestablishment of the Inquisition*, held that the main function of this obstacle to a free press and personal liberty and security was to "maintain ignorance and slavery."[70] When the Cortes dissolved the Inquisition in February 1813 and transferred its jurisdiction over crimes against the faith to the episcopal courts, the reaction was furious and instantaneous. Sixty of the 150 deputies voted against its abolition.[71] In fact, this issue reflected a deeper schism at Cadiz in which the clergy used the pulpit to vilify the constitution. One bishop called liberals "converts of the devil."[72] The foes of liberalism believed that a free press and the loss of the Inquisitorial jurisdiction meant the end of church power.[73] For some this meant the death of "Spanishness."

Church leaders of the right, having suffered what they considered the corrosive policies of the eighteenth-century Spanish Enlightenment, recoiled at the specter of the French Revolution and Napoleon. The war, the Latin American uprisings, and the dreaded epidemics seemed punishments for pagan godlessness. Many churchmen retreated into Old Testament apocalyptic rage and a thirst for theocracy to stem the tide. Thus the fight against Napoleon, which for the liberals marked a road to constitutionalism, was for the conservative clergy a prelude to revivalism. The war against the French invader made some prelates and friars patriotic in a way that was "intolerant, militant, and hostile to the secular world." Though the Cortes displayed much less anti-clericalism than did the usurper Joseph, anti-liberal churchmen turned against that body as well and their enmity shifted from the French to the Spanish foe within.[74]

A little-noted aspect of Spanish anti-liberalism in this era was the occasional resurfacing of a deep historic anti-Semitism, indirectly powered by the great myths of the Reconquista, El Cid, Santiago Matamoros, Philip II, Ignatius Loyola, and St. Teresa. This led to periodic attacks on the Jews remaining since the 1492 expulsion and to the projection of a reified "Jewish" identity upon the constitutionalists. Spanish anti-Semites, like those elsewhere, included Jews in an amalgam of their foes—masons, heretics, liberals. During debates on the abolition of the Inquisition, liberals who criticized that body for its historical persecution of Jews drew the fire of clerical malice. Later, in the years of the Trienio (1820–23), occasional anti-Semitic publications sought to weld the diabolical popular image of Jews with that of liberalism, though political anti-Semitism lacked the force it would have during later the Carlist wars. In the early 1820s, liberals and Enlightenment figures as such had become much more dangerous to the political right than the Jews and the Masons had ever been.[75]

The Constitution of 1812, capstone of the Cortes' new legal edifice, emerged from a committee of fourteen deputies, including five liberal clerics. Two of them, Diego Múñoz Torrero and Augustín Argüelles, were among its chief architects. The drafters reported out to the Cortes in August 1811, and the discussion of the document's 384 articles lasted seven months. It put lawmaking exclusively into the hands of the Cortes. The king could delay an act by suspensive veto but could not overrule it or dissolve the Cortes. Article 168 declared the sanctity and inviolability of the king's person, and articles 169–73 set out a whole range of executive powers as well as strict limitations on ceding territory, making aggressive alliances, ordering arrests, and even marrying without the Cortes' permission. Article 172—perhaps inspired by the 1791 French constitution and Louis XVI's flight to Varennes—ruled that the monarch's leaving the country without permission would be deemed an act of abdication.[76]

A small State Council chosen by king and Cortes was to monitor the sovereign's actions. The new unicameral Cortes was to meet for three months each year and be reelected every two years. One deputy represented seventy thousand voters; a literacy requirement would take force only in 1830. The cabinet ministers were to be appointed by the king but responsible to the Cortes. The constitution incorporated much of the legislation passed between 1810 and 1812: a free press, equality of citizens before a uniform code of law, inviolability of the individual, an independent judiciary, prison reform, and—in practice— economic benefits for the privileged middle-class buyers of disentailed and monastic lands.[77]

One of the many charges leveled against the constitution was that it copied the French Revolution's constitution of 1791, which created a constitutional monarchy with a unicameral legislature. Although the Spaniards borrowed some elements from that document, it in turn had taken things from U.S. constitutional history. Authors of such documents had been drawing on each other since the American revolution. The drafters of the 1812 constitution argued for its legitimacy by challenging the legality of Fernando's abdication, which had been done without consulting any Spanish body and had resulted in usurpation of the crown by a French puppet. The Spanish article on religion had no equivalent in the French constitution of 1791. In fact, Spanish liberals consistently and vocally rejected the French Revolution as a model. Their constitution also diverged considerably from the dozen or so authoritarian instruments issued to various Napoleonic satellites in Europe.[78]

Foreign inspiration can hardly be denied, especially in the broader sense of the French Enlightenment and the universalistic dimensions of the 1789 Revolution. The unwritten British constitution had some impact, partly reflecting the admiration of those Spaniards who had lived in England and the prestige of the Duke of Wellington's army that was on the point of expelling the French. From Italy came the powerful writings of Cesare Beccaria on the humanitarian treatment of convicts. The framers of the 1812 document could also allude to many medieval and recent indigenous sources and practices, many of them imagined, a practice documented meticulously by Karl Marx in a learned essay on the Spanish revolution.[79] But although the framers liked to invoke deep precedent, the reason for creating a unicameral parliament rested partly on the hostility of the Cadiz Cortes to the aristocracy.[80]

What the Spanish Serviles hated most about the constitution was that it ascribed sovereignty to the nation.[81] But as critics on the left have pointed out ever since, the 1812 constitution fell far short of democracy. Since its definition of Spain embraced both hemispheres, the constitution shortchanged some colonials by erecting qualifications for citizenship for those not of Spanish lineage (articles 18, 22, and 23).[82] Whenever land and capital change hands by fiat in a non-socialist revolution, those in the know or with ready funds have the edge in purchasing power—whether in 1790s France or 1990s Russia. When the liberal Cortes ordered the takeover of ecclesiastical and village communal lands for resale, those with money were able to buy them. This and the assault on guilds generated popular discontent, so by 1813 voters began to back the traditionalists.[83] Then of course there was the intolerant religious clause. The 1812 constitution was, like most others in Europe and America of that era, an instrument of its times, a liberal rather than democratic document, though more democratic than most. All adult males could vote except household servants, criminals, monks, and the jobless. On the technical side, Bentham bemoaned the infrequent elections and the too brief sessions of the Cortes.[84]

Foreign critiques of the constitution focused on its alleged radicalism. The great Swiss conservative juridical scholar of Restoration Europe, Karl Ludwig Haller, who believed that the state was the property of the prince, predictably spoke of the constitution's "malignity and absurdity." Some liberals, such as the Abbé de Pradt and Benjamin Constant, lamented the lack of an upper chamber.[85] Michael Quin, though sympathetic to the constitutional regime, also bemoaned the lack of a second chamber to balance the too powerful and popularly elected Cortes. Though nobles were numerous and unpopular, he noted, some competent grandees could have brought restraint and balance through an upper house.[86] Moderate Spanish liberals in 1812 and in the 1820s shared this view.

Jovellanos corresponded with British liberal Lord Holland about the possibility of a House of Lords for his own country.[87] European leftists defended and even praised the unicameral legislature of Spain as a democratic device. To Jeremy Bentham, whom the Spanish later consulted on their constitution, an upper chamber was anathema.[88] During the Liberal Trienio of the 1820s, unicameralism became one of the burning issues dividing radicals from moderates.

The drafters of the constitution stressed the need to limit the absolute power of the king, noble privilege, and ecclesiastical property. They explained the unicameral Cortes as a mechanism to deny the all too numerous and all too wealthy clergy undue influence in lawmaking. The liberal Quintana believed, as did many others, that an upper house would have been a base of reaction.[89] Thus the English model of bicameralism, though it had had many admirers in Spain, failed to take root. Cortes, rightly suspicious of an absolutist king, had to weaken his power and that of the nobles and clergy in order to get through reforms. Even many royalists agreed to curb the king, as long as they could protect their own privileges and those of the clergy.[90] The drafters wished to provide liberty of person, freedom of the press, rational administration, an honest system of justice and finances, elections, responsible government, and national education. Citing deep if sketchy historical precedent back to the time of the Visigoths, they argued that this constitution was neither invented out of thin air nor copied from foreign models. In a sweeping critique of absolute monarchy, the drafters stated that all history had proved that "there can be no liberty nor security, and by the same rule no justice nor prosperity, in a state in which the exercise of all authority is united in one sole hand." And in identifying constitutional rule with inclusiveness and a national identity based on mutual respect, the document declared that henceforth "Spaniards of all classes, of all ages, and of all conditions, will know what they are."[91]

Manuel Quintana, writing to Lord Holland, offered a brilliant apologia. Granting that no constitution could satisfy everyone, he asserted that the Spanish document, created by some of the country's most patriotic elements, hardly deserved the obloquy heaped upon it from some quarters. It was by no means the product of a hastily gathered radical caucus. The drafters labored over it for two years and the assembled Cortes debated it for seven months in a besieged city in the middle of a war. Though they may have represented only a minute portion of the population, Quintana conceded, they stood with the majority of the nation in opposing a usurper. Their constitution endeavored to respect tradition by invoking the historic freedoms of olden days; to confront the modern age by deploying the words *nación* and *libertad* again and again; and to solemnize the constitution by calling it Sagrado Código, the Sacred Codex of the nation.[92]

This code, reflecting the most progressive thought in the Spain of its time, also scored high on human rights and granted a suffrage far broader than, for example, that in Britain. The structure of the constitution did not itself cause the absence of key ingredients for moderate governance: fairness, compromise, and the acceptance of free discussion instead of personal animosities and fearful politics. A modern historian likened the motivations and practicality of the Cortes and its constitution to the two-faced Janus.

> For the radicalism of its principles, its members are revolutionaries, "Jacobins" as their enemies called them. But for their constant efforts to establish a representative regime, they are, certainly, moderates. And [are so] for being the first modern constitutionalists who realized their goals in a constitution, and for a time in real life. And so its importance and influence in Europe lasted in Portugal and in Italy, in far-off Russia, even in France. So too [did] the contradictions between its moderate intentions and its radical stance towards society's resistance to its work.[93]

Except for the arguable notion that the influence of the Cadiz experiment lasted, this is a reasonable judgment.

On January 21, 1812, the British inflicted a crucial defeat on French arms at the Battle of Vitoria. Two months later, the Cortes published the constitution. To erase the embarrassment of 1808, it chose for promulgation March 19, the day of Carlos IV's abdication and the name day of the hated King Joseph Bonaparte. Like all such solemn public rites of passage in Spanish history, the day of publication became a festival. For the moment, the Serviles and the liberals closed ranks to praise "a plebiscite of unity." In a carefully orchestrated parade, notables joined the deputies. With troops lining the road, the company marched to key sites in Cadiz and its environs to the sound of French siege guns. A Te Deum was sung at the Church of the Carmelite Order and high officials solemnly read selections from the constitution at four principal squares where portraits of Fernando VII, covered when not addressed, stood on display beneath a canopy. The ceremonies in word and picture were saturated with images of and references to the monarch. A cavalry ride past with martial music was followed by evening festivities and illumination. All this took place under a torrential rain that some saw as a bad omen. In a familiar revolutionary gesture, the celebration decree ordered inspectors to visit prisons in order to release those deemed wrongly jailed.[94]

The Cortes of 1810 inaugurated significant revolutionary changes in the country. But laws, abstract political concepts, and the five-syllable Spanish word *constitución* hardly resonated with a largely illiterate, religious, and conservative peasantry. Liberal sympathizers with the new order in the years 1808–14 attempted to win popular support by means of press, theater, iconography, songs, renaming of streets and squares, and ecclesiastical pedagogy such as sermons and political catechisms. They deployed their arts mostly in the cities, where readers and spectators could be found. When possible or relevant, they cleverly played to the anti-Napoleonic fury of the church and the people and harnessed it to the novel cause of political freedom.

In 1808, the poet Manuel José Quintana (1772–1857), who opposed the French Revolution and "the chains of absolute power" it would bring to Spain,[95] founded the journal *Seminario patriótico*, a high-toned review that established the link between liberal ideas and the patriotic struggle. He announced that the "yoke of tyranny" was to be thrown off not only by evicting the French, but by establishing a constitution. He argued that the *nation* held mastery over the country in the absence of the king[96] and, naively, that "public opinion is stronger than the repressive authority of armies."[97] Quintana, whose enthusiastic patriotic verse earned him the role of Spain's national poet of that era, made the journalism of ideas mesh with that of patriotic combat as political discourse began to swell from the Enlightenment salons and *tertulias* into a larger public sphere.[98]

Local newspapers from the very outset of the struggle employed the black-and-white dichotomies that ever accompany warfare. For example, in 1808, a Seville paper called the invaders "assassins of the North"—a geographical term laden with old meaning, from the Roman to the Gothic invasions—who were bringing tyranny, oppression, and slavery. Spaniards, on behalf of "religion and the customs of [their] ancestors" faced a "legion of Vandals." A Seville general told his readers that "the spark of patriotism has ignited in your breasts." A Granada "declamation against Bonaparte" asserted that all of Europe lay beneath his yoke while Spain had risen gloriously. These few examples typify scores, if not hundreds, of pieces employing Manichean language with an Iberian gloss.[99]

As in most of Europe, performing arts rather than print had the best chance of reaching the lower classes. Partly because of this, many Spanish secular and clerical conservatives condemned theater. Don Simón López, citing the ancients, the church fathers, and Rousseau, opposed "theaters and profane spectacles as a school for all the passions, a classroom for disease, and the occupation of the idle and the dissolute." Theater, he said, led to the "corruption of customs and the feminization of the people."[100] Traditionalists saw public expressive space as belonging exclusively to church, crown, and army. The Servile press suggested that theater, the bane of religion, should be replaced by processions of penitents. A vivid model for this idea, Seville's spectacular Holy Week reenactment of Calvary, featured hooded penitents marching alongside the three crosses.[101] Since it was customary in Spain to shutter theaters in time of war, in 1810 a clerical Cortes deputy moved to close them. Another proposed to open theaters as a Christmas gift to the people of Cadiz and to celebrate the election of a new president of the Cortes. His motion lost in a close vote and the theaters were shut down for about a year. When they reopened in 1811, the citizens of Cadiz were overjoyed. The Cortes also took measures to raise the status of actors who labored under severe social stigmatism.[102] The liberal press perceived theater as a school of good behavior, public morality, and wartime morale, and a way to raise funds for the defense of the city. The contrasting convictions of theater mirrored in miniature the clash of larger worldviews about human nature, religion, patriotism, and morality.

The Spanish stage, as elsewhere in Europe, usually presented mixed and alternating genres, though the anti-theater party apparently made no distinction between light and often vulgar works and those bristling with patriotic content. The *zarzuela*, a local version of operetta, and the *sainete*—a twenty-five-minute satirical treat or tidbit—continued to amuse popular audiences, as did the classics of Calderón and Lope de Vega. But from 1808 onward, they shared the stages of Free Spain, particularly Cadiz, with war bulletins, patriotic hymns and symphonies, allegories celebrating the constitution, and plays featuring the exploits of the guerrilla commanders, Espoz y Mina and Juan Martín Díez, known as "El Empecinado" (The Stubborn One). Pious, chauvinistic historical dramas about the Reconquista in the Iberian Peninsula, the conquistadores of Latin America, and glorious episodes from the history of Spain's current allies Russia and Britain offered much-needed morale-building and hopes for a Spanish victory.[103]

Format and esthetic quality varied wildly. As early as 1808, Cadiz audiences attended Francisco Martínez de Aguilar's one-act melodrama celebrating a recent Spanish victory, probably at Bailén. Like potboilers all over Europe at that time, it offered instead of a plotted drama a pageant designed to inspire crowds of civilians and soldiers. The author managed to capture the dual themes of the hour. His characters, each personifying provinces of Spain, intoned their vivas, oaths, and choral tributes not only to the absent king but also to reified versions of Law, Religion, and Freedom.[104] Four years later, in the same city, the Cortes was acclaimed and honored in a classic play by the Piedmontese Vittorio Alfieri (1749–1803). Retitled *Free Rome*, an allusion to Free Cadiz, it was an adaptation of the author's *The First Brutus*, one of the many cultural gestures toward classical antiquity.[105]

The master of the dramatic stage in these years, Francisco Martínez de la Rosa (1789–1861)—poet, playwright, activist, and professor of moral philosophy at the University of Granada—arrived in Cadiz early in 1811, brimming with political ideas drawn from an array of contradictory sources, including Burke and Chateaubriand, Montesquieu, Constant, and Bentham. Martínez de la Rosa believed passionately that a constitution would stabilize and strengthen the monarchy itself, the best guard against internal turbulence and foreign aggression. He hoped that a free press, despite its inexperience and inevitable excesses, would, if subject to some control, become a school for democracy and develop the public spirit of the nation. No extremist, he expressed reservations about the unicameral system and felt a need for executive supremacy over popular power.[106]

As a playwright "for the public conscience,"[107] Martínez made his place in history with the staging of *The Widow of Padilla* in Cadiz in July 1812. For liberals, sixteenth-century Spain had become the mythic touchstone that classical Rome had been for the French Jacobins: a dueling ground of tyrants and heroic martyrs. The play summons up the revolt of freedom-loving Comuneros, led by Juan Padilla, during the reign of Emperor Charles V in 1521.[108] In the dramatic climax, the rebels are surrounded by the imperial forces in Toledo's Alcázar fortress, the scene of many a siege in Spanish history—not least that of 1936. Padilla's widow stabs herself on the fortress walls, uttering the words "My liberty up to my grave."[109] Containing overtones from Alfieri, Racine's *Andromaque*, Corneille's *Polyeuchte*, Sophocles' *Antigone*, and Addison's *Cato*, the work is suffused with the language of insurrection: honor, liberty, people, "oppressed fatherland," "eternal hatred of vile tyrants." The spectators, beholding the encircled Alcázar on stage, could hardly have missed the irony that they themselves lay under siege in the makeshift wooden theater as the French shells dropped around it.[110]

However much historical precedent and suggestive pathos that might be summoned up by such dramaturgy, it could by its very nature reach the very few—even in politically overheated Cadiz. The same goes for visual high culture. The first name—for most people the only one—that springs to the mind when thinking about Spanish culture of the Napoleonic epoch is Goya. The canvases on the Madrid uprisings and the Horrors of War have been canonical for almost two centuries. And his magnificent paintings on *Sunlight of Justice* and *Allegory of the Constitution of 1812*, done in the years 1812–14,[111] made his work part of the liberal art world. But they, like the drama, could have only the most limited impact.

The Cortes tried for greater outreach in a remarkably ambitious decree of August 14, 1812, which ordered the renaming of all the main squares of Spanish towns as Plaza de la Constitución, where a stone plaque would be installed honoring the document.[112] Town squares and main streets became the sites of the kind of celebratory culture that rushes in after every modern revolution since 1789.[113] The Spanish version combined classical motifs, native themes and forms, and the novel language—verbal and visual—of constitutional life. The old ceremonial trinity of throne-altar-army was amplified as the holy mass and the military parade were joined by speeches of the new political leaders bursting with liberal propaganda followed by the more expressive and traditional popular acts of jubilation.[114]

While intellectuals were forging a link between the fight against Napoleon and the fight for liberty at home, clerics were deploying politically inspired versions of the Catholic catechism for both causes. The catechism had long been employed for non-theological purposes. When French revolutionary catechisms began coming into Spain they were banned in 1790.[115] In 1807 the Spanish church, recognizing the importance of a standard Catholic catechism, got the approval of the still extant Inquisition and sponsored a document entitled "The Child Instructed in the Divine Word." Designed for all primary schools as "instruction in faith, morality, and society," it addressed a familiar problem in Christian countries: replacing uncanonical materials and substandard teaching with "phrases, sentences, and examples of infallible truth" and the believer's obligations to God, self, and society—in that order.[116] Here we have one of many statements underpinning the importance of the written word delivered to the faithful in catechistic form. It is hardly to be wondered, given the spread of social mimicry in revolutionary times, that the catechism was soon adopted for political messages.

With the onset of the French incursion into Spain, religious rhetoric was turned against them. At least two dozen or so catechisms were published in Spain between 1808 and 1814.[117] An early example, though not strictly a catechism, reduced the struggle to a Manichean duel between good and evil by way of fundamentalist wartime propaganda. *The Beast with Seven Heads and Ten Horns*, written by a Malaga priest in 1808, employed familiar if primitive exegesis. The author dipped into the Apocalypse, which had been invoked for ages in struggles of various kinds and was here adapted to demonize Napoleon. "And there shall come out of the sea a beast," wrote the Spanish cleric, "which has *seven heads and ten horns* and upon his horns ten crowns and upon his heads the names of blasphemy." Since Napoleon came from Corsica in the Tyrrhenian Sea (called in classical times "Mar Inferno"), and since he had placed crowns on the heads of his seven satellite kings, the case seemed closed, though the analogies went on for twenty-five pages.[118]

The *Popular Instruction in the Form of a Catechism on the Current War*, published by the Royal Press in 1809, laid out the usual themes of religious anti-French propaganda. The author, a Seville priest, spoke of the need to elucidate the struggle to those who were sacrificing their property, community, and lives. "Recognizing the influence that knowledge of religion has on the success of our enterprise, we must take from it for the sake of the fatherland every part which inspires love for it and the desire for liberty and decency." The priest welded anti-autocratic rhetoric to religion: "Q: Who is Napoleon? A. In the eyes of the world, he is seen as the emperor of the French; but in the eyes of the faith, he is none other than a scourge of God [sent] to punish many kings and kingdoms." From this flowed a catalogue of the crimes of Napoleon, "the public enemy of religion," and a unique and barbarous criminal. His allies and collaborators, including those in Spain, were represented as modern versions of Old Testament villains such as Holofernes.[119]

To fight the tyrant, resistance by all possible means was required. In addition to prayer and penance, the Seville cleric specified guerrilla warfare by bands of armed local residents ("guerrillas ó partidas de paisanos armadas"), a method, he emphasized, that Spaniards had used against the Moors—with whom he regularly compared the French. The hope of heaven and the bleak prospect of eternal torment constituted the best inducement to fight: "The holy fear of God inspires in the soldier who has it a fervent wish to fulfill the essential duties of his profession." On the vital issue of civil disobedience, he took the firm line that God's will superseded the ungodly orders of the occupiers. By biblical analogy, he hinted that collaborators should be burned at the stake. The author also made a brief excursion into secular politics. Answering the query about liberty, he averred that it was the preservation of religion, non-submission to the invader, and "maintenance of our constitution [here meaning traditional bodies], our wise legislation, and our venerable customs." This devout priest also recognized the need for change. For him, the simplistic doctrine of religious hatred in no way contradicted a belief, admittedly vague in formulation, in political reform. In this way of thinking lay the germ of some clerical support for the coming liberal constitution.[120] Patriotic catechisms, along with sermons and related popular materials, transformed the resistance movement into a holy obligation and preached that opposition to tyranny justified violence.

As the Spanish struggle against the French gradually swelled from a pure crusade to preserve church and dynasty against alien tyranny to one that included a defense of liberty, the catechism began to assume a more secular shape. An anonymous early liberal adaptation composed in Cadiz in 1810 clearly reflected or anticipated the doings in the Cortes. The author of this *Political Catechism for the Instruction of the Spanish People*, saw it as the way to reach a mass audience. In brevity and vividness, it outdid the earlier ones. The opener gets right to the point: "Q: What is the Cortes? A: A national congress convened by the king to ensure the well-being and happiness of the Nation." The questioner leads the respondent to dismiss all alternate forms of rule, from aristocracy to anarchy and tyranny. The purpose of the present Cortes, the catechism explains, is to bring about national unity, giving each a stake in the country through constitutional monarchy, separation of powers, rule of law, freedom of the press, and civil liberty—the last defined as follows: "Generally it is the ability of a man to do what he wants: but in society liberty is the ability to do whatever the laws do not forbid." The document mentions God only twice, offhand, and says nothing about the church or religion. Yet, keeping radical ideas at arm's length, the author stressed obedience to the law and the inviolability of the king who was, he said, unable or unwilling to disobey the law and the constitution.[121]

In Latin America, then in revolt against Spain, all kinds of catechisms sprouted—Catholic, liberal, and counterrevolutionary. One of the more radical versions, published in Chile in 1810, promoted a republic. "Monarchy," it stated, "is the rule of only one man of the same race and origins of all others, having the same form, essence, and substance, subject to the same miseries and ailments, whether he is called king, emperor, or Caesar."[122] In criticizing the theory of divine right of kings in the light of scripture, alluding to historical "freedoms," and affirming the right of rebellion, this document constructed an anti-monarchical thesis advanced by radicals in the era, including the Russian Decembrist catechism of 1825. The *Christian Political Catechism for the Youth of the Free People of South America*, published in 1811 by Jaime de Zudáñez, justified the independence struggle by reference to a contractual doctrine that the Americas had with the king and not with the Spanish people.[123]

A *Civic Catechism and Brief Summary of the Obligations of the Spaniard* appeared in both Madrid and Seville around 1808. Given its adaptations elsewhere in Europe, its major points are worth reproducing here in their original order. The questioner addresses a child (my ellipses indicate tangential gaps in the questioning). "Tell me, my lad, who are you?—A Spaniard. . . . What and how many are a [Spaniard's] obligations?—Three: to be a Roman Catholic; to defend his religion, his country, and his law, and to die rather than allow their destruction. . . . Who is the nemesis of our happiness?—The emperor of the French. . . . How many natures does [Napoleon] possess?—Two: one satanic and the other human. How many emperors are there?—One real emperor in three treasonous persons. Who are they?—Napoleon, Murat, and Godoy. Is one more wicked than the others?—No, father, all are equally so. Whence does Napoleon originate?—From hell and from sin. And Murat?—From Napoleon. And Godoy?—From the intrigue of the other two. What characterizes the first?—Pride, evil, and despotism. And the next?—Thievery, infamy, and cruelty. And the last?—Treason, lust, and ignorance."

The catechism continues: "Who are the French?—Former Christians and now heretics. . . . What is our country?—The union or congregation of many peoples ruled by the King under the same laws. . . . What punishment awaits the Spaniard who fails his duties?—Disgrace and a traitor's death. . . . Would it be a sin to kill the French?—No sir. Rather it should be rewarded if it liberates the country from humiliation, plunder, and deception. . . . In whom must we hope [for liberation]?—From the Lord our God, from our [sense of] justice, from the skills and loyalty of our generals and officers, and from our courage and our obedience. . . . What happiness must we seek?—The security of our rights and persons, the free exercise of our holy religion, and the establishment of a government arranged according to the current customs of Spain and relations with Europe. Then we do not have this?—Yes, father, but it is disorganized by the apathy of the highest authorities who have ruled us. Who must order things?—Spain to which this right exclusively belongs with an absolute prohibition of all that is foreign.

Who authorizes this plan?—FERNANDO VII, who wishes God to restore him to the comfort of our LOVE. Amen."[124]

The *Civic Catechism*, the only one that enjoyed a wide dissemination outside Spain—in Europe and Latin America—was imitated, for example in *Catechism of a German* (1809) by the romantic nationalist Heinrich von Kleist, who adapted the Spanish example to teach the transformation of Saxon provincialism to German national consciousness.[125] Most important, it was the source of the liberation-era French novel, discussed below, that connected teaching by catechism to the resistance movement and which in turn served as the direct inspiration of the Russian Decembrists in 1825. Both the catechism and its fictional version, while revering King Fernando, contained inflammatory language about tyranny, resistance, and sacrifice—themes of the Spanish war that so appealed to revolutionaries everywhere. In 1812, it was translated in the Russian journal *Son of the Fatherland*,[126] which observed that it was distributed to schools throughout Spain.

The Cadiz constitution mandated that the Catholic catechism taught in every school should include brief instructions about the pupil's civil obligation. It is difficult to gage how catechisms were circulated and their impact. But a clue arises from the 1824 French novel *Don Alonzo, or Spain*. The author, Count Narcisse-Achille de Salvandy, officer, liberal publicist, and later statesman under Louis-Philippe, traveled in Spain in 1820 and finished the book in 1823.[127] A mixture of fiction, travelogue, ethnography, and history, with multiple plots and characters, the four-volume novel is rich in incident and had a huge success among readers. Set in French-occupied Spain, with sorties to Latin America and elsewhere, it revolves around two patriots—a resistance hero and his angelic bride. A key scene, narrated by Father Pablo, takes place in a village in Old Castile where an engagement feast is being held beside the church. The passage vividly describes how the clergyman activated the emotions of his parishioners against Napoleon by reading them a "national catechism." Salvandy adapted the catechismal sequence from the memoirs of a French officer, M. De Naylies, published in Paris in 1817. He in turn had drawn material from "a catechism written by a Spanish clergyman" that he found in December 1809 in El Escorial.[128]

Father Pablo's words were taken, with much paraphrasing, editing, and rearrangement, from the abovementioned *Civic Catechism* of 1808. Catechizing members of the assembly, the priest begins with a young boy and then queries the parishioners one by one and receives their answers. When the issue of Napoleon's natures is raised, "three" is shouted from the crowd, and the priest corrects it. In one question, Salvandy substitutes the word *république* for the *pátria* of the original. And in answer to the question "What happiness must we seek?," he inserts "That which tyrants cannot give us" and the word *constitutions*. Other revisions were clearly designed to add drama to the catechistic scene.[129] It is reasonable to assume that moments like Salvandy's catechistic recruitment occurred in partisan camps and towns.

The idea behind the Spanish political catechism of the liberation era inspired the liberal catechisms of the constitutional period after 1820 and found resonance among Neapolitan, Greek, and Russian revolutionaries. Thousands of people were inducted by catechism into insurgent movements in 1820s Europe. The last of the four horsemen, Russian officer Sergei Muraviev-Apostol, combined a Spanish catechism and a moment in Salvandy's novel as a guide to lead his troops into the finale of the Decembrist uprising of 1825.

A Spanish-Russian connection of a different order in the years of the Cadiz Cortes also fed indirectly into the Decembrist movement. More immediately, through this connection—a treaty—both the Spanish king and a major foreign power recognized the new constitution. Before and during the deliberations of the Cortes, the French, still controlling vast stretches of the country, were using Spanish conscripts and prisoners of war to fight in Napoleon's European campaigns. As part of the crisscross of nations, the José Napoléon Regiment, founded in 1809 with French and Spanish officers and mostly Spanish soldiers (some of them war prisoners), was taken to France, issued light uniforms, and then sent to Russia in 1812[130]—a less voluntary harbinger of the Spanish Blue Division that went to the Soviet front in 1942. These and other Spanish forces totaled some forty thousand men. They fought valiantly in most of the main engagements, marching to Moscow and back with the Grande Armée. As with other components of the huge multinational army, many deserted and were shot; others committed atrocities, including the execution of Russian prisoners.[131]

In the midst of the war, the Russian foreign minister, N. P. Rumiantsev, wishing to cement relations with Spain, on July 1812 signed a treaty with the Spanish envoy to St. Petersburg, Zea Bermúdez, in the small Russian town of Velikie Luki. The newly allied powers agreed to continue the war against Napoleon; and the Russians recognized the exiled King Fernando VII, the Cadiz Cortes, and the Spanish constitution of 1812, a copy of which Zea Bermúdez give to Alexander I.[132] After the tsar ratified the treaty in October, a French translation of the Spanish constitution appeared in St. Petersburg; a year later a partial Russian translation was published in the widely read patriotic journal *Son of the Fatherland*.[133] That periodical also printed a Russian translation of the 1808 *Civic Catechism and Brief Summary of the Obligations of the Spaniard*.[134] Though distant from each other, tsarist Russia and liberal Spain were now joined in a common enterprise.

As part of a propaganda campaign targeting Frenchmen, Poles, Germans, Italians, and others in Napoleon's army, the Russian High Command issued an appeal, one of several, to Spanish and Portuguese troops in the Grande Armée. It urged them to emulate the "brave guerrillas" (*khrabrye partizanay*) fighting Napoleon in Spain by deserting to the Russian lines. "Spaniards and Portuguese! At long last give up the banner of your mortal enemy, serve henceforth only the cause of your fatherland and religion, follow the example of the noble forces of your countrymen." It promised that Tsar Alexander, "the friend of all subjugated peoples," would offer them a homeward journey across the sea to their native land and allow them "to liberate it from foreign enslavement."[135] The tsar also consented to the formation on Russian soil of a unit named after himself, the so-called Alejandro Regiment—eventually three battalions—comprising the 1800 Spanish prisoners of war who were being held at Tsarskoe Selo outside St. Petersburg. They swore an oath to King Fernando VII and the constitution. The regiment left Russia in the autumn of 1813 through Vilna and Riga, and then by sea to Spain, where it retained its name.[136]

Spaniards greeted the tsar's friendly gestures with unadorned pleasure. In summer 1812, publications lauded the valor of the Russian soldier and noted the alleged character similarities between Russians and Spaniards. One asserted that Tsar Alexander "reigns over the hearts of all the inhabitants of his vast empire" and that he must become the protector not only of northern Europe but of the South. *The Spanish Bee* wrote that "Russia's war has become as national as that of Spain" (a sentiment echoed by Clausewitz).[137] Solemn masses celebrated the Treaty of Velikie Luki.[138] In September, the Cadiz Cortes ratified the treaty and thanked the tsar for recognizing the constitution of 1812. In February 1813, it decreed that the Te Deum be said, fireworks organized, and cannons fired in public recognition of "the brilliant victories of our illustrious ally, the Emperor of all the Russias, over the legions of the tyrant of Europe, and the importance of those victories for the freedom of Spain and the peace of the entire world."[139] The ultimate, and ironic, Spanish tribute to the Russian emperor came on May 5, 1814, when a Spanish statesman recommended the erection of a monument and the striking of a medal to honor the tsar as liberator of Europe.[140]

Thus on the eve of King Fernando VII's return, the Cortes and its founders had issued a constitution recognized by their king and by the emperor of Russia, and had attempted with some success to spread the liberal doctrine among the Spanish people. Right up to 1814 the adherents of liberalism failed to foresee the ingratitude of that king and the fickleness of the Russian tsar. Optimism ruled in the Cortes. Martínez de la Rosa, for one, contrasted the despot Napoleon with the beloved Fernando VII, who he believed was a true constitutional king. After the Battle of Vitoria, the flight of King Joseph, and the withdrawal of the foreign invaders, in January 1814, the Cortes moved from Cádiz to Madrid to welcome home their king.

Beloved Avenger

King Fernando had been spending his exile at Valençay in idle luxury. Once the French were out of Spain and the country safe, the king returned, arriving on March 24, 1814. According to an unauthenticated story a Spaniard told to the British Benthamite Edward Blaquiere, as the king was traveling back to power through Saragossa and Valencia, his generals advised him to tear up the constitution—which he had not read before returning from France. By this account, the king actually defended the document to these men until a deputation of bishops managed to change his mind.[141] In any case, he was greeted by a letter from a faction of the Serviles known as the Persians. This sobriquet arose from a custom, referred to in the letter, wherein the authorities of ancient Persia would promote five days of anarchy between reigns so that the people would cherish the rule of order and tranquility restored by the next monarch.[142] The substance of this manifesto-like letter advised the king to dissolve the Cortes and abrogate the constitution. The absolutist General Francisco Javier Elío, who urged and supported this reactionary coup, would later pay for his action with his life.[143]

Fernando VII became convinced that the 1812 constitution was a spawn of the French Revolution and thus of anarchy and terror. He heeded the advice of the Persians and on May 4 abolished the Cortes and its ministries. His restoration brought back old abuses and privileges and a regime of censorship, pacification, and political persecution, and the king used the mob and the secret police to manipulate public opinion. In an example of the dreary pattern of sudden lower-class shifting of opinion, crowds who had cheered the constitution in 1812 now burned it and sang in the streets: "Death to the liberals, death to the constitution, and long live Fernando, with the country and religion"; and "Long live chains / Long live oppression; / Long live Fernando / Death to the Nation!"[144]

Though the severity of the "White terror" in the Restoration Bourbon monarchies of France, Spain, and Naples has often been exaggerated, the Spanish case was vindictive by any standards. Minister of war General Francisco Eguía, a bewigged reactionary foe of Spain's resistance heroes, purged the army and ordered arrests.[145] Bands of police and clerics burned books. Dozens of liberals were flung into the filthy subterranean prisons of the Inquisition. The priest Múñoz Torrero was held in a convent, Argüelles imprisoned in Africa, and Quintana incarcerated at Pamplona for the next six years. Martínez de la Rosa later described how he was "entombed" for seven months in a tiny fetid dungeon without light whose air even the jailers could not breathe.[146] He was then remanded to the Moroccan island Peñón de la Gomera. Liberals and *afrancesados* were sentenced to jail or to hard labor in Africa, and thousands departed voluntarily for exile. King Fernando banished the Alejandro Regiment to Galicia as traitors because they had once fought on the side of the French.[147]

Quintana, describing the arrest of judges, deputies, and others who had fought for and handed back the throne to the king, later wrote, "Very soon there were not enough hands to hold them all, nor dungeons in which to throw them." Fernando had become "the blind instrument of a fanatical party incapable of governing the nation in harmony with the time and the circumstances."[148] The absolutists struck at the signs of the liberal years. Madrid mobs sacked the Cortes hall and destroyed the constitutional tablet. In Valencia, the plaque was removed and the Plaza of the Constitution became the Royal Plaza of Fernando VII. The free press disappeared, leaving only two official organs; the government closed *tertulias*, clubs, and cafés and ended their freewheeling political talk. Public life was reduced largely to religious festivals and the opera. Fernando's ecclesiastical policy consisted in restoring certain elements of church power but controlling it as well. He reinstated the Inquisition and brought back the Jesuits, expelled in the reign of Carlos III. The nation's friars wended their way back to their restored monasteries, and Te Deums observing the return of the king resounded over the land.[149]

What kind of man could stoop to such mean-spirited acts of ingratitude? Spanish testimony about Fernando's character comes to us mostly at second hand and from hostile sources. A Spanish friend of the Englishman Thomas Steele related that Fernando VII had no guiding inner principle—neither cruelty, superstition, religion, despotism, nor liberalism. He was like an empty shell, a sensualist without character who depended on those who advised him. He "took a pleasure in the ceremony, and was gratified by the state and pageantry, as a child by its baubles."[150] Another informant, allegedly close to the king at one time, wrote to Blaquiere that Fernando was a passive instrument of others—of Napoleon at times, of his current advisors at others. Blaquiere also cited a kind and generous side of the king and blamed his bad decisions on courtiers and reactionary clergy. This king of Spain was poorly educated and, judging from his actions, mendacious, paranoid, vengeful, treacherous, and probably spineless. But there also seems to be no doubt that he identified himself with Spain and sincerely believed that a constitution meant poison for both.[151]

Fernando's policy of retribution won few friends in Europe. None of the Great Powers withheld recognition of the new regime, though some held their noses. The Duke of Wellington, who looked on the constitutionalists as "dirty liberals," nonetheless refused the Spanish king's request for military aid in overthrowing the constitution of 1812. His brother, the British ambassador to Spain, Sir Henry Wellesley, condemned the absurdities of that constitution but hoped that Fernando would issue his own. The king's persecution of many who had liberated the country disgusted both men and many another Englishman.[152] Although Spain secretly joined the Holy Alliance, it was consigned to second-rate status at the Congress of Vienna in 1815 and played no active role in postwar European politics.

Aside from the economic ruin wrought by the French invasion, Fernando VII faced two major problems: the Latin American uprisings and plots against his throne at home. At the very moment when Spaniards challenged the French invader and moved toward a constitutional order, their colonies in New Spain and New Granada rose up and declared independence. Indeed, the insurgency was set off in 1808 by the French occupation of Spain. By the time Fernando VII had regained the throne, the breakaway had gone beyond the stage of defying Napoleon to a bid for compete independence. The Cadiz Cortes had sent an expedition in 1810 and two in 1813. After the restoration, Fernando escalated the size of the invading forces and offered inducements to officers. In 1815, General Pablo Morillo led the largest expedition to Latin American in three hundred years. A force of over ten thousand troops set sail for Latin America in an armada of forty-two transport ships escorted by men-of-war. There he won many victories but failed to subdue all the rebellions or win the war.[153]

The overseas imbroglio brought Spain into a new relationship with imperial Russia, which came to play the predominant diplomatic role in Madrid in the Restoration years. Dmitrii Tatishchev, minister in Spain from 1815 to 1819, had close connections with the court. Reputed to be an intriguer, Tatishchev nonetheless tried to curb the worst excesses of the Spanish king, and he kept alive the myth of Tsar Alexander as a liberal. Tatishchev on his own also floated the possibility of a Russian force to help Spain in Latin America.[154] Russian policy makers exhibited a keen interest in Latin America, and the tsar supported Fernando VII's military attempts to suppress the revolts. But Russia's main interest in Spain lay in trade and the projection of Russian sea power in the Western Hemisphere, a policy that had been developing for decades. An independent continent, inevitably dominated commercially by Britain and the United States, would work against that interest. The issue of Fernando's legitimacy remained secondary.[155]

The only concrete Russian assistance to Spain took the form of a notorious warship deal of 1817–18. The oft-repeated story held that the Russian minister and a court camarilla lined their pockets by negotiating a corrupt purchase of five Russian ships, one named *Alejandro I* and all unseaworthy, to be used for crushing the Latin American revolts. In reality, after a five-month voyage from the Baltic to Cadiz, two of the ships, accustomed to the icy waters of Russian ports, became unseaworthy in the warm waters off Cadiz because the Spaniards neglected to seal up their hulls. The king asked for and got a price reduction and two well-built replacements for the crippled vessels. Some political figures tried to discredit the military by claiming scandal. There had been unneeded secrecy but no deception. Yet the rancor did not go away: in 1820, Riego would employ the image of "rotten vessels" in his pronunciamento. After this episode, the tsar lost interest in military cooperation with Spain in pacifying Latin America, though he still supported suppressing the revolts.[156]

On the home front, Fernando VII's policies of repression led to revolutionary conspiracy. Low morale in the officer corps, a key factor in the military putsches of the Restoration years, arose from career frustration and, to a lesser extent, liberal ideology. Officers who had fought the French, including thousands of returning prisoners of war, expected posts, a chance of advancement, and perhaps even tokens of gratitude and honor. Instead, the military budget was cut due to a financial squeeze. Preferment often went to aristocratic favorites of the king, including some who had never fired a shot during the long travail of liberation. The minister of war denied promotion to liberals, war heroes, and guerrilla chiefs, and he tightened up on discipline, subjecting soldiers to the gauntlet.[157] Some of the returning prisoners of war had imbibed liberal ideas through their recruitment abroad into Freemasonry, though their enemies exaggerated the level and extent of such indoctrination.[158] Others became energized by the protests of well-known guerrilla heroes such as El Empecinado and Espoz y Mina, even though the latter, then still a Servile, protested mainly out of personal career motives.[159] The men in the ranks suffered from low pay and poor food and housing, but until 1820 they remained largely immune from politics and gave scant support to plots and uprisings.

Masonic lodges helped to spread discontent and give it a political overlay. Freemasonry, a major conduit into subversive activity all over Europe, enabled the disaffected to share their views undisturbed by authorities. Masonic networks of conservative, liberal-nationalist, and military orientation had emerged from 1808 onward, and some played a role in the early formation of Spanish Liberalism. Lodges offered clandestine sites for hatching plots in a dark and dramatic atmosphere that fed the romantic imagination but also allowed for concrete plans that went beyond the political discussion of the *tertulias*.[160] Most Spanish Freemasons hated absolutism but also feared mass uprisings, preferring the rule of the propertied and educated. They shared the conservative belief that a republic would release terror and a bloodbath.

Starting in September 1814, a half-dozen risings broke out in various cities in Spain. Civilians and officers alienated by Restoration policies, switched roles from resisting the French to a life underground. The first, the renowned guerrilla leader General Espoz y Mina, used his forces to resist the reactionary regime in Pamplona. The veteran of the War of Independence and his troops, neglected and unrewarded, had difficulty adjusting to peacetime. When the rising collapsed, Espoz y Mina escaped to France. The episode widened the schism in Spain and threw Mina into the welcoming arms of the liberals.[161]

More straightforwardly liberal in its aims, the revolt of Don Juan Díaz Porlier (1788–1815), known as "The Little Marquess," began on September 19, 1815. He had led anti-French guerrilla forces in the recent war and after the Restoration was consigned to a harsh regime of solitary confinement in an ancient fortress near Corunna. Escaping, he freed other prisoners and issued a pronunciamento to the garrison and citizens on the town square, declaring for the constitution of 1812. A moderate, Porlier intended no violence against the king. "Our aim and that of all Spain is nothing less than a monarchy submitting to just and prudent laws, formed in such a way that guarantees in equal measure the prerogatives of the Throne and the rights of the Nation."[162] In a set piece to be repeated henceforth, the troops took an oath to the constitution, followed by a parade with band music and drumbeats on the square and through the streets. Citizens shouted, "Long live the king! Long live the constitution!" At night the town blazed with illumination.[163]

Porlier then unwisely moved against Santiago de Compostela, a vibrant nerve center of traditional religion and royalism, with its thirty monasteries, a renowned cathedral, and miraculous bones. After the tomb of St. James (Santiago) the Apostle had been "discovered" in the tenth century, it became a site of pilgrimage and a well-organized tourist attraction.[164] From the Tour de St. Jacques in the middle of Paris, hundreds marched through France and over the Pyrenees to this sacred venue. The British Bible preacher George Borrow, though immune to the cathedral's rich sense of Catholic piety, described it with wonder in the 1830s. A liberal bookseller showed him a church that "was one of refuge, to which if the worst criminals escaped, they were safe. All were protected there save the negroes [*negros*], as they called us liberals."[165] In Santiago, a heartland of Catholic bigotry as well as piety, Porlier met defeat. Manacled and stripped to the waist, he was cast into a dungeon. At the trial in Corunna, when the court official read out the word "traitor," Porlier replied, "Traitor?! Rather a most loyal servant of his country." Next day, on the gibbet, he put a kerchief around his eyes and asked the priest to deliver it to his wife. The revolt had lasted but a few days. The cathedral celebrated the suppression with a Te Deum.[166]

The Triangulo conspiracy surfaced in 1816 as a plot to waylay the king by guerrillas and Madrid liberals. Vicente Richart, a well-known writer and lawyer, and two others planned to force Fernando VII to accept the constitution. They then decided instead to kill the king and his son and put some Austrian prince on the throne. Richart stole into the palace with a dagger but was betrayed. At his trial, he said that "everything is pushing society to unite in the struggle with the dynasty. The regime of Fernando VII is unbearable." The three were hanged in Madrid and their heads stuck on pikes at the Alcalá Gates.[167] As if by annual plan, on April 4, 1817, General Don Luis Lacy set off yet another revolt in Catalonia. Not a former guerrilla leader like Espoz and Porlier, he had commanded an army during the War of Liberation and was more liberal than his predecessors. He organized the garrison at Barcelona for an uprising and then issued a pronunciamento. After the collapse of his effort, his captors sent Lacy secretly to Majorca, where he fell under a hail of bullets from a firing squad.[168]

In late in 1818, Colonel Vidal plotted to arrest the hated General Elío, captain general of Valencia, at the last performance of the opera season. His colleagues were to signal the moment by shouting "Liberty and the constitution." The opera was canceled due to the death of a Portuguese royal. Their next meeting was betrayed and the conspirators were arrested. Elío called them monsters, enemies of "the throne, the laws, and religion" that had led them to the scaffold, and he alluded to the shame of such a death. He also asserted that the principle for which they conspired—that is, liberalism—would, if put into practice, bring an end to family, marital fidelity, commercial trust, law, and virtue.[169]

Juan Van Halen (1790–1864), partly due to his escape and the publication of his memoirs, became celebrated among the conspirators of this era. His Russian exploits are little known to Spaniards and his Spanish experience little known to Russians. He was born in Leon, adjacent to Cadiz. His father, a native of that city, came from a Belgian background. As a naval officer, Juan served on the French-Spanish side at the Battle of Trafalgar and in 1808 in the army opposing the French. He was captured and taken in Joseph Bonaparte's suite into exile. On returning to Spain he was briefly detained and then pardoned, and in 1817 he joined one of the revolutionary plots. It was uncovered and Van Halen was arrested for having compromising documents concealed in his cigarette pack. Charged in Murcia for Masonic conspiracy in 1817, he was consigned to a dungeon.[170]

In his memoirs, Van Halen recalled being manacled and shackled to the wall of a subterranean cell that was flooded from a nearby river. Tormented in the total darkness by swarms of insects, his only distractions were religious books and coded conversations with other prisoners through the walls. Rumors spread in the town that Van Halen had taught satanic lore and burned a statue of Christ. After an interview with the king failed to yield information about the plot, the prisoner was remanded to the Inquisition in Madrid. In the course of several protracted interrogations, conducted nightly in a darkened room where the questioners sat stony-faced at a long table beneath a sword and crucifix crossed on the wall, Van Halen was subjected to repeated rituals—questions, oath taking, and the recital of the Catholic Confiteor. When he refused to reveal the names of his co-conspirators, hooded men tied him to a torture apparatus with a wooden glove operated by a wheel that tightened the victim's flesh.[171]

With help of the turnkey's adopted daughter, Van Halen escaped and—in the true spirit of adventure novels—jailed his own jailer. Spirited through town by friends, he managed to flee the country for London. Offered the chance of seeing action in Latin America, he declined and instead went off to Russia, where he mingled with the Decembrists and campaigned with the tsar's army in the Caucasus.[172] When Van Halen's account, with its familiar features of prison literature,[173] appeared in Spanish, French, and English, some challenged its veracity. Others praised the author and accepted his version of events.[174]

Since Van Halen added to the "black legend" of absolutist Spain as a large torture chamber, it is worth recalling here the brief background. Napoleon's Bayonne constitution, the first legal document to curb torture, prohibited it along with illegal harshness and undue pressure on detainees, unless allowed by law— ambiguous, to be sure, but a step toward humane treatment. In 1811, the Cadiz Cortes almost unanimously outlawed the use of shackles, dungeons, and physical abuse or unusual cruelty to obtain confessions from accused or witnesses, a ruling incorporated into article 303 of the constitution: "Torture and physical pressure are never to be employed" (No se usará nunca del tormento ni de los apremios). On returning to Spain, Fernando annulled the law, but in 1814 he issued a royal warrant of his own that forbade torture of accused and witnesses.[175]

Of course, such a warrant, even if widely known, would not necessarily restrain the practices of local civil authorities or the Inquisition, and there is no cause to believe that prison life in Spain—or elsewhere—was a pleasant experience. Standard condemnation of royalist dungeons as places of horror notwithstanding, some of the well-filled regular Spanish prisons offered a surprisingly open forum where jailers often deferred to their potential future masters and gave them freedom to talk to visitors, read and write, conduct agitation from their cells, and even go on outside junkets to connect up with their comrades. Riego's colleague Antonio Quiroga, jailed in a Dominican cloister in 1819, played billiards, walked the streets, met with other radicals, and was elected leader of the coming revolt.[176]

The uprising that finally succeeded in 1820 owed much of its success to the independence movements that had been raging all over Latin America while Spain still writhed under the heel of Napoleonic armies. In 1815, General Morillo's forces had suffered immense losses from yellow fever. In 1817–18, a half dozen small flotillas carried reinforcements to the colonies, but the large-scale expedition of some thirty thousand troops aimed at the River Plate could not be assembled until 1819. In that year, some fourteen thousand troops were marshaled in camps around Cadiz preparing to embark.[177] But trouble was brewing in the fleet and on land. Rumors about the impossible conditions of the purchased Russian ships still circulated. The soldiers, some of whom had been encamped since 1815, became demoralized by tales told to them by revolutionary agitators and returnees of what might await them overseas: unwinnable battles, horrible torture if taken prisoner, sweltering heat, and the specter of death by a decimating tropical disease.[178]

Cadiz in 1819, as in 1810, became a hotbed of liberalism in the summer. Rebel officers joined up with civilian liberals and Latin American agents in advising the troops to refuse service in the expedition. They won the support of those driven by patriotism and a perception of Spain's impending ruin, men facing blocked careers, and soldiers alarmed by the looming terrors of the Spanish American campaign and eager to accept money distributed by colonial agents of independence or rise to the promise made by some officers of back wages, land, or early release from the army.[179] A civilian troika of Cadiz liberals backed the rebel officers. Francisco Xavier Istúriz, a capitalist and Mason, handled finance. Antonio Alcalá Galiano, son of a naval officer killed at Trafalgar, dealt with political matters. Juan de Dios Alvarez Mendizábal (1790–1853) changed the maternal Mendez portion of his name to hide its Jewish origins. A twice-captured veteran of the 1808 war, he became manager of a large Cadiz firm that did business with the army and yielded him political contacts with liberal officers. In 1819 Mendizábal gathered money and spread propaganda.[180]

Three of the leading officers in the plot hailed from distant parts of Spain: Riego, Evaristo San Miguel (1785–1862), and Antonio Quiroga (1784–1841). San Miguel and Rafael del Riego, both of Asturias, had careers that nearly paralleled in the campaigns of 1808, prisoner-of-war experience in France, return to Spain in 1814, and adoption of a liberal stance. San Miguel bore the nom de guerre of Patria. Quiroga, a former naval officer from Corunna, though outranking Riego at the time of the revolt and technically its commander in chief, was never able to achieve the popular acclaim or the notoriety of his junior colleague. The two names were constantly linked and paired in propaganda, particularly in graphic art, as well as with the relatively minor duo of Miguel López de Baños (or López Baños) and Felipe de Arco-Agüero. Like that of many revolutionaries, their solidarity did not long survive their successes.[181]

In what came to be known as the Palmar plot, Quiroga, Riego, and San Miguel enlisted the aid of the commander of the forces, General Don Enrique O'Donnell, the Count of Bisbal (or Abisbal, later nicknamed by foes "Avisbal," meaning "informer"). The plan was to approach Leon across the bridge and causeway over the wetlands, capture headquarters, and remove the governor of Cadiz. O'Donnell agreed and arranged a meeting on the Plain of Palmar near Jerez. But O'Donnell changed his mind, dissuaded from the act by another officer of Irish extraction, Pedro Sarsfield.[182] Though the generals betrayed the plot in July, the government, for reasons yet unclear, remained indecisive. O'Donnell was replaced as commander of the forces. Quiroga, Arco-Agüero, San Miguel, and a dozen others were arrested, but no blood purge occurred, as after previous plots. Riego had arrived at Palmar a few days before the arrests. Then a sudden illness took him into town and he avoided being seized.[183]

The conspirators, both those in jail and those at large, continued to conspire. Their chance arrived along with another ferocious yellow fever epidemic rolling in from Latin America. The closing of shops and public places rendered garrison duty unbearable. More important, the authorities, hoping to avoid infection of the troops, moved battalions into a string of towns outside Cadiz. Their transfer away from the harbor brought a temporary hold on the expedition, lubricated the conspiratorial network, and opened up a fresh opportunity for revolt since troops were remote from central authorities in the city.[184] The plotters prepared to free the prisoners and named Quiroga as leader, while Riego took over temporary command. At one of the small outposts, Riego unfurled the banner of revolt. The plotters scheduled the rising for January 1, 1820, and the taking of Cadiz by the next day, before the ships had a chance to sail.[185]

The First Horseman

Don Rafael del Riego y Flórez (or Riego y Nuñez) was born of poor hidalgo parentage in Tuña, near Oviedo in Asturias, on April 9, 1784—in the same year as his future archenemy, King Fernando VII. Rafael's father was a postal official and minor poet related to clergy and to local university professors. Riego's brother Miguel, a priest, became canon of Oviedo. Rafael was exposed to Enlightenment writers and, after brief study at the university, chose the army over a career in law or the cloth. He graduated from the military school at Oviedo in 1808 and began fighting against the invaders. Taken prisoner by the French in Escorial, he escaped but was then captured by patriots who at first mistook him for a French spy. Released, he returned to combat. On November 10 Riego fought in the battle of Espinosa de los Monteros, and a few days later he was caught by the enemy again and taken to France.[186]

While in captivity, Riego was moved around southern France, where he remained from 1811 to 1814. There he was subject to many kinds of ideas and influences, including Freemasonry. He learned French and some English and was exposed to Enlightenment thinkers as well as Benjamin Constant and Destutt de Tracy. How deeply he imbibed revolutionary ideas is debatable. In January, as the war was winding down, Riego escaped with other captives to Switzerland and the Rhine region and then across the Channel to Britain. Riego returned to Spain in 1814 and took the oath to the constitution shortly before Fernando VII returned to power and abolished it. Riego was then made a captain of infantry. During the era of the liberal plots, he became further involved, and by 1819 he was deeply engrossed in plans for a mutiny.[187]

On November 8, 1819, Riego, mounted on a white horse with a water-bearing dog at his side, rode into Las Cabezas to take up his command. To his battalion he said: "Love and trust your officers and we will lead you to immortality." The men shouted in reply: "Long live our commanding officer."[188] On December 27 Riego met with Alcalá and Mendizábal to make final plans. Rebel battalion commanders would take over nearby garrisons and then converge on Cadiz. After the January 1 proclamations, Riego moved on to Arcos. His column entered the town square with the band playing, and his force was able to overwhelm the larger garrison and arrest the commander. Riego uttered a proclamation and sent a message to Quiroga. He repeated the process elsewhere, and in this he parted company with many of the liberators of Latin America (and their opponents), who routinely followed their taking of a town with firing squads on the main square. Five days after the rising, he arrived at Jerez, having sent ahead orders for rations of bread, meat, and wine for his men. The authorities, too frightened to resist, nominally carried out Riego's orders, even if still loyal to the absolute monarch. Riego retained the officials but ordered the publication of the constitution, with a fine of one hundred pesos for non-compliance. The common people of the town for the most part greeted Riego's incursion with silence, not, as Blaquiere claimed, with "the utmost enthusiasm."[189] In this case and in town seizures to follow, Riego named Quiroga as leader of the national movement. Here and elsewhere, Riego parted company with many of the liberators of Latin America (and their opponents) who routinely followed their taking of a town with firing squads on the main square.

Having raised the banner in a few towns, Riego now brought his forces, amplified along the way by new joiners, to the aid of Quiroga, who had been freed by his comrades from detention. Seeking to take Cadiz by storm, Quiroga had reached León, the gateway to the city. There, on January 2, an anonymous proclamation, probably from the pen of Quiroga himself, announced that the army, under Quiroga (who was now a general), would refuse to sail overseas to the terrors and lethal climate of Latin America. It would maintain order and obedience, right the wrongs of an oppressive regime, and establish a constitutional monarchy.[190] Quiroga freed the prisoners from the arsenal. The absolutist authorities in Cadiz proper tripled the wages of their soldiers; and the clergy predicted a massacre if the constitutionalists got into the city. The archbishop of Cadiz had placards put up calling the faithful to rise "in the name of the Lord" against Riego and his "Anti-Christs."[191] The liberals, with only seven battalions and no artillery or cavalry, were unable to besiege Cadiz. Twenty-five days after Riego's act of January 1, success seemed doubtful. The insurgent forces were divided, their momentum frozen, and their cause menaced by absolutist troops coming from elsewhere. At this point Riego made a risky and momentous decision: to distract the opposing army by a forced march into the interior, a delaying action designed to set off, by its boldness, parallel risings in other parts of Spain. At dawn on January 25, Riego and his men left León.[192]

In what became a mythic ride, Riego took his mobile column of men, many unshod, for two months through the picturesque terrain of Andalusia and Estremadura, traveling past Moorish ruins and market towns, over rugged mountains, through coastal plains, and over stony clay soil. Its longest stretch lay eastward to Algeciras, north to Malaga a month later, and then twisting westward back into the interior. Like the infinitely more famous Risorgimento March of the Thousand, Giuseppe Garibaldi's 1860 liberation campaign in south Italy, Riego's exploit engaged absolutist forces all along the way and attempted to leave behind local support for his cause in the wake of the march. Combat consisted of skirmishes and occasional pitched battles that left his own and enemy dead and wounded on the ground. Casualties and desertions steadily depleted the original force of about fifteen hundred to perhaps three hundred or four hundred at the end. The march recruited few and lost many, and the citizens of the lands he crossed stood passive rather than hostile, though some resistance to requisitions occurred.[193]

The commander halted in town after town and delivered a harangue on the constitution and a pep talk on the new Spain, urging both the dwellers and his soldiers to display patriotism and observe order and discipline. Using familiar revolutionary language, Riego demonized the old order and promised a bright new dawn. In key places, he ordered military, town, and church leaders to swear to the constitution in the public square. He also corrected some abuses and abolished offensive practices of the regime as he requisitioned provisions, tobacco, shoes, and horses. Predictably, he got a mixed reception. Some garrison commanders and town leaders dissimulated and played a double game of welcome and wait, hoping for the arrival of absolutist forces or the collapse of the Riego enterprise.[194] At Vejer, one of Riego's early stops, public dancing and banquets attended by the military and townspeople went on for three days.[195] Ordinary townspeople most likely here and elsewhere divided between those caught up in the excitement of parades and festivities and those who feared the monarchy's vengeance. On the way to Algeciras, Riego received orders from Quiroga to turn back toward Leon but there found the entry blocked by government troops.

Reversing again, Riego rode to Algeciras and addressed its dwellers on February 1: "Cries of satisfaction and joy with which our National Troops were received last night convey to me your positive feelings and passionate wishes to live no longer under an oppressive system which reduces you to a condition of nonentity and of humiliation and destitution. . . . The generous shout, given for the National Army has brought the Dawning of the Nation's happiness." Spaniards, he declared, had been transformed from subjugated slaves to free men under the rule of law instead of caprice. A few days later, Riego ordered the parish priest to form up in the morning with his troops on the plaza to celebrate the constitution. Popular acclaim for Riego had erupted vigorously in Algeciras, but it proved to be sterile since it yielded not a single volunteer to join his ranks.[196]

Riego now headed northward and reached Malaga in mid-February. Though he found the streets and squares deserted and windows and doors shut, the commander issued another of his proclamations. The inhabitants showed little enthusiasm for his rhetoric. While in Malaga, enemy battalions entered the town and urban street fighting erupted, from which the constitutionalists emerged victorious but badly weakened from desertions. Once again the rebels had to take to the saddle. At nearby Antequera, Riego issued a proclamation identical to the one at Malaga. He publicly bemoaned the contrast between a land blessed by nature and its current misery and its tyrannical rule by caprice rather than law. Alluding to the struggle against Napoleon in cadences laced with anger and wounded national pride, Riego asked: "How is it that the Spaniard, so brave in battle, has become so apathetic? How is that the nation that decided the fate of Europe is today the most unhappy, the most servile of all nations?" He assured his listeners that all of Europe supported Spain's just and noble cause and urged them to unite in struggle and sacrifice for Spain so that "you will once again glitter on the global stage and will be admired by all nations."[197]

Riego unwittingly repudiated associations of Andalusia with those who gave it its name in ancient times, the Vandals. He later wrote to the king that no violence, plunder, or disorder had besmirched the luster of his march,[198] a claim supported by San Miguel. Though Riego threatened death to resisters in a few towns and made arrests, no known executions occurred during the insurgent ride of 1820. Riego released all prisoners of war who declined to swear to the constitution, though a colleague advised him to shoot them. Judging generosity to be a mark of power, Riego saw his opponents as people to be converted rather than as enemies, and he averred that blood was too precious to be spilled without major cause and due process.[199] At Malaga, Riego returned enemy prisoners—except for those who defected to his side—to their commander with a note saying that "we are brothers and compatriots" and would not fire upon or shed the blood of adversaries except in extreme circumstances.[200]

Lieutenant Colonel Evaristo San Miguel joined Riego's journey on January 27 and commanded the First Division. His account of the ride mirrors the standard war stories of the Napoleonic epoch and the liberation of Latin America—replete with examples of the valor, audacity, and patriotism of the troops; their suffering from rugged terrain, shortages, and incessant rain. The march, often at the rate of ten kilometers per hour on horseback, took the form of a triumphal parade rather than a conquest: drums were beaten and banners waved as the column entered and left each town.[201] During the voyage, San Miguel rendered a lasting service to his commander. At Algeciras, Riego asked that a patriotic song be written in honor of his pronunciamento. A first attempt at lyrics by one of Riego's officers proved unacceptable.[202] San Miguel put his hand to the job and produced the "Hymn of Riego" to a melody by A. T. Huerta. The song made reference to Spain's deep past and national legend by calling Riego and his men "the sons of El Cid."[203] An important emblem of the revolution was born. From April 7, 1820, when the new Cortes decreed it to be the Spanish national march, the hymn became a rallying cry for the liberals and it would resound long after these events by Republicans in the Spanish Civil War. But it also served as a divisive token, bitterly hated by the enemies of Riego during the three years of constitutional rule.

After Malaga, a snaky route took the column to Cordoba in early March; it apparently got a huge welcome. The harried soldiers crossed the Sierra Morena mountains and proceeded through other towns and villages to the Guadalquivir River and beyond. When Riego heard of a rising in Galicia in support of the constitution, he read the news to his men but did not discontinue the harrowing trek until the remnant arrived at Bienvenida on March 11. Commentators frequently refer to a starting force of fifteen hundred that got reduced to three hundred. The numbers, mostly speculative, did steadily diminish, and we hear of one hundred here and fifty (or forty-five) there. The figure of three hundred, though describing the size of the force at one stage, stuck in the popular imagination, possibly because allusions to the ancient Battle of Marathon were being made all over Europe in the following year when the Greeks revolted. At Bienvenida, Riego, nearly hopeless, dispersed most of his remaining men and headed toward the coast. His tiny entourage received temporary shelter in Portugal. When Riego got news of the king's acceptance of the constitution, he made his way to Seville in triumph.[204]

Although the peasantry remained inert along Riego's route, his cause was secured by the irresolute wavering of the government in Madrid and by sympathetic risings in other parts of Spain. The ultimate success of his march came not from his force of arms but from the power of example when rebels elsewhere copied his pronunciamento and frightened the king into compliance. In February, Espoz y Mina and other officers who had been exiled by the king returned from France and joined the revolution.[205] This triggered similar episodes in Galicia, where major towns revolted except for the deeply religious Santiago de Compostela. In March, Saragossa, Pamplona, and Cartagena followed suit. Murcia declared for the constitution on March 12. Among the few "counter-juntas" that emerged to stop the flow of revolt, one wondrously singled out for rejection Article 287 of the 1812 constitution, which forbade arbitrary arrest.[206] Otherwise, in what looked like a majestic wave of supporting revolts, local juntas proclaimed the constitution, mounted plaques honoring it on town squares, and released political prisoners—thus identifying that document with personal freedom.

In the face of widespread disaffection, and in an effort to halt the unfolding revolution, King Fernando VII in early March began to issue pallid remedies and a few concessions and promises. At the same time he dispatched General O'Donnell to crush the rebels. But the general, who had already turned coat once, defected to the other side. Ironically, the unit he commanded and then turned was the Alejandro Regiment, formed in Russia in 1813.[207] Beginning on March 6, events multiplied in rapid succession. On the advice of his advisors, the king summoned the Cortes. On March 7, he announced that, "following the general will of the people, I have decided to swear to the Constitution issued by the General and Extraordinary Cortes in the year 1812." The next day, he ordered the release of political prisoners. March 9—to be celebrated for the next three years—brought the abolition of the Inquisition, the appointment of a provisional junta, and the utterance of Fernando's oath to the constitution.[208]

In the oath, the king insisted on using paternalistic language.[209] "We have heard your supplications," said the king, "and, as a loving father, we have deigned to accede to what our children hold to be in the interests of their happiness." Fernando swore that "we shall always be [the constitution's] most constant supporter," while warning against utopian dreams of perfection and urging his people to avoid passion and exaltation. "Let us march openly together with our self at your head along the path of the Constitution, giving to Europe a model of wisdom, order and proper self-control."[210] This was a singular exercise in deception and a striking claim that Spain was in the vanguard of political change elsewhere in Europe. A royal oath to the constitution became a major issue in the revolutions of Spain and Naples. Insistence on it—however futile it turned out to be in both countries—was clearly drawn from the French experience. King Louis XVI's oath had been the subject of an elaborate painting by Nicolas-Guy Brenet, showing the king in Roman apparel and wearing an expression of willingness, swearing on the altar of the Fatherland, with the usual classical attributes and symbols in the background.[211]

Although a liberal victory had been achieved with little bloodshed, violence erupted in Cadiz the day after the king swore to the constitution. Crowds gathered in the streets and squares to celebrate the king's acceptance of the constitution, announced prematurely in the local press a few days earlier. Citizens began installing the constitutional plaque amid the festivities. The local military commander, General Manuel Freyre, who had pursued Riego's ragtag force for two months, doubted the authenticity of the royal decree. He entered the city with a punitive force and allowed his allegedly drunken troops to fire into the unarmed gathering. These in turn were killed by the infuriated crowd. The butchery lasted three days and claimed about five hundred lives. Only on March 12 did Freyre receive verification of the king's oath. When order was restored following the bloodbath and Freyre's departure, celebrations at Cadiz resumed, military authorities swore to the constitution, and a Te Deum was performed at the cathedral.[212]

Rafael del Riego, now informed of the king's capitulation, rode to Cadiz and joined Quiroga. In March, he wrote to his sovereign in respectful language that "Spain is the theater of one of the noblest revolutions"—the last two words doubtless sounding like an oxymoron to the king. Riego also claimed that he himself harbored no ambition and sought no celebrity. But Riego thirsted for fame and national gratitude. He and Quiroga were promoted in April to field marshal, and Riego's brief career as a national hero began.[213] His enemies at the time falsely accused him of declaring for the constitution of 1812 as an act of personal aggrandizement; others then and later claimed that it actually harmed the success of the revolution.[214] In fact, Porlier and other earlier rebels had raised the banner of the constitution and Riego himself had sworn to it in 1814 when he arrived home from captivity. He and his fellow liberals needed a symbol, a catalyst, and a concrete document that had already been tried.[215] This became also precisely the attraction for those liberals in Naples, Portugal, and Piedmont who emulated the Spaniards.

Much of the mystique surrounding 1820 concerns the term "pronuncia-mento" (*pronunciamiento* in Spanish). Riego, not the first to use it, was the first to turn it into success. The few issued in late December were general and vague: Quiroga's, drafted by Alcalá Galiano, simply denounced absolutism. Riego had crucially linked the dangerous Latin American expedition with a critique of the regime and a demand for the constitution of 1812. About a half dozen followed Riego's in early January. The last, issued on January 13 by the Army of La Isla (León) to the Spanish people, stated that the purpose of the uprising was "to reestablish the power of the laws and enable the nation to enjoy the right to manage its own interests—these are the only reasons for raising the national banner. Its first act, since it has taken such a resolution, has been to proclaim the political constitution of the Spanish monarchy."[216] After Riego's first successful military intervention in the national politics of modern Spain, pronunciamentos, for the most part delivered orally, became recurrent devices for changing regimes in the coming century and acquired the halo of romance. The method, in Raymond Carr's words, "developed the rigid form of classical drama" with certain fixed episodes: sounding out possible collaborators; commitment to the plot (*compromisos*); and the speech triggering the revolt given as a shout (*grito*, or "electrifying harangue"). The device became so common that officers in subsequent times were issued a manual on public speaking.[217] With local nuances, the other three horsemen repeated the model.

How interested were the soldiers and the mass of civilians in a constitution? The former opposed the Latin American expedition and conditions in the ranks. The latter's grievances—when voiced—lay rather in tax policy, judicial abuses, and blocked employment. Riego recognized this: in February, while still on the road, he promised a 50 percent tax reduction. Following this, tax and tithe strikes erupted in several parts of Spain—a refusal to remit monies to Madrid.[218] The success of the 1820 uprising stemmed from a combination of military mutiny, domestic grievances, and the supporting risings. But it was Riego who triggered the revolt that ushered in a three-year period of constitutional government. Gil Novales speaks of "the immense popularity of Riego and the general feeling of joy in March, 1820. A new era of life was beginning: even the king publicly seemed to embrace it in good spirits." For the moment, the church, the bureaucracy, the magistracy, and other elements of the old regime bowed to the constitutional order. Few thought that it was doomed, though many wished it so. In Madrid, hats were hurled and people danced in the square.[219] The daring of the first horseman seemed vindicated.

Trienio: Liberals in Power

On the bright sunny day of July 9, 1820, as hundreds of church and monastery bells rang, the new Cortes assembled at the Church of the Virgin of Aragon in Madrid, its first convocation in six years. The meeting took place in an oval hall, with the throne set up at the front under a large fasces. Below the king stood the table for the president. Citizens sat in the galleries. Over the king's head was the inscription "Fernando VII, Father of the country." At the first session, King Fernando grew irate at the sight of images of the executed Porlier and Lacy and of a sign bearing words from article 3 of the constitution inscribed in gold: "Sovereignty resides essentially in the nation!" The royal pique symbolized the far more serious issues that arose between king and Cortes.[220]

The term now used for the years 1820–23, the Liberal Triennium, *trenio liberal*, caught on only in the twentieth century.[221] After a long procession of Napoleonic pseudo-liberal puppet states, Spain could now boast "Europe's first indigenous liberal government—that is, one not imposed from without and upheld by foreign bayonets."[222] King and Cortes had to face each other within a constitutional framework. Fernando had not only to swallow the new system but also to work with his former victims, ex-convicts from Restoration prisons and African labor gangs. Since some of his newly appointed ministers had just been liberated, wits called it the Jailbird Government. An anonymous journalist observed at the time the inevitability of tension between Cortes and monarch. "Yesterday an absolute King in virtue of a divine decree, today a constitutional king by the will of the people."[223] It was not just the constitution that displeased the king, but its legislative reforms and the fact that it inspired copies elsewhere.

The new Cortes revived the reform agenda of the Cadiz era. One of the few items that did not generate antagonism, Spain's first penal code of 1821, remained harsh. Though eighteenth-century Enlighteners and current liberals admired Beccaria, his beliefs had never penetrated deeply into the Spanish consciousness. But at least the new code, an advance over the old, standardized punishments and even won praise from the monarch.[224] The Cortes continued efforts to build administrative decentralization and construct a rational fiscal system to replace the corporate subsets of privilege embodied in the ancient laws of the separate kingdoms that made up Spain. This meant incursions into local rights and thus resentment.[225] The same applied to limits on feudalism and monastic holdings. Laws allowing hidalgos and the nobility to sell their land ended various practices of entail and mortmain, rulings destined to be cancelled by Fernando VII in 1823.[226] Neither left nor right undertook fundamental agrarian reform.

The notoriously touchy Spanish officer corps was bound to bristle at political intrusion. The Cortes tried to take up the unsuccessful army reforms of 1812. An 1821 law addressed the built-in tensions between military and civil society and the issue of obedience versus people's rights.[227] Since it defined when soldiers were permitted to disobey anti-constitutional officers,[228] the law failed to win the allegiance of most officers. Their motivation in supporting the Riego revolt had always been as mixed as their diverse makeup: liberals, opportunists, bored adventurers, reactionaries. During the Trienio many grew increasingly offended by the anti-militarism of some Cortes deputies. Indeed, civilian liberals in the new regime suspected a standing army as an unfree institution resting on brutal discipline and a potential pool of future Bonapartes. Their open expression of hostility gained them such enmity that many officers declined to defend the government when it was militarily attacked in 1823.

Since church reform again presented a potentially volatile issue, the Cortes initially treaded softly around it. Spanish liberals, far from opposing religion, upheld the Catholic monopoly, and the 1821 proposed law code decreed the death penalty for conspiracy to establish any other church. The measure greatly upset Jeremy Bentham, an unofficial advisor of the liberal regime. Many churchmen tentatively accepted a moderate constitutional regime and the clergy did not form a solid phalanx against it.[229] According to the Englishman Blaquiere, "a very considerable portion of the clergy" expressed pro-constitutional views and the need for reform.[230] After the suppression of the regime, the Serviles—like the Franco regime much later—minimized the support of clergy for their predecessors. In fact, 54 of the 247 deputies were men of the cloth, and a tribute published in 1821 singled out seventeen of them for their "firm adherence to the constitutional system." In 1824, after its collapse, a police inquiry named seventy-one Masonic priests and ninety-five who had been members of the radical Comuneros patriotic society. Local inquiries in many cities revealed worrisome numbers of clerics, nearly a third, who had been associated with the liberals or in "opposition to the king's government"—in other words, had supported the constitution or were "declared enemies of God and of the King." They were subject to surveillance, stripped of their parishes, and sometimes punished further.[231]

The liberals were bound to take land from the church and thus weaken a pillar of the old regime. In 1821 began the hotly debated issue of liquidation and expropriation of some monastic orders and the reform and limitation of others. By year's end, citing their scandalous wealth and substandard intellectual profile and educational methods, the Cortes had closed some 324 monasteries and convents. By 1822, 801 monasteries—a bit less than half—had been abolished. With each new move, opponents voiced their opposition to the regime. The radical press reported that some priests used the pulpit to denounce the constitution and even denied absolution to liberals.[232] Although the regime's fiscal policies were designed partially to redistribute church wealth to the lower clergy, whom the liberals celebrated as vessels of popular enlightenment, anti-liberal clergy remained unimpressed. Though the Cortes itself abjured any anti-religious actions or proposals, a strong spontaneous rural and urban anti-clericalism broke out in these years against monastic property and other targets, largely motivated by economic issues.[233] Clerical malaise with the government eventually morphed into armed resistance.[234]

Appalled at its material losses, the church felt equal outrage at the wave of insulting language aimed at it during the Trienio. Feeding clerical reaction and responding to it, a new level of anti-clericalism arose during the Trienio. Critics spoke in tones ranging from Voltairean wit to profound hatred. Said one: "The clergy have no principles, no calling, no position. Clergy are devoid of letters, having no books except their breviary. They are idle and lazy, resembling country bumpkins in apparel, language, and manners."[235] Urban crowds were known to shout "Death to the Jesuits!"[236] Indeed, the Jesuit order was suppressed. The fugitive Piedmontese revolutionary Count Pecchio later observed that, whereas in Greece both the people and the church were poor, in Spain the people were poor and the church was rich.[237] Sharing this view, a Spanish priest verbally attacked his colleagues, "the fat fathers." The anti-clericalism of the 1820s crystallized previous strains of satire, intellectual critique, economic grievances, and occasional popular manifestations into a violent Spanish phenomenon that recurred again and again well into the twentieth century.[238]

The Inquisition became once again a target for anti-clericals. Juan Antonio Llorente, an ex-inquisitor who supported the French invasion of 1808, compiled the first archival histories of the Inquisition in Cadiz and Paris between 1812 and 1818, critical works that helped fashion the negative image of the body from that time onward.[239] He detailed some of its horrors, including various forms of water torture, such as pendola (drop by drop on the skull) and what is now called waterboarding—simulated drowning.[240] In March 1820, crowds in Madrid and Barcelona broke into its prisons and freed the inmates,[241] repeating the drama of the Napoleonic liberators in 1808. Some Spanish liberals indulged in symbolic retribution. Romero Alpuente, who had been jailed for three years by the Inquisition, bought for his home the chairs from which the Inquisitors had put the question. Quiroga purchased an Inquisition palace with its subterranean dungeons and an interrogation room. In this chamber, hung with black cloth, the black-clad questioners had sat at a stone table covered in black cloth on which stood black candles. Torture at this site, Quiroga claimed, took the form of water treatments and "broiling the sole of the foot" on a slow fire.[242] But in one raid on an Inquisition headquarters, the intruders found more vats of wine than torture equipment.[243] Whatever the truth of the torture stories, the liberals saw the Inquisition as the central symbol of judicial persecution and obscurantism. As long as it exerted its power, there could be no free press in Spain.

Another inherited issue, the revolt of the Latin American colonies, the Cortes addressed rather ineffectively and could never solve. The insurgencies energized the Spanish liberals and vice versa. But the two-way street between New and Old World liberalism remained clogged. For the most part, prior to March 9, 1820, Spanish rebel propaganda called for collaboration and reconciliation with Latin American freedom.[244] Comparisons, begun at the time, abound to this day between Riego, George Washington, and Simón Bolívar as agents of a triangular Atlantic wave of liberation. Certainly Riego's exploit further weakened Spain's already feeble ability to subdue Latin America—and he is still revered for that in the greater Hispanic world. At least one contemporary, erroneously or deliberately misquoting Riego, added to his Las Cabezas proclamation a nonexistent phrase about eternal liberty for the peoples of America. But in truth, Riego believed that the constitution would bring the colonies to heel.[245]

Under the new dispensation in 1820, the king and his closest associates remained committed to reconquest. The Cortes took a more ambivalent wait-and-see attitude, though clearly hoping that the colonies would remain under Spanish rule. They clung to the view that the rebels were fighting against despotism in Spain and the Hispanic world rather than for their own independence.[246] The country began to experience things familiar to warring powers of other times and places: disillusionment with the war and the body count, bitter returning veterans, a rapidly vanishing treasury—all countered by a reluctance to abandon the men on distant shores. In March 1820, the minister of war offered a pessimistic outlook by reporting huge losses among the almost forty-three thousand men who had been sent across the sea since 1811, the imperilment of troops on the ground, and a drastic shortage of vessels. The government declared a cease-fire, ended plans for a punitive expedition, and sent to the colonies a call for elections and an explanation of the new constitution. At the same time, unwilling to renounce force, it remained alert to new developments and discussed sending replacements and rescue missions for besieged forces.[247] Dissenting from this policy, some liberals in government and in the press declared for Latin American freedom or even argued that independence was a fait accompli and therefore deserving of assistance rather than suppression.[248]

Liberal management of the new government suffered from many ailments, not least of which was the lack of a united liberal front. The *afrancesados* were not welcome under the liberal umbrella, though they had similar aims and possessed political experience. Early on, the Cortes passed an amnesty for these elements, whom some looked on as nothing better than treasonous collaborators. But the amnesty denied them full citizenship rights and thus resulted in the loss of a possible set of allies, since many of the amnestied in a huff went over to the reactionaries.[249] More serious was the schism between the so-called *exaltados* (radicals) and *moderados* (moderates). One needs to apply a stern reality check when assessing the meaning of political labels during the Trienio. Contemporary participants hurled them at each other as epithets; later observers sometimes tended to simplify things by reducing the entire struggle within the liberal camp to one between reified *exaltados* and *moderados*. Both these groups called themselves patriots and liberals. And both accused the other of seeking office and privilege, among other charges. *Moderados* upheld centralization, rights of property, and order, as against social revolution and democracy. But no essential class difference divided them from *exaltados*. All changed over time; overlapping membership and fluidity marked the dynamic of partisan affiliation.[250]

Yet, for all the nuances, a broad pattern of rivalry emerged. As revolutionary regimes often do, this one quickly descended into a tripartite struggle among moderates, radicals, and absolutists. As *doceañistas*, or men of 1812, moderates were people of substance and position who adhered to the limited reforms of the original Cadiz Cortes. They included the older, cautious exiles and jailbirds, chastened by experience and immune to a principled radicalism. Since the unicameral Cortes scandalized European conservatives, many *moderados* favored a second chamber in order to avert a possible invasion by foreign powers. Though ready to return some powers to the throne, they hoped to retain the constitution's spirit and its evocative power. This solution was unacceptable to both the king and the radicals. During the first ministry of the new regime (March 1820–July 1822), the moderates predominated but—in classic fashion—were racked by absolutists and royal intrigue on the one side and radicals on the other. After July 1822, the moderates faded from the political scene.[251]

The dramatist Martínez de la Rosa embodied the moderate spirit. He had been welcomed to Malaga from captivity in April 1820 as a hero along with other released prisoners. As they disembarked from the vessel that had once taken them away from Spain, the strains of a Te Deum rang out in the cathedral and Malaga citizens pulled Martínez de la Rosa's cart amid festive street music and cannon fire. Festivities were repeated in Granada, his hometown. Martínez served as deputy to the Cortes and in March 1822 headed the cabinet. He tried to preserve some royal prerogatives and urged pardoning the Persians, moderation toward the clergy, and a universal educational system.[252] Martínez had lost some the passion of 1812. His refined manners and easy ways among aristocrats rendered him suspect to those on the left. A modern writer cited an unreferenced author who wrote that Martínez had a tendency toward seignorial manners.[253] After the July 1822 events, he resigned. A modern Spanish scholar has unfairly called the *moderados* "counterrevolutionary, pettifogging lawyers" who were shackled by the constitution and followed the line of least resistance.[254]

The radical end of the Spanish left in the 1820s, as in the 1930s, exhibited enormous variety in coloration and personnel—though it has often been reduced to a mythical monolith by the terms *exaltados* and *veinteañistas*—Men of 1820. The younger cohort who had missed 1812 formed radical clubs and militia and became the backbone of the *exaltados*. The label, originating with their opponents, came to mean to some people, among other things, followers of Riego, opponents of the *moderados*, the democratic left, radicals, and sometimes Jacobins. The term also indicated an emotional stance, as one historian saw it: "ardent love, passion, grand devotion to a cause, incorruptibility, absence of compromise with foes—the more or less open enemies of the revolution." To the Spanish left, idealism and maximalism constituted virtues; to the right, they portended simply perilous extremism.[255] Often tagged as anarchists, most *exaltados* were not even democrats, although they initiated the democratic currents that emerged in the nineteenth century. Gil Novales has called them populists, indicating a powerful but diffuse attraction to and sometimes for the lower classes.[256] Though not united around a single program, most *exaltados* sought a more liberal suffrage, local rights, and an end to the excise tax, conscription, and the American war.[257]

The ever-changing membership in radical groups at times included officers, high officials, and influential merchants with ties to émigrés and radical Latin Americans as well as provincials and civilian and military elements who felt their careers thwarted. Riego, the object of their reverence, stood as a symbolic persona rather than formal chief. Among the younger, little-known, and unseasoned leaders were the civilians Álvaro Flórez Estrada and Juan Romero Alpuente, code-named Aristarchus. Alpuente, veteran of an Inquisition prison, became a Cortes deputy and active member of radical clubs. Antonio Alcalá Galiano, a powerful orator, has been characterized by some sources as a shallow liberal and something of an opportunistic *moderado*. But he was often listed as an *exaltado*. Other names include Alcalá's Cadiz fellow conspirator Istúriz and the colorful José Moreno Guerra.[258]

Though the revolt was not a Masonic plot, as its enemies charged, some of its leaders had been lodge members. In the Trienio, most Masons, though still demonized by reactionaries, had become moderates or conservatives.[259] The more radical members withdrew and founded some 164 patriotic societies and clubs and their branches, which transformed the shape of urban political life and amplified its discourse. Begun during the anti-French war and the Cadiz Cortes, they drew on European models and indigenous ways of the *tertulia* and café and evolved from amorphous meeting places to organized sites. The polite conversation of the older venues escalated to speeches from a dais or table, matching the *grito* in volume and passion. Though based on formal membership, clubs often admitted the public. Their leaders founded journals, helped form the national militia, and organized festive meetings of homage and memory or of protest. They were mostly dominated by the *exaltados*, and Riego became a member, founder, or guest speaker at dozens of meetings. Overall, the societies aimed to guard the constitution from Serviles, *moderados*, and *afrancesados*; check on officials; fight abuses; and accelerate the pulse of the revolution.[260]

In commenting on one of the most prominent of the secret societies, the Comuneros, eyewitness Count Pecchio saw them as a miniature and concrete example of the extreme left.[261] Founded in October 1821 by Alpuente, Espoz y Mina, and others, mostly republicans, its main leader was General Francisco Ballesteros, a disgruntled older officer who had been shunted aside by the men in power. Riego did not join formally but lent his sympathy. With its aim of defending the constitution and warding off absolutism and clerical reaction, the society swore death to the foes of freedom, though it stopped short of adopting a democratic program due to the backwardness of the masses. This group became a hub of leftism and a welcoming place for exiled Italian Carbonari.[262] Like the liberals of 1812, the Comuneros or Sons of Padilla looked back to their sixteenth-century namesakes, who had inspired Martínez de la Rosa's *The Widow of Padilla*, though now Martínez de la Rosa sat at the other end of the political gallery. The society's statute also paid homage to Juan de Lanuza, an Aragonese rebel whom King Philip II had beheaded. The Comuneros were in a sense hispanicizing and radicalizing the revolution.[263]

The Comuneros sprouted as many as fifty branches, with thousands of members, including women, and a newspaper, *Eco de Padilla*. With a touch of Masonic and Carbonaro nomenclature, it set up chapters called Towers, Castles, and Forts of varying size. The center set rules for the members, mostly the urban poor, and it expected moral monitoring among them. Unlike some other secret societies, the Comuneros allowed members to withdraw. What alarmed outsiders, especially priests, about the societies was their secrecy, embodied in the mysteries of initiation. The ceremony of the Comuneros resembled a religious or chivalric rite: novices were led through ghostly and intimidating passages, declaiming codes and oaths at each stage. Emulating the Masons, Carbonari, and other such groups, the society formed a pyramid with lowly initiates—males from age nineteen—at the base and a Supreme Assembly on top. Members swore before God to defend the constitution as it stood, obey the rules, maintain secrecy, behave fraternally, and "to die sword in hand, rather than submit to tyranny."[264]

A later group, the Landaburian Society, named after a loyalist officer killed in a royalist putsch on July 7, 1822, had ties with the Comuneros. In a symbolic gesture of reversal, this anti-clerical society moved into the suppressed convent of the Church of San Tomás on the Plaza de Santa Cruz in Madrid. On three evenings a week members thronged into a hall holding some four thousand people, a site adorned with placards honoring the constitution and Landáburo. Michael Quin, a British lawyer and journalist who knew Spanish, traveled in Spain for about six months in late 1822 and early 1823. At the Landaburian Society he witnessed citizens of both sexes in the back of the hall, officers and speakers at the front, and a guard on the side. A military band played between the speeches. The audience yelled "Viva!" and shouted "Riego" as an alternative for the word "constitution." One member read a variant of the catechism in the form of a "dialogue of two school boys on the free press." The speeches attacked the higher clergy and demanded monitoring the Cortes and a retention of the unicameral constitution. Quin, a sympathizer with the *moderados*, judged the effect of this club to have been harmful.[265]

The political temperature continued to rise with each perceived government provocation or failure. Hostility intensified between radical clubs and government ministers. The stalwart liberal of 1813, Argüelles, anxious about the sudden surge to freedom of action and expression in the clubs, wrote that "the Spanish nation is, so to speak, a neophyte in the matter of liberty." Alpuente, as if to answer, declared that "the patriotic societies terrify tyrants."[266] Yet the very first society to be formed, in Corunna, had as one of its aims "to enlighten the government on matters of which it could have no awareness"—an eminently reasonable justification and one of the keystones of liberalism: the educational role—running both ways—of parliamentary life.[267] A Valencia paper described the societies as "the source of our hope, the guarantor of our peaceful existence, the anchor of our safe repose, and the rock which will shatter the haughty ships bearing the metal to forge chains for us." Gil Novales, their historian, has defended the patriotic societies as protectors of the liberty won by the 1820 revolt. The rise of provincial societies represented a momentous change in Spanish political life. For the first time in history the country had a nationwide network of bodies sponsoring secular culture and liberal or radical politics.[268]

Absolutists and their allies naturally viewed the patriotic societies as nests of dangerous republicanism and Jacobinism, and their existence also widened the gulf between *moderados* and *exaltados*.[269] The growth of radical clubs alarmed the government over matters small and large. According to Russian reportage, in November 1820 the patriotic society Maltese Cross allowed rude references to the king and ridiculed the ministers.[270] Adversaries of the clubs, with some justice, feared their extremism, lack of discipline, and unwillingness to compromise. They called street demagogues "shirtless ones" (*descamesados*). The anger, egoism, and ambitions of some of the radical leaders eventually alienated many of their own followers.[271]

The clergy nursed its own grievances against the real and perceived anti-clericalism of the patriotic societies and the press. In 1820, the Vatican declared that Spaniards owed no allegiance to the regime due to its press law.[272] In an effort to destabilize the liberal regime, Fernando VII's ambassador to the Vatican formed an absolutist Apostolic Junta, which was supported by many Spanish bishops.[273] The volume of anti-liberal complaints rose when a victorious restoration of absolutism seemed in sight. The Dominican Fr. Josef Vidal, of the theology department at the University of Valencia, indulged in deep historical vengeance. He equated the errors of the liberals with those of the Arians, Pelagians, followers of Wycliffe, Luther, Calvin, and other heretics, and he denounced "the perverse system of the political constitution of the Spanish monarchy, established in Cadiz in 1812 and reestablished in 1820."[274] As in 1812, anti-liberals, fueled by an essentially conservative and theological view of politics, sometimes revived a dash of fossilized anti-Semitism: in 1821, an absolutist group in Alcañiz was formed in order to struggle "against the Jews, the tree of Liberty, and the republic."[275]

Keeping the Faith

Given the rage boiling at the extremities of Spanish politics, it may seem unlikely that cultural promotion of the constitutional regime could have had much effect except among a choir of the converted. Yet the war of words, images, and symbolic episodes spun out by all sides yields insight into their values. We have many terms for what came flowing from the liberal imaginary: social communication, propaganda, revolutionary discourse, and so on. Symbols, signs, rituals, print, performances, speech, and artifacts provided the vehicles. Demonization of the enemy and glorification of abstract concepts, such as liberty, and concrete things and persons—the constitution of 1812, martyrs, and heroes—accounted for the themes. The language, usually couched in Manichean terms, often derived from older forms and usages. We may look back today on the political artistry of the time after two centuries of overuse as banal—but in the early nineteenth century it still had much persuasive power.

Unlike in the days of besieged Cadiz, the free press now had all Spain as its readership. Passions generated by the clubs migrated to the street in public speeches and to the pages in newspapers and flyers. Broadsheets produced by all sides contained vivid and often hate-filled messages and accusations of atrocities. The new untamed public culture, operating in a flush of freedom, often burst into invective with little regard for etiquette or balance and hurled insults and personal denunciations. The liberal and radical press defended the constitution from its perceived foes. It also assailed the aristocracy, those planning a second chamber, moderates seen to be cozy with the absolutists, and sometimes the monarchy itself. The clergy loomed as a favorite target, though some of its critics were themselves priests. They satirized excessive ecclesiastical wealth and hordes of "useless" unproductive religious; the Inquisition, and its alliance with reaction; and the church's greed, corruption, and economic oppression of the poor. Alcalá's *Eco de Padilla*, a daily with a print run of 750 that ran in late 1821, made a point of linking the old hero, Padilla, with the new one, Riego. Aside from rules against obscenity, subversion of the constitution, rebellion, and attacks on religion (not the church), the press had a relatively free rein.[276]

Although newspapers were sometimes read out loud to the illiterate, their content could hardly have reached a wide audience. Messages embedded in stage production had a somewhat better chance, at least for urban dwellers. In this revolution, as in most modern ones, some theaters reached out to get in step with the time. The Spanish romantic taste was receptive to political, social, and national themes and to a sense of struggle; and that spirit, as elsewhere in Europe, expressed itself loudly in historical drama. The sixteenth-century Habsburg monarchs continued to serve as negative models for the liberals. The works of Alfieri gained renewed resonance in Spain during the Trienio. Count Pecchio reported in November 1822 that Alfieri's *Philip II* was enthusiastically received by audiences. Likewise, Martínez de la Rosa's Alfieri-inspired *Widow of Padilla*, which had thrilled besieged Cadiz in 1812, once again won popularity when it was restaged, and another Cortes deputy wrote a historical drama about the martyr Lanuza.[277]

Lesser playwrights produced cruder and more obviously propagandist vehicles set in present times, such as *The Constitution Vindicated* and *Patriotism, or January 1, 1820*, dedicated to Riego.[278] A network of mobile troupes playing drama, popular musical theater, puppet shows, and circus-like diversions had already crisscrossed eighteenth-century Spain. In 1820, Etienne Robertson, a visiting impresario, put on magic lantern shows in Madrid, one of which was entitled *Historical Gallery and Images of National Heroes*. At the end of the parade of images that included Hernando Cortés, Miguel de Cervantes, and the French philosophes appeared Riego, Quiroga, and Arco-Agüero. The positioning of Riego at the teleological endpoint in such popular historical presentations added to the effort that helped make him the first celebrity in modern Spanish history. Since shows like this alternated with gothic horrors and sugary love scenes, they were able to attract popular audiences.[279]

Critiques of church and government joined the exalted treatments of the liberals onstage. The satirist Leandro Moratín had written the comedy *When a Girl Says Yes* in 1806. He was denounced by the Inquisition in 1815 for shady language and barbs against religious education, and he went into exile. He returned in 1820, and his naughty poke at the church went up on the boards of Spanish theaters and won new acclaim.[280] A Russian journal noted with astonishment that in late 1821 a ballet—a ballet!—called *The Inquisition* was staged in Madrid.[281] Michael Quin observed that a great number of ribald patriotic plays saw the boards. In December 1822—at the height of the crisis between king and Cortes—he attended an anti-clerical play entitled *El Trapense en los Campos de Ayerve*, a knock at one of the absolutist guerrilla clergymen. The actor portraying Trapense, outfitted in a friar's cassock, sword, and dagger, declaimed on the evils of the constitutionalists while he himself busily extorted the local population and seduced maidens. The audience greeted this mockery with raucous laughter and sang the Riego hymn between acts.[282]

The Cortes, however, preferred roping in and using the clergy to offending it. They had the king issue a decree in April 1820 that obliged the clergy to explain the constitution to the faithful on Sundays and holy days.[283] In the spring of 1820 bishops issued pastoral letters directing their flocks to keep the faith of Jesus and at the same time dwell "beneath the sweet empire of the constitution." Priests were instructed to celebrate it with Te Deums.[284] This measure revived practices of the earlier struggle against the French. Spanish illiteracy was massive, and even readers had no access to a vernacular Bible until the 1790s. In this oral culture, information came via theater, street storytellers, and sermons. At the dawn of the nineteenth century, perhaps a few thousand could attend Madrid's two theaters, but virtually all of its 156,000 inhabitants heard sermons in the numerous churches and monasteries of the city—and not only at Sunday mass but also at weekday services and multiple events in and out of doors: funerals, festivals, corridas, rosary processions. Popular preachers had books written about them and fashioned careers out of rhetorical skills. This fact in turn invited the composition of *sermones burlescos*, an underground genre that flattered as it mocked oratorical stars. For the church, sermons were the chief instrument of communication. They have been called the "first 'mass media' of the Old Regime."[285]

A battle of the pulpit broke out, and the clergy divided. A seminary rector in Segovia pretended not to have heard of the edict and refused to explain the constitution to his students. Some prelates and priests reacted to the decree so violently that the authorities exiled them. Conversely, a priest locked the church doors so that no one could leave during his constitutional sermon. A dozen or so liberal sermons found in obscure sources speak eloquently of how some clerics embraced the new dispensation. As the regime's controversies unfolded, liberal sermons were given at patriotic clubs, for honorific celebrations of Riego, and for funerals of the fallen liberals. All invoked the Bible; all but one referred with reverence to the king. Most of the sermons utilized the language of accommodation.[286]

Even before the decree on sermons, a priest in Alicante in March 1820 preached that Spaniards received their rights from Jesus Christ and that there was no contradiction between the constitution and religion. In Longroño, Augustín Barron combined dogmatic theology with praise for the martyrs and rebels, whom he apostrophized with a play on Riego's name: "The irrigation [*riego*] by your blood has restored the original greenness to the majestic tree of the Constitution and of Spain."[287] A Cadiz priest sermonized that observance of the present constitution brought Spaniards close to God and "establishes the union founded in the love of man united in society."[288] Dr. Don Ignacio María del Castillo, a scholar and canon, preached to the Seville militia who were taking the oath to the constitution in 1820. With ample exegesis from the Old Testament, he offered high praise for the constitution and for those who sacrificed themselves for it, for the law and civil liberty, and for the people and their traditions.[289]

Pastoral letters from compliant prelates took up the theme. Bishop Ysidoro of Segovia offered a defense of the constitution and its connection to religious principles. While lamenting abusive anti-clericalism and extremism, he nonetheless asserted that the constitution did not alter the faith of the nation. This cautious attempt to detach the excesses from liberal constitutionalism came in August 1822 when the tensions were high between reactionaries and liberals.[290] The archbishop of Badajoz, in a pastoral letter of the same year, repeated the mixed message, though allotting more space to the abuses of liberalism than to its virtues. These prelates at least seemed satisfied with a constitution rule as long as it provided law and order and continued respect and veneration for the church.[291]

Political catechisms, almost all written by clergy or ex-clergy sympathetic in varying degrees to the constitutional regime, revived the exhortations of a decade earlier. An ex-Franciscan radical journalist reduced the complexity of the constitution's legal language in his *Constitutional Catechism* (Cadiz, 1820) in order to reach children and peasants.[292] Another, published in Seville in 1821 for parish children, had the virtue of directness: "Q: Does the constitution bring us any good things? A: Yes sir. Q: What are they? A: It delivers us from despotism, tyranny, and ignorance."[293] Don Manuel López Cepero displayed more intellectual ambition. An enlightened dean of the Santa Iglesia Cathedral in Seville, he had been jailed by Fernando VII in 1814 for having served in the Cortes. In 1821 he produced in Madrid a *Religious, Moral, and Political Catechism*, which, claims an editor, "sacrificed the grave and magisterial language of a political lesson for simple language accessible to the ordinary person," drawing earthy examples from everyday life. In an effort to combine Catholic with civic education, López Cepero hoped "to inspire in the hearts of all children 'social' religious feelings; to attempt to form thus a Catholic citizen [*ciudadano católico*],"[294] a mission that anticipated the Christian social and related movements of the nineteenth and twentieth centuries.

We know little about audience and reception. Reading the catechisms today, one is struck by the very long answers that the pupil was supposed to learn and absorb. Nonetheless, it is worth noting that the liberals, in reviving the religious idiom for their own purposes, related the constitution not only to the faith but also to the recent patriotic war of liberation. Almost all the catechisms honored the spirit and the letter of the constitution and evinced respect and reverence for the monarch, who was held to be inviolable. A *Constitutional Catechism of the Spanish Monarchy* differed from the others in two ways: its format seemed more likely to reach popular audiences, youth, and schoolchildren, and in explaining the purpose of the constitution as stability and popular sovereignty, it announced with a touch of boldness that "the king is a citizen like everyone else, who receives his authority from the nation."[295] Though somewhat tactless, the statement actually had roots in a medieval Aragonese oath of fealty.

Beyond the discourses of the educated public and the church, other cultural devices emerged that possessed greater potential in capturing popular understanding of what the revolt of 1820 meant. As in the French Revolution, public space played a major role as a stage for kinetic display of new ideas. The most visible and accessible mode of celebrating the new regime in public was the installation of the constitutional stone—varying from blocks to obelisks to plaques on a building. The 1812 decree on renaming town squares and installing the plaques was reaffirmed. An eyewitness reported that in virtually every town there existed a Plaza de la Constitución, where a "constitution stone"—a large marble block with a coat of arms and the name of the plaza in gold—was installed in one of its buildings. Some showed the image of an open book bearing pages from the constitution carved in stone within a shield with a sheaf and scrolls. In the cradle of revolution, Cadiz, nearly all its buildings bore a plaque containing an article of the constitution.[296]

Celebrations in streets and squares followed the pattern of 1812, and on March 19 each year a Te Deum was sung in the towns, followed by a parade, speeches, and a fiesta on Constitution Square.[297] Among the first acts of the Madrid crowd in March 1820 was to bear of a copy of the constitution through the streets while seventy "Persians" were marched to monastic captivity.[298] On July 9, 1820, the citizens of Cadiz witnessed a Te Deum and an effulgent sermon in praise of the constitution as the commemorative stone was put in place. The stone was "a sign of our liberty," said the officiating priest, "recalling our happiness and our glory."[299] A sympathetic French observer described festivities in Tarragona in April 1821: in a banquet hall, to the sounds of patriotic orchestral music and song, speeches and poems resounded and guests were borne around the hall with shouts of "The Constitution forever!" and "The liberty of Europe forever!"[300]

However novel the content of the Spanish civic ceremonies, elements of old devotional practices almost always got folded into the new rituals. The reburial of liberal victims adopted the aura of sanctity in a land where reverence for the heroic and martyred dead remained potent. In 1822, a majestic monument was erected in Madrid to honor those who died during the fighting in 1820. A device beneath each name read: "He fell defending the sacred injunctions of liberty, but lives in the memory of the best people."[301] In 1822, the Cortes honored the victims of the March 1820 Cadiz massacre. Linking history to symbolism, the Cortes celebrated the martyrs of the sixteenth century—Padilla and Lanuza—along with Porlier and Lacy; Lacy's widow was granted a pension.[302] The *exaltado* press reported on ceremonies of "collaboration" between clergy and citizens. In one of these, a priest combined a Corpus Christi procession with a liberal parade and the installation of the constitution stone.[303] But the attempted alliance between the profane and the sacred in public space remained awkward. In 1820, Cadiz city officials prohibited nocturnal rosary processions, one of the most venerated of Spanish rituals.[304]

Crane Brinton, in an old but still shrewd book on the revolutionary decade in Europe, spoke about "the little things" that illuminated the French Revolution, such as toys and other artifacts made into symbols of affirmation or reversal.[305] Playing cards that had previously borne the images of monarchs and other notables came on the market in Spain, this time with pictures of Lacy, Porlier, and other forerunners of liberalism. One such pack featured Riego as a medieval caballero brandishing an oversized sword. Snuffboxes bore revolutionary scenes and excerpts from the constitution. Riego appeared on one; another bore cameo profiles of Quiroga, Riego, Lope de Baños, and Arco-Agüero, who had become a canonical foursome.[306] The usage was well established: the likeness of Benjamin Franklin, among many others, adorned snuffboxes all over Europe.

Spaniards of the liberal era, in order to "rescue" heroes—reviled, jailed, executed, or otherwise mistreated—from infamy and obscurity, also employed memory-spurring devices as old as civilization: monuments, pictures, slogans. Martyrs of the Restoration period together with Riego and El Empecinado were so treated. Some had their names engraved on the Cortes walls. Padilla was honored alongside contemporaries in order to underline the antiquity of the search for freedom. The regime sought to create visual, aural, and kinetic order out of the existing "cacophony of symbols." To celebrate the present, flags were redesigned, blessed, and waved at meetings and in plazas, and the citizens' ears were treated to the regular singing of the Riego hymn—all offering direct and subliminal messages about the present through the lens of the past.[307]

Most intriguing of all, the Spanish fan entered the universe of everyday propaganda objects. From the sixteenth century to its peak of splendor in the eighteenth and nineteenth centuries, Spanish and other European women deployed the fan for flirtation and for a whole range of social communication. A specialist has listed some forty different meanings of fan motions, ranging from "I hate you" and "I am already married" to "I am attracted to you" and "Kiss me." In earlier times, graphic representation painted on the fans had included royalty and cultural celebrities such the composer Rossini and the diva Malibran. They also accommodated bucolic scenes, conversations, warfare, mythology, orientalism, and urban life. In the years of the French occupation, Wellington and King Fernando VII featured as popular motifs. During the liberal regime revolutionary themes began to surface, probably modeled on those of the French Revolution.[308]

Two of the fans held in the Madrid Municipal Museum depicted the chief rebel leaders. That of Quiroga simply shows a bust of him atop a column around which citizens dance. The other, "Exaltation of Riego," sets the general at the center in his role as liberator, sword in his right hand spearing a serpent. His left elbow rests upon a pedestal adorned with the royal coat of arms. Riego poses in the relaxed and elevated mode of official and royal parade portraits of the time. In the background, prisoners are being released from a distant, fog-bound fortress prison, and a kneeling man prays to God in gratitude. On the left, joyous figures dance around the Spanish flag. This image pulls together frequently encountered themes of liberation: a martial protector of the new regime, the freeing of prisoners of the old regime, an act of religious thanksgiving, and the released energies of a joyful crowd of patriots—a perfect visual fusion of the new liberty and the old faith.[309]

Fans celebrating the constitution offer more complex scenarios. An "Allegory of Constitutional Liberties" features a man dressed as a Roman warrior, his shield embossed with the Spanish lion, who is "liberating" the seated lady, Spain, clothed in a chaste white garment. The act is mediated by an allegorical female figure clearly representing the constitution of 1812, now restored. In the background, a ship is arriving, labeled "Return of the Exiles"—a reference to those banished to Africa in 1814. Another, more ambivalent, shows Fernando VII taking the oath to the constitution, but without looking at it. The document is held by a woman in a medieval robe, as another female figure stands between them. Is the monarch being marginalized? The events in the background seem to have more importance than the oath: the Lion of Spain mauls a serpent as a winged monster representing the Inquisition flies away from a searing fire. On the left the people acclaim the oath amid banners and a column with the names of Riego and other heroes.[310]

It is hard to assess how much impact these artifacts had upon their consumers. Spanish fans came in all kinds and prices, and those carrying revolutionary images tended to be low-priced for wider distribution; this was probably true of playing cards and snuffboxes as well. In the visual composition of the fans, although classical motifs abound, religious ones are sometimes introduced as well in a positive or at least neutral way. However enthusiastically the populace might have responded to the liberal messages on the politicized fans, there is no question that the reaction found them loathsome and perhaps effective: in 1823, the offending pictures on fans were covered over with opaque paint.[311]

In all this cultural outpouring, one can hardly have missed the recurring prominence of Rafael del Riego as hero and focus of celebration. Formal art contributed its share of glorifying the new regime in portraits of its leaders, Riego most of all. In "El General Riego," he stands guard over the constitution of 1812, which lies in a scroll on a stone block. His young face, marked by a determined mien, tilts toward his downward-pointing left arm and a hand holding both his bicorn hat and a saber whose blade touches the block. Between the silken sash high on the waist and the black boots stretch the general's long legs, sheathed in the tight white military britches of the day. Riego's commanding figure, with the right hand tucked into his jacket, Napoleonic style, almost fills the picture from top to bottom. In the right background, his men, their weapons stacked nearby, seem to await his orders. A studio half portrait, "El General D. Rafael del Riego," shows a mature and subdued officer, now with epaulettes and minus any menacing pose.[312] As such portraits did for his contemporary Bolívar, these endowed Riego with gravitas and presented him as a masculine liberator of his country and of its jailed sufferers, a hero ready to die "sword in hand" in defense of its liberty.

Riego seemed ubiquitous in these years in person and in imaging. One of the radical newspapers took the title *Riego's Shout*. His name appeared on the stage and in sermons, his face on crowd-borne portraits. The Club of the Virtuous Shirtless in Cartagena added "Sons of Riego" to its name. Pecchio noted that at the Landaburian Society on January 1, 1823—the anniversary of his rising— Riego appeared to a roar of approval.[313] He spoke there and at many other societies on several occasions. During one of them, he tried to downplay the growing cult of personality around himself. He railed against those who called him Emperor Riego and compared him to Cromwell, Napoleon, and Iturbide, self-proclaimed emperor of Mexico. "Riego will always be Riego," he affirmed. "Riego will not change and will continue to work to secure the liberty of his country."[314]

But nothing could arrest the deluge of honors. Crowds acclaimed him the way they traditionally did kings and conquerors. In April 1820, Cadiz citizens pulled the carriage bearing Riego and Quiroga and put on days of feasting, with light shows, rifle salutes, music, dancing, and theater.[315] On July 1, 1820, exactly six months after his first incursion into Jerez, Riego entered that city to a crowd of cheering people and a welcome parade.[316] In Valencia on October 24, 1821, Riego's name day, authorities erected a pavilion in his honor. Inside a white stone was engraved in gold the words "To Citizen Rafael del Riego, restorer of liberty of the Spains, ever glorious."[317] In September 1822, the University of Granada conferred upon him a doctorate of laws and a master's degree in philosophy.[318] What worried cautious political figures in Madrid is when urban popular demonstrations in favor of Riego or denouncing his enemies seemed to take on dangerous political coloration. A pattern emerged: radical clubs praised Riego and carried his portrait through the streets, arousing mass response, which in turn led to clashes with local authorities.[319] The hero worship did not go uncontested.

As time went on, Riego became more expansive and expressive in his speeches, and his writings blossomed into richly worded and emotional patriotic rhetoric. January 1, 1820, was seen as the onset of not only a month, a year, and a decade but of a new era, and Riego made repeated references to it as a necessary ritual reminder of how things began. In justifying why he approved the rush of medals and statues, Riego explained to the Madrid militia in June 1822 that such artifacts were needed to keep alive and freshen the memory of great events. Since Riego had become the object of many of the commemorations, they caused resentment, even among former comrades. Quiroga, for one, did not appreciate all the adulation of his former subordinate.[320] But the masses continued to cheer the "revolutionary pathos" of Riego's speeches; he was thus feared by both moderates and the ultra-right. In the view of one historian, Europe also began to shudder as it would later at the name Garibaldi.[321]

What impact did any of the liberal propaganda have on the people? The masses left few or no written records, though they did leave evidence in their behavior, as witnessed and reported by contemporaries: public shows of enthusiasm on a large scale for the constitutional order in general and for Riego in particular. Yet was it not the same kind of urban crowd that had displayed indifference to Riego's ride, paraded his portrait in the early days of the constitutional regime, and then pelted him when captured by the French in 1823?

The Spanish Cockpit

The first Cortes, which deliberated until November 9, was dominated by moderates, as was the first cabinet, comprising the usual assortment of ministers—war, navy, colonies, and treasury—most of them fresh from prison. While locked in jail, they also became locked into the mentality of 1812. Though the government clashed with the king over a number of issues, a major political crisis of the year 1820 revolved around Riego and his comrades. Once they had helped restore a constitutional monarchy, the rebels opposed retaliation against their erstwhile enemies. But, as a caution, they reorganized the insurgent forces into what was variously called the Army of the South or the Army of La Isla. With components commanded by the four iconic figures, Quiroga, Riego, López de Baños, and Arco-Agüero, the army was designed to monitor unfolding developments. Riego wanted to eliminate uncalled-for harshness toward the soldiers and their subjection to blind obedience, and to treat them as citizens with full rights. He would maintain this army as a defender of the constitutional order. As he often put it, he was ready to draw his sword to protect it.[322]

On August 4, the war minister, a foe of Riego's and opponent of the 1820 revolt, dissolved the Army of the South, citing financial reasons. Interior Minister Argüelles saw that army as a potential threat. The move disarmed the revolution and reduced Riego's authority. The commanders viewed the dispersion of their units as counterrevolutionary. Riego showed restraint and obedience, though some believe that he could have once again hoisted the banner of revolt against this order of dissolution.[323] To coat the pill and get Riego out of the way, the government appointed him captain-general of the northwestern province of Galicia. On August 11, Riego, López de Baños, and Arco-Agüero wrote a letter to the king protesting the breakup of their army. In reverential terms, the signatories assured the monarch of the army's loyalty to the throne. But they argued for its retention in order to protect representative government, imperfect as it was, from the "hidden hand" of wicked advisors. They called the southern army a "shield of Your Majesty against enemies of your person and of the nation." Though an embryonic schism existed before this event, the army crisis crystallized the division of liberals into *moderados* and *exaltados*.[324]

In late August, Riego came to Madrid to argue his case against the dissolution of the army to king, government, and Cortes. His first royal audience failed to resolve the army question. But Riego was forbidden to speak to the Cortes due to a curious incident. In this, his first visit to the capital since the revolt, Riego encountered noisy acclamations on the streets and formal tributes at the Fontana de Oro club. On September 3, he attended the Principe Theater for a performance of *Henry III of Castile*. The inflammatory incident that occurred involved the then popular anti-absolutist song "El Trájala," which had appeared anonymously in 1820. The original quickly became embroidered, folkloric style, with insulting and scatological words, each singer adding new variants for the target in question. "Trájala, trájala, tu servilón" (Swallow it, swallow it, you Servile) became "Swallow it, swallow it, dog," the "it" alluding to "the precious law made for our well-being"—in other words, the constitution. One raw version of Riego's role has the Servile enemy swallowing "the curved saber of a liberal,"[325] a clear colloquial reference to fellatio.

By one account of the theater incident, the public demanded that the attending governor of Madrid, an opponent of the 1820 revolt, sing "El Trájala." When he refused, Riego left the theater, but the crowd caused an uproar and tried to assault the official. Riego was accused of setting off the riot by beating time to the song and singing his own hymn.[326] Another version had the pit honoring Riego with deafening applause and flying hats, bouquets, and mantillas. The official went to Riego's box and asked him to quiet the crowd. Riego flicked his hands at the audience who fell silent at once. "Look," he told the governor, "this is a real leader of the people." When the play ended, another outburst arose, and Riego stood at the railing and sang "Swallow it!" along with the crowd.

When the official again reappeared, Riego departed.[327] According to Evaristo San Miguel, Riego neither sang nor urged the singing, but, seeing the anger of the official, a fellow prisoner of war from years back, quietly left the theater. Alcalá and Quiroga asserted Riego's guilt in the episode. Whatever really transpired, for those who feared Riego's influence, the episode seemed to enhance his reputation as a rabble-rouser, and they inflated its importance.[328]

When the Cortes forbade Riego to address the assembly, demonstrations broke out in Madrid. Argüelles accused him of fostering public disorder and threatened to reveal a secret republican conspiracy in which Riego was allegedly involved.[329] The next day, the government canceled Riego's posting as captain-general of Galicia and sent him to his home province of Asturias. The long shadow of Bonaparte, still languishing on St. Helena, had fallen over Spain. But Riego did not harbor Napoleonic ambitions. Unwilling to stir up a revolt, he went to Asturias and wrote a defense of his behavior bristling with indignation. Highly conscious of his inherited hidalgo status, Riego displayed in the wording of his vindication an extreme sensitivity about his honor and reputation. He also employed the old rhetorical strategy of donning the garb of the simple soldier: "If I do not wield the quill with felicity, if my language does not display the stylistic grace of my accusers, if I am their inferior in this respect—they do not surpass me in love of country, respect for the truth, and accurate recounting of the facts." He followed this by a rehearsal of his valorous military deeds.[330]

The wind blew the other way in November when, after a brush with the king over appointments, the *moderados*, suspecting further moves by the king, made peace with the *exaltados*, rehabilitated Riego, and made him captain-general of Aragon. Riego served in its capital, Saragossa, from January to August 1821. This city then happened to be a hotbed of French radical exiles who were plotting to overthrow Louis XVIII and of refugees from the recently crushed Neapolitan and Piedmontese constitutional regimes. Since Riego apparently fraternized with these groups, his enemies accused him of having conspiratorial ties with the plotters. The archbishop of Saragossa accused Riego of planning to destroy the Basilica of the Virgin of Pilar—one of Spain's holiest sites. In a grotesque flourish, the indictment stated that Riego planned to lead a *Russian* force to carry out this mission. In fact, the French adventurer General Frédéric François Guillaume Vaudoncourt, then in Spain, invited Riego to join a republican plot, but he resolutely declined.[331]

The frame-up aside, Riego offended the Serviles by his friendly relations with *exaltados*. In speeches, Riego criticized the privileged classes and praised merchants, artisans, and workers as "the most essential in the nation and also the most despised." In August, when absolutist locals vandalized the constitutional plaque of a town, Riego had it restored in a festival of dedication, featuring an angel bearing a page of the constitution.[332] In August, Riego went to Madrid, where on September 4 he was dismissed for the alleged republican conspiracies. Though not charged formally, he was sent off to various places and ultimately to Oviedo near his home. To no avail, Riego again protested his dismissal in a series of letters to the Cortes and to the king.[333]

In a recurring pattern that increased the tensions between Riego and the government, each time the general was demoted or in some way humiliated, popular expression of support for him burst forth. The Saragossa dismissal led to new turmoil in Madrid on September 18, 1821. The Fontana de Oro club planned a street demonstration to honor Riego. Although the government forbade it, the march proceeded and the crowd carried a portrait of him treading on the serpents of fanaticism, despotism, and ignorance. When the marchers reached a site called Las Platerías, a standoff with the authorities took place. Though no blood was spilled, the comic opera episode became known as the Battle of Las Platerías. The political temperature rose after the August-September events involving Riego. In places, crowds called him "the heroic leader [*caudillo*] of liberty."[334] The unrest did not always relate to him alone. From the end of October 1821, in a dozen large and small towns civil disobedience and unrest broke out against unpopular local officials and polices. The government military call-up of sixteen thousand men set off massive resistance. In places, *exaltados* recruited militias, persecuted Serviles, and gave aid to the poor.[335] In Corunna, a not atypical case, grievances included the government's mistreatment of Riego, administrative abuses, and excessive tolerance of enemies of the constitution.[336]

The urban wave of turmoil lasted until the spring of 1822 in some places. Where it did not fizzle, the government repressed it, shut down patriotic societies, and curbed the press and the right of petition. The schism between *moderados* and *exaltados* continued to widen save for an occasional truce. In January 1821, some of the *moderados* had formed the Añilleros (Ring Wearers), a secret society of 1812-ers who, alienated by radicalism, wanted to introduce a bicameral constitution. At the other end of the spectrum, the Comuneros emerged in October. More ominous still, absolutist guerrilla bands began to appear in the provinces.[337]

Turmoil surrounding Riego aside, the year 1821 brought other events that further elevated political passions. Two sponsors of the Servile manifesto that had ushered in the repressions of 1814 were arrested. In January 1821, the honorary royal chaplain Augustín Vinuesa, an extreme reactionary, was convicted of conspiracy to overthrow the constitutional government. Learning that Vinuesa received a light sentence, his enemies broke into his cell and beat him to death with hammers. Since some of the mob leaders were aristocrats and one of the killers was a royal chef, some have argued, without much evidence, that the episode was an absolutist provocation to stain the constitution regime. Martínez de la Rosa condemned the murder, while some *exaltados* approved it. The unlucky

Vinuesa, treated as a hero and a martyr, became a focus for the absolutist cause and the subject of atrocity broadsheets.[338] Francisco Javier Elío, captain-general of Valencia, was arrested in May 1821 for allegedly instigating an anti-constitutional rising. Elío was sentenced to death in September 1822, though he may have been unaware of the purpose of the disorder. His real guilt, in the eyes of the judges, was his Servile manifesto and arbitrary arrests in 1814 and the repression of the Vidal conspiracy in 1818, among other things. The general was garroted on the Plaza de Real outside the town in the presence of a large crowd who shouted, "Viva la Constitución!"[339] Both episodes helped to stoke the fury of the anti-liberal right.

Both a bright ray of sunshine and a menacing cloud fell on Spain from abroad when constitutional revolts broke out in nearby states. Portugal had weathered the Napoleonic storm differently than Spain. The king fled to its colony in Brazil and the home country fell under the weighty influence of the British army, championing its old ally against the French. After liberation, King João took the throne but remained in Brazil until 1821. A junta and the British General Beresford exercised real control. Liberals from the provincial urban middle classes and a few other groups who admired the Spanish 1812 constitution had been deported during the Napoleonic war. After the restoration, their successors hatched a plot that ended in executions. In 1818, the secret society Sanhedrin appeared in the town of Oporto. On August 24, 1820, its founders, spurred by the Spanish revolt, issued a pronunciamento. Their authority then reached to Lisbon, where a Cortes proclaimed a constitution that embraced a few elements from the Spanish one. Portugal's liberal Triennium paralleled somewhat that of Spain, although King João, who returned to Portugal in 1821, was more accommodating to parliamentary rule than was Fernando VII. In May 1823, anti-liberal forces, energized by the French intervention in Spain, toppled the regime and restored King João to absolute power.[340]

A few months before the Portuguese pronunciamento, liberals in the Kingdom of the Two Sicilies (Naples)—ruled by an uncle of the Spanish king—staged a military mutiny, issued a pronunciamento, and wrested a constitutional oath from the absolutist monarch. After nine months in power, the liberal regime fell under the guns of an Austrian intervention army sponsored by the Holy Alliance. A similar revolt took place in the north Italian kingdom of Sardinia (Piedmont) in March 1821 and was quickly crushed by Austria. Both regimes had adopted the Spanish constitution. All over Europe, Carbonari, liberals, and others had been cheering the Spanish overturn. The fact that the Spanish revolution had become internationalized by the copycat revolts in Portugal, Naples, and Piedmont alarmed the Holy Alliance, and after repressing the liberal regimes in the Italian peninsula, it heightened its attention to the Iberian model. Conversely, the Madrid regime saw the successful Austrian moves as a possible threat to itself, and it angered the more radical elements.[341]

Prior to its collapse, the Neapolitan liberal regime seemed to offer advantage to Spain as a sister constitutional monarchy across the water. The Englishman Blaquiere observed in September 1820 that public attention in Madrid was divided between the work of the Cortes and the events in Naples, and a Russian journal reported on rumors in Madrid in late 1820 that in case of intervention, Spain would side with Naples.[342] When the Holy Alliance, sitting in Troppau, published a warning to revolutionary governments, the Cortes, recognizing that intervention in Naples might portend one in Spain, put the issue to a debate, shrilly amplified in the clubs and on the street. On January 4, 1821, the foreign ministry protested the Troppau Protocol to the ambassadors of the Holy Alliance and requested a guarantee of non-intervention in Spain. It also instructed its envoy in Naples to support the regime there.[343]

As the Austrian military intervention in Naples unrolled, the man who had helped install the constitution there, General Guglielmo Pepe, now in exile in Spain, appealed for help.[344] On the eve of Austrian victory, the radical deputy José Moreno Guerra announced in his rough Spanish that "Naples is a part of Spain like Catalonia and we must assist it." Some bold deputies urged military action to defend Naples and even suggested making it a staging area for further liberation. Another proposed sending aid to the Neapolitan capital even after Austrian troops had taken it. He predicted that the Austrians in Naples would experience the fate of Napoleon's Grand Armée in Moscow.[345] Nothing came of these gestures, and the Cortes resolved only to make financial and military preparations for the defense of Spain. The collapse of the two regimes in Italy opened a flow of political exiles into liberal Spain. On May 2, 1821, the Cortes offered friendship and succor to the exiled Neapolitan rebel leader, General Pepe. It also decreed financial aid for fugitive generals, ministers, and deputies from the defeated regime. Those who warned that this gesture might alienate the Holy Alliance were voted down. Henceforth, Spain's politics became complicated by its role as a haven for liberal exiles.

General Vaudoncourt, advancing views on the mutual dependence of revolutions at the time, made the naive suggestion that "ten thousand Spaniards in Italy would probably have rescued Naples from slavery." He also believed, ignoring other contingencies, that the success of the Italian constitutional regimes would have guaranteed the longevity of Spanish liberalism. But he correctly observed that "the speedy and unhappy termination of the two revolutions in Italy, has had a fatal influence on public opinion in Spain."[346] The intervention in Naples depressed and angered the Spanish left and set off public demonstrations of protest in Barcelona and Seville.[347] This unrest, as usual, helped to activate their enemies and increased ideological polarity.

Though hardly a menace to the European state system, the steadily rising star of Rafael del Riego increased the tension between *moderados* and *exaltados* and between those groups and the absolutists. In November 1821, he was elected deputy to the Cortes from Asturias and chosen by that body to serve as its president, largely a chairman's role, from February 25 to March 30. The Cortes, offering symbolic fig leaves to feed Riego's undeniable vanity, had heaped honors on his epic ride, his sword, and his hymn, which by law became an official military march. The town of Las Cabezas erected a monument in his honor. Riego and the now deceased Arco-Agüero were equated with Spanish martyrs of the recent and distant past. Riego and Quiroga received the Grand Cross of San Fernando with laurels. During his travels around Spain, Riego established twenty-two patriotic societies. Some of the Serviles in the Cortes began shouting, "Muera Riego!"[348]

Riego's brief tenure as presiding officer of the Cortes showed a mixture of hot-headedness and restraint. Martínez de la Rosa, head of government, had strongly opposed the election of Riego as president of the Cortes, who in that capacity gave preference to exaltados on committees.[349] In a speech of March 1, Riego insisted that main force was required to fend off the obstacles to change mounted by the enemies of freedom, and affirmed that "the true power and greatness of the monarch consists solely in the punctilious carrying out of the laws."[350] Yet during Riego's presidency King Fernando received him in a cordial fashion and personally introduced him to the queen.[351] Riego was also reported in the foreign press to have addressed the citizens of Madrid from his balcony, urging them to avoid disorder.[352]

Later that year, Riego reappeared at the most deadly polarizing event of the Trienio: the failed revolt in July of the Royal Guard. The royal palace in Madrid then and now offers a spectacular view of the verdant plain and the Manzanares River far below the steep west wall. To the east, however, it fronts the city and the streets that lead to the nearby and spacious Puerta del Sol and Plaza Mayor, popular gathering places. To protect the edifice and its royal residents, the king kept a unit of military guardsmen, which—as in other monarchies—was a carefully selected aristocratic body of ultra-loyal men. The suburban palace of El Pardo served as an alternate royal residence, later famous as Generalissimo Franco's home. On July 7, Pardo battalions marched on Madrid and entered the palace. Vaudoncourt heard, or believed, that the guards wished to restore Fernando VII to his full power, kill the militia, and erect gallows for the liberal leaders, with Riego as the first; failing that, they planned to flee the country with the king.[353] These desiderata may have motivated some of the officers and men. But their leader apparently desired a modification of the constitution and not the return of absolutism.[354]

Fighting began when the guards ventured into the city streets and encountered crowds in the Puerta del Sol, one of the largest squares in Madrid. In the course of events, a liberal officer, Lt. Mamerto Landáburo, was killed and a battle erupted.

Antiphonal shouts of "Long Live Fernando VII" and "Long Live the Constitution" resounded through the city.[355] The skirmishing spread to the Plaza Mayor and the Casa del Campo—the vast grounds to the west of the royal palace. The Cortes put down the revolt with the aid of the militia, the garrison, and armed urban guerrillas led by Evaristo San Miguel and Riego. The former headed the so-called Sacred Battalion—a designation possibly borrowed from units involved in the risings in Naples and Greece—which bore the image of Padilla on its flag. Vaudoncourt recalled that a unit was also formed of French and Italian exiles. Resisters to the oncoming wave of guards' bayonets shouted, "No pasarán."[356]

After the guards were defeated, Fernando VII accused Riego of acting without permission and of trying to subvert military authority.[357] In fact, he tried to restrain needless violence and probably saved the king's life. "Citizens of Madrid," he is said to have declared to an angry mob that was surging into the place, "I will not let you make an attempt on the life of the king."[358] Writing to Fernando, Riego refuted charges of troublemaking and darkly alluded to evil royal advisors in the past who had paved the way to the scaffold for Charles I and Louis XVI.[359] Though it had no legal force, this letter alone surely must have sealed Fernando's fear and hatred of Riego forever. Something Riego observed in these days led him to downplay his cult of personality. On July 7, from the City Hall balcony in Madrid, he decreed that no "Viva Riego" be shouted and no "El Trájala" be sung for him.[360] Riego perhaps had come to sense the menace to public peace of hero worship among aroused and angry multitudes and of the effect of this on his own reputation.

In the aftermath of the failed coup, politics veered sharply leftward and for the first time gave the *exaltados* control of the government, one that was too radical for moderates but not radical enough for the Comuneros. In August, two heroes of 1820 came to power: Evaristo de San Miguel headed the foreign ministry, with López de Baños as war minister. The angry Cortes deputies, seeking retribution for the palace putsch, turned on Martínez de la Rosa. He had openly opposed the clubs for their threats to the government and their harshness toward anti-constitutional clergy. The Cortes blamed him for weakness during the plot, and even of conspiring with the king to change the constitution. In October Martínez de la Rosa's ministers were jailed (he barely eluded arrest) and suffered physical abuse and threats while in captivity. The Comuneros arrested and planned to try the royal plotters of July 7 and even threatened San Miguel. The *exaltado* ministers freed the prisoners from the clutches of the Comuneros. Alpuente gave violent speeches at the Landaburian Society.[361] Plans were afoot to memorialize the July 7 bloodletting on the model of a Dos de Mayo by staging a triumphalist play called *The Seventh of July*, glorifying heroes of the day.[362]

The Dos de Mayo analogy is apt. Just as that Madrid episode marked the prelude to a nationwide war against the French, so the July 7 street fighting made civil war in Spain at least highly probable, if not inevitable. As regular as a pendulum, the right swung further out in response to the radical swing. More of the clergy opposed the constitution and the moderates for their failure to punish radical acts and the anti-clerical propaganda of the clubs.[363] Already in 1820, churchmen, peasants, and others were hatching absolutist counterplots that in a way paralleled those of the left in the years 1814–19. A Russian paper on June 11, 1820, reported that in Saragossa, five hundred peasants and others under arms gathered on Constitution Square and shouted, "Long live religion! Long live the king! We don't need a constitution!"[364] King Fernando VII complained bitterly to foreign envoys that he had been reduced to the status of a slave.[365] Monarchical-clerical absolutists who saw Fernando as a prisoner of the liberals longed to reestablish the old regime. They hated the Cortes for challenging the God-given royal prerogatives and the interests of church and nobility. The abso-lutist core in the capital threw tentacles across Spain. At first less noisy and showy than the left, the absolutists formed armed bands and secret societies and engaged in clandestine propaganda, diplomatic contacts, illegal intrigues, and infiltration of radical bodies. One newspaper claimed that anti-constitutionalists conducted subversive espionage via the confessional.[366]

In the wake of the July 7 putsch, counterrevolutionary forces erected a coun-tergovernment in the provinces. The Apostolic Junta on August 15 set up a re-gency in the Catalan Pyrenees at Seo de Urgel that was to wield power until the king was released from captivity. The regency galvanized Spaniards who felt the economic pinch and opposed the pro-urban and centralizing policies of Madrid, the loss of privilege, the taking of monastic lands, and the escalation of anti-cler-icalism, including the spontaneous execution of priests by mobs.[367] The Urgel Regency's proclamation called the government in Madrid criminal for having subverted the altar, the throne, and the peace of all Europe; despoiled and impoverished the church; and opened wide the road to atheism and anarchy. The drafters exhorted Spaniards to obey the regency alone and to take action at once in order to avoid foreign intervention, which the regency considered a last resort. As had the original rebels in 1820, the document offered money and pro-motion to troops who would desert and join the anti-constitutional cause. The signatories—the Marquis de Mataflorida, a "Persian" of 1814, the archbishop of Tarragona, and Baron de Eroles—offered no new version of conservatism but simply demanded a return to the status quo and the untrammeled power of throne and altar.[368]

King Fernando VII, still ensconced in his royal palace and surrounded by the potentially dangerous Cortes and the Madrid masses, naturally could not endorse the Urgel document and indeed had to repudiate it. A month after the manifesto appeared, he publicly rejected its authors without qualification: "Their projects are criminal; their hopes insane." The king supported the constitutional regime, praised the Cortes fulsomely, and urged the clergy and the press to condemn the Urgel criminals and bandits.[369] In October, with studied guile, the king opened the Cortes with a speech blaming the foes of the constitution for unrest and crime.[370] No one hearing the king's speeches and knowing nothing else would suspect his true attitude to the constitution regime.

In the provinces, what Vaudoncourt called "mushroom despots" sprang up all over Spain.[371] Ultra-royalist armed bands appeared in Galicia, Aragon, Catalonia, and Valencia. Navarre was dubbed "The Spanish Vendée." Priests stirred up the peasantry in a partisan war against the government. In October, a liberal deputy called the clergy "a state within a state in whose army the prelates are its generals and the Inquisition [though now non-existent] its reserve."[372] The anti-constitutionalists, known as "The Factious," began waging guerrilla war, sometimes led by veterans of the anti-French war. Adding to their popular appeal now as earlier, rebel chieftains bore picturesque names: Jaime Long Beard, Granpa, El Locho, The Vest, Caregal the One-Armed, Royo, Little Ear, the priest Querillas, Zavala Zavaletta, and the ferocious Rojo de Banderes.[373] As in the past, the movement attracted bandits such as The Thief, Baldo, and Johnny (Juanito) of Navarre.[374] Their messages were simple and clear-cut. The chieftain Romagoso said this to his band: "Comrades: my purpose in this rising is none other than to defend religion and the king. He who does not share these noble sentiments, leave my ranks."[375]

Prominent among priests and monks who led anti-government forces were Atanasio García in New Castile and Juan Cózar and Domingo Morales in Andalusia, who were caught and executed.[376] A parish priest, Mosen Ramo, captured about a hundred youths from good families who had supported the constitutionalists. He had them tied together and taken to the edge of a cliff, where they were abused with insults and laughter before being hurled over the precipice.[377] Most notorious among the guerrilla leaders, Antonio Marañon, an ex-monk and lay brother, was called El Trapense (The Trappist). Known for his extreme cruelty, he allegedly went into battle, like the guerrilla priests of 1808, holding aloft symbols of his cause: a crucifix in one hand and a whip in the other.[378] His followers, sometimes called Soldiers and Children of Jesus Christ, asserted in blood-curdling language that the liberals, whom they equated with Moors, had to be exterminated.[379] As in the case of the violent crowds in the French Revolution, opponents charged that the absolutist risings were financed from outside.[380] The Spanish historian Comellas denied this and claimed that the risings were spontaneous, that constitutionalists at the time invented some absolutist plots, and that liberal historiography exaggerated the scope of clerical reaction. Yet he himself charted some 122 popular risings (*alzamientos*) against the regime, not counting those led by royalist personages. Since many of the absolutists had resisted Napoleon, a generation that fought the French now began to fight each other.[381]

The pro-constitutionalist forces met violence with violence—and sometimes initiated it. Commanders in Aragon and Navarre meted out summary justice to the absolutists while vigilantes settled old scores.[382] The Barcelona Comuneros executed the bishop of Vich; donning the sabers, lances, helmets, and shakos left behind by Poles, Germans, Italians, and French, they held up a banner reading "Constitution or Death!"[383] Generals in the constitutional regime burned villages and slaughtered their inhabitants. Espoz y Mina, in October 1822, employed "military terrorism" to dismantle the Urgel Regency. He entered Castelfullit, a key observation point in the hills between Aragon and Catalonia, dotted with forts from the Reconquista period. Believing that the village had collaborated with the absolutists, Espoz y Mina executed the adult males and burned the homes. He left standing only a wall with a placard on it containing a chilling message—foreshadowing one of the most famous Nazi atrocities of World War II, the destruction of Lidice: "Here stood Castelfullit: villages are learning not to give shelter to traitors to the fatherland."[384] El Empecinado, fighting the French during the intervention, demanded arms from the southern town of Coria and the release of constitutional prisoners. Otherwise, he warned, nothing would remain of the settlement except a sign: "Here stood an infamous town." In Cadiz he killed innocent children. One general threw fifty-one prisoners over the side at sea.[385] In this war, wrote Raymond Carr, "both extreme liberalism and extreme royalism were popular in the worst sense of the word."[386]

To the Trocadero

When did Fernando VII began his intrigues to undermine the liberal regime? In October 1820 he implored his relative King Louis XVIII of France, with the help of the allies, to save him and his family.[387] But it seems likely that the idea entered the royal mind from the very beginning, though his public utterances resounded with praise for the Cortes. After the Austrian intervention in Naples reinstalled his uncle to an absolutist throne in March 1821, Fernando was fully alive to the possibility of repeating the operation in his own country. In any case, he played a double game by parlaying with the Cortes and the ministers for a modification of the constitution while secretly plotting for the restoration of absolute rule. On June 21, 1821, Fernando assured the Russian tsar through diplomatic channels that only armed assistance would protect the monarchy from destruction.[388] The liberal regime had few friends among foreign governments. Only the United States sent congratulations.[389] The British remained officially aloof, though a sympathetic public warmed to the constitutional regime. A London print of October 1820 showed the profiles of Quiroga, Riego, López de Baños, and Arco-Agüero as "the four distinguished founders of the Spanish Revolution," which bloodlessly put "the law above the king."[390]

King Fernando found ready audiences and allies at the conservative European courts. Foreign critics focused on flaws in the constitution. the tumult in the Cortes, and the inflammatory speeches in the clubs and street demonstrations. Louis XVIII desired a modification of the Spanish constitution along the lines of the French Charte. To this end, General Eguía held talks with the French and with Spanish exiles in France on imposing such an instrument on Spain.[391] The restored Neapolitan king Ferdinando became an unremitting enemy of the Spanish liberal regime. At Verona in 1822, he paid his respects to the powers who declared against representative government, free press, and popular sovereignty in Spain and in favor of a major role for religion and divine right.[392]

As early as the fall of 1820, the Holy Alliance, led by the three eastern autocracies—Austria, Russia, and Prussia—had convened in the Habsburg town of Troppau as part of the continuing work of the Congress System. They sent a sharp note to Madrid protesting the disorders in Spain, Naples, and Portugal. Martínez de la Rosa, still an influential figure in the Spanish government, responded with speech and brochure that constitutional movements would strengthen thrones in those nations. Unwisely, he recalled the partitions of Poland by the three protesting powers, their broken promises about constitutions, and their onetime alliance with Napoleon—noting with equal tactlessness that Britain opposed intervention in Spain. "Never," he said, "has the independence of a nation been more openly insulted."[393] From this point onward, relations between Spain and the three powers remained tense. At the time of the Austrian intervention in Naples, the Spanish government claimed that the Madrid police had foiled a plot, funded by an agent of the court, to throw stones at the embassies of Holy Alliance states in order to discredit the regime and bring on intervention.[394]

After the July putsch of 1822, the foreign ministers of the four powers (including France) warned the Spanish government of the threat to Fernando VII.[395] In November, the last congress of the Concert of Europe convened in the picturesque medieval Italian town of Verona, with its ancient marble buildings, narrow twisting streets, and scores of churches. By this time, the situation in Spain had deteriorated into a virtual civil war. The Urgel Regency dispatched a deputation to Verona, and the king of Spain sent a trusted official.[396] On November 22, 1822, the powers resolved "to destroy the representational system in every European state," to eliminate freedom of the press everywhere, and "to restore the [Iberian] Peninsula to the status pertaining prior to the Cádiz revolution." This was to be carried out by France, Spain's nearest neighbor, supported financially by the others. On the heels of this came an ultimatum accusing the Spanish revolution of inciting similar events in Naples and Piedmont.[397]

The Cortes displayed unwonted unanimity in rejecting the notes, promising to repel any attack. Evaristo San Miguel responded to the Verona notes in the

Cortes on January 9, 1823, accusing the signatories of libel and mendacity. He reminded them that the Russian tsar had recognized the constitution, that it enjoyed popular support, and that the Spanish king still wielded full executive power.[398] Michael Quin, a witness, watched as San Miguel, though possessing a weak voice, declared in stirring cadences that Spain was "secure of its principles, and firm in the determination of defending, at every hazard, its present political system and national independence," words that elicited a storm of applause. Riego and his colleagues reacted with a smile to Metternich's charge that Spain had triggered the revolts in Naples and Piedmont. Were they smiles of denial or agreement? Spectators booed and laughed at the Prussian note and displayed anger at the Russian one. Its insulting language about "*perjured* soldiers" fighting against king and country brought a jeering cry from the gallery: "Down with the tyrant!" Next day the youngest deputy, the author of *Lanuza*, also reminded his colleagues that during the Napoleonic wars the Prussian king and the Russian tsar had recognized the Spanish constitution, that it had been translated into Russian, and that Spanish prisoners had sworn an oath to it near St. Petersburg. The playwright promised a repetition of the 1808 war against future invaders.[399]

The solidarity over a foreign threat brought a temporary reconciliation between *moderados* and *exaltados*. The Cortes speeches about honor and sacrifice evoked cries of "Viva!" from the crowd, who carried speakers out on their shoulders. Madrid exploded in song, and once again the Riego hymn resounded into the night. News of the proceedings was read out to the people at the Puerta del Sol, where someone yelled, "Down with the tyrant!" and "Now for the Russian bear . . . down with the parricidal race!"—a clear reference to Tsar Alexander I's alleged role in the murder of his father, Paul, in 1801.[400] During Carnival, weeks later, mummers dressed up as Holy Alliance representatives, and Urgel reactionaries marched behind a jackass on which was mounted a man displaying the sign "Diplomatist of Verona." In the meantime, San Miguel had abandoned all pretense of diplomatic politesse as he communicated to the offending ambassadors his hope that they would leave Madrid as soon as possible.[401] War was now inevitable.

The Verona Congress assigned France the role of intervening in Spain. Another tragic episode in medical history put France in a strategically favorable position to do so. In August 1821, *Gran Turco*, a slaving brig out of Havana, brought to Barcelona yellow fever, the dread disease that had been decimating troops in Latin America for over a century, racked Spain on and off for a generation, and helped trigger the revolt of 1820. It eventually claimed the lives of about 20,000 of Barcelona's 120,000 residents. Since the fever at first hit the poorer districts, the authorities paid it scant attention; when it moved to affluent neighborhoods, they threw a quarantine around the city. By September hundreds were filling the churches, mounting processions, praying to exposed relics, and buying images of St. Roch, patron of disease victims. A small bribe could get one through the lines, even though local peasants fired at the escapees. When famine ensued, rioters sacked food shops; and the populace—egged on by *exaltados*—began accusing physicians of fostering the epidemic and even of murdering patients. Absolutist priests preached that the disaster was God's punishment for adhering to a constitution. In October a complete evacuation of the city began; in November the scourge receded, and the fever was declared officially ended on January 11, 1822.[402]

The French reacted vigorously by sending physicians and nurses into Barcelona to help the victims and stem the spread of the disease. Though some of the medical personnel deserted, others perished at their posts and became the subject of official honors and a rash of literature—including works by Delphine Gay, Victor Hugo, and Léon Halévy—that helped plant the fight against disease into romantic letters. The French government barred all ships out of Catalonia from docking at French ports, enforcing this with a sanitary fleet. It then ordered its own cordon sanitaire to be erected along the Spanish frontier, stretching from the Bay of Biscay to the Mediterranean: those attempting to cross it were fired upon. France had earlier evinced no great interest in Spanish epidemics. Now, some in the government clearly saw liberalism—Spanish or otherwise—fitting the standard definition of epidemic: a deadly communicable scourge that spreads rapidly among the population. French officials, deputies, and conservative journalists likened liberalism to pathology. A deputy in 1822 thanked his government "for having saved France both from the yellow fever and the revolutionary pestilence." Chateaubriand at the time worried about the risk of "exposing its soldiers to the dual contagion of the American disease and the Spanish revolution."[403]

Armand Carrel claimed that the French government, using the epidemic in Barcelona as an excuse, installed the cordon sanitaire along the Spanish frontier as no more than a ruse.[404] French and Spanish liberals shared that view and protested. Reliable sources refute this: at origin, the cordon was medically motivated. But it was soon used as a political instrument. It was policed by a force of some fifteen thousand troops, which in August 1821 began moving slowly by echelons toward the Pyrenees. In the summer of 1822, long after the *peste* had subsided, the cordon was transformed into an army of observation, and this in turn became an army of intervention. The French prime minister, Jean-Baptiste Villèle, justified the cordon and the army as a security measure. Yet when Spanish absolutist rebels, fleeing from government forces, crossed into France, they were in effect given asylum, medically examined, and allowed to return to fight again. This encouraged further risings in Catalonia, which in turn triggered further intervention.[405]

On the issue of intervention, France divided during the fall of 1822. The *Journal des Débats* distinguished between the current Spanish "shirtless ones" and the Cortes of 1812 that had led the heroic struggle against Napoleon, and it referred to "revolutionary tyranny" and "civil strife" in Spain.[406] The premier, Count de Villèle, showed more prudence. He hoped that if Spain adopted a modified constitution, France could avoid war.[407] He worried about finances, a possible British reaction, the specter of unrest in France, and the risk of French soldiers being infected by Spanish liberals. Louis XVIII supported him. But when the three eastern powers at Verona pressured the king, he appointed the forceful Chateaubriand as foreign minister in December 1822.[408] The new foreign minister observed that Spain had become a sanctuary for French radicals, aided by some Spaniards.[409]

François de Chateaubriand justified the coming intervention on the grounds of fear of revolution, France's national interest, and what we now call humanitarian concerns. As a great *homme de lettres*, he waxed eloquent on the issues. He offered up witty and at the same time sinister passages on the Italian Carbonari and the Spanish patriotic societies. Beyond the gothic details on the conspiracies, Chateaubriand displayed a fairly wide knowledge of their culture, rituals, and practices. Cataloging the disorders and violence that beset Spain on the eve of the French invasion, he called the liberal regime "a constitution of Spanish Mamelukes." Having become "more than ever convinced that danger surrounded the monarchy," he claimed the right to intervene in another state "in the name of human society." Chateaubriand also invoked his country's long tradition of military heroes from Clovis to Napoleon and alluded to a revision of the territorial settlement of 1815. Though friendly to Russia, Chateaubriand nevertheless showed alarm at Tsar Alexander's scheme of forming a reserve army to be deployed in Spain if desired by the powers. He considered the war on Spain his "political masterpiece," a pendant to his widely acclaimed novel, *René*. In fact, it amplified the polarization in France that led up to the revolution of 1830.[410]

French Liberals opposed restoring absolute monarchy elsewhere as an illegal violation of a nation's independence and of the spirit of the Charte.[411] A popular journalist told the troops that, after restoring reaction in Spain, the same would happen in France when they returned. A deputy said to the government: "You wish to deliver Spain back into the vengeful hands of the Inquisition and the Jesuits."[412] The opposition had no success. King Louis XVIII announced the decision to intervene on January 28, 1823. Only Lafayette and three others in the chamber opposed intervention.[413]

The commander of the intervention forces, Louis Bourbon, Duc d'Angoulême—nephew to the French king, supreme royalist, and perpetual exile—fit perfectly the mission of rescuing his distant cousin from the horrors of liberalism. His father, soon to be anointed King Charles X of France amid an orgy of medieval frippery, would lose his crown six years later in 1830. Angoulême had no war experience, but his troops were, in the words of Armand Carrel, well fed, clothed, housed, churched, and disciplined. Priestly sermons told them of their mission.[414] His army had changed its name after Verona from Army of Observation to Army of Spain. Unofficially known as "The Hundred Thousand Sons of St. Louis," it comprised some sixty thousand Frenchmen, with the rest Spanish absolutists.[415] St. Louis—that is, King Louis IX (1214–1270)—had the triple relevance of having been a pious Christian Crusader, the son of a Castilian mother, and the common ancestor of the kings of France, Spain, and Naples. The nickname of the force remained something of a joke in Spanish history. In the Civil War of the 1930s, one rival Republican faction called Juan Negrín's *carabineros* the "Hundred Thousand Sons of Negrín."[416]

In Angoulême's solidly balanced force, the majority had several years in service, though with little battle experience, except for the NCOs and officers. Armand Carrel claimed that some of these opposed the expedition, though most remained either loyal or neutral.[417] In a declaration from Bayonne of March 20, 1823, Angoulême, playing up his blood relation to the Spanish king, assured Spaniards that he intended them no harm and came to restore the power of throne and altar and bring order to the country. He blamed the revolutionary party in Madrid for igniting mutiny in France as it had done in Naples and in Piedmont.[418] The duke and his army crossed the Pyrenees on April 7, 1823.

Facing the French invaders stood a Liberal government hardly able to pay, arm, or clothe its troops properly. Should it stop the invading force by enlisting the aid of political exiles or rely on its own resources? The role of foreign refugees in the defense of Spain looms large in the story of the interrelationship of the 1820s revolutions, though it is often relatively neglected. If the conservative powers had, in a way, internationalized counterrevolution, liberals of several nations responded in kind. Pietro Gamba, Byron's Italian Carbonaro friend, observed that in August 1823, as the intervention was coming to a close, all eyes turned to Spain.[419] In fact, those eyes had been looking at liberal Spain since 1820. Edward Blaquiere believed that Spain could be the starting point of a wave of liberalism and national regeneration in the Mediterranean.[420] Foreigners' clubs, some predating the liberal regime, included the French Association in Madrid and, in Catalonia, a short-lived Carbonari group, and the Society for the Regeneration of Europe, with numerous Italian members.[421] While the Madrid government languished in its war preparation, political exiles from France, Naples, and Piedmont offered to stiffen the back of the regime.

The most prominent foreign would-be savior of the beleaguered Spanish government was Colonel Charles Fabvier. A tall, resolute soldier and a graduate of the École Polytechnique, he had joined Napoleon's army in 1805, served in Spain, and then was in Russia in 1812, where he was wounded. During the Restoration, he was implicated in the republican plot of the Four Sergeants of La Rochelle. Though his path to radicalism had been gradual, Fabvier became infected by the spirit of cosmopolitan patriotism that captured many officers in the post-Napoleonic era—a spirit reflected in the lyrics of Béranger, who sang: "Peoples—Form a Holy Alliance." Hunted by the police in France, Fabvier sought worthy causes in other climes. While Greece and Italy seemed far away at the time, nearby Spain became for him "the fortress of liberty." The spread of dissent among Bonapartists, republicans, and Orléanist officers in Angoulême's army encouraged Fabvier in the belief that he could subvert it, defend Spain, and then liberate France from the Bourbons.[422]

A Spaniard with ties to the secret societies made the initial contact with Fabvier, who hastened to London, where he met with British, French, and Italian political exiles. In December 1822, he landed on the northern coast of Spain and then made his way safely through territory racked by civil war to Madrid. There he bickered with the ministers over finances. The rosy optimism displayed by the regime alarmed Fabvier, and he complained that San Miguel acted as if he were doing the Frenchman a favor. To Fabvier it was essential to engage the French invaders on French soil. In January 1823 on the eve of invasion, Fabvier eventually reached agreement with the government, which accepted his formula that "the cause of liberty is undivided" and that all must contribute to it. Spain, menaced openly and covertly, had to be "the boulevard of liberty in Europe. Thus its safety must be the primary aim of all—and in return [Spain] must, in the interests of its security and its glory, contribute to the liberation of other nations"—Portugal, France, and Italy.[423] The decision represented an extraordinary escalation of the defense of liberty in one country to a liberal crusade in Europe.

Fabvier organized other exiles and gathered equipment. He correctly foresaw that, once over the frontier and subject to Spanish fire, the French troops would maintain discipline and defend the white flag of the Bourbons. So he focused on subverting the French Army of Spain while it still stood north of the Pyrenees. His leaflets claimed that an invasion of liberal Spain was the prelude to an invasion of France itself by the Holy Alliance. Fabvier commanded a "legion," two small units of no more than 150 men, many of them French and Italian political exiles; about a third of the total were veterans of Napoleon's armies. At his frontier headquarters on the Spanish bank of the Bidasoa River, Fabvier delivered copies of a proclamation to French troops in the front line facing him: "Soldiers, where are you going? And who would recognize in this youthful army, beneath this unclean banner, the children of the victors of Marengo and Austerlitz?" He called their leaders monks, thieves, émigrés, and traitors ready to defend Bourbon tyranny, and he called on the French troops to turn around and drive the Bourbons out of France instead of defending them in Spain. Hoping to fraternize and subvert, he flew the tricolor and raised banners inscribed with the words

France and *Liberté*. But as Fabvier's troops sang "La Marseillaise," the enemy loaded cannon. The legion met defeat and the French army entered Spain.[424]

Fabvier's attempt was not the last time international volunteers would rush to defend Spain from counterrevolution. Nor was it the end of international adventure for the liberal exiles in the Mediterranean. Fabvier's men dispersed abroad or were captured and taken to France, where most of them were eventually released. A few members of the legion stayed on in Spain to defend the constitutionalists; others went off to Portugal or the Americas. Fabvier himself began dreaming of a new crusade in Latin America or in Greece. He escaped via Lisbon to London, made contact with the Spanish Greek Committee, and, joined by other veterans of the Spanish war, went to Greece, where he held a major command in the revolutionary war.

Armand Carrel, a trained officer, onetime Carbonaro, and later a well-known journalist, had been assigned as an officer in the French forces invading Spain under Angoulême. He resigned in Marseilles and took ship to Barcelona. The Catalan seaport, accessible from Marseilles and Genoa—both hotbeds of revolutionary fugitives—became a refugee center for old Napoleonic figures, French republicans, German students, Polish rebels, and recently defeated liberals from Naples and Piedmont. Espoz y Mina, campaigning nearby, hoped to enlist them into a corps. Most scattered, but the five hundred or so remaining were fashioned into the Liberal Foreign Legion. Commanded by the Piedmontese exile Captain Giuseppe Pacchiarotti and another officer, the legion comprised no more than an infantry battalion and a squadron of lancers in which two Italian generals served in the ranks. With tricolor ribbons on their lances, they did battle at Figueres in Catalonia with the *absolutistas*. Some perished on the field of battle, and the wounded were cut to pieces by their enemy. Carrel survived and returned to France, where he was able to avoid prosecution.[425]

The most radical by far of the international volunteers, General Vaudoncourt, scorned the other French exile groups in Spain, especially "F" (Fabvier), whom he accused, rather ironically, of rashness and ambition. Like Fabvier, Vaudoncourt had fought in Russia under Napoleon. After numerous conspiracies hatched against Bourbon rule in Restoration France, he arrived in Spain in 1821. His agenda, a Spanish war of liberation to abolish the French and European reaction, led him to befriend the most radical Spaniards, scorn the moderates, and hate absolutists and the "legions of the northern despots." He inverted the Holy Alliance formula by declaring that a state (read Spain) whose political system was threatened by a neighbor (France) had the right to intervene to change the political system of that neighbor. Vaudoncourt proposed that Spain place three thousand troops on the French frontier, where they would be joined by French radicals, Napoleonic veterans, and Italian exiles. He laid out a fantastic plan to seize the medieval fortresses built to hold back the Saracens, such as Carcassonne, and the southern French cities of Perpignan, Toulouse, and Lyons. From there, they would march to overthrow the Paris government. He wrote to Riego that Spain could not remain free until France was made liberal. Riego opposed such action, fearing that this would give the Holy Alliance an excuse to intervene. Other deputies agreed.[426]

In the end, the Spanish government had to rely on its own resources, and these were weakened from the outset by excessive optimism in many circles. Speakers at the Landaburian Society announced that the invaders and the people of France loved the Spanish constitution but were being misled by degraded ministers who would be defeated by a free people. As in other liberal insurrections, optimists erroneously equated the love of liberty with military superiority. The invaders, being slaves, could not conquer Spain.[427] A common trope in the liberal age, it had been enunciated by Simón Bolivar in Latin America: "You are men, they are beasts, you are free, they are slaves."[428] Neapolitan liberals, Greek patriots, and Russian Decembrists used the same language. Patriotic rhetoric in Spain combined this argument with the myth of Marathon: "Yes, you will conquer them [the French] since one free man is worth a thousand slaves. Animated by the spirit of liberty, three hundred Greeks vanquished as many millions who sought to oppress them."[429] The empty magniloquence of defiance reached a peak in Seville in April 1823 as the town was preparing to meet the invaders: a local theater staged a female military ballet as a demonstration of the will to resist even by Spanish women. The public was not amused.[430]

In the critical months leading up to the war, Evaristo San Miguel headed the ministry from August 5, 1822, to February 20, 1823. By that time, he had secretly become a Ring wearer and thus more inclined to caution. His war minister, López de Baños, had turned to the right.[431] By rebuffing the Verona notes, San Miguel angered their authors and probably brought the intervention closer to reality, though many liberals agreed with his popular act of defiance. But he and his colleagues proved relatively lax in preparing for the invasion.[432] The cabinet deployed three army corps on the frontier under the veteran guerrilla commanders Espoz y Mina, El Empecinado, and Espinosa. It also had ships patrolling the Bay of Biscay and the waters off Barcelona to interdict communication between the French and the absolutist opposition.[433] This hardly sufficed; San Miguel even disbanded the Sacred Battalion and some militia units that were suspect for their intense radicalism, thus partially disarming Spain on the eve of invasion.[434]

Large-scale guerrilla resistance by the peasants à la 1808 might have seemed possible for the successful expulsion of the French, but in 1823 this did not materialize. On April 7, Angoulême's troops, including Swiss royal guards and men of other nationalities,[435] crossed into Spain at the Bidasoa River and various points in and near the Pyrenees. As the Sons of St. Louis marched southward toward Madrid in April and March, they found grim traces of the civil war now raging.[436] In contrast to the Napoleonic armies, the well-behaved force of 1823 paid for supplies instead of looting and met little or no resistance from the local population.[437] Michael Quin, traveling from Madrid to Seville, observed mostly indifference to the French invasion on the part of the population, except for Serviles, who hailed it.[438] When the invaders reached the capital on May 23, some Madrileños greeted them with the cry "Long live our deliverers! Death to the *negros!*" and sprinkled the Duc d'Angoulême with flowers from their balconies.[439]

The constitutional forces did offer stiff conventional military resistance. In the French campaign—by no means a cakewalk—infantry, artillery, and cavalry fought in pitched battles and men were riddled with murderous grapeshot. After taking Madrid, the French blockaded Corunna, Barcelona, and Cadiz,[440] and their warships and gunboats bombarded coastal towns and strong points. At first, Espoz y Mina's army in Catalonia turned out to be the only reliable force. Assisted by some political exiles,[441] he held on at the coasts and in the towns, but he met opposition in the mountains, where he waged a terror campaign against collaborators. With his ragtag army, he fought a six-week guerrilla campaign against three French generals.[442]

Even before the first engagement with the French, the Cortes decided to withdraw with the king southward to Seville. Fernando dallied in hopes that the French would reach the capital in time to rescue him. When in February he refused to go and dismissed the San Miguel government, the ministers put him under virtual house arrest. Hearing of the king's actions, a furious mob assembled at the palace and shouted, "Kill the king! Kill the tyrant!"—the first instance of such regicidal expression in public.[443] The crisis ended with the king forced to travel to Seville, where the crowds were even more radical than those of Madrid. The caravan, comprising a few thousand regulars and militia, departed on March 20 on the twenty-two-day journey through Granada and Malaga to Seville.[444] On April 11, 1823, Fernando VII entered the city during a rainstorm and to a mixed reception. Crowds of citizens on the balconies remained silent except for a few songs and cheers for Riego and a few for the king. The local clergy had a powerful religious sway over the population but little influence on politics.[445] On April 23, the Cortes resumed its work in Seville, and on the twenty-fourth, the king declared war on France.

As the French occupied ever large areas of Spain, the Cortes decided on June 11 to move again, this time to Cadiz. A deputation informed the king of the intended move, and when the royal personage again resisted relocation, mob violence threatened. Riego restored order. To protect him, the Cortes temporarily deposed Fernando. Alcalá Galiano invoked Article 187 of the constitution, which called for a regency "in the event that the king is unable to exercise his authority for whatever physical or moral reasons." The government declared Fernando to be in a state of "temporary delirium" (*delirio momentáneo*) and appointed a provisional regency.[446]

Those voting for this measure were later proscribed by Fernando. On June 12 the royal family left Seville and arrived three days later in Cadiz, which had remained pro-constitution in spite of the huge financial losses in trade and shipping.[447] After the Cortes departed from Seville, the lower classes went on a rampage of vandalism, apparently egged on by Serviles, destroying books, manuscripts, and other cultural artifacts.[448]

In the meantime, the command structure of the army fell into disarray due to continuous wrangling on policy and the desertion of key commanders. Generals Ballesteros and Morillo parlayed with the French and both soon defected, as did O'Donnell, who thus became a triple traitor, having in 1819 betrayed his comrades, in 1820 his king, and now in 1823 the constitutional regime. At first, the government denied Riego a command, then deployed him on various fronts. Riego was one of the few generals who carried out his orders to defend Spain and the constitution. He, Espoz y Mina, and El Empecinado refused to treat with enemy.[449] Finally Riego was assigned to the Cadiz region. That city, the birthplace of Spanish liberalism, was declared "the last boulevard of constitutional Spain."

As Spanish regulars were collapsing or in retreat, the Cortes, now desperate, in April 1823 decreed the formation of a Liberal Foreign Legion comprising units in each army of foreigners present in Spain.[450] In May this act was superseded by a new agreement. A London Spanish Committee, formed to militarily assist beleaguered Spain, appointed Sir Robert Wilson (1777–1849) as commander of volunteers. Wilson, a gallant and occasionally undisciplined officer, had served in the British army in various posts in Egypt, in South Africa, and all over Europe, including in Spain during the Peninsular War. Decorated by Tsar Alexander I, he had campaigned at Smolensk and in the pursuit of Napoleon during his retreat across Europe. After the war, Wilson gained a reputation as a radical reformer and was dismissed temporarily from the army. The Spanish government signed an agreement with Wilson, who was to serve as a lieutenant general in the Spanish army, raise his own forces, and have authority over other foreign units fighting for Spain. In explaining why he was fighting against the French government, Wilson described a motive common to many of his generation: he had fought the anti-Napoleonic struggle as a war of liberation and then saw it betrayed by the monarchs of Europe.[451]

Wilson's troops landed at Vigo, in northwestern Spain, where he took the oath to the Spanish constitution, then sailed to Corunna, where they campaigned during July and August. A Wilson volunteer, Thomas Steele, met many pro-constitutionalist citizens and anti-French guerrillas in the vicinity. With Cadiz as their destination, the volunteer force arrived at Gibraltar on September 9, 1823, and then after a delay of several days proceeded to the city, where Riego was holding out. Defended by forts and gunboats, though short on weapons, the constitutionalists settled in to face the French onslaught from warships and shore batteries that bombarded Cadiz as in 1810.[452]

The event that the French memorialized as their decisive victory in the Spanish war was the storming of the Trocadero, an ancient market and defensive structure on an island across from Cadiz. It held a garrison of some sixteen thousand men. Against them Angoulême, who had about thirty thousand troops in the area of Cadiz, sent a regiment and two battalions from nearby Puerta Santa María. While guns on both sides fought an artillery duel, St. Louis's feast day arrived, and on the last day of August the French began an assault from land and sea that lasted four and a half hours. The battle cost the defenders about 150 dead and 300 wounded.[453] Serving as a military surgeon in the French army was the future luminary of popular fiction and author of *The Mysteries of Paris*, Eugène Sue. From the moment the white banner of the Bourbons unfurled over the fort, the word *Trocadero* became incorporated into the annals of official French national-military glory. An orgy of celebration erupted in Paris.[454] After Trocadero, Cadiz fell in September, Malaga in October, and the last big town in November. Ragged bands of resisters continued to fight in the vicinity of Gibraltar into 1824.[455]

While the French were blockading Cadiz, Riego slipped through and proceeded to Malaga by sea in order to raise resistance. During his sojourn there in August and September, he released to the troops a flood of letters and proclamations full of pathos alternating with grandiose affirmations and bellicose rants, employing increasingly stronger language. One proclamation summed up the themes of 1820: a fight for honor, a need for discipline, and rejection of the cowardly and treacherous enemies of freedom.[456] The darkness and desperation of his words were carried over into action. According to an 1827 account of Riego's brief rule in Malaga, based on the church calendar kept by the bishop, his men extracted money from citizens, looted churches and confiscated their silver and gold plate for the war effort, arrested three generals and clergy who opposed the constitution, and murdered four of the captives.[457] To curb desertion, Riego offered soldiers who displayed bravery in the field furloughs, medals, and tracts of land, and issued a harsh order stating that deserters who rejoined his ranks within fifteen days would be pardoned. In one of its tortured clauses, he promised that "those who continued in their offence will be pursued in all directions, requiring that judges and families meet the responsibilities imposed by law; and then those caught will be shot without mercy."[458]

Departing from Malaga, Riego took to the hills and fought against the French. A British liberal volunteer, George Matthewes, arrived from Gibraltar with arms and other supplies arranged by Robert Wilson. But resistance became increasingly hopeless. When the French arrived in Malaga, Riego's men crossed the Sierra Nevada, incurring losses and desertions. As in 1820, numerous little towns welcomed him with church bells rather than volunteers. In one of them Riego met and captured General Ballesteros, who refused to break his oath to the French and escaped. In one engagement of heavy fighting with the French, Riego's troops suffered big losses, and a bullet wounded Riego in the knee and killed his horse.[459] Riego, in the company of three officers—a Spaniard, an Englishman, and a Piedmontese—found refuge near the village of Arquiello. Betrayed by a local inhabitant, he was captured in September by the local authorities, taken from town to town, and put in the custody of the French.[460]

Hearing of the capture, authorities in nearby Jerez ordered two days of illuminations, bell ringing, and a Te Deum, with all officials in attendance.[461] At one of the stopping points, crowds shouted, "Death to Riego!" and "Kill them, murder them! They are Jews, Jacobins, Heretics, Freemasons."[462] When a mob threatened to lynch Riego, the beleaguered captive remarked ironically to his French guards about the fickleness of the masses, "These people that you see today so violently against me, who would cut my throat without your protection, these same people last year bore me here in triumph. All night long the homes were lit up, the people danced beneath my windows and deafened me with their cries." A French regiment escorted Riego and his companions in mule carts on a twelve-day trek to Madrid. Along the way, they endured further assaults from the population and its clergy. At one point, liberal troops tried unsuccessfully to free him.[463]

In September, when defeat at Cadiz seemed imminent, the remnant of the government, having gotten King Fernando to sign an amnesty for all those associated with the liberal regime, permitted the king to cross over and join the French at Puerta Santa María. As soon as he came under their protection, he annulled the amnesty. On October 1, Fernando VII, restored to full power in Madrid, issued a manifesto proclaiming that he had been a prisoner since 1820 and had been subjected to "criminal treason, shameful cowardice, and most horrible disrespect for my royal person."[464] Rescued, he said, by God, the allies, and Angoulême, Fernando now repeated his 1814 coup and rendered the constitution void, renounced all legislation passed since 1820, and issued arrest orders.[465] To crown his triumph, on November 13 the king was drawn through the streets of Madrid in an antique chariot by a hundred men, with dancers cavorting beside the carriage as the crowds shouted, "Long live Ferdinand and religion! Death to the *negros* and the constitution!"[466]

Did Fernando VII unleash a terror? The period 1823–33, the king's final years, has been dubbed "the ominous decade." Anecdotes abound about the extent of Fernando's cruel repression. A biographer of Goya claimed that "thousands [were] executed under martial law," that "no less that 1,825 officers and men of the former constitution army were murdered in Catalonia alone," and that in 1825 "112 persons were hanged or shot within eighteen days."[467] Another relates that Prince Carlos, brother of the king and captain-general of Catalonia, danced on the gallows in full uniform as some liberals were being hanged.[468] Most of the stories lack plausible documentation and their figures draw on very old and unreliable secondary works. But there is no denying Fernando's rule of vengeance. Though it is doubtful that he uttered the words "If I am guilty of something it is not having hanged a quarter of all Spaniards in 1814,"[469] the repression he imposed in 1823–24 was real enough. History has produced few defenders of a king who in 1808 cravenly bowed to Napoleon in 1808, in 1814 arrested the men whose constitution he had recognized and who had helped wage his war, in 1820 swore on that constitution and then betrayed it, and in 1823 granted an amnesty and then broke it. Yet it must be recorded that the repressions ended rather quickly and that Fernando moved to a more moderate position—thus enraging the extreme right.[470]

Most of the liberal leaders escaped. The veteran guerrilla El Empecinado, not so fortunate, languished in a dungeon for ten months and was periodically put on display in a cage on market days to be abused by the people. On the gallows, an executioner's assistant taunted him with the very sword he had used in battle. The enraged El Empecinado lunged at the man, stumbled, and was clubbed to death while the crowds yelled "Death to the Jewish villain!"[471] There was nothing Jewish about El Empecinado but, given his murder of innocents while campaigning, much of the war criminal.

Little people suffered along with the big. A Madrid cobbler who salvaged a piece of the recently demolished constitutional plaque lit votary candles before it and a portrait of Riego. Arrested, he was made to march to the scaffold with the picture hung around his neck, where it was burned by the executioner. The bearer received a ten-year prison sentence.[472] Invoking the doctrine of *limpieza* (cleansing) to punish heresy, the authorities reestablished the Inquisition, though it staged only one execution under Fernando VII: the hanging as a freethinker of a Catalan schoolteacher in 1826.[473] A noted conservative monarchist, the Marquis de Custine, visited Spain in 1831 and later published several volumes about the country full of anti-liberal bile. But he also fretted about the stupid cruelties of Fernando VII. Custine told of a twenty-eight year-old widow who ordered a flag of liberty to be sewn in preparation of a plot. Betrayed to the police, she was condemned by Fernando to execution unless she revealed her accomplices. She refused and was drawn through the streets of Granada on a jackass and hanged. The shocked townspeople closed their shutters and emptied the streets on the day of the execution. When the next royal festival day arrived soon afterward, many houses hung black banners from the windows instead of the rich cloths customary in joyful fêtes.[474]

Spontaneous popular anger outstripped that of the central government, spurred mostly by revenge for cruelties perpetrated by supporters of the liberal regime in 1822 and during the French invasion. Vaudoncourt relates that when a militia and lower-class parade in May 1823 marched and shouted, "Viva Riego! Viva el pueblo soberano!" a bystander was killed for not joining in.[475] In the same year, a militia column massacred fourteen priests and a bishop at Mora del Ebro as counterrevolutionaries.[476] The resisters also hatched several plots against the life of Angoulême.[477] An admittedly biased Russian journal reported that when the French arrived in Madrid, constitutional soldiers attacked innocent civilians, leaving a thousand dead.[478]

The absolutists' cruelties far surpassed those of their foes. Acts of vengeance began long before the restored king reached his capital. After the liberal caravan departed from Seville, according to Vaudoncourt, violence broke out against suspected liberal sympathizers, and monks urged the crowd to kill them.[479] In parts of Spain where the French were absent, the fury went uncontrolled. Central and provincial juntas waged purification campaigns targeting militias and secret society members. The accused were stripped of honors, jailed, expelled from the capital, or sent into exile. In Cadiz, crowds sacked the Cortes building and liberal cafés and homes. On religious feast days, demonstrators led by priests burned copies of the constitution, danced on the ashes, smashed commemorative plaques, and put up crucifixes and portraits of Fernando VII. People engaged in spontaneous denunciations and officials made arrests on flimsy charges such as owning a handkerchief embroidered with the words "Long live the constitution!"[480] An angry crowd opened the grave of Felipe de Arco-Agüero, burned his raiment and the coffin, and pitched the cadaver into a sewage tank.[481]

The French, like many interventionist forces throughout history, came in for recrimination from all sides. The liberal government falsely accused the French invaders of repeating the atrocities of the Napoleonic period.[482] In fact, Angoulême's army had little cause to commit atrocities since the population welcomed them in most places. French diplomats and officers tried in vain to stop absolutist reprisals, as did Angoulême himself, who in disgust declined a victory parade in Madrid and returned directly to France. For this, some accused him of Jacobinism.[483] On hearing reports of clerical persecution, abuses, and pillage, Chateaubriand tried to curb the scope of the reactionary terror by threatening to remove French troops. Resentful of French efforts, the royal government, using the clergy as its mouthpiece, secretly backed an anti-French campaign while publicly putting on a friendly face toward its guests. In 1824, France, Britain, and Russia pressured Fernando VII through the Russian ambassador to grant an amnesty.[484]

Other foreigners honorably assisted liberal leaders to escape certain death. William à Court, a monarchist foe of liberalism, had helped constitutionalists flee from Naples in 1821; assigned to Spain, he did so again in 1823.[485] About two hundred Spanish escapees, including fifty to sixty Cortes members, sailed toward the British base of Gibraltar and were put in quarantine, meaning they had to stay afloat on ships bearing yellow flags. When the quarantine ended, the fugitives entered Gibraltar and then dispersed. Some went to nearby North Africa.[486] Those who escaped the retribution of Fernando included Quiroga, López de Baños, Argüelles, Alcalá Galiano, Mendizábal, Mina, and Romero Alpuente. Most of these, sentenced to death in absentia, landed in England; a few returned to Spain after Fernando's death. Mendizábal, who had ridden with Riego in 1820, became prime minister in 1836. San Miguel, caught by the French, was removed to France and released in 1824. He returned to Spain after Fernando's death under the amnesty of 1833.[487] Riego's wife, assisted by Matthewes, made her way to England via Gibraltar.[488] Her husband did not make it.

Why did the liberal experiment in Spain fail? Sorting out and measuring the various factors and their combination that bring down a political regime of any type is fraught with difficulties. A modern scholar made bold to summarize the judgments of anti-liberals by stating, quite rightly, that constitutional rule had no significant support in the population. For this he blames most of what went wrong on the liberals of both camps, especially the left wing, and he absolves the king of guilt.[489] Sympathetic eyewitnesses also pulled no punches in critiquing the liberal regime. Michael Quin noted the overly severe expropriation of monastic land. It failed to produce revenue because of the piety of would-be purchasers, and it generated deep resentment among the monastic clergy and among ordinary people who missed the monks' charity, the feasts, and the familiar mystique surrounding the monastery. He also cited the lack of a property qualification in the constitution and the regime's intolerance of any criticism.[490] Blaquiere, who was even friendlier to the new regime, lamented its failure to resolve the Latin American question, the grudging amnesty for the *afrancesados*, and granting immunity to the perpetrators of the Cadiz massacre in 1820.[491]

To this list needs to be added mutual alienation and feuding of those in power: radical versus moderate, civil versus military, and ego versus ego on every side. Together they caused tension and mistrust, leading to the sacking of skilled military leaders and the defection of others, legislative deadlock, and an inability either to mollify the monarch or to face up to his machinations. All observers— from Riego to his bitterest opponents—agreed that the liberal regime did not win the hearts and minds of the masses. The arch-republican supporter of the liberals, Colonel Fabvier, in his travels in the north of Spain, observed what he termed a fanatical population of a country where only the middle class wanted a constitution.[492] In an old but still valuable study, Jean Sarrailh judged that Spaniards overwhelmingly favored the absolutists and warmly welcomed the French army simply because neither the Cadiz liberals of 1810, despite a wartime common struggle, nor those of the Trienio had ever forged a bond between their regimes and the general population.[493]

But Sarrailh also recognized reasons for this that went beyond the weaknesses and policies of liberalism. The people always remained under the influence of the clergy. In 1823, a flood of addresses and congratulations to the restored king poured into Madrid. Sarrailh saw evidence of editing of these by local priests. Their language bristled with total condemnation and sweeping invective. The enemy received no nuanced judgment, no qualification, no quarter. One denunciation of June 1823 declared that for three years "iniquity, treason, rapine, usurpation, violence, and lies were enthroned in Madrid."[494] The triumphalists never called the liberals misguided, but rather characterized them as evil personified. The absolutist junta in Seville in 1823 urged the people to "destroy the edifice of anarchy and restore liberty to the king our lord," thus advancing its own definition of "liberty."[495] Satanic literature and falsified documents spoke of alleged Jewish crimes, especially in reactionary bases such as the Basque land, inner Catalonia, the lower Ebro, and Navarre.[496] As a pendant to the hate material, the victors published unctuous requests for a return of the Inquisition and of church property and privilege.[497]

A modern scholar called Fernando the embodiment of reactionary thought, a view not shared by all historians. But he rightly saw that the Spanish reactionaries who supported the king sustained a myth, an "absurd but coherent distortion of reality" that imagined a vast conspiracy against throne and altar. Its proponents saw any attempt to modify the absolutist-feudal regime as diabolical, and they taught a "radical, absolutist, intransigent, and—when needed—brutal affirmation of the unlimited power of king and church and of that class which identified its interests with those of the monarchy, that is the nobility." This belief system transformed Fernando VII, even in 1814, from the Desired One to a Holy Savior. "Long live the King! Long live religion! Eternal death to the Constitution!" ran a press slogan as constitutions were being burned all over Spain.[498]

One must also trace the difficulty of implanting constitutional life in Spain back to the decision of King Fernando VII in 1814 to abrogate the constitution instead of trying to work with it or gain its modification. Quin attributed to Fernando VII a "pride of mind that deemed the country, and all that inhabited it, created for his special use, and an imbecility of resolution that would be scarcely excusable in a boy."[499] The king's behavior after 1820 exacerbated the problem. The people knew nothing of his plots. What they saw was disorder; its cause, their priests told them, was revolution. Many priests and monks denounced abuses in the church, but the vast majority remained absolutists both in 1810 and 1820. They were the best-organized force of reaction. A French envoy reported to Chateaubriand that preachers hurled inflammatory messages from the pulpit such as "it is essential to destroy the *negros* and even their babes at the breast."[500]

What if France had not intervened and the liberals had had time to work out a new political dispensation gradually, without provocation? As it turned out, the Spanish people, having faced four kinds of "Frenchies"—Napoleon's army, the *afrancesados*, the liberals (as many ordinary folks saw them), and the army of St. Louis—found only the last acceptable. Yet in the end it was French military force that destroyed the constitutional regime. Evgenii Tarle, the distinguished Soviet historian of Napoleonic Europe, took that view. And the British dean of Spanish historians, Raymond Carr, by no means an uncritical admirer of the liberal regime, concluded that, "reduced to its own resources and without French aid, royalism could not have imposed its views on Spain."[501]

On the Plaza de la Cebada

On the morning of October 2, 1823, the convoy bearing Riego entered Madrid through the Toledo Gate and proceeded to the elite school Seminario de las Nobles, his first place of confinement. On the way to prison, mounted troops lined the route and blocked the side streets to prevent rescue attempts and to keep the crowds away. *El Restaurador*, an absolutist mouthpiece, announced Riego's arrival: "He has come to Madrid, the brigand chief, / He has come, assassin, coward, thief."[502] Conte de Torre Alta, the warden, one of the killers of Landáburo,[503] blocked out the prisoner's windows and put him in heavy shackles, attached by a short chain to an iron ring in the wall.[504] He also denied visiting rights to all except his defense attorney, Faustino Julián de Santos. It has been claimed that, after sentencing, the prisoner was poorly fed and clothed while in prison. Some have cited rumors that Riego's friends wanted to smuggle poison to him in order to spare him a shameful fate.[505] This is probably the source of the otherwise undocumented story that Riego was poisoned by his jailers, a tale redolent of Stendhal's *Charterhouse of Parma*. To Riego's request for books and a barber to shave him, his jailers granted only the first, fearing a suicide attempt. Riego told de Santos: "But, though I am brave enough to give up my life . . . , I do not intend to take it with my own hands because I cannot abandon the religious feelings that have been engraved in my heart since childhood."[506]

Riego's trial opened in a courtroom in the Palacio de Santa Cruz that now houses Spain's foreign ministry. Huge crowds assembled in the adjoining square, on the steps, and inside the courtroom, periodically letting out cries of "Death!" The treason charge against the defendant arose from his vote, along with many others, to unseat the king for a few days and remove him to Cadiz. But given the roster of other alleged crimes and the language in which the prosecutor couched them, it is clear that Riego had been on trial since day one of January 1820—the pronunciamento, the restoration of the constitution, and indeed his almost every act, real and invented. The king had drawn up a proscription list as early as 1822 with Riego's name on it.[507] Defense attorney de Santos believed that the judges bowed to the bloodlust of the crowd. This had indeed been on display on and off since the captive Riego had been brought in chains to the Madrid jail. But all other indicators—the trumped-up charges, the savage sentence demanded by the prosecution, and the actual sentence and its shaming apparatus—clearly point to vindictiveness and spite. Riego's valiant war service against the Napoleonic invasion, laid out by the defense, had no effect on the verdict and the sentence.[508]

The prosecution demanded the traditional mode of execution: "dragging" (meaning hauling through the public streets), hanging, and quartering. It was commonplace in Spain and Latin America to cart the accused to the gallows, hang and behead him, and quarter the cadaver. Quartering (actually, cutting into six pieces) involved sending the severed limbs and the head for display at places associated with the crime. The dismembered torso was thrown into a grave. The exhibiting of body parts of traitors and robbers had long been employed by authorities throughout Europe, from London Bridge to the Bosphorus. Riego's prosecutor called for "execution on the gallows, the body to be dismembered by decapitation and quartering—sending the head to Las Cabezas de San Juan, one limb to the city of Seville, another to the Island of Leon, another to the city of Malaga, and the last one in this city [displayed] at the usual places and main points where the criminal Riego has fomented rebellion and exhibited his treasonous activity."[509] The tribunal rendered a verdict of guilty and the death penalty but turned down the demand for quartering, though false stories about it circulated for years.[510] Though the king had promised amnesty at Cadiz, he rejected Riego's plea for mercy.

On November 4 Riego was transferred to the court prison to await execution. After his death, the authorities presented what was purportedly Riego's last confession and a retraction of all his evil actions, dictated in prison. According to the document it released, Riego wished to die in the bosom of Mother Church, in whose mysteries he believed. "I admit the crimes that have earned me the death penalty," that is, his role in the "constitutional system," the revolution, its fatal consequences, and his offense to the king, the church, the faith, and the people of Spain. Expressing a desire that the document be made public, it was dated November 6, 1820 at 8:00 p.m. An article written in Madrid on November 7 and printed in a Barcelona newspaper quoted other words that Riego allegedly uttered: "I am sorry, as is natural, to die on the gallows. But I recognize that I deserve much worse for the evil deeds I have done and the many more that have been committed in my name." And further: "I wish to spend many years in purgatory in order to atone for my sins."[511]

The letter, if genuine, is at first glance an astonishing repudiation of the noble if flawed career of a very brave man. Some have made a case for its authenticity.

Riego's life, his record, and his words leave no doubt that he was a deeply religious man—a very Spanish Catholic. It was customary in most Catholic countries for the condemned to spend some of their final hours in a special prison chapel. Riego requested the spiritual assistance of the Dominicans of Santo Tomás de Madrid. That order, he said, had inculcated in him the cult of the Holy Virgin when he was a boy at the San Domingo convent in Oviedo. On hand also were the Brothers of Peace and Charity. One biographer related, though without a source, that in prison Riego "experienced a violent mystical exaltation."[512] After his time with the Dominican brothers, he might have become convinced that his actions constituted crimes. The confession came after the sentence, when there was no hope of a reprieve. In any case, jail-cell and especially eve-of-execution acts of repentance were and are commonplace.[513]

Later writers doubted the letter's authenticity. Some argued that it was concocted by the priests. Others claimed that it was the product of coercion, Riego's mental instability at the time, or a mendacious promise of pardon. By one account, his jailer showed Riego the published confession that had been written by someone else in his name and then had him drugged on execution day to prevent him from shouting the truth.[514] Most of these versions smack of melodrama. Yet forced or staged repentance was common in Spanish history. Locals in these years staged repentance events of troublemakers, mostly in chapels.[515] The account by Riego's lawyer as told to his son casts doubt on the much-contested confession. When de Santos revealed to Riego the verdict and the sentence on November 5, the condemned man is said to have met it with composure and dignity, though he told his lawyer he felt puzzled and depressed by the people calling for his death. De Santos tried to console him by invoking the martyrdom and eternal glory of Lacy, Porlier, and other Spanish heroes who had suffered in the cause of liberty. The most telling of Riego's words as reported by de Santos were these: "If this is my fate, I will go to the gallows with resignation and with the assurance that *I have acted well*" (italics added).[516]

On the day of the execution, November 7—just two days after sentencing—the prisoner was led out of his cell at around ten in the morning. As de Santos—father or son—put it, Riego "was led to the scaffold, shamefully dragged through the crowd which, having not long ago borne him in triumph through those same streets of the capital, now quietly watched his death." Emerging from the prison amid the "ferocious jubilation" of some and the sorrow of the few sympathizers, Riego displayed emotion only when he saw the vehicle of shame that was to transport him to the gallows.[517] The use in most non-Spanish accounts of the term "basket" suggests a roundness whose roll and bounce would cause continuous pain to the passenger. In fact, the serón, a flat-bottomed pannier coarsely woven of esparto, a rope-like grass, served as an all-purpose wheelless carrier for coal and other items. Given the surface of old Madrid's streets, the discomfort was great enough, and the humiliation complete since it was pulled along by a burro or jackass. Donkeys had been designated in earlier times by the Inquisition to carry those accused to the stake and were often used in Spanish American executions. *Equus asinus*—an ancient symbol of a stupid, stubborn nature—often appeared as the donkey-as-dunce in old burlesque traditions of Spain and other European societies. *Arrastrar* (to drag), in a punitive sense, originally meant dragging by the feet, facedown. From the time of King Philip II traitors had been dragged to the gallows. For other crimes, nobles rode on horses or mules and lower classes on donkeys to their place of execution, while military men walked.[518]

The long procession, begun with a drumroll and led by the district mayor, moved from the prison on Calle Concepción Jerónimo down a steep and narrow decline to the broader Calle Toledo and then south past the Hospital de la Latina (no longer extant) to the Plaza de la Cebada. Contrary to another popular legend, this was a very short journey. The more or less serious pictorial representations of the procession—one set near the hospital, one at the gallows, and one somewhere in between—show officials and clergy on foot and patrols on horseback to maintain security. In one image, Riego is sitting up with a crucifix in his hands with a dolorous expression on his face. Garbed in a condemned man's black gown with a rope belt, Riego appears unshaven and with signs of acute illness. Personal appearance was, in that age of gorgeous military apparel, cherished by high-ranking officers. What might he have felt, attired for his final appearance in the tatters of shame? An eyewitness described the donkey as "wretched and emaciated" and its passenger as no better: "pallid, anemic, and looking half dead." The ministrations of the clergy were, he thought, well meant but seemed more horrible than consoling.[519]

Crowd mockery frequently afflicted those on their way to Spanish executions. One of the Goya Caprichos of 1796–97 has a woman in irons and wearing a dunce cap abused by a sadistic, insulting, and bloodthirsty mob. In Pérez Galdós' fictional account, the "vile canaille" exulted in the coming death of Riego.[520] Some of the pictorial art, done after the fact, has crowds gesturing, apparently jeeringly, at the condemned. A particularly sensational 1928 book on Riego's execution appeared in a pulp series devoted to crime, mystery, and scandal. Its lurid paperback cover depicted in vivid colors a couple doing a Spanish dance, a cheering crowd, and the corpse of Riego dangling from the gibbet. The text and cartoon illustrations got almost everything wrong, including the prisoner's basket and garb and fictitious scenes of couplets sung to guitars and castanets. One of the songs commented nastily and erroneously on the four men who had been regularly represented together as the heroes of the 1820 revolution: "Thus Arco-Agüero perished, dragged; so will Riego—soon we'll get López Bañoz [sic] and Quiroga."[521]

The Plaza de la Cebada or Barley Square was a busy, multifunctional meeting place and site of commerce, as shown vividly in Manuel de la Cruz y Cano's canvas of a fair in the late eighteenth century. Having the churches of San Andrés, Santa Cruz, and San Isidro nearby, it also became the natural venue for religious festivities, as pictured in Manuel de Chozas' *Procession of the Virgin*. On feast days, the balconies were hung with flowers and particolored carpets and tapestries of silk, chintz, or damask.[522] No such festive brightness adorned the balconies on November 7, 1823. According to Pérez Galdós, balconies were normally rented out for executions at the Plaza de la Cebada.[523] In Astur's telling of the day of Riego's hanging, the balconies were packed, but silence reigned except for the clatter of hoofs and the prayers of the priests and brothers. One onlooker described the neighborhood around the plaza as mostly lower-class, with a sprinkling of those who, "by dress and manners," were higher on the social scale.[524] Another account related that many priests and friars shared the balconies with the lay citizens.[525]

The Plaza de la Cebada had been used as an execution place from the eighteenth century until after Riego's death, when that function was moved to the much larger Plaza Mayor. The Plaza de la Cebada then became the site of a covered market—an ugly modern version of which stands there today. The procession debouched into the square at noon, having marched for two hours in a journey that is no more than a ten-minute walk. This was due no doubt to the density of the crowd and the length of the procession in front of the condemned. Allegedly, upon Riego's arrival, a marquesa whose personal hatred of the man dated from earlier years told her accompanying friend's daughter to spit on him from their carriage.[526]

According to a Spanish juridical scholar, hanging had been traditionally reserved for the plebs and for "villains" as a demeaning death. Garroting, held to be neutral, was used for nobles, and the firing squad was reserved for the military. Thus, he argued, the hanging of Riego—a nobleman and an officer—was illegal. In Spain, the garrote worked by applying a screw through a post into the nape of the neck of the sitting victim. Though painful, the shaming from defecation and urination that came with death was hidden. Joseph Bonaparte in 1809 had proclaimed the garrote for all regardless of sex or station, a measure adopted by the Cortes. In 1814, Fernando VII restored hanging (as well as public lashing), though he finally abolished it in 1828.[527] In Spain, Latin America, and Italy, shoulder hanging was used in preference to the trap door. The chief executioner would climb on the condemned's shoulders for weight while two assistants pulled downward on the legs to hasten strangulation. In this method, the agony and the mortification of gleeful hangmen pulling one's legs or hanging on one's back proved unavoidable.[528]

On the permanent scaffold, ringed by troops, the gibbet on November 7 was erected higher than the norm so that the unusually large crowd could witness the death. The shackled Riego, with some difficulty, mounted the scaffold. The friars assisted him up the stairs and several sources say that he kissed each step and held the cross fervently. Riego raised aloft the crucifix he had been carrying, in the manner of the oft-cited sixteenth-century hero Padilla, who on the gallows had said: "This is not a day to do battle like caballeros, but a day to die like Christians." Riego gave the cross to the padre along with a cloth with which he wiped his face. A black silk kerchief was put around his eyes and the noose around his neck. The hangman mounted Riego's shoulders, while helpers pulled at the legs. The executioner cried, "Long live the King! Long live religion!" These words were echoed by his assistants and, in one account, by a handful of hecklers, hired by haters of Riego to cast insults at the corpse and cheer his death. The bulk of the crowd apparently remained silent. As they watched, Riego was catapulted into eternity.[529]

3

Guglielmo Pepe

Marching into Naples

Didst thou not start to hear Spain's thrilling pæan
From land to land reëchoed solemnly,
Till silence became music?
—Shelley, *"Ode to Naples"*

General Guglielmo Pepe of the Royal Army of the Kingdom of the Two Sicilies (Naples) had no need to fight his way across the country for three months in order to install a constitutional regime. Arriving on July 6, 1820, at the provincial town of Avellino, the general issued a proclamation declaring the 1812 Spanish constitution for his country. Employing the language of wounded national pride and a summons to resurgence, Pepe echoed Riego's Andalusian pronunciamentos in words that later resonated with those of the Greek patriots and the Russian Decembrists. He contrasted his beautiful and bountiful land with its present decadence due to centuries of barbarism, servitude, and debasement; its brimming pool of talented souls with its lack of cultural status; its record of military ardor with its second-class role in Europe. Like Riego also, Pepe reminded his audience (and Europe) of the Neapolitans' early and prominent role in armed resistance against Napoleon's occupying legions. The path to reclaiming the Kingdom of Naples' rightful status, he argued, was to replace arbitrary rule with the lawful sway of a constitution. Pepe, like other liberals, understood constitutional rule as a school in which government teaches the people, who in turn add their wisdom to those who govern. Well aware already of the military threat that other powers might present to a constitutional Naples, he referred to such constitutional regimes in France, Spain, Britain, the Netherlands, and the United States, and he warned would-be enemies of his country's capacity to resist invasion. At the end of the proclamation, Pepe swore to secure the constitution for his people or perish in the attempt.[1]

A few days after the Avellino proclamation, Pepe marched into the capital, the
vast city of Naples, leading a long procession of some fourteen thousand people.
It was July 9, 1820, right after noon—a bit more than six months after Riego had
issued his pronunciamento. Though not planned that way, the column rolled
through Naples on the same day that the Spanish Cortes opened in Madrid across
the sea. At its head rode the Sacred Squadron of Nola, a cavalry unit led by Lieutenants Morelli and Silvati. General Pepe on a galloping mount, flanked by fellow
officers, followed with elements of the regular army and a noisy militia. The most
raucous and colorful unit in the parade, the six- to seven-thousand-strong Mucius

Scaevola lodge of the Nola Carbonari, trotted by in ragged formation, armed with hunting carbines and bearing the raiment, ornaments, and blue-red-black banners of their civic religion. They shouted, "Long live the King! Long live the Constitution!" A sympathetic foreign eyewitness described multicolored crowds with variegated provincial costumes and weapons enlivening the parade with symbols and emblems and badges of every sort. "The cartridge belt, the sandalled legs, the broad stiletto, short musket, and grey peaked hats" worn by some, together with the sunburned faces and warlike appearance of the marchers, made them seem to him like real-life versions of the images that Romantic painters made of brigands on their canvases. Armed to the teeth and wearing Carbonari artifacts on his cassock, the Catholic clergyman Friar Luigi Minichini rode at their head on a white horse.[2]

The solemn and jubilant procession threaded through the miles of streets of the capital. Its longest leg ran along the Via Toledo, the main north-south artery of Naples, which passed alongside the expanse of Piazza del Mercatello (nowadays Piazza Dante) and further south fed into the palace complex. The royal residence, then and now, faced the Bay of Naples on one side and the city on the other. As the procession ended, the marchers, as customary in public demonstrations, filed past the windows of the royal palace to be greeted by King Ferdinando I and his son. General Pepe left the ranks in order to join the king in reviewing the stream of humanity. Ferdinando, like his nephew in Madrid, was faced with an event not of his making or of his liking; at first he feigned illness, though later he received Pepe and other rebels inside the palace. The source of Ferdinando's discomfort was the implication of a document that rolled down the public thoroughfare with the parade, borne on "a common hackney one-horse chair, called a *curricolo*": it was a copy of the Spanish constitution of 1812. At the Largo della Carità—a nearby square—crowds proclaimed that constitution.[3] "All the houses were adorned with flags and garlands; the air rang with cries of *'Long live the king! long live the constitution!'*" Artillery salvos, drumbeats, and marching bands fed the ardor of the crowds. Pepe recalled the tremendous enthusiasm of the onlookers. A shopkeeper, employing a common allegory of freedom, handed the general a cage from which, as Pepe opened it, birds flew out.[4]

Parade theatricality, endemic to the city of Naples, became an instrument of liberal revolt. Since the eighteenth century, its theater audiences had adored the spectacle of armed troops and royal cavalry on the stage of the San Carlo Theater.[5] The secretive cells of the Carbonari, in Naples and elsewhere, were known for their staged ritual; the royal court had always deployed to the streets in their shows of power; and the Catholic Church had surpassed them all in outdoor mummery, both solemn and festive. The theater of the constitutional march of July 9, 1820, fit Naples like a glove.

Parthenopea

By copying the Spanish constitution of 1812, the Neapolitan rebels clearly signaled empathy with the then current regime in Madrid. In both countries, Bourbon absolutism had been curbed. These and other connections that unfolded in 1820–21 should not mask the differences deeply rooted in the past experiences of the two nations. The post-1789 agonies of the Kingdom of Naples had begun well before Napoleon Bonaparte imposed his brand of power upon Spain. Naples the city was much larger than Madrid and most other European cities; Naples the kingdom was heir to Etruscans, Greeks, Romans, Saracens, Barbary pirates, and Spaniards. Italian regional pride and contempt for other parts knew no bounds along the Apennine peninsula—Umbrians for Tuscans, Tuscans for Venetians, and all of them for southern Italy, which suffered then and sometimes even now a reputation among denizens of the north as "Africa." The quasi-feudal system marked by mainmort, entail, primogeniture, and a frozen land market—common old regime problems—held strong in the south.[6]

King Ferdinando IV, who came to the throne in 1759 as an eight-year-old and reigned for sixty-six years (one of the longest reigns in European history), fled from and was restored to his capital three times between 1798 and 1821. In the eighteenth century he had initiated some reforms, but, as with monarchs elsewhere, his enthusiasm was soon doused by the French Revolution. Still, a long and rich Enlightenment heritage prepared the way for the inspiration that the French Revolution had on intellectuals in Naples.[7] During the 1790s, Neapolitan Jacobin groups emerged, Club Lomo (*libertà o morte*) and Club Romo (*repubblica o morte*). Conspiracies of nobles and priests led to repression.[8]

The Borbone monarch could not so easily deal with the military menace from the north. The French established hegemony on the Italian peninsula from their invasion across the Alps in 1796 to their ejection by Austria and Russia in 1799. They founded the Cisalpine Republic, which served as a kind of model for the other republics. Eventually ten constitutions—some French-made, others native—appeared, though not all were put into effect. To expel the French, in 1798 Naples joined Britain, Austria, and Russia in the War of the Second Coalition against France. The Neapolitan army failed in its expedition to crush the Roman Republic, and Ferdinando fled to Sicily with Admiral Nelson. As the French invaded the Kingdom of Naples, Neapolitan rebels seized Castel Sant'Elmo on January 22, 1799, and ended the monarchy.

The insurgents renamed the country the Parthenopean Republic, from a classical epithet for Naples taken from Parthenope, the siren in the Tyrrhenian Sea. Its constitution was modeled on the French revolutionary constitution of Year II (1795). It provided for a bicameral legislature with an executive board and required both wealth and higher education to vote. On January 24 the French occupiers appointed a provisional government under the priest and professor Carlo Lauberg. Other leaders included nobles, clerics, professionals, lawyers, and intellectuals such as Francesco Caracciolo, Mario Pagano, and the great patriotic orator Vincenzo Russo, who had all imbibed a classical education. The revolutionary regime, emulating the French, abolished nobility, titles and ranks, primogeniture, entail, and judicial torture. A Declaration of Rights provided for security, freedom, equality before the law, a free press, and the opening of clubs.[9]

Like their French counterparts, Parthenopeans attempted the radical refashioning of revolutionary life. Most of the changes were emblematic, such as renaming streets and neighborhoods after "Humanity" and the seventeenth-century Neapolitan rebel Masaniello, along with the establishment of a new calendar, with months called Rainy, Windy, Planting, and so on. In giving the San Carlo Opera a new title, the National Theater, the new rulers meant no disrespect to the renowned saint, but were simply making a statement about its newly intended purpose as a shrine for all. The most humane of the reforms, eliminating the castration of young male singers, alas, did not survive the republic. Nor did the others.

The regime maintained a tactful posture toward the Catholic Church, though this failed to assuage the religious fury unleashed against the republic. When planting a Liberty Tree the civil authorities had a Te Deum sung in conjunction with the ceremony. Whatever they might have believed, the republic's leaders displayed special reverence for the supremely significant Saint Gennaro (Januarius), whose coagulated blood was believed to liquefy in its reliquary on certain occasions.[10] Some thirty bishops sided with the republic. Abbé Vincenzo Troysi composed a Republican Mass and Abbé Giuseppe Bellini preached a religion of liberty and equality.[11] A priest, in order to reach out to believers with a political message, published in Neapolitan dialect *The Republic Justified by the Holy Gospel.*[12] A republican catechism, probably of French origin, appeared and the 1799 constitution required that it be read to schoolchildren. The Parthenopean Republic suffered from a failure to deliver deep social reforms, French looting and taxing, and a sharp division between radical republicans and moderate constitutional monarchists—thus prefiguring schisms in Spain, Russia, and Naples itself in the 1820s.[13] The Russian Count Grigorii Orlov saw the republicans as *toujours exaltés.* To some this term, made famous later by the Spanish *exaltados,* spoke of idealism; to others it indicated impatience and hotheadedness. For Orlov, the Neapolitan republicans were "always extreme in their principles."[14]

Popular rage burst forth against the regime in February 1799, bringing three terrible waves of civil violence that exceeded all other examples in Italy during the Napoleonic era. Cardinal Fabrizio Ruffo, personally armed to the teeth, arrived from Sicily by ship and organized the Most Christian Armada of the Holy Faith, or Santafede. Peasants ran rampant, as did priests and brigands.[15] Among the latter, Fra Diavolo (Michele Pezza) and The Saber (Sciabolone) achieved notoriety by waging a ferocious guerrilla war against the French. Far from being unified, these and other counterrevolutionary forces possessed a complicated variety of motives: anti-foreignism, failure of the new government to end feudalism, grievances over evictions, town versus country, farmers versus herders, kin and class scores to settle. And virtually all social segments were divided, partly because of poor understanding of what was going on and who stood for what.[16] The counterrevolutionaries committed unspeakably hideous acts against the French and the republicans. Bishops who supported the regime were murdered; one of them had his severed head paraded on a pike. The twentieth-century philosopher Benedetto Croce observed that the Neapolitan popular resistance to the French, stronger than any other in the Italian peninsula, foreshadowed what happened in French-occupied Spain.[17] By March, Cardinal Ruffo's forces had occupied the main towns of Calabria province in the south. The departure of the French in May spelled doom to the republic and death to its organizers.

The second wave of terror broke out when Ruffo entered the city of Naples on June 13. The new horrors were committed mostly by the Neapolitan lazzaroni (or lazzari). Originally a dialect word derived from the Spanish term for "lepers," lazzaroni had come to mean the urban lower-class rebels of the 1647 revolt. In 1799 they comprised the urban unemployed, various workers, and beggars. Speaking only dialect and thus isolated from the upper reaches of society, they had little awareness of the world and even of the Kingdom of Naples.[18] They let loose ten days of frightful outrages on the upper classes and pro-French elements. Vincenzo Cuoco, a participant and survivor in exile, spoke of "barbaric atrocities that make one shudder." On public squares, the enraged crowds roasted the limbs of their victims, including women, and then threw them still alive into the flames. All this occurred under the eyes of Ruffo and in the presence of the English.[19] The cutting off and display of body parts had been prominent features of the revolts of 1585 and 1647—the Masaniello uprising—by both rebels and their executioners.[20] The traveler Baron d'Haussez observed some years later that the hot winds of the sirocco often brought a season of suicides and murders to Naples. Could this climatic phenomenon have exacerbated the fury of violence in the summer of 1799?[21]

The last and most controlled surge of counterrevolutionary violence occurred when Admiral Horatio Nelson's British fleet arrived at Naples on June 24. The exiled King Ferdinando followed Nelson back to Naples in July and insisted on a policy of extreme vengeance. The republicans had surrendered with promise of amnesty, an agreement that was promptly broken. The Borbone queen told Admiral Nelson to treat the city like a mutinous Irish town. Under Nelson's auspices, some forty thousand were jailed, and thousands more fled or were exiled.[22]

Executions on Naples' Piazza del Mercato began on Sunday July 7, 1799. Some 120 were publicly beheaded or hanged—including "13 nobles, 26 lawyers and jurists, 10 priests, 1 bishop, 6 other clerics, 16 university professors, 17 military officers, but only 7 artisans and 1 farmer."[23] Russian troops, who had also landed in the kingdom on the orders of Tsar Paul, played a minor but distinctly repressive role in Naples. Yet a few Russian officers allegedly saved some of the victims. At least one junior officer, Cuirassier Sobolev, was hanged on Mokhovaya Square in Moscow for deserting to the French.[24]

Notable victims of the terror included prominent Neapolitans such as Caracciolo, Pagano, Russo, and the poet Ciaja. Vincenzo Russo, ever the orator, intoned his last words on the scaffold: "I die for liberty. Long live the republic!"[25] Surviving officers, still flooded with emotion months after the executions, loved to recite those final words. Domenico Cirillo, a condemned physician, when asked by the judge what his occupation was now, replied: "Before you, a hero."[26] Fifty were executed in the provinces and many others were lynched. The composer Domenico Cimarosa escaped the hangman's rope but was imprisoned and then exiled for composing an anthem for the republic.[27] The two most prominent women publicly executed both hailed from the Iberian Peninsula. The Spaniard Luigia or Luisa Sanfelice was beheaded in 1800. The axe slipped and her head had to be sawed off with a knife. Her crime: espionage in defense of the republic.[28] Portuguese-born Eleonora Pimentel Fonseca served as the editor of *Neapolitan Monitor* and used the vehicle to send enlightened messages to the Naples poor in their own dialect.[29] A noblewoman, she asked to be beheaded because of her class but instead was hanged as a traitor. On the gibbet, she spoke Virgil's words: "Perhaps one day even this will be a joy to recall" (Forsan et haec olim meminisse iuvabit).[30] She has been revered ever since; at the oldest and most famous Neapolitan eating house, Brandi, a menu item still features a Pizza Eleonora Pimentel.

In explaining the collapse of Parthenopea, both contemporaries and later historians allude to popular backwardness, counterrevolutionary opposition, and the failings of the radical regime. Count Grigorii Orlov at the time characterized the Neapolitan masses as "ignorant and exasperated" and offered vivid descriptions of their "inhuman" atrocities.[31] Cuoco, who escaped into exile, wrote later that the "Neapolitan nation can be seen as divided into two peoples, divided by two centuries of time and two degrees of climate."[32] He also observed that the royalists fought the revolution by exploiting the primitive barbarism, superstition, and class hatred of the masses.[33] Those masses had no understanding of an elite radical culture based on foreign models, and the republican regime did little to bridge the gap. Croce, writing much later, argued that the people saw the revolutionaries as exploitative aliens. Though the regime's passivity and reliance on abstract formulas played a role, the regime failed to win widespread allegiance because of lack of a land reform, town-country friction, the French presence, and religious fears.[34] In any case, the collapse of the republic was complete and, in the view of one historian, "ended any hope of introducing the political culture of the French Revolution into the south of Italy."[35] As concerns 1820s liberalism, the horrors of 1799 left a lingering fear and shaped the restraint of later revolutionaries.

King Ferdinando's restoration in 1799, which reasserted monarchical, feudal, and clerical power along with repression and censorship, lasted only a few years. In 1806 Napoleon Bonaparte sent a French army to occupy the kingdom. Though facing disease and lack of food, it established the French *decennio*, 1806–15, with Napoleon's brother Joseph as king of Naples initially. Joseph abolished monastic orders and took away their property. In 1808, when Napoleon issued the Spanish Bayonne constitution, he ordered a similar one for Naples, though it never came into force. At the same time, the French emperor appointed his brother Joseph as king of Spain and gave the throne of Naples to Marshal Joachim Murat, one of Napoleon's most skillful commanders, whom Napoleon honored as the First Horseman of Europe. Murat continued or introduced the standard repertoire of Napoleonic reforms—new law codes and policies concerning taxes, administration, justice, finance, monasteries, and feudalism—with the usual mix of positive and negative results.

None of Murat's measures sufficed to end the recurrent phenomenon of brigandage. Rampant in this era throughout southern Europe and the Balkans, banditry constituted a severe problem in the Kingdom of Naples. The Vardarelli brothers in particular wreaked havoc and employed extreme violence. They robbed indiscriminately but also assisted the poorest in the population in accordance with Gaetano Vardarelli's motto: "Do the best you can for your friends, do the worst you can to your enemies." The new king hurled a campaign against the bandit menace by hiring a professional bandit-killer, General Manhès, popularly known as "The Exterminator."[36] He cleared the provinces of Calabria and Abruzzi with chilling bandit-killing raids that sometimes took the lives of innocents as well. In Calabria, the decapitated torsos and heads of bandits adorned the roads and town walls, and the rivers swelled with corpses. Manhès has been called "the greatest brigand-catcher of modern times."[37] By 1811, the campaign against the anti-French partisans was officially ended; that against the bandits was declared over in 1819, though brigandage reappeared again and again.[38] Since bandits and smugglers were more or less permanently armed, brigandage and political-social resistance often bled into each other; one historian speaks of "brigantaggio antifrancese."[39]

The bloodletting of Napoleon's legions on far-flung battlefields pulled Murat away from his capital for long absences that weakened his hold on the kingdom. During his reign, the secret society of the Carbonari appeared in the kingdom. Its members opposed Murat in favor of a restored King Ferdinando who would, they hoped, issue a constitution.[40] Murat's participation on Napoleon's side in the Hundred Days cost him his kingdom and his life. After the debacle of Waterloo, in October 1815, he tried to regain his throne by landing on Neapolitan soil to start up a guerrilla war against the returning king. His flashy uniform got him captured and he was stood in front of a firing squad.

The Two Sicilies

Occasionally called the Kingdom of the Two Sicilies in the past, Naples and Sicily had remained two separate kingdoms until 1816, though often ruled by one monarch. Both had had parliaments of varying but limited power. In 1816 the Sicilian parliament was dissolved forever. At Vienna, the powers combined the crowns of Naples and Sicily; thus Ferdinando, IV of Naples and III of Sicily, now became King Ferdinando I of the Kingdom of the Two Sicilies.[41] The largest state by far in the peninsula, the newly named kingdom formed the lower half of Italy's geographical boot, with Abruzzi, Molise, and Campania—along with the capital—as the shin and calf, Puglia as the heel, Basilatica as the instep, and Calabria as the toe.

Although the uprising of 1820 began in Nola and Avellino, its intellectual cradle and political center lay in the capital itself. Neither Bari nor Taranto nor any other provincial town assumed the role that Cadiz had played in Spain. The sprawling city of Naples possesses now and did then two spectacular views: from the bay to the city and of the bay from the heights of the town. Two grand boulevards enclose most of the ancient quarter, Old Naples, each endowed with a famous church: the Spirito Santo, site of the revolutionary parliament, on Via Toledo; and the cathedral, on Via Duomo, where Saint Gennaro's blood was liquefied in the kingdom's most important Catholic ritual. The Toledo—named for a sixteenth-century Spanish viceroy, Pedro de Toledo—housed some of the elite; the composer Rossini lived there during the Restoration and the revolution in the home of Domenico Barbaja, director of the San Carlo Theater. Stendhal, with his usual hyperbole, called it "the most populous and gayest street in all the universe."[42] The thoroughfare also provided a theatrical ramp for some of the most dramatic shows of the coming revolution—the triumphal march of the rebels to the royal palace described above and the procession of the king's cortège to the parliament for his swearing-in ceremony on October 1, 1820.

The restored Borbone king sought pomp and grandeur in his building policy. A spacious compound overlooking the sea contained the royal palace and the San Carlo Theater and was flanked by the Castel Nuovo to the east and the Largo di Palazzo Reale to the west. On that vast space, once used by Murat as a parade ground, Ferdinando in 1817 began the construction of one of the most pretentious and unattractive churches in Europe, that of San Francesco di Paola, modeled on the Pantheon. It was built to celebrate the king's return from a very long exile and to honor the sainted fifteenth-century Calabrian mystic. A smaller piazza later acquired a name that may be an absolute monarch's next-to-worst nightmare: the Square of the Plebiscite. Towering above all this to the west on the heights of Vomero stood Castel Sant'Elmo, the place where the Jacobin rebels were besieged in 1799.[43] On the Capodimonte to the north stood the summer palace. Other high places in the town were dwarfed by the twin peaks of Vesuvius and Monte.

The dense network of narrow lanes that is Old Naples lies within a U formed by the Via Toledo, the royal complex, and the Via Duomo. The quarter still retains hallmarks of an earlier age: the Spaccanapoli, which bisects it; the small squares and cafés; and most of all the huge number of massive churches— almost one on every block in some parts of the district. Two Britons visiting around 1820 reacted to the throng of Neapolitan humanity in picturesque terms: "The crowd of Naples consists of a general tide rolling up and down, and in the middle of this tide a hundred eddies of men. Here you are swept on by the current, there you are wheeled round by the vortex."[44] As in other European cities of the era, the perceived picturesque qualities of lower-class commercial street life invited "folkloric" treatment such as the illustrated albums *Shouts of London* and *Cris de Pétersbourg*. In Naples this took the form of *Grida de' venditori di Napoli* (Shouts of Neapolitan Street Vendors), a song collection arranged by Federico Ricci.[45] The journalist Matilde Serao in the 1880s saw in "the bowels of Naples"—the title of her well-known book—"beauty, power, grace, poetry, tradition," and, most of all, life.[46] Popular entertainment genres in the 1820s ranged from a street recital of Tasso's *Gerusalemme liberata* to comic improvisation, songs, and puppet shows.[47]

More than in most other major European metropolises, in Naples rich and poor dwelt (and dwell) not only in the same quarters and streets but also often in the same house, the humbler families at street level or below and thus a virtual part of the street throngs. Foreigners, especially those from northern Europe, were astonished at the teeming diurnal and nocturnal street life. The playwright August von Kotzebue in the early 1800s had a different reaction. He vividly described the homeless and the shouts and songs amidst outdoor commerce along the animated Toledo and other sites. But he also noticed the dirty, narrow alleys; the rank poverty, hunger, and beggary; and what he took to be public indecency. The affluent, he believed, remained blind to urban misery. He noted that the Neapolitan theater managers had suppressed a scene from one of his plays that showed extreme starvation, though it was clear to him that such hunger prevailed on the streets outside the theater.[48]

A crowded cultural and social calendar filled the lives of the schooled and the privileged at theaters, conservatories, the philharmonia, and musical clubs and circles. The *salotto* or salon played the role of the Spanish *tertulia*, with its mix of music and talk. Already displaying the Neapolitan melodic gift that became renowned in the nineteenth century, the songs offered laments on tormented and unrequited love, extravagant amorous declarations, threats of violent duels, romantic despair dictated by fate, and witty upbeat numbers.[49] Neapolitan high society created and lived in a culturally ebullient environment. Indeed, for those who could afford to live in a palazzo or visit from abroad, Naples became a playground. British visitors loved to quote the already long-established slogan of the city, "Vedi Napoli e poi mori" (See Naples and then die).[50] Foreign guests enjoyed its sophisticated intellectual life and classical archaeological excavations. The sculptor Canova, the composer Rossini, and the diva Colbran mingled with high society as Rossini sat at the piano and Gabriele Rossetti improvised verse. "Naples," wrote Stendhal, "is like a country home, set in a delightful landscape."[51] Of its numerous cultural treasures, the Teatro San Carlo, erected in 1737, reigned as the most renowned.

At the epicenter of high society as well as of political power sat the restored absolute monarch, Ferdinando I. In a bust of the king, Canova dressed his subject in Roman garb, a standard mode of imperial flattery in that age. But Ferdinando possessed neither the grandeur of the most vigorous Romans nor the disgraceful decadence of those who followed Augustus. In the running portrait given by Harold Acton, a virtual court historian who revered the dynasty his ancestors had served, Ferdinando comes across as banal in every way—an intellectually uncurious man obsessed with hunting, procreation, tradition, and the perquisites of his throne. Ferdinando believed in charms to ward off danger. "Though far from spiritual," writes Acton, "he was an assiduous, even a bigoted, observer of religious rites." The king's dedication to the worldly church proved endless as he built monasteries, endowed churches, and handed over all kinds of power to the clergy and to Rome. One of the last monarchs in Europe to wear the eighteenth-century wig and pigtail, he astonished his court when in 1818, in connection with an illness, he was persuaded by doctors to cut it off. Self-indulgent to the core, Ferdinando declined to leave one of his perpetual hunts even when his dying brother implored him to come.[52]

The arch-conservative Austrian Friedrich Gentz, Metternich's secretary, judged Ferdinando to be weak, beset by volatile mood swings, empty and without an intellectual center or a strong will, alien to work, unable to read more than one page at any given time, terrified of political change, and subject to extreme behavior. Lady Blessington, an English socialite, found the king witty but uneducated.[53] But he was not, as cliché had it, lazy and coarse. Ferdinando always mistrusted intellectuals and was called "the lazzarone king" because he seemed to share a certain "national characteristic" with the commoners[54]—especially a love of mass festivals and of devouring macaroni in public. The king's plebeian manner, doubtless sincere, served as a conservative political asset. Ferdinando frequently provided his subjects with royal spectacle and mass feeding celebrations. Since these sometimes alternated with public executions, liberals called the Restoration the era of "feast, flour, and gallows."[55]

The king in Naples faced a familiar dilemma of post-Napoleonic absolutisms, including Spain. The French-imposed regimes almost everywhere had brought efficient laws, police forces, armies, and bureaucracies and had eroded the power and privilege of nobles, church, and provincial notables. The monarchs restored to their thrones in 1814–15 had a choice: keep most of the useful Napoleonic legacy—in this case Murat's reforms—and risk alienating the church and the nobility, which were their anchors, or "de-bonapartize" and lose the support of an influential and valuable sector of the population, those who had served King Murat.[56] Restored monarchs who wanted to eat their absolutist cake had to do so from a Napoleonic plate. To manage the new administrative landscape, the king needed the so-called Muratists, in some ways equivalent to the *afrancesados* of Spain. The Muratists were ready to oblige because, though they had served the French, they did not have to don a cloak of shame like their Spanish counterparts and there occurred no reprisals over a constitution.

Ferdinando's restoration compared favorably with that of his nephew in Spain. Even in comparison with the French Bourbon Restoration, the Neapolitan monarch more resembled Louis XVIII than Charles X, the notorious reactionary whose policies set off the 1830 revolution.[57] Ferdinando managed for a time to coexist peacefully with those who had served his predecessor, and he retained many of them in his service. In 1815 British statesmen and Prince Metternich, a virtual arbiter of continental European politics, feared a reprise of the 1799 bloodbath, so they pressured the king to avoid persecution or mass firing of Muratists, and to retain the reforms of the previous era. The Austrian statesman believed that violence, even punitive violence, disturbed public order. Ferdinando, now a widower, was no longer chained to a wifely avenger, as in 1799,[58] and for a time he adhered to the moderate advice of Metternich.

King Ferdinando began with a promise not to seek vengeance, but he made a sharp turn in January 1816 by appointing as minister of police the Prince of Canosa. One of the most articulate European ideological foes of liberalism, Canosa, despising rule by the multitude, praised the rule of a king responsible only to God.[59] He later wrote a book on the role of the Catholic faith in ensuring popular tranquility and the security of thrones. In 1799 he had been rescued by Cardinal Ruffo from a death sentence. As ambassador to Spain in 1815, he admired Fernando VII for bringing back the Inquisition and the Jesuits and abolishing the constitution of 1812.[60] In Naples, Canosa assaulted suspected enemies on the left with the help of a right-wing group of religious zealots who resembled the Sanfedisti of 1799. The Calderari (Braziers), whose origin is contested, swore a bloodcurdling oath to defend the Catholic Church and vowed "eternal hatred of Freemasons and Carbonari."[61] The Calderari had fought the French as guerrillas and, like Spanish guerrillas, had often attracted brigands to their ranks. Canosa used them as a counterweight to the still existing Carbonari and licensed thousands of firearms for them in what came to be called a "war of the sects."[62] Canosa ignited an orgy of repression from January to June 1816, ordered thousands of arrests, and allowed royalist émigrés to settle private scores.[63] He ordered Calderari to slay revolutionary suspects. Canosa played on the lingering hatreds of some Calderari who were counterrevolutionary veterans of 1799.

The royal government also enlisted another organization to fight opposition—the fabled Camorra. So named since the eighteenth century, it was Naples' younger version of the ancient Sicilian Mafia, part guardians of the people, part criminal secret society. The Camorra, which dealt in protection, extortion, prostitution, gambling, and smuggling in the densely populated poverty-ridden quarters of the capital, constituted in effect a countercommunity. In an urban environment where honest and efficient law enforcement was weak or absent, they generated security for some and insecurity for others—including the prison population.[64] After the fall of Murat, the Camorra became a sect-like organization with a catechism, rites, hierarchy, and frightening initiations. Members wore a special costume of short jacket, bell-bottom trousers, and a hat cocked to one side. Organized according to the twelve sections of the city, for a time they adopted some of the rituals of the Carbonari. Politically, Camorristi were devoutly Borbonist and emulated from below the dignified, privileged, parasitic life of the highest ranks of society, and they were honored by the popular masses.[65]

Canosa's violence proved too much for the Austrian and Russian ambassadors, who, like Tatishchev in Madrid, preferred moderation. The virtual prime minister, Luigi de Medici, fired Canosa in June 1816. De Medici's good sense was able to check the "gallows profession" of Canosa. All secret societies, left and right, were declared illegal. He then pursued a policy of *amalgama*—working with both the Muratists and the ultra-royalists to solve the problems of the state.[66] In 1819 when the Spanish ambassador Pedro Labrador urged him to arrest some liberals, Medici refused, and the envoy was replaced by the liberal Luís de Onís.[67] With the fall of Canosa, according to Orlov, came a reign of peace and order, though still marred by epidemics, undernourishment, and banditry.[68] But grievances remained. Arbitrary, confused, and poorly defined law enforcement resulted in innocents being condemned. Conversely, amnesty was granted to dangerous criminals. Colletta tells of a vicious brigand who smashed the head of his own newborn child and was pardoned by the king.[69] A few days after the revolt began in July 1820, common people shouted from their windows: "No more arbitrary taxes! No more arrests on a whim!"[70]

In 1818 the king signed a concordat with the papacy that restored a good deal of power to the church. The government reinstated Catholicism as the only legal religion in the kingdom, reopened some monasteries, returned some of the monastic land taken by Murat, and established ecclesiastical censorship and control over much of civic life. Miracles, rituals, processions, and worship of saints took on a medieval coloration. One historian claimed that "the Kingdom descended into the murk of a religiosity of the purely Spanish type."[71] Though this is exaggerated, the state heavily backed the social power of the church, and some intellectuals became alarmed at what they saw as the marriage of throne and altar and the latter's censorship powers.[72]

The slowly brewing opposition to the king was partly fed by his adherence to the Holy Alliance in September 1815. A relatively harmless allegiance on its face, it would help shape the outcome of the Neapolitan revolution. Of more immediate import, a separate treaty with Vienna, reflecting as it did Metternich's obsession with control, required the maintenance of twenty-five thousand Neapolitan troops to defend "Italy"; the appointment of an Austrian commander of the Neapolitan military; a temporary Austrian occupation of the country at the king's expense, a drain on Neapolitan finances; and, by a secret clause, a ban on tampering with the absolute monarchy.[73] The treaty was a gross infringement on sovereignty.

Muratists who hoped to work with the king in a moderate direction also expected rewards in the form of promotion or retention of rank. But Ferdinando sought to countervail the efficiency of the Muratists with the loyalty of his trusted courtiers, the so-called Fedeloni or loyalists, and he tended to promote the latter and assign the former to inferior posts. Muratist bureaucrats became disenchanted with this staffing policy. The military experienced the familiar post-Napoleonic frustrations at blocked advancement—as in Spain and many other places. Junior officers, passed over for promotion, resented the preference given to geriatric senior officers who had spent a decade in Palermo with the king.[74] But the Muratists' aspirations for change were modest and moderate.

The classical rift in the mindscape of revolutionaries that opened in 1820 between the *moderados* and *exaltados* in Spain had its counterpart in Naples. In both cases, moderates were caught "between two fires."[75] The elitist and moderate Muratists, veterans or admirers of the defunct regime of King Joachim Murat, had no taste for democracy and preferred the French Charte to the Cadiz document of 1812. Unlike the restless spirits who emulated the rebel heroes of antiquity, Muratists rather revered the stoic discipline of that classical era. On the practical level, never far beneath the surface, they wanted more than they were getting from the restored absolutist regime. The chief figures—Guglielmo Pepe, Pietro Colletta, Michele Carascosa (the name is found with variant spellings), and Lorenzo de Concilj—often found themselves in mutual conflict for various reasons, and their liberal aspirations, personal goals, and distaste for lower-class revolt clashed or clouded their motivations.

Unlike in Restoration Spain, no blood flowed from the handful of amateurish Neapolitan plots to overthrow the king or implant a constitution in the first half decade after 1815. The grievances grew incrementally rather than by way of dramatic clashes. But the king's government was well aware of swelling resentment in the country. Luigi Blanch, conservative and veteran of the Russian campaign of 1812, urged a moderate reform program to loosen the rigid absolutism and defang the Carbonari, but his wish was probably too optimistic.[76] On the far left, the Carbonari were not going to be silenced by piecemeal reform from the top. They were not just waiting in the wings; they were eagerly preparing for the right moment.

Charcoal Burners

The origins of the Carbonari—the "charcoal burners"—remain shrouded in legend. Where did they come from? Observers and historians have been asking this question ever since the sect emerged into the public eye. The Carbonari's own mythic accounts claimed genealogies ranging in time and place from the era of Philip of Macedon to medieval Saxony, Valois France, and Elizabethan England. An 1820 document alluded to the intellectual origins of the Carbonari in 1799. A recent Italian study pushes the birthplace back to a Neapolitan lodge in 1786.[77] In the modern scholarly consensus, the Carbonari originated as an anti-French movement in the Kingdom of Naples at least as early as 1807, though others argue that the original Carbonari were a French anti-Napoleonic movement that formed earlier and then spread to Italy.[78] The political significance of the term Carbonari is as dark as the charcoal from which it was derived. It might have designated the sellers of charcoal or the fire they sat around. In Italy, political malcontents and disaffected clergy fled from their enemies into the Apennine forests and took up the trade of charcoal burners—an important artisanal occupation in southern Europe. It seems clear that by 1816 the south Italian Carbonari had become a popular sect that freely borrowed some forms, terminology, and rituals from the Freemasons, and that it had shifted from an anti-Napoleonic current to an embrace of a wide if fuzzy range of liberal goals.[79]

A modern scholar speaks of the appeal of Carbonarism's "complex, mystery-laden, and picturesque ceremonial."[80] The secrecy and the rituals of the Carbonari have ever fascinated observers. These and the doctrines and organizational forms varied from year to year and lodge to lodge. Clandestine societies of the Restoration and other eras—though drawing from common vestiges of antiquity, religion, Freemasonry, military organization, and neo-pagan imagery—were bound to vary by culture. The common thread in this age consisted of conspiracy and quasi-liberal or national goals, sometimes blended. The Carbonari met usually in forests at a lodge called *vendita* (plural *vendite*, with variant spellings), meaning "shop" or "market," a place where charcoal was sold. Members called each other *cugino*, "cousin," and employed crossed thumbs for a secret handshake. At meetings, a hatchet became a gavel, a tree stump a table; a skull and daggers served as decor along with the colors of black, blue, and red, standing for coal, smoke, and the glow of flames.

Lodges or chapters diverged slightly in decor. The seal of the *vendita* in the town of Chieti showed two floral columns flanked by a vase and a Hebrew menorah, above which hung a sun and a moon. At the base were arrayed the familiar Masonic tools—hammer, trowel, carpenter's square, and level. The seal of the Achilles Disciples in Vacri contained an image of the lodge or cabin with a holly trunk, rising sun, globe, dagger, and axe.[81] A surviving illustration of a *vendita* meeting from an undisclosed source shows an elongated Neapolitan barn with the Grand Master, the Orator, and the Secretary sitting at tree-stump tables, flanked by two rows of seated members, and with four others on chairs facing the presidium—resembling somehow a tribunal.[82] In one account, the thrilling secret rituals proceeded in a candlelit barn adorned with "a linen cloth, water, salt, a cross, leaves, sticks, fire, earth, a crown of white thorns, a ladder, a ball of thread and three ribbons" of blue, red, and black.[83]

The Carbonari initiation ceremony, dramatized in order to display gravitas and to elicit emotional commitment, arranged the novice's movement to each stage of the rite as a journey and a test of morals, courage, and loyalty to the society. The blindfolded initiate listened to verbal incantations and underwent inquiries and trials. Drawing from ancient notions of original sin, a pristine state of nature, and a golden age of history, one speech asserted that the freedom and equality of olden days had been destroyed by the strong, and that the secret society would be the bearer of reason and the agent of rescue.[84] A Neapolitan Carbonari catechism cited biblical villains as metaphors for tyrants, corrupt satraps or priests, and money grubbers.[85] Carbonari catechisms bore only a superficial resemblance to the political catechisms of Spain. For the Neapolitan inductee, they served as a test on what he had seen during initiation and an explanation of the symbols. The rite concluded with an oath of secrecy administered with warnings of bloody retribution in case of betrayal. Catechismic oaths of Pasquale Tavassi's Free Pythagoreans, uncovered by Russian agents, allegedly mandated eternal hatred of tyrants and their extirpation by any means.[86]

In the stew of Carbonari sources and inspirations, clearly the Christian theme prevailed, especially its "mysterious and picturesque" element. The Carbonari injected into the language of the gospels vague notions of democracy and natural rights, combining the magical cult of St. Theobaldo, patron saint of the society, with modern and plebeian themes. As a Catholic "sacred drama," so familiar to and beloved of the observant masses, the initiate's walk suggested the stations of the cross and even the Via Dolorosa itself. During the initiation ceremony for one of the upper ranks, a Christ figure was introduced as the liberator of mankind from slavery.[87] A contemporary observed that the bonding power of Carbonarism lay in its "secrecy, symbols, and a genius for novelty," and that the key to its success lay in its capacity to endow ideas with forms and rituals that captured the imagination, thereby transforming "the rational side of freedom into religious passion."[88]

In contrast to the Spanish Comuneros' metaphorical use of strongholds for their units, the Carbonari employed rustic imagery. The jurisdiction of a *vendita* was called a "forest" and that of a group of cabins a "province." Rank-and-file cousins were not to know those of other *vendite* and were privy to few secrets of loftier members. At the acme of a pyramidal structure stood the Supreme Vendita, headed by a *capo bianco*. To avoid sending messages through the postal system, members communicated verbally or by messenger, using passwords and signs. The apparatus, seen as mere rigamarole by the Carbonari's foes, was perceived by other observers then and now as quintessentially "Romantic" because it generated a sense of peril through rites and artifacts, adapting military and espionage techniques to social intercourse and peacetime politics.[89]

In spite of the intimidating initiation, the sect posed no serious barriers to membership. The charter of one local chapter affirmed that "any free man of good behavior who has the means, a job or a craft that can support himself and his family, has the right to be a Carbonaro."[90] In the years of growth from 1817, thousands of *vendite* gathered officials, small and medium landowners, minor professionals, merchants, artisans, urban employees, and eventually militiamen and officers. As in Spain, the Neapolitan clergy accommodated a wide spectrum of political colors. Many Carbonaro priests, monks, and friars resented the ecclesiastical hierarchy in the way that junior officers resented senior ranks and courtiers. The Carbonari contained hundreds of priests, some of whom held meetings in churches and monasteries.[91] The Carbonari, though stronger among the rural bourgeoisie, also sought an alliance with the peasantry. In fact, their use of Christianoid rituals and catechisms represented an effort to try to reach the masses and thus avoid the isolation that had resulted in the popular bloodbath of 1799.[92] For this reason, Carbonari messages upheld monarchy and religion. In parts of Italy, even women had their own chapters.

A major target for Carbonari recruitment was the regular army, which, in the view of one general, suffered from poor pay, leadership, discipline, and training, as well as a lack of horses.[93] Conscription was widely hated. Though the Neapolitan regulars faced no harrowing punitive expedition, as did the Spaniards, their loyalty to the present system began to erode. A complex relationship arose among Carbonari, bandits, the army, and the militia. Like the Calderari, the Carbonari appealed to some elements prone to violence and, in spite of their elevated aspirations, criminals, including brigands, infiltrated the lodges. At the same time, Carbonari recruited among the militia, comprising self-equipped landowners deployed on an ad hoc basis to fight brigandage, escort dignitaries, and keep order.[94] From 1817, militia regiments were garrisoned in each of the kingdom's twenty-one provinces. These troops, propertied elements who took an oath not to join the sects, nonetheless made good soil for Carbonari enlistment.[95] General Pepe, a militia commander, allowed Carbonari into his units to assist in bandit-hunting. Though informers reported on heavy Carbonari infiltration of the militia, the authorities failed to face the issue vigorously.[96] How large was the Carbonari movement before the revolt? As usual for secret societies, estimates vary widely. The Russian minister in Naples gave the number of sixty thousand and a modern specialist cites the same number.[97]

What did the Carbonari want? Like Freemasons, they held broad humanitarian values and aspired to moral regeneration; a few individuals adopted provocative classical tags such as Brutus and Diomedes,[98] and *vendite* in Abruzzi took names such as Spartans and The Horatii at the Bridge.[99] Out of their secret social gatherings emanated vague dreams with Christian overtones; in everyday life, the membership denounced carousing in taverns, gambling, and adultery.[100] The movement attempted a partial withdrawal from official society and its institutions, and counterposed an alternative world for which the structure of the Carbonari stood as its embryo. Carbonari nourished a vague and spontaneous dream of local community, untouched by the intrusive forces of the capital. The Carbonari in the mainland kingdom became the magnet for all discontent. The contemporary conservative Luigi Blanch noted that they were driven by "a communal and provincial spirit" opposed to the whole array of alien forces—baronial power, incipient capitalism, and the French administrative system.[101]

Apparently, grievances crystallized into a Carbonari political program around 1816–17, though even then it remained vague. When political vocabulary entered Carbonari discourse, it was voiced in biblical cadences. A member called the Carbonari a Masonic-like sect with an evangelical doctrine serving political ends. To them, Jesus had been the victim of a cruel tyranny. They called their enemies "wolves," meaning "tyrants, foes of public liberty."[102] Carbonari taught that burning charcoal cleaned the air and kept wild beasts at bay. Their motto, "to clear the animal kingdom of wolves," meant to clear the country of foreigners and despots.[103] Some provincial lodges debated the relative merits of the Spanish and U.S. constitutions.[104] Only a few groups had republican and egalitarian ideas. The radical but weakly documented Jacobin-like sects—with names such as Universal Republic and Liberty or Death—flaunted as their symbols fasci, axes, Phrygian caps, and the Thunder of Jupiter to strike at thrones. Often enough, the term "republic" implied a local community rather than a national republican polity.[105]

The inflow of information on events in Spain from the adoption of the 1812 constitution in Cadiz onward gave political focus to both the Carbonari and the liberal officers who supported them. Neapolitan aspirants to a limited monarchy had three models within their immediate ken. The first, under Murat's reign, originated in Bayonne on March 30, 1808—a few weeks before a similar one was created for Spain. Hardly more than a vague draft calling for a national parliament (unicameral and authoritarian, favoring noble landowners and clergy), it remained a dead letter like its Spanish twin. In 1815, when time was running out, Murat issued a fuller variant of the Bayonne draft.[106] The second model came out of the British occupation of Sicily (see below). The third and most important was the Spanish constitution of 1812.

In arguing the unsuitability of the 1812 constitution for Naples, some have pointed out that it was not *officially* translated until after the uprising, in July 1820, and that few had actually read it.[107] In fact, from 1812 to 1821 it was published or had appeared in clandestine versions in Messina, Milan, Rome, Turin, Piacenza, and Naples, some in several editions. Translations in Messina and in Milan were made by sympathizers with Spain's national resistance against Napoleon and aimed at liberal readers. Neapolitan officers who served with the French during the Peninsular War brought back news of the Cadiz Cortes and its constitution long before the outbreak of 1820.[108]

Even to those who did not or could not read it, the Spanish constitution served, by its very existence, as an anti-absolutist totem. General Pepe claimed that "all honorable citizens" were inspired to oppose absolutism by the fact that the Neapolitan king had sworn to it as heir to the Spanish throne. Pepe conceded that few people actually knew the contents of the Spanish document, but insisted that all believed that it was born of a liberal body—the Cortes—"unexposed to the seductions of the court."[109] Discounting Pepe's obvious exaggeration, it is clear that while its details remained vague, the 1812 constitution was enthusiastically taken up as a model by Freemasons, Carbonari, and some army officers.[110]

The next phase of Spanish input began with the failed risings of 1814–19. Spanish events were no mystery to Neapolitans and it seems clear that the Carbonari were well aware of the pre-1820 Spanish putsches aimed at restoring the constitution of 1812. In May 1817 Stendhal noted that in Calabria people never ceased speaking about Spain and he heard a priest defending "the present inquisitions and massacres in Spain."[111] The patchwork of aborted Carbonari plots in the years 1817–20 paralleled the military attempts in Spain—though none reached its level of outright revolt and repression. Canosa's 1816 campaign against the Carbonari actually helped augment their ranks, and in 1817 there began a continuous struggle for a constitution. After the Austrian troop withdrawal, Carbonari membership swelled and they dug in and spread out.[112] The city of Salerno, south of the capital, had the best organized and most dynamic Carbonari center, the High General Vendita, which created a national body, the Supreme Executive Magistracy, and kept the leadership from the older Naples chapter. A leader, the physician Rosario Macchiaroli, launched a moral crusade and published a penal code that was aimed at popular vices—[113] a kind of purifying movement designed to strengthen the will of its members.

In May 1817 the Salerno conspirators, in order to unite Carbonari from all provinces, summoned their first large-scale meeting in the ruins of Pompeii, disguised as an antiquity outing to provide security[114] and perhaps also to evoke an atmosphere of impending menace. The organizers' plan for a September rising did not pan out. In December they distributed hundreds of printed and manuscript manifestos containing demands for the Spanish constitution and sent a copy of the Spanish constitution to the king along with demands for its implementation.[115] In January 1818, according to Father Minichini, the Carbonari named the Spanish constitution as the instrument of change. Their goal, to transform Neapolitans into "active citizens," would be reached through a constitutional monarchy, universal male suffrage, freedom of speech and religion, education and civic rights for women, and a level of local and provincial self-government—though some Carbonari wished for complete federal autonomy.[116] A handful of plans and plots followed over the next two years.

Riego's mutiny in early 1820 raised hopes exponentially for change in the Neapolitan kingdom. Some Italian historians have reasonably argued that the Spanish events did not cause the revolution in Naples, which had been stewing for years, but rather just triggered it.[117] Cause or trigger, the upsurge of unrest in the kingdom after Riego's ride leaves no doubt about its impact. "The example of Spain," wrote Colletta, "had great influence on the Neapolitans, from the resemblance between the people both by nature and habits. Never was there greater excitement in the meetings of the Carbonari, and never did their numbers and strength increase so rapidly."[118] In the years 1818–19 they had managed to enroll a few generals into their schemes. In 1820, learning from Spain the need for army support, they intensified recruitment.[119] News about the Spanish king's oath to the restored constitution in March 1820 created as much of a sensation among Neapolitans as had the uprising in January. The Spanish example of 1820 had special relevance for the Neapolitans since the two nations shared one family as their dynasties. Thus King Ferdinando recognized the Spanish constitution in order to ensure his possible succession to the throne of Spain as uncle and heir to a still childless King Fernando.[120] The combination of events let loose a flow of anonymous letters to the king asking him to apply the Spanish constitution to his own realm.[121]

The commerce and mutual fertilization between Restoration Spain and Naples across the Tyrrhenian and western Mediterranean seas in the years

1815–20 could certainly have brought to Naples copies of the constitution, and many educated Neapolitans would have had little trouble reading it in Spanish. Giorgio Spini rightly concluded that the enthusiasm in Naples for the Spanish liberal struggle long preceded Riego's ride and that in 1820 "a revolutionary wave pushed off from Spain bearing like a ship the Constitution of Cadiz." And with it disembarked the very method of imposing this constitution with its lexicon of pronunciamentos, *giunte, capi politici (jefes políticos), liberali,* and *servili.*[122] Later in life, Pepe refuted the charge of Chateaubriand, one of the architects of the Spanish intervention, that the Spanish liberals had foisted their constitution on the Italians. Pepe affirmed that the Spaniards had never forced or even offered their constitution as a model for Naples. Only after the revolt did Spanish liberals congratulate the rebels in Naples on their success. Nonetheless, he wrote, the Spanish revolution "captured the admiration of all European liberals and above all those in the Kingdom of Naples."[123]

The Second Horseman?

The ride from Nola to Avellino in July 1820, it might be argued, constituted the real analogue of Riego's exploit, though it was far shorter and unopposed; one might also claim that its leaders, Father Minichini and Lieutenants Morelli and Silvati, were the original heroes of the Neapolitan revolt. It is a fair argument. Yet it was General Guglielmo Pepe who took up the cause and fashioned it into a winnable enterprise. Pepe admired Riego's rapid exploit and the possibility of emulating him in Naples, rather than the constitution of 1812, which he disliked. Pepe (1783–1855) was born a year before Riego, at Squillace in Calabria province. His parents, *nobili patrizi* by social station, had many children, three of whom became officers. The austere eldest sibling, Florestano, tried to temper the passion of his younger brother.[124] The fourteen-year-old Guglielmo arrived in the capital in 1797 and two years later entered military school under the Parthenopean Republic. The youngster fought to defend it and was arrested. A police profile of Pepe in 1800 described him as age twenty-two (though he was only seventeen) with dark brown hair and eyelashes, a rather prominent nose with a small mole below it, a normal chin, and a small beard.[125]

For serving in the Parthenopean resistance, Pepe was exiled, and when he returned to Naples two years later he was again apprehended and sent to prison on Marettimo, a tiny fog-bound island off the coast of Sicily. There he was consigned to an ancient castle's cistern, set in the hollow of a cliff and used as a dungeon. For three years the young man endured, in his words, "an existence whose recounting would make humanity shudder." The physical conditions of the prison were truly miserable by any standard, though Pepe was able to purchase some privileges and receive books.[126] Pepe eventually became, in a way, like his Spanish counterparts of 1814 and 1820—a jailbird who later served his jailer. Released by Napoleonic troops in 1806, Pepe joined the French army at first as a soldier. When Joachim Murat ascended the throne, Pepe became his loyal servitor. In light of later events, two ironies appear in these years. Under Joseph, Pepe rode against Calabrian anti-French rebels, the kind of grassroots, anti-foreign resisters that Pepe would one day hope to use against Austrian invaders. Ambivalent about this role, Pepe hated the idea that the rebels wanted a Bor-bone restoration, and yet, as a native Calabrian, he admired their patriotism. The other irony arose from his campaigning as a colonel under Murat in Spain in 1811–12.[127] A decade later he would became an active champion of that coun-try's independence.

Pepe has been variously characterized as "ever the man of revolution," "a vol-canic and theatrical personality," and a man driven more by the "impulse of the heart than by way of subtle speculation."[128] The view of Pepe as a perpetual revo-lutionary arose also from his later years of relentless struggle in the Risorgi-mento. But he was not a consistent radical; his role in 1799 had been marginal. In 1814 and 1815 Pepe, along with his colleagues, pressed Murat to grant a constitution. Murat's fall and the return of Ferdinando made this idea no longer viable and they had apparently become lukewarm toward constitutional rule after 1815. Their shifting motivations and actions in the years 1818–20 remain obscure. Apparently, for Pepe and Colletta, the revolt seemed "inevitable but not necessarily desirable."[129] Within a few years, however, Guglielmo Pepe was plot-ting for a constitutional regime.

What motivated him? And to what end? Aside from the personal satisfaction and glory essential to most activists, Pepe wanted for the Kingdom of Naples a moderate constitutional monarchy where talent could rise and reform be enacted. He actually thought the Spanish constitution absurd.[130] Like *moderados* and others in Madrid, he preferred the bicameral legislature of the French Charte but believed that some kind of constitutional order was inevitable. To achieve his goals, Pepe worked for a military coup led by a junta of the Muratists rather than a Carbonari revolution from below. In his memoirs, Pepe stressed the desire to retain order and control throughout the insurrection as a duty to his country, and to complete the revolt quickly so that the king could not summon his "dear Austrians."[131] Pepe therefore looked upon the Carbonari with mixed feelings and hoped to harness their force rather than simply unlock it. Pepe became a Car-bonaro, if ever, only after the revolt of 1820. Evidence remains contradictory and unclear.[132]

During the Restoration, Pepe secured a place in the royal armed forces as one of the Muratists whom King Ferdinando saw it necessary to retain. In 1818 he appointed Pepe a divisional commander with the rank of field marshal. His militia of ten thousand self-equipped men destroyed brigand bands in the provinces of Avellino and Foggia that had continued to terrorize life and property for some time.[133] Pepe co-opted local Carbonari into the anti-bandit campaign; many of his militia officers already belonged to or sympathized with them.[134] Pepe claimed that as early as 1819 he considered a plot—how seriously is hard to say—to use this force to abduct the Austrian emperor and Metternich at Avellino during a review of five thousand men held during their state visit.[135] Due to bad roads, the review did not take place. Pepe's apparent desperation to bring off a military coup as soon as possible was fueled by his concern about the concurrent activity of those Carbonari outside his ranks. Soon after news of the Spanish revolt, a newly energized Salerno Carbonari delegation approached Pepe. Seeing him perhaps as a second Riego, they offered him leadership over the movement. Pepe declared his patriotism but declined the offer and urged caution.[136] Henceforth, two parallel forces—Pepe and the Carbonari—began to converge on the moment when Neapolitan despotism was to be overthrown.

The essentially leaderless Carbonari did not take Pepe's advice to act prudently. They launched a half dozen plots, mainly in Naples and Salerno, while failing to unite the nationwide organization. In late April 1820 a Naples branch of the Carbonari agreed to arrest the king and force him to grant a constitution. The detention of Ferdinando and his family was designed to prevent his flight from the country. The Naples group and those in other provinces concocted yet fresh plans that failed to materialize.[137] In June a Salerno plot offered the leadership to a Muratist colonel, who declined, causing it to collapse. Yet another one in that city went up in smoke due to the premature appearance in public of Carbonari in their colors shouting, "Constitution or Death!"[138] The conspiratorial plans of the Carbonari were unhinged by vagueness, amateurish preparation, squabbles among the plotters, counterorders, leaks, and betrayals—all of which revealed their need for a firm military organizer.

Pepe did no better with his own schemes. In April 1820 he resumed his attempt to confront the king. The final details were to be worked out during the royal review and annual maneuvers in April and May at Sessa Aurunca, a huge concentration of troops that further enabled Carbonari recruitment. Large-scale massing of troops in peacetime—Cadiz in 1819, Sessa in 1820, and Ukraine in 1825—enabled mutineers to more easily gain followers and connect with other officers who were normally scattered in their command outposts. After the maneuvers ended, Pepe devised yet another plan to marshal a military demonstration of ten thousand men before the king on June 25 and beseech him to issue a constitution. Pepe would release a pronunciamento designed to avoid disorder. This scheme also fell through due to an informant.[139] Pepe's intended armed pronunciamento in the very presence of his king had no counterpart in Spain where the revolt had been set off halfway across the country from the Spanish king's residence in Madrid.

Though information about possible Carbonari risings had been filtering into the government and the court for some time, it was only after the Sessa encampment that Medici began to order some arrests in Salerno, but did little else. In the meantime, the Carbonari continued their plotting. Pepe was plagued with doubts about success after all the previous failures.[140] He came up with a new idea for starting a revolt in late June in Apulia and Calabria and a plan to proclaim a constitution at San Severo. When this scheme also collapsed, Pepe went from Avellino to Naples on June 27 to see if he had been discovered.[141] While he was there, a real rising began—not in Salerno, Naples, or Avellino, but in the little town of Nola.

Midnight Ride

Nola—today an hour away from the center of Naples by car—lies between the volcanoes and the Apennines and once served as a Roman fort. Here the Carbonari normally met in the *vendita*, but also availed themselves of a coffee shop operated since 1816 by a shady Neapolitan policeman's son who had been cashiered from the army for immoral behavior. There gathered a dozen of the most devoted followers of Minichini. The Carbonari chapter adopted the name Mucius Scaevola,[142] "The Left-Handed," after the stoic Roman hero of legend who burned off his right arm to show his contempt for torture. The Scaevola image of national heroism had been constantly invoked from France to Russia for a generation. The Grand Master of the lodge in 1820, Father Luigi Minichini, became suddenly one of the most colorful figures in the drama of the Neapolitan uprising. Born in Nola 1783, he took holy orders, left the church in 1809, spent two years in Britain, returned home, and reentered the church. Accused of poisoning a parishioner at Mass, he was jailed in 1816. By 1818 he had regained his freedom. Along the way, Minichini became a fervent Carbonaro and "a ferocious enemy of the church."[143]

Minichini, like most revolutionaries a tangle of seeming contradictions, emerged in 1820 as a thirty-eight-year-old Catholic friar and a leader of one of Europe's most feared and celebrated revolutionary organizations. Once described as "a character in a novel,"[144] Minichini made a visual splash. The jarring contrasts in his personal appearance as bandit and holy man seemed to reflect his continuing dual identity. A tall man with a full, bushy beard, the radical padre presented a bizarre spectacle as he rode into provincial towns "wearing glasses, arrayed in clerical garb, armed with a fowling piece, and mounted on a purloined steed [*destriero*]."[145] Odd as Minichini appeared to some contemporaries, he was one of numerous Carbonaro priests and a type familiar in southern Europe and Latin America: the guerrilla monk of Spain, the Greek Orthodox warrior priest, and the Mexican revolutionary Padre José María Morelos, who while saying the Mass supplemented his clerical vestments with a general's hat, firearms, and a sword.[146] Europe was filled with radical or populist clerics and ex-clerics whose political awareness meshed with religious training. During this turbulent era, the clergy embraced all kinds of persuasions and denounced each other as well.[147]

The fact that Minichini's feast day matched that of St. Theobald, the Carbonari's patron saint, may have given him additional sway among the local lodge members. Observing the progress of the Spanish revolution from a distance, this passionate cleric found inspiration in Riego's spectacular march through Andalusia. He became convinced that the Carbonari, already active among the middle classes, needed to win over the army and use it—as had the men of Cadiz—to gain power. Minichini began serious agitation in the army only in March 1820, after the success of the Spanish revolt seemed assured.[148] As luck would have it, he encountered officers who met his needs exactly.

Two lieutenants stationed at Nola visited the Scaevola *vendita* and offered to join the cause: Second Lieutenant Giuseppe Silvati, a native of the capital, and Lieutenant Michele Morelli, a Calabrian, both veterans of the Napoleonic wars. Morelli presented a striking contrast to the particolored priest. A stern and handsome young professional soldier, he wore the mustache of a cavalry officer and a high collar, a single epaulette, and a double row of buttons on his tunic. Morelli was described as having a dark complexion and deep dark eyes—hardly unique to a Calabrian—and being very lean, with steely muscles. Morelli allegedly was proud, loyal, generous, contemptuous of danger, admired by his fellow officers, and dear to his men. Though not highly educated, he spoke French. Born of an old patrician family in 1792, at age sixteen Morelli joined Murat's army and later fought in the Russian campaign of 1812 and in 1815 against Austria. He was accepted into the cavalry of the restored monarch in 1816. Stationed at Nola, Morelli rode against the Vardarelli bandits. At some point he became a Carbonaro.[149]

Morelli and Silvati commanded a squadron in the Borbone cavalry regiment that was barracked in an old Orsini palazzo dating to 1465. According to Pepe's account, Morelli and Silvati got word to be ready for Pepe's orders, and the two officers then decided to travel to Avellino, Pepe's headquarters. The *vendita* agreed unanimously to go as well. According to a biographer of Morelli, however, the original decision to move came from the Nola *vendita*; Minichini played the key role in recruiting, organizing, and deploying the Carbonari, and Morelli determined the participation of the troops. Morelli selected as their next destination the army post of Avellino over Minichini's choice of a closer Carbonari center. Although Avellino also held an active nest of Carbonari, Morelli knew the commander there and trusted the garrison more than his small but fiery Carbonari contingent. The ride began on July 2, shortly after midnight. The 140 or so troops were roused from bed, armed, and put in formation along with Minichini's twenty or thirty Carbonari on the square. The column exited the town led by the two officers and Minichini. According to an eyewitness, Morelli began the march by commanding, "Mount up. The hour of freedom has struck. Those who love their country, follow me." They rode off at lightning speed.[150]

As dawn broke on a warm Sunday, residents of settled areas awoke to cries from the column of rebels. On this much romanticized early morning ride, the gun-toting and black-garbed priest Minichini rode along on a white horse to the sounds of occasional band music and shouted slogans. Flying the Carbonari flag, the cavalrymen shouted "Long live God, long live the king, long live the constitution!"—prudently ordering deity, monarch, and document in an acceptable hierarchy. When the bugler sounded, the horsemen shouted, "Viva paesani, allegri! viva la libertà e la costituzione" (Hoorah countrymen, Rejoice!; long live liberty and the constitution). Two different insurgent cultures traveled in tandem: celebrators and military leaders. Riego had ridden largely unencumbered by civilian revolutionaries and had taken great care to maintain order among his troops. Morelli likewise kept his men in line. And, like Riego, he controlled news of the revolt, in this case by detaining a carriage on its way to the capital.[151] What kind of reception did the marchers get along the way? They encountered a vendor of sweets who was gathered into their ranks though he had little or no understanding of their aims.[152] While the peasantry remained indifferent to the marches, some military units broke ranks and joined the column.[153]

Halfway to Avellino, the group reached a high point in the Apennines from where they could see both the Tyrrhenian and the Adriatic Seas. When they arrived at Monteforte, a strong hilly position not far from their destination, they found a few hundred new supporters, and still others were summoned by a tocsin.[154] Lieutenant Colonel Lorenzo de Concilj, Pepe's chief of staff, a Muratist and apparently a Carbonaro also, was an acquaintance of Morelli's. At that moment he served as the temporary garrison commander at Avellino. When he got news that troops were approaching his city, he sent a messenger asking Morelli to delay their arrival, and ordered the town of Monteforte to feed the marchers and their mounts.[155] De Concilj stiffened security in the city, sent a messenger to Pepe, and informed other units, using the recently introduced semaphore telegraphy system. Morelli, leaving Minichini with some provincial militia to guard Monteforte, proceeded to Avellino. He entered at the head of his motley column of cavalry, militia, Carbonari, and other civilians.[156]

Apparently the town greeted the newcomers with enthusiasm. Military, civil, and ecclesiastical authorities applauded the arriving force, which held aloft Borbone and Carbonaro banners and marched to the sound of a trumpet. In a solemn church ceremony attended by the bishop, the marchers and the locals swore an oath to the Spanish constitution. Lieutenant Morelli declared his loyalty to the royal family and to law and order.[157] In the midst of the tumultuous meetings, someone proclaimed De Concilj to be the new Quiroga and Morelli the new Riego—an accurate prediction at least of their fates.[158] Winning the constitutional allegiance of Avellino, admittedly already a Carbonari stronghold, proved crucial to the success of the rising. Most important of all, a continuous abdication took place. Minichini had deferred to Morelli over the itinerary; at Avellino, Morelli submitted to De Concilj's command; and De Concilj in turn obeyed the orders of his superior—General Pepe. Power flowed upward from the initiators to the consolidator.

De Concilj informed other units that the constitutional regime had been proclaimed in Avellino, General Pepe in turn spread the news and prepared to enter the scene. Proclamations issued throughout the provinces were greeted with uproarious demands for "the constitution of the Cortes" and with exclamations of "Long live the king! May he grant us a constitution!" The rebel forces maintained order and abjured violence or looting. Desertion from the king's army spread with alarming speed.[159] A newly composed Carbonari hymn declared, "Despotism's destroyed / Tyranny has perished / And aristocrats will no more tread on us." In Bari province, a priest delivered a sermon on the virtues of the constitution. Complete unanimity eluded the movement. In the same province, moderates preferred to wait for confirmation from the king, but their opponents wanted to declare it at once; some opted for the Spanish constitution, others that of the United States. In Foggia, a Federal Republic of Daunia was declared, and in Potenza a Republic of Eastern Lucania—both referring to ancient geographical names. Their leaders refused to obey government decrees until a constitution was issued.[160]

On the evening of July 2, the royal retinue attended a soirée and then repaired to the San Carlo Theater. The "vague but alarming" rumors arriving about troops moving from Nola to Avellino, seemed to indicate nothing more than a familiar act of desertion. The next two days widened the picture.[161] When it became clear that a rising was in process, the commander of the armed forces, Austro-Irish general Count Nugent summoned his military council. Seeing Pepe as the only one who could quell the revolt, they at first decided to send him to handle the disorder in his military district. This would have been equivalent to the king of Spain's dispatching of General O'Donnell against Riego. The ministers, court, and king, distrusting Pepe, opposed the order. Medici would have had him thrown in irons. Three other generals were sent instead: Carascosa from Naples and Campana and Nunziante from Salerno as backup.[162] The rebel forces barred Carascosa's march, a lukewarm effort marked by desertion, and only a few skirmishes occurred. Insurgents cut communications between

capital and provinces and spread their own pleas for support by means of run-
ners and bonfire messages from the hilltops. When Campana and Nunziante
learned that other regions had joined the movement, they returned to Naples.[163]
The confusion and bungling of orders reflected a panic felt in the ruling circles;
the royalist generals' efforts proved halfhearted and their motives obscure. In all
probability, they felt intimidated by the scale of the defections of entire units
over to the rebels.

When Pepe in Naples got the news from Avellino on July 2, he had to decide
whether or not to lead the revolution and move its power from the provinces to
the capital. Playing a perfect ruse (or what a hostile historian called "double
dealing"),[164] Pepe pretended to suppress the revolt while joining it. When pro-
rebel officers warned him of his possible arrest and gave him details on the
rising, Pepe on the night of July 5–6 made his decision. Under Nugent's nose, he
converted three regiments to the cause and set off. Pepe's recollections of his
secret messages and schemes to get to Avellino undetected contain accents of
melodrama.[165]

As Pepe reached Monteforte, he related, women from their windows
applauded, shouted his name and the words "Long live the constitution," and
assured him that their men were ready to fight for the cause. The militia and his
officers wept tears of affection and said to him: "If we were told that you, our
father, had been imprisoned in Castel Sant'Elmo, we would have sworn to go
and free you that very night." Refuting Carascosa, who later claimed that the
people did not know what they were revolting for or against, Pepe told of the
popular slogans shouted by the people.[166] These may have been rudimentary
words viscerally delivered, but they nonetheless expressed concisely some of the
core values of a liberal revolution: political participation, personal liberty and
security, and equitable taxation. According to Colletta, at Monteforte Pepe did
what the Spaniards had done: promised his troops promotion.[167] When General
Pepe entered Avellino with his men, he uttered the proclamation that opened
this chapter.

As news from Avellino reached Naples, the king was on a vessel in the harbor
welcoming his son home from Sicily. The king feared for his life and wanted to
remain in safety onboard but was persuaded to return to the palace. On July 5
crowds demonstrated in Naples. Five Carbonari gained entrance to the palace
and demanded that the 1812 constitution be adopted for Naples within two
hours and warned that otherwise the revolution would envelop the palace and
threaten the royal family. The king at first promised only to prepare a constitution. When the rebels demanded specifically the Spanish constitution, he
agreed.[168] The next day Ferdinando again promised a constitution within eight
days and appointed his son Francesco as vicar-general, acting ruler of the realm.
The Carbonari pressed them again. The ministers and generals persuaded the

vicar to accede to the demand. On July 7 he announced that "the constitution of the Kingdom of the Two Sicilies will be the same as that adopted by the Kingdom of Spain in 1812 and that was approved by His Catholic Majesty [Fernando VII of Spain] in March of this year."[169] While mentioning that the king of Spain had recognized the constitution in 1812 and in March 1820, he omitted what that monarch had done in 1814. On the same day, the Spanish version of the constitution appeared in the *Journal of the Two Sicilies* and was posted on the walls of the capital. Carascosa returned to Naples, according to Craven, with an actual copy of the constitution, which he had supposedly received from Pepe's men. Calm returned to the city.[170]

The elite knew that to punctuate any major change in the political sphere, a solemn ceremony was required. Though Pepe made his pronunciamento in Avellino at roughly the same moment that the king in Naples agreed to a constitution on July 6, he was widely considered the leader of the revolt—even by the court.[171] The planned July 8 parade was delayed by one day and the prospect of provincial multitudes pouring into the capital caused nervous anxiety among some.[172] A minor spat over what flags were to be borne ended with a compromise: the Borbone banner would have a Carbonaro ribbon attached to it. On July 9 came the triumphant procession of Pepe and the Carbonari into Naples, representing the first full public showing of Carbonari culture. All the leaders of the Nola-Avellino affair featured prominently. Pepe led his troops, Fra Minichini tried to position himself in a conspicuous place in the march, and the unit led by Morelli and Silvati was dubbed the "Sacred Squadron,"[173] a term later used by Spaniards and Ypsilanti's Greek volunteer fighters.

The parade ended by debouching from Via Toledo into the Largo di Palazzo, the ceremonial center of the city, where social classes converged during festivities. It had long served as a site of social reliability and loyalty to the absolute monarch and as a mark of government control of the urban masses. During festivities, popular gatherings outside the palace represented a kind of personal link between people and their king and an emblem of the prosperity and contentment of the kingdom.[174] On that July day, did the huge square get converted into a popular celebration of constitutional monarchy? It might have seemed so, since the king's son and now vicar wore the Carbonaro trefoil cockade, stood on the balcony to receive the throngs, and ordered everyone in his entourage to don the cockade.[175] To the politically unlettered, this doubtless looked like an endorsement; to those who remembered Paris in the 1790s, it darkly suggested something like coerced behavior.

After the parade, Pepe had an audience with the vicar, who thanked him and praised the constitution. Then King Ferdinando, ill or feigning illness, received him in the royal boudoir and did likewise.[176] Pepe acted the great persuader in these days. In a letter to the vicar he showed proper deference but also, as if giving a lesson, pointed out to the prince the bloodlessness of the recent events and the obedience of the people. He got the Carbonari to return to their homes and on July 16 composed a proclamation asserting to the military, with ample exaggeration, that the constitution had been approved unanimously by the nation.[177] In every respect, Pepe was trying to smooth edges, assuage the fears of the royal menage, and maintain tranquility among the people. In statements and letters of the time and in later memoirs, he asserted that the constitution was created not by a military coup but by a unanimous national popular movement that the military joined. Like Riego, Pepe assured his king that he had no political ambitions or aspiration for promotion. To disarm those suspecting him of these, he announced that he would retain his military post only until the new parliament assembled. And he kept his word. Pepe hoped to go to Spain as a diplomat. He also declined a very large monetary award from the government for his services.[178]

On July 13 King Ferdinando repeated the gesture that his nephew King Fernando had made in Madrid four months earlier. Inside the royal chapel, surrounded by family and civilian and military leaders, including Pepe, the king of Naples swore a solemn oath to preserve the Catholic faith and no other and to uphold the constitution of 1812, with certain unspecified modifications. Following the conventions of swearing, he declared that if he betrayed this oath, "the people need not obey me" and that he would be answerable to God—not quite asking to be cut in pieces, as in some of the Carbonari oaths, but rigorous enough.[179] It seems indisputable that Ferdinando had no intention of keeping his promise. The revolution had taken a week—as opposed to two months in Spain—and not a single drop of blood was shed.

Who made the July uprising in the Kingdom of the Two Sicilies? The newspaper L'amico della costituzione on July 24 put it tersely if a bit simplistically: "The army followed the people and not the other way around as in Spain."[180] A modern historian offers a more elaborate view. Piero Pieri agreed that the revolt had been prepared by the Carbonari and begun by a nucleus of regular army people. But the rising owed its success to the support of the provincial militia, largely linked to the Carbonari. The social makeup of much of the revolutionary movement was rural petty bourgeois who were radical only for the moment. Essentially conservative, they had upper and middle bourgeois as leaders.[181] Wrote another eminent scholar: "The Neapolitan revolution of 1820 was not, as has been repeated over and over, a simple military pronunciamento, but was rather, at least initially, a movement that had a large base in the country."[182] Somewhat differently, a modern biographer of Morelli, in summarizing the various roles of the actors, argued reasonably that Morelli, assisted by Minichini, had begun the rising, that the surrounding population had responded to the march, that De Concilj and Pepe had ensured its success nationally, that the revolt reflected most middle-class desires, and that masses remained largely spectators without full comprehension of what had happened.[183] The fight for a constitutional monarchy succeeded due to the combined efforts of Minichini, Morelli, Silvati, and De Concilj, and behind and in support of them ranged a variety of social groupings. But it was Pepe's adherence that marked a turning point.[184]

Under the Sacred Codex

For the constitutional King of the Two Sicilies, the first step was to name an interim government. Unlike the Spanish monarch, Ferdinando did not have to appoint jailbirds to his first ministry under the new order. The exception, Pepe, a veteran of confinement in a dungeon, had suffered in an earlier generation. During the three months before elections took place, a hybrid system wielded authority. Francesco, Duke of Calabria, now vicar-general of the kingdom, shared power with a fifteen-member Provisional Giunta, a weaker version of the Spanish Junta. Comprising mostly Muratists, it included Giuseppe Zurlo, Francesco Ricciardi, Giuseppe Parisi, Melchiorre Delfico, and Pepe's brother Florestano.[185] In the new cabinet Carascosa was appointed minister of war. Pepe became supreme commander, a post he agreed to hold temporarily. Both the Giunta and the government tried to slow down the revolution. When the cabinet appointed a committee to prepare an official translation of the Spanish constitution, the king ordered that no substantive changes be made to it so that the liberals might not encroach further on his power.[186] Delfico and Giulio Rocco prepared the translation and published it July 24, with minor adaptations and nomenclature altered to fit the Neapolitan kingdom.[187]

During the summer, officials drafted election rules, adapted from those of the Spanish constitution, and a well-conducted election took place in September. Adult males, except for jobless, propertyless, and dependent elements, voted indirectly for electors, who in turn chose the deputies to parliament. In terms of suffrage rights alone, Naples, like Spain, became one of the most liberal nations in Europe. The voters elected ninety-eight deputies (of whom twenty-six were Sicilians). Information on the seventy-two mainland deputies yields one cardinal, nine priests, twenty-four landowners, eight pedagogues or scholars, eleven magistrates, two bureaucrats, nine physicians, five soldiers, and three merchants.[188] Of these only six were aristocrats. Provincial notables featured heavily.

On October 1, to celebrate the dawn of a new political era, a solemn and meticulously staged ceremony marked the public swearing-in of the king and vicar and the opening of parliament. On this Sunday morning, the royal cortège was protected on all sides by hussars, mounted militia, and halberdiers as it moved up Via Toledo from the royal palace to the Church of the Spirito Santo. The streets were strewn with flowers, birds were set free along the route, and the crowds again gave voice to vivas.[189] Inside the church, a railing separated the assembled deputies from the audience, which could witness all the proceedings. The parliamentary deputation greeted the royal family and accompanied Ferdinando to the throne. Modest in oratory, as he was in all things intellectual or literary, the king once again swore a solemn oath to uphold the constitution. A cannon salute followed and the city was flooded with illumination. Deputy Matteo Galdi produced a learned and overheated rhetorical string replete with classical allusions, putting the day's event in the context of global, natural, geological, and Biblical history. At a more topical level, he presented the 1812 constitution as a universal model, the perfect fusion of popular rights and royal prerogative—an orderly, balanced, symmetrical pyramid of power offering a social compact between king and subjects.[190] The ceremony had faintly resembled that of March 19, 1812, in Cadiz, when the Cortes published the constitution amidst general revelry and solemnity. Both featured a downpour that some saw as a bad omen.[191]

Having opened in the Church of the Spirito Santo, the Neapolitan parliament continued to hold its sessions there until its demise in March 1821. This church still stands on the western side of the Toledo near a small square. Now squeezed by flanking structures, its neoclassical facade seems unimpressive. But if one regards its length from the adjoining courtyard or, from inside, its height and volume, the effect is staggering. The ten chapels, five on each side, are bathed in light from multilevel windows. This grandeur of the setting ought not suggest that the edifice was intimidating. Naples was and is full of massive churches. Nor was the ecclesiastical venue an innovation. Churches had long been used (and abused) for other purposes, such as coronations and solemn masses to celebrate military victory. Insurgent political bodies aped the practice, from the Spanish Cortes of a few months earlier in Madrid to the 1848 Frankfurt parliament at the Paulskirche. When parliament convened, the Provisional Giunta dissolved and, as in the Spanish constitution, parliament chose a Permanent Deputation of seven as a watchdog over the executive between parliamentary sessions. The king found this body and the unicameral legislature obnoxious.[192] In November 1820 the parliament departed from the Spanish model by adding a second chamber, the State Council,[193] which made it more conservative.

The fledgling parliament generated much verbosity. British envoy William à Court observed in disgust how much time the deputies spent debating the issue of whether God was the legislator of the universe.[194] Parliamentary speakers indulged in high diction, neoclassical declamation, and flamboyant speechifying—in the sarcastic words of a historian, abandoning themselves "to metaphors, to dazzling images, to hyperboles, to classical references, to bombast, all evoking sentiment."[195] This mode of delivery may seem absurd to admirers of an austere rhetorical style, but it is hard to imagine how in that time and place speakers would be able to win over their peers without using flowery locutions and passionate imagery.

No real political parties emerged, because the deputies believed—wrongly in the case of Spain—that the Spanish instrument induced harmony and a general will, rather than divisive factions.[196] Indeed, the absence of openly disputatious parties spared Naples much of the intemperate and counterproductive sectarian divisions and outbursts of the Spanish Cortes. Benedetto Croce noted that few youths appeared in the parliamentary ranks and that most of the leaders were men of the Murat era or earlier, enlightened and rational in approach rather than exalted, disinclined to ideological transports. Nor did the Carbonari's "cold Masonic theology and its cold symbolism" produce enthusiastic ferment.[197] Most of the heat came from public intervention. The gallery at first limited itself to cheers for popular speakers but soon escalated into disapproving shouts at those who displeased them. Colletta called this public "ignorant rabble." Of course, rough groupings emerged in parliament. Colletta neatly named three main forces—ultra-liberals on the left, a large middle group of the uncommitted, and moderates on the right.[198] Though overly schematic and ignoring the spectrum of opinion between these categories, the characterization is useful. As in Spain, moderates tended toward revising the constitution, while their opponents insisted on upholding the present one.[199]

A few deputies stood out for restraint in matters of substance. Giuseppe Poerio, seen by admirers as a man of talent in the midst of mediocrity, radiated moderation and firmness, in spite of the ridicule some have poured on his ornate oratory.[200] The Muratist Gabriele Pepe (1779–1849), Guglielmo's cousin, had fled Naples after the 1799 revolution and served with the Napoleonic army in Spain under Murat. Called "an antique soul, fated to live in modern times," Gabriele Pepe remained an anti-absolutist and a champion of Italian unity.[201] On the evidence of his speeches, Matteo Imbriani was one of those deputies whose vision transcended flowery appeals to heavenly reason and universal justice. He saw liberty through a double prism. Special interests had to be subordinated to the general will, which was expressed in laws and institutions. But, he stressed, to ordinary people liberty meant not abstract ideas but serving their needs—eating, doing business, earning a living, and securing one's hearth and home, free of disturbance or abuse.[202] These men and those like them added sobriety to the legislature even though they were not always able to bring their ideas to fruition.

Outside the walls of parliament, voices also rose to discuss the meaning of the new politics. Press freedom followed automatically from the adoption of the Spanish constitution; and a decree of July 26[203] made way for a flood of newsprint, as happened whenever liberal regimes came to power in this era. Myriads of brochures and new pro-constitution dailies and biweeklies appeared in the capital alone. The moderate press dominated through organs such as *Annals of Patriotism, Light,* and *The Independent.* The *Neapolitan Minerva,* associated with Poerio, ranked as the most prominent. Imbriani had his *Voice of the People. Friend of the Constitution,* bearing the motto "Moderation and Constancy," had Colletta as a contributor. The *Voice of the Century,* the *Impartial,* and others also had a reputation for temperance.[204] Press wars broke out briefly at first. Conservatives voiced their views in the *Anti-Journal.* The radical *Voice of the People* criticized the government and other papers; and *Friends of the Fatherland* launched a vendetta against Giuseppe Zurlo, who had called for the suppression of the Carbonari in 1813.[205] But the level of journalistic friction almost never reached that of Spain or showed disrespect for the king.[206] Mostly the newly unchained press lamented the misery, poverty, and foreign domination of their country and proclaimed confidence in the new dispensation.[207]

A discourse about the constitution broke out also in broadsides, catechisms, odes, speeches, and songs—as well as "dialogues and lessons" in dialect. Slavish acceptance of the 1812 document was by no means the norm; in open debate, writers argued and suggested amendments. The chief elements of consensus were found in its limitation of royal power, the broad suffrage, and the expansion of local government.[208] Publishers rushed into print with translations of and glosses on the Spanish and other constitutions. One offered up as precedent the Magna Carta and the constitutions of the United States, Poland (1791), the Ligurian Republic (1797), Spain (1812), and Sweden-Norway (1814).[209] Enthusiasts of the Spanish document called it "the sacred codex." Among the many optimistic paeans to it, that by an otherwise obscure Neapolitan lawyer named Fiorilli reached a level of exaltation. Titled *The Best Possible Political Constitution for All Peoples from a Rational Viewpoint,* it offered a veritable blueprint of reason taken to the limits of a geometric utopia.[210] Another enthusiast heaped praise upon the Spanish rebels of 1820 as "a handful of brave men concentrated on the Island of Leon," and described their constitution as a model of moderation and generosity.[211] A slightly more critical contribution refuted what it deemed to be the intolerant clause that excluded all faiths except Roman Catholicism.[212]

A rash of popular "catechisms" appeared that, as in Spain, sought to plumb the deeper moral meanings of the new order. An Italian translation of the 1820 Spanish *Constitutional Catechism of the Spanish Monarchy,* with notes applicable to Naples, pitched to the less educated and stressed popular sovereignty by declaring that "the king is a citizen like everyone else, who receives his authority from the nation."[213] A Neapolitan original, *Constitutional Catechism*—inspired by the July fever of enthusiasm, according to its anonymous author—offered a guide against prejudice for "the instruction of the common people." Its interrogatory form took on a potentially disquieting issue of freedom and revolution. The constitution, it argued, was a simple and practical instrument that delivered freedom as a refuge between slavery and anarchy by dividing power among the monarch (to whom was owed profound respect), the ministers, and a parliament unhindered by divisive political parties. The catechism proclaimed that civil liberty, a free press, and public education posed no threat to religion, which was stoutly defended in the new system. Rather, the fruits of liberty purified religion by fighting superstition and hypocrisy. The arguments, couched in familiar patriotic terms, reflected a moderate attempt to persuade readers that the changes of the moment implied no desertion of the well-grounded traditions of throne and altar.[214]

In a related genre, *A Conversation Among Three Students on the Present Situation* compares the seminarians of Nola to the European youth who ardently love king and country, such as the patriotic German Burschenschaften and liberal French students. The Neapolitan characters identify themselves as religious opponents of despotism. They assert that governments are made for the people and not the other way around, and they praise the moderation of the recent turnover. Though the pamphlet appeared on September 11, more than a month before the powers assembled at Troppau, it reflected the fear of intervention already hanging over Naples. The students voice the hope that Tsar Alexander "remembers the acclaim he received on the Seine and on the Vistula when he was the apostle of constitutions."[215]

A story was told of a conversation between lazzaroni on July 7, at the outset of constitutional victory. One asked the meaning of the word *costituzione*. Another replied, "*Cauzione*" ("caution," in this sense implying security and guarantee)—a plausible reduction of a six-syllable word to a four-syllable one.[216] Droll anecdotes of folk etymology are told in almost every modern revolution. The liberal tales and catechisms stressed moderation and caution and a mood of satisfaction with the new order. The Neapolitan intelligentsia were offering optimistic assessments and, as in Spain, using catechisms to fuse religious and secular messages in hope of reaching the masses. They tried to reproduce on a vernacular level those ideas being nourished on the floor of parliament and among Neapolitan diplomats. Of course, for the most part, the authors were talking to each other. Despite their earnest intentions, one must wonder whether tracts alluding to Tsar Alexander or the Spanish victories would find wide readership among the common people. Neither the Spanish nor the Neapolitan elites betrayed much understanding of the masses. As prisoners of language, they possessed their own thought processes and reading habits. Nonetheless, their motives and efforts to include the broader population in a political discourse represented a move toward national enlightenment that, if given time, might have borne fruit.[217]

In the universe of high-style imaginative writing, the revolution found a champion in one major poet—Gabriele Rossetti (1783–1854), a genial improviser who became the bard of the revolution of 1820 and was later overshadowed by his two children, Dante Gabriel and Elizabeth, founders of the English Pre-Raphaelite school of poetry, painting, and criticism. Gabriele, the son of an Abruzzi blacksmith, attended Naples University until his studies ended with the French invasion.[218] Though he held a lifelong affection for "kindly Joachim" Murat, Rossetti showed a fickle side when he—like so many Europeans—turned against the French he had once admired, and when he later blasted King Ferdinando, whom he had once loyally served. Before and after 1820 the poet worked as librettist at the San Carlo. Rossetti joined the Carbonari in July 1820 and befriended General Pepe, a friendship he later called "the noblest honour of my life." He improvised verses at the Caffè d'Italia in Naples prior to the uprising, urging the king to grant a constitution. Rossetti wrote sixty or so manifestos and numerous patriotic odes to constitutionalism.[219] One of them celebrated the revolt: "From the walls of Nola / The free cohort / Shouting—'To Monteforte!' / Raise the banner and ride!"[220] Another voiced the belief in a harmonious new order: "And one could hear a new allegiance preached / Of two great forces in a single sway: / Popular liberty and kingly power / Conjoined in amity by a lasting link"[221]—the link being a constitution.

The Neapolitan constitutionalists had much less time than their Spanish counterparts to deploy propaganda and build hero cults. Like the republic of 1799, the new regime gave Latin names to the provinces. Suggestions for nomenclature for the new constitutional order included Regno Italico Meridionale for the kingdom and Parthenope for the capital; some wanted to call the parliament a Cortes.[222] Landmark moments such as Minichini's midnight ride, the July 9 march past on the Via Toledo, and the opening of the elected parliament generated talk among the public but—since the regime lasted less than a year—apparently nothing in the way of commemorative events. Pepe and the two lieutenants were praised by government and parliament, but no cult of personality rose around them. Minichini, however, became the object of poetry, song, and sculpture. Copies of his portrait sold by the thousands in the streets of Naples.[223] As with the much grander cult of Riego, this fueled animosity toward him. Luigi Minichini was seen as such a troublemaker in Naples that Pepe ordered him to Sicily. Even a relatively sympathetic biographer admitted to Minichini's delusions of grandeur, extreme arrogance, and demagogy.[224]

A leading historian of Naples has shown that opera—Naples' principal cultural product—did not generally foster revolution in this period of history. Though little is known about the political role of the San Carlo in 1820–21, the whole setup—opulence, decor, royal patronage, ceremonial display, hierarchical seating, censorship, and the audience preference for the music and production over staged ideologies—fed into the grandiose image of absolutism rather than undermining it. Although opera music certainly spilled over into salons, it is not clear that it poured out onto the streets of Naples.[225] Giuseppe Zurlo, the chief security minister of the king, said that theater kept the population out of mischief. The visiting Kotzebue had noted the arrogance of the royal family, who regularly arrived late at the theater while the public waited, and he spoke of the brutal conduct of the mounted dragoons toward the public outside and inside the theater.[226] The castration of boy singers for the opera had been banned by the revolutionaries of 1799 but reinstated after the republic fell. The French liberal Baron Louis Bignon in 1821 critiqued Neapolitan society under Ferdinando as one seduced by pleasure and supplying castrati to all Europe's theaters.[227]

When the ancient Giovanni Paisiello died in 1816, he was succeeded as director of the San Carlo Theater by Domenico Barbaja, a sturdy royalist and Milanese ex-waiter and gambler who since 1809 had been the chief impresario of the city.[228] Barbaja projected his own brand of majesty and iron authority. Stendhal—informed, gossipy, and maliciously exuberant—recounted how Barbaja retained the diva Colbran in spite of her failing voice because the king wished it. Stendhal insisted that the public would much prefer having Colbran fired than receiving a constitution. Visiting the just-rebuilt San Carlo in 1817, he said that this theater "binds the people in fealty and homage to their sovereign far more effectively than any *Constitution*."[229]

The Teatro San Carlo, the largest in all of Italy, outshone the other four capital houses in prestige and volume. Founded in 1737, it stands next to the royal palace and boasts twenty-five hundred seats. Its interior had royal property written all over it. The theater's curator relates that, aside from the two-tiered box reserved for the king and his family, the loges had mirrors mounted on their walls at such an angle so that the occupants could gaze only at the reflected image of the monarch, since they were forbidden to look directly upon his person.[230] According to the British diplomat and royal sympathizer William à Court, at least one constitutionalist, "Colonel Pepe," perceived that the San Carlo was closely associated with autocratic culture and made a motion in parliament that would have brought about the abolition of that theater.[231] The story is unsupported.

When the 1820 uprising triumphed, the theatrical life of the old regime seemed to invite some liberal reform and symbolic innovation by the new. As one theater historian put it succinctly, Barbaja's throne also shook. As in royal theaters elsewhere in Europe, insubordination to the management could result in being jailed. But a new rule book issued in September 1820 relaxed discipline for San Carlo Theater personnel.[232] At San Carlo, those currently incarcerated were released and put back to work; punishments of this sort were henceforth abolished "as a result of the reform which guarantees individual liberty."[233] On July 13, a few days after the constitutional march, the San Carlo Theater was opened free of charge to the provincial troops, who, still armed to the teeth, overflowed the pit, causing a sensation though no incident.[234] But, as in Madrid, the nation's premier theater did witness political statements. Whenever General

Pepe appeared in it, the theater burst into applause—a reason he did not attend very often. In contrast, when the unpopular Colletta arrived, the audience booed and the embarrassed general left the theater.[235]

Unlike later Risorgimento impresarios, opera managers did not indulge during this brief liberal season in direct revolutionary propaganda. Indirect allusion was another thing. On December 3, 1820, Rossini, musical director of the San Carlo, produced *Maometto II*, which floated the theme of Greek struggle against the Ottoman Turks in the fifteenth century. Audiences long had the habit of reading performances of historical stage works as commentary on contemporary politics, and the San Carlo repertoire had often staged plays and operas about evil tyrants.[236] Since the Greek uprising had yet to begin, that parallel could not be made. But Bruno Cagli claims that *Maometto* was probably inspired by the July Neapolitan uprising since it was no trick to substitute Italy for the Greeks and Austria for the Turks. Fearing that the script was too bold, Rossini toned down some of the patriotic-sounding lyrics.[237] In any case, whatever message remained was lost on the audiences and the opera bombed.

It has been claimed that Rossini was drafted into the National Guard, perhaps in a musical capacity. Stendhal says that he composed a "War Hymn to the Constitutionalists," which was sung after the end of an opera on February 12, 1821. By that time the maestro had left Naples. Rossini, eminently flexible, had composed a "Hymn of Independence" when Murat in 1815 declared Italy's independence from Austria. In 1822, at the behest of Metternich, he produced "La Santa Alleanza," a cantata performed at the Congress of Verona—where the death knell of the Spanish liberal regime was sounded. Rossini also hobnobbed with Fernando VII of Spain in 1831.[238]

In the realm of non-musical drama, Neapolitans seem to have possessed some of the bravado of the politicized Spanish stage, particularly when the sword of intervention hung over their heads. In the final months, some theaters in the kingdom put on "'Carbonarist' dramas" and patriotic rallies during the approach of the Austrian army[239]—as the Spanish liberals had done at Cadiz when besieged by the French a decade earlier. One of the last appeared in February after the news of a coming invasion arrived. We do not know the content of the play innocuously titled *Love of Country*, but audience reaction spoke volumes. When the actor playing an enemy of freedom spoke his lines, spectators drowned him out with cries of "Death to the tyrant, long live liberty!" He had to stop acting, move to stage front, and declare his agreement with them before he could continue.[240] Interestingly enough, politics did manage to enter one of Naples' four conservatories. The Sicilian Vincenzo Bellini, studying there at the time, composed a patriotic hymn for the liberal regime which he later disowned.[241] None of this artistic bravado stemmed the tide of the invasion. Cultural works produced in time of revolution in this era and in these lands tell us only a little about their impact on broad audiences[242] and consequently on how effectively they served the revolutionary regime. What they do reveal are the values of the producers—their *imaginaire politique*—or at least the values they wanted to express and disseminate.

The new government and parliament had to face an array of domestic issues in the few months allotted to them by history before the onslaught of the Austrians. They did so, predictably, with mixed results. Middle-class professionals, nobles, and priests divided on various issues, and the free press heated the polemics. People of means feared the appetites of the dispossessed, who might desire some gains from the revolution. The regime's need for broad support and stability slowed the reform process.[243] The political ideas informing the parliament drew on European liberalism, notions borrowed from Spain, the Muratist legacy, and traces of the Neapolitan enlightenment. But it failed—for want of time and will— to implant the central ideas of Naples' most eminent philosophe, Gaetano Filangieri. In the famous *Legislative Science* (1780–85), he had highlighted the scandalous gap between the "immense scale" of the capital—the city of Naples—and a countryside of poor agriculturalists: a hypertrophied head on a meager body. Filangieri's solution was to revivify that ailing body by breaking up and parceling out the great landed holdings, energizing the provincial economy, dissolving the structure of privilege, and localizing justice, culture, and administration.[244]

The regime for a while enjoyed wide support among many parts of the population—peasants, the army, midsize landowners, the urban middle class—but interests clashed as well. The parliament had only five effective months, October to February, to make its mark on the kingdom. That body received a mass of petitions, varying in content and focusing on taxation, banditry, and administrative confusion.[245] The stress on mostly local and even personal issues revealed, in the view of Alfonso Scirocco, certain popular hopes in the revolution. The deputies responded particularly on two fronts: reform of local administration in the direction of more autonomy, and adjustment of the constitution in line with Neapolitan conditions. Responding to landowners' requests, they lowered the land tax.[246] The body did little for the peasants, however. As in 1799, it failed to introduce significant land reform, and it delayed division of noble and church lands. Most peasants waited patiently for something from parliament. There were land seizures in one district, but they ended with the peaceful withdrawal of the peasants.[247] A Russian newspaper claimed that the lack of significant agrarian reforms led some Carbonari to establish contact with bandit gangs on the highway between Naples and Rome.[248]

The lag in reform, real and perceived, naturally aggravated the Carbonari, who had a more ambitious agenda. Though absent from the governing process, they made great inroads into the political landscape outside the walls of parliament.

Legalization brought them into full public life, and they widely distributed pamphlets, brochures, protocols, and catechisms.[249] Now well organized, they grew rapidly, and the proliferating lodges and deluge of new members made them the largest non-clerical and non-governmental grouping in the state. The city of Naples alone had ninety-five lodges, one of them allegedly containing twenty-eight thousand members. The Carbonari had become a huge semi-public body that attracted people of all ranks, some out of interest, some out of conforming to fashion.[250] In the provinces, they represented almost a "state within a state."[251] Carbonari infiltrated courts, prisons, and warships. In regiments they organized soldiers into lodges, thus diluting the authority of the officers.[252]

Late in 1820, responding to the threat from abroad, the Carbonari met in a General Assembly, which unified the separate Carbonari chapters for the first time. Not just a network of clubs as in Spain, the Assembly comprised provincial delegates and thus paralleled the national parliament. Though not a shadow government ambitious to take power, the Carbonari Assembly, along with the free press, aspired to keep order and monitor parliament.[253] This early species of insurrectionary political watchdog clearly resembled the clubs of revolutionary France and Spain; it also—if one stretches a bit—foreshadowed in some ways the Petrograd Soviet of revolutionary Russia in 1917. Since Carbonari political views ranged leftward from those inside parliament, they maintained a continuous check on it from the galleries inside and by means of street demonstrations: their aim was to prevent any significant shaving down of the 1812 constitution.[254] The Carbonari spectrum was rich and diverse. The Salerno chapter was more radical than that in Naples, and even within chapters, divergence of opinion prevailed, though the Soviet historian Koval'skaia exaggerates somewhat the gulf among the Carbonari.[255]

In particular, the Carbonari targeted Zurlo and Ricciardi (who hated all constitutions and parliaments), vetoed most reform legislation, and bred factionalism. As early as July 9, demonstrators in Naples, unhappy with the appointment of those two as Giunta members, displayed their wrath on the streets. Nonetheless, at that point the Carbonari curbed the temper of the crowds and brought order again.[256] But the mutual rancor did not go away. Ricciardi, the minister of justice, assailed the "patriotic societies" as disruptive, sappers of army discipline, and the cause of the rise in crime.[257] Some in power wanted to abolish secret societies, but Pepe opposed this and may have eventually joined the Carbonari himself.[258] He tried to bridge the gulf between them and the Muratists. Ultra-radical offshoots of the Carbonari appeared, sectarian splinter groups calling for a republic. The Russian archives reveal that the tsarist ambassador to Naples may have exaggerated the extremist tendencies of the Carbonari, reporting to St. Petersburg the presence of *vendite* named Robespierre and Louvel (the latter the assassin of the Duc de Berry in France in 1819). Yet one extremist chapter, on the eve of Austrian intervention, is known to have proposed the elimination of the royal family,[259] the only case until the Russian Decembrists of a regicidal program in the 1820s revolts.

The religious issue, which so vexed the Spaniards and which had helped doom the Parthenopean Republic, did not cause serious trouble to the parliamentary regime. The king's oath at the royal chapel included the promise not to permit any other religion in the kingdom. This was taken directly from article 12 of the Spanish constitution. Nor did the liberals, following the lead of the 1799 leaders, reject what was viewed as a notorious superstition in the eyes of foreigners: the liquefaction of the blood of Saint Gennaro, a mythical fourth-century martyred bishop whose ritual had been celebrated since the seventeenth century. When Vesuvius erupted, believers would sometimes file past the statue of the saint and consult his facial expression.[260] Michael Kelly, an Irishman visiting Naples in 1779–80, noted that worshipers would ritually curse the saint if the blood did not liquefy. The Countess of Blessington, witnessing the ceremony in the early 1820s, reported that the officiating priest held the vial of blood for a long time—often near the flame of a candle. She also noted that the habit of stylized shouts and name-calling at the saint from the crowd still endured.[261] In spite of these opinions, shared no doubt by many enlightened Neapolitans, the regime made no assault on religion or "superstitious" practices.

To some churchmen, this did not suffice and tension between them and the regime remained. The former endeavored to keep the government's hands off ecclesiastical affairs. The archbishop of Naples, Cardinal Luigi Ruffo, opposed the press law as an insult to God, church, religion, morality, and virtue. Pressed by Pope Pius VII, he decried press criticism of the church and the weakening of the Catholic hierarchy's censorship powers. Addressing the vicar, he "fulminated against the extravagance of modern opinions and against the wickedness of men."[262] Churchmen also opposed the Ecclesiastical Affairs ministry's prohibition of bishops from interfering in matrimonial matters, and they fought motions to lower bishops' pay, reduce clerical tithes, and suppress religious orders in Sicily. As in Spain, the more conservative clerics resented the regime's efforts to reduce their power and siphon off some of the church's revenue for other purposes. Not surprisingly, the Carbonari, who had been put on the Pope's excommunication list for all of Italy in 1814, remained there.[263] Another thorny issue involved toleration of non-Catholic faiths. The slightly modified constitution issued on January 29, 1821, continued to prohibit all public worship except that of the Roman Catholic Church, but it did allow private worship by non-Catholics,[264] a measure especially obnoxious to the church and not approved by the vicar. Ruffo announced that religious toleration would lead to degeneration, immorality, and vice.[265] Parliament rejected this position.

How did the clerical deputies in parliament regard these clashes of church and state? Did they feel the conflict between their affiliation with the church, the fact of their having been elected, and a secular environment that at the very least had the potential to pass anti-clerical legislation? Guido de Ruggiero argued that parliamentary clergy were too new to constitutional politics to take a position.[266] The Neapolitan clergy at large, as in Spain, divided over political issues. The lower ranks also tended to be hostile to liberal policies, yet some of them joined the Carbonari.

As if purely domestic problems on the mainland were not enough, the new government also faced one that partly resembled Spain's relations with insurrectionary Latin America. During the British occupation of Sicily, while the king and his family were living there in exile, the aristocracy, unhappy with Ferdinando's carpetbagging court, urged the occupation authorities to create a new constitution for Sicily along British lines that would strengthen its autonomy. Under the benevolent gaze of Lord William Bentinck, commander of British forces in the Mediterranean and de facto ruler of Sicily, the old but powerless Sicilian parliament in 1812 forged a document roughly based on some aspects of the British unwritten constitution. The king retained executive power and the Chambers of Peers and Commons (Pari, Comuni) made laws with his assent; ministers were accountable to parliament, and an independent judiciary operated. Feudal estates came to an end and personal security was extended to all subjects. Ferdinando signed it and thus in effect separated the two kingdoms under the same dynasty.[267] When he returned to power in 1815 and proclaimed the Kingdom of Two Sicilies as a single state for the first time, all constitutional schemes were rejected and Sicily lost its army, flag, and local administrative autonomy.

The establishment of the Spanish constitution by the liberals in 1820 on the mainland put these two constitutional models of 1812 into opposition once again. Aristocratic elements in Palermo, defying the liberal regime in Naples by opting for the more conservative Anglo-Sicilian constitution of 1812, wished to restore the autonomy of Sicily with Palermo as its capital. When movements in a half dozen provincial towns declared for the Spanish constitution, the Palermo rebels stood ready to crush them. A ribbon war erupted between the Carbonari colors and the yellow of Sicily. The anti-Naples crowds shouted, "Long live the constitution! Long live independence!" and released criminals who then jailed government troops. Mobs massacred their opponents, burned homes, and assaulted forts.[268] This brief civil conflict looked like a war of independence from the mainland and a struggle between a British-inspired Spanish constitution and a French-inspired one, both dating from 1812. Behind the documentary façade lay deeper class rifts and regional conflicts between Palermo and the Sicilian hinterland.

In Naples, anti-Sicilian riots broke out, and the government, declining to accommodate, responded to the resistance by sending to the island in August an army of fourteen thousand men under General Florestano Pepe. Reluctant to use force against the Sicilian rebels, the commander arranged a truce that allowed Sicily to keep its separate constitution. In October, he recommended autonomy for Sicily. The Naples parliament rejected the proposal and replaced Pepe with Pietro Colletta, who failed to reach accommodation with the rebels.[269] Complicating matters, Minichini arrived on the island to wild acclamation in some towns. His flamboyant manner of speaking and his pushy authoritarianism earned him so much bad blood that his life was thought to be at risk.[270] The issue remained unresolved by the liberal regime.

If enemies of constitutional monarchy in Naples sought evidence of its violence, they would have found little. In contrast to Spain, only one outrage occurred on the mainland of the kingdom: the murder of a police official. Francesco Giampietro was killed in February 1821, on the day of popular disorders after the staging of *Love of Country* at the San Carlo. He had been a vigorous persecutor of the Carbonari. Though unique, this homicide generated fear of a radical bloodbath.[271] But no reactionary jacquerie by the lower classes occurred, as during the Parthenopean Republic. Relative stability prevailed and the poorest in the country did not attack the liberals as they had in 1799 because the new government was not beholden to a French invader who plundered and showed no respect for home or altar. The incidence of crime and disorder declined notably in the constitutional period, according to Pepe.[272] There also occurred one violent case of desertion involving three hundred infantrymen over an unwanted posting. General Giuseppe Rossaroll, then governor of Capua, suppressed it: some sixty men were shot in the fray; and seventeen died from flogging.[273] But the event had nothing to do with the nature of the regime.

Muratists and Carbonari enjoyed a short honeymoon. The former—mostly moderate conservative soldiers, administrators, bureaucrats, and realists—saw the chance of harmony and the consolidation of the achievements if they could placate the European powers. Preferring the Charte, they nonetheless agreed to a constitution that they saw as too democratic for the Naples of its time. The Carbonari represented real interests of the lower ranks of the bourgeoisie, artisans, and some lower and midlevel officials with a desire for lower taxes, the end of the draft, and reform of local government—shading over into more radical ones who desired federal rule and in some cases a republic and redistribution of the nation's wealth.[274] As in Spain, the secret societies not only had helped plan the revolution but were determined to maintain control of the resulting regime. They built and sustained awareness of problems of bureaucracy and elite rule.[275] The farmers, artisans, and petty tradespeople among them shared few values and

interests of the provincial bourgeoisie. Discord among classes, societies, government, and parliament did not dissolve under the constitutional regime. These
issues remained—and would continue to remain long after the crushing of the
1820 liberal experiment.[276]

Richard Craven, who left Naples in the summer, saw foreign intervention as
the most serious threat to the new order. In a fair-minded backward look, he
outlined other perils in store for constitutional Naples: a surfeit of military influence, petty jealousies among those who wrought the turnover, and an inexperienced electorate. He recognized that even some of the enlightened new leaders
worried about the free press and the free movement of people across provinces.
Craven also shared some of the liberal biases against the south of Europe and the
Europe-wide concerns about the political participation of uneducated masses
who were exposed to "forms of religion considered so favourable to despotic
power." Conceding all this, Craven favored allowing the experiment to continue
and wished it success, hoping that a moderate course would prevail.[277]

Austrian Bayonets

"Two squadrons of cavalry overturn a throne, and throw all the world into inexpressible troubles," wrote Prince Metternich in July 1820, shortly after the revolt.
"It will not go in Naples as it did at Madrid. Blood will flow in streams. A semi-
barbarous people of absolute ignorance and boundless cruelty, hot-blooded as
the Africans, a people who can neither read nor write, whose last word is the
dagger—such a people offers fine material for constitutional principles."[278] Aside
from Metternich's "orientalist" (or meridionalist) view of southern Italians and
his misreading of comparative violence in Spain and Naples, the phrase about
throwing "the world into inexpressible troubles" clearly indicates that he looked
on the constitutional regime in Naples as prelude to a disastrous domestic revolutionary regime whose poison would inevitably spread, and that he had pretty
much made up his mind to eliminate it.

Tsar Alexander I of Russia played a key role in the decision to intervene in
Naples. But Metternich, after much potential friction and persuasion of the
other Great Powers, came to dominate policy. Like other conservative statesmen, he bristled at a combination of incidents such as the assassination of August
von Kotzebue for his close association with the tsar and of the Bourbon dynast,
the Duc de Berry; the Spanish, Neapolitan, and Portuguese overturns; and the
mutiny of a Russian regiment—all in suspiciously close sequence. Beyond that,
the Austrian chancellor had a vital concern about Habsburg sway in northern
Italy—the annexed provinces of Lombardy and Venetia and a few nearby petty
despotisms described so brilliantly by Stendhal in *The Charterhouse of Parma*.

The mutually reinforcing concerns caused him to see disturbances as leading to a domino effect, with one successful liberal revolt causing the next. Having lived through an age of brute force and cynical diplomacy, Metternich had no compunction about acting on his fears.[279] For good measure, King Ferdinando employed his ambassadors in Vienna and Paris as sub rosa channels to Metternich and very early on began undermining the constitution.[280]

Although only Sweden, Switzerland, the Netherlands, and Spain recognized the new regime in Naples,[281] the constitutionalists initially had a few other diplomatic friends. The Piedmontese minister in Naples told his government that the political changes there intended by "the better elements of the country" would probably lead to stability.[282] Even the Austrian ambassador reported to Metternich as late as October that the constitutional idea had taken root in the nation, including clergy, nobles, military, middle classes, and above all the legal profession.[283] But these assurances were exceptional and ineffectual. Counterrevolutionary diplomats worked both ends of the line: royalist Neapolitan ambassadors at some European courts sabotaged the regime, as did most of Europe's envoys in Naples—in both cases acting as the king's ventriloquists. William à Court defamed the revolt to the British foreign minister, Castlereagh.[284] The Russian embassy in Naples became a regular factory of rumors floated by the tsar's minister General Stackelberg. One claimed that Pepe and the Carbonari were planning to unseat Ferdinando and offer the throne to a European royal, and that among their candidates was Grand Duke Mikhail of Russia, brother to the tsar.[285]

Reports of the anti-constitutional diplomats flowed into the Congress of Troppau (now Opava), a spa in Austrian Silesia where the Concert of Europe convened in October 1820. Metternich showed much more concern about the Apennine than about the Iberian peninsula. The Neapolitan constitution violated the secret provision of the treaty which precluded any limitation on the monarch's powers. On November 19 the congress issued a protocol signed by Austria, Prussia, and Russia which held that "the powers bind themselves, by peaceful means, or if need be by arms, to bring back the guilty state into the bosom of the Grande Alliance." Guilty states were defined as those "which have undergone a change of government, due to revolution, the results of which threaten other states."[286] The Austrian emperor wrote from Troppau to his brother monarch King Ferdinando that the situation in Naples was threatening the rest of the peninsula and perhaps even all of Europe. Other monarchs wrote to him as well and invited the king to the next international conference, at Laibach.[287]

The Congress of Laibach (now Ljubljana in Slovenia), also on Austrian imperial soil, met from January to May 1821. The dignitaries could not stomach the 1812 constitution. But Castlereagh opposed intervention on principle and remained ready to join France and Russia in pushing for a more moderate one.[288] Their proposals met defeat and Metternich convinced Alexander I of the need to move into Naples and end the constitutional regime. By then, the tsar needed little convincing and the discussion became not whether but how to intervene. Alexander proposed that a joint Austrian-Russian army descend into the Neapolitan realm. But Metternich and Castlereagh preferred a single national invasion force, and in the end, after some debate, Austria was given the assignment on the basis of geography and long-term interests. The Marquis de Lafayette later dubbed the proceedings of the conference the "brigandage de Leybach."[289]

Ironically, the most persistent diplomatic voice in defense of the Naples constitutional regime turned out to be Antonino, Duke of Serracapriola, the long-time legate in St. Petersburg for the King of Naples. He had a record of forty years at court, multiple Russian connections (including his father-in-law, Prince Aleksandr Viazemskii), keen rhetorical skills, and an impeccable reputation as a conservative unsympathetic to the men of 1820. Almost alone among Naples' ambassadors to support the constitutional regime,[290] Serracapriola firmly opposed Austrian intervention. He told the Russian foreign minister, Capodistria, that Metternich was using slander to ensure Austria's control of Italy. Serracapriola's superiors in Naples trusted his ability to engage "the noble and generous feelings of His Majesty the Emperor of Russia in our favor." They instructed him to tell the tsar that the new regime in Naples would in no way injure the long-standing friendship of the two states. In an uncharacteristic display of liberal language quite alien to him, Serracapriola said that the Neapolitans were animated by the love of freedom and ready to die for it. "Conciliation, persuasion, and firmness," he wrote to Capodistria, "in introducing the stable principles of a constitutional monarchy constitute the happiness of the people, and not bayonets." For his efforts to prevent intervention, futile as they were, the venerable Neapolitan statesman fell into disgrace when Ferdinando regained absolute power.[291]

A decisive moment of the conference came with the arrival of King Ferdinando himself. This monarch had turned his private face against the constitutional regime from the outset, long before violence arose in the liberal regime of Spain. His identification of constitution with bloodshed had older sources. His cousin Louis XVI and his sister-in-law Marie Antoinette had perished on the guillotine, and the Parthenopean Republic had forced him into the first of his involuntary exiles. Though the liberal regime of 1820 was a comparative paragon of moderation, Ferdinando, like many conservatives of that era, conflated liberals and Jacobins. It also seems clear that he handed over de jure power to his son, the vicar, not just out of fear but to relieve himself of constitutional responsibilities and give him a legal loophole to deny his "oath."[292] Ferdinando's animosity to any limits on his prerogatives and his correct belief that he could rely on Metternich to intervene doomed the new regime. In September 1820 the king wrote to Vienna via Stackelberg revealing his hatred of the constitutional order. According to another letter found in the Russian archives, Ferdinando informed the tsar that he had sworn on the constitution "in order to save myself from an assassin's dagger."[293] The opportunity to travel to Laibach and commune with Europe's arbiters presented him with a golden opportunity.

The invitation came on December 6, and the next day the king wrote to parliament announcing that he was going to Laibach, where he planned to amend the constitution and thereby save it. The king's message was read out in parliament: "I declare to you [deputies] and to the entire nation that I will do everything so that my people may enjoy a wise and liberal constitution."[294] The king, aware that a revised constitution was still on the agenda at Troppau and Laibach, adopted it as his plan B, though his optimal goal was to abolish it altogether. The very mention of introducing a more conservative constitution brought loud protests from the floor of parliament and louder ones from the street in the form of demonstrations by Carbonari and large-scale rioting in the city amid cries of "Either the Constitution of Spain or war!"[295] The parliament, after a stormy debate, rejected any modifications of the constitution but agreed to let the king go to Laibach on the condition that he would uphold the present constitution—an unwise decision, as it turned out.[296] In response, Ferdinando renewed his vow to the Spanish constitution.

On December 14 Ferdinando embarked on a British vessel, the aptly named *Vengeur*, and traveled by sea and land to Laibach. Thus in both 1799 and 1820, the same king fled from insurrection in a British bottom. After considerable delays on the voyage, he arrived at Laibach on January 7, 1821. There he appealed to the powers, and on January 25 the congress made its decision to intervene. Ferdinando wrote to Naples that the powers required an end to parliamentary rule. He told his son to allow the Austrians troops to enter the kingdom peacefully in order to avoid bloodshed. The vicar replied that he would bow to parliament.[297] The missive reached Naples in February along with letters from three powers. The ambassadors of the Holy Alliance in Naples read to the vicar the note to which the French adhered and the British registered no objections.[298] On February 4, 1821, the Austrian legions crossed the Po River and marched relentlessly southward, heralded by a lengthy proclamation besmirching the "obscure fanatics" of Naples who, it averred, had upended all institutions. On the thirteenth Naples declared war.[299]

The king's son Francesco, still vicar-general of the kingdom, now had command. His motivations and his role still remain unclear. Some have seen him as nothing more than a pure time-server. Like his father, it has been argued, he pretended ardor for the constitution. Pietro Colletta, a contemporary, believed that Francesco was caught between fear of his father and the Carbonari. In any case, on February 13 the vicar informed parliament of the intervention and declared his loyalty to the constitution.[300] He took charge of the defense of the country at once and appointed Carascosa for the western sector, Guglielmo Pepe for the eastern, Florestano Pepe as chief of staff, and Colletta as minister of war. During the campaign he regaled the troops with words of encouragement and relayed detailed military orders to Pepe.[301] The public embrace of the war was not the same thing as genuine commitment, and the behavior of those in power was questioned for years after the event. In the higher latitudes of government, those uncomfortable with the new order or fearful of the intervention sought to subvert that order in the name of defense. Ricciardi wanted to abolish the free press, the secret societies, and Carbonari organizations in the army. Zurlo and Carascosa urged a coup that would abolish parliament, in order to stave off the intervention. Pepe and Poerio opposed this on the grounds that it would bring civil war.[302]

Parliament reacted in quite another way. As the Austrians were marching through the Papal States, some deputies exhibited anger and bravado. In an emotional speech, Giuseppe Poerio denounced the intervention as illegal. Parliament's address to the king waxed poetic, admitting that the kingdom would face "desolated fields, smoking huts, great heaps of dying and dead." But while the enemy would possess "servile discipline, oppression and numbers," Naples could count on morality and on "the law of nations, public opinion, the justice of our cause, national freedom."[303] Justice and morality helped not at all. The Neapolitan optimists had not grasped the fact that patriotic swagger was useless against bullets. The Spaniards would learn two years later that free men could indeed be defeated by invading "slaves." Many in parliament believed—or claimed to believe—that the king was being held captive by the Austrians against his will.[304]

Initially the Carbonari, who dubbed the enemy "barbaro tedesco,"[305] responded to the menace with élan. Minichini had Via Toledo festooned with tricolor ribbons and called the people to arms, declaring that the nation had been betrayed.[306] As early as September 1820 the Russian painter Silvester Shchedrin saw signs of war preparation. While studying in Rome, he visited the Kingdom of Naples to paint landscapes. He noticed groups of citizens near the city of Naples dressed in Carbonari tricolor and shouting for constitution and freedom. Villagers elsewhere slept with windows open and arms at the ready for the Austrian invasion.[307] The Naples *vendita* threw a banquet for the generals and had Rossetti improvise patriotic verses.[308] Some Carbonari scolded parliament for its lack of defensive preparation. Others sailed along the coasts of the neighboring Papal States to recruit volunteers. A number, however, deserted at crucial moments or even purchased exemption from the draft.[309] Little violence accompanied the days of panic and emergency. Naples' street crowds threatened death to traitors among the deputies; outside the parliament, crowds shouted, "The Spanish constitution or death."[310] No fatalities ensued except that of Giampietro.

As the first object of a Holy Alliance invasion, the Neapolitan regime could not rely on any defeated revolutions nearby to spew out numerous political refugees who might come to defend it. Lord Byron offered financial assistance, and Robert Wilson volunteered his services and two thousand Englishmen, but these offers were accepted too late.[311] Pepe floated one of his many military fantasies. He envisioned drawing the Ottoman Empire (as a traditional enemy of Russia) and Portugal into a war of liberation, with troops landing at Trieste and Livorno and Carbonari suborning the Austrian armed forces.[312] The Spanish ambassador to Naples, Luís de Onís, tried strenuously to ward off the Austrian attack and hounded his government in Madrid to render help. De Onís came to distrust the key figures in the Neapolitan government, including the generals, the ministers, and the vicar—all except Pepe, a personal friend whose courage and integrity he admired. He appealed to Carascosa, who was of Spanish ancestry, to take greater defensive action, with little luck. And the vicar seemed only too ready to open the gates of the city to the invader. The prince did not want to subject his kingdom to the experience of the bloody Spanish war against Napoleon. The Neapolitans, he believed, lacked the morality and the character needed to bring such a resistance to success. De Onís could only encourage Pepe and use his diplomatic connections to keep him informed about the Austrian advance.[313] The Neapolitans had to fight on their own.

The constitutional army was outnumbered on the ground but not hopelessly so at the outset. Its roughly forty thousand men faced about sixty thousand Austrians. The Neapolitans had the advantage of defending their own terrain, but their army suffered from desertion, friction between Muratists and Carbonari, poor finances, and weak popular support due to tardy reforms. The soldiers, poorly armed with hunting rifles, lacked overcoats, blankets, and packs for a winter war in high terrain. Some twelve thousand well-armed men who might have turned the tide or held the enemy at bay were bogged down in Sicily. Pepe deployed numerous provincial militiamen, but these were hardly a match in fighting capacity for the Austrian regulars.[314] Pepe proposed an offensive drive against the enemy, but Carascosa and others opposed it and decided on a defensive war by means of forts and other strong points, garrisons, massed formations, and guerrilla bands.[315]

On February 20 Pepe took up his post as commander of Second Corps in the eastern sector near the snowy Gran Sasso d'Italia, the highest peak in the Apennines—the place where Mussolini was temporarily jailed after his fall from power in 1943. Pepe established headquarters at L'Aquila, the picturesque medieval town that would be ravaged by an earthquake in 2009. Troops promised him—including three hundred Abruzzian volunteers who wished to emulate Leonidas—never materialized.[316] At his side rode Colonel Vincenzo Pisa and an international trio of perpetual revolutionaries: the Poles Marszewski and Szulc and Maurice Persat, a Frenchman who had served with Bolívar in Colombia. All three would later help defend the Spanish liberal regime in 1823 and then head off to fight in Greece. These volunteers, however, could have little impact.[317] The province of Abruzzi formed a stony flank from which to menace the Austrians who might march down the western coast to the capital.[318]

In a proclamation to his troops, Pepe said: "The enemy is advancing, but why? Are we the first to grant ourselves free institutions? Why do they not move against Spain or Portugal? Are we to become just by chance the Helots of Europe, we who have taken the classical names of our forebears?" Pepe also referred to the eight million Italians who were waiting to see if the Neapolitans could defend their independence and the liberty they had won.[319] Pepe chose to attack. Contemporaries and historians have questioned his tactics. Colletta called Pepe's decision to attack rash, uncoordinated, provocative, and hopeless. "Pepe, a fantasist and a risk-taker," wrote Candeloro, "deluded himself that a bold, improvised personal action could reverse the situation."[320] But then another commander of Italian ancestry had baffled Europe for almost two decades by launching hopeless charges.

Pepe was no Bonaparte. On March 7 his attack on the Austrians near the Rieti valley turned into a seven-hour battle. His withdrawal to reorganize and strengthen positions became a full retreat that ended in disorganized confusion. Henceforth the Neapolitans could no longer offer stout resistance. Like many a defeated general, Pepe found abundant reasons for the disaster, including false rumors, conflicting orders, and the treachery of his fellow generals and the vicar. Some commanders refused to fire on the Austrian units because they heard wrongly that the King of Naples was among them.[321] Carascosa and Colletta dispersed the heavily Carbonari troops assembled at Monteforte, thus denying Pepe reinforcements. Like some Spanish generals in 1823, these two were clearly leaning toward accommodation with the invaders. But the fact remained that Carbonari themselves often deserted, mutinied against their officers, and even attacked other soldiers who continued to fight. Colletta claimed that the Carbonari drove non-members toward the front instead of serving, a charge that Pepe refuted. By March 11 Pepe had reached the capital in an effort to reorganize.[322]

On March 19, a rump of parliamentary deputies assembled to listen to a moving speech by Poerio and to issue a statement: "We protest the violation of the rights of peoples. We intend to hold fast to the rights of the nation and of the king. We call on the wisdom of His Royal Highness [the vicar] and his august parent, and we give over the cause of the throne and of national independence into the hands of that God who rules over the destinies of monarchs and of people." The parliament dispersed. On March 23, the Austrians occupied the city. Orlov related that they were welcomed with enthusiasm. They had suffered only fifty-four casualties.[323]

What could have been done after the fall of Naples? The idea of protracted popular resistance in a guerrilla war began to take hold. Historians and contemporaries often refer to the recurrence of Calabrian insurgency: in 1799, during the French Decennium, at the defeat of Murat in 1815, and in later struggles. The Russian press reported in May 1821, months after the fall of Naples, that Austrians were sending mobile punitive columns into Apulia and Calabria against armed bands.[324] An article in *Friend of the Constitution* titled "War Cry of the Neapolitan Nation" revived the idea and summoned Calabria to lead the resistance, alluding to that province's recent irregular war on Murat's puppet state.[325] Count Bianco de Saint-Jorioz, a participant in the Piedmontese and Spanish struggles, recalled in a booklet *On the National War of Insurrection by Bands* (1830) that the Calabrians had mounted the first large-scale popular resistance to the French and thus taught some lessons to the better-known Spaniards—namely, that national spirit was more important than the numbers and training of regular troops.[326] This Calabrian experience was repeated in the Risorgimento: guerrilla war raged in that region during the 1848 revolution for two months before being defeated.[327] But those contemplating guerrilla war in 1821 had very little guidance about how it actually worked.

The Spanish model seemed to offer more specifics. The *Minerva napolitana* article on Spanish guerrilla warfare described in the previous chapter supplied rich detail and concrete methods of struggle by irregulars against a foreign invading army.[328] Grigorii Orlov, a longtime resident of the kingdom, had already predicted in the previous autumn that if Austria invaded, the Neapolitans would resist, as the Spaniards and the Russians had done in the Napoleonic era: with fire and sword. The Austrians, he thought, would reach Naples but would find it hard going further on due to mountains and ravines where a small band could hold up entire regiments.[329] None of these scenarios took note of the vital fact of British and Russian armies in those campaigns, and they tended to exaggerate the potentialities of a guerrilla.

General Pepe's scheme, combining the two models, might have succeeded. The Spaniards in their war against Napoleon had retreated southward, eventually to Cadiz, and Pepe saw his Cadiz in Sicily. He also recalled from experience that in the years after 1806, the French had endured a difficult time subduing the guerrilla war in Calabria. He argued later that if the army, the parliament, and the royal family had withdrawn down through the boot and then, if needed, across the Straits of Messina, the Austrians could not have prevailed. The enemy, he believed, would have to garrison Naples and thus dilute their force. As the Austrians pursued the fleeing Neapolitans, coastal parties and inland guerrillas would launch constant raids on enemy lines.[330] Pepe was prepared to continue the fight in Calabria inch by inch, hill by hill, wood by wood.[331] The southern resistance option was not a product of the *calabrese* Pepe's romantic local pride. He knew the ground, knew its people, and knew their recent history.

But, although a few bands were deployed by military commanders, no spon-taneous guerrilla struggle of the Spanish type arose to resist and expel the for-eign invaders. A motion in parliament echoing the *Minerva* article came to nothing. One reason had to do with timing: the military underestimated the speed of the Austrian forces. More fundamentally, the regime had not given potential volunteers a good enough reason to die. The masses had lost their ini-tial patriotic fervor and enthusiasm for the regime, partly due to a lack of funda-mental reforms, partly as the result of routine indifference to politics once the celebrations and dancing ended. And the government had no money to subsi-dize fighters. All this certainly weakened the chance to unleash a successful Spanish-type guerrilla war.[332] But did it doom such a war? In any case, the magic power of the monarch still had force. On February 23 the still absent King Ferdi-nando denounced the constitution, promised to restore order, and instructed his people to greet Austrians as friends.[333]

One final act of would-be resistance took shape in Sicily, where part of the army had remained. A week or so after the surrender of the Neapolitan army, local Carbonari leaders urged General Giuseppe Rossaroll to continue the struggle. In agreeing, he justified his act by recalling the wording of the king's oath—that his subjects should not obey his orders if he broke his word.[334] Ros-saroll commanded a division of troops and a Messina fortress, which he tried to turn into an anti-Borbone stronghold after the Battle of Rieti. He hoped to gather all the garrisons of Sicily and Calabria and march north to expel the Austrians. But his Carbonari friends who had urged him on failed to lend support.[335] Spain and Greece became Rossaroll's next revolutionary destinations.

Did the Neapolitan revolution commit political suicide or was it murdered by outsiders and the king? In opting for the former verdict, one could easily catalogue the weaknesses of the regime: the rift between the Muratists and the Carbonari, paralleling that between the Spanish *moderados* and *exaltados*; fail-ure to win mass support by means of major social reforms; the war in Sicily. But does a repertoire of infirmities automatically indicate heart failure and death? Those who sympathized with the constitutional order preferred to di-agnose that death as unnatural, brought on by the invasion of a superior mili-tary force. We are back to the Spanish example. If one postulates that the invasion sank the revolution, this implies that it could have survived in the absence of intervention. And this in turn takes us inevitably to a counterfactual: how long could it have survived, in what form, and with what results for sub-sequent history? These queries are of course unanswerable, but it is at least reasonable to argue that, given time and space for developing and learning, the liberal experiment project might have been able to proceed. Habsburg armies did not allow this.

The picture is clouded by the unsurprising fact that, as in almost all failed revolutions, mutual recriminations flooded the pages of the protagonists' memoirs. Of the two best-known autopsies by participants—Colletta's and Pepe's—the former, an eminently readable account of the revolution, was called a "historical novel" by the Borbonist police official Pasquale Borelli.[336] Though this judgment is exaggerated, Colletta certainly embroidered and attributed faulty judgment or stupidity to all parties concerned except himself. In his usual sweeping (and self-serving) manner, Colletta blamed the king, the vicar, Pepe, the Holy Alliance, the Carbonari, the Neapolitan people, and the constitution, which should have given more power to the king and less to the masses. On many of these points, Colletta hit the mark, though the list is so big as to be useless. His one curious suggestion about what might have turned the tide on one of the battlefields—a religious rite—anticipated in a way the final episode of the Decembrist uprising in Russia. He wrote that instead of letting deserters depart, an altar should have been erected in the field, as the ancient Romans had done. This sanctified gesture and the raising of the colors, he claimed, surely would have inspired the faithful to honorable battle.[337]

Pepe in exile, less judgmental than Colletta, published in November 1821 a long apologia addressed to his king, who had charged that the Austrian defeat of the Neapolitan army proved that the constitutional regime had had no base of support. Pepe replied that this defeat no more proved a lack of popular aspiration for liberal rule than the defeat of Ypsilanti by the Turks proved a lack of Greek popular desire to unburden themselves of the Ottoman yoke.[338] He further argued that the radical and unpopular 1799 Parthenopean regime had been destroyed by a popular uprising precisely because of its republicanism, foreign sponsorship, and rule by an alien faction. None of these features applied to the constitutional monarchy of 1820–21, which had remained bloodless and moderate, one in which neither the parliament nor the free press discouraged popular affection for the king. Pepe refuted the accusation that his revolt was a military revolution; rather, army leaders had merely reflected the wishes of the great majority of Neapolitans and adopted a constitution that the king himself had actually recognized as heir to the Spanish throne.[339]

And as to the role of Pepe himself? His colleague Colletta wrote that Pepe "placed himself at the head of the revolution, without possessing any of the qualities necessary for so great a work . . . In this, he was urged on by an ardent desire to benefit the people, as well as the hope of gaining fame and power for himself."[340] A century later, Croce, who was mildly sympathetic to the 1820 revolution, called Pepe "a rash and light-headed general."[341] The American historian George Romani, the first to devote a monograph in English to the Neapolitan revolution, had contradictory thoughts about Pepe. With some truth, he repudiated Pepe's sometimes inflated claims to have been its chief instigator. But at the end of his book Romani called him "the sole idealist among the Muratists" and "without question, the hero of the Neapolitan Revolution of 1820–21."[342] The restored government of Ferdinando certainly shared the notion of Guglielmo Pepe as a central figure. He was condemned to death in absentia for his role in the uprising, and the 1822 judgment emphatically declared Pepe its principal leader.[343] A fair judgment would have Pepe share this status with Fra Minichini and the two lieutenants who paid with their lives.

Pepe's role aside, Benedetto Croce, writing in the 1920s, enumerated the countless failings of the 1820 regime: inexperience, unawareness of the effects of the "ultra-democratic" Spanish constitution, ideological confusion, the embarrassing presence of the Carbonari as a state within a state, and the propertied classes' and small landowners' lack of concern about the government's success. Yet none of these disabilities separately or together sufficed to stifle the revolution. "The Austrian intervention," he concluded, "was the real and only cause of its failure."[344] The eminent liberal historian Guido de Ruggiero endorsed that view. "The final collapse of this régime," he maintained, "was due not so much to its incompetence—the Neapolitan parliament of 1820 and 1821 showed remarkable political capacity—as to international action expressing itself through Austrian bayonets."[345] Though the regime might have fallen under the weight of mismanagement or lassitude, the evidence supports the belief that the fate of the revolution fell from its own hands into that of the European powers. The liberal moment in Naples had offered jury trials, administrative decentralization, relief of some local fiscal burdens, basic political participation, and even a limited degree of religious toleration. The regime lasted too short a time to accomplish more than this but, as Alfonso Scirocco rightly put it, it constituted "a great experience of participation in political life."[346]

From the very outset, the Spanish connection took on a special meaning in the Neapolitan revolution. Commentators then and some historians later argued strenuously that the role of Spain had been minimal or nonexistent. Like the Greek rebels of 1821 who distanced themselves from the revolts in Naples and Spain, cautious Neapolitan liberals did so from the Spanish case, which was already attracting negative attention from the powers. A modern scholar stressed, as did many before him, the local roots of the revolt, such as the pre-1820 plots, in order to play down the Spanish impulse. But since no serious investigator has ever read Naples as merely a pale copy of Spain,[347] these arguments, by rightly stressing those obvious differences, were beating a dead horse, and there can be no denying numerous interconnections and similarities.

What were they? Both Mediterranean Catholic and Latin kingdoms, headed by absolute Bourbon princes who were, after long exile, restored in the wake of Napoleon's defeat, suffered from structural social and economic woes. Their restoration policies, though differing in harshness, engendered the growth or revival of secret societies and disaffection among officers and soldiers. A combination of these elements rose up and, in the form of pronunciamentos, imposed the Spanish constitution of 1812 upon their ruler and ushered in a parliamentary monarchy. The victorious liberals could neither agree among themselves nor work productively with the more radical clubs and secret societies. They nevertheless tried to push through liberal programs that, they believed, could see their countries evolve peacefully along a progressive path with the participation of their people. They faced varying degrees of suspicion and outright opposition from clerical and lay figures. Most of all, they found themselves menaced by monarchs who betrayed their oaths and foreign powers determined to intervene.

Piazza del Mercato

The Austrians entered Naples on March 23, 1821, but the king, age seventy, remained in Florence for a time out of fear of returning to his own country. Restored to the throne for the third time, King Ferdinando justified his multiple perjuries, deception of parliament, and collusion with the Great Powers to overthrow it: he asserted that the rebels would have killed him had he not sworn the oath to the constitution—a more than doubtful proposition.[348] Emulating his nephew in Spain after 1814, the king revoked all laws passed by the parliament and other acts taken during the nine months of constitutional rule.[349] Before returning to his capital, the king brought back the reactionary Canosa and initially gave him a free hand to exact vengeance. The minister set about this with relish. He forbade all meetings, disarmed civilians, set up boards of inquiry, and purged the bureaucracy of constitutionalists and Carbonari. Canosa cracked down on the rebels of 1820 in Naples and even proposed an international police force to ferret out radicals all over Europe.[350]

Canosa revived a traditional form of punishment: *frusta*, whipping of the accused performed as a public ceremony along the city streets. At midday, the victim—hands bound, stripped to the waist, barefoot, festooned with Carbonari emblems and cap, and mounted on a jackass—was led down Via Toledo, guarded by Austrians and Neapolitan police. At each note from a bugle, he was scourged by the executioner from behind with a knout studded with nails. Three such incidents occurred in Naples and one in Salerno.[351] Combining the pain of the whiplash and the humiliation of riding an ass, *frusta* also was meant to induce in the bystanders a contempt for the victim. On city squares, the public hangman incinerated books banned by the Papal Index, especially works by the philosophes confiscated from private homes and bookstores. A Russian journal reported the burning of forty-five volumes of Voltaire, seven of Rousseau, and eighteen of d'Alembert. Added to the flames were numerous copies of a *Catechism of Christian*

Learning and Civic Duties. This work, though not one of the political catechisms of 1820, might have been an adaptation or translation of a Spanish catechism. Colletta claimed that it had been officially in use by the church since 1816. But since it mentioned the name of Bossuet and used the word "citizen," copies were now banned and burned and their owners were arrested.[352] All domestic and imported printed matter fell under state control, including "invitations to private parties, posters, leaflets and theatre programmes."[353] Theatrical censorship grew more severe after 1821.[354]

A royal decree of April 1821 ordered house searches, courts-martial, and the death penalty for anyone joining the Carbonari, leading some members to have their beards and long tresses shaved by barbers in order to avoid arrest.[355] The government initiated Inquiry Boards (Giunte di Scrutinio), pallid counterparts to the Spanish Inquisition.[356] The repressions of 1821–22 exceeded those of 1815 but paled before the butchery of 1799. Metternich wished to avoid massive retribution, and when the terror threatened to get out of hand, he and the powers intervened in the name of order and tranquility. The Austrian commander of the occupation army, General Johann Frimont, turned out to be far from the "barbarous German" the Carbonari had feared. No Haynau or Jelačić appeared in this Habsburg army to wreak sadistic vengeance on revolutionaries. Frimont pressured the regime to forgo savage reprisals—as would Angoulême in Spain—and to replace Canosa.[357] The king was also induced, against his better judgment, to issue an amnesty for certain categories of "offenders." However, when a liberal revolt occurred in the Kingdom of Piedmont, the powers agreed to a harsher dispensation and the machinery of persecution continued to grind. Police harassment and denunciations by government informers became common. The clergy were put under surveillance and bishops called for the return of the Jesuits.[358]

The enigmatic Vicar Francesco, more tolerant than his vengeful father, allowed some of the leaders to escape abroad. Foreign diplomats also assisted defeated rebels. Sir William à Court, the British envoy in Naples, despite his loathing of the revolutionaries, helped to organize their exit. Both men wished to avoid repeating the 1799 bloodbath. A Russian diplomat in Naples actually asked his foreign minister, Nesselrode, to give sanctuary to the Neapolitan Italian exiles, which the minister flatly refused.[359] In one way or another most of the leaders of the revolt and the constitutional regime escaped with their lives.

Lieutenants Morelli and Silvati were not among them. They had received heroes' laurels during the march into Naples on July 9, 1820, with the Sacred Squadron and were later honored by parliament. From November to January 1821, Morelli served in Sicily with Pepe's brother and was decorated. Returning to the mainland, he was ordered to deploy the Sacred Battalion against the Austrians. Though present at Rieti, he did not partake of the battle. Morelli and Silvati and the remnants of their squadron repaired to Monteforte for a final stand, but desertions depleted their ranks. They then tried to form a guerrilla unit.[360] The two officers and about five hundred soldiers and irregulars fled eastward. When it became clear that the cause was lost, they embarked on a flimsy boat and headed for Greece. A storm tossed them ashore at Ragusa (Dubrovnik), where suspicious authorities jailed them and sent them to Ancona, north of the kingdom of Naples. There, the prisoners' dialect gave them away and they were sent under guard to Naples. Escaping from their convoy on the way, they headed further south, but in August they once again fell into the police net.[361]

In 1822 Morelli and Silvati endured a three-month trial along with forty-one others accused of treason. Four of the seven judges rendered a death sentence for thirty and prison or the galleys for the remainder. Citing the amnesty of 1821, the court reduced the death sentences to life, except for Morelli and Silvati. To avoid being used in a "spectacle for a stupid rabble and for a cruel king," Morelli took a dose of poison in his cell. Silvati declined to do so, and Morelli ended up vomiting and in convulsions.[362] The barbaric punitive shows of early modern times in Naples had peaked in 1799 with the ferocious bloodletting amid cackling crowds. At least partly due to the influence of Filangieri and Beccaria, butchery and quartering were abandoned in the nineteenth century.[363] But public executions remained in force in 1821. Writing fifteen years earlier, the observant Kotzebue described how a condemned prisoner was taken to a chapel in the Vicaria Prison and consoled there for three days by White Penitents. On the day itself, overflow crowds menaced by dragoons jammed the square and stood on balconies and roofs. The condemned man received last rites in a nearby church and was then led to the gallows to the sound of the continuous prayers of the Penitents. On the gibbet, three men shoulder-hanged the victim.[364]

The massive circular Piazza del Mercato lay in one of the poorest and most volatile quarters of the city and stood as the endpoint of a huge agricultural intake and daily fish delivery. It also served as the city's main site of public execution.[365] On September 12, 1822, it became the arena of another dismal act of revenge. Here, where Pimentel, Sanfelice, and scores of others had been dispatched a generation earlier, the two condemned officers were marched to the scaffold barefoot in black garb, faces covered. Silvati stayed serene and resigned, Morelli defiant to the end. According to Pepe, Morelli wanted to address the "glum and silent crowd," but the drums of the invader drowned him out and the two were executed.[366] Silvati had received the sacraments and got a Christian burial. Morelli allegedly replied to an offer of religious consolation: "Oh! Had your Christ been just, he would have sent down the lightning bolt which the king invited when he swore an oath to comply with the constitution." Morelli died *empio* (impious or unredeemed), was denied a church funeral, and by law had to be buried by police outside sacred grounds.[367]

Those spared the hangman's noose, with shaved heads, dressed in prison garb, and chained in pairs, were shunted off to rocky penal islands such as Santo Stefano and Pantelleria[368]—a custom, called *confino*, lavishly employed by Mussolini in the twentieth century. On Santo Stefano, eight miles in circumference, the convicts were locked in a four-story oval-shaped fortress twice the size of the San Carlo Theater. It housed fifteen hundred inmates, with twelve to fifteen prisoners to a cell. The politicals were separated from each other and mixed in with ordinary criminals, shackled to the wall, fed a Spartan diet, and made to sleep on the stone floor. They were released from the prison, but not from the island, in 1825; later some of them were set free under King Francesco.[369] The repression did not end with the hanging of Morelli and Silvati. In 1822 sixty-six officers were tried for taking up arms against state and sovereign, and twenty-nine of them were condemned to death but soon pardoned; the rest were sentenced to twenty-five years in prison. The *Official Gazette* of the kingdom made bold to announce, "The sentencing of such brave officers has cast a shadow of mourning over our beautiful capital." After a protest by the Austrian ambassador, the journal was closed and copies of the issue burned.[370] In the murder case of police chief official Giampietro, eighteen went to prison and two were executed. Increase or revival of Carbonari activity led to more arrests and executions in the early 1820s.[371]

The influential account of Colletta greatly exaggerated the number of death sentences carried out. At one point he claimed that an execution took place every day.[372] Gleijeses, among other historians, argued that Colletta's accounts of cruelty all sprang from his imagination, inflamed by his hatred of the Borbones. In the twentieth century, Harold Acton wrote that Colletta's version of events after the king returned described scenes of "violence, persecution and cruelty which would have delighted an Elizabethan audience at the Globe."[373] Repression continued for years, but in response to later episodes of radicalism in subsequent reigns. King Ferdinando—thrice evicted and thrice restored—died in peace at age seventy-three on January 24, 1825.[374] The Austrian occupation force of 35,000 men departed in December 1826.

Addio Alla Patria

Since Spain, having engineered the first revolt of the 1820s, had gained Europe-wide publicity and favor among liberals, its story overshadowed the Neapolitan one.[375] Partly due to the brevity of the liberal regime in Naples, Europeans voiced less ardor for it. The poet John Keats, while moored in the harbor off Naples in late October 1820, dreamed only of ancient "Greek galleys and Tyrrhenian sloops" and of a lost love. On shore he attended the San Carlo but saw almost nothing of the city and recorded none of the political events.[376] Stendhal was turned off by the "childish stupidity" he saw in the conspirators of Naples and Piedmont.[377] The poet Giacomo Leopardi (1798–1837) poked fun at the facial hair of the "liberaloni."[378] What did attract attention was the continued internationalization of constitutional struggles. Hearing of the short-lived Piedmontese uprising, Lord Byron, then living in Ravenna in the Papal States, somewhat jocularly noted in April 1821 that "the Spanish business has set all Italy a constitutioning. . . . You can have no idea of the ferment in men's minds, from the Alps to Otranto."[379]

In the northern kingdom of Sardinia-Piedmont, with its capital at Turin, a group of officers, aristocrats, Carbonari, and students attempted in 1821 to end the absolutist sway of the House of Savoy. A major figure in the overturn, Count Santorre Annibale Derossi di Santarosa (b. 1783), had enjoyed an enlightened education and, while pursuing a military career, had become a liberal.[380] He and his friends bristled under arbitrary rule in Piedmont and Austria's dominance of the peninsula, and they found inspiration in the Mediterranean revolts of 1820. "The Revolution in Spain," he recalled, "sounded like a clap of thunder throughout Europe," and the Piedmontese took action in solidarity with the beleaguered constitutionalists in Naples in March 1821. On March 9–10, a provisional government proclaimed the Spanish constitution of 1812 in the garrison town of Alessandria.[381] Santarosa, a devout monarchist and believer in a bicameral parliament, thought the British-inspired Sicilian constitution of 1812 a better model. But he deferred to his friend Count Pecchio, who spoke these revealing words to him: "Till the talisman of the Spanish constitution is displayed, the majority of the Italians will not stir."[382] Santarosa organized the army in the brief military brush with Austria.

The Piedmontese king Vittorio Emanuele I abdicated in favor of his brother Carlo Felice. But since the latter was absent, Carlo Alberto, a relative of the king and second in line for the throne, became regent. This young prince, a neurotic and complicated personality, performed a remarkable political dance. After cooperating with the provisional government for a time, Carlo Alberto lost his nerve and fled. Carlo Felice emulated Ferdinando of Naples and appealed to the powers at the Laibach conference for intervention. Austrian forces quelled the movement and terminated the constitutional government in Piedmont. For flirting with the rebels, Carlo Alberto was later punished symbolically by being made to ride with the French interventionist army to Spain in 1823.[383] Santarosa, taken prisoner, was rescued by a Pole who later fought on the Turkish side against Santarosa in Greece.[384] He and other escapees joined the detritus of the failed Neapolitan revolution. The unlucky ones ended up in Austrian captivity.

The Austrian state also played host to the captured Neapolitan moderate constitutionalists. They were jailed in Naples for a time, but the authorities decided to expel them from the country in order, claimed Colletta, that they suffer the pangs of exile. They were shipped off to various Habsburg prisons. Poerio, Colletta, and Guglielmo Pepe's cousin Gabriele, after serving time in Graz, Prague, and Spielberg dungeons, were released.[385] "Culture," wrote a well-known popular historian of the city, "in a real and important sense, emigrated from Naples together with the exiles from the revolution of 1820–1821."[386] In fact, a bubbly cultural life continued in the city right up to and after unification. But Naples did lose to exile Gabriele Rossetti, the Poerios, and Pietro Colletta. Among those who abandoned the active struggle, Giuseppe Poerio and his son remained in exile. One critic has called his son Alessandro "perhaps the greatest poet of the Risorgimento."[387] Colletta, still considered one of the major historians of Naples, wrote his influential book in Florence in 1824, published posthumously.[388]

The die-hard revolutionaries, however, created a veritable flood that gushed forth from Italy for decades. Refugees from the 1820–21 revolutions shared the bitter bread of exile. The more moderate tended to settle in Switzerland, Paris, or London in order to write, while the more committed radicals moved on from those places to fight in Spain. Guglielmo Pepe, Minichini, De Concilj, Carascosa, Rossetti, and Florestano Pepe escaped from Naples—all but the last two condemned to death in absentia.[389] Santarosa hopscotched through Europe and ended up in England. By the 1820s London had become an international center of Iberian and Italian exiles. At times one could see Pepe, Minichini, Argüelles, and Galiano at the London opera. British liberal circles offered a warm welcome and the government even offered pensions to all former members of the Spanish Cortes. Some declined. Uprooted Italians found themselves in London, Norwich, Nottingham, and Ireland. But the aura of heroism soon faded and many émigrés were reduced to teaching Spanish or Italian.[390] Political squabbles, the bane of exile life, occasionally punctuated the days away from home ground. Pepe fought two duels during his time in Britain. In one, Carascosa called him out in 1823 for what he had published concerning the Battle of Rieti. Pepe wounded the challenger.[391]

Gabriele Rossetti became the lyrical voice of tormented exile. After the collapse of the liberal regime, he had been hidden, disguised as an English officer, for three months on one of the frigates of a British fleet moored in the bay. He sailed on it to Malta and then made his way to Britain. Once settled, Rossetti blasted the Holy Alliance as the "terrible scourge of our time / the shame of Europe, a three-headed monster."[392] The poet reserved his darkest bile for King Ferdinando, "that Bourbon void of faith," "crime-stained king," and "felon king." Rossetti addressed him with the oft-quoted inflammatory verses:

> Traitor! From the moment
> When you broke your vow
> One hundred daggers
> Point avidly at your heart.[393]

Fra Luigi Minichini, who stayed briefly in England, lost the ragged mien that had so impressed his followers and terrified or repelled his foes. In an undated portrait, he looks neither ferocious nor grotesque, but rather resembles Franz Schubert and a thousand other good European bourgeois of the time. His eyeglasses apparently caused some consternation among zealots, for one of them protested a portrait of him: "A hero of our time / Which knows no equal to him / Is now the butt of ridicule / Hidden behind spectacles."[394] During the Austrian invasion, Minichini, like Morelli and Silvati, tried too late to assemble a guerrilla force.[395] His exile road took him briefly to Spain, the Isle of Jersey, Birmingham, and Paris. Along the way he converted to Protestantism. The old radical eventually landed in Philadelphia, where he taught Italian.[396] One biographer wrote that when Minichini passed away in 1861, he "was able to bring to the grave the consoling thought of having, with his rebellious and sectarian activity, carried a small stone to the edifice of Italian unity."[397]

Santarosa had first fled to France, where he was briefly jailed on suspicion of subversion. Released after two months, he went to London in October 1822 and later moved to Nottingham. His home there became a haven for veterans of the Piedmont revolt, including Arrivabene, Count Porro, and Count Pecchio, who would later join him in Greece. Like most émigrés, Santarosa suffered from the humility of inaction, recollections of the short-lived freedom of his country, and a "persistent nostalgia for the homeland" to which he could not return.[398] Unlike those Italians who fought both in Spain and in Greece, Santarosa declined the Spanish route and chose instead the role of philhellene.[399]

For liberal activists, Spain seemed the obvious next stop. Like those European communists a hundred and more years later who had been defeated in the 1920s, they found a new battleground. More than a thousand Italian volunteers fought there in 1821–23, and hundreds died.[400] The Madrid regime, having expressed its solidarity with the Italian rebels, was ready to receive them. At a March 1821 session, Cortes deputies demanded help for Naples. The Spanish ambassador in St. Petersburg, M. G. Salmon, informed a Russian diplomat that if the Holy Alliance intervened in Naples, Spain would assist the latter.[401] But internal political crises in Spain precluded any action. When the shooting stopped, the Cortes condemned the intervention and offered asylum and financial support to certain Neapolitan figures who were subject to repression.[402] Austrian repression had thrown together the outcasts of Naples and Piedmont on the waterfronts of Genoa, Livorno, and other places. Those revolutionaries who inscribed the Spanish constitution on their banners and had eluded dungeon and fetters now set out to assist their role models. Giuseppe Mazzini—a major prophet of the Italian Risorgimento—recalled how, as a sixteen-year-old, he strolled with his mother along the docks of Genoa in 1821. There they witnessed the heart-rending sight of the political exiles. "The insurgents crowded together, seeking refuge at the seaside in Genoa—impoverished and without means, wandering in search of aid to get them to Spain, where the revolution still remained victorious."[403]

Barcelona became the main port of entry into Spain for those in flight. A Russian journal reported an overflow of exiles there by June 1821. Some three hundred of them were Italians, mostly Piedmontese with some Neapolitans and others, mingling with the waves of French radicals and Bonapartists that were greeted by the government agents.[404] General Pepe had embarked for Barcelona on a Spanish vessel provided by De Onís and arrived in April with Minichini, Vincenzo Pisa, and the Piedmontese Count Pecchio.[405] De Concilj was there already. An influx of Carbonari ensued. The captain general of the province, Villa Campa, against whom Pepe had fought in the Napoleonic wars, welcomed his old adversary with affection. After a few days Pepe proceeded to Madrid, where he met with other exiles from Piedmont. On May 2, 1821—Dos de Mayo—a group of *exaltados* addressed Pepe in a letter as a friend of liberty and offered fraternal greetings and assistance.[406]

Pepe did not linger long or accomplish much during his first sojourn in Spain. Seeking greater international support, he traveled to London in August 1821 with Colonel Pisa. Working two fronts, Pepe first wrote to Capodistria in November 1821 that he had wanted merely a revolt in Naples and not a revolution. Nurturing a naive belief in Alexander I, he asked the Russian diplomat to intercede with the tsar, "a great monarch" who had already granted constitutions to France and Poland. Pepe even asked, *mirabile dictu*, if he might visit and enlighten the Russian emperor about the Kingdom of Naples.[407] Unsurprisingly, this line of inquiry bore no fruit. Turning to more familiar material, Pepe met with Robert Wilson, Lord Holland, and other liberals, and he founded on paper the Constitutional Brotherhood of Europe in order, he hoped, to transcend the divided efforts in the Italian Peninsula and elsewhere.[408] According to a London police report of May 1822, the Brotherhood's charter was adorned with signs of nails, a cross, the sun, the moon, battle-axes, thorns, a spear and a sponge, shamrocks, a jug, a house, a basket, a beehive, a ladder, and a liberty cap.[409] Pepe, now more deeply radicalized, apparently had yielded to the charms of Carbonari symbolism.

After an interlude in England and Portugal, Pepe returned to Madrid, where he witnessed the palace guard putsch of July 1822.[410] During his visits to the Iberian peninsula, Pepe returned to his dream of a Calabrian campaign, this time to overthrow the restored monarchy. One of his fantasies involved a request to the insurgent Greek government for a thousand men. A British police spy of May 1822 reported another: a planned expedition to Dalmatia with Italian exiles and Irish and Scottish volunteers to start a rising of a thousand Montenegrins, ostensibly to help the Greeks. They would then sail by night to Calabria.[411] Pepe's more serious though still far-fetched scheme was a variant of French plans hatched in Spain by Fabvier and Vaudoncourt. Coauthored by Pepe and the irrepressible liberal the Marquis de Lafayette, it called for an invasion of France by Spanish forces in order to overthrow Louis XVIII and thus protect the future of Spanish liberalism.

Pepe had admired Riego from afar and wrote him from Paris in March 1822 that all who serve the cause of liberty were automatically friends, even though they had never met.[412] When they did meet, Pepe presented his French invasion plan at a meeting in Riego's home attended by a dozen other influential Spaniards, including Ballesteros, Quiroga, Istúriz, Alcalá Galiano, Flóres Estrada, and Romero Alpuente. Pepe explained that an absolutist France was deploying money, intrigue, and military might to annihilate Spanish liberty, and he advised them to prepare for an intervention since the Spanish people would not repeat the guerrilla experience of 1808. Thinking perhaps of his own people's experience with Sicily, he urged his Spanish colleagues to free the Latin American colonies, bring back the expeditionary forces, and work with Lafayette to overthrow King Louis XVIII. Pepe observed much mutual jealousy among his listeners and he could get no agreement. Some arrived hours late, and others had been advised by foreign envoys not to heed Pepe. Most of these men of the left refuted Pepe's arguments, and some averred that neither freeing Latin America nor overthrowing a French king would be acceptable to the Spanish masses.[413]

Pepe found the Spanish to be, in his words, "rich in pride and short on intellect," meaning political acuity. He warned them of the hazard of royal perfidy and tried to convey to them the lessons of his own land. Instead of learning from that disaster, they were wont to say behind his back, "We are not Neapolitans." But Pepe's argument is not convincing. Neither in Naples nor in Spain could the leaders' knowledge or suspicion of the king's double game—as if that awareness did not exist—necessarily have saved their regimes from foreign invasion. His solution, to invade France, could never have won sufficient support, and it could hardly have succeeded. Pepe, however, remained on good terms with Riego. After the Spaniard's demise, Pepe wrote that "General Riego was always faithful to the cause of liberty."[414] Pepe chose not to enter the fray in Greece, but instead went into exile to fight again and again for a Calabrian campaign and in later Risorgimento battles. Pepe's loyal aide Colonel Pisa and the adventurous Rossaroll both fought the French intervention in Spain. Pisa was captured and spent two years in a Madrid prison, after which he went to London and then to Greece.

Rossaroll, though not captured, followed Pisa's route.[415] General Pepe exits from the story at this point, but his name would be honored again and again by revolutionaries in faraway Russia.

The Piedmontese, whose constitutional order had lasted only thirty days, were shorter on revolutionary experience than the men of Naples but not on valor. In Catalonia the Piedmontese exile Captain Giuseppe Pacchiarotti's Liberal Foreign Legion fought valiantly against the French and lost. Pacchiarotti died of wounds.[416] Others worked the political front. Count Pecchio, a political reporter and advisor rather than a combatant, provided a gossipy account of events in his several memoirs. He held out little hope of exporting Spanish liberalism. In 1824 he refuted the notion of "revolutionary contagion" adopted by the interventionists and stressed instead the indigenous sources of the Italian uprisings over their alleged Spanish origin.[417] Like most other exiles in Spain, Pecchio lamented the low level of preparation and supported the commander of the armed forces, General Ballesteros, who was pushing for vigorous defense measures.[418] Captured and expelled from Spain, Pecchio arrived in London for the second time in August 1823.[419]

By 1821 the liberal emigration had divided geographically and politically over where to go, whether to continue the struggle, and whether to wed the Italian cause to Spain, Greece, or even France. As to Spain, General Santarosa wrote in October 1823 of Riego, just prior to the latter's execution, that he had "attempted a very great thing and did it with courage." He also admired Pepe, whom he met in London, where he served as second in Pepe's duel with Carascosa. "Naples is also my country," wrote Santarosa, and he pronounced Pepe "a fine man . . . bursting with good intentions." But Santarosa did not share Pepe's plans to defend Spain and had no faith in a combined Hispania-Italia liberation, partly because he opposed the Spanish unicameral parliament.[420] Some of his compatriots bitterly criticized him. A March 1, 1823, "manifesto" of a Piedmontese lancer unit in Barcelona accused Santarosa of bad faith by refusing to aid the beleaguered Spaniards.[421] Demoralized by this assault, he decided to head off to Greece. By that time Santarosa had developed a vision of a Grecia-Italia liberation, an idea rooted in his profound love for Greece as "a second fatherland" and sharer of the classical tradition.[422] As a biographer put it, the decision was "more than a gesture of solidarity for the nation oppressed by the Turks, more than a decision, reached in the name of liberty, it was an act of desperation, done in order to recapture the lost energy and to put an end to all the calumny. 'Only a heroic act could save him and pull him out of the humiliating position into which he had fallen.'"[423] In his romantic soul the myth of a decent and good Greek people got mixed in with his own fantasies about the destiny of Italy.

With the collapse of the constitutional regime in Madrid, the Italian legionaries and those associated with the defeated Spanish liberals had to rethink their future. Between the summers of 1823 and 1824, as King Fernando's Spanish vengeance raged and the constitutions of Portugal, Naples, and Piedmont were reduced to ashes, the once-again homeless Italian exiles who had fought there asked themselves what to do as they left Iberian shores. The police hounded them.[424] Some went to Marseilles. Others sailed to Britain. In both places, the news of the Greek insurrection filled the press and heated up political conversations. Freedom, as the exiles of the 1820s understood it, had perished in Naples and Spain. "Yet, Freedom!" in Byron's words. "Yet the banner, torn, but flying, / Streams like the thunder-storm, *against* the wind."[425] Off they went, heroes and renegades, from one end of the Italian boot to the other to recapture that banner for the Greeks of the Ottoman Empire.

4

Alexandros Ypsilanti

Across the River Pruth

One common cause makes myriads of one breast,
Slaves of the east, or helots of the west;
On Andes' and on Athos' peaks unfurled,
The self-same standard streams o'er either world.[1]

The National War Museum in Athens holds a brilliant romantic rendering in oil by Theophilos Tsoukas of Alexandros Ypsilanti's landing on February 22/March 6, 1821, on Moldavian soil, the first act of the Greek War of Independence. In the dramatized scene, the hero steps off the boat from the raging waters of the Pruth River. Flanked by his companions and welcomed by an Orthodox priest, Ypsilanti plants his right foot on the bank and raises the banner of freedom in his right hand, the stump of his left arm folded in his sleeve. Ypsilanti, like Admiral Nelson and thousands of others, had incurred a life-changing injury in the Napoleonic wars. But the artist erred in preserving the right arm, the one the general had actually lost. Or did Tsoukas deliberately choose to put the banner of revolt in what was after all the symbolically more appropriate limb?

The Pruth River rises in the Carpathian Mountains and flows south to the Danube. In 1821 it divided Ottoman Moldavia, now part of Romania, from Russian Bessarabia—modern Moldova. General Ypsilanti, an ethnic Greek prince in Russian service, crossed the river on the first stage of a journey of liberation: to free all the Greek-speaking and other Balkan lands from the five-century-long Ottoman Turkish rule. Accompanying him were two of his brothers, several comrades, and some fifty armed men.[2] The boat landed at Sculeni (Gr. Skouleni; Russ. Skulyany), opposite a Russian quarantine station. One of Ypsilanti's agents sent two hundred Arnaut horsemen to the Pruth to welcome and guard him. As in parts of Spain and Italy, banditry made travel without armed guards in these lands perilous. Arnauts, ferocious mercenaries, originally Albanian bodyguards for the Romanian nobility, were now infused with Christian Greeks, Bulgarians, and Serbs.[3]

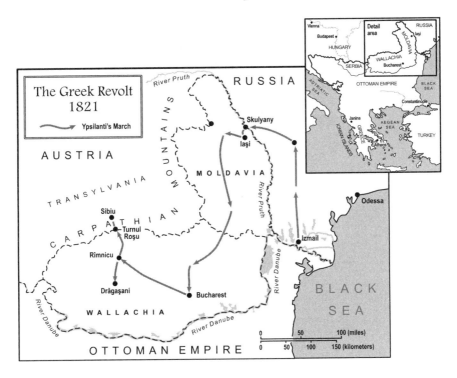

The party rode to the Moldavian capital of Iași (Jassy), about twelve miles away, with Arnauts guarding the road and the city's streets. Late that night, Ypsilanti met with Mikhail Soutsos, a Greek who was the hospodar (Ottoman-appointed governor) of Moldavia. The following day, Ypsilanti began to issue statements outlining his intentions. In his most far-reaching proclamation, "Fight for faith and motherland," he declared that the Greeks would take up arms to free themselves from the Turkish yoke. He wrapped his appeal concretely in a pan-European context. Like Riego, who claimed that all Europe was on his side, Ypsilanti asserted that Europeans had long struggled to affirm their liberty and were now waiting for the Greeks to do so as well. With his usual misplaced optimism Ypsilanti predicted that "our tyrants, trembling and pale, will flee before us"; and he misleadingly suggested that "a mighty empire"—clearly Russia—stood ready to assist. Referring to a recent example of success in popular movements, he spoke of Spain, "who first and by herself put to rout the invincible phalanxes of a tyrant."[4] Ypsilanti may have been thinking also of Riego in general terms, but here he was clearly alluding to the Spanish resistance to Napoleon. In any case, he would not have publicly linked his revolt to liberal overturns in Spain and Naples in words that would be heard by the Russian tsar.

The Russian journal *Messenger of Europe* observed that Ypsilanti's manifestos were bathed in "pietistic solemnity."[5] Indeed he deployed a style that then enjoyed a vogue in liberal and national rhetoric. Ypsilanti played the antiquity card by enumerating heroes of the classical age as the glorious ancestors of the contemporary Greeks. He began with a clarion call to the inhabitants of Moldavia and to Greeks everywhere to rise up against the Turkish overlords along with subjugated people of the Balkans. To the present ruinous conditions in which the Greeks lived—despoiled maidens, demolished homes and churches, and enslaved villagers—he contrasted a coming order under an elected parliament. Ypsilanti urged his co-nationals to offer their blood and treasure to the cause, and he directed priests to broadcast its message. In a dark warning, the general echoed the literature of the anti-French struggle in Spain (and also anticipated a Decembrist proclamation): "Those who disobey and turn a deaf ear to this present appeal will be declared bastards and asiatic germs, their names, as traitors, anathematized and cursed by later generations."[6]

Ypsilanti's insurgent commencement resembled in some ways those in the other Mediterranean states in 1820–21: the military "man on horseback," a pronunciamento brimming with emotion and colorful imagery, an indictment of oppressors, and a promise of deliverance. Ypsilanti's men, emulating the ancient warriors Miltiades and Leonidas, began letting their beards grow and vowed not to shave until they had taken Constantinople.[7] In this adoption of facial hair, they were also unknowingly emulating the Carbonari and other European leftists. There can be little doubt that, as a historian wrote, Ypsilanti "believed in a Russian war and in the justice of the rising on the part of the great power next door; and he dared to believe that on this hung the fate of his people." Most of all, Ypsilanti "actually believed in a triumphal march through the principalities, Bulgaria, and Macedonia into Greece itself,"[8] in spite of the distance of more than 650 miles from Iaşi to Athens as the crow flies. Though there is no direct evidence, he may have been inspired by, among other things, Riego's ride through Andalusia. But Ypsilanti and his legions parted company with the rebels of Spain and Naples in several ways. He lingered long in his initial base, Iaşi, before riding forth into action. Ugly episodes of gratuitous violence stained the movement. And, though his own rising failed ignominiously, in other hands it eventually yielded a spectacular success.

Voices of Awakening

The Ottoman Turks had established a firm foothold in Anatolia and the Orthodox Christian Balkans by the fourteenth century. In 1453 they captured and sacked Constantinople, eventually renaming it Istanbul. The Ottoman legions went on to subdue and rule much of the modern Muslim Middle East and North Africa. Greeks, Romanians, their Serb and Bulgarian Orthodox Slav coreligionists, and Catholic Croats—among others—fell under the Ottoman sultan's sway for centuries, an era that the Greeks call the *tourkokratia*. The Turkish ruler gave Orthodox Christians status as a religious community with a certain amount of self-administration under the authority of the Patriarch. The Greeks resided for the most part at the base of the Balkan peninsula, in Rumelia, in the Morea or Peloponnese, on numerous archipelagos surrounding the mainland from the Adriatic to the Aegean, and on the coast of Anatolia. Though Greek Christians were not systematically persecuted by the Turks, they were subject to unequal taxation, recruitment of their children, exploitation by corrupt local bosses, and periodic retribution for real or imagined disobedience.[9]

Modern Greek nationalism arose originally outside the Ottoman Empire. The low educational level of the common people under Turkish rule and relatively little contact with the rest of Europe, except for mariners and merchants, meant that the ordinary Greek, though endowed with some level of religious and ethnic consciousness, felt nothing like national identity. On the eve of liberation, to peasants or shepherds the word *patrida* meant their own region. The Greek rebel leader Theódoros Kolokotrónis asserted that his fellow villagers in Epirus knew nothing of other settlements an hour away, and they called the Ionian island of Zante "Frangia"—that is, the land of the Franks, or Europe.[10] A kind of collaborative elite emerged, comprising Greeks who originally lived in the Lighthouse District of the capital (and thus were nicknamed "Phanári" or "Phanariots"). These performed vital functions of Ottoman administration, sometimes at the very highest level. After failed risings in the principalities of Wallachia and Moldavia by native Romanian princes, Phanariot Greeks became the hospodars there from the eighteenth century to the early nineteenth. Western and secular notions began to find shelter in the Phanariot schools established throughout the Balkans to offset the hegemony of church teachings. But to critics, the Phanariots remained wedded to the Byzantine heritage.[11]

Among Greeks of the diaspora, deep (though hard to measure) currents of history, mythology, culture, and religion flowed gradually into a Greek national consciousness.[12] The diaspora began to develop some signs of a common heritage long before the Enlightenment, indeed from the moment the Turks conquered Constantinople. Venice, Naples, Trieste, Toledo, Amsterdam, Vienna, Budapest, Odessa, and many other places became centers of Greek life. In Naples, second only to Venice as a major Italian exile base, Greeks plotted against the Ottoman Empire, enlisted in the Neapolitan armed forces, and acted as spies. On a different level, the early modern Greek diaspora founded schools to keep the culture alive.[13] The Greek awakening remained limited to a few hundred or so mostly isolated figures, who produced newspapers, translations, and scholarship on classical Hellas and on current political and ethnic yearnings. To this one must add the frequent travel by Greeks between their ancestral homeland and

Europe and the early wanderings of European cultural proto-philhellenes who published observations on Greek life under the Ottomans.[14]

National awakening drew nourishment from ideas of the Enlightenment and the French Revolution and from literary romanticism. Abstract notions of freedom and enlightenment intermixed with themes of the classical tradition, a Byzantine revival, the defense of Orthodox Christianity against Muslim infidels, and opposition to Turkish despotism—all promising some kind of national regeneration.[15] The most prosperous and influential diaspora Greeks resided in the big emporia. Affluent merchants and shipowners drew on commercial organizational principles and economic needs. Merchant communities there, in the words of one historian, were "miniature national societies established and fashioned to their own requirements."[16] They patronized institutions that endeavored to keep the flame of Hellenic memory alive.

As in all such currents, proponents divided into thinkers and actors—those who advocated a gradual flowering of education toward a distant goal, and those who plotted for freedom in the near future. The intellectual ferment of the eighteenth century flowed into a conspiratorial secret society movement of the early nineteenth.[17] The poet Rhigas Pheraios (1757–1798) received his education in Wallachia and worked for Phanariot circles in Bucharest. Rhigas encountered Enlightenment ideas, which led him to a quest for both Greek and Turkish freedom from Ottoman rule. As a child of Danubian chancery politics and a skillful linguist, he came to believe that Christians and Turks were all "children of God and descendants of Adam" who were deserving of equal treatment. Living in exile in 1797, Rhigas wrote the revolutionary "Thourios," a patriotic hymn that offered a catalogue of martyrs and appealed for pan-Balkan cooperation in the struggle against the sultan's regime: "Bulgarians, Albanians, Armenians and Greeks, / blacks and whites all with the same fling, / for freedom the sword let's all gird / . . . / Let's light all a flame to all the Turkish world / to light up from Bosnia up to [Arabia]." An oath, enfolded in the hymn, promised a fight against tyranny and mandated being burnt to a crisp by the sun in the event of betrayal.[18]

In a revolutionary proclamation of the same year, Rhigas delivered a scorching indictment of Ottoman anarchy and tyranny. In the attached "Rights of Man" he demanded for the Greeks human rights, equality, personal security, and a natural freedom that abridged no one else's.[19] Rhigas called for complete religious toleration; freedom of press, speech, and assembly; due process of the law; universal education; and mass participation in elections in a republic with a bicameral parliament and a five-person executive.[20] Rhigas' programs, almost unique among Greek writings of this era in its lack of anti-Turkish hostility, called for Greeks and Turks to fight against the despotism that oppressed them both—the Ottoman state. Greeks, he wrote, had a sacred duty to rise up against and punish tyrants. He envisioned a society where all would prosper beneath the umbrella of a constitution whose models were those of the United States and France. Long before the Spanish liberals, Rhigas also dreamed of placing copies of his constitution, engraved on copper plates, in every Greek town and village. Three thousand copies of Rhigas' inflammatory writings were produced in 1797 for distribution in Greece. The revolt failed to materialize. Rhigas Pheraios was arrested in Trieste by the Austrian authorities in 1798, turned over to the Turks in Belgrade, and murdered by his guards.[21]

Adamántios Koraïs (1748–1833), though inspired by the same patriotic passion as Rhigas, abjured revolution. His parents ran a silk business in the Anatolian port city of Smyrna (Izmir). When Koraïs moved to Amsterdam and then to Paris in 1788 he also switched his metier from commerce to medicine while plying scholarship on Greek national subjects and promoting the standardization of the Greek language. Claiming that most Greeks were prone to envy and strife and that gradualism and education were the way to freedom, Koraïs hoped to delay an uprising until the middle of the nineteenth century. He saw the diaspora merchants' alleged indifference to the Greek cause, the egoism of the Ionian aristocracy and the mainland Phanariot and landowning oligarchy, and the Greek Orthodox Church as major obstacles to a genuine liberation. His anticlerical belief that the church was intellectually obscurantist and a source of popular resignation in the face of the Turkish yoke led him to rail at a corrupted clergy for obstructing his program.

In an outline of Greece's future independence at the end of the long preparatory road, Koraïs, drawing on Rousseau, Condorcet, and Montesquieu, set out a program of constitutional government and rule of law. He envisioned a small and modest Jeffersonian middle-class state of harmony and Christianity marked by liberty and popular participation, governing a people engaged mostly in agriculture. Koraïs grudgingly conceded that a constitutional monarchy like that under the French Charte rather than a republic suited this state. Fearing both the power of the elite and the fury of the masses, he invested hope in the middle classes, assisted by people of learning, humility, and virtue. The peasants, whom he admired, would come into their own politically through universal education. The Orthodox Church, autocephalous and run by a synod, would need to reduce its wealth and practice toleration, while defending itself from excessive missionary work by other cults.[22]

At a more active level, two personalities, both Greeks in Russian service, bracketed their people's modern struggle for independence: Ypsilanti, the Russian general and revolutionary of 1821, and Ioannis Capodistria, the Russian foreign minister who became Greece's first president in 1830. The Capodistria family (from Capo d'Istria; Gr. Kapodistrias), of Greek stock from Trieste, had become Italian-speaking Orthodox residents of the Ionian Islands. Ioannis

Capodistria trained as a physician at the University of Padua. A liberal at heart but an aristocrat by birth, he longed for freedom without revolution; constitutions conferred from above, not from below; and consultative governance with limited powers wielded by conservative aristocrats and educated voters. At least partial consent of the governed was required, he believed, in order to avoid revolution. He was ready to apply this scheme to all of Europe, including Spain and Naples and the republics of the Ionian Island (1800–7) and Switzerland. In 1816 he told his sovereign, Tsar Alexander of Russia, that the continent could be saved from revolution by granting constitutions resembling the French Charte to all of Europe. For these moderate ideas, he was called the "scourge of Europe" by Metternich and a "mongrel minister" by Castlereagh.[23]

Capodistria's outlook was partially shaped by the Adriatic world of the Ionian Islands off the coast of Greece. After the expulsion of the French in 1798, a kind of condominium ruled for the next two years under Russian and Turkish admirals. In the Mediterranean, this was very much the age of national naval chiefs who held sway in Gibraltar, Malta, Naples, and Sicily. In the Ionian islands, between 1800 and 1806, three different constitutions came into play that were revised, rebuffed, or recalled by the Russians or the Turks. Thus for a time, the Ionian Island became a miniature state anchored off the Ottoman coast and known as the Republic of the Seven Islands. After the Treaty of Tilsit in 1807, Ionia reverted to France and brought to an end an era of constitutional experiment in the Greek world. This was Capodistria's political training ground. Like Koraïs, whom he had met a few times, Capodistria viewed education as the only road to a still distant Greek independence.[24]

Ottoman Greece itself experienced little genuine thirst for independence and even less theoretical speculation about it. True, an Athens schoolteacher in 1813 urged pupils to adopt names such as Pericles, Themistocles, and Xenophon.[25] But the Greek Orthodox hierarchy remained passive and even hostile to a national struggle. In 1798 the patriarchate issued a Paternal Exhortation condemning Rousseau, the idea of liberty, and disobedience to the constituted authorities—that is, the Ottomans. In 1819 Patriarch Grigórios dismissed science and rationalism in his encyclical *Enlightenment as the Handmaid of Irreligion*.[26] Two years later, when the 1821 insurrection broke out, he would be hanged by the Turks.

The Friendly Society

The city of Odessa—the Cadiz of the Greek uprising—was founded in 1794 on the Black Sea coast after the Russians conquered its hinterland from the Turks. It bore a Hellenic name and the region had been home to Greek colonists since antiquity. In the newly created imperial city, diaspora Greeks came to form a large segment of its population, and they dominated shipping, the grain trade, and the restaurant and hotel businesses. A Greek school opened in 1817. Dimitrios Inglesi, of a prominent merchant family, served as mayor (1818–21) at the time of the uprising.[27] This dynamic multinational city became the site of organized conspiracy with the formation there in September 1814 of a Greek underground group known as the Friendly Society (variant transliterations: Filiki Eteria or Philiki Etaireia). The society was founded by three lower-middle-class diaspora Greek Odessites—in David Brewer's curt characterization, "a hatter, a bankrupt and a recent ex-student." All came from a business background: Nikolaos Skouphas, who was an Odessa merchant, Athanasios Tsakalov, who was the son of a Moscow fur merchant, and Emmanouil Xanthos (Xantos), a merchant's factor who had been a Freemason in the Ionian Islands. They modeled the Society roughly along Masonic lines, as was standard in European secret societies of the time. The new society aimed to unite Greeks of all persuasions inside and outside Ottoman territory in a rising of all Balkan Christians under Greek leadership.[28]

The founders and members came not from the big established merchants of the eighteenth century but from a new generation of merchants and intellectuals, motivated variously by the ideas of 1789, their educational background, the languages they used in trade, and the arbitrary actions of the Turks. By 1821, membership in the Friendly Society had reached almost eleven hundred. In a sampling of a bit over nine hundred of its members, one scholar found that over half were merchants: about 35 percent professionals, clergy, and notables; almost 12 percent military and naval men; and a mere 1.3 percent from the artisan and peasant classes. Over three-fourths of these were, when joining, from Russia and the non-Greek Balkan lands.[29] According to Alexandros Ypsilanti's brother Nikolaos, a member, the Friendly Society's program was written in "simple, Greek popular jargon that could reach every shepherd," and its emissaries preached among people of all classes.[30] But this strategy of social communication had little success in drawing in the lower classes.

Though culturally specific in many ways, the Friendly Society resembled Spanish, Italian, and other secret societies of the time in arcane organization and ritual. The far-flung cells varied in their terminology. One source speaks of a chapter's chiefs, coadjutors, and priests, and each chapter had its own codes, signs, passwords, and handshakes. Others list pupils and brothers at the lower end, with priests, shepherds, and senior shepherds above them and a Supreme Council or Invisible Directorate at the top.[31] The society admitted only men considered to be true Greek patriots who would submit to the rites of catechism and whose adherence would supersede all other bonds. Some of the novices brought with them bands of irregular fighters. The society gradually morphed into an "apostolic" organization, that is, divided into twelve districts in various locales whose chiefs directed recruitment. The twelve "Apostles," though mostly merchants, included at least one government official and, allegedly, an ex-priest.[32]

George Waddington, a Greek-speaking English cleric who lived in Greece during the War of Independence and had access to Friendly Society documents, offered keen insight on some of the links between Greek Orthodox religious rituals and those of the secret societies. Recruits were given a copy of the oath to study for two days. The highly clandestine initiation seemed to recall the mysterious and evasive gatherings of early Christians who were subject to Roman persecution. At midnight the inductee knelt before a table bearing an icon and a taper. After thrice making the sign of the cross, he touched the icon with his right hand as he held the taper in his left, saying: "This taper is the only witness which my afflicted country accepts, when her children swear the oath of their emancipation." The priest invoked God and the Society's laws as the newcomer crossed himself again and recited the "catechism" and the main oath. An 1849 painting by Ph. Tsoios in the Athens War Museum replicates this description exactly: as a priest officiates, the white-haired initiate, wearing the fierce mustache of a mountain warrior and attired in a red bolero jacket, a white tunic, and a green sash, presses his left hand against his heart as he swears.[33]

The founders had devised a catechism for initiates that exuded a sacral quality but differed from that of the Greek Orthodox Church in content and in its use of the demotic instead of the Hellenic or old Greek, incomprehensible to the worshipers.[34] The church catechism itself consisted mostly of lengthy statements rather than a question-and-answer format.[35] Unlike those of Spain and Naples, the Greek political catechism served as a questionnaire about personal reliability, not ideas. The interrogator asked about work, family, major life events, views on the future, and friends or loved ones who had been imprisoned or executed. The lengthy oath bound the juror to remain loyal to the Friendly Society, perform all assigned tasks, keep all secrets, "nourish in [his] heart undying hatred towards the tyrants of my country," and be ready to destroy them in the fight for freedom. He was to respect other religions; assist the sick, the poor, and the weak; and maintain a total dedication to the future liberty of Greece. Political oaths in that era were taken with deadly seriousness about the promises of lethal consequences for betraying them. Clergy who swore in new members required initiates to promise to give their lives under torture rather than betray the cause.[36]

To a far greater extent than in Spain or Naples, the Greek secret society engaged in the social mimicry of the indigenous church and soaked its language and ritual in religious imagery: the participation of a priest, the solemnity of the setting, the sacramental quality of taking the oath while genuflecting, and the mystical surroundings augmented by icons and lighted tapers. The initiation, which lasted several days, had the newcomer repeating key words and making the sign of the cross. Into this exalted and even ecstatic atmosphere, the organizers inserted simplified political messages: God hated tyrants, the Orthodox Greeks languished under a tyranny, and true patriots and Christians—through loyalty, reliability, silence, and unconditional obedience—must be constantly armed and ready to respond to the first call to liberation.[37]

For those outside the Society and some members as well, secular culture also emerged as a motivating factor. Sources on how Greeks were drawn into the struggle for independence are sparse. One realm of endeavor, theater, became a motivator of young urban idealists. Wealthy Greek merchants in Odessa, generous to their own, contributed lavishly to cultural institutions, including a theater in 1814 that glorified the Hellenic past and lamented Ottoman rule of the present. In this, the first modern Greek "patriotic" theater, only talented males appeared onstage at first; then came Greek-speaking foreigners, including an English amateur philhellene man and a Russian woman. Its repertoire included works by Sophocles and Greek translations of Alfieri, Voltaire, and Metastasio as well as those by contemporary Greeks, such as *The Death of Demosthenes* (1818) by the twenty-one-year-old Nikolaos Pikkolos. The productions drew loud applause from an audience that appreciated listening to Greek-themed plays spoken in their own language.[38]

Greek theaters appeared in Iaşi and Bucharest as well. Around the time of the founding of the Odessa theater, the daughter of the hospodar of Wallachia established in its capital, Bucharest, her own private stage in the princely palace. She had Racine, Voltaire, Alfieri, and Metastasio translated into Greek. Bucharest exchanged repertoires with the Odessa theater, and the spectacle of Attic masterpieces and European adaptations spoken in modern Greek apparently produced the same delirious reception and "tears of pride and joy" as in the Russian city. In 1818 a new public theater opened to a broader audience, with women in the cast. One of its founders was an Orthodox bishop, a surprising fact given that church's negative view of theater and actors, but one illustrating the increasing engagement of clergy in patriotic activity. A play such as *The Death of Caesar*, with its obvious regicidal content, had to be renamed *Julius Caesar* in order to steer carefully between liberation designs and Ottoman suspicions.[39]

A historian of this theater made what may seem an exorbitant claim: "Under these conditions, it was natural that the first sparks from the furnace of revolution which was to ignite Greece had smoldered in the hearth of culture where the frail elements of persecuted Hellenism had to rally. In fact, the insurgent movement of Ypsilanti derived more or less directly from the revival of drama in the little court of Bucharest in 1815." Exaggerated, yes. But a direct connection certainly emerged between the halls of drama and the fields of battle. Some of the Bucharest playwrights joined the Friendly Society. And when Ypsilanti's march began, some actors and spectators joined him and fell at the Battle of Dragoşani.[40] The unknown author of a letter to Ypsilanti on the eve of his exploit, though skeptical of the Friendly Society's success, conceded that in the principalities "the youth is taught the Greek tongue, and accustomed to see the deeds of our forefathers represented on the stage."[41]

In 1816 Skouphas moved his group to Moscow, and two years later, in response to growing success in Greece, he himself relocated to Constantinople. Odessa, birthplace of the Society, remained the hub of a secondary network. Cells popped up all over western Europe, Russia, and the Ottoman Empire as preparations for a revolt got under way. In Russia, the Society had made contacts with Greeks in Moscow, St. Petersburg, Odessa, Taganrog, Kherson, Kishinev, and other towns. From key organizational points emissaries were posted throughout the Greek mainland and islands. The Apostles carried the "gospel" of a rising throughout the Balkans. Tsakalov, a founder, recruited and conducted propaganda in the Morea.[42] Although the patriarch of Constantinople declined to join the Friendly Society, a multitude of priests and prelates did so.[43]

The huge influx of clergy into the liberation movement offers little cause for surprise. Churchmen had supported the overthrow of an alien intrusion in Naples and Spain under the French. Greece endured centuries of perceived oppression. The apathy lamented and sometimes exaggerated by Rhigas and Koraïs sprang from a lack of any hope for change. When the revolt of 1821 began, certain clergymen saw it as an emancipation of Orthodox Christianity from the infidel rule of ungodly Muslims. The Friendly Society program did not offer a sophisticated critique of the *tourkokratia* nor a detailed political blueprint for the future. It presented a flat condemnation of Ottoman rule and demanded a national community of all Greeks.[44] To deceive the Turkish authorities in correspondence between cells, society agents cleverly masked their intentions by encoding plans with such innocuous phrases as "to found a school," which meant "to prepare the revolt."[45] The society also scattered hints at a Russian intervention on behalf of Greek independence,[46] even though older Greeks could recall the cruel Turkish retaliation let loose in the past after the failed Russian expedition of 1770 sent by Empress Catherine II.

What the forces of independence needed was foreign assistance and a leader of some stature. The desire for and even expectation of Russian intervention on their behalf lay deeply embedded in the mentality of educated Greek society, as expressed in traditional prophecies of liberation by "a fair-haired nation (*xanthon genos*) from the north."[47] This prophecy seemed validated by the numerous Russo-Turkish wars of the eighteenth and early nineteenth centuries and Russia's efforts to legalize its right to protect Christians in the Ottoman Empire. The liberators initially attempted to enlist Ioannis Capodistria, still serving as foreign minister of the Russian Empire, a title he shared with Nesselrode. The Friendly Society approached him on four different occasions—twice in the Russian capital, once in Kishinev, and once in Corfu. Capodistria emphatically and contemptuously declined the final bid, made by Xanthos in St. Petersburg in January 1820.[48] The Friendly Society then offered the leadership to General Alexandros Ypsilanti.

Journey of the One-Armed Prince

The family of Prince Alexandros Ypsilanti (1792–1828) claimed descent from a Byzantine imperial dynasty and was part of a distinguished community of Phanariot Greeks who had been coming into Russian service for generations. The Ypsilantis had served the Ottomans since the eighteenth century. The grandfather had been dragoman to the sultan and hospodar of Wallachia. In 1805, the Turks, suspecting his loyalty, executed him. His son, Konstantinos, while serving as a hospodar, conspired to liberate the Balkans. Deposed after his father's death, he sought haven in St. Petersburg and in 1806 marched with Russian troops into Bucharest during one of the Russo-Turkish wars. But his plan to free the Balkans was overturned by the Treaty of Tilsit, signed by Napoleon and Tsar Alexander I in 1807. To escape the fury of the sultan for collaborating, Konstantinos Ypsilanti fled with his family to Kiev. Highly connected in Russian official and court circles, he gained his son Alexandros admission to a good St. Petersburg school and in 1808 a commission as coronet in the tsar's aristocratic Household Cavalry Regiment, a unit—though known for its fidelity to the monarch—that eventually yielded the Decembrist conspirators Mikhail Orlov, S. G. Volkonskii, and Mikhail Lunin.[49]

At the Battle of Austerlitz against Napoleon in 1805, the regiment had lost nearly half its forces. Though Alexandros Ypsilanti joined only in the wake of Austerlitz, he basked in membership of this heroic and celebrated unit. In July 1812, during the Grande Armée's invasion of Russia, young Lieutenant Ypsilanti showed reckless courage at the Battle of Polotsk and was decorated several times. In 1813 at Bautzen, a bitter engagement with the retreating French, he was again honored for valor. He transferred to the Grodno Hussar Regiment and fought at Culm, near Dresden. There in August a cannonball tore off his right arm—a misfortune that would contribute to his mystique. Hailed for his bravery in these campaigns, young Ypsilanti came out of the war a colonel. He attended the Congress of Vienna and moved easily in high society. Tsar Alexander appointed him aide de camp. At age twenty-five he attained the rank of general, young for the Russian army even in that era, and took command of a division in the Pskov region. Fluent in French and Russian and possessing a charming manner,

Ypsilanti, now relieved from combat duty, won admiration for "his youth, sociability, romantic appearance, and honourable mutilation."[50]

The affluent Ypsilanti family owned estates in Ottoman Moldavia, and the
father lobbied against that empire to the tsar. Alexandros thus lived amid
dreams of Greek liberation. In 1816 he apparently swore to his dying father
that he would liberate Greece. He met Capodistria and reveled in the works of
the martyred Rhigas. After the war's end, Ypsilanti mingled in a Masonic lodge
with several future Decembrists, including Pavel Pestel, and was acquainted
with others through family and social connections. Years later, on the eve of
his death, Alexandros Ypsilanti recalled that he had been invited to join one of
the Decembrist secret societies but had declined, he said, in order to save himself for the Greek struggle. By 1820, the turning point in his life, Prince Ypsilanti had become a man of stature, well known in the Greek diaspora in Russia
and elsewhere.

The Friendly Society, lacking the adherence of Capodistria to its cause, found
in Ypsilanti their supreme leader. Since Ypsilanti already had two brothers in the
Society, Xanthos offered him the post. The general consulted with Capodistria
and allegedly took away from the meeting the minister's encouragement. Stories
about their conversations conflict. Although Capodistria refused Ypsilanti permission even to speak to the tsar, the general went ahead with his plans.[51] In
April 1820 Ypsilanti agreed to head up the revolt and was designated the leader,
with the title of *genikos epitropos* or general commissioner. Given a new nom de
guerre, "Kalos" (good), Ypsilanti became Alexander the Good. In summer 1820
Ypsilanti got a two-year leave of absence from the Russian army and began his
peregrinations, meeting with key Friendly Society figures.[52] In Odessa he gained
financial support from prominent Greeks. In the Bessarabian town of Ismail,
Ypsilanti, with the aid of Georgeos Kantakouzinos, a retired colonel in the Russian army and a Society member, set up a base, collected money, sent out envoys,
and held planning meetings.[53]

From Ismail, Ypsilanti wrote to his agents, "In the present critical circumstances, when nations all over Europe are struggling for their national rights and
for *the limitations on the power of tyrants*, the brilliant star of a flourishing Greece
is also in the ascendant" (italics added).[54] This statement seemed to suggest a
linkage of national struggles in Greece to the fight for constitutional rule against
"tyranny"—read absolutism—in Spain and Naples. Ypsilanti could voice a sug-
gestively radical view in private correspondence that he could not in public utterances since he hoped to gain support from other states. Although in October
1820 the leader issued a proclamation to the Greeks urging them to prepare to
liberate themselves without foreign aid, he finally realized that they would
require outside help. At that stage, he dreamed of possible assistance from the
United States (still a beacon of liberty for Europeans) and even from King Louis

XVIII of France. But, given the history of the Eastern Question, he trusted most of all in the support of the Russian tsar.[55]

At a conference in the autumn, the conspirators fashioned a concrete plan. Ypsilanti began with a scheme to invade Greece through Moldavia and Wallachia, and then pondered sailing from Trieste, on the Adriatic Sea, directly to the Peloponnese, in southern Greece, there to raise the banner of revolt. This plan and a few others came unraveled due to close calls and betrayals by or of Society members. Ypsilanti reverted to the route through the principalities and then southward into Greece. The arguments for this Balkans-first strategy, given the hazards of sailing with an army to the Peloponnese, seemed compelling: the precedents of Serb revolts in 1804 and 1815 that had won a measure of autonomy, the Ypsilanti family legacy and contacts in the Greco-Romanian world, proximity to Russia and the history of Russia's treaty rights in the region, the nearness of potential south Slavic allies, and the Turkish diversion against Ali Pasha. In addition, a Romanian military leader, Tudor Vladimirescu, had joined the Friendly Society and was expected to assist. Ypsilanti also saw the operation as a feint to deflect the Turks from the Morean peninsula, which would rise independently. The plan was approved by the Friendly Society leaders in October 1820.[56]

By December 1820, Ypsilanti had transferred headquarters to Kishinev, capital of the Romanian-speaking province of Bessarabia, which Russian arms had won from the Turks in 1812. This city, close to Ottoman Moldavia and inhabited by numerous Greeks, proved an ideal base. Ypsilanti established a press there and maintained correspondence far and wide throughout Ottoman and diaspora lands.[57] The most famous of the proclamations that opened the struggle, "Fight for faith and motherland," was actually composed in Kishinev, not by Ypsilanti but by a Friendly Society member, Georgeos Tipaldos.[58] In late 1820 and early 1821, homeland and diaspora Greeks arrived in Kishinev to confer with the leader, and advance agents moved in a frenzy from town to town to enlist more supporters, particularly the Moldavian hospodar Mikhail Soutsos at Iași. Ypsilanti also tried to gain a promise of military aid from the Russian commander in Kishinev, General Mikhail Orlov, a Decembrist revolutionary sympathetic to the Greek cause.[59]

The planners assumed that uprisings of Balkan Christians would break out and that Russia would intervene on their side once the Turks crossed the Danube and began to suppress the initial revolt. With this scenario in mind, Ypsilanti made contact with, besides Soutsos of Moldavia, Prince Miloš Obrenovič of Serbia and the Serbian rebel Stefan Živkovič, then living in Russia.[60] Another potential ally or at least a diversion was the autonomous chieftain of Janina, the Muslim Albanian Ali Pasha, who in 1820 was veering back and forth between support for the Greek rebels and betraying them to the Turks. He finally opted for the

Greeks, declared his own region independent from the Ottoman Empire, and summoned a council of klephts in 1820 at Preveza. Turkish forces along with local auxiliaries attacked Ali but failed to capture him.[61]

Much has been said about the poor preparation of the Ypsilanti expedition, but this was not for lack of trying. The Friendly Society issued manifold orders to Balkan peoples of all nationalities, local Society chapters, and Greeks in south Russian towns.[62] In classic conspiratorial form, Ypsilanti himself sent out "feelers"—not very different from the *trabajos* of the Spanish plotters—to sound out potential allies. He posted packets of letters and manifestos to Baron Stroganov, the Russian representative in Constantinople, asking him to forward them to Society members all over Greece. Since that diplomat opposed the uprising, this was a risky gesture. Yet the baron forwarded letters to the few who needed to be warned of the impending event so that they might flee the capital if danger arose. In one touching missive to a relative, Ypsilanti wrote shortly before his expedition: "Farewell good friend. We'll meet again I hope in our liberated fatherland."[63] Ypsilanti was destined never to see that liberation or either of his two fatherlands again.

The choice of Moldavia as a jumping-off point made some sense: an autonomous vassal state governed by a Phanariot, a heavy Greek presence, and the home to many Friendly Society members.[64] Its capital, Iaşi, lightly garrisoned, was also far from regular Turkish forces. On February 21/March 5, Ypsilanti departed from Kishinev and, after crossing the Pruth, arrived in Iaşi the next day. Ypsilanti's party did not "invade" Moldavia, as is sometimes claimed. He crossed the frontier post from Russia to Ottoman Moldavia legally, "as a simple traveler," with a passport signed by Nesselrode and accompanied by a small party of brothers and friends, including his adjutant, Vencheslav Gornovskii—a friend from Ypsilanti's days in the Grodno Hussars. Other associates entered separately, giving as their reason for travel family and property affairs. The party was met on the other shore by the horsemen sent by the Friendly Society of Iaşi.[65]

Iaşi, the capital of Moldavia, with its population of some thirty thousand to forty thousand and its wooden streets and buildings, was said to be more pleasant than Bucharest.[66] Ypsilanti's arrival, in a Russian general's uniform, did not surprise the city's elite. A few days earlier, the Orthodox metropolitan and some Romanian-speaking boyars (nobles) questioned Hospodar Soutsos about rumors of an uprising. He reassured them and had them take an oath in support of it.[67] Ypsilanti, after settling in at the home of an aristocratic friend, met with the hospodar. He used every means to persuade him that his master, Tsar Alexander I, was backing his plans and that a corps of thirty thousand men would occupy Moldavia, detach it from the Ottoman Empire, and keep Soutsos on his princely throne.[68]

Ypsilanti began issuing specially targeted proclamations, in addition to that which opens this chapter. One he addressed to the Moldavians: "Pay heed, residents of Moldavia. With God's help and grace, I have come to free you from the yoke under which you have lived. With this goal before my eyes, I and my compatriots and friends are here as needs be. On my part and that of my compatriots who are here under my command, I grant you citizenship and a guarantee of security for your persons and your authority." Ypsilanti assured the Moldavians that Prince Soutsos would remain their paternal leader and told them not to tremble should Turkish troops appear. As in later declarations, he alluded to Russia without naming it: "a fearsome power is ready to punish their brazenness and annihilate them."[69] He also addressed the Wallachians in a vague manifesto that repeated language about release from subjugation and flattered its readers by alluding to Romania's ancient past as the Roman province of Dacia.[70] Ypsilanti's communiqué from Iaşi to the Friendly Society was written in accents of joyous deliverance: "Finally the radiant and long-awaited moment has dawned! Behold, the object of our activity and efforts over many years has come to pass. The Band of Brothers will for us ever be the only sacred solution along the road to our spiritual happiness. Friends and comrades! You have demonstrated the power of pure and warm-hearted love of the fatherland."[71]

While in Iaşi, Ypsilanti sought to sacralize the revolt in deed as well as word as the Spanish and Neapolitan liberals had done, by celebrating the Holy Mass. He and his revolutionary associates on February 24 organized a military review of his forces, after which they repaired to the Orthodox Church of the Three Hierarchs. In accordance with the rites of the Friendly Society, Metropolitan Veniamin girded Ypsilanti with a saber. Local dignitaries and dwellers attending the mass took a solemn oath to launch the struggle and then witnessed the blessing of the red, white, and black banners of liberation.[72] Combining themes, one banner contained both the slogan "Long live freedom," a cross, and the ancient device associated with the Roman-Byzantine Christian Emperor Constantine, "In hoc signo vinces"; its reverse held the image of a phoenix rising from the ashes.[73] The oath taken by the troops was even sterner than that of the Friendly Society initiation. They swore to kill their own brother if he turned traitor. As true Christian believers, they vowed "never to look upon the Turks, our enemies, except with hatred and contempt" and "not to lay down arms until my country is delivered and its enemies exterminated." Those who broke this oath were to perish without the final sacraments of the church.[74]

The wording of his last oath reflected one of the aspects of the Ypsilanti expedition that helped doom it: gratuitous anti-Turkish atrocities. The first outrage occurred a day before Ypsilanti entered Moldavia. Galaţi, the main port of the province, perched on the Danube about 150 miles from Iaşi, was a largely Romanian town with a small community of Turkish residents and an Ottoman garrison. Ypsilanti's captain there, Vasilios Karavia, an Ionian Greek and Friendly Society member who had previously served in Russia, commanded Society members and Arnaut mercenaries. At his behest, they looted and burned the town, butchered Turks in their beds, and dragged the remainder to the river, where the men were forced to watch as their families were slaughtered on the moored boats. The men were then tortured and drowned.[75] A French chronicler suggested that Ypsilanti, a man of discipline, might have ordered the deed due to false information he received. Some believed that he had wished Karavia to disarm the garrison and kill only resisters.[76] Still others claim that Ypsilanti himself planned this and other outrages in Moldavia while still in Kishinev. In any case, he promoted Karavia to general for his grisly deed.[77]

Ypsilanti also allowed or ordered a massacre in Iaşi soon after his arrival. Hospodar Soutsos maintained a bodyguard of fifty Turkish soldiers. By one account, Soutsos persuaded them to disarm and then, with Ypsilanti's permission, had them slaughtered. A Serb eyewitness claimed that Ypsilanti decreed the massacre and dismissed him for making that charge, which Ypsilanti denied, stressing rather the need for order and discipline.[78] These episodes came to pale beside the large-scale sadistic horrors perpetrated by both sides in the nearly decade-long Greek War of Independence. But they also had an immediate impact on Ypsilanti's enterprise. Fearing Turkish retaliation—all too fresh in the memories of residents of the principalities—thousands of Greeks started a mass influx into Russian Bessarabia and Ukraine.[79] The massacres and the leaders' perceived approval of them undermined the discipline of the liberation army and led to uncontrolled bloodlust and pillage.

Before setting out on his southward march to Wallachia, Ypsilanti wrote to Tsar Alexander at Laibach on February 24/March 8. Though he anticipated a negative reaction, given the tsar's now public position on the Spanish and Neapolitan revolutions, Ypsilanti nevertheless beseeched him to "cleanse Europe of these bloody monsters [the Turks], and deign to add the title liberator of Greece to all the great designations that European renown has already bestowed upon you."[80] In his reply of March 14/26, the tsar called Ypsilanti's revolt "a shameful and criminal action of a secret society," a view that the tsar held until the end. Capodistria echoed the monarch. He worried that this revolt might set off mass atrocities against the Greeks and also ignite liberal revolutions in Europe.[81] Ypsilanti did not share these rejections with his men. For good measure, the Orthodox patriarch of Constantinople issued an anathema on Ypsilanti. Thus the enterprise faced opposition by the tsar, his foreign minister, and the head of the Greek church.[82]

Ypsilanti, undeterred, marshaled his initial multiethnic forty-five-hundred-man army of liberation, At its peak, it may have reached seven thousand men and included Russian, Ukrainian, Romanian, Bulgarian, Serbian, Montenegrin,

Albanian, and Greek volunteers.[83] Many, veterans of earlier Balkan risings who had cooperated with invading Russian armies, saw yet another chance for a final liberation from the Turkish yoke by joining Ypsilanti and—they thought—the Russian tsar. Though it is not always clear about the ethnic identity of many in these regions, Bulgarian scholars stress the pan-Balkan makeup of the liberating army. The Greek intellectual impact on the emergence of Bulgarian national consciousness had deep roots.[84] Certainly ethnic Bulgarians played a major role in the ranks of Ypsilanti's army. Most came from outside the Bulgarian provinces of the Ottoman Empire—from south Russia, Bessarabia, and the principalities. Many had entered the Friendly Society and in 1821 they joined Ypsilanti's movement.[85] Since apparently only about two thousand of the forty-five hundred men in the general's forces were Greek, this made the initial episode a diaspora revolt.

The Greek diaspora in Russia responded with energetic measures. Odessa, as an entry point for Greek ships, rapidly ingested news and people. Ypsilanti's proclamations were read aloud there to the cheers of the listeners.[86] Greeks in southern and Black Sea towns welcomed tens of thousands of refugees onto Russian soil and gave them food, shelter, and schooling. Ransom money was raised to redeem captive slaves. Clergy, merchants, nobility, the military, and peasants made donations. A Russian resident recalled that "Odessa harbor was filled with ships bearing Greek émigrés, fleeing for safety." The vessel carrying the body of patriarch Grigórios V, whom the Ottomans had hanged in Istanbul, brought seventy Greek refugees who benefited from private and government charity.[87]

Greek volunteers arrived from all over the Ottoman Empire and from south Russian and Ukrainian towns. In 1820—even before the revolt got started—a Russo-Greek official and merchant had donated forty thousand rubles' worth of his wife's jewelry to Demetrios Ypsilanti for the purchase of five thousand rifles for the Greek rebels.[88] Alexander Pushkin, during a stay in Kishinev in March 1821, watched Greeks crowding in streets, shops, and taverns selling their possessions for almost nothing in order to buy rifles, sabers, and pistols as they spoke of Themistocles and Leonidas and enlisted as volunteers for Ypsilanti.[89] When volunteers from Bessarabia began pouring in, Xanthos assisted them with clothing, weapons, and even bribe money to pay the Cossacks on guard at the Pruth border crossing.[90] Similar scenes were enacted elsewhere in the Russian Greek diaspora. Enthusiastic Orthodox priests—like so many Friar Minichinis or Spanish guerrilla priests—arrived on horseback, armed and carrying crucifixes in their hands.[91] Not all Ottoman Greeks—clerical or lay—rushed to the banners of Ypsilanti. A few recalled the mishandled 1770 Russian campaign, and many knew of it.

The members of the most dedicated unit in Ypsilanti's force, the Hieros Lochos (Sacred Battalion or Legion)—originally called Mavrophorites (Men in

Black) because of the color of their uniforms—were inspired by Greek antiquity and bore the sign of the skull on their headgear and the words "Liberty or death."[92] Taking final form during Ypsilanti's southward movement, it numbered between about five hundred to one thousand. The battalion comprised mostly young, well-off, and allegedly "pure" ethnic Greek volunteers, including many pupils and students enrolled in foreign universities.[93] Many, perhaps most, were merchant sons from Russia, Italy, and Germany. A noted historian suggests that the large number in the Sacred Battalion who came from Odessa might have been inspired by the Greek schools and the historico-patriotic performances at the Greek theater in that city.[94] Imbued with youthful enthusiasm, they were the only troops who did not plunder, and they won acclaim for their discipline, idealism, and courage.[95]

On the eve of departure from Iaşi, Ypsilanti repaired to a nearby monastery, where he donned a short black tunic, the death's-head cap, and the tricolor cockade. His force, devoid of artillery, initially included about eight hundred horsemen, some six hundred Arnauts, and two hundred "Cossacks"—meaning about seventy-five actual Cossack deserters from Russia and the rest dressed like them. Leading a largely equestrian caravan, he headed south to start an uprising in Wallachia. In order to remain close to the Habsburg border in Transylvania as a possible escape hatch, Ypsilanti chose a westward route, though it stretched longer than the more direct eastern road. Along the way he brought some discipline to his troops but stopped to encamp frequently. At Focşani, Karavia brought him a few ship's cannon and two hundred more men. After a week of inertia there, he continued creakily as more reinforcements filtered in. Only after a month did the column reach the environs of Bucharest.[96]

Unlike Riego riding through Spanish Andalusia or Pepe marching toward Naples, Ypsilanti was invading alien country. The once independent Romanian principalities of Moldavia and Wallachia had been made tributaries in the fifteenth century by the Ottomans, who allowed them to retain their Romanian princes as hospodars. As a result of local subversion, the Turks ended native rule and handed over the administration in 1721 to the Phanariots. A swarm of Greek officials, priests, prelates, and monks arrived, where they held sway in finance, justice, education, and religion.[97] The Romanian population of Wallachia, which Ypsilanti was poised to enter, was dominated by the Phanariot community and a laughably proud and indolent Romanian boyar class. The peasants were prone to apathy, drink, and superstition—though they were not enserfed like their Russian counterparts.[98] The British consul in Bucharest in 1820 wrote of the corruption, bribery, and extreme subjugation and exploitation of the population by the Phanariots and the boyars. Though measuring degrees of oppression is difficult, it is noteworthy that a British historian of the Greek uprising maintained that the Romanians were worse off under the Phanariots than were the Greeks under the Turks.[99]

Thus, when the abject Romanian peasants espied a troop of Ypsilanti's Greeks on horseback, what else could they imagine them to be but agents of another harrowing descent on a village in pursuit of plunder?[100] The ragged marchers moved through a landscape of thick forest and numerous rivers dotted by monasteries, old Ottoman forts, and the occasional palace or boyar manor house. The intervening villages lay helpless in the path of looters. Since Ypsilanti's troops were always short of supplies, they resorted to plunder or "requisition."[101] According to hostile sources, bands often acted on their own, and some of the armed men of the Friendly Society and the Arnauts ravaged the principalities, looted, perpetrated atrocities, and recruited by force. They also confiscated wealth from some Greeks there and thus cost the revolt support. Only the Sacred Battalion trained and maneuvered; the rest loafed and pillaged.[102]

Already at Iaşi Prince Ypsilanti had displayed a frigid pride and arrogance toward the Romanian boyars, made them dance attendance, acted like an emissary of the tsar, and behaved as though he already wore the crown of Greece on his head.[103] On the road, Ypsilanti exhibited inertia and near apathy, seldom showing himself to his men. He put on airs and amused himself in a royal manner. In his camp near Bucharest, he again wasted precious time on acts of triumphal ritual and useless pomp. He even looted a monastery in order to hire a comedy troupe and fit out a theater there.[104] In April Ypsilanti's men, halting near Bucharest, learned that the tsar had repudiated Ypsilanti, news that Russian diplomatic agents in the Ottoman Empire were busily distributing. Hearing this, the Moldavian boyars and metropolitan also renounced Ypsilanti; Soutsos abdicated and fled to Bessarabia. Thus Ypsilanti's secure rear base evaporated, and he was forced to send troops in a vain attempt to regain control of Moldavia. This might have been a moment of truth for Ypsilanti, a chance to abandon what looked like a hopeless adventure. By now, a major insurrection had broken out in Greece proper and a war of liberation was under way. He could rightly have taken credit for initiating the struggle and retired honorably from the field. But the man's poor judgment and wavering had taken him to the point of no return.[105]

Even before Ypsilanti entered Wallachia, that province already erupted in turmoil. The dwellers of its capital, Bucharest, on hearing of his expedition and the massacre at Galaţi, became frightened of retribution from the nearby Ottoman garrisons on the Danube. In mid-March they filled the streets of the city, terrified and wondering whether or not to leave Bucharest.[106] One of the Soutsos clan witnessed chaos as the city was plunged into anarchy. Nobles deposited their valuables and furniture in churches and sought sanctuary there. Others joined a mass exodus toward Habsburg Transylvania in fear of Turkish repression and of the "hordes" of Ypsilanti's rebels.[107]

In provincial Wallachia, a different story unfolded when a Romanian revolutionary made his appearance: Tudor Vladimirescu, a wealthy minor boyar of humble origin. Tudor (the name is a form of Theodor) was born in the town of Vladimiri (thus his name) around 1780, probably a free peasant. He had fought on the side of the tsar in the Russo-Turkish War of 1806–12 and received the St. Vladimir Cross—thus feeding the myth that he took his name from the medal— and had assisted the Serbian uprising of 1811. Vladimirescu became a Russian officer and was enlisted into the Friendly Society by Georgakis (Georgaki) Olympios from Thessal.[108] Described by an early British historian of the revolt as "ambitious, cruel, and suspicious,"[109] Vladimirescu found himself eventually caught between Turks and Greeks and ended up in Romanian historiography as a revolutionary martyr.

As a potential ally of the Ypsilanti incursion, Vladimirescu, together with some of the boyars, in January 1821 led a body of troops from western Wallachia in a rising that was anti-Turkish, ant-Phanariot, and partly anti-boyar. While they were marching to Bucharest, peasant disorders erupted, aimed at the boyars, ex- cepting those in Tudor's camp. To disarm the Turks' suspicions, Tudor wrote to them that he was rising against Phanariot and boyar oppression. In March, now in Bucharest, Tudor learned that the tsar had repudiated Ypsilanti's expedition and that his soldiers had been plundering. When the two leaders met near the capital in early April, their relations were far from harmonious. Angered by the outrages of Ypsilanti's men against the Romanian peasantry and feeling betrayed by news about the tsar's lack of support, Vladimirescu began negotiating with the Ottomans.[110]

An on-the-spot French observer claimed that in Wallachia as early as 1820, word of the revolts in Spain and Italy and of Ali Pasha's anti-Turkish moves—all allegedly "fomented by the spirit of liberty"—made an impression on many Wal- lachians. He implied that this "spirit" merged with the existing discontent with Phanariot rule among some Romanians.[111] In any case, Tudor Vladimirescu aimed to become the leading power in Wallachia, introduce tax reforms favoring the peasantry, and summon an all-class national assembly. To the peasantry, Tudor stressed the anti-boyar side of the uprising, and to the Ottoman author- ities he stressed its anti-Phanariot aspects. Initially he lulled the Turks while working for Ypsilanti's cause. But his request for the approval of the Ottoman sultan led to debate over his ultimate motives. In some readings, this was a ruse to reassure the Turks so that later he could gather forces among the Romanian boyars and peasants to revolt against the Ottoman Empire. Greek and Romanian historians still disagree over his true motivations.[112]

A triangular ethnic conflict, all too familiar in the history of eastern and east- central Europe, now erupted involving Ypsilanti's Greek and Slavic forces, the insurgent Romanians, and the Turks. Neither common faith nor shared ani- mosity to Turkish rule of the first two could dispel mutual distrust. At its base lay a social problem that conditioned the national issue. Vladimirescu saw the

Ottomans as a distant foe, to be handled in the future. As a spokesman for the thoroughly exploited Romanian peasantry, he aimed his revolt at the boyar land-owners and, especially, at the Phanariot ruling order. Vladimirescu may have seen a Greek victory as portending a Phanariot neo-Byzantine regime and a per-manent all-Romania orgy of looting. Ypsilanti's Moldavian and Wallachian proc-lamations had given no sure sign that the Phanariot hospodar system would be abandoned.

In May 1821 Ottoman forces responded to the two uprisings by invading Moldavia and Wallachia. At Galați they conducted a retributive slaughter. Bucharest was spared a general massacre, but in the countryside butchery ran rampant. In one monastery alone, reported the Frenchman Raybaud, they slew some three hundred men, women, and children. The ubiquitous Blaquiere, fresh from Spain, heard stories of children being hung by their feet on trees and Friendly Society members impaled on stakes.[113]

Earlier Ypsilanti had withdrawn to Tîrgoviște, about fifty miles to the north-west. Tudor departed Bucharest in a different direction. As the Ottoman menace loomed, Tudor Vladimirescu and Alexandros Ypsilanti accused each other of treason. On May 23/June 4 Ypsilanti's accomplice Olympios captured, tortured, and executed Vladimirescu. By other accounts, the bloodthirsty Karavia shot him, dismembered the corpse, and threw the remains into a river or a latrine. In justifying the murder to Ypsilanti, Olympios called Vladimirescu a traitor for breaking the Friendly Society oath. Some of Vladimirescu's army joined Ypsi-lanti's ranks.[114]

Having disposed of an enemy by murder and avoided a possible Romanian peasant jacquerie,[115] Ypsilanti now had to face his most competent adversary, the Turks. As he retreated, one of his advisors urged him to resort to guerrilla war-fare. Spain, which Ypsilanti had mentioned in his early pronunciamento, was clearly the inspiration. But it is almost impossible to imagine that partisan action on the Wallachian plain could have yielded success, given the terrain and the population through which the Greek-led army moved. After preliminary skir-mishes in this mode, Ypsilanti chose pitched battle, the mode of warfare he knew, but which proved equally fruitless. The Greeks retired to Drăgășani where on June 18 (NS) Ypsilanti fought his only battle against the Turks. He now com-manded some four thousand infantry and twenty-five hundred cavalry plus four cannons, as against eight hundred Turkish horse. First Olympios and then Niko-laos Ypsilanti commanded the Sacred Battalion. They and Karavia's five hundred cavalrymen faced off against the enemy, while Ypsilanti remained in the rear. Karavia fled the field, and the battle was lost. Of the survivors, most met death later in the field or in captivity. Some four hundred of the five hundred Greek youths in the Sacred Battalion perished.[116]

In an epilogue of resistance, Georgakis Olympios and Yannis Pharmaki, an aide to Ypsilanti and Society member, led the remainder of the forces in an epic march to the spectacular seventeenth-century Secu monastery in Bukovina. In a last stand there, Olympios died and Pharmaki was taken prisoner, tortured, and executed. The Turks took Iași on June 25 and wiped out the last resistance at Sculeni, where the uprising had begun. After the defeat at Drăgășani, Ypsilanti took a different route. He crossed the Carpathian Mountains and proceeded to a small town in Habsburg Transylvania. In his final proclamation, Ypsilanti assigned blame for his defeat to his colleagues, falsely announced that Austria had declared war on the Ottomans, and celebrated this fiction with a Te Deum. Other survivors of his campaign scattered as refugees to Austria, Turkey, and Russia. Some moved down into Greece proper to fight in the new outbreaks that had already occurred.[117]

Austrian forces jailed Ypsilanti in Munkács, Hungary, until 1823, and then transferred him to the old Theresienstadt Fortress in Bohemia at the request of his mother. In 1827, with the intercession of Tsar Nicholas I, Ypsilanti was released with his brothers to a town of his choice within Habsburg control. He chose Verona but died of illness in Vienna en route on August 1, 1828, in a well-known inn once frequented by Beethoven. On his deathbed, Ypsilantis bewailed his lengthy prison time and voiced the hope of regaining freedom for Greece.[118] Shortly before his death, the would-be liberator heard about the independence of Greece. The brothers were allowed to return to Russia, though put under surveillance, and led a quiet life there. Nikolaos died in Odessa in 1833; Georgios visited Greece in 1845 and died in Bucharest in 1846.[119]

Few mourned Ypsilanti's death. His surviving brothers and comrades-in-arms blamed him for the failure of the revolt and for their incarceration, and they behaved very badly toward him in prison. Capodistria, during his brief tenure as president of the new Greek state, promised to render official honors to Ypsilanti but did not do so. The defeated rebel received no memorialization on the order of those in Spain for Porlier and Lacy. The only recognition given at the time—besides admiration from various revolutionaries—was a brilliant military parade held by his one successful brother, Demetrios, on the Plains of Megara on May 15, 1828.[120] Only later was Ypsilanti enshrined in the Greek national mythos. The first literary eulogy to Ypsilanti employed the fashionable idiom of the Romantic prisoner languishing in chains. Ivan Kozlov (1779–1840), a blind Russian poet who translated Byron, Ariosto, Schiller, and Mickiewicz, had vague liberal leanings but never joined a Decembrist group. In 1823 he wrote "Captive Greek in a Prison," an elegy imagining, in the spirit of Rossetti, the prisoner Ypsilanti contrasting his dream with his fate. "Sacred native land, my delightful land! Dreaming of you always, I hasten toward you in my soul. But alas, they hold me here in bondage, and I am not able to fight on the field of battle! Day and night I am tormented by your fate. In my heart the sound of your chains has echoed."[121]

In spite of his Balkan pedigree and the resistance tradition of his forebears, and despite his own valorous army record, Ypsilanti turned out to be an almost complete bankrupt in the realm of military insurrection. A critical British historian of the mid-nineteenth century argued that at each point Ypsilanti had gone wrong: taking Iaşi instead of the stronghold of Ibrail, lingering too long at halting spots, heartlessly massacring unarmed Turks, and refusing to give Romanians relief from Phanariot oppression. Most of all, he not only failed to get Russian support but lied about its imminence. Though short on artillery, Ypsilanti disposed of a large supply of arms and money and men, but he had his generals commanding small company-size units and mounted no daring attacks.[122] A German scholar suggested that, after the tsar's repudiation of Ypsilanti's reckless enterprise, he should have either given up, taken the blame, and saved his men, or plunged across the Danube to Bulgaria, kept open volunteer lines from Bessarabia, and continued to inflame the Greeks—even if that risked falling in battle.[123] A French observer thought that Olympios would have made a better commander, since he had led anti-Turkish bands in the Russo-Turkish war of 1806–12.[124]

Such speculative after-the-fact tactical critiques lack credibility in this case. It is hard not to agree with modern British historians who see the expedition as hopeless from the start. William St. Clair called it an "ill-judged and badly executed revolt." Douglas Dakin pronounced it "ill-conceived, ill-prepared and ill-conducted." Dakin added that Ypsilanti "had lived in a world of fantasy and misplaced optimism." A Balkan rising, Russian support, assistance from Tudor Vladimirescu, and even a hoped-for revolt in Constantinople—all predictably failed to occur.[125] In the opinion of Sergei Turgenev, a Russian diplomat then serving in Constantinople and brother of a Decembrist revolutionary, Ypsilanti, in having the Metropolitan of Iaşi bless the banners of rebellion, hoped to ignite a popular and religious war. But he had been drunk with the idea of being the liberator of his country, unable to foresee the obstacles, unschooled in the situation on the ground, and vainly hoping for Russian aid.[126]

In contrast to some of his portraits, Ypsilanti did not cut an imposing figure; he was short, skeletal, bald, nearsighted, and of an aged visage—Ypsilanti spoke with a twang and comported himself awkwardly. He also seemed to radiate different impressions to different people. An American admirer called Ypsilanti courageous, honest, patriotic, kind and generous—though surrounded by many who lacked these virtues.[127] Others have been less kind in their judgment of the one-armed prince. Alexander the Good had come nowhere near being Alexander the Great. Phillips, noting Ypsilanti's "vanity, incapacity, and weakness," denounced him for his deviousness and lies about Russian and Austrian assistance.[128] Finlay rendered an even more acid verdict. Conceding the prince's courage in the Napoleonic wars, he saw him as excessively vain and proud, sluggish, indecisive, deceitful, a timid leader, and a poor judge of character. His ignorance of Greek reality, wrote Finlay, was matched by his ambition for a throne. Granting Ypsilanti private virtues, Finlay nevertheless declared that he "was a contemptible leader and a worthless man."[129]

At least one modern historian has tried to undermine even Ypsilanti's tattered achievement in 1821. Dennis Skiotis correctly stressed the importance of Ali Pasha of Janina for the onset of revolt. His activity and the Turkish reaction to it, the argument goes, triggered both the Ypsilanti and the Morea uprisings. Skiotis notes that since Ali and his plotters delivered no high-sounding proclamations, they were later marginalized by historians who credited the launch of the independence war to the wrong people.[130] Skiotis had a point, but he underestimated the importance of symbolism and publicity. The Ypsilanti march and its collapse became a cause célèbre in Europe, and the inflammatory language of his proclamations spread like wildfire. The message reached poorly educated Greeks in remote places well after his defeat, as demonstrated, to take one example, in the semi-fictional memoir *Loukis Laras*.[131] Echoes from the Ypsilanti ride reached many throughout the Greek lands and were joined to tales about the bishops and guerrilla chiefs of the Morea, solidifying the fact that this was a pan-Hellenic enterprise and not just another adventure of Ali Pasha's warriors nor a bandit raid.

Did events in Spain and Naples reverberate among the Friendly Society and on Ypsilanti's exploit? Mladen Pantschoff believed that Ypsilanti's deed was stimulated by the Spanish and particularly the Neapolitan revolutions, though he offered no concrete evidence. In regard to the Italian Carbonari connection, the ever vigilant Prince Metternich claimed to have found correspondence between them and Ypsilanti, a charge that the general denied. In making his case, Metternich suggested that the whole Greek episode was a plot to disrupt the friendship between Austria, a consistent breaker of revolts, and Russia, which could be tempted by Eastern dreams.[132]

Although Metternich exaggerated, many connections existed between the Carbonari and the Greek insurgency. At least two Greek secret societies were formed in Italy between 1800 and 1806. Many Ionians and Epirots had spent time in Italy.[133] Konstantinos Rados studied in Pisa and became a Carbonaro before the outbreak of the Greek independence war. Michael Spyromelios, whose grandfather had served the Neapolitan king as a mercenary, studied military science in Naples. He returned to Greece in 1819 and joined the rebellion in 1821. Carbonari in the southeastern reaches of the kingdom could easily cross the Adriatic. Among the many false rumors of 1821, one had it that Minichini and other veterans at one point did so to attend a gathering of the Friendly Society at Preveza in Epirus.[134] The Englishman George Waddington reported with alarm that "the revolution of Naples was mistaken, by [the Greeks'] eager and inexperienced eyes, for the beacon of liberty. Greece beheld the signal, and rose."[135] But the real impact of Neapolitan and Piedmontese revolutionaries began only after the fall of Ypsilanti—and it was, except for the Carbonaro who coauthored the first Greek constitution, military rather than political.

Evidence of influence from Spain, aside from the few items noted above, is even more fragmentary. Educated diaspora Greeks and Slavs living in major European centers had full access to news from the insurgent Mediterranean. But Greece proper is far from Spain and, lacking a real press, its people had little news about the outside world on a regular basis was hard to come by. Though Greek mariners were not unknown in Spanish ports, news of Madrid events did not seem to play a role in the Balkans. It is possible, though I have seen no evidence, that the Sephardic Jews of Salonika, Smyrna, Istanbul, and elsewhere, given their Spanish-based language (Ladino) and their contacts throughout the Mediterranean, might have known—and perhaps spread—that news. In any case, interaction between the two peoples in this era lay rather in the nature of their independence struggles: both waged guerrilla wars with the help of outsiders, the Spaniards to reclaim their state from 1808 to 1813, the Greeks to create one.

In a State of War

Almost simultaneous with Ypsilanti's ride and closely linked to it, a protracted war of independence, marked by geographical and social diversity, broke out in Greece proper. The chief Greek-inhabited lands consisted of a mainland north of the Corinthian isthmus, the Morea or Peloponnesian peninsula to its south, and the surrounding island groups. Of special strategic import were the islands off the eastern coast of Morea—Hydra, Psara, and Spetsas, near the uprising's early capitals and home to numerous maritime merchants and shipowners. These regions yielded not only particular realms of combat but also particularist economic interests and political outlooks. On the social landscape could be found well-connected Phanariots of Constantinople, religious orders, sea captains, peasants, shepherds, and a diverse elite bearing the infelicitous label "primates"[136] or notables, which included landowners, other rural dignitaries, and shipowners. The rugged mountains of the mainland and the Morea offered shelter to malleable elements such as klephts (bandits sometimes turned into patriotic fighters and led by chiefs or captains) and armatoles (Ottoman employees who guarded the mountain passes against the klephts but who sometimes merged with the resistance). A regional group, the Maniots, dwelt near the rocky shores of Morea's southernmost finger-like peninsula.

Apostles of the Friendly Society had honeycombed the Greek lands as agents of rebellion and had already organized notables, captains, and a large percentage of the clergy in Greece proper for revolt on the eve of Ypsilanti's ride.[137] One of

them, Archimandrite Grigórios Phlessas (called "Papaphlessas"), faintly reminiscent of Fra Minichini, went around armed and was known for his shady
morals and record of petty theft. An early leader of the Friendly Society, he had
been present at Ismail, one of Ypsilanti's bases, and arrived in the Morea in
December 1820. Headstrong and loudmouthed, he became for a while a rival to
the emerging Morea leadership and later died a valiant death on the battlefield.
In late January, Papaphlessas, uninformed about Ypsilanti's Moldavia plan, urged
the notables to rise against the Turks. These men, skeptical of the chance of
success, preferred to wait and gather more information.[138]

Elsewhere, less patient rebels launched in mid-March the first armed clashes
with the Turks at Kalávrita—future site of a horrific World War II massacre.
Soon after Ypsilanti's Balkan incursion, the Turkish authorities, hearing of unrest
elsewhere, in March summoned Orthodox notables to Tripolitsa to turn over
their arms. But the Greeks sniffed danger and instead proceeded to Agia Lavra,
the Holy Monastery. There on March 25/April 6, 1821—a month after Ypsilanti
crossed the Pruth—the fifty-year-old Bishop Germanos of Patras, a Friendly Society member since 1818, raised the flag of insurrection and declared Greece
independent. This, and not Ypsilanti's crossing, became the official date of the
Greek uprising.[139]

Separate and isolated incidents of Greek defiance and violence against Turkish officials began, some perpetrated by bands of peasants and klephts.[140] A local
chief, Petrobey Mavromichalis (1765–1848), led one of these at a gathering at
"Spartan headquarters" near Kalamata. His proclamation of March 23/April 3,
1821 read in part: "Reduced to a condition so pitiable, deprived of every right,
we have, with unanimous voice, resolved to take up arms, and struggle against
the tyrants . . . in one word, we are unanimously resolved on Liberty or Death."
The proclamation made an appeal to Europe for direct assistance in arms and
money to support the struggle.[141] The revolt spread from the Morea to the islands
of Hydra, Psara, and Spetsas and by 1822 to the Greek mainland regions around
Missolonghi, Thebes, and Athens. Stalemates alternated with the renewal of
bloodshed. The Turks crushed risings in Thessaloniki and Macedonia and
defeated Ali Pasha in February 1822. In the summer, the Greeks defeated a
thirty-thousand-man army in the Peloponnese.

The Turks had forbidden the bearing of arms by Greeks and other non-Mus-
lim communities, except for designated military and security units. This may
have explained, as so many foreigners observed, the sudden ostentatious blos-
soming of weaponry on the persons of many ordinary Greeks—a display of rifles, one or two pistols, and a jatagan (a vicious-looking curved Balkan sword).
Dramatic posturing matched the staginess of the dress. The Italian volunteer
Count Pecchio noted that, as in many other liberation struggles—Spain's, for
example—an almost universal passion and spontaneous enthusiasm prevailed

but that the fever eventually subsided.[142] Gaudy uniforms and showy battlefield practices in any case did not always enhance the quality of the war fighting. As both the British and the Spaniards had learned while fighting side by side in the Peninsular War, it was not easy to marshal irregulars into formation or for pack animals to stagger under the weight of heavy guns on their limbers across rugged mountains. Once the philhellene volunteers began to pour in from Europe, pitched battles occurred, but there arrived no large-scale professional foreign army, like Wellington's in Spain.

Guerrilla activity came naturally in this war. And, as in the Spanish and Calabrian resistance of the Napoleonic era, it occasionally intersected with brigandage. But the Greeks had a much longer klephtic tradition of irregular blows against the occupying power. Klephts (from the Greek meaning "to rob")—the local counterpart of Ukrainian haidamaks, Romanian haiduci, Bulgarian haiduts, and Serbian hajduks—ran in bands of about fifty and sometimes of two hundred to three hundred. Depending on the moment, they acted as plain thieves, Robin Hoods, patriotic bandits, or all of these at once. Klephts veered more toward national than social banditry. Many inhabited the Agrapha, or uninscribed Greek highlands where no one was "written" or recorded by the state—in other words, not taxable. They sometimes protected Christians from Muslim raids. The line between klephts and armatoles often blurred when the latter crossed over.[143]

The Friendly Society, wrote Marion Sarafis, "gave form and content to the natural instinct for rebellion of the Greek mountain fighters, the klephts or 'bandits.'"[144] Did it? If content meant a crude and concise edition of Greek independence, yes. But the Friendly Society was a paragon of organization compared to the klephtic bands and their captains. About their rebellious propensity, however, there is no doubt. Klephts and armatoles converted themselves into guerrilla warriors in an asymmetrical war of armed bands—*klephtopólemos*. Living for centuries under an alien and often oppressive government, they suspected all central authority, including the newly emergent Greek ones, and had only a foggy notion of the state. Commanders responded primarily to local needs—as their descendants would do as partisans in Nazi- and Italian-occupied Greece of World War II.[145] They hoarded resources, resisted coordination, and acted like satraps and warlords, sometimes igniting local goat and sheep wars in the midst of the liberation struggle. Mountain politics, being exceedingly personalized, often defied any kind of command and control and sometimes degenerated into sheer banditry.[146]

At the moment of extreme discontent, when conditions were ripe for armed resistance, guerrillas would shout, "Sta vouná" (to the mountains). Lightly armed with musket, sword, pistol, and dagger, they employed their rough-and-ready intelligence network, knowledge of terrain, occupation of the high ground, genius for cover and concealment, control of the passes, and ambuscade to defeat the lumbering units sent against them. Greek irregulars who dressed in traditional fustanella skirts, vests, daggers, and bandoliers and sang the verses of Rhigas around the campfire caught the Romantic imagination of admirers. When adapted to the bigger conflict, klephts and other warriors tended to disdain the "Frankish" (European) ways of war, with their infantry squares and bayonet charges. But their own combat methods too often included firing from the hip, premature retreat, plunder, and abandoning their European comrades at crucial moments. Guerrilla contempt for outsiders and a behavior that sometimes seemed like cowardice or even treasonous collaboration angered both the government and the foreign volunteers who had come to fight and die for a free Greece.[147]

Theódoros Kolokotrónis (b. 1770–1842) emerged as one of the iconic bandit heroes, and his autobiography, self-serving and fantasy-laden as it may be, certainly conveys the spirit of what European and diaspora Greek observers perceived as wildness in the Greek struggle. Like the Serb rebel Karadjordj, a livestock owner, he lived as a klepht in his youth and then became a mercenary. The Friendly Society took him in as a member in 1818. After the revolt, he led the storming of Tripolitsa and later served for a time in the Capodistria government of independent Greece. Kolokotrónis' book offers scenes of endless treachery, spectacular heroism, wondrous escapes, towers of human heads, and the fluidity between klephts, armatoles, and resistance captains.[148]

The Greeks engaged in a holy war with the ready participation of the clergy as preachers, leaders, combatants, and even executioners. The sultan responded by ordering the Shaykh-al-Islam to issue a fatwa announcing jihad (holy war).[149] In the wake of successful risings, Orthodox priests would celebrate victory with an icon-bearing thanksgiving procession. After the Greeks took Kalamata, twenty-four of them officiated at an outdoor mass with five thousand armed men in attendance. "Never was the *Te Deum*," wrote Finlay, "celebrated with greater fervour, never did hearts overflow with sincerer devotion to Heaven, nor with warmer gratitude to their Church and their God." Turkish prisoners who had been promised to be spared were later killed.[150] When Greek peasant rebels entered Athens to aid their comrades, they shouted, "Freedom, freedom; Christ is risen." Thus was celebrated once more the familiar wedding of Christianity with a war of national independence—as in the Spain of the Napoleonic era.[151]

Atrocities committed in this war on both sides far exceeded in numbers and cruelty anything seen in the other revolts of the 1820s. The massacres in Galaţ, Iaşi, and elsewhere during the Ypsilanti campaign produced bloody Turkish reprisals in the principalities. Sadism begat sadism. In one of the first acts of violence in Greece itself, rebels seized several score Turkish sailors and roasted them one by one over a fire on the beach.[152] The most spectacular individual reprisal by the Ottomans took the life of the seventy-year-old patriarch of Constantinople, Grigórios V. The fact that the patriarch had denounced the rebellion and excommunicated Ypsilanti proved embarrassing to the Greek rebels. But it meant nothing to the Turkish officials who held him accountable for the acts of his co-religionists. After Grigórios officiated at Easter eve service in the St. Georgios Cathedral in Istanbul, they hanged him on the central doors of his patriarchal palace. Some of the city's Jews were coerced into dragging his corpse through the streets of the capital and throwing it into the Bosphorus. The body was retrieved by believers and sent to Odessa, where the Russian tsar ordered a special solemn mass.[153] Horrendous massacres of Greeks ensued in Cyprus, Crete, Smyrna, Rhodes, Salonika, and Adrianople. The best-known of the devastations, on the island of Chios, took the lives of uncounted thousands, cut down and displayed with their severed heads between their legs; an estimated forty-one thousand were enslaved, mainly women and boys.[154]

Mutual reprisals led to a long sequence of bestial acts. Greeks massacred some twenty thousand Turkish men, women, and children in the first few weeks, the butchery often urged on as holy work by priests.[155] In October 1821 the rebels laid siege to the fortified town of Tripolitsa in central Peloponnese, an Ottoman stronghold with thick stone walls, bastions, and minarets. Upon taking the city, the Greeks slaughtered some eight thousand people, Turks and Jews.[156] During the course of the war, both sides took hostages, raped, enslaved, and perpetrated almost unimaginable brutalities as acts of terror, vengeful rage, or deterrence. Hanging, impaling, beheading, dismembering, skinning alive, disemboweling, and otherwise torturing to death prisoners and civilians became commonplace. The national custom among hill people of roasting goat and mutton on a spit was easily extended to living humans. A German volunteer tells of "three Turkish children being slowly burned alive over a bonfire while their mother and father were forced to watch."[157] By a miracle of miscommunication, most Europeans who did not visit Greece during the war, though regaled with poetry and painting about Turkish cruelty, knew almost nothing of the Greek abominations.

The early phases of the war bled into each other. In the first four years or so, the rebels recorded some notable victories in various locations. In 1825 a new menace arose in the person of Ibrahim Pasha of Egypt, underling and ally of the Ottoman sultan. In February 1825 he dispatched a large Egyptian fleet filled with fighting men who regained Crete and then invaded the Peloponnese, where Ottoman troops began to win battles. In the same year, the Turks reversed the positions in Athens and laid siege to the Acropolis. In the meantime, a civil war had erupted among the Greeks and the whole enterprise reached its lowest point.

How did the would-be leaders of thirteen million Orthodox Greeks conduct their search for a state? The burgeoning country was geographically divided and marked by social-political and cultural diversity. Islanders and mainlanders distrusted each other, as did civilians and the military. The social rift was at least as great as those in Spain and Naples and the poverty greater. Turks owned twice as much land in the Morea as the Greeks, and the bulk of the Greek-owned lands belonged to the notables. After the collapse of Ypsilanti, the Friendly Society retained some influence in Russian diaspora towns, saw it erode in the Danubian principalities, and lost much of it in Greece proper, where landed magnates of the Morea and shipowners of the islands wielded power and initially resisted the surge to revolt.[158] Of the founders, Skouphas had died in 1818 and Tsakalov fell in battle at Drăgășani fighting for Ypsilanti. Only Xanthos survived. European diaspora Greeks such as Alexandros Mavrokordatos, Demetrios Ypsilanti, and Teódoros Negris had to face major prejudice and suspicion of their European customs, language, and even apparel. Class and sectional differences, explosive outbursts of the masses, and unrestrained warlords set up blocks to unity.[159]

State building in time of war is an agonizing process. In the uneasy movement toward the marriage of national liberation and liberalism, both the Spanish and the Greek courtship took place during wars of independence. For the Greeks, it presented massive problems, especially when a civil war unrolled within the larger war. "The Greek independence struggle," wrote an eminent Greek historian, "offers the armed manifestation of the European liberal idea."[160] But "liberal" ideas stuck on bayonets seldom retain their original meaning. Greek constitutional thinking and political life unfolded against and was conditioned by the warfare between insurgent Greeks and the Ottoman armed forces, frightful atrocities, a civil war, and even hostility toward the foreign volunteers. Like the mythical race of giants who tried to reach the gods by piling the mountain of Pelion upon Ossa, the builders of a fledgling wartime state toiled under the most adverse circumstances. Changing allegiances and even capitals required improvisation, and the form and content of founding documents had to be adjusted to the national struggle. Given the overhanging presence of the Holy Alliance, to whom rebellion was anathema, Greek lawmakers exercised caution in fashioning their new political institutions. Indeed, Greek politics—from this war through the irredentist claims of the nineteenth century to the ill-fated Megali Idea or Grand Scheme culminating in the post–World War I Smyrna disaster—constantly adjusted to international aspirations and defeats.[161]

Although the locals had had some experience in self-government, including even a "senate" in the Morea, this was of little help in forging a national polity. The founding fathers generally brought with them political lessons they had grown up with, largely drawn from the Enlightenment and the American and French revolutions. They studiously avoided mentioning contemporary Spanish and Italian liberals. Yet, like the former, the Greek constitutional architects sought the advice of Jeremy Bentham, the era's guru of constitutional life. The first post-rising native-language newspaper, *Greek Chronicle*, launched by a devout Benthamite, Colonel Stanhope, in January 1824, featured a masthead reading "The greatest happiness of the greatest number," and Greek deputies in London approached Bentham for comment on the constitution of January 1822.[162] Mavrokordatos offered him gushing thanks for his advice, and Ioannis Orlandos and Andreás Louriótis of the Greek Committee in London addressed Bentham in a letter as "our father and protector of Greece."[163] Bentham praised the Greek constitution precisely for seeking that "greatest happiness" and noted Greece's advantage over Spain in having no colonies.[164] In November 1823, referring to the recent repression of Spanish liberalism, Bentham bluntly warned the Greeks against monarchy. "Give yourselves to a king? Know that, if you do so, you give yourselves to an enemy."[165] The advice was well received, but Bentham also criticized several aspects of the new constitutional order, which in any case was in constant flux.

Regarding one of the most famous Greek guerrilla captains, Odysseas Androutsos, a historian half jocularly wrote that he "was certainly the most unusual Benthamite ever to burn a village or slit a throat."[166] Indeed, the profound gap between the teaching embedded in the English philosopher's almost impenetrable prose and the punishing realities of insurgent Greece ensured that his impact would not be great. Bentham's agent Edward Blaquiere, who had come to Greece after the Spanish debacle, delivered Bentham's "Observations" to the Greek legislature in 1823. That body received them with enthusiasm, though they were not published, except for a few selections in the *Greek Chronicle*, since there was no other press as yet in Greece. Few of Bentham's ideas had any direct application at this time.[167]

In the real world of Greece, one of the first national political leaders to take the stage, Demetrios Ypsilanti, traveled from Bessarabia through Habsburg territory to Trieste and then proceeded to Hydra in June 1821. He arrived as chief of the Friendly Society and representative of his brother, whose movement was in the process of collapsing. Demetrios saw himself as the natural leader of the revolution, the army, and the emerging state. He commanded the assault on Tripoli and continued his military activities with valor through the war. Politically, however, Demetrios paid dearly for his brother's disastrous defeat in a case of failure by association—failure of Alexandros on the battlefield and failure to secure the allegedly promised Russian support. His plans for the emerging state were also opposed by local interests and political rivals. After several months of military campaigning, Demetrios' power and influence slipped away.[168]

A leading role was assumed by Ypsilanti's antagonist Alexandros Mavrokordatos, a vastly superior politician who was deemed one of the major founders of modern Greece. Born in Constantinople of a high-ranking Phanariot family, he had lived since 1818 in the diaspora, where he felt at home amidst European trappings—languages, manners, style of dress. For a while Mavrokordatos was close to the circle of the poet Percy Bysshe Shelley in Pisa. After the uprising began, Mavrokordatos made his way in July from Marseilles to Greece and arrived just as the influence and authority of Demetrios Ypsilanti was waning. One of the architects of a "non-radical" image, he worked intensively to oppose the Friendly Society and what he took to be its Carbonari conspiracies, and he constantly tried to curb the suspicions of the Holy Alliance about associations with the rebels of the Iberian and Italian peninsulas.[169]

In the course of 1821 a dozen directories, mini-parliaments, councils, assemblies, and senates sprang up, joining the traditional self-government organs of Ottoman times—all claiming some degree of revolutionary authority. The fall of the Turkish stronghold at Tripolitsa made possible the formation of a provisional government in the Morea, at Epidaurus, some twenty miles southeast of Corinth. Though no more than a large Balkan peasant village,[170] it became the founding site of the new state. On January 13/25, a National Assembly chaired by Mavrokordatos declared Greece's independence in the prologue to the constitution. The declaration, using language clearly borrowed from Rhigas[171] and justifying national liberation in religious terms, opened with these words: "In the name of the Holy and Indivisible Trinity! The Greek Nation, freed by immense sacrifices from under the yoke of the odious Ottoman tyranny which it could no longer bear, today proclaims, through the organ of its legitimate representatives, gathered in a National Assembly before God and man, *its political existence and its Independence.*"[172]

A few days later, Mavrokordatos added to it a clever gloss in a proclamation addressed to his people, but clearly composed with an eye on readers among the European diplomatic corps. Aside from the familiar themes of eternal Turkish cruelty and tyranny, the ancient Hellenic heritage of the Greeks and their affinity with the "Christians of Europe, our brothers," Mavrokordatos stressed that the Ottoman sultan, far from being a legitimate monarch, was rather a "hated brigand come from faraway lands." Thus, he argued, the Greek struggle was in no way a "war of faction or sedition" (read political revolt) but rather a national war, a holy war. While again distancing the Greek experience from the liberal rebellions of recent years, Mavrokordatos stressed that his people sought only the common rights to a decent life enjoyed everywhere else by the peoples of Europe.[173] A careful observer would have noticed the verbal similarity of that part of the appeal to those of Riego and Pepe.

The indirectly elected Epidaurus assembly charged a committee to draft a constitution: Mavrokordatos as chair, the former Ottoman diplomat Theódoros Negris, and the Italian philhellene Vincenzo Gallina (1795–1849), a former Carbonaro from Ravenna and a friend of Byron's. Fleeing Italy after the repressions of 1821, he had come to Greece. Gallina later played an important role in the formation of a supreme court and served as secretary of the foreign minister. He was eventually decorated and made a member of the Assembly for his services to the young state.[174] Gallina's principle contribution was his role in drafting Greece's first constitution. As a Carbonaro, Gallina was well aware of the Neapolitan (and thus Spanish) constitution, but his Greek document did not take it as a model. After several years in Greek service, Gallina, disturbed at the growing power of the guerrilla leaders in the Morea, left for Odessa. Unable to get there, he lived for some years in Georgia and died on a visit to the Holy Land in 1842.[175]

The Greek founders, though they carefully avoided identification with the European revolutionary constitutionalists, outstripped them by opting for a republic. Benthamism might have provided intellectual fuel for some of the founders, but the real reason for republicanism was the fact that the Greeks, having no monarch of their own except the sultan whose rule they were rejecting, and no immediate prospects for one, had to begin with a republican instrument. The Greek constitutional struggle, though it unfolded in the midst of war, as in Cadiz in 1810, differed from the Spanish experience in that no native dynast sat somewhere poised to return and reimpose absolutism. In Greece the ground was fresh if shaky. On it stood Alexandros Mavrokordatos as president, Negris as foreign minister, Ypsilanti as chair of the legislature (a ceremonial post), and Petrobey Mavromichalis, the hero of Kalamata, as its vice president.[176] Mavrokordatos and his colleagues faced the daunting task of coordinating the military forces, uniting the people, and freeing the country. Addressing Europe, Mavrokordatos stressed his country's national aims and not "demagogic and revolutionary principles," and he assured the British foreign minister, George Canning, that the Greeks were not inspired by the Carbonari.[177]

The Epidaurus Provisional Constitution of 1822 and the regime it created showed several faces. It drew partially on the French constitution of Year III (1795), and its language was thoroughly Western. Its designation as merely "provisional" and the Greek leaders' correspondence with European powers suggested that the future was open to alternative forms. And its first visual symbols, flags with a cross hanging over an upturned crescent or a severed Turkish head,[178] reminded everyone that the new Hellenic Republic was a state engaged in war. The constitution placed limits on the central power wielded by a president, an executive of five, and a cabinet of eight. A strong unicameral legislature was elected annually. It banned aristocracy and asserted that only merit determined preference. It introduced legal equality, an extensive suffrage, meritocracy, and a progressive tax policy. It also provided for habeas corpus, a swift trial, personal security, a free press, transparent government organs, and the abolition of torture. The new regime was, in the context of the time, fairly "democratic," though women and non-Greeks were not enfranchised—a point that Bentham deplored.[179]

Chapter I, article 1 declared Orthodoxy to be the established religion and made belief in Jesus of Nazareth as the Redeemer a requirement for being defined as a Hellene (Greek). Unlike the Spanish constitution of 1812, the Greek one specified toleration of other faiths, including the allowance of ceremonies in public. Muslims and Jews were to have civil but not political rights.[180] Unlike in Spain or Naples, anti-clericalism was hardly to be found either in the Friendly Society or among the leaders and fighters of the new Greek nation. Most of the clergy closed ranks around the anti-Turkish struggle. Greek authorities thus had no intention of confiscating monastic lands. Instead they decided on the dispossession of the Turks. A reform known as *ethnika ktímata* or "national property" arranged for their lands to be put into a land sell-off program. This would clearly favor the rich or the well-connected, as almost always happens in such state-sponsored transfers, whether by the French Revolution or the Spanish Cortes. Some Greek combatants hostile to the plan wrote the words "land sell-off" on a piece of paper and—like Espoz y Mina in Spain, who executed the constitution—used it for target practice. The measure was withdrawn.[181]

In January 1822 European liberals became excited by the Epidaurus constitution, all the more so due to the repressions in Italy less than a year earlier and the portents of similar actions to come in Spain.[182] The prophet of liberation Adamántios Koraïs did not share their joy, however. Koraïs at first believed that it had come too soon and that it invited menace from the Turks and from the Holy Alliance. Later, as triumph loomed into sight, he reminded his fellow Greeks that winning a war was the easy part, keeping the victory the hard part. Though Koraïs made his peace with the insurgent forces, he flooded them with advice and criticism. He picked away at the Epidaurus constitution for its unicameral form, lack of a suspensive veto power, limited catalogue of civic rights, and other technical flaws. More important, his belief in Enlightenment values of toleration led him also to lament the exclusion of Jews and Muslims from political citizenship, which he argued was not only an unjust act of a new freedom-loving state but one that would lose, as Spain had done in 1492, "a valuable part of its population."[183]

In fact, much deeper rifts in Greek society doomed this first constitutional order. The trappings of parliamentary life could not eliminate class and regional interests. Epidaurus essentially created an oligarchy of notables. Elites, particularly those of the Morea, virtually compelled to join a war that many of them feared, could not turn back once it had begun. But they expected to retain the power and privilege they held under Ottoman rule.[184] The Epidaurus regime lasted until the next National Assembly and neither it nor its successors were able to solve the endemic problem of local power and rivalry. Most of the pre-Epidaurus bodies dissolved (often temporarily) in deference to a national government; but the forces that created them did not.

In looking back at the political environments of liberal Spain and Naples, it is clear how much wartime Greece differed from them. In Spain, the Masonic cells that had helped seed the uprising persisted and were amplified by more-radical patriotic societies after 1820. In Naples, the Carbonari spread like wildfire and even set up a national organization. In both cases secret and open societies intervened in national politics in the parliamentary galleries, in the streets, and in provincial towns. Nothing like that happened in Greece because the Friendly Society lost much of its influence after the debacle of Alexandros Ypsilanti, as did his brother, who tried to sustain that influence. What Epidaurus did accomplish, however, was to fashion at least the façade of a central government, which—though it remained largely on paper—allowed the Greeks to claim to the world that they had or would soon have a state and were not just a ragged collection of warriors.

The second National Assembly met in Astros, not far from Tripolitsa, in April 1823 to revise a constitution that satisfied nobody, but the new one they wrote did no better. The election of Petrobey Mavromichalis by a large and loose assortment of delegates marked a shift of power to a temporary alliance of Morea notables and captains that was also destined to disintegrate. In addition to tension between the executive and legislative bodies, the personal rivalries, distaste for a central government, native Greek suspicion of diaspora politicians, and regional interests persisted and worsened. Local countergovernments dug in but were themselves afflicted by schisms. Normal politics gave way to a "politics of the chiefs, that is to say, of money, weapons, families, and force."[185] The notional "Greece" established at Epidaurus had become a collection of little Greeces ranging at various points from the Morea to Missolonghi in the west to Athens in the east and to the islands. No amount of institutional tinkering or personal political assertion brought relief. As one scholar put it, "Even if the leaders of insurgent Greece had been masters of statecraft, they would probably have proved unequal to the task of creating a state in the midst of a desperate struggle to wrest recognition of the nation's right to independent statehood."[186]

As in Spain, political life was impeded by civil war—two in fact, in 1823–24 and 1824–25—over issues rooted in structures that preceded the war for independence and were exacerbated by rivalry over foreign money and arms coming in from abroad. Armed civil strife shredded what passed for a government and greatly debilitated the larger patriotic war. During these years of internecine warfare, independent captains, acting like warlords, at various times plundered Greek villages, collaborated with the Turks against their own people, siphoned off supplies and rations targeted for the general struggle, and refused to assist other Greek fighters beleaguered by the enemy. Kolokotrónis was imprisoned, and other captains were killed or narrowly escaped death. A combination of Turkish bad luck and incompetence; the undeniable bravery and fortitude of the

Greek resisters, even though divided; and the difficulty of the terrain prevented the rebels from going down to defeat. But it was only a frightening new wave of Muslim forces that managed to bring the Greek insurgents together.[187]

The new menace arrived by ship from Egypt organized by Mehmet Ali, a satrap of the sultan's who agreed to assist his liege lord in crushing the Greeks. Commanded by his son, Ibrahim Pasha, a flotilla sailed from Egyptian shores bearing four thousand infantry and five hundred horse and made a landing on February 24, 1825, at Methoni at the southwestern tip of the Morea. Finding the beachhead inadequate for resupply, Ibrahim moved north to a complex around the Bay of Navarino, guarded by fortresses and the island of Sphakteria. In the first, and lesser-known, Battle of Navarino, Mavrokordatos, his Greek forces, and philhellene volunteers defended the stronghold, which fell in May, Mavrokordatos barely escaping with his life. Ibrahim's troops fanned out from their base and began the bloody reconquest of the Morea. In a panic, the faction that had jailed Kolokotrónis released him, and the war ground on, resulting in the fall of Missolonghi in the spring of 1826 and Athens in the summer. Turkish and Egyptian reprisals mounted and a rumor began to float about Ibrahim's plan to "de-Hellenize" the Morean peninsula by annihilating part of its Greek population of one and a half million, taking the rest to Egypt and there converting some to Islam and enslaving others.[188]

In the spring of 1827, in the midst of the war against the Egyptians, the Third National Assembly convened at Troezen and established the first really effective and stable government to deal with the military crisis. To obviate the usual outbursts of rivalry over command, it was given to outsiders: the army to General Richard Church, the navy to Admiral Thomas Cochrane. Ironically, the man who had both dampened and spurred the revolt, Ioannis Capodistria, was offered and accepted the presidency of the new state for a term of seven years. He arrived in 1828. A new constitution was eventually superseded, but its liberal bill of rights survived into nationhood.[189] Salvation of the beleaguered Greeks came eventually through intervention by the Great Powers, but in the meantime the war became enlivened and complicated by the arrival of a remarkable cohort of "Frankish legions"—European and American volunteers who came to be known as the philhellenes. Among them were exiled remnants of the Mediterranean liberal revolutions.

Brothers of the Sword

In this era, travelers and philhellene volunteers from Europe often voiced their disappointment at finding in Greece no one who resembled the heroes chronicled in their schoolbooks. This was sometimes taken wrongly to mean that the entire Greek population comprised only barbarous savages with no knowledge of their ancient heritage. In fact, the invocation of classical motifs continued during the war by diaspora Greeks was taken up by those on the ground. The name "Hellenes," abandoned for centuries and replaced by "Romans" or "Christians," was revived in the years prior to 1821. When the war began, it came to designate "fighters," and the word "Hellenic" to mean brave.[190] At one of the first insurgent capitals, Nauplion, the assembly hall was described by Admiral Codrington as dirty and ramshackle building, lacking a ceiling, with unsteady floors and stairs and starlings flitting in and out.[191] Yet in that humble little town, public entertainment followed the Odessa-Bucharest theatrical tradition and filled its stages with classical patriotic verse, war hymns, and amateur drama.[192]

An intriguing aspect of Greek cultural expression during the independence war—the wedding of pagan classical and Orthodox Christian themes—flowed naturally from the dual heritage of ancient Hellas and Byzantium. Admiral Yakovos Tombasis' May 1821 proclamation employed the familiar dualistic litany about a downtrodden people—Orthodox Christians and the descendants of Miltiades and Themistocles—and he had it nailed to the main mast of all his vessels.[193] The theme echoed in numerous declarations and appeals and was incorporated into the work of the diaspora poet Dionísios Solomós, whom Goethe called "the Byron of the East."[194] His 1823 "Hymn to Liberty," the first poetic work to address Greeks as "free people," was a lengthy Romantic and chauvinistic epic on the Greek war of liberation. To its religious thematics, it added a reminder of the three hundred Spartans of Thermopylae and glorified the recent siege of Tripolitsa without mentioning the Greek atrocities.[195]

European observers on the ground and from afar took their classicism unadulterated by Byzantine Christianity. The Greek uprising seized their attention, which overwhelmingly favored the rebels. philhellenism—the admiration of things Greek—had deep roots in European intellectual history dating back to before the Renaissance. Its most recent popularization, based largely on aesthetic considerations, began with the excavation of antiquities at Herculaneum and Pompeii in the eighteenth century and its wide advertisement in the works of the German critic Johann Winckelmann. Enthusiasts often conflated Rome and Greece in their adulation of the classical age. Diaspora Greeks won sympathy throughout Europe by dressing up their programs for Greek independence in the language of classical revival and the regeneration of the descendants of Plato and Alcibiades. The cult of antiquity in the French Revolution had vigorously appropriated the mythos of that distant era and turned it to radical purpose in a classical masquerade of naming children Solon or Lycurgus and in the antique ceremonies of Jacques-Louis David.[196]

While the struggle that began in 1821 divided opinion among European statesmen, it had irresistible appeal to the educated public. The main attraction was the dream of recovering the glory that was Greece. Publicists, writers, and artists caught the fever: Guizot, de Vigny, Lamartine, Alexandre Dumas père, and Delacroix, among others.[197] Both the liberal Benjamin Constant and the conservative Chateaubriand were swept up in a wave of French Grecophile passion. Fighting an Islamic foe added to the appeal for some. When the papacy adopted a neutral stand on the rising, the arch-Catholic Chateaubriand protested that it should rather declare a crusade for the faith and for humanity.[198] European interest in the Greek revolt far exceeded interest in those of the western Mediterranean, though their view of it remained distorted from the outset.

Mental philhellenism escalated to physical participation almost immediately after the banner of revolt was held aloft in early 1821. Then a bigger wave began after the English poet Lord Byron set an example for the restless and romantic youth of post-Napoleonic Europe by traveling to Greece in 1823 and dying at Missolonghi in 1824. Byron's charisma and the legend of his sacrifice still inform many modern accounts. The poet, damping down his recent radicalism, set an apolitical tone that was adopted by many philhellenes. According to his constant companion while in Greece, Pietro Gamba (an erstwhile Carbonaro), Byron believed that the Greek revolution "had little or nothing in common with the great struggles with which Europe had been for thirty years distracted, and that it would be most improvident for the friends of Greece to mix up their cause with that of the other nations who had attempted to change their form of government, and by so doing to draw down the hatred and opposition of one of the two great parties that at present divided the civilized world."[199] Byron therefore hoped that politicians of all persuasions would unite around a cause that represented the remnant of the classical world and Christianity ranged against barbarism.

Lord Byron's countrymen responded handsomely. Edward Blaquiere headed a Greek Committee in London, which floated loans dedicated to the Hellenic cause. Greek Committees appeared soon in France, Hungary, Sweden, Denmark, Spain, and Portugal. The coffers of benefit societies rang with donations from private and public sources. A Byron Brigade of thirty philhellene officers and between a hundred and two hundred men was formed after his death. Before and after the Byronic punctuation mark, volunteers from almost every country in Europe and from the United States and Latin America sailed to Greece to serve, defend, and nurture a struggling people. Long before Byron arrived on the shores of Hellas, eight shiploads of philhellenes out of Marseilles landed there between November 1821 and August 1822. Poets, Byron-worshipers, scholars, clerics, Romantics, liberals, and all sorts of other people joined the crusade.[200]

Into Greece flowed many currents feeding philhellenism: a revival of raw *Türkenfurcht*, Romanticism, classical aesthetic sensibilities, religion, humanitarianism, liberal rights, and hostility to Metternich and the Holy Alliances' intervention in Spain and Italy.[201] David Brewer aptly points out the colorful variety of the crowd who came to make Greece free: "a clutch of eccentrics: a Bavarian china manufacturer intending to set up a factory in Greece, an out-of-work French actor, a dancing master from Rostock, and even a Spanish girl dressed as a man."[202] But this breezy description should not hide their seriousness: the "Spanish girl" he alludes to may have been the wife of the Italian philhellene Torricelli, who was killed at the Battle of Peta (she died at Missolonghi), or the Spaniard José de Oñate's wife, an active combatant.[203]

Of the 1,100 to 1,200 philhellenes who went to Greece, about 940 were identified by nationality in a standard British account.[204] Among the aesthetes, adventurers, soldiers, and revolutionaries, often embodied in one person, the number of German volunteers much exceeded those of all the others, though their role has been left in the shade by mainstream historiography. Britain has always been in the spotlight because of Byron's soaring reputation and British financial and intellectual support from many quarters of society. The Italian contingent was by far the most political. Some volunteers entered Greek units as individuals, but most served in European formations such as Regiment Baleste, Sacred Company, Battalion of Philhellenes, Byron Brigade, Army of Liberals, or Company of Philhellenes. philhellenism reached as far as the Greek colonies in British Calcutta and Dacca in India, where Greek settlers and others sent support to the rebels.[205]

A titled Swedish philhellene noted the wide variety of national origins among his comrades-in-arms and claimed that "we forgot completely about nationality and lived together as friends."[206] But others also noted discord among countrymen and between, among others, Germans and Frenchmen.[207] After the first wave of recruits, roughly from March 1821 to late 1822, came the Byronic and post-Byronic cohort between early 1823 and mid-1825. Distinct from these, though overlapping in time, radicals and exiles from failed revolutions in southern Europe fleshed out the ranks of the philhellenes. Europe would see nothing quite like this until the Spanish Civil War of the twentieth century with its Lincoln, Garibaldi, and Thälmann brigades.

If the philhellenes of western Europe were mostly admirers of classical Greece, with an admixture of other motives, the Balkan Slavic volunteers who joined the fight saw the Greeks not so much as modern embodiments of the ancient Hellenes but rather as co-religionists in a Balkan struggle; with the Greeks they shared a faith, often the same schoolrooms and churches, and a common life under the Turks. Support came in the form of arms, food, medicine, and shelter for victims, refugees, and fighting men. Some Balkan military volunteers became prominent commanders. Many of the "Greek" partisan bands who fought the Turks comprised many ethnic groups, and most of their members were young people between the ages of eighteen and thirty.[208] Among them, the Bulgarian fighters, for example, did not match the profile of the

Romantic European, but they nonetheless participated in both phases of the struggle for Greek independence.[209]

In terms of providing combat volunteers, the Russian effort both at the time and in subsequent historiography was overshadowed by the philhellenes of western Europe. Though they produced no highly publicized units and no Byronic celebrities, Russians enlisted in the Greek war despite a ban issued by Tsars Alexander and Nicholas.[210] Contrary to received opinion,[211] volunteers from Russia fought in both phases of the uprising and equaled numerically the volunteers of some Western counterparts. The fifty or so Russians and Ukrainians, all absent from one otherwise carefully compiled list, would have ranked fifth on it after the Germans, French, Italians, and British and ahead of nine other nationalities. Aside from these, in 1824 an apparently lone Russian volunteer appeared at Byron's camp and caused a minor rumpus, though we have no traces of his origins.[212]

Who were the Russian volunteers? During the Ypsilanti campaign, Colonel Vasilii Sultanov with a unit of 150 men saw action in Moldavia. His adjutant, Arkhip Kulikovskii, a retired staff captain living in penury in Odessa, had responded to a philhellene appeal and taken his son Silvester and twenty-two others to Iaşi. Routed by the Turks, Sultanov squabbled with his men and the unit disbanded. Kulikovskii, his son, and three others escaped to Austria, where they were interrogated. Volunteers identified as Russians in this and other outfits included Pandelie Sheremet, Nikolai Tideev (Tidejow), and Ivan Filippov. Those who fled back into Russia congregated at the little town of Orgeev. There in June 1821 Russian officials compiled a list of 1,002 returnees of various nationalities, half of whom were Greek, the rest mostly Balkan peoples and a smattering of Gypsies, Poles, converted Jews, and west Europeans. The sixteen Russians and fifteen Ukrainians listed by name and rank or social affiliation included two serfs, Captain Kulikovskii, and one Cossack, with nothing on the status of the others. They came from the Russian, Austrian, and Ottoman Empires. One, Petr Markevich, hailed from Vasilkov—site of the last Decembrist rising.[213]

The record of those who fought in greater Greece offers a bit more detail and color. At the outset of the rising, Ivan Afanasiev, a mariner and specialist in fire ships, found himself among the islands and took part in the burning of several Turkish vessels. Foma Androvich commanded a Russian schooner and ran guns and matériel from Trieste to the Greeks. Mikhail Doktorov arrived at Hydra from Moscow in June 1824. Mark Vulidzevich, a merchant sea captain, brought arms and goods from Livorno. Captain Iosif Berezanskii (variant spellings) had served sixteen years in the Russian cavalry and artillery. As "co-religionists and philhellenes," he and two brothers went off with 180 men of unspecified nationality to fight against Ibrahim Pasha in the Peloponnese and against the Turks in

Crete. Wounded, Berezanskii pleaded poverty, retired, and remained in Greece. One brother perished at Peta; another lost a leg and returned to Russia in 1825. Georgy Kalamos of Chernigov Province, Russian by origin in spite of his name, went to Greece as a gunnery specialist on land and sea. He fought for seven years, was captured, and was released or escaped. The Russian Ivan Katevskii, a teacher in Moldavia, was taken prisoner in the Ypsilanti rising, then escaped and went off to Hydra.[214]

The Decembrist Lohrer recalled that news of the Greek rising inflamed the youth of his circle. One of them, Nikolai Raiko (Raio in the Greek sources), allegedly the son of an illegitimate child of Catherine the Great and Prince Grigorii Orlov, embodied his grandparents' schemes of a liberated Greece, though in a vastly different way. Raiko spent a number of years in Florence and returned to Russia in 1815. An artillery officer with Decembrist sympathies and a friend of Byron's, he traveled to Greece in 1824, reaching the summit of a long-held dream. He fought at Chios under General Fabvier and became a general and later military governor of Patras. When Raiko returned to Russia, Capodistria recommended he be given a medal and a colonel's rank, but the angry tsar ordered him to the Caucasus, the dumping ground for disobedient officers. Returning to Russia proper after his frontier service, Raiko began handing out his visiting card: "Raiko, General Feldzeugmeister [artillery commander] of an Overseas Region." In official circles, Raiko earned the reputation as a Carbonaro either for his "crime" of going to Greece or for his Italian experience.[215]

Greeks divided over the issue of foreign volunteers who were driven by the politics of international liberalism. Some diaspora figures freely made the connection between Greece and the rebels of Spain and Italy. Dionísios Solomós' "Hymn to Liberty," a poem replete with gory massacres, "sobs, and groans, and clanging chains," fulminated against the great powers for their lack of assistance. It also hailed other liberal struggles, blasting the Austrian eagle's claws dipped in the blood of Italy and praising Latin American freedom. Of liberal Spain—at that moment under attack—he wrote in May 1823: "While the Spanish lion roars / From his proud ancestral tower, / Every thundering tone he pours / Seems to welcome Freedom's hour."[216]

Liberation poetry was one thing. But to the authorities in Greece, politically active liberal volunteers coming to Greece presented a dilemma. On one hand, the Greeks valued the expertise of professional officers and revolutionary fighters. On the other, they worried about taking on volunteers who previously had been involved with political revolt. Aware that the Holy Alliance kept constant check on the doings of liberal exiles in a shadow war of conspirators and spies, they feared it would see the presence of such volunteers in Greece as evidence that the Greek struggle was a variant of the revolutions in Naples and

Spain.[217] The concern was well founded. Aside from Metternich, Tsar Alexander and his minister Nesselrode, sitting at Laibach in 1821, tended to see the Greek revolt as a direct continuation of the Spanish rising.[218] Even to the British foreign minister, Viscount Castlereagh, the Greek revolt was a new example of an "organized spirit of insurrection which is systematically propagating itself throughout Europe"[219] and which "in its organization, in its objects, in its agency, and in its external relation is in no respect distinguishable from the movements in Spain, Portugal and Italy" and thus "deeply tainted with revolutionary danger."[220] Greek officials therefore, in cultivating foreign support, always stressed national independence and denied being part of an international revolutionary movement.

The Greek government reacted selectively to the well-meaning veterans of the recently suppressed constitutional regimes. Military volunteers often had to produce a character testimonial and other documents about prior service and a sum of money to support themselves.[221] Kolokotrónis in his memoirs made a dutiful bow to European influence when he proclaimed that "the French Revolution and the doings of Napoleon opened the eyes of the world." But at the time of the struggle he was careful to distinguish the Greek revolt from other kinds. At one point during the civil war he deflected some of the rebels from massacring property-owning notables. Outsiders, he warned, instead of seeing the rebels as fighters for freedom against the Turks, would call them "bad men and Carbonari."

> Our rising was totally different from any which had ever taken place in Europe before our day. The revolutions of Europe had always been against their rulers—they were civil wars. Our war was more just than any of them—it was a nation rising up against another nation—it was a war with a people whom it never desired to acknowledge as ruling them.[222]

He and other leaders, in understandably setting themselves off from the political radicalism of Restoration Europe, were also slapping the face of those political refugees who had come to risk their lives for Greece. Kolokotrónis gives them no credit.

The Benthamite activists Blaquiere and Bowring acted as cautious enablers of political exiles. Prior to 1823, they and Bentham had been in touch with Adamántios Koraïs. Then Louriótis arrived in Madrid seeking support there. But it was the collapse of the Spanish liberal regime that changed their focus to Greece. Blaquiere viewed Greece as a continuation of the liberal cause now lost in Naples, Piedmont, and Spain. He arrived there in March 1823 as the death of liberalism in Spain rapidly approached, and he became friends with Alerio Palma and Count Pecchio. But in public and in print Blaquiere prudently distinguished the Greek cause from the others as a revolt against an illegitimate government.[223]

In spite of misgivings, the insurgent Hellenes did allow numerous political refugees into their war. Some signed up through the London and Madrid Greek Committees and the network of continental émigré communities. Exiles and stragglers from battlefield defeat in Spain made their way to Marseilles. The French port became a major embarkation point for Greece until November 1822, when no more philhellene ships were permitted to sail, either because of anticipated Holy Alliance pressure or to save the lives of further volunteers—given the stories that were coming back about conditions in Greece. The French general Fabvier, veteran of the Spanish fight against the 1823 intervention, became a key figure in organizing exile volunteers. After the collapse in Spain, he gathered a troop of men from emigration circles willing to harness their energies to a new campaign for liberation on the far side of the Mediterranean.[224] Arriving in Greece, he commanded a company of Greek regulars and a unit of foreign volunteers. By 1825 many of his comrades had spent their best years struggling against Bourbon dynasties. At one point Fabvier, fighting a rear-guard action against the enemy, chose as his fortified base a volcanic peak on the Peloponnesian peninsula of Methoni, near Navarino, approached by a narrow isthmus. Recalling the last holdout of Spain's beleaguered constitutional forces in 1823, Fabvier declared that this would become the Cadiz of Greece.[225]

The Spanish cause and its defeat produced many a volunteer for free Greece, but few of them were Spaniards. In early modern times the rulers of Spain (and Naples) had used their Greek residents to subvert the Ottoman Empire, and the sixteenth and seventeenth centuries had witnessed many examples of Greco-Spanish collaboration against the Turks. Spanish interest in the eastern Mediterranean declined after that. Its revival took the form of literary and philological philhellenism in the early nineteenth century. The cult of Byron nourished it among intellectuals and political and military figures. The stalwart liberal Francisco Martínez de la Rosa penned these verses sometime in the 1820s.

> Noble sons of Sparta and Athens,
> Heed the voice of the fatherland,
> And by bursting your dishonorable chains
> Forge the weapons of combat.[226]

Spanish philhellenism did not proceed much beyond the verbal. The leaders of the Trienio, though sympathetic to the Greek cause, could contribute very little to it except recognize that both their movements posed a threat to the Holy Alliance. The Madrid press proudly printed Ypsilanti's 1821 appeal to follow the example of Spain's defeat of the usurper Napoleon. Liberals hoped that the Greek revolt would divert the Russian tsar from interference in Spanish affairs.[227] A Philhellene Committee was formed in Madrid in late 1822 or early

1823—much too late for any serious action. It then moved to London.[228] The Greek agent Andreás Louriótis sought loans in Spain and Portugal, but those countries had no funds to give. He went on to England in 1823; by the summer of that year, the Spanish regime was about to fall.[229]

The one concrete offer of military aid came from members of the Spanish government on December 18, 1821: a proposal to send three hundred Italian political exiles in Spain to fight in Greece (by some accounts this group included Spaniards also). The offer, signed by Morales, Palmas, and Vurinos, noted that the volunteers expressed a desire to emulate Leonidas—thus the number three hundred—and that though the entire Spanish people wanted to join the struggle, they were prevented by the need to consolidate their own freedom at home. The Greek government declined the offer. A Spanish expedition to fight in Greece, even if comprising volunteers, would have added weight to the concerns of the Holy Alliance about an international Mediterranean conspiracy.[230] After the French 1823 invasion, of the fleeing Spanish survivors, only a handful went to Greece.

Active Spanish philhellenism, such as it was, came into being near the end of the liberal regime. Bowring reported in October 1823 that the Spanish Committee had sent a hundred thousand cannonballs and two thousand firelocks to the Greek Committee.[231] Information is almost nonexistent on most of the nineteen or twenty Spanish philhellene volunteers, and scanty even on the half dozen or so on whom we have data. Victorio Lascaris of Saragossa, born in Spain in 1801 of Byzantine heritage, had sailed the eastern Mediterranean and joined Greek and Spanish secret societies. Lascaris fought at the Greco-Turkish naval Battle of Lala in June 1821 but left no trace of his activity after that; he died in Spain in 1872. The others arrived after the Spanish liberal regime had perished. Juan Torribio Ibañez, a cavalry officer, served from April 1825 until the following January, when he requested passage money to leave for health reasons—a frequent request during that disease-ridden war. Miguel Fernando Rivero and Serafim de Lanzana arrived late in 1826, served with Fabvier at the siege of the Acropolis in Athens, and were dead by 1827. Colonel Veleiras, possibly Portuguese but identified only as a Spanish philhellene, arrived in Greece from France in 1826 and was enlisted in the military.[232]

José García de Villalta (1800–1864) seems to have been the most ideologically motivated of the Spanish volunteers. He was, in the words of a Greek newspaper, "a great journalist of that era, [a man] of liberal principles." A supporter of the constitution, he fled Spain in late 1823 or 1824 for England and then shipped to Greece soon afterward. Though García de Villalta had some artillery training, it is unclear what he did in the war. He returned to Spain as governor of Galicia during the Carlist wars, was arrested and sentenced to death, and escaped. Eventually he became Spanish ambassador to the Kingdom of Greece. When he died in Athens, García de Villalta was honored in parliament and in the press as a philhellene. On the occasion of his passing, a Greek newspaper proclaimed that, had France not intervened in Spain in 1823, that country would presently be leading a more tranquil existence.[233]

Of quite a different stripe, Lieutenant Juan Maria Lhufrior, evidently a Catalan, had been a reserve officer in Spain from 1811 to 1820. He arrived in Greece on May 7, 1825, served at Nauplion, was arrested over a fracas with his fellow officers, and resigned. He wrote two letters in pidgin French in January 1826 blasting the Greek government and his military superiors for mistreating officers. Revealing his politics, he stated that officers in an absolute monarchy were not arrested unless they were state criminals—that is, liberals. In a curt and cold reply, General Fabvier told him that he was happy to release a "completely useless" officer.[234]

Italian philhellenism proved to be more vital to the Greek cause. The Greek diaspora in Italy, which escalated in 1453 with the Ottoman conquest of Constantinople, planted "little Greeces" in Ancona, Trieste, Venice, Padua, Livorno, and Pisa that earned high esteem from their Italian neighbors.[235] When the modern philhellene craze began, major poets such as Giacomo Leopardi, Enrico Mayer, and others wrote verses in praise of the Greeks or translated Greek patriotic materials, as did the exiled patriot Rossetti. The cultural bloodline that connected Romantic literature to political sensibilities meant that liberal intellectuals also favored the Greek David over the Turkish Goliath.[236] While Eugène Delacroix's canvas *Massacre on Chios*, shown at the Paris salon of 1824, became the iconic artwork dealing with the Greek revolt, Italian artists produced more graphic representations of the Greek war than those of any other culture. They offered the extravagant Romantic idiom for the Greeks and a demeaning Orientalism for the Turks.[237] The many pictures of crammed boats cutting through churning waters with a warrior holding up a banner in his right hand are reminiscent of the canvas of Ypsilanti crossing the Pruth, which may well have been influenced by the Italian works that preceded it.

Italians had a long tradition of receiving and welcoming refugees from Muslim powers and raising money to redeem hostages and slaves.[238] With the outbreak of the war in 1821, Italians of many persuasions offered asylum, charity, ransom money, and platforms for philhellene arms shipments and Greek military expeditions against the Turks. The city of Naples, with its small Greek colony, was among those extending aid, though northern cites predominated, particularly Livorno, Genoa, and Pisa.[239] As volunteers, Italian officers and soldiers appeared in Greece as early as 1821.[240] Medical personnel came to serve in the field and in base hospitals.

How many fought? How many died? A memorial raised years after the war at Nauplion listed the names of 280 philhellenes who perished in the war, 42 of whom were Italian. In 1821–22 alone, some 62 Italians arrived, 19 of whom died in battle, and many more flowed in. William St. Clair recorded 137 Italian phil-hellenes who fought in Greece—the third-largest contingent after that of the Germans (342) and the French (196). Probably all the estimates are low, since many fighters were never counted or recorded.[241] There exists no complete list of Italian volunteers. They hailed from Piedmont, Naples, the Papal States, Lombardy, and Venetia. In terms of social background, their ranks comprised simple citizens, educated men, physicians, and nobles—including at least six counts, Santa Rosa, Porro, Palma, Ciappe, Pisa, and Gamba—leading some to talk of the incursion into Greece of "Carbonari counts." Officer ranks ran from private to general, including a large contingent of veterans of the Napoleonic wars and of the recent revolutions in Naples and Piedmont.[242]

Refugees from the Neapolitan and Piedmontese revolutions who went directly or via Spain to fight for Greece formed the living link between the Mediterranean uprisings, as they were the only national contingent that fought in all three. In one wave alone, that of 1825–26, all of the sixty to seventy Italian exiles who went to Greece had fought in Napoleon's army, participated in Piedmontese or Neapolitan revolts, and served the liberal regime in Spain—and thus had been "three-time losers."[243] Italian liberals mythologized the Greek war as part of an international Holy Alliance of Peoples.[244] Their sympathy for the Greek uprising sprang from a rough identification of the Austrian and Ottoman Empires as despotic oppressors of Italy and the Greeks, respectively. Aside from a religious solidarity with other Christians that probably motivated some volunteers, many were driven by a clearly affecting notion of a common Greco-Roman cultural ancestry. Palma, Santarosa, and Pecchio all recorded their view of Greece as historically and culturally linked to Italy.[245]

The very fact of exile played an important motivating role. One gets the feeling, though it is never quite voiced, that in going to Greece the Italian fugitives had nothing to lose. Of those from the Neapolitan and Piedmontese revolutions, a dozen faced real death sentences in Italy and about half that number the possibility of such.[246] Unable to return home, some had gone to fight in Spain, others to England or France, where they waited or worked for the next opportunity.[247] Other motives included raw ambition and the reach for glory and prestige. Some of the professional officers also wanted to practice their martial skills once again in the only place then available—except for distant Latin America. Their preference for familiar pitched battle led to friction with Greek guerrilla fighters.[248]

Among the Italian political exiles who became philhellenes, those from Naples and Piedmont predominated. The virtual coincidence of the onset of the Greek war with the Austrian suppression of the Neapolitan and Piedmontese constitutional regimes eased the decision of some exiles to cross over into

Greece. Guglielmo Pepe, however, was not among them. Like other Italian and Spanish liberals, he closely followed events in Greece and the Balkans. From Madrid he was corresponding in July 1821 with Giuseppe Pecchio about the unrest in Moldavia.[249] He and Rossaroll were among the few Neapolitans who had served in Greece earlier—a brief spell at Corfu when the French held sway in 1807–8.[250] But Pepe's heart still beat for Italy, and his dream for it remained undying. Though he did not venture forth to fight in Greece, he saw that war-torn land as yet another source and staging area for his own liberation plans.

Frustrated in his efforts to mobilize the Spanish liberals, Pepe turned his eyes eastward. He came to believe that the insurgent Greeks would look with favor upon an "extension of liberty in Europe, especially in nearby Italy."[251] During his sorties back and forth between Spain and Portugal in 1822–23, Pepe corresponded with Mavrokordatos, then the Greek foreign minister. "The power of treason," he wrote in December 1822, "has caused my country to be reinterred into slavery." Pepe tried to broker a Greek expedition outfitted, armed, financed, and manned by liberal Spain and Portugal, with Italian volunteers. In the course of the correspondence, Pepe also revived a variant of his Montenegrin scheme. He asked Mavrokordatos to send a thousand selected Greek fighters across the Adriatic to Calabria with the goal of restoring the constitution. His letter of December 1822 was sent to Greece through Colonel Rafael Poerio, brother of the deputy.[252]

Seldom in the history of international brotherhood has the understanding of solidarity been stretched to such lengths. The Greeks at that point were engaged in a full-scale war. But Pepe was no monomaniac, obsessed by Naples alone. His political panorama always included Italy as a whole, and his services in Spain and willingness while there to engage in an overturn in France reveal a man of capacious political sympathies toward the cause of liberalism in its many forms. Mavrokordatos understandably could not participate in Pepe's plan. In a letter of May 4/16, 1823, he drew another line between the Greek rebels and those of the western Mediterranean. The minister expressed his personal admiration for Pepe but told him that accepting his proposal would mean a deviation from the principles on which the Greek movement was founded—that is, national liberation, not radical revolution or international adventurism in solidarity with liberals.[253]

The indomitable Giuseppe Rossaroll (1775–1825) also tried to organize a Greco-Neapolitan operation. Born in Naples of Swiss origin, he was among the most adventurous of the Neapolitans who fought in Greece. He had served the Parthenopean Republic as a captain, after which he was exiled to France. He then joined Napoleon's army, saw action at Marengo, and served with Murat in Russia. Under a Neapolitan death sentence after the failed Messina resistance, he followed a familiar pattern by fleeing to Spain to oppose the French intervention.[254]

After that effort collapsed, Rossaroll went to England and thence to Greece. Once there, he formed the Army of Liberals and fashioned yet another fanciful Adriatic stratagem: to use the Ionian Islands as a base for Italian forces, which, after securing a Greek victory, would restore one of Murat's relatives as a constitutional monarch of Naples. But the fifty-year-old warrior died at the siege of Nauplion in 1825. His sons continued to fight on for the Greek cause. One, Cesare, plotted against the king of Naples in 1833 and was sentenced to twenty years in irons. Released by revolution in 1848, he was killed in combat in 1849.[255]

Count Vincenzo Pisa, a former Neapolitan major, veteran of Marengo, and Carbonaro supporter of the constitutional regime, followed a familiar route. After the invasion of Naples, he tried unsuccessfully to launch insurrections in other Italian towns, was condemned to death in absentia, and fought for liberal Spain. Armed with a letter of recommendation to the Greek government, Pisa set sail from London in 1826. In Greece Pisa became a colonel, commanded a company of philhellenes, and saw action, including the siege of the Acropolis. Wounded in the leg during one of the campaigns, he became one of the few Italian officers who stayed on in Greece and became Hellenized. Some years after independence, Pisa gained the rank of general in the Greek armed forces.[256] In one of those curiosities of the Greek war, Pisa found himself campaigning on the same side as a man he had fought against and saw as a destroyer of liberty in Naples and Sicily: General Richard Church, the Irishman who had served King Ferdinando in Naples as a bandit hunter in 1817–20 and suppressor of secret societies.[257]

The Piedmontese, whose constitutional order had lasted only thirty days, had less revolutionary experience than their southern cousins, but they outnumbered them as armed volunteers in Spain and Greece. Radicals from the north Italian and Papal States came with them. Count Giuseppe Ciappe of Genoa started the journal *Friend of the Law* on the island of Hydra. Gioacchino Prati died at Missolonghi. Sergeant Antonio Forzano lost an eye in Spain and then lost his life in Greece in 1825. Vincenzo Aimino, another sergeant with an almost identical profile, died in battle at Nauplion.[258] Although more perished from disease and deprivation than in battle, many Italians lost their lives and incurred wounds in major engagements. Two battles in particular—at Peta and at Navarino—claimed the lives of Italian volunteers. The sickening fate of Andrea Dania and Pietro Tarella at Peta attests to the terrible risks that volunteers took in fighting for another people's freedom. Among the early volunteers, they had shared the familiar career pattern and political trajectory: soldiering on Napoleon's far-flung battlefields and proscription for their role in the Piedmont revolt. Dania, a valorous but brash Genoan cavalry officer, commanded various units of philhellenes. Tarella had campaigned with the French in Spain, in Germany, and at Waterloo. In Greece he served under Demetrios Ypsilantis.[259]

A disastrous bloodletting occurred at the Battle of Peta in July 1822, caused by poor philhellene leadership and the desertion of their Greek allies. Among the sixty-seven philhellenes who fell were thirty-four Germans, nine Poles, three Swiss, one Hungarian, six Frenchmen, one Netherlander, one naturalized French Mameluk, and twelve Italians. At least five of the Italian volunteers killed—and probably more—were revolutionary exiles.[260] Dania and Tarella commanded units at this battle. The lucky ones perished on the battlefield, but the philhellene prisoners suffered a terrible fate. The vengeful Turks forced their captives to carry the severed heads of their comrades from the field to the Ottoman camp. Two were beheaded and twenty of the prisoners, including Dania and Tarella, were impaled.[261] This mode of execution involved slowly tapping a long sharpened stake up through the rectum into the bowels and out through the shoulder in a way designed to keep the victim alive for hours in unspeakable agony until death came. Samuel Howe, a philhellene surgeon not much given to lurid imagery, described seeing victims "suspended upright in the air upon stakes driven through the whole length of their bodies, still alive perhaps, and writhing with all the horrid pangs of impalement."[262]

The vessel *Little Sally* departed England for Greece in November 1824 and landed at Nauplion on December 10.[263] From it disembarked the Piedmontese liberals Collegno and Santarosa. In a tribute to Giacinto Collegno, Massimo d'Azeglio, a major Piedmontese figure of the Risorgimento, recalled the restless life of his dear friend, from the fires of Moscow to the liberation of Greece. Born in Turin of an old family, Collegno, after the Napoleonic occupation of that city, went to France, graduated from St. Cyr, and saw action in Vilna, Bautzen, Dresden, and Leipzig. Thus, like many other Italians, he unknowingly faced future Decembrist rebels on the field of battle. By 1821 Collegno had joined the Carbonari and took part in the Piedmontese revolt, for which he was executed in effigy in Turin and all his earthly possessions were confiscated. After brief sojourns elsewhere, Collegno landed in Lisbon, where he tried in vain to persuade the Portuguese regime to defend the constitutionalists in Spain. Collegno then joined Fabvier and fought at Bidasoa in April 1823. From Spain, Collegno returned to England and then traveled to Greece with Santarosa.[264]

Collegno's diary, begun on April 20, 1825, offers a detailed account of the siege of Navarino fortress, where he and Santarosa and other Italians fought alongside Greeks, Englishmen, and Americans. In the course of battle Collegno was captured and released by Ibrahim.[265] Ever the literary officer, the Italian philhellene invoked scenes from Byron's *Childe Harold*, which, he said, paralleled his current milieu. Quite un-Byronic, however, were his remarks about the classic conflict between professional officer and guerrilla: when Collegno, a military engineer, laid out his defensive requirements, the Greek officers laughed at him. Collegno eventually became disillusioned with his Greek fighters, though not with their cause. After distinguishing himself at Navarino, Collegno returned to Italy under a pardon, became a noted geologist, and died in 1856.[266]

Count Santorre di Santarosa, after the failed Piedmontese revolt and a spell of exile, chose Greece over Spain as his next stop. The London Greeks sent along with him open letters to government leaders praising Santarosa and sealed ones warning them not to accept his service. They were as usual concerned about attracting the negative attention of the great powers by hiring on a well-known revolutionary exile to their cause. In November Santarosa departed from London on board the *Little Sally*, the next month landing at Nauplion, where his request for a command remained unanswered.[267] While waiting, Santarosa visited Athens. Standing in the Agora, he sang aloud verses from Aeschylus' *The Persians*: "O sons of Hellas! Set free your fatherland, your children, wives, homes."[268] Back in Nauplion, Santarosa became disillusioned with the current sons of Hellas who administered the country. In a letter of April 1825 he described the simple people of Greece as worthy folks who blended superstition with religion, but he deemed the ruling classes a corrupt hybrid combining the "oriental manner" and European wickedness.[269] Still lacking a commission, Santarosa, stirring "with the enthusiasm of a Crusader," donned Albanian garb and volunteered as a soldier in the ranks.[270] By April he was present at the defense of Navarino during its siege by Ibrahim Pasha.

The philhellenes at Navarino and elsewhere experienced shock in discovering that some of their former French, Polish, British, and Italian comrades were fighting as mercenaries for the Turks against the Greeks. Among them were Colonel Giovanni Romei, a condemned exile from the Neapolitan revolution. Santarosa denounced Romei in a blistering letter and voiced his own dual view of the Greek struggle: "Compatriot! . . . Your behavior is severely and sharply condemned in Europe by all those in whom lives the feeling of religion, by all those in whom lives the desire for the progress of civilization."[271] When Romei, mantled in Turkish garb, eventually surrendered to the philhellenes, Santarosa's comrade Collegno took him into captivity and made a wry comment in his diary: "And so it turned out that a Piedmontese major condemned to death in 1821 for love of the Italian cause was put in charge of a Neapolitan colonel, also condemned to death in the same era for the same reason."[272] Santarosa was killed in battle on May 8, 1825, at Sphakteria. The body was never found. Having been dubbed by some the soul of the Piedmontese revolution, Santarosa now became the chief icon of the Italian philhellene military volunteers. The French liberal philosopher Victor Cousin, an admirer, later erected a memorial at Sphakteria to Santarosa "who died for the independence of Greece."[273]

After the siege ended, a kind of nostalgic epilogue took place in another part of Greece. On June 9, 1825, Collegno found himself in the company of philhellenes, his old comrade-in-arms General Fabvier among them. Their paths had crossed often in the past: in a Napoleonic corps in 1813, in Paris in 1822, and in Spain in 1823. The company celebrated by singing arias, romances, and patriotic hymns of many nations. When "La Marseillaise" was struck up, Fabvier fell into a somber mood, as the French anthem brought back memories. His and Collegno's thoughts turned from Greece back across the sea to the beleaguered Spain of 1823. Recalling the Battle of Bidasoa, Collegno, the thirty-one-year-old veteran of international revolution, mused about "how many victims had fallen on that day to the sound of this solemn song!"[274]

The great majority of European philhellenes returned home and were fêted as heroes, especially the British and Germans, and the veterans of recent wars had been able to display their reverence for Mars once again. The French Foreign Legion, founded in 1830, just as the Greek war ended, would swallow others like them into its maw for the next century and a half. But the Italian soldiers of the Mediterranean revolutions for the most part remained homeless exiles, men without a country. Although some issues had divided the Italian volunteers, it seems abundantly clear that their devotion to foreign causes was fueled by the agony of exile and defeat in their homeland, which in turn fed a thirst for compensatory heroism.

The revolutionary nomads helped to finish what General Ypsilanti had begun, and some gave their lives doing it. They came to Greece as ex-revolutionaries but brought no revolution with them. They reacted with disgust to Greek atrocities and the intermittent mercenary behavior of Greek, Turkish, Egyptian, and Albanian fighters. Most of them stuck it out nonetheless and became living precursors of Mazzini's doctrine of the brotherhood of nations by folding their own brand of liberalism into nationalism in a time before these two enormous currents of thought and feeling were divorced later in the century. Pietro Gamba, a close friend of Byron, had been expelled from Ravenna in the Papal States for Carbonaro activity in 1821 and died in Greece in 1827. In an 1825 memoir he proudly enumerated the dozen nationalities of the philhellenes in Byron's camp and saw their exploits as "a crusade in miniature." Many Italians shared this view. Another philhellene, Colonel Brengeri, perhaps expressed most simply and most poignantly the link between them. A political refugee from the Papal States, he departed from Livorno in August 1821 to fight in Greece in order to liberate, as he later wrote, "some day my own country which groans under the priestly yoke."[275]

Hellas Reborn

Thanks to the diligence of scores of scholars—particularly diplomatic historians—the Greek rising has become the best-known of the revolts of the 1820s—so well known, in fact, that a brief sketch will suffice here. While foreign intervention had crushed the rebels in Spain and Naples, it saved the Greeks, but only through a gradual and difficult process. The insurgent government sought recognition and support from all the powers. In 1823 the British foreign minister, George Canning, fearing Russian influence in the Balkans, recognized Greeks and Turks as belligerents. In 1825 a group of leaders in Greece even proposed to make it a protectorate of the British crown.[276] But, in spite of Russia's repudiation of the Ypsilanti adventure, many Greeks continued to see the tsar as their natural ally by virtue of a common faith. In April 1821 some Peloponnesian rebels penned a letter, thought to have been ordered by Petrobey Mavromichalis, to Alexander I, addressing him as a co-religionist and a philhellene and requesting arms and other support as an alternative to slavery and continued tyranny under the Turks. The language of the missive attests to the trust in a liberator from the north.[277] Since a Greek Corps had served in the tsar's army and other Greeks were enrolled in various Russian services and branches during and after the Napoleonic wars, some of them might have expected a gesture of gratitude as well.[278] The gesture was long in coming and was hardly rooted in gratitude.

In April 1826 the Duke of Wellington came to St. Petersburg to congratulate Nicholas I on his succession. While he was there, an Anglo-Russian Protocol became the first instrument leading to diplomatic intervention. Thus between the last ride of the Decembrists and their execution, Greece was on the way to independence. In order to interdict what looked like the shaping up of a genocide, the two powers demanded that both sides submit to mediation. The Greeks acceded, but the Turks declined. Tsar Nicholas reverted to the old Russian Balkan policies of interest, expansion, and the protection of Orthodox Christians. In October the Treaty of Akkerman forced the Turks to withdraw from the principalities. More than a year of bitter fighting in Greece passed before another act of intervention came. In July 1827 the Treaty of London, with France now included, demanded an armistice. When the Ottomans again refused, the signatories agreed to use coercion by sending a combined fleet to blockade the resupply of Ibrahim's arms and men from Egypt. In the near-accidental Battle of Navarino in October 1827, the warships of Russia, Britain, and France destroyed the Turko-Egyptian naval forces. The French press made some rather odd comparisons. A liberal paper had equated the fall of Missolonghi to the Turks with the crushing of the Spanish and Neapolitan liberals. A conservative, still hankering after French military grandeur, celebrated Navarino as a new Trocadero.[279]

The war continued and Russo-Ottoman friction increased. In April 1828 the Russian Empire, as much over a squabble about the Danubian principalities as to help the Greeks, declared war on Turkey and, after major holdups, reached the town of Adrianople (Edirne), near the Turkish capital, in 1829. In the meantime, Capodistria, who was still the Greek president, appointed Demetrios Ypsilanti commander in eastern Greece, where he managed to defeat the Turkish force in September 1829, thus ending the military operations roughly at the moment when the Russians had done so. By the ensuing treaty, achieved in September, the sultan's government agreed to end the war with the Greeks and grant them autonomy, among other concessions. In February 1830 the three powers declared Greece an independent monarchy under their guarantee. The new state contained only about one-fourth of the Greek population of the Ottoman Empire. The revolutionary decade that had begun with Ypsilanti in 1821 ended with a murder rather than an execution: in October 1831 Capodistria was assassinated. In 1832 the Ottoman Empire recognized Greece as a fully independent state. From Bavaria, its first king, Othon—the Greek rendering of Otto—landed in February 1833.[280]

Three contrasting groups had, at least initially, linked the Greek uprising with the Mediterranean revolts: the Holy Alliance, poets such as Pushkin and Byron (though Byron later tried to downplay the association), and many of the revolutionary exiles themselves—especially the Italians. But neither the efforts of the philhellenes nor those of the Greeks themselves had been able alone to bring success to the cause. The Greeks won—just as Spain and Naples had lost—by way of foreign intervention. No Russian Cossacks, no Habsburg bayonets, no Sons of St. Louis came crashing down into the Balkans to crush the Greek rebels. Ironically, the *Appeal to the French People* of October 1821, written by a philhellene former law student in France, sought volunteers for Greece by adding to the usual tropes of classical nobility and Christian solidarity a nice French touch: "Are you no longer the descendants of the Crusading St. Louis?"[281] Those who wielded state power in Europe had come to draw a clear line between, on one hand, the fight for national independence from what they saw as an alien yoke and, on the other, liberal constitutional struggles in Spain, Naples, and elsewhere.

Intervention on behalf of the Greeks presented a scenario as yet unseen: one or more of the Great Powers taking the part of rebels instead of crushing them. In this victory, traditionalists came to view the Greek struggle, unlike the international crusade for liberalism, as one of legitimate nationalism: strong, tribal, self-centered, natural, and eventually capped by a monarch from a European dynasty. The actions of the three powers, whatever the mix in their motivations, also represented one of the first great humanitarian interventions in history by responding to a possible near genocide—a policy followed later in the century by European interference in Syria and Bulgaria and taken up periodically in the twentieth century down to our own times.[282]

‖ 5 ‖

Sergei Muraviev-Apostol

Into the Steppe

The heavy-hanging chains will fall,
The walls will crumble as a word;
And Freedom greet you in the light,
And brothers give you back the sword.
—Pushkin, "Message to Siberia," 1827[1]

"At 2:00 in the afternoon of a winter day on a town square, Jesus Christ was proclaimed the only universal tsar."[2] The town: Vasilkov; the day: December 31, 1825; the proclaimer: Lieutenant Colonel Sergei Muraviev-Apostol, prominent member of the Decembrist conspiratorial movement and the last major leader still at large. Son of a Russian ambassador to Spain, he had been an avid follower of Riego and the Spanish liberal regime. In late December 1825, after the collapse of the insurrection attempted by his comrades in St. Petersburg, he made use of two printed artifacts dealing with the Spanish struggle against Napoleon. One was a Spanish catechism of 1808 that had been translated into Russian in 1812. Using its format as a model, but modifying the content to fit Russian conditions, Muraviev-Apostol and a fellow officer crafted an Orthodox catechism that cited Christian scriptures in a diatribe against tyranny in general and against Russian tsars in particular. The second was a French novel, Narcisse-Achille de Salvandy's *Don Alonzo*, published the year before. The colonel and his comrades chose to make a last-ditch stand in order to salvage the uprising that later became known as the Decembrist revolt.

On that day Muraviev-Apostol ordered his troops into formation. On the snow-clad square facing the cathedral in the tiny Ukrainian town about a thousand men fell into formation. Muraviev-Apostol enlisted the local priest to read out the catechism to the assembled troops. Virtually all the fourteen questions and answers contained a message of treason: "Q: What are the Russian people and the Russian army unhappy about? A: That the tsars have stolen their

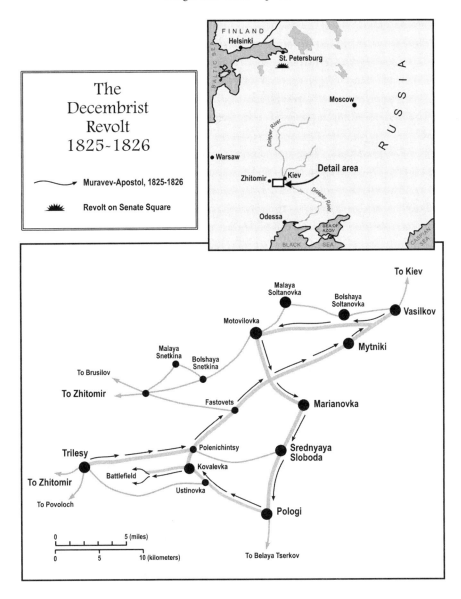

freedom. . . . Q: What does Holy Scripture enjoin the Russian people and the Russian army to do? A: To repent of their age-old servility and, taking up arms against tyranny and misery, swear: let there be for everyone a single Tsar in heaven and on earth—Jesus Christ." After reciting passages on the monarchy's misuse of the church and deception of the people, the priest ended with the catechistic reply to the question, "What then should the Christ-loving Russian army do?"

In order to liberate their suffering families and their country and to fulfill the sacred Christian law, it must say a heartfelt and hopeful prayer to
God who fights for justice and visibly protects those who staunchly put
their trust in Him; it must join together and take up arms against tyranny and restore faith and liberty in Russia. And on whoever who stays
behind, as on Judas the Traitor, let there be a curse and anathema.[3]

Muraviev-Apostol, like Riego, put family and country as the objects of salvation.
He told the troops that henceforth they should serve the heavenly tsar and not
the earthly one. The soldiers responded with cheers. In spite of the curse at the
end of the catechism, their commander then, like his Spanish model, offered the
chance for dissenters to drop out of the formation and remain in Vasilkov. At that
moment, none did so. Muraviev's breathtaking plan was to gather more units,
engage any foe sent against him, and march via Kiev and Moscow to the capital,
where he would install a revolutionary government. By one account, when he
gave the command to march out of town, the men fell in behind him with flags
unfurled and broke into song. Some townspeople saw them off, shouting, "May
God assist you!"[4] The insurgents rode through several towns and villages from
December 31, 1825, to January 3, 1826. Though this four-day march into the
jaws of defeat hardly constituted an epic, the journey lasted longer and was richer
in movement, action, and battle than the more famous rising on Senate Square.

How could a seasoned officer such as Sergei Muraviev-Apostol have believed
that success was within reach? The answer brings us back to the onset of the
revolutionary era in Spain. A few days earlier, after being released by his comrades from arrest, Muraviev-Apostol, referring to Rafael del Riego, told them
that the Spanish officer had "crossed the country with three hundred men and
restored the constitution. So how could [we] fail to accomplish our mission
when all is in readiness, especially the army which is rife with discontent."[5] Years
later, D. K. Petrov, one of the few Russian scholars conversant with the Spanish
side of things, stressed Muraviev-Apostol's decisiveness and the boldness of his
struggle for a constitution by way of forced marches. "The Decembrists," he
wrote, "in their dreams and conversations loved to compare themselves to Riego,
but only one of them actually resembled the Spanish hero closely. That was S. I.
Muraviev-Apostol."[6]

The Tsar Faces South

Some historians have made an enigma of Tsar Alexander I. Contemporary Europeans often "orientalized" him for his alleged "Asian cunning," though he was a
fluent French-speaker of mostly German blood who saw himself as one of the

European brotherhood of kings. Unlike the frivolous despots and nauseating hypocrites Fernando and Ferdinando, Alexander could and did say truthfully that he once shared the values and ideals of the men who would try to overthrow him. Certainly more intricate and interesting than the Spanish and Neapolitan monarchs, Alexander, like many complex people, brimmed with contradictions and obsessions that changed with the passage of years and the rush of events. A certain psychic malaise went back to his youth, when he had been subject to the tension between his father, Tsar Paul, and his grandmother Catherine the Great, and to his ambiguous role in the assassination of his father.

No simple line divided the early reforming tsar from the reactionary one of Alexander's later years. Like Hamlet, he felt perpetually rent by conflict and "plagued by doubts and suspicions." In domestic and foreign policy, his own insecurities pulled him between ideals and his view of realities. Shifts and ambivalence arose from the constant struggle between his belief in both enlightenment and stability.[7] Empress Catherine II had urged her grandson to be, among other things, *liberal'nyi*, probably meaning open to reason and compromise. Early in his reign Alexander wrote a troubled missive to one of his advisors: "Incredible disorder reigns in our affairs. There is stealing on all sides. All branches of the government are poorly administered. There is order nowhere and meanwhile the empire strives only to extend its borders. In such a state of things, it is hardly possible for one person to administer a state, and all the more correct the deeply rooted abuses."[8] With a few minor tweaks, these same complaints can be found in the writings of many of the Decembrists.

Alexander's Swiss republican childhood tutor La Harpe had planted seeds of liberalism that grew in the environment of his companions in reform. In the first years of his reign, the tsar promoted progressive measures and made a few major reforms in government structures and university life and minor ones in serf-master relations. In 1808, when in Spain the idea of a constitution was still germinating, Alexander set his minister Mikhail Speranskii to fashion one for Russia. About a decade later, in a speech to the Polish Diet, the tsar made an elliptical reference to Russia getting a constitution also, and then in 1819 ordered one drafted by an official from his reforming days. These schemes came to naught, yet hope for a Russian constitution persisted among those who witnessed what one scholar called the tsar's "constitutional Saturnalia"[9] in Europe. Alexander, fascinated by acts of statesmanship no less than Napoleon, combined a sense of his own awesome power with the equivalent belief in his benevolence. The persisting dreams of youth turned him into a perennial constitutionalist right up to the year 1820. This towering autocrat played a major role, sometimes with the aid of his foreign minister Capodistria, in planting or endorsing constitutional rule from the Atlantic and the Mediterranean to the Adriatic and Baltic Seas.

The first such gesture took place in the Ionian Islands in 1803–6 and then in Sardinia. In 1812 Alexander recognized the Spanish constitution. When peace descended, he favored the French Charte of 1815 that created an elected parliament and made the restored Bourbon a constitutional monarch. The tsar also encouraged constitutions in the Germanies. When in 1813 he sent Capodistria to set up a Swiss confederation with a new constitution, he told him: "You love republics, and so do I."[10] Closer to home, in spite of the nearly hundred thousand Poles who had accompanied the Grand Army of Napoleon into Russia in 1812, the tsar presented Poland in 1815 with a constitution for a kingdom within the Russian Empire that allowed the inhabitants use of their own language for official business; established an army, a civil service, and a court system; and provided for habeas corpus, an independent press, and religious freedom. The bicameral Diet had no power to initiate legislation, and the tsar, as king of Poland, retained a veto right over its resolutions and could prorogue it at will. Yet it was elected biennially by something between 106,000 and 116,000 voters in a population of about 2.5 million. In France only 80,000 of 25 million citizens voted under the Charte.[11] For the Grand Duchy of Finland, recently wrested from Sweden in war, the tsar confirmed its eighteenth-century corpus of laws, which provided at least a good deal of autonomy.

Alexander's promotion of constitutions from above created a protective shield against the potentially restless furies of the European masses and their ideological leaders, a familiar top-down approach of many conservative statesmen. The imposition of representative government in those places where it was new rather than restored followed the Russian traditions of reform from above, dating back at least to Peter the Great. In this sense, Alexander's constitutional orgy is one of the first examples—and far from the last—of Russian statecraft impinging on the domestic politics of other nations. But the capstone of Alexander's constitutionalizing—becoming a constitutional monarch himself in Poland—illustrates how he differed from other conservative statesmen who abhorred parliaments altogether, even those imposed from above.

The distinction did not impress the tsar's Decembrist critics. Might they have withdrawn their animus had he granted a constitution to Russia in these years? For them, the fact remained that a whole array of peoples won more political rights than those possessed by Russians. Much of Europe applauded that fact. After 1812 the Russian emperor seemed to radiate an aura of sacred hero and redeemer. His February 1813 proclamation in Germany of his role as the agent of liberation from Napoleonic oppression was infused with religious rhetoric. The Spanish liberals saw him in this light. A eulogizing versifier at Oxford called Alexander "the pure and steadfast ray of Freedom's morning star."[12]

Tsar Alexander's excursions into state building assume a stark irony when set against his reaction to the revolutionary wave of constitutionalism in the 1820s.

Observers then and later were puzzled by the drive of a "reactionary" to sponsor in so many places elections and parliamentary life. Historian Giuseppe Berti, like some other students of the era, offered the too simple explanation that Alexander's "reforms were for him more an object of self-indulgent talk than a real political objective."[13] Alexander I was never really a liberal in the early nineteenth-century sense of the word, but he did not abandon his own brand of reform until 1820. Opposed to constitutions wrested spontaneously from below by "the people" led by secret societies and revolutionaries, Tsar Alexander offered them prudentially—as gifts from a benevolent donor to deserving peoples.

The tsar began to hear alarm bells in the years before 1820—and they were not all rung by Prince Metternich. Scholars long conducted a rather unreal debate about the scale of the Austrian chancellor's influence on the tsar. To take only one school of thought, some of the early Italian writers on the Risorgimento quite naturally floated the notion that their nemesis Metternich turned the "liberal" Alexander into a reactionary. Giuseppe Berti, though exaggerating Alexander's hypocrisy, argued persuasively against this one-sided position, as have many other scholars. Alexander's shift to intervention, he wrote, was due not only to Metternich: "In reality a hundred motives, and above all pressing concerns of domestic politics, propelled the tsar into renouncing that snare for the unwary,"[14] that is, his constitutional dreams. More specifically, the eruption of "popular" constitutions eventually turned him against all constitutions. One of his officials, Alexandre Stourdza, claimed at the time that his master's actions were driven by his "own fears and anxieties" rather than by Metternich's warnings and inventions.[15] Metternich's input cannot be dismissed altogether, but motives other than the Austrian chancellor's famous charm or logic drove the tsar to side with him.

By 1815 Alexander had become seized by triumphal pride and a sense of mission, overlain with pious religiosity induced partly by his association with Baroness Julie de Krüdener. Scholars and contemporaries saw proof of Alexander's descent to political and even geopolitical mysticism in his brainchild, the Holy Alliance. Conservative cynics smirked at it; liberals saw it as a warrant for counterrevolution. Alexander himself seems to have conceived it as a benevolent and even progressive instrument. He felt a powerful urge, reinforced by an inner spiritualism, to save Europe from the folly and terror of 1789 and Bonapartist imperialism. He believed that the Holy Alliance would provide such a firm barrier of European security against revolution that even constitutions could be granted and spread.[16] The founding document spoke of Christian justice, charity, and peace. Metternich made some revisions in the final version, but it was Alexander I's original that was read out on the anniversary of its adoption to congregations all over Russia from 1815 until his death.[17]

The emperor's repressive impulses continued to cohabit with his moderately progressive ones. In an 1818 speech to the Polish Diet, he warned of "subversive doctrines which today menace the social system with a terrifying catastrophe." Where he saw them is not quite clear. But in 1819 he became fearful of "revolutionary rumbling" and alarmed by the murder by a German nationalist student, Karl Sand, of the dramatist August von Kotzebue, a part-time political informer for Russia. When the relatively liberal foreign minister Capodistria went on leave to Corfu in 1818–19, his influence declined for a time.[18] The year 1820 brought political firestorms around the Mediterranean that created anxieties in and out of Russia. In January the Spanish officers rose in revolt in Cadiz. In February a republican in Paris assassinated the Duc de Berry, heir to the throne of France. In July Neapolitan rebels emulated those of Spain. The tsar's obsession with the evil of a recently defeated foe who had ravaged his country blinded him to the doings of malodorous restored monarchs in Spain and Naples. When revolts erupted in those countries, Alexander—out of deep-seated fear and under the influence of recent events—donned the mask of counterrevolution. Planting a Charte on the French people was one thing. The revolts in Spain and Naples and elsewhere involved a military initiative and the coercion of the monarch.

The rapid succession of changes in the two Bourbon kingdoms in 1820 and their apparent similarities raised the anxiety level of European power brokers. Naples became the first to attract a strike force from the Holy Alliance. But intervention was no foregone conclusion. The Russian tsar played a complicated hand in postwar Italy. His diplomats did sponsor anti-Austrian activity in Italy in the post-Vienna years, mostly to counterbalance Austrian power and promote moderate reform, not to advance liberal revolts—though Russians on the ground delivered mixed signals. One envoy in Italy believed that reform and not brute force would weaken the Carbonari.[19] But the Russian ambassador to Piedmont showed such sympathy to the secret societies that he was transferred and, after the rising of 1820, forced to retire.[20] Even some Carbonari considered the tsar a kind of patron and allegedly met with Russian agents. When Capodistria visited Italy in 1819, Metternich suspected him, based on overheated reports, of supporting the Carbonari.[21]

After the 1820 liberal triumph in the Kingdom of Naples, a fog of conflicting information and misinformation about it oozed through European chanceries. One eyewitness, a colonel in Russian service, described the overturn as quiet and bloodless, and Count N. Pahlen believed the new regime had won unanimous support of all social classes.[22] Eventually the negative outweighed the positive. The July uprising, ostensibly copied from the Spanish experience, generated fear of an international plot to overturn thrones and spread the venom of revolution. The Russian conservative Fedor Rostopchin warned in August that the new governments in Naples and Spain threatened Russia and needed to be uprooted.[23] Reports by the Russian mission in Naples on the spread of Carbonarism and secret societies in Russia were passed on to the tsar. In September one of them spoke of Carbonari infiltration of the Austrian army and of "links among Jacobins of all shades in all countries."[24] Along with other powers, the imperial Russian court refused to receive the new Neapolitan ambassador, and for good measure Russian art students on scholarship in Rome were put under surveillance, lest they be attracted to the Italian liberal movements.[25]

Unnerved by this information, the Concert of Europe convened at Troppau in the fall of 1820. Since the Neapolitan drama was unrolling uncomfortably close to Austria's Italian sphere of influence, Metternich assumed the lead. Tsar Alexander, for his part, on October 23 (NS) wrote to a Russian princess that he had reread Chapter 2 of the *Apocalypse* and that he and his colleagues were seeking "a remedy against *the empire of evil* which is spreading rapidly and by every *occult means* used by the *satanic spirit* directing it."[26] In November he told the chair of the State Council, I. V. Vasil'chikov, that the conference would take measures against "the fires lapping at the south of Europe" by intervening in Naples with a force that would serve as a legitimate escort to a legitimate monarch seeking back his throne, and that this would also have a decisive effect on Spain and Portugal.[27]

The key domestic event shaping the tsar's support for intervention in Naples was the October mutiny of the Semenovskii Regiment, a much honored and decorated unit of 1812 veterans and the tsar's favorite. Its commander in 1820, Colonel Schwartz, a fierce martinet, employed excessive cruelty and arrogance toward his men by subjecting them to unprecedented humiliation and physical punishment. The "mutiny" was an organized non-political complaint about their commander. But politicized elements attached themselves to it and radical proclamations denounced not only army abuses but noble serf-owners and even the tsar. Like their Spanish colleagues in this very year, some Russian officers opposed draconian discipline and sided with their defiant men in the dispute. Though the officers opposed a revolt at this point and tried to end the mutiny peacefully, they were blamed for it. Transferred to other units, some of them formed the nuclei of the Decembrist conspiracy in the south. Miniature copycat disorders broke out in other units from 1820 onward, peaking in 1825.[28] When and how to elevate mutiny into insurrection remained a burning issue in Decembrist tactical debates.

During the Semenovskii mutiny, an anonymous inflammatory leaflet scattered among troops in the capital blamed all Russia's evils on the tyrannical tsar and the nobility and demanded their overthrow and the establishment of a representative government.[29] The linking of a parliament with the military against an absolute monarch suggested alarming parallels with the recent outbreaks in southern Europe. Viktor Kochubei, minister of interior and Russia's chief policeman, spoke with a colleague in November about the growth of Russian secret societies whose revolutionary aspirations would unleash a reign of barbarism and murder in Russia resembling the Mongol invasion of the thirteenth century. He worried about the "many empty-headed young people who were attracted by news of the events in Spain and Naples and would wish, if one can believe their windy speeches, to do something similar here." Kochubei censored details of the Neapolitan revolution that might induce "an undesirable mood among the army officers."[30] *Messenger of Europe* and *Neva Observer* added venom to their coverage of the Italian overturn. The latter dubbed the Carbonari a "horrible sect" of criminals who aspired to destroy order and bring on chaos.[31]

The Semenovskii mutiny, though the largest, was only one of more than a dozen or so in the years 1821–25. Other forms of disorder, including petitions and riots, began earlier. A large-scale revolt in the Military Settlements at Chuguev in 1819 had to be subdued violently by regular troops under the reactionary Count Aleksei Arakcheev, the tsar's chief minister. Factory serfs seethed with unrest from 1817 through the early 1820s, with one of the uprisings, in 1823, being crushed by more than twenty-five hundred government troops. In 1820 came industrial strife in Perm, a Don Cossack rising, and fighting in Ekaterinoslav Province.[32] Metternich, in order to heighten the tsar's anxiety, wrote him in August that the unrest on the Don was triggered by Russian knowledge of the Neapolitan overturn.[33]

News of the turmoil in Russia arriving at Troppau in November gave final shape to Tsar Alexander's hostility to the Neapolitan constitutional regime. Organizing intervention, however, caused division among the powers. The Austrians, backed by Prussia, wanted action as soon as feasible. Alexander and Capodistria preferred joint to unilateral Austrian intervention, when and if needed. Capodistria agreed that the king of Naples should be returned to his throne peacefully, not aided "by a roaring cannon or by an Austrian bayonet tinged with Neapolitan blood." The tsar, still clinging to the notion of imposing suitable constitutions, and seconded by Capodistria, favored a Charte-like constitution for Naples and its restored king. This was rejected.[34] The three eastern powers met with King Ferdinando at Laibach and made the decision to intervene, with an Austrian army as the invasion force and a Russian corps in reserve.[35] The tsar recalled General Ermolov from the Caucasus to head up the force. Ermolov fell ill and arrived at Laibach after it was all over.[36]

During and after the crushing of the Austrian intervention in Italy, his officials assured the Russian emperor of its wisdom. Governor-General Filippo Paulucci of the Baltic provinces, a Piedmontese by origin, wrote to him in April 1821 of people in those provinces "whose spirits have become excited by widespread constitutional ideas and the revolutions in southern Europe, and who admire the conduct of military men who assume the role of lawmakers of their countries."[37] Vasil'chikov reported that "the news about the Piedmontese revolution has generated the greatest sensation here, my dear friend. Reasonable men are in despair, but the vast majority of youth is delighted with what has transpired and do not hide their way of thinking."[38] The *Messenger of Europe* celebrated the crushing of the Neapolitan constitution by printing in translation a French royalist diatribe claiming that the Neapolitan revolt had been a criminal venture enjoying no popular support.[39] Lingering fear of the Carbonari proved useful in justifying repressive actions at home. In August 1822, when interior minister Kochubei ordered the shutting down of all Masonic lodges, Senator E. A. Kushelev wrote to the tsar denouncing the Masons and noting that "in many kingdoms, especially in the Kingdom of Naples and other Italian lands, secret sects and societies, particularly Carbonari sects, had given rise to freethinking, revolutions, uprisings, and bloodshed."[40]

The tsar was caught by surprise and embarrassed by the Ypsilanti expedition, which began while Habsburg legions were marching through Italy.[41] Given the moment, it is hardly astonishing that by the spring of 1821 Tsar Alexander was looking darkly at an anti-Ottoman rebellion in the Balkans and in Greece. Though Russia severed relations with the Ottoman Porte after the hanging of the Greek patriarch, it took no military action. Rather, Alexander came to believe that the Semenovskii mutiny and the Spanish, Neapolitan, and Greek revolts all sprang from the same source: European secret societies with a conspiratorial center in Paris. In August 1822 the tsar told the French ambassador, La Ferronais, that of all the revolutionary plots then afoot, the Greek rising, with its "criminal aspirations," had been the most cunningly prepared.[42]

Two of the tsar's most loyal officials tried to disabuse their master of his simplistic linkage of Greece with insurgent Spain and Naples. Capodistria denounced Ypsilanti's adventure but then supported the Greeks once the bloodshed began to take its toll on them. He hoped that the tsar would be provoked into occupying the principalities of Moldavia and Wallachia and pulling the other powers into a war for Greek independence. Capodistria echoed many who saw in the Christian Greek struggle against the Turks an anti-Islamic crusade comparable to Russia's own breaking of the Mongol yoke in the fifteenth century.[43] But he was reassigned in May 1822 and his influence quickly waned.[44] Alexandre Stourdza, Ypsilanti's cousin and a devout monarchist, vigorously refuted the tsar's view of the Greeks. It was impossible, he argued, to equate their rising with those in Spain and Naples, where citizens had rebelled against a lawful monarch. The Greeks, in contrast, were fighting "for their lives, their property, and their faith."[45] These arguments fell on deaf ears.

Greek and Russian residents of Odessa were outraged to the point of war fever by the execution of the patriarch. The Russian government sent an ultimatum ordering the Porte to restore the ruined churches and punish the killers of the Orthodox prelate; when this went unanswered, it severed relations with the Ottoman Empire in July 1821 but did not go to war. Negotiations stumbled on until 1825, when the tsar, recognizing that his people were pressuring for war, began to experience a turnaround and considered using force against the Turks to bring about a settlement. The tsar apparently believed the stories of a Turko-Egyptian "de-Hellenization" or "barbarization project." France and Austria withheld support for the tsar, and he told his diplomats that he would no longer work with the Austrian chancellor.[46] What might have happened if Alexander had gone further in the summer of 1825 and sent troops into Greece? Would the Decembrists have rallied to him and modified their ambitions? As things played out, the tsar died two years before Russia intervened.

Russia's policy in Spain in the 1820s became a burning issue between the Decembrist rebels and their sovereign. Their esteem for the Spanish, shared by many educated Russians, originally sprang from the Napoleonic occupation of the Iberian Peninsula. Curiosity had been quickened by news items, political tales, and capsule histories sold in bookstores that heightened the admiration.[47] According to what police snoops heard in salons, coffee shops, and merchant circles, the French occupation of Spain in 1808 reinforced a widespread discontent in Russia with the Tilsit treaty in which Tsar Alexander allied with Napoleon in 1807. A. Ia. Bulgakov, a high-ranking opponent of Tilsit, former envoy to Spain, and a longtime admirer of Spanish culture, contrasted Spain's resistance to Russia's apparent appeasement. When the Spanish general Palafox in 1809 sent a defiant letter to Marshal Lefebvre refusing to surrender, Bulgakov, in an ecstasy he claimed was shared by many, wrote in his diary: "What a nation are these Spaniards!"[48]

Guerrilla warfare had a particular appeal to some professional soldiers, such as Staff Captain P. S. Kaisarov. As early as February 1811 he praised the "undisciplined militias" of Spain and implied their relevance for Russia in case of an invasion.[49] The more famous Denis Davydov, poet and a partisan leader in 1812, though no radical, had friends among the Decembrists. His lengthy 1821 retrospective essay on partisan war lauded the Spanish guerrillas: "Their activity in 1809 will serve as an example to every unit commander of how one must use the local terrain where combat occurs and direct the fury of the peasants rising up in vengeance." He stressed emotion, hatred, a passion for independence, and the "*organized disorder* of armed inhabitants in a kind of war—more than any other—marked by the Spaniards' indomitable nature and the local situation." The gorges of the Spanish highlands, he wrote, "concealed in their depths the keen-eyed, intrepid, and fearless fighters whose glory is indelibly printed in all the chronicles and in all hearts that beat for their fatherland."[50] The author singled out two legendary guerrilla leaders, El Empecinado and Espoz y Mina, the first of whom would be executed in Spain a few years after Davydov's essay appeared.

Russians who had served in Spain spoke of a new kind of war, as did figures of all political stripes. In February 1812 the liberal La Harpe pointed to Spain as a model for a people's war. He said to the tsar: "Look, my sovereign, at Spain and Portugal! These important recent examples convincingly demonstrate what courage, persistence, and energy can do against superior forces."[51] Conservatives Fedor Rostopchin and Admiral Shishkov dwelt on Spanish spirit and bravery in their fight against enslavement. The latter wrote of "the bright never-to-be-extinguished spark of Liberty"[52]—a word that was constantly conflated with "liberation" from the Napoleonic yoke. In January 1812 Tsar Alexander wrote to a Spanish representative that the drawing away of Napoleonic forces northward would help Spain.[53] Yet that very deployment soon pitted the tsar's troops against Spaniards, joined by Portuguese and Italians, on the battlefields of Russia.

Russians not only praised the Spanish mode of warfare but invoked it as a model for Russian resistance. A few months before the 1812 French assault on Russia, a high-ranking staff officer urged that the "people must be armed and incited, as in Spain, with the aid of the clergy."[54] A Russian army bulletin of late September informed the troops that "this war is becoming a popular one resembling the struggle in Spain. Russian peasants, armed with pikes, encircle the French, who are plundering and defiling churches."[55] Indeed, similarities became apparent, down to the level of cruelty—though this was often reciprocal. Like guerrillas in Spain, Russian peasants committed unspeakable atrocities on French prisoners.[56] The guerrilla craze reached the Russian theater by way of an 1813 heroic drama, *The Kirilovites, or Enemy Invasion*—using a play on the Russian name Kiril and the word "guerrilla"—complete with chorus, ballet, and battle scenes. In one episode the peasant partisan leader named Strong, using a bit of folk etymology, tells Brigadier Goodthoughts why his men are called *kirilovtsy*: "In some distant land which our enemy is also ravaging, all the inhabitants, young and old, who are rising against them also call themselves kirilovites [*kirilovtsy*, or guerrillas]. . . . Our Russian kirilovites, following the example of the Spanish, are teaching a lesson to the uninvited guests."[57]

"Partisan war," an elastic term, in its original sense indicated actions by a party or part of a unit, a detachment, as in "a party of sappers." Or it could mean civilians fighting, sabotaging, or harassing an occupying or invading force (or its stragglers)—alone or in conjunction with the military. The Russian term *partizan* was used in 1812 in all these ways. Regular troops, militia, Cossacks, and peasants engaged in it. As in the Spanish case, peasants exhibited no developed patriotic mentality; rather they acted to defend home and Orthodox religion and to wreak revenge for depredations.[58] As in Spain also, the clergy high and low thundered against Napoleon as the Horned Beast and urged peasants to kill prisoners. When Russian peasants captured an ethnically mixed group of enemy troops, they informed their prisoners how they had been told that the invaders had come as Antichrists to smash their icons. The Spanish and Italian captives were particularly pained on hearing this.[59]

A few days after the June invasion, the tsar wrote to Barclay: "I hope that on this occasion we show as much energy as the Spaniard."[60] In July the Russians went beyond the rhetoric of a common goal and signed the Treaty of Velikie Luki, which recognized the Spanish constitution of 1812, the very instrument that Tsar Alexander would come to hate. At Tsarskoe Selo on April 20, 1813, the new Alejandro Regiment, comprising Spanish prisoners of war, attended mass at a field altar and, in the Spanish manner, paraded past a portrait of King Fernando VII. The special envoy to Russia, Don Eusebio Bardaxi, announced that the king and the Cortes would guarantee all Spaniards civic freedom. Zea Bermúdez then read out a few articles of the constitution of 1812 and ordered the troops to swear fealty to it. The men knelt and shouted, "Long live Fernando VII, long live the nation and the constitution." After the ceremony, the dignitaries toasted the Spanish Cortes, the allied crowned heads, and the military leaders of Russia and Spain, including Spaniards such as Espoz y Mina.[61] Thus in 1813, Spanish officials on Russian soil, in swearing the oath, did what their colleagues had done at Cadiz a year earlier and what Riego's followers and his king would do seven years later.

From the summer of 1812, Russian interest also extended to the new Spanish regime and elicited a flurry of comparisons between the two countries.[62] French and Russian translations of the 1812 constitution appeared in print, and one of the 1808 Spanish catechisms was published in *Son of the Fatherland*.[63] According to Faddei Bulgarin, an alert observer, excerpts from this or other Spanish catechisms appeared at the time in many journals and other places and in his own memoirs of Spain.[64] From 1812 to 1814 a kind of spiritual brotherhood emerged between the Spanish and the Russian resistance to Napoleonic tyranny, as well as a mutual sympathy between the Russian autocracy and a Spanish constitutional monarchy, legitimized by official treaty and ceremonial oaths and blessed by public opinion.

But when Fernando VII returned from exile in 1814 and rescinded the constitution, that bond was broken. While the Russian press for a time condemned Fernando's coup, Tsar Alexander withdrew recognition of the constitution and banned its publication.[65] The emperor made no comment on this except to tell the Spanish king that the long and bloody war against Napoleon had been about the return of legitimate rulers.[66] In 1822 the Russian foreign minister, Count Nesselrode, replying to Spaniards' criticism of the about-face, displayed cynical contempt for their belief in the Velikie Luki treaty. He offered an acid comment on the constitution of 1812 and a feeble and mendacious argument that the treaty recognizing it had been based on the needs of war and not on a principle of diplomacy. There had been no other government in Spain to ally with at the time, he asserted, and so when King Fernando returned to power, previous agreements lost their force.[67]

Yet Spanish liberals in 1820 found it hard to believe that their former ally would support an intervention. Their diplomats worked strenuously for approval. In April 1820 the envoy in St. Petersburg brought a letter to Nesselrode from King Fernando, playing the game of temporary compliance, reminding the tsar of the 1812 treaty. In June he wrote to Alexander that he was "never freer than on the day I took the oath of loyalty to the constitution."[68] The radical Cortes deputy Moreno Guerra declared that this document was "the same as that which in 1812 was solemnly published on the shores of the Neva." An optimist in San Miguel's *El espectador* in early 1821 asserted that the tsar would not intervene in Spain because he was occupied with Balkan events.[69] *El constituciónal* in April 1820 went so far as to call Alexander I "a great monarch, an ardent defender of constitutions" who would threaten the governments of Austria and Prussia with the dissolution of the Holy Alliance if they failed to fulfill their promises for "liberal systems."[70]

In 1820–23 Tsar Alexander and his envoys pursued a tortured policy in Spain that included support of Fernando as autocrat, pallid attempts to curb his more repressive policies, and an on-again, off-again determination to intervene. At times the tsar's discomfort at the incursion of the Spanish military into politics, the occasional violence, and the perceived incidents of disrespect for the king made Russia for a time the most hostile of the powers to the new Spanish regime. Count Nesselrode worried that the new government could not keep in check the "revolutionary 'volcano.'"[71] On May 2, 1820, he delivered to Zea Bermúdez a sharp note, written by Capodistria and reflecting the tsar's concerns, criticizing the Spanish constitution, condemning the revolt, and hinting that the powers might take some action.[72]

The revolt in Naples in July, which seemed to be copying Riego's exploit, fed the Great Powers' anxiety over Spain. By the time of the Laibach conference, Alexander I was declaring Spain to be "the tribune to which all the revolutionists of Europe have recourse, as to a vehicle from which they can disseminate their pernicious doctrine."[73] Through 1821, Alexander sent King Fernando via his ambassador assurances of friendship and offers of armed assistance.[74] When the Madrid government turned leftward under Martínez de la Rosa in 1822, the tsar called for an international army to intervene.[75] A major Russian organ, *Messenger of Europe* joined the anti-liberal chorus denouncing the "shirtless ones" and the "well-known troublemaker" Riego and comparing the exodus of Spanish émigrés escaping horrors to those who fled from Robespierre's terror.[76]

The new Russian envoy in Madrid, Count M. N. Bulgari, a nephew of the Phanariot turned Russian poet and official Antiokh Kantemir, became the tsar's chief source of intelligence. Bulgari could not make up his mind. In March 1820 he reported ambiguously that the Spanish constitution offered some good, but much bad as well, though he hoped that it might save the monarchy from those threatening it. The constitution, he thought, had brought both order and widespread joy but would also require a long and painful process. He warned that if the European powers exerted force to preserve the monarchy unchanged, this might spell the end of the Spanish throne.[77] Tsar Alexander adopted a tactic of wait and see, cooperation with the new regime, and secret plotting with the king on the possibility of sending an army into Spain. After the royalist putsch in Madrid in July 1822 and the subsequent turmoil in the country, Russian hostility to the regime sharpened. In August the tsar expressed alarm but blamed the clumsy Spanish counterrevolutionaries who were worsening the king's situation. He feared that a French intervention might induce violence akin to the anti-Napoleonic struggle and might also make the Spanish revolution "contagious."[78]

As with Naples, the Russian emperor, either on his own or at the suggestion of Metternich, linked Russian domestic unrest to the events in Spain.[79] Some months after the Spanish rising, Stepan Gushchevarov (or Gushevarov), a company clerk in a St. Petersburg Jaeger Guards regiment, offered while tipsy a garbled comparison, asserting that if the Semenovskii affair was not settled in favor of the mutineers, "all the Guards will rise up and make a revolution. This is not Spain. Over there, it's the peasants and lower-class people who rebel, and they can be pacified. But here all the Guards will revolt." Gushchevarov was sent to the Schlüsselburg Fortress prison and later reassigned. This and other incidents constituted evidence to Russian officials of foreign instigation and the harmful effects of press coverage of Spain and of officers talking in front of their men.[80]

By the time of the last counterrevolutionary congress at Verona in late 1822, Tsar Alexander had become convinced of the need for intervention in Spain. On the eve of the invasion, not happy at the exclusive assignment of the French, he offered to ready his own force on the Polish frontier to assist in case of need.[81] This was declined and the French marched into Spain alone. Their triumph there did not gain popularity in Russia, particularly among those who likened it to the Napoleonic invasion. To counter this, conservative journalist Faddei Bulgarin stressed the contrast between Angoulême's army of intervention and the invaders of 1808.[82] Bulgarin had fought against the Spanish resistance in the Napoleonic wars and republished a memoir on it in 1823, stressing popular loyalty to King Fernando.[83] Though Bulgarin failed to mention it, several of its guerrilla heroes had been or were to be executed by the restored monarch.

After the dissolution of the liberal regime in Spain, an aura of triumphalism arose in Russia's highest circles. The French ambassador, La Ferronais, gave a lavish ball in October 1823 to celebrate the victory of French arms and the restoration of the absolutist king. The walls were adorned with monograms of the tsar, King Louis XVIII, Fernando, and the Duc d'Angoulême. Beneath the Spanish king's name appeared poetic lines that neatly inverted the rhetoric of tyranny and freedom that the defeated rebels had employed:

> Freed from your shackles, Vanquisher of tyrants
> Heaven reserves, O Ferdinand, a prosperous fate for thee.
> Your people will find anew a father in their king
> Just as you will again find in your subjects your children.[84]

Cognitive dissonance divided the Spanish and Neapolitan moderate constitutionalists from the intervening powers. The former, with a few exceptions, wished their countries to become peaceful and stable members of the European community. The latter came to see an inevitable slide from the 1789 constitutional monarchy in France to two decades of military slaughter, ruined cities, and toppling hierarchies and traditions. An inexorable lunge into horror, they feared, would happen to other constitutional regimes brought into being by rebel forces. The tsar, while still clinging to top-down constitutional dreams for other peoples, had undergone a fundamental shift in his view of humanity. In prior times he had occasionally evinced a broad verbal commitment to enlightened humanitarianism. At the Aix-la-Chapelle congress of the Great Powers in 1818, the Russian emperor, speaking about the slave trade, had referred to Africans as "men capable of being brought to as high a degree of proficiency as any other Men."[85] But after the uprisings of 1820, he told the French ambassador that constitutions would work for advanced nations but—referring to Spain, Portugal, and Italy—were not appropriate for the "ignorant peoples of both peninsulas."[86]

The close interrelationship and apparent similarity in inspiration of the 1820s revolts frightened Alexander I, who imagined an interlocking conspiracy that menaced orderly civilization. Did one exist? Often cited as the only "evidence" for such a center is a letter in the Madrid archives from General Ballesteros to Lafayette of August 1, 1821, calling for the coordination of revolutionaries in all countries and the spurring of secret societies in Russia.[87] In fact, dozens of such letters circulated from France, Britain, Spain, and other places—though none name a "central headquarters." Many activists in Spain and Naples, republicans among them, wished to extend liberalism all over Europe and overthrow absolute monarchies. Some of these plans, however, were driven by the fact of intervention already accomplished in the Italian states in early 1821.

By 1826, the armed forces of the French, Austrians, and Russians had divided up the counterrevolutionary labor by suppressing revolts. Though it was his successor and brother Nicholas I who dealt with the Decembrists, Emperor Alexander I played a key role in the restoration of absolutism in Spain and Naples. That and his refusal to come to the assistance of the insurgent Greeks played a major part in infuriating the Decembrists and feeding their revolutionary longings.

Praetorian Anger, Decembrist Dreams

The Men of December have achieved epic status in Russian history for their attempt to seize power and transform Russia in December 1825 and January 1826 in what is sometimes called the first Russian revolution. After its failure, the authorities arrested hundreds of conspirators—alleged or real. The average age of the 123 who stood trial was 27.4 years.[88] A remarkable cohesion among the rebels derived in part from mutual acquaintance, noble status, and shared service in the Napoleonic wars. Family relationship and military comradeship played a greater role in this conspiracy than in those of the Mediterranean, with their much larger civilian contingents. Bestuzhevs and Bestuzhev-Riumins appeared in both the Northern and Southern Societies, as did members of the Muraviev clan, which also embraced the Muraviev-Apostols, three of whom, brothers, fought in the final Decembrist battle. Major-General N. N. Muraviev and two relatives founded a training course in the Russian army that produced twenty-four Decembrists; and they fathered future leaders of the movement. Some of these, in turn, created a military society with thirty members at its peak, all Guards officers, that fed into the first Decembrist grouping, the Union of Salvation. N. N. Raevskii fathered two Decembrists and two daughters who married Decembrists: Mikhail Orlov and Sergei Volkonskii.[89]

Like Spaniards and Neapolitans in the half decade following the Napoleonic wars, Russian officers of a liberal bent endured their own "restoration" of autocracy and the old order. Their acute malaise paralleled that of Neapolitan officers and the disillusionment felt by Spanish fighters and former prisoners of war toward the "insipid social life" in Madrid.[90] Decembrist Mikhail Fonvizin, nephew of the great writer, summed up the experiences and the grievances of his generation: the contrast of Europe with Russia; abuses at home, especially the bloody repression in the Military Settlements; shame and anger at the tsar's granting of constitutions to other countries but not to Russia; a youthful spirit enhanced by associations with Prussian officers of the Tugendbund, French liberals, and secret societies; and reading about international politics—all of this feeding into a quickly swelling river of political resentment.[91]

Russian officers, the majority from noble landowning and serf-owning families, had grown up in partial awareness of the pathologies of life in their county. But those who had spent years campaigning across central and western Europe had not failed to notice the neatness and prosperity of small towns and farms even after a generation of wartime ravages, and they had imbibed the fresh air of relative efficiency, spontaneous activity, and a certain level of civic freedom. Back home they encountered their opposites almost everywhere. Above all rankled the shame of serfdom, the bondage of half of Russia's men, women, and children to private noble landowners, as well as the spectacle of other rural dwellers liable to state service and living in squalid villages, isolated from civilization. Though many Russian peasants lived better than their counterparts on Spanish holdings and Calabrian latifundia, as serfs, they lacked the juridical freedom of their European counterparts and were locked in a hereditary caste. Mikhail Lunin and many of his Decembrist colleagues deplored the bondage of millions of their compatriots, deprived of civil rights; they also condemned the evils of military settlements, where agriculturalists were enthralled in semi-military service.[92]

As military men, the future conspirators felt a sense of ignominy at conditions in the army. For the lower classes, a virtually lifetime service was so severe that some recruits were known to murder passersby at random along the road—even children—in order to gain prison or exile instead of military duty.[93] Some officers resigned in protest at the dishonorable treatment they and their men received through gross mistreatment or sadistic punishments. After the suppression of the Semenovskii mutiny, reassigned officers from that regiment, including Colonel Sergei Muraviev-Apostol, would provide key leadership in the Southern Society. Hardly any Russian officer remained unaware of the risings and mutinies of the post-1815 years.

During the investigation after the uprising of 1825, the accused often spoke of being politically aroused by official corruption and judicial abuse, hardly unique to Russia, but which Decembrist officers saw as flourishing on a large scale. Aleksandr Bestuzhev told the tsar flatly of his anger that justice had been openly for sale. A. I. Iakubovich, Vladimir Steinhel (Shteingel), and others condemned bribery and arbitrary law enforcement procedures. Peter Kakhovskii wrote to Tsar Nicholas about "the total absence of law and of equity in the judicial process."[94] Others condemned the reactionary policies of Count Arakcheev and the obscurantist repression of thought by anti-intellectual officials such as M. L. Magnitskii who scoured universities for subversion, and by high churchmen such as Archimandrite Fotii, who persecuted Masonic lodges.[95]

Even more rankling was the gap between the actions and the implied promises of Tsar Alexander I during the war of 1812–15. To disillusioned officers returning from it, the general aura of liberation and reform and the European monarchs' slogans about freedom from despotism and aggression now seemed exposed as empty rhetoric. Kakhovskii asserted that during the final campaigns, the wartime leaders "preached freedom to us [and issued] manifestoes, appeals, orders! They deceived us and we, good-hearted folk, believed them, not sparing our blood or treasure." Aleksandr Bestuzhev, while a prisoner of Tsar Nicholas I in 1826, wrote to him that in 1812 "the government itself pronounced the words: 'liberty, liberation!'" as a pendant to the tyranny of Napoleon. Bestuzhev recalled that officers began to ask: "'Did we liberate Europe in order to be draped in its chains? Did we confer a constitution on France so that we dare not talk about it, and did we purchase with our blood preeminence among nations only to be degraded at home?'"[96] Sergei Trubetskoi testified later that, influenced by the granting of the Charte to France, the promises of constitutions to other states, and the freeing of the serfs in the Baltic lands, he felt that the time was ripe for a revolt in Russia.[97]

Like their sovereign, the Decembrists were quick to link domestic with international issues, though reaching different conclusions. The Decembrists' feeling of mortification about the state of their country was amplified by a sense of guilt about their role in liberating Europe, only to see it turned over to reactionary monarchs.[98] Understandably, they failed to discern the immense difference between their notion of liberation and that of the tsar and other European crowned heads who wished to cleanse Europe of Napoleonic occupation and restore a traditional order. Decembrists perceived no nuances in their emperor's policy, but saw rather rank betrayal and ingratitude. Officers who had exhibited exemplary patriotism in battle against Napoleon transformed their love of country into a critique of those who governed it. Wounded national pride, humiliation, and the longing for reform—through a constitution, they hoped—mingled together in their minds,[99] as it did in Riego's and Pepe's.

Notions of self and a predestined role fortified the Decembrists' indignation concerning the condition of Russia. It would be vain to speak of a common Decembrist social mentality. Yet there can be no doubt that many Decembrists indulged the pan-European passion for antiquity with its republics and its martial and civic heroes.[100] Classical learning worked in two ways. At the obvious level, it helped supply the vocabulary of the Decembrists for their support of the Greek patriots of 1821. When combined with a devout religious sensibility, it amplified their commitment to rebellion, sacrifice, and even secular martyrdom.

Tales of the Greco-Roman world and neoclassical works in the original and in translation circulated widely in Russian journals.[101] The cult of the Roman Mucius Scaevola—the hero who had inspired the Nola chapter of the Carbonari—gave rise to a legend about a Russian peasant who, branded on the arm with the Napoleonic monogram, chopped off the offending member. The idea made its way into popular prints and statues during the 1812–13 campaign.[102] Plays featuring struggle against tyrants had seen unimpeded production at the Russian court under the nose of Empress Catherine II in the eighteenth century because she saw her rule as enlightened rather than despotic. The genre was suspended for a while during the French Revolution but revived under Tsar Alexander and harnessed to nationalist propaganda.[103]

The poet Kondratii Ryleev, a Decembrist leader and an emotional man in life and in art, steeped himself in the classics and in their reworking by Voltaire and Racine, which fostered his oft-expressed anticipation of a heroic martyr's death, as in the poem "The Citizen." The Napoleonic invasion raised Ryleev's historical consciousness, which was further fed in the theaters of Paris during the Russian occupation of 1815. Ryleev became known for his florid declamation. He believed that the sacred purpose of poetry was "to remind youth of the deeds of our ancestors, to acquaint it with the brilliant epochs of our history, to bring together love for the fatherland with the first impressions of memory."[104] A personal devotion to "civic courage" led him to choose the words as the title of one of his best-known poems, which cited examples of that recurrent virtue from Russian as well as Greek and Roman history. Verses that glorified the heroic resistance of the Russian medieval prince Vadim of Novgorod and others became in a sense national glosses on classical heroes such as Cato. Ryleev's tales in verse alternated between images of the proud hero in dungeons and chains and the righteous murder of tyrants.[105]

Nikita Muraviev, a leader of the Northern branch of the Decembrists, studied ancient history at the feet of his father and kept Tacitus and Plutarch on his reading desk. Drawing ascetic sensibilities from the classics, he once asked his mother if Cato and Aristides had danced.[106] Lunin's writings contained abundant references to classical figures, especially Greek philosophers and writers who were sent into exile. He loved to quote Cincinnatus and Epaminondas.[107] Kakhovskii discerned a direct link between his bookish heroes and those of his own time. "From childhood, through studying the history of the Greeks and Romans, I became inflamed by the heroes of antiquity. The recent [1820–21] overturn of governments in Europe strongly affected me."[108] Decembrists in the Society of United Slavs took the nicknames "Protagoras," "Scipio," and "Cato," the last widely celebrated for his self-sacrifice in the face of tyranny.[109]

It was a Roman tyrannicide that most captured the Decembrists' imagination. Whether drawn from Plutarch, Shakespeare's *Julius Caesar*, or Voltaire's *Brutus*, the figure of Marcus Junius Brutus (85–42 BCE) loomed over other classical figures as a model—both for his killing of Caesar and for his honorable suicide at Philippi. Ryleev pronounced his name on several occasions, and he also drew on dreams of tyrannicide from Russian history and legend, as in "Rogneda": "With what eagerness I would look at the spurting blood, / With what delight I would look, tyrant, on your corpse!"[110] Alexander Bestuzhev (Marlinskii)—destined to become one of the most popular Russian writers of the early nineteenth century—memorized Shakespeare's Brutus speech.[111] Alexander Pushkin wrote of his friend Peter Chaadaev: "In Rome he would have been a Brutus / In Athens a Pericles. / Here he is a hussar officer."[112] Though neither Pushkin nor Chaadaev joined the Decembrist movement, they shared the admiration for classical heroes with their Decembrist friends. Tsar Alexander himself, who later spoke of the values he had once had in common with the Decembrists, apparently read or possessed a copy of Voltaire's *Brutus*.[113]

Like their Spanish, Italian, and Greek counterparts, most Decembrists clung to or returned to the faith of their fathers.[114] In the eclectic Romantic age, admiration for classical ideals had no intrinsic conflict with religious piety. Many Russian Freemasons, dissatisfied with the ritualism of the Orthodox Church, sought a blend of religious faith and rationalism. In the case of Ryleev, pious evangelism and the classical ideals of patriotism and virtue dwelt harmoniously within his spirit.[115] Baron Andrei Rosen remained a devout Lutheran.[116] Pestel, after a five-year lapse from that faith, returned to it. Sergei Muraviev-Apostol found in faith the key to motivating his men to revolution: later, chained to a fortress wall after the uprising, he found solace in the Bible.

The vaunted legend of the Decembrists predated those woven by their admirers after the suppression; it was fashioned by the revolutionaries themselves as they worked and dreamed of an end. Classical lore and religion fed into intimations of martyrdom. Decembrists and those who wrote about them often, in the words of one scholar, "plotted their life stories as tragedies."[117] Premonitions of mortal sacrifice appeared long before the uprising. According to recorded memory verging on folklore, three Decembrists heard predictions of their fate from the same person. While in Paris after the war, Ryleev went with some comrades to the then famous fortune-teller Mlle. Le Normand. Inspecting his palm, she recoiled in horror and refused to reveal Ryleev's fate. On being pressed, she said: "You will not die a natural death!" When he asked about perishing in battle or in a duel, she said, "No, no, much worse than that; question me no further."[118] To Sergei Muraviev-Apostol, Le Normand allegedly predicted that he would be hanged. He replied: "You must be mistaking me for an Englishman. . . . In Russia we have abolished capital punishment."[119] When the same woman told Lunin that he would be hanged, he replied: "I must do my best to fulfill the prophecy"— one that remained unfulfilled.[120]

How much the conspirators brooded over these alleged predictions of doom remains unknown. But on the day of the rising in the capital, Decembrist Aleksandr Odoevskii with eyes aglow, declared: "We shall die, oh, how gloriously we shall die."[121] Echoing the sentiment, the high-spirited and exalted Ryleev, in one of his displays of romantic anguish, seemed to recognize the nearness of death when he announced that "our chances of success are indeed slim."[122]

The first glimmerings of the Decembrist movement appeared in the secret societies, mostly Masonic or quasi-Masonic lodges similar to those that dotted Europe in that era. Russian lodges took in a broad membership and adopted exotic names, such as Three Virtues and Flaming Star. The first important formation and a precursor of the Decembrist movement proper, the Union of Salvation (1816–17), had a membership of officers and other men mostly of noble rank. One of the latter, Pavel Katenin, did not graduate to active Decembrism. But as an erudite classical scholar and dramatist, he provided in his hymn of revolution one of the earliest expressions of what became the Decembrist language of anti- tyranny:

> Misfortune rules o'er the fatherland,
> Bent to thy yoke, O evil one!
> If despotism oppresses with heavy hand
> We'll oust the tsar and topple his throne!
> Freedom! Freedom! Rule us till the end of days.
> Tremble, tyrant, for thine hour has come.
> Better to die than live as slaves—
> We swear, each and ev'ry one![123]

The successor to the Union of Salvation, the Union of Welfare, modeled itself partly on the Tugendbund or League of Virtue, founded in 1808 by Germans in Königsberg as a patriotic secret society noted for its high moral tone. The Union of Welfare in early 1818 established a kind of central committee called the Root or Core Council and adopted a rambling, authoritarian, and repetitious constitution, the Green Book, derived partly from the Tugendbund, Rousseau, and the New Testament. The new union declined to adopt the more esoteric rituals and oaths of other European secret societies. It lacked the harsh threats to members that some Decembrists would later employ and refrained from the talk of poisons and daggers that characterized Carbonari, the Greek Friendship Society, and some of the Spanish radical clubs. But it did share their moralizing posture. Accepting only Christians of good repute, it exalted virtue and required conformity and obedience enforced by surveillance, informants, shaming, and expulsion. In puritanical tones, the union took aim at literature that had no moral message. It also exhorted members not to free their serfs but to treat them kindly.[124] The union resembled a national charity organization and a reserve army of reformist watchdogs and whistle-blowers. If mobilized and deployed, it would have—in the vision of its organizers—flooded the country with pious teachings. Activists and individualists of a romantic sensibility could not have felt very comfortable amidst the boring ethical and aesthetic constraints of this body.

Due to internal squabbles and fear of the government, which knew about the Union of Welfare, it was fictitiously dissolved in Moscow in January 1821 at the first all-national underground congress ever held in Russia; there would be many more. During the half decade when the early lodges had discussed literary, moral, and welfare-related issues and abstract political affairs, a core of radical elements had emerged. From the Carbonari, they adopted a rule of limited acquaintance with other members. After the union dissolved, almost immediately members and outsiders began organizing new underground societies with greater political ambitions. Shared objectives for the future included some level of political participation, personal security for citizens, judicial reform, and improvement for or emancipation of the serfs. But they divided over crucial issues: How were they to come to power? Would the common people participate in a revolt? What were they to do with the tsar? What kind of a state and society would they create? Out of these concerns and divisions, two distinct revolutionary secret societies were born: the Southern in 1821 and the Northern in the autumn of 1822.

Nikita Muraviev represented the moderate wing of the St. Petersburg Northern Society, which in turn contrasted in its moderation with the Southern Society. But the Northern group, ever shifting in emphasis, harbored some very radical figures who came to sponsor a republic and regicide. Muraviev, chief theoretician and author of its draft constitutions, had studied the political systems of ancient Greece and Rome, France, and Britain. An assiduous researcher, he had an intimate knowledge of the United States federal constitution, which he admired, and those of all its then twenty-three states.[125] His personal library contained works on the Enlightenment, including those by Beccaria and the Neapolitan Filangieri, and on the French Revolution; books on economics by Jean-Baptiste Say, David Ricardo, and James Mill; and political tracts of the Abbé de Pradt, Destutt de Tracy, Benjamin Constant, Louis Bignon, and Bentham. Works dealing with the recent European revolutions included Pecchio's memoirs of liberal Spain, studies of the Cortes, and original and translated editions of the Cadiz constitution; on the Neapolitan revolution by Guglielmo Pepe; and on Greece and the Ottoman Empire.[126] The ideological introduction to Muraviev's first draft rings out like a pronunciamento, critiquing autocracy and making oblique reference to the recent revolutions.: "All the European peoples are gaining laws and freedom. More than any of them, the Russian people deserve to have both."[127]

Muraviev's constitutional drafts of 1821–22 may be fruitfully examined together. They reflect his approving view of American federalism, the division of powers, and checks and balances—though he preferred a constitutional monarchy to an elective presidential system. In the first draft, the Russian nation contained thirteen federal states and two regions, each with a bicameral legislature and the power to tax. The national lawmaking body, the Narodnoe Veche or National Council—the name drawn from medieval terminology—was to be elected indirectly by male property owners, with voting power weighted according to income or wealth. At the top sat a monarch, the emperor. The second draft called for a provisional government of non-Decembrist high officials thought to be sympathetic to the cause, with Prince Sergei Trubetskoi as temporary "dictator." This would usher in a constitutional monarchy along fairly moderate liberal contours. The Narodnoe Veche would comprise a Supreme Duma and a Chamber of National Representatives with power to override the tsar's veto.[128]

All Russians, broadly defined, were to enjoy civil rights—those of legal equality, a free press, a jury system, habeas corpus, free assembly and association, and a more humane prison system, including the end of subterranean dungeons. Those defined as citizens by virtue of gender, age, and property or income status enjoyed political rights—to vote and to be elected. These provisions, together with the abolition of all juridical distinctions of social class and all forms of serfdom, constituted a radical break with the Russian past. So did the clause on religion: toleration was to prevail, and restrictions on Jewish electoral rights were dropped in a later version. Muraviev's constitution would have launched a political transformation of Russia even with its conservative political structures, weighted franchise, and preservation of private landed property for the current owners—the nobility—but would not have solved the peasant problem.

Although Nikita Muraviev did not follow the pattern of Naples, Portugal, and Piedmont in adopting the Spanish unicameral constitution, his projects did share—directly or indirectly through other sources—several features of the Spanish instrument. In one version, article 2 stated, "The source of supreme [or sovereign] power is the people, to whom belongs exclusively the right to make fundamental laws for itself"[129]—a close match to chapter I, article 3 of the Spanish constitution.[130] The latter allowed the monarch a three-time veto power of suspension, whereas Muraviev allowed only two if opponents of a bill could muster sufficient votes. As in the Spanish case, the monarch could be replaced by a regency in case of his physical or mental illness; his powers to make war or cede land were similarly constrained, and he had to take a solemn oath of fidelity to the constitution. Crucially, article 105 mandated that the emperor could not, on pain of abdication, leave the country without permission. This measure was probably prompted by Tsar Alexander's frequent absences in the company of the Holy Alliance.[131] Muraviev might also have had in mind the treasonous journey of Ferdinando of Naples.

On the issue of the people's personal freedom, chapter I, article 1 of Muraviev's second draft almost literally reproduces the Spanish constitution's chapter I, article 2: "The Russian people are [or the Russian nation is] free and independent; they are [or it is] not and cannot be the property of any person or any family." Muraviev's cryptic "I.K." in the footnote clearly shows that he was alluding directly to "Ispanskaia konstitutsiia"—the Spanish constitution.[132] Muraviev's project, like the Spanish one, required for citizenship a knowledge of the country's language within twenty years.

But the two documents also diverged on many issues other than the bicameral and federal structures. Apart from dealing with matters peculiar to Russia—
the military settlements, the Table of Ranks, and serfdom, which were all to be
abolished—the Russian project, in glaring contrast to the intolerant constitution of Catholic Spain, stated that "no one may be disturbed in the exercise of his
religion according to his conscience and feelings, as long as he does not violate
the laws of nature and morality."[133] This decision speaks volumes about the
relative political influence of organized religion in those two societies. So deep
was the power of the Catholic Church in Spain that the liberals, however much
they applauded tolerance, would not dare challenge the confessional monopoly.
The Russian Orthodox Church possessed no Inquisition, and Catherine the
Great had greatly reduced monastic holdings a half century earlier. This is not to
say that, had the Decembrists managed to install a liberal regime, they would not
have faced massive resistance from parts of the clergy.

The acknowledged leader of the Southern Society, Colonel Pavel Pestel (1793–
1826), came of German stock, the noble son of a onetime governor-general of
Siberia.[134] According to the recollections of one of their serfs, the family treated
them very well, gave them land, and forgave arrears.[135] In 1812, as a young officer,
Pavel was wounded at the Battle of Borodino and fought at Leipzig. In September 1818 he was posted to the headquarters of the Second Army at Tulchin, a
village about 250 kilometers southwest of Kiev, the property of the Polish nobleman Count Mieczesław Potocki. There Pestel joined the Union of Welfare.
In November 1821, after the Southern Society had already taken shape, Pestel
gained the rank of colonel and the command of the Viatka Regiment, based in
an awkward location about 60 kilometers north of Tulchin, the Society's headquarters. This region, peopled by Ukrainian peasants, Polish nobles, and Jews,
had few Russian noble families. Though lacking in social amenities, the posting
afforded much opportunity for political talk.[136]

The personality of Pestel, a bachelor, remains enigmatic. No family memoirs
exist. Both contemporary testimony and memory conflict as to his style as a
commanding officer and as leader of the Society: to some he was contentious,
ambitious, cryptic, secretive, Napoleonic, cerebral, and intolerant; to others,
learned, decisive, brave, and a clear and original thinker. Even a close associate,
Sergei Muraviev-Apostol, had moments of opposition to Pestel. Like a much
later authoritarian revolutionary, the Bolshevik Leon Trotsky, Pestel lacked a
personal power base and gave off an aura of arrogance. Another detail links the
two: when Aleksandr Poggio suggested that Pestel would head the Provisional
Government, he replied: "It is difficult for me, having a non-Russian name."[137]
Pestel was well aware of the widely held view of Russian high-ranking officers
with Germanic names as hardheaded disciplinarians.

Pestel rejected the Northern Society's scheme of a constitutional monarchy on a number of grounds. In conversation Pestel voiced republican views as early as the first months of 1820, before news of the Spanish uprising reached Russia. One source of Pestel's republicanism, the first Russian republican constitution, had been written by Mikhail Novikov of the Union of Salvation.[138] But Pestel later testified that his reading of Destutt's *Commentary on Montesquieu* in the spring of 1820 turned him from a constitutional monarchist into a republican since, as his mentor argued, any one-man hereditary rule was bound to become a despotism. Like many republicans, he saw constitutional monarchies as favoring the rich.[139] In Pestel's major project for Russia's future, *Russkaia Pravda* (Russian Justice), voters would periodically elect a Narodnoe Veche and a Duma of five members, and would choose for life members of a Supreme Council meant to oversee the other bodies.

Pestel had a special loathing for serfdom, Russia's biggest social problem, and yet initially he faced it with moderation. The first draft of *Russian Justice* noted the distinction between benevolent and cruel serf owners, exhorted the latter to change their behavior, offered them consultation on the peasant question, and spoke of reaching a "satisfactory conclusion"—the freeing of the serfs—by "only gradual steps" after a period of fifteen years. The second draft decreed immediate emancipation.[140] It also employed more menacing language. The "destruction of slavery and serfdom is enjoined to the Provisional Supreme Administration as its most sacred and unfailing duty." Failure to do this expeditiously would bring eternal shame. In Pestel's world, enemies—including open critics—of serf liberation were to be arrested and punished severely.[141]

Pestel envisioned that after the liberation, privately owned land would be expropriated and combined with state and church lands. Half of the total would be parceled out to the peasants or any tiller of the land; the holdings would be inalienable and reclaimable by the state in case of the user's unlawful activity. The state would dispose of the other half for various purposes. Schemes of state-managed redistribution of land had been in the air since the French Revolution.[142] A somewhat analogous but much less radical half-and-half scheme had been legislated, though never implemented, in liberal Spain in the early 1820s. There, half the municipal lands—the commons—taken over by the state were to be sold, and the other half distributed to ex-soldiers and landless peasants. The amount of Spanish land thus affected and the attendant social upheaval were minuscule compared to the vast scope of Pestel's solution.[143]

Living in a multiethnic state, Decembrists were much attuned to the nationality issue. Many of them, including Aleksandr Odoevskii, Mikhail Bestuzhev, and Sergei Muraviev-Apostol, had to learn Russian as a second language, after French; not to mention those of Baltic German background. Pestel, one of the latter, not only denied Russian provinces autonomy in a federal system, as in Nikita Muraviev's plan, but opposed any kind of autonomy or cultural identity for non-Russian nationalities. In the new order, all national and ethnic groups—Russian or otherwise—would be directly subject to a central state made up of fifty-three provinces. Pestel chose as the future capital Nizhnii Novgorod, to be renamed Vladimir after the sainted tenth-century prince, the Christianizer of Russia. The city, a geographical center, major trade emporium, and communications link with Russian Asia, laid claim to patriotic traditions dating from the Time of Troubles, when its citizens in 1613 helped expel the hated Polish invader.[144]

The Russian Empire housed the largest concentration of Jews in the world— a Judaic-worshiping and Yiddish-speaking Ashkenazic community constricted to the Polish lands and the Jewish Pale of Settlement. Though a Jewish enlight- enment current, the Haskalah, came flowing into their midst from western Euro- pean Jewry, the majority clung to traditional piety and made a living as best they could under the discriminatory restrictions of the Russian government. Both by choice and by legal necessity, the Jews formed a kind of caste, visually and socially distinct from the Catholic and Orthodox Christian Slavic population around them in Poland, Ukraine, Belorussia, and Lithuania. Although Pestel promised a qualified religious freedom, he defamed the Jews of the Russian empire as clannish, alienated from the larger community, heretical by faith, and unable to assimilate. His solution? Fundamentally "reculturing" and assimilating the Jews by consultation with "the most learned rabbis and the wisest Jews." If that failed, they would be escorted out of Russia, perhaps to a region in Ottoman Anatolia—an early example of "compulsory Zionism"—in such huge numbers that the Turks would be unable to prevent them from entering.[145] One shudders in imagining what would have happened along the road if Pestel, in power, had carried out his intention to relocate by force an entire people.

Pavel Pestel's blueprint, much more radical than the constitutions adopted in Spain, Naples, or Greece, envisioned a centralized, unitary republic with a Jaco- bin-like state organization. Moving the capital far away from European contact, de-nationalizing its minorities, and expelling the Jews (a likely scenario) would have entailed massive changes in Russian society and polity. His plan for a tem- porary dictatorship and the sudden emancipation of the serfs certainly would have required violent enforcement. Pestel foresaw this and provided for a police force of about 113,000—in striking contrast to the future and much maligned Third Section of Tsar Nicholas I, which had four thousand agents a decade later.[146] Pestel's ominous vision contained much that presaged modern authori- tarian polities and at the same time seemed to provide a leap backward from progressive European currents.

In some places, Pestel's language hardly differs from Nikita Muraviev's—and, like it, clearly draws from the Spanish model. Article 7 of the second draft of Russian *Justice* reads: "The people of the Russian empire is not the property of any person or family. On the contrary, the government is the property of the people and it is established for the good of the people; the people do not exist for the good of the government."[147] Article 7 also echoes passages from the Spanish document: "The sovereignty resides essentially in the nation, and for the same reason to it alone belongs the right to establish its fundamental laws"; "The object of the government is the happiness of the Nation, and so the aim of all political society is nothing other than the well-being of the individuals who comprise it."[148] Nothing in Pestel's Article 7 contradicts the Spanish positions. But there is no evidence of direct borrowing, much less quotation. One can find language close to both the Russian and the Spanish formulations in American and French documents and in the works of Destutt de Tracy, Bentham, Bignon, and a handful of other liberal constitutionalists of the era. Pestel may have gotten his notion of supervisory organs of control from the Spanish constitution.[149] Pestel, in his *Russian Justice*, diverged even more widely than did Nikita Muraviev from the Cadiz model in its republican form of government, a new capital at Nizhnii Novgorod, and radical nationality policies.

Pestel's scheme at first evoked opposition from his own society in 1822, though they accepted it a year later at a conference in Kiev, with some probable dissent. In 1824, however, the more moderate leaders of the Northern Society rejected it, and Pestel undertook revisions.[150] Given the divergences in temperament and program between the two societies, by the time the Southern Society allied with the Society of United Slavs in September 1825, the gulf had widened.

The third component of the Decembrist movement, the Society of United Slavs, began its life with a meeting between Julian Lubliński and the Borisov brothers. Lubliński, a frail twenty-year-old Polish nobleman, deist, and revolutionary, devoured books and taught himself new languages. "Reading the works of Cesare Beccaria and Gaetano Filangieri," he testified, "made me recognize the force of the love for mankind."[151] He was arrested in Warsaw and transported, shackled, to his hometown, Novograd-Volynsk, in 1823. There he met the brothers Andrei and Petr Borisov, who had arrived a few years earlier as junior officers. Petr Borisov testified later that his radical ideas had come from classical biographers: "Reading Greek and Roman history and the lives of great men by Plutarch and Cornelius Nepos instilled in me from childhood a love of liberty and Democracy [*Narododerzhavie*]." Borisov felt the need to be a useful person and became scandalized by the harsh punishment of Russian soldiers and the subjugation of the serfs.[152] Lubliński and the Borisovs founded the Society of United Slavs; they were joined by Ivan Gorbachevskii and a few dozen others.

The new Society contrasted with the Northern and Southern Societies in its lower social ranking—minor nobles, junior officers, clerks—and in a ritual machinery reminiscent of the Carbonari and Friendly Society.[153] "Upon joining the United Slavs," ran the initiation oath, "in order to free myself from Tyranny and to restore the freedom that is so precious to humanity, I solemnly swear on this weapon to a mutual love which I hold Divine and from which I await the fulfillment of all my desires." The new member swore to uphold these aims, sword in hand, and to submit to "a thousand deaths" and "any infernal torments" rather than betray the society.[154] Even granting the fact that many European secret society oaths resembled each other, that of the Slavs shows a marked Carbonari influence. A juxtaposition of its oath and that of the second stage of the Neapolitan Free Pythagoreans reveals almost identical phraseology in describing freedom and tyranny, swearing on a weapon, declaring mutual love of the members, faithfulness and secrecy, and willingness to suffer the eternal torments of hell for breaking the oath.[155] The Slavs resembled Italian and Greek secret societies also in working constantly to expand, though on a far smaller scale—in contrast with the other Decembrists, who limited membership.[156]

The United Slavs embraced some of the chief aims of the Southern Society: a post-revolutionary republic and the abolition of serfdom. But they also advanced a vague plan for a union that would bring the Slavic peoples—and those thought to be Slavic—into a loose confederation of democratic republics. Mikhail Bestuzhev-Riumin, a key figure in the Southern Society, considered the Slavs enthusiastic and energetic, though lacking in order and clarity.[157] In many ways, they proved to be the most daring of the three societies in their greater receptivity to regicide and in a desire to reach out to the masses, including even the workers of Kiev.[158] The Slavs inevitably learned of the existence of the nearby Southern Society. After long and tortuous negotiations, including much exaggeration on the part of the Southerners about their strength and connections, the Slavs with some reluctance agreed to a merger, which took place in September 1825.

Aside from questions about the contours of the future society, there emerged those of how to take power and—for republicans—the fate of the tsar. As to the first, the Decembrists had two main precedents from Russian history. One was the "palace revolutions" of the eighteenth century, wherein courtiers had used force, usually with the help of elite Guards regiments, to replace one monarch with another without changing the fundamental nature of the regime or the social order. Such coups had enthroned Anna Ioannovna in 1730, Elizabeth in 1740, Catherine II in 1762, and Alexander I in 1801. None was driven by an ideological revolutionary program, prepared by secret societies brimming with ideas; none enlisted the common people. The Decembrists, seeking a much deeper transformation in Russian society and politics, could hardly be satisfied with this mode of revolt.

The second precedent, the Pugachev rebellion of the 1770s, remained a terrifying specter in Russian society. The onetime Cossack Emel'ian Pugachev had led serfs, state peasants, soldiers, Cossacks, bonded factory workers, and non-Russian ethnic groups in a massive three-year-long popular revolt that had taken the lives of thousands of noble landowners and state officials, among others, and had shaken the foundations of the state. The poet Alexander Pushkin had it only half right when he called the *pugachevshchina* a "senseless and merciless" revolt. Pugachev and his followers, far from being aroused by a blind and motiveless fury, each had a purpose, however limited and unencumbered by sophisticated revolutionary theory.

Spaniards and Neapolitans had each suffered dual agonies of popular violence: the Spanish and Calabrian guerrilla wars against Napoleonic forces, and popular counterrevolutionary assaults on radical and liberal regimes—1799 in Naples and 1822–23 in Spain. All in a way had posed a threat, real or potential, to liberal ideas and their bearers. Russian rulers and army commanders, while welcoming the peasant partisans of 1812, had worried about the movement turning into an anti-landlord jacquerie. Decembrist officers shared the ambivalence about 1812 and even more so about the Pugachev uprising. Aleksandr Poggio called its leader a "citizen bandit" and a "Russian Spartacus," praising his attempts to liberate millions of "brother slaves," but condemning him for excessive bloodshed. "He began as a citizen, humanely, but ended as a bandit—inhumanly."[159] All the great lower-class upheavals of the seventeenth and eighteenth centuries had drawn upon the folk notion of "popular monarchism," the peasant belief that the tsar shared their aspirations for freedom but was shielded from realities by officials and landowners. This allowed a series of pretenders or false tsars to win massive support by claiming to be or to speak for the legitimate monarch.

Reaching out to lower-class elements of the populace posed a problem for the Decembrists—and for all Russian radicals who followed them. In 1820, Spanish rebel agents in Cadiz had worked "to prepare the minds of the soldiers" at a critical moment for the Spanish army: the overseas expedition.[160] After winning over his own soldiers, Riego had ridden out to capture the allegiance of townsmen on the way. General Pepe, by inducting Carbonari into his militia, had radicalized a branch of the armed forces. Both the Spaniard and the Neapolitan had the limited goal of establishing a constitutional monarchy—not upsetting the entire social order. The Decembrists, unlike the Spanish liberals, had no looming foreign expedition as a negative motivator of troops. Without this element of pressure, the Russian conspirators proceeded with caution on the issue of popular involvement. Virtually all the conspirators opposed a peasant jacquerie. Despite sympathy for peasants and factory workers, both civilian and military Decembrists remained anxious about their potentially anarchic character.

What of the soldiers whom the Decembrists would lead to liberty? How were they to get troops to follow them in a rebellion against the tsar without preparing them or allowing spontaneous energy to flow forth? Initially some officers adopted a long-range approach by teaching classes approved for soldiers: the Bible society and the Lancaster method of mutual instruction, allowing pupils to tutor newcomers. The high-ranking General Mikhail Orlov, in his classes at Kiev, taught that faith did not contradict enlightened ideas about freedom, and he interlaced his lectures on religion to soldiers in other classes with talk about slavery and despotism, freedom and constitutions.[161] When Orlov transferred to Kishinev in 1820, he had Major Vladimir Raevskii, a fellow Decembrist, run the courses. In penmanship and grammar drills, Raevskii insinuated the words "liberty," "equality," and "constitution," and the names Brutus, Cassius, Washington, Mirabeau, Quiroga, and Riego. After Raevskii's arrest in 1823 for this activity, pupils revealed a tale he told them that Quiroga "made a revolution in Madrid and when he entered the city, the most prominent ladies and all the common people threw flowers at his feet." One pupil claimed that his teacher spoke of George Washington marching into Madrid.[162] When the risings in St. Petersburg and Vasilkov began in 1825, it became painfully clear to the rebels how little political terminology meant to their soldiers.

Raevskii, called the "First Decembrist" due to his early arrest, also wrote a pamphlet, *About the Soldier*, in 1822. This and his teaching reflected not the spontaneous wishes of mutineers but rather his wariness of them. Raevskii described the soldier he knew as a part of a caste defined by *"poverty, hard work, and death,"* a man who saw officers as "tyrants whom he fears and hates." Raevskii, perhaps in turn fearing soldiers in their present brutalized state, gave noncoms and men in the ranks only superficial and abstract kinds of political ideas.[163] In their recurring debates over the issue, the Decembrists ventilated a whole range of solutions, including paying, ordering, flattering, deceiving, and even beating the men—and using their loyalty to commanders and playing to their religious faith.

Among the most glaring differences between the Decembrists and the liberals of the Mediterranean was the fate of their monarch. For the Spanish and Neapolitan constitutional monarchists, by definition regicide was never an option. In Russia, the first discussion of the issue of regicide arose in the Moscow branch of the Union of Salvation in 1817, some of it in the form of literary posturing. Pavel Katenin, ever in a classical mood, responded to the debates with a partial translation in 1818 of Corneille's *Cinna* (1643), which pits the anti-tyrannical would-be assassin Cinna against Emperor Augustus, though Corneille's play actually sides with that ruler. In one of his speeches, Cinna says: "Heaven in our hand has placed the fate of Rome, / And its salvation hangs on one man's doom."[164]

The Northern Society leaders, committed to a constitutional monarchy, for the most part opposed regicide. For Nikita Muraviev and his colleagues, the question became, at various points, which of the three Romanov brothers—Alexander and, after his death in 1825, Constantine or Nicholas—would sit on the throne after the uprising.[165] But dissident chords sounded among more radical Northerners. Kondratii Ryleev unleashed gory fantasies. His poem was based on a folk verse told of a blacksmith who possessed three knives—one for the nobles, one for the clergy, and one for the monarch. What of his actual intentions? As with most Decembrists, Ryleev modulated his views over time and circumstance, and conflicting testimony about them, including his own, further fogs our understanding. The most judicious treatment convincingly shows that in the end Ryleev came to favor a republic, the murder of the tsar, and the extermination of the royal family.[166] The striking thing about this revolutionary is his admission to the court that "the extermination of the entire imperial family" would have united all factions in an act of extreme bloodshed, removed elements—the Romanov grand dukes, for example—who might mount a counter-revolution, and thus avoided "internal strife and all the horrors of a popular revolution." And yet while Ryleev entertained the possibility of regicide, he also feared it could let loose a spontaneous uprising of the masses, "civil strife, and all the horrors of a popular revolution."[167]

Another Northerner, Lieutenant Dmitrii Zavalishin of the navy, had favored the liquidation of the imperial family precisely because of the Spanish example. He told a fellow officer that "the requisite for an uprising is the extermination of the imperial family; he said that a revolution in any case must start with the head, and he brought in the example of Spain as proof that half measures did not work." Zavalishin told another officer that Spain "had so easily effected a revolt, and a few men had forced the king to grant a constitution to the people. But afterward the Spanish acted foolishly; relying on his word, they let the king out of their hands." Arguing with moderate colleagues, Zavalishin charged that their approach would bring internecine strife and cause "some pure patriots, like Riego, to perish."[168] Several members expressed willingness to assassinate the tsar. While the Northern leaders initially refused to countenance regicide, members began asking themselves, "What if the tsar does not agree to a constitution or—as the Spanish example had shown—such agreements were unreliable?"[169] The Society agreed to expulsion or regicide only if the tsar refused to accept the constitution or, after accepting it, betrayed it.[170]

In the Southern Society, matters were clearer on regicide, thanks to the influence of Pestel. But his insistence that the imperial family be killed in order to foreclose future claims by legitimists met opposition. At Southern Society meetings from 1822 onward, Pestel endeavored to reach consensus. Testimony after the revolt diverged widely as to who consented and who opposed the bloody act. In an oft-quoted passage from Aleksandr Poggio's testimony, Pestel began ticking off the number of royals to be executed; when he got to the count of thirteen, he began to blanch at the notion of killing the grand duchesses and their children.[171] Specifics remained undecided, as did the question of who would carry out the job.

Pestel's radical republicanism and what was known of his dreams of regicide deepened the rift between the Southern Society and the Northern Society. His leadership style amplified their differences. Northerners began to see Pestel as a "Southern Napoleon."[172] Ryleev, unlike Pestel, despised the French emperor. Eventually some of Pestel's own colleagues in the Southern Society and the Society of United Slavs shared this view. Thus the Decembrists, divided by personal issues, also remained far from united on key substantive questions. For answers and resolution, many looked at the lessons coming out of revolutionary Europe, from Andalusia to the Morean peninsula.

Revolutions in the Mail

"Where there is mail, there is revolution!" exclaimed Nikolai Turgenev, the Decembrist scholar, in reference to the early 1820s.[173] Certainly the reverse held true. Even with the pre-electronic communications technology of 1820, news seemed to flash across Europe—in newspapers, with travelers, by diplomatic couriers on the road or at sea. The French press and a half dozen Russian periodicals regularly carried tales of events in Spain, Naples, the Balkans, and elsewhere. News of the assassinations of Kotzebue and the Duc de Berry added to angst or jubilation among readers. Tatiana Passek, a highborn lady, recalled heated conversations about the upheavals of 1820 in salons and even at balls.[174] Information filtered through the press or rumors usually came in distorted form, either incomplete or wrong. Clearly the details had less weight for sympathetic readers than the slogans, symbolic shorthand phrases, and mythic and even poetic locutions of the rebels.

The police spy M. K. Gribovskii informed Tsar Alexander that the Russian members of secret societies "could not hide their stupid glee at the events in Spain and Naples."[175] Many Decembrists confirmed this glee in their testimony after arrest or later in memoirs. Given the hatred for European radicalism by their new emperor (and at times interrogator), Nicholas I, the Decembrists' claims about their pan-European revolutionary inspiration can hardly have been exculpatory. In their circles, Decembrists grumbled at Tsar Alexander's perceived treasonous collusion with Metternich in suppressing revolutions, a betrayal not only of the peoples of Europe but of his own ideals of liberation as acted out in the defeat of Napoleon.

Naval officer Mikhail Bestuzhev (1800–1871), a man of extraordinary versatility and broad culture, told his examiners that early ideas about different lands had dawned on him during his voyages and in talks with officers of several nations; and he testified flatly that "the uprising occurring almost everywhere in Europe, about which one could get ample news from Russian newspapers, was what deepened the ideas and ways of thinking that I had already developed."[176] Another well-read and well-traveled young mariner, Aleksandr Beliaev, never joined the secret societies but took part in the revolt in St. Petersburg on December 14. He later offered a neat summary of the impulses shared by his generation and leading to its disaffection. Veterans of the recent wars dreamed of applying what they had seen in western Europe to Russia via reform of their own country, which they saw as besotted by serfdom, military cruelty, corruption, injustice, and waste. Beliaev stressed the factors that led him to revolt: yo-yo swings at home between promises of reform and realities of repression, the scandalous liquidation of Riego in Spain and the Carbonari in Italy, the imprisonment of Silvio Pellico, and the poetry of Ryleev and Pushkin.[177]

In similar terms, Baron Vladimir Steinhel, a veteran of the 1812 war and Northern Society member, complained in a letter to Nicholas I after the revolt that he had helped to plan that Tsar Alexander's 1817 promise of a constitution had raised the hopes of Russian liberals. "Then suddenly events in Spain and Naples and the simultaneous rising of the Greeks produced a sharp break in the tsar's intentions but also inflamed minds with dreams of freedom for Russia."[178]

Petr Kakhovskii, too young for the Napoleonic wars and retired early from the army, was an impoverished nobleman who had traveled in the Caucasus and lived in Europe. Back in St. Petersburg, he came into contact with the Northern Society. In testimony, he lamented that "the prisons of Piedmont, Sardinia, Naples—all over Italy—and Germany were filled with shackled citizens." He blamed Tsar Alexander for the uprisings. "Was it not he who fanned the flame of liberty in our hearts; and afterward, was it not he who brought about such cruel repression not only at home but all over Europe?" In correspondence with his prison investigator, Kakhovskii linked the unfolding events of a dramatic quarter century to the American and French revolutions. He and his colleagues were deceived, Kakhovskii wrote, by the talk of liberation and freedom in the wars of 1812. But instead of granting freedom, the rulers of Europe "thought only of retaining their unlimited power, preserving their rickety thrones, and extinguishing the last spark of freedom and enlightenment." To the people they offered instead "chains and dungeons."

> Peoples, having tasted the sweetness of enlightenment and freedom, aspire to them; whereas governments, guarded by millions of bayonets, try to push them back into a pall of ignorance. But all their efforts are

futile. Impressions once received can never be effaced. Liberty is that torch of intellect and bearer of warmth to life! It has always and everywhere been the attribute of peoples who have emerged from primitive ignorance. And we cannot live like our ancestors—as barbarians or slaves.

He wrote that Tsar Alexander had "assisted Fernando to suppress the legal rights of the people of Spain and failed to foresee the evil that this wrought on all thrones." From that moment, Europe exclaimed that there would be "no agreements with kings [tsari]."[179]

Kondratii Ryleev believed that the tyranny of the Napoleonic empire had been replaced by a new version—the European restoration. In an 1824 fragment on Napoleon, Ryleev commented on the events of his own time: "The peoples have perceived this and already Western and Southern Europe have made attempts to throw off the yoke of despotism. The kings united and by force tried to suppress aspirations to liberty. They triumphed, and now a deathly silence hangs over Europe, but it is like the temporary silence of Vesuvius"—the reference to Naples' volcano doubtless voicing the hope for a new eruption.[180] Baron Andrei Rosen (Rozen), a German-speaking officer born in the Baltic provinces, became a key figure on the day of the uprising. In retrospect, he linked foreign to domestic repression, and explained in his memoirs that the secret societies arose because of the policies of Tsar Alexander I: "The savior of Europe, restorer of Poland, liberator of the Baltic serfs, sponsor of enlightenment, spreader of the gospel, suddenly, heeding the slanders of Metternich, began to crush all popular movements for material and intellectual betterment." He reneged on Polish promises, put a brake on progressive movements at home and abroad, and refused to help the insurgent Greeks.[181]

In addition to Muraviev-Apostol, several officers in the Southern Society bore witness to the impact of foreign events. Nikolai Basargin, a moderate liberal officer, joined the Union of Welfare in 1817 and then the Southern Society but had minimal involvement. Though he withdrew in 1822 and knew nothing of the plot to seize power, Basargin was sentenced to twenty years' hard labor in Siberia (later reduced) and loss of rights. Writing in middle age, he recalled that the international situation in the post-Napoleonic years caused acute dissatisfaction among youth and was the main impulse for the formation of secret societies. The victory over Napoleon had raised hopes that remained unrealized. Basargin lamented the repressions in Spain, Naples, Piedmont, and Germany and, like many Decembrists, bemoaned what he saw as the tsar's capitulation to Metternich.[182]

General Mikhail Orlov of the Kishinev section of the Union of Welfare, soon to become part of the Southern Society, recalled that in 1820 his circle debated the merits of various constitutions, finding that of Britain (unwritten) too aristocratic and the French Charte worthless. "American federalism, the Spanish events, and the Neapolitan revolution played a major role in all our conversations." Ever cautious, Orlov lamented that his colleagues seemed to reject gradualism and took theory as a starting point. His also stressed that political arguments took place not only in secret societies but also in public places, streets, theaters—everywhere.[183]

Pavel Pestel observed that "the events in Naples, Spain, and Portugal had at the time an enormous impact on me. I found in them, to my way of thinking, irrefutable evidence of the ephemerality of monarchical constitutions and quite sufficient reasons not to believe in any constitution accepted by a king. These last considerations greatly fortified in me a republican and revolutionary frame of thinking."[184] Like Kakhovskii, Pestel reviewed in his testimony the panorama of the previous twenty-five years, which demonstrated "how many thrones were overturned and new ones set up; how many kingdoms destroyed, how many new ones created; how many kings were expelled, returned or summoned back, and again forced into exile; how many revolutions occurred—how many *coups d'état* carried out. All these events familiarized the minds with revolutions, *with the possibilities and the means of making them*" (italics in original).[185] The italicized sentence revealed not only that Pestel was inspired by the European revolutions and angered at their failure, but that he saw in them clues on how to make a revolution in Russia.

Pestel's comrade Lieutenant Colonel Aleksandr Poggio was one of two sons of Vittorio Poggio, a Piedmontese who had resettled in Odessa. Aleksandr also presented a sweeping survey of the events he had lived through in his formative years, from the wars against Napoleon to the revolutions and Restoration-era suppressions and the broken promises of sovereigns, including his own. Poggio in a key passage of his testimony revealed how Russia's foreign policy fed his radical stance:

> In 1819 and 1820, many—and not just we [Decembrists]—spoke of the cruel pacification of the Chuguev [military settlement] inhabitants. In 1820, the Spanish business occupied many. . . . Then came Naples, Piedmont, and Greece; the disgraceful situation in those places also captured much attention. But this [attention] was not brought about by the [secret] Society, but rather, I'm telling you, by the government itself. Our government, by turning all its attention to foreign policy, attracted our attention to it as well."

He explained that his path to political subversion began by "tracking all the policies of our government, seeing . . . the suppression of the constitution in Spain," among other abominations.[186] As Poggio put it bluntly in his memoirs, the tsar had become the upholder of the business of "gallows, firing squads, and dungeons."[187]

The sheer scale and scope of the rebellious wave in Europe invited grandiose similes even from those lacking any sympathy for the rebels. The reactionary Filipp Vigel recalled that at first he and his friends remained indifferent to what happened in such a distant land as Spain. Then the flame burst into a wildfire driven by the wind across Europe. "Portugal, Naples, Sardinia [Piedmont], and then in the following year, Greece burst into flames." Fire gave way to pernicious gale force for Vigel, as he likened the eruption to "the gusts of a storm arising on the banks of the Tagus which by year's end—though in attenuated form— echoed on the shores of the Neva."[188] Vigel's storm moved the Decembrists to react emotionally to eruptions in the Mediterranean.

Speaking at the time or recalling later the Mediterranean events, the Decembrists tended to put Naples, Greece, and Spain in reverse order of importance, though it was the intervention in Naples that first aroused their ire. Tsarist minister Kochubei endeavored to control news about Italian events for fear of infecting officers. Nonetheless, *Son of the Fatherland* and other papers sometimes provided accurate and, initially, favorable information. In tsarist Poland, the Warsaw journal *White Eagle* welcomed the Neapolitan liberal regime as "a new dawn of genuine freedom," linking it to the Spanish experience.[189]

Personal connections with Italians amounted to little. The Union of Welfare had a secret branch, Heirut (Hebrew for "freedom"), organized by Fedor Glinka. Grigorii Peretz, apparently the only one in the movement who came from a Jewish background, was a member. The branch condemned the Holy Alliance's posture toward Spain and Italy. A "professor," Mariano Gigli, had fled to Russia from one of the Italian Carbonari plots in 1817–18 and joined this group; a witness later testified that Gigli inducted him into a secret society whose goal was "preparing the people to accept a constitution." The group dissolved in 1822 and Gigli allegedly died in a madhouse soon afterward.[190]

Aleksandr Poggio at his trial confessed esteem for General Pepe, who had struggled "for the independence of all Italy from the German [Austrian] yoke." Vladimir Raevskii praised the organizers of the uprisings in Italy and hoped to emulate them in Russia.[191] Ivan Liprandi, an officer of Spanish origin whose father had entered Russian service, joined the Union of Welfare. In 1820 he requested permission to leave as a volunteer "of the national Italian army" in Naples. For this he was reprimanded and forced out of the military.[192] Soviet historian Nikolai Druzhinin believed that the Neapolitan revolt made a particularly strong impression on the Decembrists because of its organized form, its lack of bloodshed, and—yes—its "holiday-like" mode of changing regimes.[193] The overturn there had taken only four days, as opposed to two months in Spain.

Given these sympathies, foreign intervention in Italy was bound to anger the Decembrists. Mikhail Fonvizin, a seasoned war veteran since 1805 and a moderate member of the Northern Society, condemned the Great Powers for suppressing the Neapolitan constitution "as if an independent nation had no right to change its form of government." His wrath induced exaggeration: Fonvizin asserted that "a hundred thousand Austrians invaded Neapolitan territory, destroyed everything they pleased, and established in Naples an Austrian military administration."[194] Sergei Turgenev, brother of a Decembrist, wondered whether a constitution in Naples was really a menace to civilization.[195]

The temperature of the Decembrists rose upon learning of Tsar Alexander's readiness to send a Russian unit into the Italian peninsula. At army headquarters in Tulchin, younger officers reacted ambivalently to the prospect of invading Italy. Though eager for action and travel to Europe, they opposed the goal of the mooted expedition.[196] The ever vigilant Vasil'chikov reported in March 1821 that while the men in the ranks were calm, officers were feeling rage at the prospect of marching against Naples. "The revolution in the spirit is already accomplished," he said. Vasil'chikov, perhaps unaware of the connection between Riego's revolt and the hated expedition to foreign shores, believed that combat would squelch "the revolution in the spirit." The Guards regiments, he suggested, should be deployed at the front: "A few good battles will calm their young heads and inure them to severe discipline."[197] What might have happened had a Russian force been sent off toward Italy and had Russian Riegos in this intervening army seen a chance to emulate the Spaniard and turn an unpopular expedition into a revolution?

Sergei Muraviev-Apostol, unlike his comrades, blamed the Neapolitan regime for not defending itself. Disturbed by the battle of Rieti and the suppression that followed, he wrote a scorching letter to his father two months after the defeat. "These vile Neapolitans, I wish a sultan on them. What harm they have brought to the cause of all Europe! Napoleon said that it is but a small step from the sublime to the ridiculous. Greece and Naples offer proof of that. It would be interesting to know what has become of the eloquent [Neapolitan] parliamentary orators, the valiant generals, and the brilliant armies. What a great misfortune not to know how to defend such a sacred thing as one's independent country   The greatest shame came in surrendering to the Austrians. We should leave them to their sad fate and raise our voices in prayer for the Greeks."[198] All in all, the Italian revolutions had less direct resonance among the Decembrists than did the Spanish; even its 1821 suppression was often simply linked in their minds to the 1823 intervention in Spain. The Greek war for independence, however, elicited a strong emotional response.

The Decembrists reacted to events in Greece as did a broad spectrum of Russian society. Russians felt a special empathy for the rebels who shared their Orthodox faith. Facing few censorship barriers on the matter, discussion of the Greek events freely unfolded and philhellenism cut across political lines, embracing court, society, radicals, and figures as diverse as devout monarchists, conservative and liberal intellectuals, religious mystics, diplomats, and generals.

What a historian calls a "war party" began informally to take shape among people of various persuasions. The future prophet of Slavophilism, Aleksei Khomiakov, tried to enlist in the Greek struggle at age seventeen but was forbidden to do so. The conservative Faddei Bulgarin recorded his view that the filthy Carbonari could not be compared to the holy bands of Greek patriots fighting what he called a "popular war."[199] Another conservative interventionist perspective surfaced. In the fall of 1825, an army officer resuscitated the "war as social stability" scenario that had been floated in 1821 for Italian intervention. He sent an anonymous memo to the tsar that spoke of a dangerous dissident mood among Russian officers and soldiers; he proposed that a war "against the barbarous and bloodthirsty Ottomans" would be popular in Russia and would serve to "avoid setting off eruptions like those which occurred a few years ago in Southern Europe."[200] When General Ermolov was summoned from the Caucasus to prepare the army for the suppression of the Italian rising in the spring of 1821, false rumors flew that it was actually to be deployed to the Balkans in order to liberate the Greeks.

Troops and officers of the Second Army stationed in the south contributed to a Greek benefit fund, and its commander sang the praises of the descendants of Achilles.[201] Sympathy for their co-religionists led some to believe that the St. Petersburg flood of 1824 reflected divine retribution for not intervening in Greece.[202] The Greek rebels were correct in predicting wide support in Russia for their endeavor, but wrong in their assessment of what those in power would do.

Poets voicing admiration for the Greeks employed the affecting imagery of the dungeon and depicted an entire people languishing in chains. The classical revival fed the philhellene fever as it did elsewhere. N. I. Gnedich spent twenty years on the first Russian translation of *The Iliad*, and his rendering of Rhigas Pheraios' "War Hymn" appeared in *Messenger of Europe* in 1821.[203] Alexander Pushkin devoted many verses and commentaries to praising Ypsilanti's exploit. After its collapse his unfinished poem celebrated those who perished at Sculeni and at the Secco Monastery. Pushkin never traveled to Greece but, like many who did, eventually turned cynical toward the real Greeks he met, though he continued to hope for Greek freedom.[204]

The few score Russian and Ukrainian volunteers in the Greek war had no known liberal agenda. Not a single Decembrist is known to have gone to Greece to fight for its independence and no Russian equivalent of a cohort of revolutionary or ex-revolutionary philhellenes appeared. Decembrists, like other European philhellenes, wrote verses and dreamed of a sojourn in the land of the Hellenes. Wilhelm Küchelbecker's "Greek Song" of 1821 announced in rather wan verse that "Peoples asleep until now / Awaken, gaze forth, and rise up. / O bliss! The hour, freedom's joyous hour has struck.[205] Ryleev's "On the Occasion of Byron's Death" recognized present-day Greece as the fatherland of Themistocles, cursed "the tyrant of the luxuriant Orient," and saluted Byron, who "withered in the flower of his youth in the sacred struggle for the freedom of the Greek."[206] Ryleev expressed his regret at being unable to fly to the Morea. Kakhovskii, on returning from Europe, planned to follow Byron's example but instead joined the Decembrist plotters. I. D. Iakushkin also made preparations to go to Greece but was deflected by the task of feeding hungry peasants in the Smolensk region. Zavalishin began studying Greek to ready himself for the journey.[207] None went. Doing so would have entailed punishment or permanent exile from Russia and discarding plans for revolution at home.

As in the rest of Europe, Decembrists' sympathies extended solely to Greek victims, not to Turks. Basargin accused the Holy Alliance of putting the principle of legitimacy before the suffering of the Greeks. Küchelbecker praised the forces that stormed Tripolitsa in 1821, without a word about the Greek atrocities perpetrated there. Nikolai Turgenev worriedly wrote of news and rumors about outrages against the Christian population of the Ottoman Empire. Fedor Glinka, even while languishing in the Peter and Paul Fortress in 1826 for his ties with Decembrists, composed verses on the Greek victims. The list could be extended.[208] The Turks of course lacked a public relations establishment and produced no Delacroix who could represent on canvas the Greek atrocities. Decembrists, like other readers, relied heavily on the British and French press reports.

Decembrists saw larger issues raised by the Greek revolt. Aleksandr Poggio, with family connections in the great port of Odessa, dreamed of a Greek victory as a future spur to Black Sea trade.[209] General of Engineers Gavriil Batenkov, a severely wounded and decorated veteran of 1812 and a member of the Northern Society, testified at his trial that in 1825 his feeling for the Greeks led him to ponder the dire plight of Russia.[210] Nikolai Turgenev likened the *tourkokratia* to the Tatar yoke of Russia's Middle Ages. He favored national liberation but not Russian intervention, which would deflect attention from the burning issue of serfdom. "Do many of our peasants," he asked, "live better under their masters than the Greeks under the Turks?"[211] The lot of Raevskii, who was languishing helplessly under solitary confinement in a fortress, perhaps led him to use extravagant language about "the fiery dawn in the East" in a letter to his friends, urging them to enlist under "the holy banner of the field of martial glory."[212] Mikhail Orlov looked on the Greek war as part of the general European struggle for freedom. Though dismissive of another rebel, Riego, he urged his wife in March 1821 not to laugh at Ypsilanti: "He who lays down his life for his country is always worthy of respect, whatever the outcome of his undertaking."[213]

Most Decembrists wanted Russian intervention on the side of the Greeks. Nikolai Lohrer recalled that when news arrived of the revolt, his fellow officers believed that the tsar would "extend a helping hand to co-religionists" and deploy the army into Moldavia.[214] Ryleev addressed the popular Caucasus commander, General Ermolov, in verse: "Hasten to save the sons of Hellas / You, genius of the northern hosts! / . . . Like a modern phoenix from the ashes, Greece is now reborn / . . . All through the ancestral lands of Themistocles, / are now raised freedom's flags."[215] Kakhovskii, in his testimony, railed against Alexander I for failing to help "our Greek coreligionists, who were several times encouraged by our government to rise up against Muslim tyranny." Steinhel testified that Russian society and the Greeks resident in Russia were dismayed when the Ottoman Greeks were left to their fate and ties that had lasted eight hundred years were broken.[216] Mikhail Lunin, from his exile in Siberia after the Decembrist revolt, looked back critically at the government's failure to assist an oppressed people, in contrast to the secret societies that had "pleaded the cause of the Greeks, abandoned by almost all the European powers."[217] The failure of the Russian emperor to intervene added one more article of indictment against him in the eyes of the Decembrists.

Of the two preeminent leaders of the Southern Society, located not far from Ypsilanti's staging area, Sergei Muraviev-Apostol wrote to his father on April 21, 1821: "Judging from the latest news, the Greeks . . . are conducting themselves as befits the courageous descendants of Miltiades, Leonidas, and other heroes; they are strong and their resolve is firm: to prevail or die. . . . If this be true, they will triumph and then we will laugh not at the expense of the poor Greeks, whose cause and desperate plight is so deserving of respect, but at . . . the Turks." The Russian officer was particularly impressed with the role of women in the revolt, which meant that the Greeks would have to win the struggle or perish. A few weeks later he wrote that "the devotion of the Odessa Greeks" reminded him of the revolutionary wave in Latin America, which he hoped would reach European shores. In a key phrase that may have shaped his own later determination, he exclaimed, "If inexorable fate brought them defeat, then such a defeat would be nonetheless magnificent!" Muraviev-Apostol, perhaps musing on his own possible fate, announced that "Ypsilanti is on the road to immortality." He also correctly traced weaknesses in the Greek camp to fights over political details, a judgment that may have strengthened his constant pleas for unity among the Russian secret societies.[218]

The Decembrist leader who engaged most closely with the Greek revolution in a policy sense, Pavel Pestel, did so in a tortuous way—officially as a virtual informer to the tsar on Ypsilanti and the Friendly Society, and to his own comrades as a promoter of Greek freedom and a pan-European revolution. When Ypsilanti began his march, the tsar needed an agent to inform him about it and the larger Balkan situation. Pestel's superior officer chose him. Between February and June 1821 Pestel thrice visited the quarantine station on the banks of the Pruth—Ypsilanti's jumping-off point. Pestel met with Russian consuls and with Soutsos, who provided him with information on its plans, apparently with the hope of enlisting him. Exaggerating the size of the movement, Pestel reported back that if there were eight hundred thousand Carbonari in Italy—a gross inflation—then there might be even more Greeks enrolled in a political organization.[219] Pestel's final report to the tsar also described the Friendly Society's rituals and its role in the Ypsilanti rising.[220]

These reports, begun during the Austrian suppression of the Neapolitan regime, might seem like a betrayal of the Greek struggle. In fact, although Pestel promoted a vigilant and forward policy by the Russian state, he also backed Greek aspirations as well as those of Tudor Vladimirescu, highlighted Turkish rather than Greek atrocities, and warned the tsar against Austrian ambitions. To his superiors, Pestel stressed the massive backing behind the revolt and saw Ypsilanti as mostly a rallying point. Pestel underlined the Greek rebels' religious motivation over conspiracy and, like many who underplayed the revolutionary character of the rising, compared it to the Russian liberation from the Muslim Tatars rather than to the revolts in Spain and Naples.[221] Pestel simultaneously passed on to colleagues in the Southern Society some of Ypsilanti's proclamations that he had translated into Russian. These deeply impressed a number of the Decembrists. In conversation with a member in September 1824, long after his mission had ended, Pestel "praised the unyielding actions . . . of the Greeks . . . for the restoration of their fatherland."[222]

Pestel privately fashioned a broader theory that tied the Greek insurgency to a Decembrist program and to a European realignment. He believed that a successful revolution at home would trigger a victorious Russian liberation war on Turkey that would produce a kind of Greek satellite, a scheme redolent of old Russian efforts dating back to and before Catherine the Great's "Greek project." Though Pestel initially envisaged a "Greek kingdom," he later saw it as part of a "federated union of Balkan nations [or peoples]," as protectorates of Russia, bound by its foreign policy and adapting its political form. The new Russian republic would become the hub of a network of East European republics, from the Baltic to the Aegean. In regard to Greece's liberation, Pestel wrote that it would "demonstrate Russia's departure from an aggressive system in favor of one featuring a protectorate."[223] Given the terms of Pestel's scheme and his authoritarian character, it is difficult to see how much independence any of the federation's members would have enjoyed.

Ranging even further into European geopolitics, Pestel foresaw a Russian war with Prussia and Austria over the Balkans.[224] The consequent collapse of the Holy Alliance would defang the interventionists and thus pave the way for a "permanent" revolution throughout Europe, here meaning a continuous wave of insurrections that would topple the remaining autocrats of Europe.[225] Much speculation and contradiction arose as to which would come first, the Russian revolt or the war with Turkey, and some uncertainty remains whether Pestel invented this plan alone or—in one view—in consultation with the Friendly Society.[226] Pestel had managed to construct a scenario for international revolution that foreshadowed the much vaunted theory of permanent revolution unveiled early in the following century by the Russian Marxists Parvus and Trotsky. While Pestel's scheme also resembled the ambitions of General Pepe and other exile adventurers in Mediterranean lands, the Russian's requirement of international wars and his weakly hidden imperial design added more than a dose of realpolitik to their idealism. As to a possible European intervention to crush the Russian revolution, Nikita Muraviev not Pestel had the answer: there would be no risk because "our neighbors will fear that the same thing might happen in their lands"—that is, revolution. Echoing the dubious Spanish and Neapolitan responses, he said that "an army defending freedom can repel anyone."[227]

Apart from sympathetic vibrations and geopolitical dreams, how closely did the Decembrists connect with the Greek rebels? Ypsilanti was personally acquainted with Pestel, Sergei Volkonskii, Mikhail Orlov, Sergei Trubetskoi, Nikita Muraviev, and others.[228] His brothers had all served in Russian Guards regiments and were thus fellow officers of many Decembrists. Interaction was especially intense in the south. Kishinev in Bessarabia, adjacent to Moldavia, served as a local hub of both the Decembrists and the Friendly Society. Pro-Greek feeling ran high among the military based in the south. An official investigation of 1825–26 found that most of the officers in the 33rd Jaeger Regiment had joined the Friendly Society in Akkerman and Kishinev.[229] Sergei Volkonskii in 1821 said that the army was tempted by the hope of going to the Danube to free the Greeks from the cruelties of the Muslim.[230] General Orlov, who had conversions and mutual planning sessions with Ypsilanti and the Friendly Society in Kishinev in 1820, was eager, if Russia went to war with the Turks, to deploy the forces under his command—a division with sixteen thousand men, thirty-six guns, and six Cossack regiments.[231]

Nothing came of any of the Decembrist schemes to align themselves with the Greek war of independence, which, waged close at hand and possessing many historical and cultural ties to Russia, offered the most promising opportunity for the Decembrists to link it to their own revolutionary designs. Russia's engagement with the Turks occurred only after the Decembrists had fallen and its agent was the state. It turned out that distant Spain ignited the most frequent and passionate feelings of the Decembrists and presented some of them with what looked like a model and a precedent.

At the beginning of the 1820 uprising in Spain, the Russian patriotic journalist Fedor Glinka, who had ties to the Decembrists, tried to sketch out parallels between the Spanish and the Russian experience: centuries of rule by Muslim invaders—Moors and Tatars; far-flung empires—the Americas and Siberia; and pretenders installed by foreign armies—a False Dmitrii brought in by the Poles in the seventeenth century and the puppet Joseph Bonaparte imposed by the French.[232] But these tenuous parallels with Spain offered Russians no connections comparable to the Byzantine heritage and the Orthodox faith they shared with Greece. What lured Russian radicals to the Spanish cause was political, not cultural or historical. Spain's constitutional regime served as the touchstone for the Decembrists' reading of the 1820s upheavals; it lasted three years, acted out a parliamentary life, unveiled problems associated with a post-revolutionary order, and suffered suppression by its king and a foreign power—both backed by the Russian tsar.

Decembrists' admiration for liberal Spain emerged during the first Cortes and resurfaced with the Restoration. Referring to the return of Fernando VII in 1814, Major-General Count M. A. Dmitriev-Mamonov, a founder of the Union of Welfare, commented on the Spanish king's persecution of the liberals: "To save T [tyrants] is to prepare and forge shackles heavier than those that one wants to throw off. What of the Cortes! Dissolved, tormented, condemned to death and by whom? By the swine whose crown they saved!"[233] At an 1819 meeting of the Green Lamp Society—a reading circle close to the Decembrists—the Russian official Aleksandr Ulybyshev described Spain under the Restoration as "burdened in the triple chains of political dependence, internal despotism, and the Inquisition—waiting for the hour of liberation."[234]

Beginning on January 13, *Russian Invalid*, using the Madrid press as its source, reported details about the events of 1819, the expedition, and the outbreak and development of the 1820 uprising. *Invalid* was read by officers, officials, tradesmen, soldiers, artisans, and even literate peasants. Other papers and journals followed events in the European press. Lacking signals from the government and knowing that the tsar had recognized the 1812 constitution, some reports initially took a cautiously positive tone.[235] The Spaniard Van Halen recalled that even officers of the Special Caucasus Corps in remote Tiflis and other towns got regular news from the French papers and letters on European events.[236] By March, the rising, Fernando's assent to the constitution, the end of the Inquisition, and the counterrevolutionary massacres in Cadiz and other towns had become known to readers.[237] But the reports were fragmentary and conflicting, and those who praised the peaceful transition usually ignored the few bloody events.

Some important intellectuals marginal to or outside the Decembrist orbit offered a range of sometimes ambivalent responses. The philosopher and publicist

Petr Chaadaev, encouraged by the absence of a bloody social explosion in Spain, called the outbreak there a good argument for revolution, and added cryptically that it touched somehow on Russia.[238] The conservative historian Nikolai Karamzin wrote to the poet Viazemskii in April 1820 that "the history of Spain is very curious. I fear only phrases and bloodshed. The Cortes constitution is pure democracy—or something like it. If they build a state, I promise to go on foot to Madrid and take 'Don Quichotte' or 'Quijote' along with me."[239] Viazemskii wrote: "I am happy for Spain, but at the same time I fear that the tempting example of the Spanish army might lead some among us into sin." He feared a possible Pugachev rebellion, though he still longed for a Russian constitution.[240]

The young Guards officer Aleksei Khomiakov often appeared at meetings in Ryleev's home attended by Decembrists in the 1820s where the Riego model was held up as the means to bring a constitution to Russia through a military rising. Khomiakov curtly refuted their views. In November 1824 he declared that the Spanish revolution was a crime against the people; the army's business, he said, was to defend the state and not change the system. All military mutinies were immoral, said he, and of all revolutions, the mutiny was the most illegal. Its supporters, he insisted, far from being liberal, wished to replace the monarchy with the "tyranny of an armed minority."[241] The Neva Observer, a short-lived journal, displayed both scorn and foresight about Spanish events. Referring to disorder and clerical uproar over the monasteries a year after the uprising, it refuted the allegedly received wisdom that "the Spanish constitution was a model of reason and politics" and saw its single chamber as a soaring comet doomed to crash.[242]

Decembrists viewed things differently. Almost all accounts by and histories of them agree that the Spanish events, as they understood them, helped to radicalize them—though this happened in various ways. The news from Spain energized those mentioned elsewhere in these pages and many more. Küchelbecker, a Russian poet of German ancestry, wrote rather piously in The Neva Observer that "Spain, in its struggle for freedom and independence, and for the sacred rights of its people stands as a great and edifying example for posterity."[243] This kind of generalized language, however, hardly reflected the heating of the blood among the active Decembrists, whose remarkably similar testimonies about Spain resembled a chorus. These men were fired up by examples of personal bravery, the apparent successes of the regime in Spain, and its destruction by the Holy Alliance.

Riego and his comrades remained distant objects of the Decembrists' admiration. But they had another Spanish hero closer at hand, a full-fledged victim of persecution by Fernando VII and the Inquisition: Juan Van Halen. After escaping from prison, he had gone to London and procured a letter of introduction from a Russian diplomat. In St. Petersburg by 1818, the Spaniard had established contacts with Guards officers and met a number of Decembrists.[244] Though a revolutionary and jailbird, he made high society connections, won the support of Zea Bermúdez, and gained a post with the Russian army on the Caucasus front. There, in what wits called "warm Siberia," he served as a major in the Nizhnii Novgorod Dragoon Regiment in Chechnya and Georgia from September 1819 to late 1820.[245] When the Spanish revolution erupted in 1820, an aide to the tsar congratulated Van Halen and told him he could now either "send the Inquisition to hell" by returning to his "*cara patria . . . and olla podrida*" or continue to serve with Ermolov.[246] Van Halen remained.

Van Halen's account of his stay in Russia, replete with ethnographic and geographical detail, likened the state of the Spanish people under Fernando to Russian serfs. The Spanish officer received news of events on the ground in Spain, which he shared with his Russian comrades. "Tiflis [Tbilisi] soon became for me a second St. Petersburg," wrote Van Halen. In the Georgian capital, he related, Ermolov organized a well-stocked library full of foreign newspapers and journals which were eagerly devoured by the members.[247] He befriended several Decembrists. A fellow officer, having heard the news from Leon and of the mounting of a constitutional stone in Madrid, addressed Van Halen in a letter as "Dear Constitutionalist," assuring him that nowhere else in the world did the Spanish exploits raise such a furor as among Russians.[248]

A dubious source from a Freemason group in Simbirsk—far from the Caucasus—had it that a Van Halen (Van-Galen) had been sent by Spanish Masonic circles to establish ties with the Russians.[249] The Russian envoy in Spain, Bulgari, made a similar allegation. When the tsar got wind of this, he ordered that an armed guard arrest Van Halen and escort him across the frontier to Habsburg territory. Aware of the danger this would bring to the Spanish revolutionary, General Ermolov disregarded the order and arranged a safer exit for him. Van Halen made his way back to Spain, married Quiroga's sister, fought against the 1823 intervention under Mina, led troops in the Belgian revolution of 1830, and fought against the Carlists in Spain.[250]

The new Spanish liberal regime and its constitution intrigued Decembrists, many of whom owned copies of it.[251] The day after the news of the revolt reached Nikolai Turgenev in Germany, he wrote in his diary: "Glory to you, glorious Spanish army! Glory to the Spanish people! For the second time, Spain is showing what national spirit means and what love of country means. The rebels—to the extent we can believe the papers—are conducting themselves in a wholly noble way." He noted that they have explained their plans to the people and were willing to die so that their ideals may live on. "Perhaps Spain is demonstrating the possibility of something that up to now we thought impossible."[252] Ryleev, captivating his fellows during their conversations about Spain, flatly declared that Russia also needed a constitution and a military revolt.[253]

The sharpest impact of the Spanish revolt on the Decembrists and a focus of their rage came in 1823 with the intervention. If the Great Powers had not engineered the destruction of the constitutional regime in Madrid, the Decembrists might have come to see more differences between Russia and Spain over time and their inspiration might have eroded. As it happened, the repression and the execution of Riego inflamed their passions. They recalled 1812, when Tsar Alexander had glorified the Spanish fighters against the tyrant Napoleon. Kakhovskii, in a kind of counterindictment, charged that "the Holy Alliance forgot that it was Spain which first resisted the power of Napoleon; and Emperor Alexander came to scorn the regime he had once recognized, saying that in 1812 circumstances had required that he recognize the constitution of Spain." Kakhovskii noted that in return for saving the king's throne, the heroic Spanish people had been repaid in blood when Fernando VII and the tsar had broken their word and "the army of France disgraced itself by invading Spain."[254] Kakhovskii offered a lament: "Unhappy Spain! There the Holy Beneficent Inquisition has been established once again, and effeminate people with bent backs drag logs to feed the fire of an auto-da-fé."[255]

The news of Riego's arrest aroused further dismay among officers in and out of the Decembrist movement. According to General Batenkov, even the most moderate people condemned as cowardly Fernando's treatment of Riego.[256] In 1823, Tsar Alexander, freshly arrived from Europe, where he had sanctioned the French intervention in Spain, reviewed the troops in the camp at Tulchin in Ukraine. Afterward he attended an officers' mess, where he sat at the center of the banquet table. Having just received by courier a message from Chateaubriand, Alexander announced to his men. "Messieurs, je vous félicite: Riego est fait prisonnier." The company displayed a demonstrative silence except for one who said, "Quelle heureuse nouvelle, Sire!"—thereupon losing the respect of his fellow officers.[257]

Recounting the incident in verse, Alexander Pushkin confused news of Riego's arrest with that of his execution.

> They told the tsar that now at last
> The rebel leader Riego's hanged.
> "I am very glad," a zealous toady said.
> "The world's now rid of one more scoundrel."
> All fell mute with downcast eyes—
> Surprised by the unexpected verdict.
> Riego sinned against Fernando.
> Agreed—but he was hanged for that.
> But pray tell, it is decent, in a fit of ire,
> For us to curse the hangman's prey?

> The tsar himself, so kind a man,
> Wished not to approve it by a smile.
> Bootlickers and yes-men! Try preserving
> In your meanness just a shred of nobility.[258]

Mikhail Orlov reported a similar episode. He angered the company at a dinner when he said that "Riego was a fool and not worth mourning."[259] The hanging occurred on October 26, 1823, in the Russian calendar, and apparently one just could not avoid hearing about it among some circles. Lieutenant Aleksandr Gangeblov, while in the Corps of Pages, joined a study group in 1823 to discuss world history. Within a short time, the discussion had moved from ancient times "to Riego, recently hanged in Spain."[260]

Kakhovskii, under question after the collapse of the Decembrist revolt, recounted that his radicalism had gained an edge from the news of the humiliating spectacle of Riego's execution. He described the Spaniard's end in accents of indignation and sorrow: "Poisoned and half-alive, that saintly martyr, a hero who had renounced the throne offered to him, a friend of the people, savior of the king's life, was now by the king's order pulled through the streets of Madrid in the cart of shame harnessed to a donkey, and hanged like a criminal."[261] The probably false poisoning story was widely accepted in Europe; and at least one Decembrist, Aleksandr Bulatov, believed that Riego had been quartered.[262] Kakhovskii muddled some of the facts about Riego and the king's voyage from Madrid to Cadiz in 1823, but his perception of treachery and barbarism in the public execution of Riego clearly fed his thirst for revolt.

Other victims of Fernando's repressive campaign elicited sympathy from Russian officers. In the summer of 1824, the Russian frigate *Swift* sailed into Spanish waters. Among its crew were the Decembrists Aleksandr Beliaev, a junior officer, and Lieutenant Nikolai Bestuzhev, Mikhail's brother, the fleet historian. They landed in British Gibraltar near which the liberal resistance to the French still smoldered. Beliaev met veteran rebels Lopez Bañoz, Navarez, Espinosa, and Lieutenant Colonel Catayano Valdés, who had just landed at Tarifa with a new pronunciamento. British and Russian officers joined them in singing the Riego hymn. We "raised our glasses to the immortal hero and to freedom," recalled Beliaev; the experience "infused me with love of liberty and readiness for any sacrifice." He felt disgust at seeing vessels manned by the once freedom-loving French bombarding Tarifa and killing Spaniards who had recently tasted liberty.[263] Bestuzhev saw royalist troops executing unarmed Spanish liberals by shooting them in the back like thieves and bandits. According to Nikolai Grech, the spectacle filled Bestuzhev with hatred for the despotic Spanish government.[264]

The accumulating rancor over the counterrevolutionary bloodshed in Spain edged some of the Decembrists into resuming talk of regicide. The Spanish and

Neapolitan rebels had taken the word of their sovereign on faith and had been betrayed. Could a constitution work under a Romanov tsar? More and more after 1823 grew a reluctance to trust any monarch, even if he were to agree on a limitation of his powers. Alexander Poggio admitted that his thoughts about regicide had first been born in 1817, but he stressed the impact of the 1820s events. He recalled that, after telling Matvei Muraviev-Apostol of the death of Riego, he said to him: "He has met his death; he, the very man who abolished the Inquisition and torture and liberated many of its victims, those who had declared a constitution in 1809 [sic] and had shed their blood to save it and their country from the Napoleonic yoke." Poggio, in ritual fashion, denounced Tsar Alexander, who had earlier recognized the constitution. Muraviev-Apostol replied that "Riego himself was to blame: he should have founded a republic and never put his trust in the oath of a tyrant." In 1826, explaining himself to the investigators, Poggio wrote: "Be not surprised at the way we likened Russia to Spain, even though we lacked its Inquisition and its tortures—in a word, those [modes of] persecution: but in our deliberations we denied this [difference] and looked into the future. This is how we came to our present ruin."265

The conspirators' furious response to the suppressions and Tsar Alexander's role in them radicalized the Decembrist goals and accelerated their timetable. Though Russian conspirators idealized the uprising in Spain and often ignored its complexities, its power sufficed to ignite enthusiasm and a sense of solidarity. The inspiration sprang from their perception of a heroic uprising against tyranny carried out with a minimum of violence, a liberal constitution, royal betrayal, and defeat only at the hands of a foreign invader. What appealed to the Decembrists was a kind of Spanish formula: a rapid blow performed by officers without bloodshed.266 The more ambitious Decembrists also belonged to an international confraternity dedicated to overthrowing absolutism all over Europe. Pestel's elaborate plan to trigger the liberation of Europe in the wake of a Balkan rising, the most developed of this aspiration, was not the only one. Kondratii Ryleev came to believe that Europe could only be freed by a revolutionary Russia. Mikhail Bestuzhev-Riumin, when initiating the Society of United Slavs into the Southern Society, announced that its imminent aim was "to liberate Russia and perhaps all of Europe. The Russian army will support the upsurge of all peoples. As soon as it proclaims freedom—all the nations will rejoice. A great deed will have been done, and they will call us the heroes of the age."267 These visions suggested that, with the collapse of autocracy in the three Eastern powers, Naples and Spain would be avenged and liberated. Together with the scattered Russian testaments of solidarity with the insurgents of Spain, Naples, and Greece, they added up to a picture of emerging international revolutionary consciousness, anticipating in a way Mazzini, the Pan-Slavs, the Polish slogan "For your freedom and ours," and even the early Bolsheviks.

Decembrists did not play the role of activist political exiles who roamed from revolution to revolution to liberate lands other than their own, like the French, Italians, Poles, and others who fought in Latin America and in Spain in 1823 and the radical philhellenes. As conspirators in their own country, the more radical among them hoped to turn Russia into a base, a motherland, so to say, of international revolution. How secure would that base have been had the Decembrists come to power? Ryleev and others alluded to the example of Russia's decisive defeat of Napoleon in 1812. That experience, he wrote, "serves as the best proof that a revolution [in Russia]—unlike those in Naples, Piedmont, and . . . Spain cannot be stopped by a foreign force."[268] But here one must ask the question: if such a revolution had succeeded and an army—say, of Austrians and Prussians—had intervened, would the Russian masses have supported the revolutionaries, as Ryleev believed, or would they have welcomed an "eastern Angoulême"? The Spanish experience offered no encouragement. There the people, who had resisted Napoleon far longer and more strenuously than had the Russians, failed to aid the beleaguered constitutional government in 1823.

Generally, the experience of the south European revolutions of 1821 taught different lessons: to the moderate Northerners, they seemed to indicate that constitutional monarchies worked, if not crushed by interventions; to the Southerners, the treachery of monarchs proved otherwise. Though couched in somewhat schematic terms, Professor Nechkina's verdict stands: "The West European revolutionary events were an important component in the general situation from which emerged the further ripening and development of the Decembrist movement."[269] But something more concrete needs saying. Key figures in the Decembrist movement were inspired by the heroic revolt of dissident officers in Spain and Naples— their pronunciamentos, their limits on the king's powers, and their efforts to convert their people to a liberal cause through religious language. Their sympathy for the Greek rebels was further molded by admiration for an insurgent underdog struggling for freedom from tyranny, in this case national subjugation. The perceived treason of the European monarchs and the reactionary interventions and reprisals escalated the Decembrists' determination and led them into martyrdom. The final theme that binds them together arose from the contrast between the seeds of liberty and the hard ground on which they had to be planted.

On Senate Square

Tsar Alexander I died unexpectedly on November 19, 1825 (OS). Due to a secret protocol in his will naming Nicholas instead of Constantine as heir to the throne, the succession remained in suspense until Nicholas, previously unaware of the will, finally realized that his older brother would not accept the throne.

Though the oath to Grand Duke Constantine had already been taken in important ceremonies in Petersburg and Moscow, Nicholas decided on December 10
to assume the purple. Since Constantine, as viceroy of the Kingdom of Poland,
resided in Warsaw, the resultant delay and confusion convinced the Northern
Society that this could be their moment. By mid-December, when it seemed that
the crown would be fitted to the head of Grand Duke Nicholas, the conspirators
had decided to strike. But where?

Did Spain or Naples offer clues? For Spanish liberals, Cadiz and Leon had
been the birthplace of the constitution, an operational base in 1820, and a last
stand in 1823. Fuzzy knowledge of this inspired Kondratii Ryleev to see Kronstadt, an island naval base near the capital, as a "Russian Leon." He urged naval
officers and Northern Society members Konstantin Torson and Nikolai Bestuzhev to spread agitation in the fleet in order to create a staging area for the uprising from which to seize St. Petersburg and its bastion, the Peter Paul Fortress.
Thinking of the Spaniards at Leon and Cadiz in 1823, Ryleev also imagined that
Kronstadt could serve as an escape hatch for the Russian rebels in case of failure.
They would ready a ship and defend the "fortress of the revolution," in emulation
of Quiroga and Riego. In addition, Kronstadt would be a barrier to the departure
of the royal family. In any event, wiser naval heads dissuaded Ryleev from the
scheme.[270]

Like Generals Pepe and Fabvier, who conjured up a "Cadiz" in Sicily and at
Navarino, Ryleev had become enchanted with the notion of a Spanish-style revolutionary stronghold. His analogy, born of a misreading of Leon's role in 1820
and 1823, was faulty in every way. Kronstadt was a real island surrounded by
water; Leon and Cadiz lay on a promontory halfway across the country from its
capital. The site gave birth to the Cortes in 1810 and to the 1819 plots against the
gathering armada. But Riego launched his revolt from a small provincial town.
Crews of the Baltic fleet faced no dangerous overseas expedition. In 1823, Cadiz
and Leon collapsed, defeated by the French.

Thus, the action more sensibly began at the center of the capital, the grandiose city of Peter the Great and site of previous overturns carried out by Guards
officers. The huge Winter Palace, residence of the imperial family, stood between
Palace Square and the Neva River and on its embankment, directly across from
the Peter and Paul Fortress, the city's main defensive point and chief prison. The
Admiralty extended from the palace several blocks along the river to Senate
Square. Nearby in several directions were quartered the Guards regiments, set to
protect the throne; private palaces and mansions, cathedrals, and theaters. Various units were barracked across the river on Vasilievskii Island to the north.

On the days leading up to the revolt, the conspirators met constantly at the
home of Ryleev on the Moika River. They were propelled into action not only by
the confusion of the interregnum but also by news that they had been infiltrated

by police informers. The late emperor's brothers, Grand Dukes Constantine and Nicholas, both known to be iron-fisted drillmasters, hardly fit the role of constitutional monarch. But Constantine remained far away, and by December 9, the rebels knew about his refusal of the throne. So they chose to depict Nicholas as a usurper and place his brother in the role of the legitimate monarch in the eyes of their troops. The decision to advance Grand Duke Constantine as the rightful heir thus in a way made him an unwitting and unwilling "pretender." Abandoning any open demand for a republic at this stage, the rebels, in order to deceive the soldiers, presented them with a "false tsar." His fate if the revolt had succeeded remains an open question.

Ryleev and the Bestuzhev brothers spent two evenings making the rounds of barracks to talk with the soldiers. They told troops they met that the late tsar's will, reducing military service, had been suppressed. They got little response. On the eve of the rising, the last meeting took place amid an orgy of emotion and incantations about the rebels' imminent death. The poet Ryleev had emerged as the natural leader—the "soul" and the "mainspring," as some called him later. He unleashed his energy and rhetoric in the cause of enlistment, stiffened the will of some, and announced that their effort would probably fail and that he himself would perish. Ryleev remained grounded enough to try to have an informer assassinated and to commission Kakhovskii to kill the tsar on Senate Square.[271]

The setting for the mutiny of December 14, 1825, offered visual and kinetic theatricality. How different this urban theater of revolution was from the modest squares in Las Cabezas, Avellino, Iași, and Vasilkov. Senate Square—site of the Bronze Horseman and surrounded by the ice-locked Neva River, the Admiralty, the Senate and Synod buildings, and St. Isaac's Cathedral, still under construction—came to life that day as the troops gathered to give their oath to the new monarch. A wintry sun blazed through the falling snow, catching the glint of metallic helmets and scabbards and equestrian caparisons. The emperor and his entourage on one side of the immense plaza and the massed ranks of the rebel units on the other provided an illustrious cast for the unfolding spectacle. The fourteenth of December became embedded in history as *the* day of the rising. In the aftermath, Tsar Nicholas referred to the plotters as "mes amis de quatorze" and never as those of the thirty-first, the day of the Southern revolt.

Some 2,850 men led by thirty officers and six civilians formed up on Senate Square in the morning of December 14. The organizers failed to win support in the Finland and Semenovskii regiments and gained only segments of the Moscow, Marine, and Grenadier regiments and very few of their officers. The rebels stood against potentially more than three times as many.[272] The Bestuzhev brothers told men of the Moscow regiment that Grand Duke Constantine, the real tsar, was in chains. But the hard-core conspirators found themselves still reluctant to reveal to the men in the ranks and other members of the lower

classes their plans. Officers told their men to shout "Constantine and the constitution!" An urban legend persists that some soldiers who shouted "Konstantin i
Konstitutsiia" believed it meant Constantine and his wife. True or not, the tale is
not so farfetched. When in 1860 Giuseppe Garibaldi's Red Shirts in Sicily cried
"Viva l'Italia," some of the locals thought that "Italia" was the wife of the Piedmontese king Vittorio Emanuele.[273]

The new emperor, Nicholas I, stood at the head of government troops at first
along the Admiralty boulevard and later before the riverside face of the Isaac
Cathedral construction site. The two formations faced each other for hours
through the winter day. The insurgent side sent up hurrahs for the constitution
but took no mass action. Their chances were badly bruised by the defection of
Sergei Trubetskoi, recently chosen by the Northern Society as "dictator" of the
movement. Trubetskoi had prepared a proclamation calling for a provisional
government, freedom of worship, legal equality, a jury system, public trials, the
"abolition of the right of ownership extending to people," and the end of military
conscription and of the Military Settlements.[274] Instead of heading up his forces
and reading them the proclamation, however, this high-ranking grandee from an
ancient family lost his nerve: he went to the other side, swore an oath to Nicholas, and, after wandering the streets in a fugue of despair, retired to the Austrian
embassy. His failure to take command deprived the rebels of a prestigious presence on the square.

Inside and outside the rebel cause, the day was blemished by two assassinations. General Mikhail Miloradovich, governor-general of the city and one of the
most highly decorated officers in the tsar's forces, tried to persuade the rebels to
disperse. Peter Kakhovskii, whom Ryleev had seen as the movement's Karl
Sand,[275] came forward and shot Miloradovich to death. Of the two other officers
who attempted to parlay, one was killed, the other missed the bullet.

But even given these dark auguries, achieving some kind of overturn was not
impossible. The new emperor's admirable reluctance to shed the blood of his
soldiers led him to delay military action until dusk. In the intervening hours, the
insurgents might have been able to win some of the assembled government
forces over to their side. Even more hopeful was the sullen mood of many civilian bystanders, who seemed to favor the defiant ones. The Decembrist leaders,
in addition to the other weaknesses derived from poor planning and defections,
declined to take up these options. Eventually, Nicholas' advisors prevailed and
three artillery pieces were deployed against the closed ranks of their adversaries.
The snow turned red with blood on the square, in neighboring Galernaia Street,
and even on the Neva River as the shot tore through the rebel units and brought
the mutiny to an end.

Did Riego's shadow fall across Senate Square on December 14? Only in the
most inconsequential manner. In Steinhel's later testimony, quoted endlessly in

the literature, portraits of Riego and Quiroga were on display in one of St. Petersburg's shops in the weeks running up to December 14.[276] Aleksandr Bulatov, a recent recruit to the Northern Society and a regimental commander, boasted to his brother that "if I am part of the action, then Brutuses and Riegos will appear among us, and perhaps they will surpass those revolutionaries."[277] Bulatov was quoting the final words of Ryleev's "The Citizen," which had warned that some of his comrades might suffer a failure of nerve: "They will repent when the people, / Having arisen, / Finds them in idle languor's embrace, / And, seeking liberty's rights in the stormy revolt, / Finds among them neither a Brutus nor a Riego."[278]

Sergei Trubetskoi and other Decembrist leaders did indeed fall into "idle languor's embrace" on December 14. But Ryleev's stirring verses mispredicted what really transpired on that day. The "people" did not rise, nor were they ever inducted on a broad scale into the plans and aims of a revolution. The Petersburg putsch—what else can it be called?—suffered from lack of a rigorous and coordinated plan and an undisputed leader, a paucity of committed men and artillery, and most of all from the firmness shown by the tsar's troops—in spite of verbal harassment from civilian bystanders. The episode on Senate Square, framed as it was by the magnificence of the capital and marked visually by the blood on the snow, has captured the imagination and the attention of all general accounts down through the years. St. Petersburg formed the heart of the revolt and was home to the Northern Society, two of whose leaders perished on the scaffold. This day-long scene of confrontation stands in stark contrast to the mobile drama played out over a week on the steppes of southern Russia, with its pronunciamento, forced marches, and plots to capture cities and mobilize troops.

The Last Horseman

The revolt in the south has been less successful in capturing the imagination of readers about the Decembrist uprising. Its leader, the man who closed the gap between the Slavs and the Southerners and who raised the last banner of revolt in 1826, Lieutenant Colonel Sergei Muraviev-Apostol (1796–1826), has been piously called—with a play on words by a Soviet biographer—"the Apostle Sergei."[279] He might justly be called "the last horseman" of this revolutionary era. Russian society felt shock that a man from such a distinguished family should rise against the tsar and be executed. In fact, no fewer than six Muraviev-Apostols were implicated in the Decembrist movement—and a clutch of Muravievs as well, all in some way related. Later members of the family became loyal servitors. N. N. Muraviev (1809–1881) earned the sobriquet "Amurskii" for his activity in the Amur Basin when governor of Siberia. M. N. Muraviev (1796–1866), briefly arrested and acquitted as a Decembrist, gained notoriety as

"Muraviev the Hangman" for his role in the brutal suppression of the Polish revolt in the 1860s.[280]

Muraviev-Apostol's mother, daughter of an Austrian general in Russian service, came from a Serbian background. His father, the nobleman Ivan Muraviev-Apostol, descended on his mother's side from Danilo Apostol, a Ukrainian hetman. As the owner of four thousand serfs in Poltava Province and thousands more in other provinces, the father was able to pursue, in the Russian manner, a career as court favorite, tutor to royalty, and diplomat, and also have a vocation as a cosmopolitan literary traveler, classicist, dramatist, and translator. After a diplomatic stint in Hamburg, he served from 1801 to 1805 as minister to Spain, where he lobbied against Napoleon. When Manuel Godoy began appeasing Napoleon, Muraviev-Apostol was no longer welcome in Madrid, and he returned to Russia in 1807.[281]

Ivan Muraviev-Apostol had stopped in Paris on the way to Spain and enrolled his children at a lycée—or, as some sources say, took the children to Spain and then sent them back to Paris.[282] Sergei, his older brother, Matvei (b. 1793), and the youngest, Ippolit (b. 1806), lived in France even during a bitter war with Russia between 1805 and 1807. Sergei excelled, learned Latin, and mastered French—which remained better than his Russian. One of his schoolmates was the future poet Alfred de Vigny. A story was told later that Napoleon, visiting the school, noticed Sergei's strong resemblance to himself, like that of a son. Though existing likenesses of the Russian do not lend weight to this tale, it was used against him near the end of his life.[283] In 1809 he returned to St. Petersburg, thoroughly gallicized but full of fervent Russian patriotism—a familiar combination of that era among aristocracies everywhere. At home, Sergei followed the news of the Spanish struggle against Napoleon. On the death of his mother, the boy went to live in Moscow with his aunt and his cousin—the soon to be renowned leader of the Northern Society, Nikita Muraviev.[284]

After military training, Sergei had become a second lieutenant by May 1812—just at Russia's most menacing moment of the century. Napoleon invaded in June. The young officer's baptism of fire occurred at the battle of Vitebsk on July 11–13, and he fought at Borodino and Krasnoe, where he received the Golden Sword for bravery—not the last of his decorations for valor. After campaigning in Germany and France, in 1814 the seventeen-year-old received his captaincy.[285] Military service in the Napoleonic wars was a formative experience for the most prominent Decembrists, as it was for Riego, Pepe, and Ypsilanti. After the war, Muraviev-Apostol ended up in the elite Semenovskii Regiment. By all accounts, he loved the men who served under him, and he enjoyed a reputation for kindness; his soldiers sometimes wrote to him for advice.[286] M. A. Fonvizin, Decembrist officer and nephew of the famous writer, recalled decades later that Muraviev-Apostol possessed "a pure character . . . a bright mind, deep religiosity, and a noble spirit." He was "loved, respected by all." Others confirm that judgment.[287]

At war's end, Muraviev-Apostol shared the dissatisfied mood of other returning officers. In 1816, the flat he shared with a brother became the founding site of the Union of Salvation. The original membership comprised Nikita and Alexander Muraviev, I. D. Iakushkin, Sergei Trubetskoi, and the Muraviev-Apostols. In 1817, he joined a "Military Society." Sergei, like many of his fellow officers, abolished or lightened physical punishment in his command—a feature of the philanthropic impulse in the first secret societies. Years later, his surviving brother, Matvei, told Leo Tolstoy about Sergei's remarkable lenience toward his men; the conversation inspired the novelist to write the article "Shameful," denouncing corporal punishment.[288]

In the wake of the Semenovskii mutiny, Muraviev-Apostol and other officers and men were dispersed to different units. At a banquet while on assignment in the Baltic, Sergei was feted for his honorable behavior during the turmoil.[289] But his mood may be gauged by the fact that when he encountered the equally learned Vigel in Petersburg in early November, he uttered the Latin phrase "Vivere in sperando, morire in cacando" (To live in hope and to die in shit).[290] The authorities frowned upon the affection between Muraviev-Apostol and his men, and an imminent arrest was rumored. Instead they posted him far from the capital, in Ukraine, where, as a lieutenant-colonel, he eventually became a battalion commander in the Chernigov Regiment of the Southern Army. He met secretly with former soldiers of the Semenovskii Regiment and spread discontent among them. Everyone knew that the Semenovskii mutiny had helped tip the tsar toward intervention in Naples.[291]

Sergei Muraviev-Apostol's brothers, Matvei and Ippolit, became Decembrists, as did his cousins the Muravievs. Among his closest comrades Sergei counted Mikhail Bestuzhev-Riumin. Born in 1801 in a village in Nizhnii Novgorod province to an eminent serf-owning family, Bestuzhev-Riumin was among the youngest of the conspirators and the youngest to be hanged. Schooled by a native tutor, he became well versed in French literature. Voltaire's tragedies, he reported, awakened his first liberal impulses. In Moscow in 1816, he enrolled in a Chevalier Guards regiment; in St. Petersburg, he frequented the salon of Aleksei Olenin, a meeting place for luminaries of art and literature. After a difference of opinion with his commander, Bestuzhev-Riumin transferred to the Semenovskii Regiment.[292] Thus the two disgraced officers ended up together in the southern reaches of the empire. Suspected and carefully watched, they felt deeply humiliated by their treatment. They spent the next five years in and around the little town of Vasilkov, near Kiev, where troops were quartered in villages and town residences in winter.

The annual Contract Fair in Kiev filled the ancient city with thousands of visitors and traders, turning it temporarily into the liveliest city in the empire and thus a natural magnet for officers in the Southern Army, bored out of their minds by peacetime garrison duty. There in 1822, Pestel persuaded Muraviev-Apostol to join the Southern Society, formed a year earlier. The decision was driven by Pestel's arguments for a republic and by Muraviev's bitter experience in the Semenovskii affair.

From 1823 onward, concrete plans for a revolt began to take shape, some involving annual bivouacs, maneuvers, or inspections. This was the kind of event—one that brought masses of troops together out of their scattered billets and garrisons—that had seemed promising to Quiroga and Riego for recruitment purposes at the Plain of Palmar and to General Pepe at Sessa Arunca for that reason and as the site of a possible coup or abduction of the monarch. Muraviev-Apostol, Bestuzhev-Riumin, and their colleagues also decided to play capture-the-king. Temporarily stationed at the Bobruisk fortress, and learning of the tsar's intention to review their troops, they planned to arrest him, force him to abdicate, and hold him under guard. They would then "march at once to Moscow, recruiting soldiers along the way and winning popular support by means of proclamations."[293] The plan was abandoned not because the tsar failed to appear, a notion found in some older accounts, but due to lack of agreement and insufficient means for carrying it out. Pestel persuaded his colleagues that the revolt was premature and that in any case it should begin with the killing of the tsar and not his arrest.[294]

In late 1824 Muraviev-Apostol, Bestuzhev-Riumin, and their comrades advanced the more radical Belaia Tserkov' plan, after another site of an imperial troops inspection planned for 1825. There, officers dressed in soldiers' greatcoats would kill the tsar at night, signaling the rebels to march off to Kiev, Moscow, and St. Petersburg. Muraviev-Apostol, on reaching the capital, would arouse the Northerners and organize a revolt. The plan was aborted by the emperor's cancellation of his review.[295]

In the Southern Society, one of the issues that continued to vex discussions in the years leading up to the uprising was the fate of the imperial family. A key meeting took place on November 24, 1823, on an estate at Kamenka in Ukraine. The small gathering came to celebrate the name day of Vasilii Davydov's mother and became a strategy session of Southern Society leaders: Pestel, Sergei Muraviev-Apostol, Mikhail Bestuzhev-Riumin, Sergei Volkonskii, and Davydov. When the talk turned to Spain, the conspirators criticized liberals who had given too much power to King Fernando. They resolved not to follow "the foolish example of Spain and to guard against the possibility of failure."[296] The "foolish example" of course was trusting in a constitutional king. Matvei Muraviev-Apostol thought that "Riego himself was to blame. He should have founded a republic and not believed the oath of a tyrant."[297] Riego had been hanged on November 7 (NS; November 19 in the Russian calendar), five days before the meeting. In this atmosphere, the talk of Spain led naturally to the issue of how to deal with the Russian dynasty. Here the testimonies diverge.

According to Prince Volkonskii's account, Mikhail Bestuzhev-Riumin, Muraviev-Apostol, and the others agreed to the extermination of the royal family. Denying this, Muraviev-Apostol testified that the issue, first raised at the Kamenka meeting, was postponed for further discussion and never resumed. He confessed to having agreed to the murder of the emperor, but neither he nor the others present condoned slaying the royal family. Prince Volkonskii, he said, had erred in tying this extreme measure to the Spanish example. The colleagues had spoken of Spain, Muraviev-Apostol admitted, but as proof of the need to introduce a constitutional system in Russia by means of a provisional government. They did not think the Spanish liberals had erred in preserving the life of the king and the entire royal family. Their mistake was only in their continued faith in a monarch who had already betrayed the constitution (that is, in 1814). Volkonskii, Muraviev-Apostol said, had mistaken the talk of removing any member of the Russian dynasty from the post-revolutionary government for the family's physical liquidation. Muraviev-Apostol added that had he favored the murder of the royals, he would have supported a rising in the capital, where that family lived.[298]

In fact, Sergei did accede to the extermination of the royal family at Kamenka. After the ventilation of the Spanish tragedy, he felt it his duty to tell his comrades that he had changed his mind and that it was necessary to destroy not only the tsar but the entire Romanov dynasty.[299] Muraviev-Apostol's conversion to regicide resulted from Pestel's persuasive powers and the example of Spanish royal treachery, but his vote for the family's annihilation had no particular Spanish dimension, since the Carlist wars would not begin until ten years after the Kamenka meeting. At the trial in 1826, Muraviev could not or would not admit being a party to such brutal slaughter.

The next stage of the conversation in the south on regicide occurred in late August and September 1825, during the summer encampment of several divisions and brigades of the Russian army at Leshchin, a hamlet of Zhitomir district, Volynia province. The discussion again took a "Spanish" turn and pitted some of the United Slavs against the original Southerners. Petr Borisov testified that on August 30, 1825, Sergei Muraviev-Apostol, referring to the Spanish example, told him and a few colleagues that no member of the Russian imperial family would agree to the demands of the people, but neither he nor Bestuzhev-Riumin talked of killing the royal family or even the emperor.[300] In Gorbachevskii's account, Muraviev-Apostol, in this first meeting with Borisov and himself, indirectly raised the issue of what to do with the tsar. He wondered "if they thought that the sovereign would agree to grant a constitution and that, having done so, would observe it to the letter." Arguing the impossibility of trusting the tsar, he alluded to King Fernando's treatment of the constitution in Spain.[301]

Earlier editions of Gorbachevskii's memoirs have one of the Borisovs and a few other members of the United Slavs opposing all palace revolutions and regicide and rejecting a scenario resembling the "fate of Charles I, Louis XVI, the exile of James II, and the captivity of Fernando VII."[302] But in a copy of the original manuscript of the memoirs, found in the archives in 1930, Borisov and company were said to have condemned "the murder of Paul I and in general all palace revolutions, *but approved* [italics added] the fate of Charles I and Louis XVI, the exile of James II, and the captivity of Fernando VII." The substitution of one word, *ne* (not) for *no* (but), had thus changed the entire sense of the statement, endorsing at least the execution of two previous European monarchs.[303] The garbling aside, Gorbachevskii did favor killing the tsar and said that liberty was "bought neither with tears nor with gold, but with blood." Thus the Southern Society, some of the United Slavs, and even some Northerners endorsed regicide, though many still opposed it. In fact, some of the Slavs were among the most eager volunteers for the suicide and assassination squad.[304] The exact division on the matter of exterminating the royal family remains obscure. Crystal clear, however, is the way Spanish events were so frequently invoked on this issue and the way the hatred of Fernando was transmuted into a desire to kill the tsar.

During September 1825, another recurrent issue came to a head. Put in its starkest form, it was the question of whether to launch a pure officers' revolt, leading passive soldiers, or to instruct the troops on the aims of the conspiracy. Several methods and various levels of inclusion had been tried. Burned by the arrest of Raevskii for his radical schooling, some leaders opted for a limited program of carefully cultivating officers on the coming revolt; they in turn would prepare their commands for "blind obedience." Pestel had opposed agitation in the ranks and maintained strict punishment and discipline. When a visit by the tsar was imminent, he increased severity, thus identifying it with the monarch.[305] Pestel saw the army as a state *in ovo*, aimed at defending the new order both from counterrevolution and from mass revolution.

Some of the United Slavs questioned a purely military seizure of power by officers. At the Leshchin encampment, Peter Borisov challenged the intentions of a post-revolutionary authoritarian government ruled by the military. Mikhail Bestuzhev-Riumin, a close associate of Pestel in the South, felt insulted at the slur on the honor of his comrades who were willing to buy freedom by killing their monarch. But Borisov replied somewhat angrily that Caesar had fallen under the blows of assassins and then a young Octavius made himself the new master of Rome.[306] The Slavs displayed more revolutionary enthusiasm and democratic tendencies than the other groups, but they too opposed a massive uprising. What they endorsed was propaganda and enlightenment of the troops, but not of the broad lower-class population.[307] They believed that revolution required slow, gradual education into morality and enlightenment.

Among the most vocal on this matter was Ivan Gorbachevskii (1800–1869), born in Nezhin, Ukraine, grandson of a priest, and son of a poor but high-ranking official who was accused of embezzlement and fired from government. Ivan, a learned man who translated Voltaire, Rousseau, and Schiller, donated all his land to his serfs.[308] As a member of the United Slavs, Gorbachevskii and a few others met in Leshchin on September 15 in the tent of Sergei Muraviev-Apostol, with Mikhail Bestuzhev-Riumin present as well. Muraviev-Apostol and Gorbachevskii talked in a corner by themselves about "the preparation of the soldiers." Gorbachevskii endorsed a systematic agitation among the ranks. He wanted gradually to reveal to them the aims of the societies, have them understand the reason for the rebellion, and get their commitment to it on the basis of its advantages for them. In somewhat contradictory fashion, he wanted "not to hide anything from the soldiers, but endeavor with great caution to explain to them all the advantages of a revolt and gradually introduce them to all the secrets of the society, but of course without revealing its existence, so that they would fight not in a moment of fervor but steadily—for their own ideas and for the rights they seek." He was convinced that "sincerity and openness would work better with the Russian soldier than all the cunning Machiavellianism."[309]

M. P. Bestuzhev-Riumin put it tersely in September 1825, as the Slavs were uniting with the Southern Society. Omitting the movement's regicidal plans, he said, "Our revolution will be like the Spanish Revolution—it will not shed one drop of blood, for it will be carried out solely by the army without the participation of the people."[310] This elitist military approach to regime change had wide support among officers. Gorbachevskii ironically recalled his fellow officers' views on leading soldiers into revolution. Colonel Thiesenhausen said that all he had to do was "form up the regiment, open a few casks of wine, hand out some money, get some song-books, and move forward with the shouted command 'After me!'" Others thought that some extra chunks of bacon fat in the men's kasha would do the trick. Colonel Ental'tsev, an artillery officer, asked Gorbachevskii why an artillery brigade, composed mostly of Society of United Slavs members, was given an explanation of the meaning of the revolt. When Gorbachevskii replied that it was so that the men knew what they were fighting for and were ready for it, the colonel told him it was unnecessary: "If my unit did not follow me, I would drive them forward with a club."[311]

According to the Gorbachevskii account, Sergei Muraviev-Apostol said on September 15 "that it would be not only useless but even dangerous to reveal to the soldiers anything whatever about the goals of the Society; that they were in no position to understand the advantage of a change in government; that a republican form of government, equality of social classes, and the election of officials would be to them as the riddle of the Sphinx."[312] The debate begged the question of exactly at what point, as the revolt began, the leaders would unveil their real intentions. But it did raise the larger dilemma of liberal revolutionaries of that era—one that would face Russian and other radicals right through the nineteenth century and into the twentieth. To "trust" that soldiers would be able to follow and absorb—to say nothing of support—a revolt based upon European notions of freedom and a constitutional order would be to share subversive plans with men who largely came from the illiterate peasantry. This entailed a risk that the troops might report those plans to the authorities—or, worse, would rise against and slaughter the conspirators in the name of the tsar. But to keep in the dark the future shock troops of the uprising on whom the leaders would have to depend required either a future and equally perilous disclosure of the leaders' true aims or an elitist dictatorship in the event of success. Muraviev-Apostol opted for greater secrecy and chose to reject giving crucial information to the men. Instead, he hoped to win them over with the argument for their material gains and for religious truth.

The historian Nechkina, in a slightly scolding tone, correctly noted that "in the most leftist group of the Southern Society, not one member went further than a timid recognition of the 'right' to self-liberation of the masses from its yoke, while at the same time denying their 'right' to violent means, to the 'path of bloodshed.'"[313] But on the matter of informing soldiers, the Gorbachevskii memoirs give the mistaken impression that Muraviev-Apostol flatly opposed agitation of any sort among the troops. In fact, he told some of his former Semenovskii troops of a coming revolt "against the tsarist regime," but probably without details of the future political settlement.[314] He also used demoted and embittered former officers to establish links with the commune soldiers.[315] And in the Bobruisk and Belaia Tserkov' schemes, he had already considered using propaganda materials, including a condensed version of the Pestel program, in order to apprise "the people" of the movement's general intentions.[316]

What ultimately distinguished Muraviev-Apostol's final act of propaganda policy from all others in the movement was its focus on religion. Authors of previous subversive proclamations, including those written during the Semenovskii mutiny of 1820, had put God on their side, but almost as an afterthought.[317] Pavel Pestel, though a skeptical deist himself at the time he sketched the second version of Russian Justice, planned to draft the Orthodox clergy into the state administration as the "most respectable part" of the government. He sought to restore the balance between a powerful black clergy (the monks who ran the church) and the suffering, poorly educated white clergy (the parish priests), and to extend and modernize theological training in order to produce what he called "sacred servants required for the common good."[318] Like Napoleon, another skeptic, he believed that the people needed a faith, a church, and an organized clergy. This notion also figured in naming his new capital after St. Vladimir, the Baptizer of Rus.[319]

Sergei Muraviev-Apostol, though he also saw religion's role as a pacifier of the masses to avoid the horrors of 1789, was a true believer. According to Gorbachevskii's recollection of the Leshchin meeting, Muraviev-Apostol averred that "the best way to deal with Russian soldiers is through religion. We need to awaken their fanaticism, and Bible reading can instill hatred for the regime." He told Gorbachevskii that in the Bible "'several chapters contain a direct prohibition by God on choosing a tsar and obeying him. If the Russian soldier learns these divine teachings, then, without the slightest hesitation, he will agree to take up arms against his sovereign.'" Muraviev-Apostol spoke of the simplicity of the common people, reached into his case and pulled out a piece of paper as he uttered these words to Gorbachevskii: "Religion will always be a strong motivation for the human heart; it points the way to goodness, leads to great and valorous deeds of the Russian—who in your view is indifferent to religion—and awards him the martyr's crown." The paper also contained a translation of the Old Testament chapter dealing with the selection by the Israelites of King Saul[320] (Kings 1:8; actually 1 Samuel 8:5–18). This biblical excerpt, where God allegedly showed his people the perils of monarchical rule, would be the one that Muraviev-Apostol used in his catechism.[321]

Gorbachevskii, anticipating radicals such as Belinskii and Bakunin, replied to Muraviev-Apostol that priests and monks had little influence on the Russian people and that there might be more freethinkers in the army than believers. He and his comrades also reminded Muraviev-Apostol that the masses had been brought up with the New Testament teaching that those who opposed their king thereby offended God and religion.[322] Except for details, Muraviev-Apostol confirmed the gist of this meeting when he reported to the Investigating Committee that, in case of a rising, "our best hope and succor must be adherence to the faith, which is so strong among Russians; and that is why in our every action we must endeavor to not to weaken that [devout] feeling." He told the skeptical Gorbachevskii that pure liberty dated only from the birth of the Christian faith and that its rejection in the French Revolution had caused untold misery.[323]

Whatever their differences, religious feelings had animated the leaders of both the Slavs and the Southerners when they merged and took an oath a few days before the conversation between Gorbachevskii and Muraviev-Apostol. Gorbachevskii described the "open-hearted, solemn, and terrifying oaths, accompanied by shouts," played out in an exalted atmosphere of blissful commitment. Each swore on an icon, kissed it, and passed it on amidst tearful addresses and mutual embraces. High emotions prevailed in an atmosphere of mystical romanticism, youthful idealism, and ecstasy.[324] The description leaves no doubt that the Southern conspirators easily equaled the Greeks, the Carbonari, and the Spanish radicals in their level of exaltation. By the time the bivouacking troops had broken camp, two main features of a possible revolutionary strategy had been enunciated, though not yet combined: Bestuzhev-Riumin's concise statement about emulating the Spanish manner; and Muraviev-Apostol's commitment to religious motivation of the troops—both to be reflected in a the use of a revolutionary catechism.

The Catechism of Revolt

In the Russian Orthodox church, the Greek-based term "catechism" (*katikhizis*) sometimes alternated with the Russian equivalent, *oglashenie*—teaching orally by rote memory. Originally used as a preparation for baptism, it grew into a condensed theology of basic principles, with elements of what the Catholics call the Confiteor (I confess)—the profession of faith, but in a dialogical form. Russian Orthodox catechisms of this era feature many components of faith that are found in Western Catholic counterparts.[325] One version adjures the faithful to "honour all who in diverse relations stand to us in the place of parents; as the Sovereign, who is the common father of the whole people and empire; spiritual Pastors and Teachers; Elders; Guardians and Benefactors; Governors and Masters."[326] Catechists in effect took an oath of allegiance to their God and to all other authority figures.

During the Spanish war of resistance, the purely patriotic and the quasi-liberal catechisms transcended their religious content. Both liberal and anti-liberal catechisms had appeared during the Triennium. Revolutionary catechisms had been widely adopted by the Neapolitan Carbonari and the Greek Friendly Society. In all cases, the trick was to weld one's message to a Christian theme in the hopes of capturing the allegiance of believers familiar with the genre. Some Decembrists reasonably viewed this as a plausible way to communicate with the masses in Russia as well. Ryleev remarked that "such works are the most useful of all in influencing the minds of the people."[327] Nikita Muraviev began one and invited Ryleev to finish it. But the latter never got around to it.[328]

Nikita Muraviev's "A Curious Conversation," also known as "Catechism of a Free Person," used the question-and-answer form to place God on the side of good, justice, and freedom. As in the Spanish catechisms, the author explained that Russia had once possessed freedom and a lawful order—in this case exemplified by the Russian *veche* or medieval assembly. In the dialogue, the respondent added the familiar image of rulers as "wolves in sheep's clothing" acting like Tatar khans and a Turkish sultan, violating God's will by gradually enslaving a once free people. "Evil power cannot come from God," says the respondent. All people have the right to resist abridgement of their freedom. Freedom, in Muraviev's words, meant the right "to do whatever does no harm to someone else."[329] The last line, long established in the discourse on freedom, also echoed one of the Spanish catechisms that declared civil liberty as the "ability of a man to do what he wants: but in society liberty is the ability to do whatever the laws do not forbid."[330]

In December 1825, Muraviev-Apostol, who owned a copy of the "Curious Conversation," joined with Bestuzhev-Riumin to create a politically charged "Orthodox Catechism" to rally the troops.[331] The source of this catechism has been the subject of much speculation and occasional distortion. For example, A. Trachevskii's oft-cited 1872 history of Spain noted correctly that "many little catechisms" on patriotic themes had appeared in Spain during the Napoleonic era. He cites a passage from what he takes to be one of them.[332] A comparison of texts shows that his quotation is a compression and paraphrase of passages both from Salvandy's 1824 novel, *Don Alonzo*, and from the original or the Russian translation of the 1808 *Civic Catechism*.[333] These works and all others of the era fulminated against Napoleonic tyranny but exalted the captive King Fernando.

A retrospective attempt to link Colonel Riego directly with the Spanish catechism and thus to Muraviev-Apostol was made in 1939 by the Soviet writer Grigorii Revzin in his semi-fictional biography of the Spanish hero. Revzin has Riego attending a guerrilla camp site where a "Father Pablo" is holding a catechism lesson. This scene was lifted, with minute modifications, from Salvandy's *Don Alonzo* and inserted into the biography of Riego as if it had been a real event in his life during the war against the French. Revzin at least is faithful to the original catechisms by reporting the resistance's loyalty to God, king, and Spain, and in describing the use of religious language to cement this trinity in the minds of its listeners.[334]

What inspired the Russian officers to take up the Spanish example? Two works came into play concerning the form, content, and use of a text in the final episode of the Southern uprising: a Spanish catechism and the French novel. In terms of form, Bestuzhev-Riumin testified after the fact that "the idea of such a work [catechism] had been around society for a long time and was suggested by a catechism for the people composed in 1809 by Spanish monks."[335] The reference to monks and the year 1809 seems to allude to the catechism that indirectly made its way, in bowdlerized form, into the Salvandy novel *Alonzo*. That catechism almost certainly was a copy or variant of the 1808 Seville *Civil Catechism*, whose Russian translation appeared in *Son of the Fatherland* in 1812. Various Spanish catechisms and adaptations appeared in Russia during the Napoleonic wars,[336] and it seems likely that Bestuzhev-Riumin and Muraviev-Apostol were acquainted with the Spanish genre well before the discovery of Salvandy's novel.

But as to content, except for a few inflammatory diatribes about resistance to tyranny, none of the Spanish examples of that era, fictionalized or genuine, offered the kind of political message that the conspirators needed.

Who wrote the revolutionary catechism? At his examination, Mikhail Bestuzhev-Riumin testified that he and Muraviev-Apostol had composed both a proclamation and the catechism. After arrest, Muraviev-Apostol affirmed that Bestuzhev-Riumin had contributed only a small portion. The first version was probably written in early December. When the two men were menaced by arrest on December 27, they destroyed it in order to keep it from the gendarmes, and later recomposed it from memory on the eve of the revolt.[337] The catechism, couched in a familiar rote devotional style and selectively citing the Old and New Testaments, charged all monarchs with usurping the throne of God and indicted the Russian tsar for bringing suffering instead of freedom to his people. One of the replies cited the Apostle Paul on freedom: "You shall not be slaves of man." Another declared the only government in accord with God's laws to be "one where there are no tsars." The catechism ended with the passage quoted at the opening of this chapter.

The "Orthodox Catechism" touched on themes that had appeared in numerous Spanish anti-Napoleonic catechisms. Like them, it castigated a tyrant for contravening God's laws by taking power and purloining the people's freedom; and it consigned to eternal damnation collaborators and those who failed to fight tyranny.[338] Politically, Muraviev-Apostol substituted the Russian tsar for the Spanish puppet Murat or his puppeteer Napoleon. The parallels seem clear, though it must be allowed that Muraviev-Apostol could have gotten some of these formulations from other places. As a strategy, he masked overt references to other revolutions behind a veil of Christian Orthodox teaching—even in the title of the catechism. He captured the cadences and rhythms, the pieties, and the menace of standard religious catechistic literature. The official catechism of the Russian Orthodox Church at that time warned that the person who does not live by God's law "perishes throughout eternity."[339] Muraviev-Apostol's echoed this in his message to the troops in the final sentence of the catechism about anathema and damnation for those who remained aloof from the struggle. He was expressing both his own religion and the adjurations of the Spanish clerics.

Employing religious imagery and exegesis against one's enemy was nothing new. The tsars, like all European monarchs, did it regularly and had done so with great intensity during the war against Napoleon. In taking up this approach, Sergei Muraviev-Apostol analogized Russia with Spain under the Napoleonic yoke, where the priests joined the rebels against the tyrant Napoleon. For all its flaws and deceptive elements, the "Orthodox Catechism," marrying freedom and religion to agency, struggle, and sacrifice, is a far cry from the amorality found in the "Revolutionary Catechism" of Sergei Nechaev and Mikhail Bakunin a generation later.[340] An early historian of Russian constitutions went so far as to include Muraviev-Apostol's "Orthodox Catechism" as part of that history.[341] It was also the only agitational document known to have been unveiled to a public during the uprisings, north and south. The catechism provided the answer in a long debate about the use of propaganda aimed at the common soldier. Considered inflammatory by the Russian government, it was held secret until 1906.[342]

It was Salvandy's novel *Don Alonzo*, however, that provided the propaganda method that the two Decembrists adopted. Sergei Muraviev-Apostol's brother Matvei testified that Bestuzhev-Riumin got the idea of a catechism while doing guard duty in December 1825 at Bobruisk and put some of his ideas on paper. He had gotten hold of *Don Alonzo* and drew a vision from it.[343] A passage in the novel describing how a priest used a catechism to arouse potential resistance fighters against tyranny led the Russian officers to adopt the catechistic format as a transmitter of simple ideas to the troops. They decided to use a Russian priest to play the role of Father Pablo in the novel. The Soviet historian Nechkina, alluding to their republicanism, correctly rejected the Salvandy passage as the inspiration for the political substance of the "Orthodox Catechism." But she also underplayed the role of any Spanish source at this juncture.[344] Yuri Oksman in the 1920s had also challenged the Spanish inspiration of the catechismal form, citing instead various military manuals and other simple teaching materials sometimes called catechisms.[345] Both err in dismissing the Spanish element from the catechism, though it certainly drew on Russian sources as well. In the end, the combination of religion and resistance served as the catalyst that attracted the two Russian officers to a Spanish precedent.

Two successive disasters catapulted Sergei Muraviev-Apostol into action. Pestel's role, still strong in spite of police spy surveillance and some resistance to his leadership in the secret societies, ended with his arrest on December 13, a day before the Northern uprising. News of the latter collapse reached the Southern Society only on December 23, a shock that radically changed everything. Pestel's mantle fell to Muraviev-Apostol and a few comrades and resulted in a flurry of plans. It took almost two weeks before the St. Petersburg call to arms reached the south. False rumors about the alleged success of the Northern Society led the Southerners to move. When word of the Senate Square debacle reached the Chernigov Regiment, Muraviev-Apostol was absent in Zhitomir.

A real-life melodrama of pursuit, arrests, rescues, and counterarrests ensued.[346] On the night of December 24–25, the Chernigov Regiment held a Christmas ball. Two gendarmes covered with snow appeared there with an official arrest order for Muraviev-Apostol, addressed to regimental commander Colonel Gustav Goebel (Gebel). Gendarmes searched Muraviev-Apostol's home in Vasilkov and took his papers. Several Society of United Slavs members got wind of the arrest plans and pursued Goebel, who was chasing the Muraviev-Apostol brothers and Bestuzhev-Riumin. Goebel and his gendarmes, stopping to rest at a house in Trilesy, stumbled on the brothers and arrested them. The next day, responding his earlier note, several members of the Society of United Slavs rescued the prisoners and in turn took their captors into custody. Goebel related that these officers, including Sergei Muraviev-Apostol, assaulted him with bayonets before he managed to escape from their clutches.[347] Muraviev-Apostol in vain ordered him followed and killed. The much-disliked Major S. S. Trukhin, another prisoner, was tossed into a crowd of soldiers, who beat him and tore off his epaulets. Muraviev had him jailed. Though the colonel had ordered the killing of Goebel, Muraviev forbade revolutionary outrages and threatened death to any soldier who abused the citizens.[348]

Spain had remained high in Muraviev-Apostol's consciousness. He often talked and wrote to his father about it, followed events, and praised what he believed was the unity of the revolutionaries and the Cortes' concern for the people. A letter of July 22, 1822 (OS; August 4, NS), focusing on the positive, displayed no awareness of the July 7 (NS) royalist putsch in Madrid that nearly a month earlier had effectively shattered any remaining solidarities in Spanish politics.[349] Riego's execution in 1823 had depressed Muraviev-Apostol. One of the most quoted of Muraviev-Apostol's utterances in his saga of resistance was, according to the testimony of Baron Ven'iamin Soloviev, made in the apartment of a junior officer in late December. "On arriving, Muraviev ordered a company formation; and in the meantime recounted an example from the history of Riego who crossed the country with three hundred men [again the mythical number] and restored the constitution. So how could [we] fail to accomplish our mission when all is in readiness, especially an army which is rife with discontent."[350] This sentence is occasionally cited as being spoken when Muraviev-Apostol set off from Vasilkov into battle, thus glamorizing and distorting the context. In the actual situation, the words had more meaning than if he had flung them to his troops on their way to battle. In addressing officers who would understand the reference, Muraviev-Apostol was revealing how concretely he believed in the viability of emulating the man who had ridden through Andalusia almost exactly six years earlier.

After Muraviev's little Riego speech, Soloviev and others rode for an hour to Vasilkov, where before dawn on December 30 they were arrested by loyalist troops. At 5:00 p.m. (or 3:00 in other sources), Muraviev-Apostol arrived with a grenadier and a musket company. He occupied the town, took command of the units stationed there, freed the prisoners, organized food requisition, and posted guards at the town gate. During the night Muraviev-Apostol, with the aid of Bestuzhev-Riumin and a handful of members of the Society of United Slavs, prepared to strike for power. First he ordered his officers to marshal the troops into formation for the next day. Then, with the help of Mikhail Bestuzhev-Riu-min, he recomposed from memory and in French the "Orthodox Catechism." He sent for two regimental clerks and he and Bestuzhev-Riumin took turns dic-tating to them in Russian, reading aloud the text of the catechism from a paper written "in a foreign dialect." The clerks, assisted by other literate men, produced eleven copies.[351] On the following day, the leaders went out onto the square of Vasilkov to meet their men.

Vasilkov, on the Stugna River, was fabled in the chronicles as a place where Kiev Rus princes conferred on the eve of battle with the Cumans in 1093.[352] A blizzard had blanketed the tiny town in snow. For December 31, Muraviev-Apostol had ordered a 9:00 a.m. reveille, but the men did not form up until 11:00, 12:00, or 2:00 p.m., depending on the source, in front of the Cathedral of St. Theodosius. The formation comprised five companies of the Chernigov Reg-iment and sixty armed musicians. There a solemn ceremony took place, the like of which Russia had never before seen. Muraviev-Apostol had asked a young priest, Daniil Keizer—recently appointed regimental chaplain—to read the cat-echism to the men. Stressing the natural alliance of church and people, Mura-viev-Apostol, according to Gorbachevskii, said to the chaplain: "The Russian clergy . . . have always sided with the people; have ever been, in times of national misfortune, bold and unselfish defenders of the people's rights." The priest replied: "I am ready to die with you for the common good." But Keizer had concerns about his family, should the effort fail and he end up in prison. Mura-viev-Apostol gave him two hundred rubles to help in this eventuality and said, "Neither Russia nor I will ever forget your services." Needless to say, in later tes-timony Father Keizer presented himself as a much more passive figure.[353]

Church deacons and other witnesses testified later that Father Keizer asked Muraviev-Apostol what kind of "mass to say" and that Muraviev-Apostol replied: "Perform something shorter." One of the deacons told Muraviev-Apos-tol that prayers were needed; Mikhail Bestuzhev-Riumin added that a catechism should be read. It seems likely that Keizer, in his admittedly imperfect under-standing of what was happening, conflated "something shorter" and the word "catechism" into the so-called Short Catechism, the standard work for religious instruction in the Orthodox faith.[354] He sent a deacon to fetch it, and Keizer then took prayer books and the catechism to Muraviev-Apostol at headquarters, where the officers had gathered. The sight of loaded weapons frightened the priest. An officer took the church catechism away from him, saying that they had their own.[355]

The scene of the insurgent drama was set: a battalion on the square, by-standers talking to each other, and a rigged-up altar. Muraviev-Apostol rode into the square and, still on horseback, flanked by officers who were armed with pistols and daggers, he had the men form a circle, informed them briefly of the aim of the uprising, and spoke of the nobility of sacrifice for a great cause. Men and officers responded resoundingly. At Muraviev-Apostol's direction, Keizer donned his ecclesiastical garments and intoned a series of prayers—the Laudation and the Lord's Prayer. Unlike the fictional Father Pablo, the Russian priest did not catechize his listeners but simply recited it to them. Accounts diverge sharply. Gorbachevskii claimed that Keizer read the catechism loudly.[356] Keizer himself related that an officer handed him a paper he had never seen before—apparently the "Orthodox Catechism." The terrified chaplain understood nothing in it but intoned each of its passages as they were read to him by another officer standing behind him. Yet another account says that since Keizer spoke in a tremulous voice, Bestuzhev-Riumin took the catechism from him and finished reading it audibly. At the conclusion of the reading, Muraviev-Apostol, clearly wishing to underline the religiosity of the moment, had the priest chant, "Many years of life to all Orthodox Christians."[357]

What effect did the reading have? After the fact, everyone seemed to know how the catechism had been received, though they had no power to read minds. The deacons, under interrogation, claimed that the soldiers understood nothing of it except—except!—that there should be no tsars and that in the past the church had misled the people.[358] In fact, this was the kernel of the document. The catechism resounded many times with the words "tsar" and "tyrant" or their derivatives. Gorbachevskii, though not present, claimed that the religious service made a strong impression on the troops.[359] The soldier Ignatii Rakuza testified that when "they" read the catechism, he heard it, but could not recall its content; the lower ranks, he said, could hardly hear what was being read.[360] How many of the several hundred men standing in formation on an open square could have heard and absorbed the catechism, however it was read? But then again, even if only a few did, given the lightning speed of scuttlebutt in any army, how many could have remained totally unaware of its overall message?

Muraviev-Apostol and Bestuzhev-Riumin had also written a "Proclamation of the Southern Society [Appeal to the People]," which was not distributed among the soldiers or the population and apparently not read to the troops on the square, though Muraviev-Apostol clearly recited some catchphrases from it. It may also have been partially read to the soldiers as they rode out of Vasilkov. A copy was found on Bestuzhev-Riumin. Its language seems to imply, as some have argued, that the army alone would handle the revolt and that the "people" were to remain inert and orderly and not participate in the upheaval.[361]

After the catechism, Muraviev-Apostol again spoke to the troops, promising them a shorter service and basic changes in soldiers' lives. He also told them that other units would join. Judging from fragmentary sources, Muraviev spewed forth short phrases from both the catechism and the proclamation. A local veteran reported that Muraviev-Apostol, sitting atop his horse, shouted to the troops that "there are no tsars, they are merely made-up stories, lads, and there is only the heavenly king and Jesus Christ." The men responded in rote form, "Happy to give our last drop of blood," and Muraviev-Apostol had them shout the three hurrahs.[362] A deacon reported that the commander said, "Lads! Be loyal and serve only the king of heaven above—Jesus Christ: anathema and damnation to him who betrays or deserts me."[363] Muraviev-Apostol at this point offered dissenters the chance to drop out of the formation and remain in Vasilkov. After the speeches, Father Keizer officiated at a Te Deum and the benediction, followed by more hurrahs from the soldiers and, according to Gorbachevskii, the shouts of townspeople: "May God assist you!"[364]

We cannot be sure how the soldiers who followed Muraviev-Apostol were affected by the catechism and their commander's shouted words, which together constituted a pronunciamento. Some of the men had not been able to hear. Those who did cheered and followed him out of town. What of their level of understanding and motivation? Some hated the harsh conditions of service and the corruption of higher commanders. Gorbachevskii surmised that the cheering arose out of trust and personal admiration for their chief. On the day before the rising Muraviev-Apostol, in full view of the troops, had paid the regimental punishment officer twenty-five rubles to go easy on two miscreant soldiers who were to be whipped.[365] Gorbachevskii also admitted that those who planned to defect, get drunk, or misbehave in other ways clearly needed the control of officers who put sentries at the door of taverns along the way.[366] The positive response of some of the men in the ranks, attested to by witnesses, may have been rooted in a blend of martial anticipation and spiritual exaltation created by the familiar jointure of signals from chaplain and commander on the eve of an engagement. For others, it resulted surely from simple habits of obedience. Yet it is hard to believe that all of the nearly one thousand men riding under Muraviev-Apostol for the next few days were merely misled or mystified.

Further confusing the issue of the reception was Muraviev-Apostol's shift from God as Russia's rightful monarch to Grand Duke Konstantin Pavlovich. Did Sergei Muraviev-Apostol cease agitation via the catechism and execute a dramatic switch by preaching allegiance to Constantine? He testified to the authorities as follows: "Seeing that the reading of the Catechism produced a poor impression on the soldiers, I decided again to act in the name of Grand Duke Konstantin Pavlovich."[367] According to the report given by General L. O. Roth after the revolt, Muraviev-Apostol, in order to prevent his troops from swearing to Nicholas, misinformed them that Constantine had not abjured the throne.[368] In one version, Muraviev and his comrades, observing while on the road that the soldiers had no concept of freedom in the absence of a tsar, were obliged to act in the name of Constantine.[369]

Nechkina refuted the notion of a reversal. She argued that Muraviev's state-ment contradicted his actions. If he really thought the catechism was ineffective, he would not have sent an agent to Kiev to spread copies of it.[370] Nechkina's logic falters here, since the Kiev agent was on his way early in the morning, hours before the reading of the catechism. But her skepticism is well placed. Incidents along the road in the next few days allude to a continued use of the catechism and/or the "Appeal to the People." A fellow officer noted during the ride out of Vasilkov how Sukhinov and a few others, "often reading the catechism to the soldiers, spoke to them of freedom [vol'nost']."[371] Yet a different version of this same testimony tells that when the soldiers contradicted Sukhin's teaching about no need for a tsar, "he told them that they were going to support Tsar Constan-tine."[372] It seems reasonable to suppose that the leaders were keeping two arrows in their quiver. There is no question that they were deceiving their men on the issue of Constantine as well as in their false claims about mutiny in other units. In this regard, Muraviev-Apostol was repeating the ways of Ypsilanti.

On December 31, Muraviev-Apostol, mounted on his horse, gave the com-mand to march off, and the priest blessed the column as it rode out of Vasilkov, flags unfurled, crying hurrah.[373] The insurgents' march lasted from December 31, 1825, to January 3, 1826, and covered a distance of less than fifty kilometers through rural settlements with names such as Slopes and Three Forests. Though this was hardly an epic, the zigzag journey through the snow was much longer and richer in movement, action, and battle than the standoff on Senate Square. Muraviev-Apostol had with him about a thousand men, some five hundred fewer than Riego's or Ypsilanti's forces at their peak and much smaller than Pepe's three regiments plus Carbonari.

The column halted from December 31 to January 2 at Motovilovka, a village and estate complex. Here an officer read aloud to the peasants a "proclamation to the people" (proklamatsiia narodu), which Muraviev's biographer believes was either the catechism or the "Appeal to the People."[374] Muraviev proclaimed freedom for the serfs in the areas he occupied; at Motovilovka, in the presence of other serfs, he freed his own personal serfs.[375] Gorbachevskii relates that when Muraviev-Apostol was making his round of the guard posts, the villagers came out of the Motovilovka church and welcomed him. They joyfully wished him a happy New Year and surrounded him, uttering the words "May God assist you, our kind colonel and our liberator."[376] Tellingly, before departing from the next town, Pologi, Muraviev left a copy of the catechism in the hands of a church elder so that he would explain its contents to the congregation.[377]

The report of Lieutenant Lishin, an examiner for the tsar's forces, told a dif-ferent story. He claimed that the locals failed to respond to the rising, but rather helped hunt down the leaders. The catechism, he reported, contained "harmful teachings aimed at the local population. . . . As the peasants came out of church,

[Muraviev-Apostol] read the catechism to them, attempting to instill in them its pernicious rules. The villagers replied: 'We do not understand anything and do not need to [meaning 'do not want to'].'"[378] The local Polish nobleman and owner of the village of Motovilovka, Józef Rulikowski (Iosif Rulikovskii), who was generally friendly to the rebels, insisted that the peasants paid no attention to the events around them. A military inquiry reported that "even in those places where Colonel Muraviev-Apostol appeared and proclaimed freedom, the inhabitants never deserted their obligations [as serfs] and only had conversations about them, which completely ceased once the revolt was over."[379]

Distributing clearly scandalous republican documents in these two towns does not square well with the notion of a genuine shift by Muraviev to Grand Duke Constantine, unless he himself sent out two different messages, one for his troops and one for the peasantry and townspeople. That Muraviev-Apostol intended actually to change his allegiance to a potential Tsar Constantine for other than tactical reasons and thus adopt the Northern Society's program of a constitutional monarchy cannot be credited. Perhaps he decided at the last minute that, for Russians still steeped in popular monarchy, the invocation of a human "tsar" or "tsarevich," as used by previous pretenders, would have more resonance than the abstract reference to God. The most reasonable explanation for the ambivalence is the need to keep all options open. In any case, the leaders, in their proclamations to the "people"—the peasants—merely wanted their sympathy and passive support and not a rural uprising.

How did the mutinous column behave? Historians and their sources diverge on this question. The military historian General Mikhailovskii-Danilevskii later made two claims about Muraviev-Apostol's march: that the commander acted the Napoleon, with arms folded on his breast (a posture he had allegedly cultivated since the incident with the French emperor at the lycée), and that his troops, out of control, engaged in violence, looting, and drunkenness.[380] Lishin, an officer loyal to the tsar, also reported that Muraviev-Apostol planned to pillage the home of a local countess. Documents often ignored or glossed over by historians sympathetic to the rising tell of drunken raids, extortion of Russians and of Jewish merchants and tavernkeepers by soldiers and officers, and demands (sometimes accompanied by death threats) for cash, food, and vodka.[381]

Muraviev-Apostol—like Riego and Pepe and unlike Ypsilanti—forbade his men to loot. When Rulikowski reported that soldiers had entered his home demanding vodka, the colonel put guards on his door. He threatened soldiers who mistreated Jews. But he could not control all of them all the time. Some of the abuses occurred in outposts distant from his headquarters. Nor could he prevent desertions of officers and men, which had already begun in Motovilovka. He did, however, threaten at least one officer with death if he refused to obey orders. The post-Soviet historian Oksana Kiianskaia has gone far in correcting the traditional one-sided picture of the Southern uprising. Leaning largely on sources hostile to the revolt and on interrogated soldiers and peasants, she drafts a bleak scenario of deceived and suborned troops, drunken brawls, and poor leadership. She credits Muraviev-Apostol with valor and stoicism but removes the halo.[382]

In fact, wishful thinking, lies, cover-ups, self-justifications, and the desire to please authorities or comrades or posterity can be found throughout the thousands of pages of testimony and memoirs on both sides of the conflict. Muraviev-Apostol clearly violated his code of honor by attacking his unarmed fellow officer and commander, Goebel. In deceiving his troops with exaggerated promises of support from other units, he went far beyond Colonel Riego's general reference at the outset of rebellion to Quiroga as commander of a new or national army, and beyond General Pepe's claims about the universal support of the constitution. Muraviev's overreaching declarations to his men paralleled Ypsilanti's statements of a guaranteed Russian support for the Greek liberation. Mendacity in time of armed hostilities, whether war or revolution—including lying to one's own forces—was hardly invented by the Southern Society. Ultimately one may choose a judgment: did Muraviev-Apostol betray his ideals and his men, or did he act pragmatically according to circumstance?

On January 2, the troops moved through a few hamlets to Pologi on the way to Belaia Tserkov'. There Muraviev-Apostol expected to join up with the 17th Jaeger Regiment, but it had been transferred. He had won over part of a musket company but not the three hoped-for regiments and a grenadier company. The commander of one of the regiments, aside from breaching his agreement to join the uprising, ruptured communications between Muraviev-Apostol and the units readied for revolt by the Society of United Slavs by destroying his note to them. At Pologi the morale of the soldiers, darkened by uncertainty, began to sink, and desertion increased. As to the next destination, several variants presented themselves to the leader. Muraviev-Apostol opted for a westward swing in the direction of the Slavs' encampments. On January 3, the rebel troops reached Kovalevka and then continued over the open steppe to Ustinovka, near Trilesy, to meet their fate.

On that day, the rump of the Chernigov Regiment encountered and engaged Russian imperial forces, led by German-born General Heismar (Geismar) and French-born corps commander Roth, stiffened by cannon and cavalry. On spying their ranks, Muraviev-Apostol felt joy because he mistook them for troops sympathetic to the revolt.[383] But the authorities had deployed only the most loyal units. When he realized what faced him, he rolled out the pretender theme and told his men that usurpers had "stolen the throne of Constantine and these men have joined them." He had assured his own men that the opposing troops would not fire on them. By one account, when government artillery sent off rounds, one of Muraviev-Apostol's soldiers tried to bayonet him, crying,

"You have lied to us."[384] The commander, struck in the head by shell fire, collapsed in a pool of blood. His brother Ippolit, presumably thinking that Sergei was dead, killed himself on the battlefield. When that young officer had arrived in Vasilkov to join his brothers near the church, Baron Soloviev had a vision of the Muraviev-Apostols as the three Horatii brothers at a temple in ancient Rome about to die for freedom.[385] And before he rode off, Ippolit had embraced, exchanged pistols, and sworn with a friend to die for "liberty or death."[386]

General Mikhailovskii-Danilevskii was told in Vasilkov in 1829 that the Chernigov troops owed their defeat to drunkenness. Other witnesses from the government army claimed that the rebel soldiers were undisciplined, intoxicated, and armed with unloaded and inferior weapons. Government volleys of shot and shell, he said, made them throw down their arms while hussars stabbed and slashed at the "pitiful herd." The prisoners taken in the field were marched to the village of Trilesy—the officers jailed in a tavern and the men in peasant cabins under guard—and then to Belaia Tserkov'. From there the officers were moved to Mogilev, First Army headquarters.[387] According to Lishin, the captured lower ranks under questioning claimed that they had been misled and knew nothing of Muraviev-Apostol's aims[388]—hardly conclusive evidence, given their situation and the understandably evasive habits of lower classes at the mercy of superiors.

Tactical errors have been attributed to Muraviev-Apostol. He had delayed offensive action by declaring a day off on New Year's in order to regroup and see what developed. This was hardly an Ypsilanti moment—the Greek had lingered for weeks along the road, and Riego had paused many times during his trek. But the gap did curb the momentum and allowed time for the marshaling of government forces. In moving toward Trilesy, the Russian commander had chosen a track over the plain rather than a more secure route through villages, thus exposing his column to artillery. The more serious critique involves the larger direction of the rebel march—westward instead of northeast to Kiev. The leaders of the Society of United Slavs called for an immediate raid on Kiev, where several sympathetic officers might assist. Gorbachevskii critiqued Muraviev-Apostol for not heeding this advice. Some historians agree. Muraviev-Apostol himself had sent an advance agent to Kiev with a few copies of the catechism.[389] A Soviet biographer of Muraviev-Apostol persuasively argued that since the rebels did not really know the situation in Kiev, it would have entailed too much risk to lead a thousand men there.[390] Muraviev was bold but not wildly impetuous: he needed supporting units and he needed information. He thus opposed charging into Kiev without a preliminary reconnaissance.

What chance did the Southern Decembrists have of making a revolution? The short verdict must be very little. Had the uprising on Senate Square prolonged itself, the Southerners might have had a plausible target—a vulnerable St. Petersburg—though this speculation is not very convincing. In Russia, a huge country afflicted by poor communications, it took weeks for messages to make their way between St. Petersburg and the southern outposts. The Southern Society suffered not only from the Petersburg failure but also from the infiltration of informers, the relative efficiency of the loyalist commanders, and the refusal of potentially crucial support regiments and other units to rally behind the rebels of Vasilkov.

An early and relatively obscure biographer of Muraviev wrote in 1920 that "if Pestel was the chief of the Southern Society, then Sergei Muraviev was its soul." Pestel was here cast as a "cold theoretician."[391] What of D. K. Petrov's above-noted verdict that among Decembrists, only Sergei Muraviev-Apostol resembled Riego? Both were young veterans of the Napoleonic wars, ambitious, a bit headstrong; both were equipped with energy, a thirst for limited government, and great sympathy for the men in the ranks. But this could be said of hundreds of their contemporary officers. An adventurous man, Muraviev placed his faith in sudden direct action. Riego was not his only model. He believed that, as with Ypsilanti, after a signal at the right moment and a bold and sudden "push," a mass revolt would follow. He relied on a revolutionary mutineer mentality, believing that a single spark could ignite his men.[392]

Sergei Muraviev-Apostol attempted to combine revolutionary aims with sympathy for the people whom he wanted to reach. Even up to the very last moment, he was never ready to share with the men his most intimate radical plans. He befogged his own agenda by alternating the Grand Duke Constantine figure with his Christianoid republican pronunciamentos. Spain had offered him the spectacle of a heroic officer, a mendacious king, a reactionary intervention and reprisal, and—for a day or so—an instrument for winning over the soldiers through religious inspiration. He also followed his chief model Riego into martyrdom and legend. In a friendly poetic duel with V. L. Davydov at Kamenka in 1823, Muraviev-Apostol had composed his own epitaph.

> I will pass my days on earth,
> Ever dreaming and alone,
> With no one having known me.
> 'Tis only at the end of life,
> That in a burst of light,
> One may see what one has lost.[393]

Isle of the Dead

Hundreds of arrested survivors of the Northern and Southern insurrections were initially committed to the Peter and Paul Fortress, the city's very first building, a recurrent symbol of oppression, and the recent stockade for the

Semenovskii mutineers. The "underground dungeons and casemates" that Nikita Muraviev's constitution would have abolished[394] now became the conspirators' home. In his memoirs, Aleksandr Muraviev, brother of Nikita, called the Peter and Paul Fortress a "hideous monument of absolutism, [that] faces the Monarch's palace, like a fateful warning that the one can exist only because of the other."[395] Inmates had to wear manacles weighing nine kilograms and shackles weighing twelve.[396] They also endured the torments of solitary confinement, vermin, lack of books for most, and the occasional absence of drink and food. Incarceration in the dreaded fortress affected the Decembrist inmates in different ways. Though many of the recollections are draped in the garments of the Romantic prisoner, there is little reason to doubt their accuracy.

Torture had been officially abolished in the eighteenth century and was not applied to the incarcerated officers. In spite of this, some prisoners, including Aleksandr Beliaev, feared they might suffer physical torture.[397] He may have heard Spanish atrocity stories while serving nearby at Gibraltar in 1824. A mariner who had sailed around the world, he now found himself locked in a tiny space almost underground in the Peter and Paul Fortress. Years later Beliaev would put the incarceration of Silvio Pellico high on the list of the reactionary misdeeds that had awakened his generation. Now he shared the Piedmontese prisoner's experience.[398] Nikolai Lohrer also summoned up that romanticized prisoner. He recalled that in his cell in the Peter and Paul Fortress, the sun hardly reached his "dungeon" even at noon. "Silvio Pellico in the Spielberg," he said, "was apparently no better off than me."[399]

In his memoirs, the grounded seaman Mikhail Bestuzhev described his cell, eight by six paces in area, whose window behind thick crossed iron bars was covered over with a substance that blocked the light. He related in detail how, though communication between cells was forbidden, the detainees used an elaborate prison code consisting of knocks on the wall corresponding to letters on a grid.[400] Bestuzhev was later sentenced to eternal exile at hard labor. As an old man in the 1860s, recently amnestied and returned from Siberia, he compared his experience in the Peter and Paul and Schlüsselburg fortress prisons to that of Silvio Pellico in the Spielberg. He titled his memoirs in direct imitation of *Le miei prigioni* and copied its format.[401] Like so many Decembrists, he also sought a literary parallel in this case, a verse by Vasilii Zhukovskii, inspired by Byron's *Prisoner of Chillon*:

> Wild strode I 'cross dungeon cell
> Where a kind of coldness dwelt,
> And out from danky walls there gave
> A frigid chill as from the grave.[402]

Of the many Decembrist prison writings, Mikhail Lunin's is among the most intriguing. Though his voluminous correspondence is full of sophisticated political observations, he also came armed with the ability to refract his sojourn in captivity through the dingy light of the Romantic prisoner. During a voyage on the Baltic Sea years earlier, he had become fascinated by the ruins of the notorious castle prison of Hammershus on Bornholm Island, from which had sprung tales of Count Corfitz Ulfeldt, a seventeenth-century Danish political oppositionist sent there with his wife for conspiracy and treason.[403] The fictions of Ann Radcliffe offered another image. Lunin likened one of his prisons to her bleak dungeons. "To have some notion of my present situation one must read *The Mysteries of Udolpho* or some other novel by Madame de Radcliffe. I am plunged in darkness, deprived of air, space and food, surrounded by bandits, murderers, and counterfeiters."[404] Did this tough and determined man who shared with Pestel the belief that there were those who obeyed and those who commanded, and who had laughed out loud on hearing his twenty-year sentence,[405] come to see himself as a victim of a powerful and evil man—the tsar as stand-in for Radcliffe's icy aristocrat?

Mental agony over the sheer fact of incarceration and isolation took its toll. The one successful suicide in the fortress, Aleksandr Bulatov, smashed his head against the stone cell wall. Nechkina and others have concluded that the suicide stemmed from Bulatov's remorse at missing the opportunity to kill Tsar Nicholas on the day of the uprising.[406] Alongside this stands his extremely slavish testimony to the investigators. In an abject letter to the tsar's youngest brother, Grand Duke Mikhail Pavlovich, and in addressing the tsar, he employed the overheated language of perdition and eternal hellfire. Bulatov was also among those who believed that Riego had been quartered. Though he might have feared this kind of hideous execution, Bulatov's suicide seems to indicate that he had not been pleading for his life. That he killed himself out of remorse seems likely, whether that remorse arose from failure to act decisively on December 14, his "criminal activity" in the uprising (as he testified to the examiners), or both is open to question.[407]

Hagiographers have stressed Kondratii Ryleev's defiance. Reacting to imprisonment, Ryleev offered his own verse, which a fellow prisoner claimed to have found scratched with a nail on a metal dinner plate:

> Prison my honour cannot take,
> A noble cause has brought me here.
> And in my chains no shame I fear,
> I wear them for my country's sake.[408]

When it came to religion, however, Ryleev and many others continued, revived, or reconverted to a genuine Christian piety—Orthodox or Lutheran—after their arrest. In his prison cell, Aleksandr Beliaev, never a Bible reader, found solace in religion, immersed himself in scripture, and wept over the words of Christ.[409]

Of the Decembrists who turned to—or back to—religion in their hour of woe, Pavel Pestel's case was unusual. He had already regained his faith at Easter in 1825. After ten days in the fortress, he began to feel the weight of failure. Pestel regretted his membership in the society, asked that his parents be spared the shame of a harsh punishment for their son, and offered to serve the tsar. Brave at first, Pestel weakened and gave names, though apparently this was not held against him by his fellow conspirators, many of whom did the same. Pestel cloaked himself again in the persona of an officer loyal to the tsar. When his alternate world collapsed, he turned inward to piety. His father visited Pestel, and they knelt and prayed.[410] In any case, the condemned man's conversion—so redolent of the Riego scenario—naturally aroused suspicion in some quarters. Soviet historians discounted Pestel's contrition. One argued that, when Pestel saw his days were numbered, he more or less faked his devout stance in letters to his parents in order to console them and spare them further grief.[411]

Tsar Nicholas ordered the chaplain of the fortress, Archpriest Petr Myslovskii, to confess all the Orthodox detainees who desired it. Pastor Rheinboth of St. Anna's Evangelical Church on Liteinyi Prospect handled his fourteen Lutheran co-religionists. According to Myslovskii, during the several hours spent with Pestel, the Protestant pastor was driven to tears by the prisoner's self-justification, refusal to hear the mysteries of the faith, and insistence on discussing points of dogma and politics.[412] On one point, Myslovskii's account contradicts those that record Pestel taking the sacraments and a blessing from his Lutheran pastor.[413] Describing the scene on the scaffold, Myslovskii seemed to be pushing Pestel a bit further away from Lutheranism into the arms of Orthodoxy. According to that priest, Pestel fell on his knees and said to him in a firm voice: "Holy father! I am not of your faith but was once a Christian and would very much like to be one now. I fell into temptation—but who has not. From the bottom of my heart I beseech you: forgive me my sins and give me your blessing as I enter on my distant and terrible journey."[414]

Sergei Muraviev-Apostol, after a few weeks of confinement on the road, arrived in St. Petersburg on January 19 and a few days later was put in the Alekseevskii Ravelin of the Peter and Paul Fortress—a notorious dungeon complex that had housed many a political prisoner and would hold many more in the future. His heavy chains removed, he was brought before the tsar, weakened from his wound and the shackles and hardly able to stand. Tsar Nicholas had him seated and asked him how a bright and talented officer had come to involve himself in such a crime. According to the tsar, Muraviev-Apostol openly revealed to him what he thought to be the many miseries of Russian life and how he and his comrades had planned to come to power and change the system. The great mythologist of the Decembrist movement, Alexander Herzen, floated a story about Muraviev-Apostol's defiant behavior. Standing in chains before General

Osten-Sacken (Ostenzaken), who alternated his rage at Muraviev-Apostol with honeyed words, the prisoner allegedly spat at him and turned away.[415] Similar tall tales proliferated: that the prisoner refused to shake the tsar's proffered hand, and that he disdained an offer from the emperor to forgive and forget and to take Muraviev into his service to work together for the good of Russia.[416]

At subsequent interrogations, Muraviev gave a full account of the conspiracy, though certainly masking some details and lying about his own agreement to exterminate the royal family. But he voiced no regrets and said no prayers for forgiveness. He tried to claim sole authorship of the catechism to lighten the punishment of his friend Bestuzhev-Riumin. In the opinion of his examiners, Muraviev "evidently took upon himself all that others blamed him for, unwilling to justify himself by refuting their testimony."[417] The tsar allegedly promised to spare his life. Believing this, Muraviev, like Pestel, in vain asked his sovereign to send him back into service, specifically to a hazardous frontier post along the Caspian and Aral Seas or in southern Siberia.[418] This scenario, loaded with contradictions about freedom and colonial conquest, became one of the great cover stories for European expansion by "decent men" and failed heroes.

Little remained of Muraviev-Apostol's family. Though he had dreamed of a perfect wife, he had never married—perhaps because of his perilous work in the secret societies. His father had always been an icy despot, an egoist, and an "arid-spirited scholar."[419] And yet Sergei, his favorite, wrote him regularly, though contact diminished somewhat after the father's remarriage. The revolt cost him three sons: one a suicide, one hanged, one exiled. Ivan Muraviev-Apostol composed an elegy in classical style comparing his sons to three trees that were planted, flourished, and were doomed by Zeus. He visited Sergei and Matvei in the fortress in May 1826, though no record of the encounter remains aside from a rumor that when the father offered to send Sergei a new uniform (he still wore battle dress), the son replied: "No need . . . I will die with the spots of blood that I shed for my country."[420] The sons wrote letters of remorse to the father, who went abroad before the execution and died in St. Petersburg in 1851.[421]

The Decembrists stood trial—that is, submitted to closed questioning by the tsar in the Winter Palace and by the Investigating Commission, first in the palace and then in the fortress. It convened 146 times from December 17, 1825, to June 17, 1826, questioned 579 men, and indicted 121. It then delivered its findings to the Supreme Criminal Tribunal, which included the once prominent reformer Mikhail Speranskii.[422] Of the 579 men recorded in 1827 as having been involved with the Decembrists, almost 79 percent were officers in service; of those for whom there is relevant data, almost 90 percent had some formal schooling, and a third had seen action. Of those tried, about 70 percent were age thirty or under.

Incomplete data show that the vast majority of the 289 men who were sentenced were or had been in the army.[423]

Emotion, flamboyant expression, religiosity, and repentance marked some of the Decembrists' postures and even led to embraces and tears—by both Decembrists and Tsar Nicholas.[424] The prisoners provided a copious body of oral and written testimony. Responses to the charges varied. Some indulged in slavish recantation and mutual denunciation. Others openly defied the tribunal and proudly admitted their deeds and plans—including regicide. Aleksandr Muraviev recounted that naval officer Vasilii Divov, age nineteen, went nearly mad and confessed to dreaming while in captivity of stabbing the tsar. Nikita Muraviev, architect of the constitutional monarchy project, declared to the committee that he had turned republican by the time of the hearings.[425]

In its final verdict on the causes of the uprising—published in several languages—the Investigating Commission found no direct personal bonds between the Decembrists and the activists of Spain and Naples and elsewhere. From this, they deduced the absence of links with the European revolutionary movement,[426] despite ample testimony to the contrary. Tsar Nicholas's reading of the foreign role in the revolt was more complex and more accurate. Even before it ended, he made a pronouncement on the matter. On December 20 (OS; January 1, 1826, NS), at the traditional New Years' reception for the European diplomatic corps, Nicholas conceded that the long-brewing conspiracy had originated with officers serving abroad who imbibed revolutionary teachings. A few brought back false notions. "Evildoers and madmen" dreamed of revolution, which, he said, thank the Lord, had no future in Russia. Some soldiers were tricked into the plot only due to their unwavering fidelity to their oath, but the army remained loyal. The tsar set Russia off from the West: "It is impossible to compare this rising [in Russia] with those of Spain and Piedmont." In a sense the tsar was depicting his country as a well-run, conservative regime in command of a loyal soldiery who remained immune to the plotting of officers infected by harmful European doctrines.[427]

After the interrogation process by the Investigating Commission ended, the tribunal members read the transcript, confronted the prisoners for the first time, and passed sentence. Of the 121 major convictions, five were condemned to hanging and quartering, thirty-one to beheading, and the rest to various terms of hard labor in Siberia and loss of rank and property. Before the trial, the emperor had told La Ferronais that he would show no mercy to the rebels: "This example is necessary both for Russia's sake and for Europe's."[428] In an additional extraordinary judgment, 800 troops of the Chernigov Regiment were sent as punishment to the Special Caucasus Corps, marched unarmed, and escorted by a dense convoy of armed security forces drawn from loyal units.[429]

Thus began a vast dispersion of the conspirators to numerous prisons inside European Russia and to Siberian penal settlements. Nikolai Bestuzhev, veteran of the Mediterranean cruise, was taken from the Peter and Paul Fortress by cutter to the island of Kronstadt for a civil or mock execution before a panel of admirals. He removed his uniform before it could be torn off, then knelt as the executioner broke a sword (previously filed down) over his head. Bestuzhev was returned to the fortress and exiled to Siberia, where he died in 1854.[430] Wilhelm Küchelbecker spent ten years of solitary confinement in the Peter and Paul, Schlüsselburg, Dünaburg, Revel (Tallinn), and Sveaborg (Suomenlinna) fortress prisons.[431] Sergei Muraviev-Apostol's brother Matvei served his time in Siberia and, like all other surviving Decembrists, was amnestied in 1856 in honor of the coronation of Tsar Alexander II, son of Nicholas. He returned to European Russia and died age ninety-two in 1886.[432]

Tsar Nicholas commuted the sentence of decapitation for the thirty-one prisoners to hard labor, and that of execution by quartering to hanging. This arrangement enabled the monarch to make a merciful gesture, since he had no intention of shedding blood. But those condemned actually had to hear the sentence of a horrendous death by quartering first before learning of the commutation to the noose.[433] Those sentenced to be hanged included two Northerners, Kondratii Ryleev and Peter Kakhovskii, and three Southerners, Pavel Pestel, Mikhail Bestuzhev-Riumin, and Sergei Muraviev-Apostol. Mikhail Bestuzhev-Riumin had in his cell the icon on which the Southerners and the Slavs had sworn at Leshchin in September. He gave it to his guard before execution, and the guard sold it to Lunin, who kept it through the years.[434] Pestel had expected the firing squad, and when, in chains, he spotted the gallows at Kronwerk, opposite the fortress, he allegedly exclaimed, "Don't we deserve a better death?" Referring to the war records of many Decembrists, he added: "It seems that we never dodged bullet or shell. Could they not then shoot us!"[435] Muraviev-Apostol, bitterly regretting his recruitment of Bestuzhev-Riumin, asked his forgiveness.[436]

On July 13, 1826, after a delay of a few hours to complete construction of the gallows, the five were hanged at about 6:00 a.m. The hour of dawn was chosen perhaps in emulation of the 5:00 a.m. execution of Karl Sand at Mannheim in 1819, done so out of concern about mass student unrest.[437] The most memorable moment of the execution occurred when the ropes broke and three of the condemned plummeted to the ground: Kakhovskii sustained no injury, Ryleev cut his head, and Muraviev-Apostol broke both his legs. The three had to be hanged again. From this arose the alleged comment—urban folklore or gallows humor?—by one of the fallen, variously attributed, that "poor Russia does not even know how to hang properly."[438] This observation, if made, ignored the fact that, since no professional executioners were available in Russia, hangmen had to be brought over from Sweden.[439] Compared to the barbarous public spectacles in

Spain and Naples, the execution was restrained and moderate. That night, under cover, the bodies were taken to Golodai Island and buried.

Appendix: "Vozzvanie K Narodu" (Appeal to the People), 1825

God has taken pity on Russia. He has sent death to our tyrant [Tsar Alexander I]. Christ has said: Be not slaves to men for you are redeemed by my blood. The world has not paid heed to his holy command and has plunged it into an abyss of disaster. But our sufferings have moved the Almighty. Today he is sending us freedom and salvation. Brothers! let us repent of our age-old servility and let us swear: for us there shall be but one tsar in heaven and on earth—Jesus Christ.

All the misfortunes of the Russian people have sprung from autocratic government. It has collapsed. With the death of the tyrant, God has manifested His will that we cast off from ourselves the chains of slavery that are contrary to Christian law. Henceforth, Russia is free. But as true sons of the Church, we shall not engage in any kind of outrages. Without internecine strife we shall establish popular government based on the law of God that declares: let the first among you serve you.

The Russian army will restore a popular government based on sacred law. No evil deeds will be committed. And so, may our devout people remain at peace and tranquility and pray to the Almighty for the most expeditious accomplishment of our sacred cause. May those who serve at mass, who up to now have been kept in poverty and scorned by our impious tyrant, pray to God for us, as we restore the temples of the Lord in all their splendor.[440]

The Torn Cloth of Memory

What! Shall reviving thralldom again be
The patched-up idol of enlightened days?
Shall we, who struck the Lion down, shall we
Pay the Wolf homage? proffering lowly gaze
and servile knees to thrones?
                    —Byron, *Childe Harold's Pilgrimage*

Libera me, Domine.
Free me, O Lord, from eternal death.
                    —The Catholic Requiem Mass

Byron's "What!" encapsulates the indignant posture—close to rage—of those who had fought against Napoleon only to fall beneath the sway of Bourbons, Hapsburgs, Hohenzollerns, and Romanovs. Robert Wilson described a motive common to many of his generation: he had fought the anti-Napoleonic struggle as a war of liberation and then saw it betrayed by the monarchs of Europe.[1] Unlike the Napoleonic commanders who rode into conquered realms with, metaphorically, legal codes and semi-constitutions in their field packs, the leading rebel officers of 1820, unbacked by a state, were riding with liberal or national ideals on their banner. They shared certain traits of the age's Romantic personality: stormy, fanciful, impetuous. All officers, they were born within eleven years of each other between 1785 and 1796, but in regions as diverse as northwestern Spain, southern Italy, Constantinople, and St. Petersburg. Their adventures that began in provincial towns met failure in even less familiar locales: the Trocadero, Rieti, Dragoșani, and Trilesy.

But did bigger and historically significant unities bind the products of this season of revolution? Poets such as Byron and Pushkin who saw underlying impulses of the Mediterranean (and Latin American) revolts were not simply engaging in lyrical hyperbole. As one modern scholar put it, revolutions "ran through the three peninsulas of the Mediterranean as in a system of communi-cating vessels."[2] An eminent Soviet historian went even further: "Analogous conditions produced analogous phenomena everywhere from the Guadalqui-vir to the Neva."[3]

Pavel Pestel saw things exactly that way at the time. And his colleague Alek-sandr Poggio asserted after the collapse of the Decembrist revolt that it would nonetheless have great significance for the next wave of European revolutions.[4] A secret society in Naples followed the events in St. Petersburg of 1825 and won-dered why the revolution did not proceed.[5] Many of the activists conceded and indeed promoted the connection, as didsc, from a radically different angle, some statesmen and diplomatists of the Holy Alliance who saw the specter of an inter-national conspiracy exacerbated by mutual contagion.

Though divided by geography, religion, and outcomes, the mechanical simi-larities of the four uprisings, I think, have been made clear in the previous pages: the impact of the Napoleonic wars, assorted grievances, secret society prepara-tion, military initiators, the pronunciamento, liberal aspirations, heroic postures, inner conflicts, cultural and religious adaptations. Those that failed fell under the guns of the Austrian, French, and Russian armies.

Surely the most spectacular and long-lasting character of the revolts was their internationalism. "Liberty can be upheld by liberty only;—the revolution of one country can be countenanced only by a similar revolution in other countries."[6] The Italian liberals and their more radical compatriot Buonarotti joined the Poles as forebears of itinerant revolutionaries—Blanqui, Garibaldi, Bakunin, Rosa Luxemburg, and Che Guevara, to name a few. International not only in their wanderings from one liberation struggle to another, the men of the 1820s nursed visions of permanent revolution. Ypsilanti hoped to ignite the entire Bal-kan peninsula by his march into Greece. Pestel dreamt that a Russian revolution and resulting republic would automatically destroy the Holy Alliance and set off revolts across Europe. Many Spaniards saw eruptions in Italy and Portugal as natural aftershocks of their own upheaval. Pepe, the eternal revolutionary, encased his plan in a European constitutional brotherhood and made constant appeals to struggling colleagues in other nations for help in liberating Naples once again.

The risings of the 1820s eventually found a hallowed space in a heroic tele-ology of successful national or political struggle: for the Greeks, as the rebirth of a nation; for the Neapolitans, a place on the bumpy road of the Risorgimento; for the Decembrists, co-optation into a highly mythologized history of contin-uous liberation struggle that triumphed in the Bolshevik Revolution of 1917. The Spanish pronunciamento, sometimes copied by the political right, became subject to alternate praise and condemnation.

Where Is Ypsilanti?

Among the four insurgencies, if the Decembrists registered the only complete failure by not getting into power even for a moment, the Greeks, after suffering the
initial defeat of Ypsilanti, gained ultimate victory in the independence war. That
war became the largely uncontested foundation tale of modern Greece, celebrated
without interruption over the past almost two centuries. Phanariot rule in the
Romanian Principalities came to an end and the Greeks focused on building,
maintaining, and expanding their small new state under a foreign dynasty. Argu-
ably the greatest Greek statesman of the twentieth century, Eleutherios Venizelos
(b. 1864), whose first name means "liberator," had a father who had fought in that
struggle and three uncles who died in it. In 1919, after World War I, with the in-
viting specter of a collapsing Ottoman Empire, Premier Venizelos benefited from
the philhellene sympathies of the peacemakers at Paris and got a victory that had
turned to ashes by 1922.[7] Other connections to the liberation struggle, loosely
invoked, were the pronunciamentos and military coups, including the "operatic
dictatorship of Pangalos" of the 1920s, that punctuated the twentieth century.[8]

The war of independence made its way into every realm of cultural expression.
The focus of most Greek historical novels has been on that war, the Disaster of
1922, and World War II. Of the first, apparently none zeroed in on Alexandros
Ypsilanti—at least as of 1965. The first fictional representations—*The Brave
Youth*, published anonymously in Malta in 1835, and Stephanos Xenos, *Heroine
of the Greek Revolution* (1842)—dealt with individual heroic struggle far removed
from the campaign in the Principalities. The same holds true for the other early
efforts that center on Ali Pasha or the Ottoman court, and of the many philhel-
lenic works in the later years of the nineteenth century. A twentieth-century
novel, *Greek Dawn*, revolved around Ioannis Colletis.[9] By then, the saga of the
Greek liberation war had been fully sacralized in high and popular culture and
historiography, Silent films joined the chorus of adulation in the 1920s with *The
Last Days of Odysseas Androutsou* (1928) and *The Banner of '21* (1929) and with
sound films of the 1930s.

During the German and Italian occupation of World War II, Greek resisters
found it natural, if not mandatory, to invoke 1821. Less appealing at first was
1789, due to Greek resisters' scorn for the capitulationist France of 1940. Later
various local leaders adopted the nom de guerre Robespierre (or Rovospiere) to
sow terror among their enemies.[10] More often, partisan captains took names
such as Ypsilantis, Botsaris, and Kolokotrónis. The Communist guerrilla leader
Aris coupled the raging inferno of the 1820s with the battle of Stalingrad, and his
EAM movement put on dramas of resistance featuring the ghost of Karaiskakis
returning to inspire the peasants. Angelos Sikelianos, a fifty-eight-year-old poet,
identified March 25, 1942, with March 25, 1821:[11]

The swallows of death threaten to bring you
Oh Greece, a new spring, and from the grave a gigantic birth.
Vainly is the guard of the Romans on watch around you.
Soon you will rise up in a new Twenty-One.

Greece has been generous with historical and topographical reminders of the heroics of the 1820s. The beautiful War Museum in central Athens devotes a good deal of space to that theme, and many city streets bear names of the great patriotic warriors and state builders of that epoch, including Alexandros Ypsilanti. But that impetuous general has always had to share the memoryscape with the more successful warriors and the martyrs of mainland Greece. Like Riego, Ypsilanti got his face in a deck of playing cards: he appeared as the ace of spades in 1829; and much later a sculptured bust was erected in Athens. A Soviet historian saw him as a threefold hero for his loss of an arm in defense of Russia, his 1821 ride, and his friendship with the Decembrists.[12] Contrary to some popular opinion, the town of Ypsilanti, Michigan, was named not after him but after his brother Demetrios, around whose bust citizens celebrate his memory periodically. Perhaps the unkindest cut to the memory of Alexandros is the fact that twentieth-century Turkish scholarship, leaning mostly on nineteenth-century works, marginalized him as a deluded Russian general and his ride as a sideshow.[13]

From Pepe to Garibaldi

In present-day Naples, the Corso Giuseppe Garibaldi begins in the south at Piazza Guglielmo Pepe, a geography that might suggest that the 1820ers were the pioneers for the 1860ers. Some have adopted this linkage. Writing in 1943 during the last months of Mussolini's rule, the anti-Fascist liberal Luigi Salvatorelli penned these words: "The uprising of 1820 and 1821 (the revolutions in Naples and Piedmont) represented the first genuine revolutionary initiative of the Risorgimento."[14] Aurelio Lepre, in contrast, argued forcefully that 1820 did not launch the Risorgimento, a movement that required an all-Italian national consciousness. Regional solutions were doomed to fail.[15] The debate goes on, perhaps unresolvable. After all, one could with some reason also push back the origins of the Risorgimento to the Neapolitan Parthenopean Republic of 1799.

Unlike the other contemporary uprisings, the Neapolitan one has apparently found no place in fiction, a major site of cultural memory. In a recent work, Alberto Banti has compiled what he calls the canonical Italian works produced during the Risorgimento, circa 1801–49, "fundamental texts" including scholarship, poetry, novels, memoirs, and operas. Much of the fiction deals with the distant past; of those books concerned with the nineteenth century, only a handful are about the first decades. Silvio Pellico, Mazzini, and Garibaldi are clearly the bright stars in this constellation. For Naples are listed the poetry of Alessandro Poerio (Gabriele Rossetti is oddly missing) and the nonfiction works of Cuoco, Colletta, and Pepe (the memoirs).[16]

Among the many historical novels about the Kingdom of Naples, running from Dacia Maraini's *The Long Life of Marianna Ucrìa*, set in the early eighteenth century,[17] to Giuseppe di Lampedusa's *The Leopard*, dealing with the end of the old regime in Sicily, none seems to have taken up the theme of 1820. Several specialists in Italy have assured me that no historical novel of the Neapolitan revolution of 1820–21 exists, though I still harbor hope of finding one. The piece of fiction, to my knowledge, that comes closest to evoking the Carbonari milieu in the 1820s is Roberto Rossellini's script for his 1961 film *Vanina Vanini*, though it is set in the Papal States rather than Naples or Piedmont. In its level of histor-ical detail—in spite of its depiction of a Carbonaro *vendita* in a salon—the film surpasses the original Stendhal story, which is hardly more than a sketch.[18] That this historical melodrama flopped seems to reinforce the general impression that episodes of that era do not have much resonance with modern audiences—or readers—especially when compared to the high Risorgimento.

Other ways preserving memory have at least rescued three of the initiators of the Neapolitan revolt. Today in Nola, a charming valley town with a half dozen picturesque squares and churches, a narrow street bears the names of the polit-ical martyrs Morelli and Silvati; a bit further from the center, another is named after Fra Minichini. Though buried in obscurity and relatively neglected in his-tory, in 1920 Morelli was honored at his birthplace by a memorial stone on the centennial of his ride to Avellino. Other monuments followed in the 1930s and 1960s. The Piazza della Libertà in Avellino honored all the participants in that event.[19]

Guglielmo Pepe has gained much more traction in historical memory not only because of his stature as a general and his key role in the uprising but also because he survived to write voluminously about his experiences and to partici-pate in later struggles. Pepe tried again in vain to revive the Calabrian expedition during the 1830 revolution in France by requesting from Lafayette two thousand men, ten thousand muskets, and two frigates.[20] He participated in the 1848 rev-olutions in Naples and Venice and was rewarded for his troubles with yet an-other death sentence in absentia and another sojourn in exile until his death in 1855.[21]

For all his revolutionary energy and his devoted contributions to the Nea-politan and Italian cause, General Pepe has not risen very high in the ranks of historical prominence in his own country or elsewhere; nor, outside Italy, has the liberal regime he helped to enable won much attention in the chronicles or in expressive culture. Yet that insurgent regime, in many ways, outshone those of Spain and Greece in its tranquility and humanity. Pepe stubbornly and wrongly in his memoirs maintained that the Naples revolt had universal support among Italians.[22] But Benedetto Croce's later verdict on the constitution, its moderation, and its potential role as a school of politics was far from fanciful, especially when one notes the fact that the Neapolitan parliament of 1820 was the only body elected (though indirectly) by universal male suffrage in all of nineteenth-century Italian history.[23]

A final note: A number of critics—conservatives and liberals, Spanish, English, Austrian, and Russian—sneered at the defeated Neapolitans of 1821, implying weakness or cowardice. This habit, often applied in northern Europe to Latin enemies or partners, resurfaced in World War II in commenting on the massive surrender of Italian troops in Africa and elsewhere in the face of Allied attack. Among both the Allies and the Nazis, a kind of myth of Italian cowardice emerged. Yet after Italy's surrender, when the partisans faced the occupying German forces, they fought and died in proportionately huge numbers. In the 1820s, the band of Neapolitan and North Italian officers and men who fled their lands for political reasons also fought bravely and selflessly in Spain and in Greece— and many died there as well.

How Losers Can Win

The Decembrist revolt, the only rising of the 1820s snuffed out by domestic forces alone, helped promote among European liberals an image of Russia under Alexander I and especially Nicholas I as a land of darkest tyranny. Though in many ways refuted in serious historical treatments, this image may still be met in popular accounts. At the very least, a wide-ranging major reassessment is in order for readers and scholars both, who should set early nineteenth-century Russian rule against the regimes of restoration and post-liberal Spain and Naples. In both Mediterranean lands, despotism, neglect of the poorest and weakest elements, a church ridden obscurantism and censorship, gaudy and wasteful court life, unspeakable prisons, and executions at least matched the pathologies of Russian life, even under serfdom. But as frequently happens, the stronger a potentially threatening state becomes, the greater its reputation as an evil empire. As the century wore on, neither Spain nor Naples offered such a threat to the great powers whose presses dominated European public opinion, conservative or liberal.

Negative thinking about the Russian tsars helped augment that of their foes—the defeated rebels of 1825–26. European rebels sang the praises of the Decembrists. Mazzini and the Young Italy in 1844 saluted the memory of the men "who gave their lives for the liberation of the Slavic peoples, thus becoming citizens and brothers of all who struggle for the cause of Justice and Truth on earth."[24] Polish exiles exhibited a particularly unselfish and clear-eyed rejection of the national hatred that had divided Russians and Poles over the centuries. They saw the Decembrists as brothers-in-arms in the cause of freedom and celebrated their uprising each December 14.[25]

At home, by no means everyone extended sympathy to the defeated rebels. Pestel's brother, Vladimir, renounced the cause and found favor and advancement under his tsar, as did a few of the ex-Decembrists. Leading cultural figures denounced the uprising. Emerging Slavophiles, such as Aleksei Khomiakov, parted company with the insurgents. Another, Ivan Kireevskii, though he shared the Decembrists' angst about Russia's backwardness, took no part in the movement.[26]

But the mystique of the Decembrists began to gather force almost at once. Martyrdom, individual or collective, can turn defeat into a moral victory. Witness the Serbians' seven-hundred-year memory of their rout by Turkish forces at Kosovo Pole on St. Vitus Day in 1389, or the celebration of a Roman crucifixion in Judea. The spectacle of young noblemen campaigning to liberate Russia and Europe melted the hearts of many a family. The surviving convicts sent off to Siberia and elsewhere differed from the Italian and Spanish exiles, who escaped to another land where they lived sheltered in safety and freedom. The Decembrists had and needed no community of escaped political exiles to stoke the fires of their sacrifice. Those came from within. Adding to the pathos of hundreds herded off to the vast eastward reaches of empire was the sight of their wives, who abandoned families and a privileged life to join their men in what was for many perpetual banishment from the centers of power and culture.[27]

Setting a tone of lamentation and of hope, Alexander Pushkin in 1827 launched the Decembrist myth and mystique in his fabled "Message to Siberia," excerpted at the head of the previous chapter. Matching it in emotional and lyrical power came the reply by exiled convict Aleksandr Odoevskii in the same year:

> The sound of your prophetic harp,
> Impassioned, came to us at last.
> Swiftly our hands reached for the sword,
> But found that shackles held them fast.
>
> Yet, singer, fret not: we are proud
> Of these our chains as of our fate.
> Locked in our prison cells, we scoff
> At the rulers of the state.

Our grievous toil will not be lost,
The spark will quicken into flame;
Our people, blindfolded no more,
A new allegiance will proclaim.

Beating our shackles into swords,
Liberty's torch we will relight,
and she will overwhelm the Tsars,
While nations waken in the night.[28]

The chief draftsman of the Decembrist legend, Alexander Herzen, was also the founder of the Russian variety of socialism known as populism, a pioneer of liberalism and rationalism, and a gigantic figure in the history of the Russian intelligentsia. His emigration journal *The Polar Star*, took its name from an almanac that had been published by Ryleev and others. Its masthead was adorned with cameo-like heads of the five hanged Decembrists. Herzen took up the cult as a teenager by swearing an oath to their memory on Sparrow Hills in Moscow in 1830. By midcentury, writing from exile, he had fashioned a picture of a community of heroes containing elements of their own classical self-images, combined with those of Christian martyrs and brave medieval knights.[29] The appeal of these characteristics—real and embellished—to the emerging intelligentsia was enhanced by the fact that the Decembrists, like themselves, had been afflicted and motivated by a sense of the backwardness of their native land. The apparent ascetic virtues of the leading figures of 1825 were passed on to the radical men and women of the 1860s and 1870s and even to the Marxist generation of the pre-revolutionary decades.

Russia produced no Pérez Galdós in the nineteenth century to chronicle in novel after novel the political upheavals of the past. Lev Tolstoy planned one, to be called *The Decembrists*, first sketched out in four chapters in the 1860s but never completed. The author opposed the sanctification of the Decembrists by Herzen and others, and constructed his own ideal Decembrist: an aristocrat and mystic, led astray by wrong ideas, and then chastened and ready to return to society—which many did in the amnesty of 1856. Tolstoy eventually incorporated its themes into *War and Peace*, some of whose heroes skirted around the movement.[30]

When the Bolsheviks came to power, they got busy incorporating the Decembrists into their own schema of revolutionary history, which traced a line from the revolt of 1825 through the various strands of radicalism up to the teleological triumph of Bolshevism. So strong was the mystique of the fallen officers that even anti-Soviet Russian émigrés adhered to it. The authorities in Leningrad renamed a bridge, a square, and several streets after the Decembrists.[31] Other towns followed suit. In the jubilee year of 1925, Kiev celebrated the southern events.[32] The early Soviet Society of Political Exiles and Prisoners published Decembrist documents and memoirs, adorning their publications with logos of broken chains and a darkened cell in a dungeon, along with the profiles of the five executed Decembrists.[33] A well-known directorial team, Leonid Trauberg and Grigorii Kozintsev, in 1927 created the silent film *The League of the Great Cause*, based loosely on the revolt of the Southern Society, though Muraviev-Apostol was overshadowed in the drama by another, semi-fictional, officer.[34]

Stalinist high-culture managers crowned Pushkin in 1937 as the national poet, and wishful-thinking ideologues falsely implied or even claimed that he had joined the ranks of the Decembrists. Heroics and distortion aside, Soviet historians retained a certain ambivalence toward their alleged ancestors, as they did for all non-Marxist revolutionaries. In patronizing tones, they praised the Men of December, but liked to use the term "noblemen revolutionaries" in preference to the equally accurate "tsarist officers" to remind readers of the class-based and pre-Marxist nature of this doomed historical enterprise. A slump in Decembrist studies ensued during the Stalinist 1930s and World War II, reflecting ambivalence toward a movement that could be a respected ancestor but also a conspiratorial model.

Ambivalence turned to anxiety toward the end of the war. Fear of a new "Decembrist-type mood" emerged in 1945 as the Red Army, overflowing into Germany and east-central Europe, became exposed to a European standard of living, even among the ruins. A remarkable military report from the Soviet archives described how the Decembrist officers had rightly recognized the contrast between a prosperous Europe of 1812–15 and the misery of tsarist Russia. But, the report observed, "nowadays, it is a very different thing. Perhaps some landowner's estate is richer than some collective farm. From this, a man who is politically backward draws a conclusion in favour of a feudal economy against the socialist variety. This kind of influence is regressive. This is why a merciless fight is necessary against these attitudes."[35]

The commissar's fears were not entirely unwarranted. Some educated Red Army officers experienced the same kind of postwar hopefulness as had the Decembrists. One believed that a new social and cultural revival would open up as had happened after 1812. During the post-Stalin Thaw and after, the Russian intelligentsia fashioned a kind of cult around the Men of December. In 1967, a renowned theater director mounted a trilogy which led off with a drama about the Decembrists. The guitar poets Bulat Okudzhava and Alexander Galich both honored the rebels of 1825 as heroes who sacrificed their lives for the good of Russia. The popular historian Natan Eidelman, oft cited in previous pages, wrote book after book about the Decembrists, encoding their revolt as an epic struggle for freedom and a cryptic subtext for intellectual dissidence.[36]

In a cultural universe parallel to the muted and elliptical defiance of the intelligentsia, the Decembrists became permanently inscribed in Soviet musical performance alongside Spartacus, serf rebels, and Paris Communards. The Soviets had already produced two Decembrist operas before the war. The first, with music by Vasilii Zolotarev in 1934, was followed by one produced at the Workshop of Monumental Theater, which, astonishingly, employed the music of Giacomo Meyerbeer's *Les Huguenots*, an 1836 French grand opera about the persecution of French Protestants in the sixteenth century.[37] It must be wondered how the producers, in the land of atheism, dealt with the melody of Bach's eminently Lutheran hymn, "A Mighty Fortress Is Our God," which was quoted several times in Meyerbeer's opera.

In 1953, after a quarter of a century of intermittent work, Yuri Shaporin finished his opera on the Decembrists, which was premiered at the Bolshoi Theater in Moscow several months after Stalin's death. The work opens on a Russian gentry estate, where—in a well-worn convention—serfs sing in chorus. But unlike happy serfs in most nineteenth-century Russian operas, Shaporin's are lamenting their hard existence. The Northern Society Decembrists Ryleev, Kakhovskii, and Aleksandr Bestuzhev and the southerner Pestel sing and act in stark contrast to the Tsar Nicholas character, a cruel, hypocritical sensualist and coward who is given cheap and vulgar melodies. The libretto is all heroism and a good deal of rhetorical bombast, with the usual sacrifice of historical richness for alleged dramatic effect. Privileging Petersburg life with a climax on Senate Square, the story thus omits Sergei Muraviev-Apostol and his exploits in the south.[38]

The Soviet scholarly community continued to pump out huge batches of histories, biographies, documents, and popularized tales. Well over 7,000 works on the Decembrists appeared in the near half century between 1929 to 1976, and an untold number since then.[39] One scholar reckons that up to 1994, some 18,355 publications on the subject had appeared, making the Decembrist movement numerically one of the largest topics in Russian historiography.[40]

Inevitably, with the onset first of glasnost in the 1980s and then independence in the 1990s, revolutionary icons of the past were shattered by a new wave of scholars. Not only did the Bolsheviks suffer from this, but all radicals whose efforts had allegedly led to the disaster of 1917. A generation of serious historians has attempted to challenge the rosiness in some of the Soviet pictures of the movement and to introduce what a western scholar calls a "post-Herzen-Lenin" approach—scholarly and objective.[41] Oksana Kiianskaia, one of the new historians of the Decembrists, wishes to end the practice of historiographical "state command" that produced for the Decembrists a "triumphant genealogy," and to do so without committing the opposite sin: blackening the entire movement as evil.[42]

Some of the demythologizers seemed to take gleeful pleasure in their work. The most detailed of these for the Decembrists was the 2006 book by S. E.

Erlikh, *History of a Myth: Herzen's Decembrist Legend.*[43] He demonstrated that the Russian intelligentsia and even anti-Soviet dissidents had swallowed this legend. But what was the legend? Erlikh's method, the inverse of Herzen's, was to selectively focus on all the negative aspects of the movement, its failures, moral lapses, and deceptions, such as using soldiers as tools for their own purposes. As a corrective to the Herzen story that had been canonized and reinforced by Soviet pieties, the work is unobjectionable but hardly revelatory, since many historians in and out of Russia had been giving nuanced and critical readings of the movement and the uprising for decades.

As the noted Russian historian Boris Mironov put it succinctly, "Ehrlich has convincingly unmasked the mythic essence of the Decembrist concept. But to fight against a myth is a labor of great difficulty. In spite of all its fantasy, incongruity, and inadequacy, any myth fulfills an important social role, and it persists until the moment when that role is fulfilled. So the myth of the Decembrists will perish when the need for it disappears. I fear that the people of Russia will have need for this myth for a long time, and it is thus destined for a long life."[44]

If popular and monumental culture do more than trivialize but also keep memory alive, then Mironov is no doubt correct. The indefatigable S. E. Erlikh tells us of thousands of "Decembrist" sites on the Internet, though some of them are city streets or logos of business firms. A St. Petersburg café serves a Ryleev Salad. Places in fifty-seven cities in Russia, Belarus, and Ukraine still bear Decembrist names. Museums operate in the larger cities and particularly in Siberian sites of exile. In 2000, the Moscow government agreed to preserve the Muraviev-Apostol mansion in that city.[45]

Western historians have recently shown an interest in alternative history, as reflected in the What If? series. But Russian books and websites playing the subjunctive mode on the Decembrists offer not so much thoughtful and plausible scenarios about what might have happened as bizarre science fiction tales without the science.[46] To take only two of many examples. In Ilya Dissident's (pseud.) *Novel of the Five Who Were Pardoned*, published online, Ryleev and Kakhovskii are sent to the Caucasus. The other three sicken, die, or commit suicide. Pestel has homoerotic yearnings for Bestuzhev-Riumin, and Sergei Muraviev-Apostol dreams of the plots and characters later attributed to Gogol and Dostoevsky. L. P. Vershinin's *First Year of the Republic* plunges Russia into an 1826 civil war between monarchists (Whites) and republicans (Blacks), transforms Bestuzhev-Riumin into a modern Vlad the Impaler, and features a peasant "Riego Regiment." These tales are wild variants of the counterfactual first laid out in 1975 by Natan Eidelman in a chapter of his *Apostle Sergei*, a fantasy that possessed at least a hint of plausibility.[47]

In the last full year of Mikhail Gorbachev's refreshing glasnost, a comic book on the Decembrists appeared, called *1825: The Conspiracy*. A decade later, Colin Meloy formed an Oregon rock group, which he called the Decemberists in honor of the Russian revolutionaries, but with an additional *e* for clarity. How can they lose? But this and a recent Western work give little space to events to Muraviev's revolt in the South.[48]

From the very moment of the revolt, the Northerners captured the spotlight. In standard iconography, Senate Square is the emblem of the Decembrist revolt. Most general accounts describe Muraviev-Apostol's belated sortie into the steppe, but almost always as a postscript, and a hopeless one at that. Of the biographies of its leader, few provide the international context, and none does him justice.

But if scholarship constantly bends the story toward St. Petersburg, that minor distortion fades in comparison with how local peasants saw, experienced, and "remembered" what had happened in those wintry days of 1826. In trying to link popular unrest in Ukraine with the rising of the Southern Society, historian V. S. Ikonnikov around 1905 examined two dozen or so court cases involving lower-class defendants who made inflammatory statements in public in the two years after the collapse of the revolt. One announced in his cups that the "arrestees" (i.e., the rebels) would be freed, a tsar would be crowned, and the Polish nobles and the Jews would be wiped out. In another case, a witness overheard soldiers saying that Grand Duke Constantine and not Nicholas was their tsar. In Vasilkov, the launchpad of the rising, a drunken peasant told soldiers to raise a revolt "like that of the Chernigov Regiment" and kill the "devilish Yids and Polacks." Most of the cases simply transformed the combination of rumor, grievances, and alcohol into threats against Polish landowners and Jews—prime targets in times of unrest in this region since early modern times.[49]

Folkloric memory took an even further leap into fantasy. During an 1884 interview, an ancient peasant survivor of the events gave, with the aid of *horilka*— Ukrainian hard spirits—a compressed account in the three-part manner of a folktale or saying. He related that during the uprising, a gentleman appeared, asked for the elder, and told him to gather the village and go to the church and swear. They did. A few days later, another one came and repeated the orders. When told they had already sworn (to Constantine), the visitor ordered fifty lashes for the peasant elder. Then arrived an angry and shouting general asking him about the oath. The peasant told him: first they had sworn to Constantine and then to Nicholas. Lifting up the back of his shirt, he informed the general that he knew what was coming.[50]

Unhorsed and Remounted

After Riego's execution, King Fernando remained another decade on the throne until his death in 1833, surviving assaults from both political flanks. Those from the right, the Apostólicos, embittered by his easing up on repression, formed a prelude to the bloody Carlist wars that afflicted Spain intermittently for decades. From the other side, Espoz y Mina, who had escaped to England, launched in 1830 an unsuccessful liberation raid into Spain across the Pyrenees. An eighteen-year-old Russian living in France, M. A. Kologrivov, joined it; after its failure, he was sent back to Russia and made into a common soldier. Juan Van Halen had returned to Spain in late September 1823 to fight the Apostólicos. Afterward he went into exile again, participated in the Belgian revolution of 1830, and then campaigned against the Carlists.[51] The final incursion of liberals occurred in December 1831, led by José María Torrijos and sixty men. He was defeated and executed. Surviving Spanish liberals now endured the pangs of exile as had their Italian colleagues. As a Russian observer in the 1840s put it, they could be seen "in the bazaars of the Levant, the streets of English towns, and on the shores of American rivers."[52]

Riego's ghost also haunted the chief lands of emigration. The three years of hope hovering over Spain had won many friends across liberal Europe. Soon after the execution of Riego, British radicals, the London *Times*, Lafayette in France, and dozens of sympathizers around Europe and in North and South American raised voices lamenting Riego's death as the symbol of Spanish martyrdom.[53] Liberals of the London Spanish committee protested against the Holy Alliance and France; and against the British government for failure to support Spain. Blaquiere excoriated Fernando VII as a tyrant and called Angoulême's army "mercenary hordes."[54]

Riego's execution set off a storm of protest on the cultural front including lithographed ex-votos in liberal Europe. W. M. Praed, a minor British versifier, called Riego the man "whom Tyranny drew on a hurdle / that artists might draw him on stone."[55] John Cartwright, the British radical, called for thirty-eight days of mourning for Riego and the erection of a monument to him. In 1825 H. M. Milner's drama *Spanish Martyrs, or the Death of Riego* reached the stage of the Royal Coburg Theater in London. Mazzini and Garibaldi both added their tributes to Riego. Across the Atlantic, in 1824, the émigré Spanish journalist Félix Mejía published in Philadelphia a five-act tragedy entitled *There Can Be No Union with Tyrants . . . or Riego and Spain in Shackles*. In the new republics of Latin America, songs, pictures, streets, and squares honored him.[56]

Riego's rehabilitation in his own country came only a dozen years after his death, under Queen Isabella, Fernando's daughter. The bitter dispute about her succession over that of her uncle Don Carlos fueled a dynastic civil war. The Carlists, an extreme anti-modern, anti-urban, deeply religious, and anti-liberal movement, lent its support to Carlos, whom a noted historian has called "a sixteenth-century theocrat who passed among his followers as a saint."[57] The threat from the far right led the monarchy to an accommodation with the liberals. An amnesty brought back thousands of exiles to Spain; liberals of 1812 and 1820

(Martínez de la Rosa, Toreno, and Mendizábal) briefly headed ministries; and a constitution modeled partly on the French Charte was issued in 1837. The new political climate allowed Spaniards at home to join the foreign chorus who were praising Riego and to revisit his historical reputation.

On October 31, 1835, the Queen Regent and prime minister Juan Álvarez y Mendizábal, Riego's old comrade-in-arms, issued a decree announcing that he had been wrongly condemned. Fanaticism was blamed for Riego's ignominious punishment and he was restored to his good name, reputation, and memory. The family received a state pension and enjoyed the special protection of Queen Isabella and the Regent.[58] Canon Miguel Riego came from England in 1835, seeking the remains of his brother. He had no luck, since corpses of criminals and politicals had been thrown together indiscriminately.[59] In 1836, Cadiz citizens beheld a reenactment of the military operations of 1820, and for the third time they intoned the oath to the constitution and installed the stone plaque in an attempt to revive the spirit of 1812 and 1820. The March celebrations were accompanied by a critique in the press of the late king. One paper called him an ungrateful monarch who had caused the nation's misfortunes by accepting aid from another tyrant—Louis XVIII—and by bringing in a hundred thousand "Janissaries" and all the oppression that followed.[60]

Twenty years later, the most remarkable of the cultural tributes to Riego's memory in this era took place. A "historical drama" called *The Triumph of a Free People in 1820* was staged in Madrid. Unlike most of the martyr-centered plays and books to come, it portrays Riego as an active personal savior, thus echoing rescue tales of the romantic period, from Beethoven's *Fidelio* to Poe's "The Pit and the Pendulum"—both set in Spain—and blending gothic with melodrama. In this play, the goal of Riego, an "angelic soul" and an honest and unambitious man, is "to break the infamous yoke that oppresses us and to redeem the beloved country." His exploit at Las Cabezas de San Juan is described, and Riego himself speaks of the glory of martyrdom that awaits him.[61]

The authors of *Triumph of a Free People* make Riego a noble righter of wrongs who saves innocents from destruction. The plot features a prototypical villain, the president of the Seville Inquisition, who, obeying stage conventions, utters evil asides. He targets Riego's liberal friend, whom he calls "a Jewish Mason," arrests him and his beloved and subjects them to interrogation in a subterranean dungeon. The robed members of the Holy Office tribunal, amid torchlight and the sound of tocsins, sentence the young couple to death. As they are being tortured on the wheel and the rack, Riego arrives in Seville with his men to release the victims and destroy the infernal machinery of torment. When a mob crowd calls for death to the Inquisitors, Riego addresses it as "liberal people" and adjures them to "show mercy. He blesses the lovers, and the crowd breaks into the building and liberates the prisoners.[62] As in Risorgimento rescue dramas,

Riego fights for freedom, upholds justice, rescues a maiden, and shows Christian mercy to his enemies.[63]

Laurels continued to fall on Riego's memory through the nineteenth century. Writing in the 1870s, Joaquín Costa, an early Spanish historian of the revolution of 1820, compared Riego to old-time victims of Spanish tyranny, including Padilla and Count Egmont. He was also among the first scholars to compare Riego to his contemporaries Pepe and Ypsilanti: "The cry of liberty sent forth by Riego and Quiroga in Andalusia was echoed not only in Spain but in Naples, Piedmont, Portugal, Brazil, and Greece."[64] In Spain, portraits of the dead hero enjoyed immense popularity throughout the nineteenth century. Political figures in the Cortes and intellectuals in print argued over his virtues and vices. Enemies called him a traitor for his alleged role in "losing" Latin America.[65] Popular idioms came into the language in the wake of Riego's death, such as "to be more liberal than Riego" and "to be braver than Riego." Patriotic songs, funeral marches, and even flamenco verses celebrated his memory.[66]

Anti-liberals had their own fictional take on Riego and his like. Cecilia Böhl de Faber (pseud. Fernán Caballero), an early realist writer, produced novels ridiculing the adherents of the *trienio*. The novella *A Servile and a Liberal* (1855) transpires in 1823, when a liberal officer in flight from the French arrives at a castle owned by absolutists, whom he playfully insults by singing lines from the "Hymn of Riego" ("Guerra á muerte á la tirania"), comparing Fernando VII to Nero, and calling his host an Ostrogoth. But at the end of the story, the impious protagonist, now a general, has—as in the official version of Riego's last days—converted to religion and tradition.[67] A half century later, the well-known Spanish Basque novelist Pío Baroja offered an unattractive portrait of Riego imbibing revolutionary ideas as a prisoner in a small French town and then imposing them on Spain. In a dark and smoky café the "good Spaniards, Catholics, and royalists" spar with the liberal slanderers of the king, led by Riego and the San Miguel brothers.[68]

Memory of, or at least attention to, Riego seems to have faded in the later nineteenth century and a lengthy hiatus in his mythologizing and demonizing ensued. In 1916 at Las Cabezas de San Juan, the locals commemorated the building from whose balcony he had spoken in 1820. With the centennial of 1920, a revival occurred: celebrations and new biographies. Ginés Alberola wrote in one that "with Riego begins the Hegira of the armed revolutions of our century."[69] An anarchist writing under the pseudonym Cánovas y Cervantes added one more hagiography to the pile.[70]

In 1931, with the dawn of the Second Republic, interest in Riego escalated further. On July 14 of that year, deputy Don Niceto Alcalá Zamora—soon to be president—stated to the Cortes in his inaugural address that the "Spanish republic is the grand-daughter and great-grand-daughter of Riego, Torrijos, and all those who perished due to the treachery of Fernando VII." A former laboring man and a priest, Don Zoilo Méndez García also praised Riego—while differentiating him from Marx—as a prophet and activist for freedom and justice for the humble people of Spain.[71]

Another burst of biographies appeared in the early 1930s. For some reason, Diego San José's *Martyrology of the Reign of Fernando: Victims and Executioners of Absolutism* offered hagiographies of Torrijos, Van Halen, Empecinado, and—perhaps for some balance—even the absolutist Elío, but not Riego.[72] In 1932, a year before she died, Carmen de Burgos or Columbine, a well-known Andalusian feminist, produced her *Glorious Life and Unhappy Death of Don Rafael del Riego: A Crime of the Bourbons*, a popular and semi-fictional treatment.[73] The fullest biography of Riego, though written almost eighty years ago, is still that of Eugenia Astur (Enriqueta G. Infanzón), one of the first to dig into crucial documentation.[74]

The Spanish Civil War provided a perfect battleground for the soul of Riego. The beleaguered Republic made the "Hymn of Riego" its national anthem and named a street and a square after him.[75] José Antonio Balbontín's avant-garde agitprop play *Song of Riego* appeared in Republican Madrid at the Teatro del Pueblo in August 1936. Replete with modernist touches, it included women as freedom-fighters and proletarian propaganda speeches by Liberty, "the bride of Riego." Abuses and distortions of the religious spirit by a corrupt church are brought into play in the prison scene of 1823. Riego is "consoled" in his cell not by Dominicans but by the notorious absolutist guerrilla El Trapense. When he tells Riego that the "the Brothers of the Lord are as numerous as the sands of the sea," Riego call this Spain's misfortune. The Riego character—like some real-life leftists in 1936 who tried to bridge religion and radical politics—loves the Christ of peace and freedom, with his sympathy for the poor, the oppressed, and the exploited, and not the Christ of empty ritual. Far from agreeing to sign a letter of repentance urged by the Trappist, Riego says to him: "I would rather burn in hell with Robespierre and Rousseau than be with you in heaven."[76]

For General Francisco Franco's Nationalists, Riego's name was anathema. In 1942, Dr. Gregorio Marañon gave a lecture in German-occupied Paris on the theme of Spaniards in France. He portrayed Riego as an untalented man who by a stroke of luck became the liberal leader and whose long reputation rested upon a mediocre song (the "Hymn of Riego").[77] The "mediocre song" he alluded to caused a comic and embarrassing moment for the Franco regime. When the Nationalist soldiers and Falangists of the Spanish Blue Division arrived in Germany in July 1941 on their way to help the Nazis on the Russian front, their hosts welcomed them at the station with a band playing the "Hymn of Riego," apparently the only Spanish march in its repertoire.[78] After the victory of Franco in 1939, Riego and all he stood for remained almost taboo in Spain in public life until the dictator's death in 1975. "Underground" leftists cherished it in privacy. Ironically, Riego's major contribution to revolutionary history, the military-political pronunciamento, was last employed in a 1981 putsch by ultra-reactionaries—known as the *inmovilistas* or "the Bunker"—who attempted to curb the restoration of democracy.[79]

The chief historian of Riego's post-Franco place of honor in Spanish scholarship, Alberto Gil Novales, wrote in 1980 that Riego "suddenly achieved fame and an immense popularity never matched in Spain by any other figure in Spanish modern history."[80] At a 1985 conference devoted to the Riego bicentennial, Gil Novales spoke of him as a man, "noble and with dignity, at times incautious perhaps, but never for personal gain, always faithful to his ideas and to the Cadiz constitution."[81] In another memorial publication, the historian wrote that "Riego, in his life and in his death, was the symbol of liberty and the independence of his country. . . . To honor Riego means to honor the best of ourselves as Spaniards of conscience."[82] These and many other writings on Riego by Gil Novales represent a virtual academic monument to the revolutionary leader.

Riego's birthplace and the site of his pronunciamento have had their own celebrations and streets or squares named in his memory. The city where he died, however, has been less attentive, perhaps because of the sheer length of the roll call of Spanish heroes, kings, soldiers, priests, and creative figures. He is certainly well represented in documents, books, iconography, and artifacts at the Military Archive, the National Library, and the City Museum. But I have seen no statues. On the busy Plaza de la Cebada one finds not a hint that this is the place of Riego's execution. In a lame attempt at an unscientific "public opinion survey," I made my way in 2005 to a rather shabby precinct south of Atocha Railway Station. An undistinguished acacia-lined street about six blocks long bears his misspelled name: Calle de Rafael de [*sic*] Riego. I found neither a mark of commemoration nor anyone who knew what his name stood for (including—surprise—a Russian shop-owner).

None of this can be seen as unusual. Memory, as we all know, is fickle and selective. Heroes come and go, shunted around by the winds of history and politics. Boredom with stone and cement reminders of the past sets in easily as generations wind their way down the ages. Historians must be content that the four horsemen are remembered at all in their different ways and degrees of prominence. What the citizens of modern Las Cabezas de San Juan, Avellino, Iaşi, and Vasilkov will probably never know, much less remember, is how, long ago, their little towns were, for a moment, part of a single story in European history.

NOTES

Preface

1. Deborah Cohen and Maura O'Connor, eds., *Comparison and History: Europe in Cross-National Perspective* (New York, 2004), ix–xxiv and passim.
2. Crane Brinton, *Anatomy of Revolution* (New York, 1938).

Chapter 1

1. *PSS*, V:210–11.
2. John L. H. Keep, *Soldiers of the Tsar: Army and Society in Russia, 1462–1874* (Oxford, 1985), 267.
3. Paul Schroeder, *The Transformation of European Politics, 1762–1848* (Oxford, 1994), 586.
4. Even specialized works sometimes omit the 1820s revolts altogether: J. Klaits and M. Haltzel, eds., *The Global Ramifications of the French Revolution* (Cambridge, 1994); Jeremy Black, ed., *Revolutions in the Western World, 1775–1825* (Aldershot, 2006).
5. Kathleen Bulgin, *The Making of an Artist: Gautier's Voyage en Espagne* (Birmingham, AL, 1988), 12: Carrie Douglas, *Bulls, Bullfighting, and Spanish Identities* (Tucson, AZ, 1997), 105.
6. Both cited by Giuseppe Pecchio in *Journal of Military and Political Events in Spain During the Last Twelve Months*, trans. Edward Blaquiere (London, 1824), 12.
7. M. A. Dodolev, "Rossiia i ispanskaia revoliutsiia 1820–1823 gg.," *ISSSR* 1 (January-February 1969): 118; Dodolev, *Rossiia i Ispaniia 1808–1823 gg.: voina i revoliutsiia v Ispanii i russko-ispanskie otnosheniia* (Moscow, 1984), 196.
8. Bulgin, 13. See also Douglass, *Bulls, Bullfighting, and Spanish Identities*; Ruth McKay, *"Lazy, Improvident People": Myth and Reality in the Writing of Spanish History* (Ithaca, NY, 2006); and Julian Juderias, *La leyenda negra: estudios acerca del concepto de España en el extranjero* (1914; Madrid, 1954).
9. Tommaso Astarita, *Between Salt Water and Holy Water: A History of Southern Italy* (New York, 2005).
10. *Memoirs of Prince Metternich, 1815–1829*, ed. R. Metternich, trans. A. Napier (1881; New York, 1970), III:386.
11. Martin Malia, *Russia Under Western Eyes* (Cambridge, MA, 1999), 85–165.
12. See Jane Schneider, ed., *Italy's "Southern Question": Orientalism in One Country* (Oxford, 1998).
13. Astarita, *Between Salt Water*, 71.
14. W. Gaunt, *Bandits in a Landscape: A Study of Romantic Painting from Caravaggio to Delacroix* (London, 1937).
15. Eric Hobsbawm, *Bandits* (London, 1967).

16. Robert Hughes, *Goya* (London, 2003), 123.
17. See the literature cited in the introduction to James Collins, *The State in Early Modern Europe*, 2nd ed. (Cambridge, 2009), ix–xxv.
18. Stendhal, *The Charterhouse of Parma*, trans. R. Howard (New York, 2000), 479.
19. Santorre di Santarosa quoted by Guido de Ruggiero, *The History of European Liberalism*, trans. R. G. Collingwood (Boston, 1959), 296.
20. Jerry Miller, ed., *Conservatism: An Anthology of Social and Political Thought from David Hume to the Present* (Princeton, 1997), 136–45.
21. For the constitutional landscape of Europe in this era, see chapter 5.
22. Quoted in a review of Alan Wolfe, *The Future of Liberalism* (New York, 2009) in the *Washington Post*, March 1, 2009.
23. Franco Venturi, "Destutt de Tracy and the Liberal Revolutions," in Venturi, *Studies in Free Russia*, trans. F. S. Walsby and M. O'Dell (Chicago, 1982), 125–26. The works of all three were published in Russia in several editions: ibid., 73–75.
24. Benjamin Constant, *Principles of Politics Applicable to All Governments*, ed. E. Hoffman, trans. D. O'Keefe (Indianapolis, IN, 2003), esp. 77–78, 85–93, 114, 120, 419.
25. Alan Wolfe, *The Future of Liberalism* (New York, 2009), 127–28.
26. Brian Head, *Politics and Philosophy in the Thought of Destutt de Tracy* (New York, 1987).
27. Venturi, "Destutt de Tracy and the Liberal Revolutions," 59; Emmet Kennedy, *A Philosophe in the Age of Revolution: Destutt de Tracy and the Origins of "Ideology"* (Philadelphia, 1978), 237–38, 245–49; quotation, x.
28. M. F. Orlov, "Zapiski o tainom obshchestve" in *Memuary dekabristov*, ed. M. V. Dovnar-Zapol'skii (Kiev, 1906) I:1–26; quotation, 10.
29. William St. Clair, *That Greece Might Still Be Free: The Philhellenes in the War of Independence* (London, 1972).
30. F. Rosen, *Bentham, Byron, and Greece: Constitutionalism, Nationalism, and Early Liberal Political Thought* (Oxford, 1992), 294.
31. Philip Schofield, *Utility and Democracy: The Political Thought of Jeremy Bentham* (Oxford, 2006), 208–15; quotation, 209 n. 40.
32. Louis Bignon, *Du congrès de Troppau, ou examen des prétensions des monarchies absolues à l'égard de la monarchie constitutionelle de Naples* (Paris, 1821), ix, x, xi, 44; quotations, 3. Other political writers who figure in the liberal current of the day include the Abbé Dominique de Pradt, diplomat, publicist, and later bishop. In 1819, Pradt was already predicting a revolution in absolutist Spain due to its poverty and a government he likened to that of the Ottoman Turks. He also believed that representative government acted as an agent of peace among nations. Dominique de Pradt, *L'Europe après le Congrès d'Aix-la-Chapelle* (Paris, 1819), 215–17, 304–24.
33. Jeremy Bentham, *Security Against Misrule and Other Constitutional Writings for Tripoli and Greece*, ed. Ph. Schofield (Oxford, 1990), 103.
34. Sophocles, *The Theban Plays*, trans. E. P. Watling (London, 1974), 139.
35. Harry Hearder, *Italy in the Age of the Risorgimento, 1790–1870* (London, 1983), 175.
36. Frederick Artz, *Reaction and Revolution, 1814–1832* (New York, 1934), 151.
37. Chateaubriand compared Spanish liberalism to yellow fever in 1822. Nesselrode, decades later, still believed that liberal ideas constituted a "moral disease" and were thus communicable: *Krasnyi arkhiv*, 4–5/XXXIX–LC (1938): 185.
38. Eric Hobsbawm, *The Age of Revolution, 1789–1848* (1962; London, 2003), 138.
39. George Rudé, *The Crowd in the French Revolution* (Oxford, 1959), 191–209; quotation, 196.
40. Benito Pérez Galdós, *La segunda casaca* (1876; Madrid, 2003), 127.
41. On the emotional drives of revolutionaries, see the richly documented and vigorous studies with wide chronological scope by James Billington, *Fire in the Minds of Men: Origins of the Revolutionary Faith* (New York, 1980), and Adam Zamoyski, *Holy Madness: Romantics, Patriots, and Revolutionaries, 1776–1871* (New York, 2001).
42. David Brewer, *The Flame of Freedom: The Greek War of Independence, 1821–1833* (London, 2001), 57.
43. Theodore Lyman, *The Political State of Italy* (Boston, 1820), 398.

44. M. V. Nechkina, *Dvizhenie dekabristov* (Moscow, 1955), I:305.
45. John Stanley, "The Polish Military in the Napoleonic Era," in *Armies in Exile*, ed. David Stefancic (Boulder, 2005), 3–51.
46. For the influx of foreigners in the French armed forces, see Eugène Fieffé, *Histoire des troupes étrangères au service de France* (Paris, 1854), vol. II.
47. St. Clair, *That Greece Might Still Be Free*, 32.
48. Zamoyski, *Holy Madness*.
49. Georg Schuster, *Die geheimen Gesellschaften, Verbindungen, und Orden*, 2 vols. (Leipzig, 1906); Norman MacKenzie, ed., *Secret Societies* (London, 1967).
50. Arthur May, *The Age of Metternich, 1814–1848*, 2nd ed. (New York, 1963), 119.
51. Diego Martínez Torrón, *Los liberales románticos españoles ante la descolonización americana, 1808–1833* (Madrid, 1992), 44.
52. Chadwick, *The Popes and European Revolution* (Oxford, 1981), 545.
53. Robert Palmer, *The Age of the Democratic Revolution* (Princeton, 1959–64), II:358–59; quotations, 358.
54. Karen Carter, "Creating Catholics: Catechism and Primary Education in Early Modern France," Ph.D. dissertation, Georgetown University, 2006.
55. Robert Holtman, *The Napoleonic Revolution* (Philadelphia, 1967), 130; *Catéchisme de toutes des églises de l'Empire français* (Clermont, 1806), 75.
56. Zamoyski, *Holy Madness*, 27, 98.
57. CNC (minus title page), 482, p. 106. The master copy is *Catéchisme à l'usage de toutes des églises de l'Empire français* (Paris, 1807), in CNC, 484, of which the one cited in the above note is a variant.
58. Emilie Delivré, "The Pen and the Sword: Political Catechisms and the Resistance to Napoleon," in *Popular Resistance in the French Wars: Patriots, Partisans, and Land Pirates*, ed. Charles Esdaile (London, 2005), 166–67.
59. Maria de las Nieves Muñiz Muñiz, "Romanticismo italiano e romanticismo spagnolo," in Annarosa Poli and Emmanuele Kanceff, eds., *L'Italie dans l'Europe romantique* (Moncalieri, 1996), I:642.
60. W. B. Carnochan, "The Literature of Confinement," in Norval Morris and D. J. Rothman, eds., *The Oxford History of the Prison* (New York, 1995), 435.
61. "Prisons," in Maurice Lévy, *Images du roman noir* (Paris, 1973).
62. Francisco Goya's engravings of torment and shackled prisoners, though often cited for his period, mostly became public later. Gwyn Williams, *Goya and the Impossible Revolution* (New York, 1976), 112–15; Hughes, *Goya*, 137. Greeks and Russian, interestingly, fell outside this wave of imagery. The horrors of incarceration in Turkish prisons paled before the striking atrocities perpetrated on the ground by both sides in the Greek independence war. Public awareness of Russian convict life—especially in the Siberian penal system—arose only in the reign of Alexander II (1855–81).
63. Quoted in Jacqueline Howard, "Introduction," in Ann Radcliffe, *The Mysteries of Udolpho: A Romance* (1794; London, 2001), xxxvi n. 5.
64. Ann Radcliffe, *The Mysteries of Udolpho*; Howard, "Introduction," vii–xxxix.
65. Armand Carrel, *Oeuvres* (Paris, 1857–59), V:81.
66. Mikhail Lunin, *Pis'ma iz Sibiri*, ed. I. A. Zhelvakova and N. Ya. Eidel'man (Moscow, 1967), 257.
67. Tr. from English in Liliane Abensour and Françoise Charras, eds., *Romantisme noir* (Paris, 1978), 165.
68. Ludwig van Beethoven and Joseph Sonnleithner, *Fidelio* (New York, 1935).
69. Edgar Allan Poe, *The Annotated Tales*, ed. S. Peithman (New York, 1981), 120–33.
70. Though certainly Britain was far ahead of the continent in prison reform in this era. Barry Hollingsworth, "John Venning and Prison Reform in Russia, 1819–1830," *Slavonic and East European Review* 48, no. 113 (October 1970): 537–56.
71. Charles Laumier, *Histoire de la révolution d'Espagne en 1820* (Paris, 1820), 168.
72. Robert Harvey, *Liberators: South America's Savage Wars of Freedom, 1810–1830* (London, 2000), 95–96; Paul Johnson, *The Birth of the Modern* (London, 1991), 634.
73. Zamoyski, *Holy Madness*, 86–87, 290–91.

74. John A. Davis, "Cultures of Interdiction: the Politics of Censorship in Italy from Napoleon to the Restoration," in *Napoleon's Legacy: Problems of Government in Restoration Europe*, ed. David Laven and Lucy Riall (Oxford, 2000), 252.

75. Carnochan, "Literature of Confinement," 447.

76. Victor Brombert, *The Romantic Prison: The French Tradition* (Princeton, 1978); Paul Austin, *The Exotic Prisoner in Russian Romanticism* (New York, 1997).

77. *The Complete Poetical and Dramatic Works of Lord Byron* (Philadelphia, 1883), 112.

78. For the cult of Cato and the literature on it, see Susan Morrissey, *Suicide and the Body Politic in Imperial Russia* (Cambridge, 2006), 53–54.

Chapter 2

1. The text of Riego's speech is in Rafael del Riego, *Rafael del Riego: la revolución de 1820, día a día—cartas, escritos, y discursos*, ed. A. Gil Novales (Madrid, 1976), 34–35. For the event, see Zoilo Méndez García, *Historia documental de Riego* (Luarca: Heredera, 1932; reprint, 1995), 47–48, drawn partly from records of two of Riego's officers. Apparently Riego spoke sometimes on foot. For obvious reasons, the Riego iconography almost always has him on horseback when he issued pronunciamentos. See Francisco Domingo Román Ojeda, *Riego: "Héroe de Las Cabezas"* (Las Cabezas de San Juan, 1985), 60–62 (illustr. 64).

2. Riego, *Revolución de 1820*, 35. In my translations, I have retained Riego's use of capitalization but have modified slightly the punctuation for greater clarity.

3. Riego, *Revolución de 1820*, 36–37.

4. Ibid., 34. The term *ambiciosos* in this context meant those with an inordinate thirst for power rather than a natural aspiration for personal success.

5. Edward Blaquiere, *An Historical Review of the Spanish Revolution* (London, 1822), 288.

6. Raymond Carr, *Spain, 1808–1975*, 2d ed. (Oxford, 1982), 16; Robert Hughes, *Goya* (London, 2003), 123; Richard Ford, *Gatherings from Spain* (1846; London, 1906), 201–30 (qu. 213); Michael Quin, *A Visit to Spain*, 2d ed. (London, 1824), 277, 280, 289, and passim.

7. Carr, *Spain*, 55; Ford, *Gatherings from Spain*, 227–30 (an execution); John Moore, *Ramón de la Cruz* (New York, 1972).

8. Carr, *Spain*, 39.

9. Carr, *Spain*, 45–47, 45 n. 3, 197. The extent of that commitment has been questioned by some scholars. See Henry Kamen, *Imagining Spain: Historical Myth and National Identity* (New Haven, 2008), 74–95.

10. Hughes, *Goya*, 333–40.

11. Henry Kamen, *The Spanish Inquisition: A Historical Revision* (New Haven, 1998), 304.

12. Marie-Danielle Demélas-Bohy, "La guerra religiosa como modelo," in *Revoluciones hispánicas: independencias americanas y liberalismo español*, ed. François-Xavier Guerra (Madrid, 1995), 143–64 (qu. 162).

13. Richard Herr, *The Eighteenth-Century Revolution in Spain* (Princeton, 1958).

14. Charles Esdaile, *Spain in the Liberal Age from Constitution to Civil War, 1808–1939* (Oxford, 2000), 13–14.

15. Richard Herr, "The Spanish Road to Parliamentary Democracy," in Isser Woloch, ed., *Revolution and the Meanings of Freedom in the Nineteenth Century* (Stanford, 1996), 71–72.

16. Text in *Constituciones españolas y extranjeras*, ed. Jorge de Esteban (Madrid, 1977), I:57–72; Karl Marx, *On Revolution*, ed. Saul Padover (New York, 1972), 591.

17. Carr, *Spain*, 85.

18. Charles J. Esdaile, *The Wars of Napoleon* (London, 1995), 81–82; Brian Hamnett, "Constitutional Theory and Political Reality: Liberalism, Traditionalism, and the Spanish Cortes, 1810–1814," *JMH* 49, no. 1 (on-demand supplement, March 1977): D1071–110.

19. Richard Hocquellet, *Résistance et révolution durant l'occupation napoléonienne en Espagne, 1808–1812* (Paris, 2001), 84–96; Herr, "Spanish Road" in Woloch, *Revolution*, 74.

20. Between 1950 and 2001, at least fifteen hundred titles on it appeared, as many in recent years. Hocquellet, *Résistance et revolution*, 171–73, 351 n. 834.

21. Hocquellet, *Résistance et revolution*, 171–73 and passim.

22. Charles Esdaile, *Fighting Napoleon: Guerrillas, Bandits, and Adventurers in Spain, 1808–1814* (New Haven, 2004); Carr, *Spain*, 108–9; Hocquellet, *Résistance et révolution*, 177; Nikolai Nevedomskii, "Tri poslednie glavy iz istorii gveril'iasov," *Sovremennik* XXVII, no. 3 (1842): 1–56 (September pagination).

23. "Della guerra di parteggiani" in *Minerva napolitana* (1820), cited in Franco Della Peruta, "La guerra di liberazione spagnola e la teoria della guerra per bande nel Risorgimento," in *L'Italia del Risorgimento* (Milan, 1997), 11–29 (13 14).

24. Hocquellet, *Résistance et révolution*, 178.

25. Franco Della Peruta, "War and Society in Napoleonic Italy: The Armies of the Kingdom of Italy at Home and Abroad," in *Society and Politics in the Age of the Risorgimento*, ed. John Davis and Paul Ginsborg (Cambridge, 1991), 26–48; see 47.

26. Della Peruta, "Guerra di liberazione spagnola," 11–12; Eugène Fieffé, *Histoire des troupes étrangères au service de France* (Paris, 1854), vol. II.

27. Nevedomskii, "Tri poslednie glavy," 40.

28. Della Peruta, "War and Society," 42 (qu.), 43, and passim.

29. Della Peruta, "Guerra di liberazione spagnola," 12–13.

30. Niegolewski, *Les Polonais à Somo-Sierra en 1808 en Espagne* (Paris, 1854); Fieffé, *Histoire des troupes étrangères*, II:235–42 and passim; Adam Zamoyski, *Holy Madness: Romantics, Patriots, and Revolutionaries, 1776–1871* (New York, 2001), 273; John Stanley, "The Polish Military in the Napoleonic Era," in David Stefancic, ed., *Armies in Exile* (Boulder, 2005), 3–51; Vladimir Lamanskii, *O slavianakh v Maloi Azii, v Afrike, i v Ispanii* (St. Petersburg, 1859), 367–68 and n. 1.

31. Della Peruta, "Guerra di liberazione spagnola," 12. For Dębowski, see *Wielka encyklopedia powszechna*, II:873; *Nowa encyklopedia powszechna*, II:53.

32. Antony Beevor, *The Spanish Civil War* (1982; London, 2004), 210.

33. Hocquellet, *Résistance et révolution*, 176 and n. 427; Hughes, *Goya*, 6 (qu.), 295.

34. Esdaile, *Fighting Napoleon*, 193–204 and passim.

35. Esdaile, *Wars of Napoleon*, 219–24.

36. Ibid., 220–21.

37. Esdaile, *Spain in the Liberal Age*, 17.

38. Esdaile, *Wars of Napoleon*, 130, 139; Esdaile, *Fighting Napoleon*, 188–91.

39. Esdaile, *Wars of Napoleon*, 224.

40. Carr, *Spain*, 47.

41. Esdaile, *Fighting Napoleon*, 93.

42. Hamnett, "Constitutional Theory," D1090.

43. A. Ramos Oliveira, *Politics, Economics and Men of Modern Spain, 1808–1946*, tr. Teener Hall (London, 1946), 26; Jean Sarrailh, *Un homme d'état espagnol: Martínez de la Rosa, 1787–1862* (Paris, 1930), 35 (qu.).

44. Ramón Solis, *El Cádiz de las Cortes: la vida en la ciudad en los años 1810 a 1813* (Madrid, 1969), 23–27, 60–130.

45. Vladimir Romanov, "Otryvok iz pokhodnykh zapisok v Ispaniiu," *OZ*, II/3 (1820), 27–41 (34). He was arrested in 1826 as one of the Decembrists.

46. Solis, *El Cádiz de las Cortes*, 3–43, 134–38; Juan Francisco Fuentes, "De la sociabilidad censitaria a la sociabilidad popular en la España liberal," in *Sociabilidad y liberalismo en la España del siglo XIX: homenaje al profesor Alberto Gil Novales*, ed. Juan Francisco Fuentes and Lluís Roura i Aulinas (Lleida, 2001), 207–224.

47. Ford, *Gatherings from Spain*, 347.

48. Solis, *El Cádiz de las Cortes*, 320–30; Fuentes, "Sociabilidad censitaria." See also the historical novel by Benito Pérez Galdós, *Cádiz* (1874; Madrid, 2001) for the vivid atmosphere of street and salon life.

49. James Billington, *Fire in the Minds of Men: Origins of the Revolutionary Faith* (New York, 1980), 135.

50. Owen Chadwick, *The Popes and European Revolution* (Oxford, 1981), 532.

51. Solis, *Cádiz de las Cortes*, 134; Richard Herr, "Flow and Ebb, 1700–1833," in Raymond Carr, ed., *Spain: A History* (Oxford, 2000), 198.

52. Herr, *Eighteenth-Century Revolution*, 326 n. 42; José A. Ferrer Benimeli, "Masoneria e iglesia en España," in *Libéralisme chrétien et Catholicisme libéral en Espagne, France, et Italie dans la première moitié du XIXe siècle* (Aix-en-Provence, 1989), 68.
53. Esdaile, *Spain in the Liberal Age*, 25.
54. Solis, *Cádiz de las Cortes*, 228–29. Picture of the theater in Miguel Artola Gallego, *La España de Fernando VII*, 3rd ed. (Madrid, 1983), 472. The Cortes moved several times in order to avoid French artillery and an epidemic of yellow fever.
55. Artola Gallego, *La España de Fernando VII*, 454 (ill., 451).
56. Solis, *Cádiz de las Cortes*, 204–14, 237–39.
57. Herr, "Spanish Road," in Woloch, *Revolution*, 85.
58. C. W. Crawley, "French and English Influences in the Cortes of Cadiz, 1810–1814," *Cambridge Historical Journal* VI, no. 2 (1939): 186.
59. *CDO*, I/1, 1 and 163–64.
60. *CDO*, I/1, 6–7 (September 25, 1810). See also *CDO*, I–IV, passim.
61. *CDO*, I/1, 14.
62. *CDO*, I/1, 55, 64, 133 (qu.), 77–79.
63. *CDO*, I/1, 199; Juan Sisinio Pérez Garzón, "Ejército nacional y Milicia nacional," in Gil Novales, ed., *La revolución burguesa en España* (Madrid, 1985), 181–84.
64. *Constitución de Cádiz de 1812* (n.d., n.p.), articles 356–65.
65. Sisinio Pérez Garzón, "Ejército nacional y Milicia nacional," 183–85 (qu. 185); Esdaile, *Spanish Army*, 154–193.
66. *CDO*, I/1, 31, 107 (qu.); Constitution of 1812, article 12.
67. Joaquín Varela Suances, "Los modelos constitucionales en las Cortes de Cádiz," in Guerra, *Revoluciones hispánicas*, 263.
68. Carr, *Spain*, 115.
69. Article 366; *CDO*, I/2, 162–63.
70. Cited in Román Ojeda, *Riego*, 21–22.
71. Hamnett, "Constitutional Theory," D1104.
72. Herr, "Flow and Ebb," in Carr, ed. *Spain: A History*, 199; Solis, *Cádiz de las Cortes*, 74 (qu.).
73. Esdaile, *Wars of Napoleon*, 227.
74. William Callahan, "The Origins of the Conservative Church in Spain, 1793–1823," *European Studies Review* 10, no. 2 (April 1979): 197–203 (qu. 201).
75. Gonzalo Álvarez Chillida, *El antisemitismo en España: la imagen del judio, 1812–2000* (Madrid, 2002), 96–118.
76. *CDO*, I/2, 132–35; Carr, *Spain*, 97.
77. Suances, "Modelos constitucionales," in Guerra, *Revoluciones hispánicas; Preliminary Discourse Read in the Cortes at the Presentation of the Constitution by the Committee of the Constitution, to Which Is Added the Present Spanish Constitution* (London, 1823); Esdaile, *Wars of Napoleon*, 225–26.
78. Alfred Blaustein and Jay Sigler, eds., *Constitutions That Made History* (New York, 1980); Hamnett, "Constitutional Theory," D1064, 1097, 1104.
79. Marx, *On Revolution*, 615–19.
80. Carr, *Spain*, 44.
81. Luis Sánchez Agesta, *Historia del constitucionalismo español* (Madrid, 1955), 89.
82. A. F. Zimmerman, "Spain and its Colonies, 1808–1820," *HAHR* 4 (November 1931): 452–55; John H. Elliott, *Empires of the Atlantic World: Britain and Spain in America, 1492–1830* (New Haven, 2006), 439.
83. Hamnett, "Constitutional Theory," D1107–9.
84. Philip Schofield, *Utility and Democracy: The Political Thought of Jeremy Bentham* (Oxford, 2006), 212ff. There is some evidence that the Spanish liberal movement helped swing Bentham leftward (ibid., 137).
85. George Romani, *The Neapolitan Revolution of 1820–21* (Evanston, 1950), 94–98 (95 n. 81, 97 n. 83).
86. Quin, *Visit to Spain*, 166.
87. Carr, *Spain*, 94.
88. Romani, *Neapolitan Revolution*, 95 n. 81.

89. W. N. Hargreaves-Mawdsley, ed., *Spain Under the Bourbons: A Collection of Documents* (Columbia, SC, 1973), 269.

90. See Suances, "Modelos constitucionales," in Guerra, *Revoluciones hispánicas*, 250–51, 256, and passim, for a discussion of the English and French models.

91. *Preliminary Discourse*, 14 and 16 (qu.) and passim.

92. Quintana in Hargreaves-Mawdsley, *Spain Under the Bourbons*, 261–75.

93. François-Xavier Guerra, "El ocaso de la monarquía hispánica," in *Inventando la nación—Iberoamérica, siglo XIX*, ed. Antonio Annino and François-Xavier Guerra (Mexico City, 2003), 139.

94. Solis, *Cádiz de las Cortes*, 254–59; *CDO*, I/1, 175.

95. Letter to Lord Holland, 1823, in Hargreaves-Mawdsley, *Spain Under the Bourbons*, 262.

96. Esdaile, *Wars of Napoleon*, 218.

97. Hocquellet, *Résistance et révolution*, 265.

98. Albert Dérozier, *Manuel Josef Quintana et la naissance du libéralisme en Espagne*, 2 vols. (Paris, 1968–70).

99. *Colección documental del Fraile, Archivo General Militar, Madrid*, I: excerpts from *Gazeta ministerial de Sevilla*, June 1808 and July 23, 1808, and *Diario de Granada*, June 5, 1808.

100. Cited in Solis, *Cádiz de las Cortes*, 338–43 (qu. 341, 342).

101. Felipe Fernández-Armesto, "The Improbable Empire," in *Spain: A History*, ed. Carr, 148.

102. Solis, *Cádiz de las Cortes*, 338–40, 354–55.

103. Ibid., 345–51.

104. Francisco Martínez de Aguilar, *Melo-drama en un acto, que en celebridad de la victoria conseguida por las armas españoles en la Andalucía* (Cadiz, 1808).

105. Ermano Caldera, "Presenza italiana nel romanticismo spagnolo," in *L'Italie dans l'Europe romantique*, ed. Annarosa Poli and Emmanuele Kanceff (Moncalieri, 1996), I:328.

106. Sarrailh, *Homme d'état espagnol*, 7–70, 145–52, and passim.

107. Francisco Martínez de la Rosa, *Obras dramáticas*, 2d ed. (Madrid, [1947]), xi.

108. Stephen Haliczer, *The Comuneros of Castile* (Madison, WI, 1981).

109. *La viuda de Padilla*, in Martínez de la Rosa, *Obras dramáticas*, 45–115 (qu. 115).

110. Sarrailh, *Homme d'état espagnol*, 37–38.

111. Hughes, *Goya*, 269–71; N. Glendinning, "The French Revolution in Spain and the Art of Goya," in *The Impact of the French Revolution on European Consciousness*, ed. H. T. Mason and W. Doyle (Gloucester, 1989), 117–32.

112. *CDO*, II/1, 52–53.

113. Mona Ozouf, *Festivals and the French Revolution* (Cambridge, MA, 1988); James Von Geldern, *Bolshevik Festivals, 1917–1920* (Berkeley, 1993).

114. Gonzalo Butrón Prida, "Fiesta y revolución: las celebraciones políticas en el Cádiz liberal (1812–1837)," in Gil Novales, ed., *La revolución liberal* (Madrid, 2001), 160–64.

115. Karen Carter, "Creating Catholics: Catechism and Primary Education in Early Modern France," doctoral dissertation, Georgetown University, 2006; Emilie Delivré, "The Pen and the Sword," in *Popular Resistance in the French Wars: Patriots, Partisans, and Land Pirates*, ed. Charles Esdaile (London, 2005), 161–79.

116. *Proyecto al catecismo universal y su compendio, intitulada: El Niño instruido por la Divina Palabra* (Madrid, 1807). See also *Catecismo para el uso de todas las iglesias del Imperio frances* (Madrid, 1807). Ordered published by Napoleon to standardize and restore the faith, it was a translation of *Catéchisme à l'usage de toutes des églises de l'Empire français* (Paris, 1807) in CNC, 484. Article 366 of the Spanish constitution of 1812 required elementary schooling to include reading, writing, and arithmetic in addition to the Catholic catechism and knowledge of civil obligations.

117. Delivré, "The Pen and the Sword," 171. The ones I have read are from the Military Archives in Madrid and, when noted, from Ramón Espinar Gallego, ed., *Catecismos políticos españoles arreglados a las constituciones del siglo XIX* (Madrid, 1989); and, in brief excerpts, from Alfonso Capitán Díaz, *Los catecismos políticos en España, 1808–1822* (Granada, 1978).

118. *La bestia de siete cabezas y diez cuernos, o Napoleon Emperador de los Franceses: exposición literal del capítulo XIII del apocalipsis* (Malaga, 1809), 1, 3.

119. Un Presbitero, *Instrucción popular en forma de catecismo sobre la presente guerra: la consagra al exército y al pueblo de España* (Seville, 1809), iii–iv (qu. 1, 5).

120. *Instrucción popular en forma de catecismo*, 1, 31, 33 (qu. 13, 25, 49).

121. *Catecismo político para instrucción del pueblo español* (Cadiz, 1810), in Capitán Díaz, *Catecismos políticos en España*, 114, 127 (qu.), 129. A similar catechism appeared in *El observador* in September 1810: Hocquellet, *Résistance et révolution*, 274–75. In 1811 came another, in Cadiz, noted in *Advertencias al catecismo civil de D. Andres de Moya y Luzuriaga por D. Hugo de Lema y Rull* (Cadiz, 1811). A *Catecismo político arreglado a la Constitución de la monarquía española* was published both in Cadiz and in Palma in 1812: Gallego, *Catecismos políticos*, 107–37. See also Isabel de Madariaga, "Spain and the Decembrists," *European Studies Review* 3, no. 2 (January-October 1973): 150 n. 32.

122. Walter Hanisch Espindola, *El catecismo político-cristiano—las ideas y la época: 1810* (Santiago de Chile, 1970), 24–29 (qu. 24).

123. José Andrés-Gallego, "La pluralidad de referencias políticas," in Guerra, *Revoluciones hispánicas*, 139–40.

124. *Catecismo civil, y breve compendio de las obligaciones del Español* (n.p., c. 1808), in Gallego, *Catecismos políticos*, 17–20. Madrid and Seville origins are noted in various sources.

125. Heinrich von Kleist, *Sämtliche Werke* (Frankfort-am-Main, 1991–97), III:479–91. See Delivré, "The Pen and the Sword," 166–67; Ol'ga Orlik, *Dekabristy i evropeiskoe osvoboditel'noe dvizhenie* (Moscow, 1975), 20.

126. *SO* 1 (October 1812): 53 and note. See Chapter 5 for additional documentation.

127. Narcisse-Achille de Salvandy, *Don Alonzo, ou l'Espagne: histoire contemporaine*, 4 vols. (Paris, 1824). My source: *Don Alonso, ou l'Espagne: histoire contemporaine*, 6th ed. (Paris, 1857), II:142–49 (the setting). All quotations are from this edition. The spelling of the protagonist's name was changed here to Alonso. Data on Salvandy in *GDU*, VI/2 (1870): 1078 and XIV/1 (1875): 148–49.

128. De Madariaga, "Spain and the Decembrists," 151.

129. Salvandy, *Don Alonso*, II:149–52. The term "constitution" here and in other Spanish documents of the era often related to traditional charters and laws.

130. Paul Boppe, *Los españoles en el ejército napoleónico*, tr. A. Salafranca Vázquez (1899; Malaga, 1995), 171–211; Paul Austin, *1812: The March on Moscow* (London, 1993), 107, 368 n. 2; Paul Austin, *1812: Great Retreat* (London, 1996), 48; Fieffé, *Histoire des troupes étrangères*, II:144–52.

131. M. P. Alekseev, "Etiudy iz istorii ispano-russkikh otnoshenii," in *Kul'tura Ispanii: sbornik* (Moscow, 1940), 398 n. 3; Austin, *1812: Great Retreat*, 433–34 n. 12; M. A. Dodolev, "O vliianii ispanskoi revoliutsii 1808–1814 godov na vneshniuiu politiku evropeiskikh gosudarstv," *Novaia i noveishaia istoriia* 2 (March-April 1968): 40.

132. Lamanskii, *O slavianakh*, 368; Dodolev, "Rossiia i voina ispanskogo naroda za nezavisimost' (1808–1814) gg.," *VI* 11 (November 1972): 39; *Diplomatisches Archiv für die Zeit- und Staatengeschichte* (Stuttgart, 1821–26), III:386–87.

133. *Constitution politique de la monarchie espagnole publiée à Cadix*, tr. Abbé Vialar (St. Petersburg, 1812); Orlik, *Dekabristy i evropeiskoe osvoboditel'noe dvizhenie*, 20.

134. "Grazhdanskii katikhizis, ili Kratkoe obozrenie dolzhnostei ispantsa," *SO* 1 (October 1812): 53–60; Dodolev, "Rossiia i ispanskaia revoliutsiia 1820–1823 gg.," *ISSSR* 1 (January-February 1969): 113–22 (113 qu.).

135. *Listovki Otechestvennoi voiny 1812 goda: sbornik dokumentov*, ed. R. E. Alt'shuller and A. G. Tartakovskii (Moscow, 1962), 38–39 n. 2.

136. Orlik, *Dekabristy i evropeiskoe osvoboditel'noe dvizhenie*, 20–21; Ana María Schop Soler, *Las relaciones entre España y Rusia en la época de Fernando VII, 1808–1833* (Barcelona, 1975), 410; Lamanskii, *O slavianakh*, 368.

137. *Noticias sobre el exército de los rusos y el de Napoleon en la Polonia* (Seville, 1812); *Españoles* (Cádiz, 1812); Esdaile, *Wars of Napoleon*, 246.

138. Schop Soler, *Relaciones entre España y Rusia*, p. 5.

139. *CDO*, II/1, 62–64, 193–94.

140. Matías Jorge de Arcas, *Memoria sobre la alianza de España con Rusia, y la gratitud que los españoles deben al Emperador Alexandro* (Madrid, 1814).

141. Blaquiere, *Historical Review*, 619.
142. Sarrailh, *Homme d'état espagnol*, 48 n. 2.
143. Pérez Garzón, "Ejército nacional y Milicia nacional," 185, 192; Esdaile, *Spain in the Liberal Age*, 38–40.
144. Carr, *Spain*, 120; G. I. Revzin, *Riego* (Moscow, 1939), 228; Capitán Díaz, *Catecismos políticos en España*, 100; Hughes, *Goya*, 325 (qu.).
145. Esdaile, *Spain in the Liberal Age*, 46.
146. Sarrailh, *Homme d'état espagnol*, 50; Herr, "Spanish Road," 92.
147. Ana María Schop Soler, *Un siglo de relaciones diplomáticas y comerciales entre España y Rusia, 1733–1833* (Madrid, 1984), 411 n. 18b.
148. Letter to Lord Holland, November 20, 1823, in Hargreaves-Mawdsley, *Spain Under the Bourbons*, 270, 275.
149. Carr, *Spain*, 118–19, 126; Marx, *On Revolution*, 621; Callahan, "Origins," 205–6.
150. Thomas Steele, *Notes on the War in Spain* (London, 1824), 197–98 (qu. 198).
151. Blaquiere, *Historical Review*, 615–24.
152. Charles Webster, *The Foreign Policy of Castlereagh, 1812–1815* (London, 1950), 310–13.
153. Margaret Woodward, "The Spanish Army and the Loss of America," *HAHR* 48, no. 4 (November 1968): 589–95; John Lynch, *The Spanish-American Revolutions, 1808–1826* (New York, 1973), 206–8 and passim.
154. Patricia Grimsted, *The Foreign Ministers of Alexander I: Political Attitudes and the Conduct of Russian Diplomacy, 1801–1825* (Berkeley, 1969), 282–83; Schop Soler, *Siglo de relaciones*, 413; C. M. Woodhouse, *Capodistria: The Founder of Greek Independence* (London, 1973), 155.
155. Russell Bartley, *Imperial Russia and the Struggle for Latin American Independence, 1806–1828* (Austin, 1978), 9–11, 104–5, 131–44; Schop Soler, *Relaciones entre España y Rusia*, chaps. 1–2.
156. Schop Soler, *Relaciones entre España y Rusia*, 5–7; Enno Krahe, "Strange Bedfellows: Alexander I and Ferdinand VII, 1812–1823," in *The Consortium on Revolutionary Europe, 1750–1850*, ed. Ronald Caldwell et al. (Tallahassee, 1994), 7; Manuel Morán Ortí, "Políticas liberales, políticas absolutistas (1810–1833)," in Guerra, ed., *Revoluciones hispánicas*, 83.
157. E. Christiansen, *The Origins of Military Power in Spain, 1800–1854* (Oxford, 1967), 19–20.
158. Jean-René Aymes, *Los españoles en Francia (1808–1814): la deportación bajo el Primer Imperio* (Madrid, 1987).
159. Charles Esdaile, *The Spanish Army in the Peninsular War* (Manchester, 1988), 196–97.
160. Carr, *Spain*, 127; Artola Gallego, *España de Fernando VII*, 616–617.
161. Artola Gallego, *España de Fernando VII*, 619–23, Esdaile, *Spain in the Liberal Age*, 46–47.
162. Artola Gallego, *España de Fernando VII*, 624.
163. Revzin, *Riego*, 280.
164. Richard Fletcher, "The Early Middle Ages, 700–1250," in *Spain: A History*, ed. Carr, 75–76.
165. George Borrow, *The Bible in Spain* (1842; London, 1913), 244–50 (qu. 249).
166. Callahan, "Origins," 206; Blaquiere, *Historical Review*, 225, 235–38 (qu. 235); Artola Gallego, *España de Fernando VII*, 623–25.
167. Revzin, *Riego*, 287 (qu.); Artola Gallego, *España de Fernando VII*, 625–27.
168. Esdaile, *Spain in the Liberal Age*, 47–48; Artola Gallego, *España de Fernando VII*, 627–29.
169. Artola Gallego, *España de Fernando VII*, 632–33; Elío document cited in Blaquiere, *Historical Review*, 655–56 (qu. 655).
170. Juan Van Halen, *Narrative of Don Juan Van Halen's Imprisonment in the Dungeons of the Inquisition at Madrid* (New York, 1828), 43–54 and passim. Additional details in N. Belozerskaia, "Zapiski Van-Galena," *IV*, June 1884, 651–78, and Artola Gallego, *España de Fernando VII*, 631.
171. Van Halen, *Narrative*, 83–106; Belozerskaia, "Zapiski Van-Galena," *IV*, May 1884, 402–19.
172. M. A. Dodolev, *Rossiia i Ispaniia 1808–1823 gg.* (Moscow, 1984), 163–65; Dodolev, "Van-Galen v Rossii (1818–1820 gg.)," *ISSSR* 2 (March-April 1980): 145–57.
173. See Victor Brombert, *The Romantic Prison: The French Tradition* (Princeton, 1978), 9 and passim.
174. [José Joaquín de Mora], *Mémoires historiques sur Ferdinand VII, roi des Espagnes*, tr. M.G.H. (Paris, 1824), 218.

175. Francisco Tomás y Valiente, *La tortura en España*, 2d ed. (Barcelona, 1994), 135–38 (qu. 138). On the Black Legend, see Chapter 1 and Sebastian Balfour and Alejandro Quiroga, *The Reinvention of Spain* (Oxford, 2007), 33.

176. Carr, *Spain*, 124 n. 2, 125; E. V. Tarle, "Voennaia revoliutsiia na zapade Evropy i Dekabristy," in *Sochineniia* (Moscow, 1957–62), V:14.

177. Michael Costeloe, *Response to Revolution: Imperial Spain and the Spanish American Revolutions, 1810–1840* (Cambridge, 1986), 77–83; John McNeill, "Yellow Fever, Empire, and Revolution," paper presented at the Helsinki University Collegium for Advanced Studies, October 15, 2004; Artola Gallego, *España de Fernando VII*, 634–35.

178. Tarle, "Voennaia revoliutsiia na zapade Evropy i Dekabristy," 13; Blaquiere, *Historical Review*, 280–81.

179. Artola Gallego, *España de Fernando VII*, 635–36; Emilio Fernández de Pinedo, Alberto Gil Novales, and Albert Dérozier, *Centralismo, ilustración, y agonía del Antiguo Régimen (1715–1833)*, 2d ed. (Barcelona, 1982), 288; Christiansen, *Origins of Military Power*, 21.

180. Román Ojeda, *Riego*, 44–45; *DBTL*, 18–19, 30.

181. Román Ojeda, *Riego*, 44–45; *DBTL*, 233–34, 544–45.

182. Charles Laumier, *Histoire de la révolution d'Espagne en 1820* (Paris, 1820), 154–61; Blaquiere, *Historical Review*, 275.

183. Artola Gallego, *España de Fernando VII*, 635–36; Esdaile, *Spanish Army*, 197–98; Fernández de Pinedo, *Centralismo*, 289; *DBTL*, 233; Blaquiere, *Historical Review*, 284.

184. Alberto Gil Novales, *El Trienio liberal* (Madrid, 1980), 2; Blaquiere, *Historical Review*, 282–85.

185. Méndez García, *Historia documental*, 42–47; Manuel Moreno Alonso, *Blanco White: la obsesión de España* (Seville, 1998), 362.

186. The fullest life of Riego is still Eugenia Astur [Enriqueta G. Infanzón], *Riego: estudio histórico-político de la Revolución del año veinte* (1933), intro. A. Gil Novales (Oviedo, 1984), 11–33. There is no modern scholarly biography, though the many works by Alberto Gil Novales provide the best information (see Bibliography). Popular treatments include the semi-fictional Carmen de Burgos (Colombine), *Gloriosa vida y desdichada muerte de Don Rafael del Riego: un crimen de los Borbones* (Madrid, 1931); S. Cánovas Cervantes, *El pronunciamiento de Riego: otra vez la constitución de 1812* (Madrid, 1930); Raúl Pérez López-Portillo, *La España de Riego* (Madrid, 2005), a broad survey of the period; and Francisco Domingo Román Ojeda, *Riego: "Héroe de Las Cabezas"* (Las Cabezas de San Juan, 1985), an homage that contains valuable selections from original documents. A special case is the Russian work by G. I. Revzin, *Riego* (Moscow, 1939; Spanish translation as *Riego: héroe de España*, tr. V. Lepacó de Puiggrós [Montevideo, 1946]). Inspired by the Spanish Civil War, this book, though based on some important sources, has no notes, is padded with Spanish history, offers a vulgarized Stalinist bias, and contains many fictionalized or imagined conversations. I have used it with care. A second Russian edition came out in Moscow in 1958.

187. Pablo Casado Barbano, "El pensamiento político-militar de Riego," in Alberto Gil Novales, ed., *Ejército, pueblo y Constitución: homenaje al General Rafael del Riego* (Madrid, 1987), 186–87; Aymes, *Españoles en Francia*, 33, 79, 166 n.; Gil Novales in Riego, *Rafael del Riego*, 12.

188. Román Ojeda, *Riego*, 48 (qu.), 53–67, 73–75.

189. Blaquiere, *Historical Review*, 289–94 (qu. 94).

190. *Diplomatisches Archiv*, III:73–74.

191. Blaquiere, *Historical Review*, 291–93; Revzin, *Riego*, 313–14.

192. Tarle, "Voennaia revoliutsiia," 15; Moreno Alonso, *Blanco White*, 363; Blaquiere, *Historical Review*, 296–305.

193. Evaristo San Miguel, *Memoria sucinta sobre lo acaecido en la columna movil de las tropas nacionales al mando del comandante general de la primera division, D. Rafael del Riego* (Oviedo, 1820).

194. Riego, *Revolución de 1820*, 40–68 and passim.

195. Moreno Alonso, *Blanco White*, 363.

196. Riego, *Revolución de 1820*, 46 (qu.); Laumier, *Histoire*, 231.

197. Riego, *Revolución de 1820*, 66–67; Laumier, *Histoire*, 239–40; San Miguel, *Memoria sucinta*.

198. Román Ojeda, *Riego*, 106; Riego, *Revolución de 1820*, 68.

199. Riego, *Revolución de 1820*, 38 and n. 21; Gil Novales, *Trienio liberal*, 4–5.

200. Riego, *Revolución de 1820*, 64. See also Blaquiere, *Historical Review*, 312.

201. Román Ojeda, *Riego*, 83–96; Riego, *Revolución de 1820*, 39–71; *DBTL*, 30; San Miguel, *Memoria sucinta*.

202. The author, Fernando Miranda de Grado, was later condemned in absentia to the garrote in 1826: *DBTL*, 434.

203. D. K. Petrov, *Rossiia i Nikolai I v stikhotvoreniiakh Espronsedy i Rossetti* (St. Petersburg, 1909), 59–60 n. 2; Revzin, *Riego*, 324.

204. Román Ojeda, *Riego*, 90–96; Riego, *Revolución de 1820*, 67: Blaquiere, *Historical Review*, 311–12; Esdaile, *Spain in the Liberal Age*, 49; Gil Novales, *Trienio*, 4–5.

205. *Diplomatisches Archiv*, III:98–99; Orlik, *Dekabristy i evropeiskoe osvoboditel'noe dvizhenie*, 56 (Russian press coverage); M. V. Nechkina, "Dekabristy vo vsemirno-istoricheskom protsesse," *VI* 12 (December 1975), 10; Tarle, "Voennaia revoliutsiia," 15.

206. Fernández de Pinedo, *Centralismo*, 289–91; Esdaile, *Spain in the Liberal Age*, 49.

207. Esdaile, *Spanish Army*, 198; De Madariaga, "Spain and the Decembrists," 143 n. 3; Frédéric François Guillaume Vaudoncourt, *Letters on the Internal Political State of Spain during the Years 1821, 22, & 23*, 2d ed. (London, 1825), 134.

208. Artola Gallego, *España de Fernando VII*, 661 (qu.).

209. Diego Martínez Torrón, *Los liberales románticos españoles ante la descolonización americana, 1808–1833* (Madrid, 1992), 43.

210. The oath is in Hargreaves-Mawdsley, *Spain Under the Bourbons*. 249–50 (qu. 250).

211. François Furet and Mona Ozouf, eds., *Dictionnaire critique de la Révolution française* (Paris, 1988), facing 576.

212. Blaquiere, *Historical Review*, 322–29; Revzin, *Riego*, 358; Tarle, "Voennaia revoliutsiia," 16.

213. *Diplomatisches Archiv*, III:123–25 (qu. 124), 317.

214. Charles Wentz Fehrenbach, "Moderados and Exaltados: The Liberal Opposition to Ferdinand VII, 1814–1823," *HAHR* 50, no. 1 (1970): 60–61.

215. Blaquiere, *Historical Review*, 285–86, 220, and Gil Novales, *Las Sociedades patrióticas (1820–1823): las libertades de expresión y de reunión en el origen de los partidos políticos* (Madrid, 1975), I:21 and n. 23.

216. Miguel Artola Gallego, *Partidos y programas políticas, 1808–1936* (Madrid, 1974–75), I:207–8.

217. Carr, *Spain*, 124; and Carr, "Spanish History from 1700," in P. E. Russell, ed., *Spain: A Companion to Spanish Studies* (London, 1977), 159.

218. Fehrenbach, "Moderados and Exaltados," 60–61 and nn. 37, 41.

219. Alberto Gil Novales, "La contradicciones de la revolución burguesa española," in Gil Novales, ed., *Revolución burguesa*, 52. See the contemporary print of popular jubilation in Madrid in Artola Gallego, *España de Fernando VII*, 672.

220. Quin, *Visit to Spain*, 57; Revzin, *Riego*, 365–67.

221. Gil Novales, introduction to Astur, *Riego*, viii.

222. Paul Johnson, *The Birth of the Modern* (London, 1991), 659.

223. Cited in Antonio Moliner, "Opinión pública y anticlericalismo en la prensa exaltada del Trienio liberal," in *Sociabilidad y liberalismo*, ed. Fuentes, 73.

224. Gil Novales, *Trienio liberal*, 34; *British and Foreign State Papers, 1821–1822* (London, 1829), IX:811–12 (king's speech, 1822).

225. Hamnett, "Constitutional Theory," D1071.

226. Jaime Vicens Vives, *An Economic History of Spain* (1955; Princeton, 1969).

227. Pérez Garzón, "Ejército nacional y Milicia nacional," in Novales, ed., *Revolución burguesa*, 185.

228. John Bergamini, *The Spanish Bourbons* (New York, 1974), 174.

229. William Callahan, *Church, Politics, and Society in Spain, 1750–1874* (Cambridge, Mass, 1984), 132; Jeremy Bentham, *Letters to Count Toreno on the Proposed Penal Code . . . of the Spanish Cortes* (London, 1822), 2, 102–9.

230. Blaquiere, *Historical Review*, 435.

231. Gérard Dufour, ed., *Sermones revolucionarios del Trienio liberal, 1820–1823* (Alicante, 1991), 41–47 (qu. 41, 43); Chadwick, *Popes and European Revolution*, 543.

232. Moliner, "Opinión pública y anticlericalismo," 85.
233. Callahan, *Church, Politics, and Society in Spain*, 132–34.
234. Enrique Martínez Ruíz, ed., *El peso de la Iglesia: cuatro siglos de órdenes religiosas en España* (Madrid, 2004), 604–9; Callahan, "Origins," 215–216; Gil Novales, *Trienio liberal*, 16.
235. Cited in Alberto Gil Novales, "Iglesia nacional y constitución, 1820–1823," in *Libéralisme chrétien*, 109–25 (qu. 117).
236. Callahan, "Origins," 212–216; Callahan, *Church, Politics, and Society in Spain*, 122.
237. Giuseppe Pecchio, *Relazione degli avvenimenti della Grecia nella primavera del 1825* (Lugano, 1826), 52.
238. Callahan, *Church, Politics, and Society in Spain*, 131–35 (qu. 131).
239. Chadwick, *Popes and European Revolution*, 531; Kamen, *Imagining Spain*, 127–29.
240. Cited in Blaquiere, *Historical Review*, 415–20.
241. Callahan, *Church, Politics, and Society in Spain*, 133–34.
242. Alpuente: Pecchio, *Journal of Military and Political Events in Spain during the Last Twelve Months*, tr. Edward Blaquiere (London, 1824), 20–21; Quiroga: as told to Steele, *Notes on the War in Spain*, 344–45.
243. Bergamini, *Spanish Bourbons*, 174. There is some disagreement over how much hostility arose from the abolition of the Inquisition: Callahan, "Origins," 212–16; Chadwick, *Popes and European Revolution*, 533.
244. Riego, *Revolución de 1820*, 37 n. 20.
245. Gil Novales, "La fama de Riego," in *Ejército, pueblo y Constitución*, 369; Gil Novales, "La independencia de América en la conciencia española, 1820–1823," *Revista de Indias*, January-December 1979, 254–55.
246. Alfredo Ávila, *En nombre de la Nación: la formación del gobierno representativo en México, 1898–1824* (Mexico City, 1999), 103, 190–91.
247. Costeloe, *Response to Revolution*, 85–100.
248. Gil Novales, "Independencia de America," 235–65.
249. Gil Novales, *Trienio liberal*, 16–17.
250. Fehrenbach, "Moderados and Exaltados," 53–55; Esdaile, *Spain in the Liberal Age*, 52–53. See Blaquiere's confusing attempt at categories in *Historical Review*, 592–614.
251. Carr, *Spain*, 130–31; Quin, *Visit to Spain*, 196–97.
252. Sarrailh, *Homme d'état espagnol*, 101–2, 105–15, passim.
253. J. Lucas-Dubreton, *Madrid* (Paris, 1962),181.
254. Morán Ortí, "Políticas liberales," in Guerra, *Revoluciones hispánicas*, 84.
255. Alejandro Mosquera, *Rafael del Riego*, intro. R. Villanueva Echevarría (La Coruña, 2003), 28.
256. Gil Novales, "Contradicciones de la revolución burguesa española" in Gil Novales, *Revolución burguesa en España*, 52.
257. Stanley Payne, *A History of Spain and Portugal* (Madison, 1973), II:432.
258. Sarrailh, *Homme d'état espagnol*, 103; Giuseppe Pecchio, *Semi-Serious Observations of an Italian Exile During His Residence in England* (London, 1833), 129; Artola Gallego, *Partidos y programas políticas*, I:209; *DBTL*, 18–19, 579–80.
259. Gil Novales, *Trienio liberal*, 25.
260. The fullest study remains Gil Novales' magisterial *Sociedades patrióticas*: see I:5–15, and both volumes, passim. See also Georg Schuster, *Die geheimen Gesellschaften, Verbindungen, und Orden* (Leipzig, 1906), II:378–79.
261. Pecchio, *Journal*, 72.
262. Christiansen, *Origins of Military Power*, 26; Gil Novales, *Trienio liberal*, 25–26; Orlik, *Dekabristy i evropeiskoe osvoboditelnoe dvizhenie*, 57.
263. Fernández de Pinedo, *Centralismo*, 297.
264. Vaudoncourt, *Letters*, 386–92, reproduces the Comunero charter and oath, complete with misspelling (qu. 391); Esdaile, *Spain in the Liberal Age*, 54; Quin, *Visit to Spain*, appendix, i–ix; Schuster, *Geheimen Gesellschaften*, II:382–83.
265. Schuster, *Die geheimen Gesellschaften*, II, 384; Quin, *Visit to Spain*, 66–81; Gil Novales, *Sociedades patrióticas*. I, 681–733. For picturesque atmospherics, see Pérez Galdós' novel *Fontana de Oro*.
266. Dérozier, *Quintana*, I:638.

267. Artola, *Partidos y programas políticas*, I:209n.16.
268. Gil Novales, *Sociedades patrióticas*, I:19 and passim.
269. Ibid., I:14–15; Gil Novales, *Trienio liberal*, 11.
270. *VE* 2 (January 1821): 152.
271. Schuster, *Die geheimen Gesellschaften*, II:80, 384.
272. Dufour, *Sermones revolucionarios*, 7.
273. Léon-François Hoffman, *La peste à Barcelone* (Paris, 1964), 39 n. 1.
274. Fr. Josef Vidal, *Idea ortodoxa de la divina institución del estado religioso contras los errores de los liberales y pistoyanos monomacos* (Valencia, 1823). For a similar assault, see *Aviso al verdadero y legítimo pueblo español sobre la conducta de los españoles falsos bastardos ó sea aviso a los blancos sobre el proceder de las negras* (Madrid, 1823), by "a Spaniard." Spain's greatest historical novelist Pérez Galdós has a plausible character in one of his novels look upon liberalism as "as a form of horrendous heresy more worthy of the hellfire than those of Luther and Calvin." Benito Pérez Galdós, *La segunda casaca* (1876; Madrid, 2003), 11.
275. Álvarez Chillida, *Antisemitismo en España*, 114.
276. Carr, *Spain*, 132–33 and n. 1; Manuel Morán Orti, "La 'Miscelánea' de Javier de Burgos: la prensa en el debate ideológico del Trienio Liberal," *Hispania sacra* 41 (January-June 1989): 237–44; Moliner, "Opinión pública y anticlericalismo," based on a sampling of seven important periodicals.
277. Pecchio, *Journal*, 30–33; Ermano Caldera, "Presenza italiana nel romanticismo spagnolo," in Poli, ed., *Italie dans l'Europe romantique*, I:328; Maria de las Nieves Muñiz Muñiz, "Romanticismo italiano e romanticismo spagnolo," in Poli, ed., *Italie dans l'Europe romantique*, II:641–58; Francesc-Andreu Martínez Gallego, "El rescate del Héroe: el pantéon sincopado del liberalismo español (1808–1836)" in Manuel Chust and Víctor Mínguez, eds., *La construcción del héroe en España y México, 1789–1847* (Valencia, 2003), 270.
278. Martínez Gallego, "Rescate del Héroe," 270.
279. J. E. Varey, *Títeres, marionetas, y otras diversiones populares de 1758 a 1859* (Madrid, 1959), 27 and passim.
280. John Dowling, *Leandro Fernández de Moratín* (New York, 1971), 115–23.
281. *VE* 2 (January 1821): 157–58.
282. Quin, *Visit to Spain*, 104–5.
283. Dufour, *Sermones revolucionarios*, 37.
284. Callahan, "Origins," 211.
285. Dufour, *Sermones revolucionarios*, 7–18 (qu. 7).
286. Ibid., 35–40 and passim.
287. Ibid., 66–67, 101–11 (qu. 101), and passim.
288. Cited in Román Ojeda, *Riego*, 113 and n. 22.
289. *Exhortación que en la Santa Iglesia Patriarcal de Sevilla hizo a los cuerpos de infantería y caballería de la milicia voluntaria local al tiempo de presentar el juramento solemne de defender la constitución* (Seville, 1820).
290. *Pastoral del obispo de Segovia* (Segovia, 1822).
291. Mateo, Archbishop of Badajoz, *Carta pastoral que dirige el ilustrísimo señor D. Mateo Delgado y Moreno, arcobispo de Badajoz* (Badajoz, 1822).
292. Capitán Díaz, *Catecismos políticos en España*, 93, 94, 108.
293. *Cartilla de explicación de la Constitución política de la monarquía española*, cited in Román Ojeda, *Riego*, 114 and n. 25.
294. Capitán Díaz, *Catecismos políticos en España*, 97–98, 99 n. 116, 108 (qu. 98, 108). Capitán Díaz also mentions three others: *Political Catechism Dedicated to the Immortal Quiroga* (Pamplona, 1820); *Historical-Political, Religious-Constitutional Catechism* (Madrid, 1822); and *Christian-Constitutional Catechism* (Majorca, 1823).
295. I cite the Italian translation: *Catechismo costituzionale della monarchia spagnola* (Naples, 1820), 7. I have not seen the original Spanish and it is absent from Capitán Díaz, *Catecismos políticos en España* and Gallego, *Catecismos políticos*.
296. Quin, *Visit to Spain*, 37 n. and 327–28; Mercedes Gutiérrez Nogales, *Rafael del Riego: datos biográficos, romancero, y documentos* (Seville, 1988), 27.
297. Butrón Prida, "Fiesta y revolución," 165, 173–74.

298. Bergamini, *Spanish Bourbons*, 174.
299. Román Ojeda, *Riego*, 114.
300. Vaudoncourt, *Letters*, 7.
301. Orlik, *Dekabristy i evropeiskoe osvoboditel'noe dvizhenie*, 68–69.
302. Gil Novales, *Trienio liberal*, 48–49.
303. Moliner, "Opinión pública y anticlericalismo," 88–89.
304. Jeremy Bentham, *Collected Works* (Oxford, 1983–2000), X:52.
305. *A Decade of Revolution, 1789–1799* (1934; New York, 1963), 142–51. The best collection of such items is in the Musée de Carnavalet in Paris.
306. On display at the Museo Municipal de Madrid. Most are undated; the Riego cards are marked 1822.
307. Martínez Gallego, "Rescate del héroe," 263–71 (qu. 265).
308. Carmen Priego Fernández del Campo, "El abanico, útil de seducción, código de lenguaje, e imagen pictórica," *Abanicos: la colección del Museo Municipal de Madrid* (Madrid, 1995), 33–50. See also Anna Kolesnikova, *Bal v Rossii: XVIII–nachalo XX veka* (St. Petersburg, 2005), 170–75. In the 1790s, Spain prohibited the import of fans and other artifacts from France related to the revolution: N. Glendinning, "French Revolution in Spain," 118.
309. *Abanicos*, nos. 45 and 46. The obverse of the latter displays a bit of folksy humor: Cupid on a donkey is waving a banner with the words "Good news—long live the Constitution!"
310. *Abanicos*, nos. 50 and 51.
311. *Abanicos*, 151.
312. Both undated: Museo Municipal de Madrid.
313. Riego, *Revolución de 1820*, 154; Gil Novales, *Sociedades patrióticas*, I:360; Pecchio, *Journal*, 44–45.
314. Casado Barbano, "Pensamiento político-militar," 189.
315. Butrón Prida, "Fiesta y revolución," 176–77 and n. 48.
316. Núñez Muñoz, "Pronunciamiento de Riego," 108.
317. Gil Novales, *Sociedades patrióticas*, I:338.
318. Riego, *Revolución de 1820*, 182–83.
319. Vaudoncourt, *Letters*, 74–76; Gil Novales, *Sociedades patrióticas*, I, passim; M. P. Alekseev, *Ocherki istorii ispano-russikikh literaturnykh otnoshenii XVI-XIX vv.* (Leningrad, 1964), 123 n. 316, citing numerous Russian press reports.
320. Riego, *Revolución de 1820*, 178–79; Román Ojeda, *Riego*, 115. Quiroga eventually chose to align with the *moderados*: Gil Novales, *Trienio liberal*, 18–19.
321. Schuster, *Die geheimen Gesellschaften*, II, 80.
322. Casado Barbano, "Pensamiento político-militar," 188–91.
323. Fernández de Pinedo, *Centralismo*, 295.
324. Rafael del Riego et al., *Representación hecha al Rey y a las Cortes* (Cadiz, 1820), 14 (qu.); Riego, *Revolución de 1820*, 85–87; Fehrenbach, "Moderados and Exaltados," 63–64. Arco-Agüero died of a fall from his horse in September 1821. Vaudoncourt, *Letters*, 72.
325. Gil Novales, *Trienio liberal*, 19–20; Román Ojeda, *Riego*, 110–12.
326. Mosquera, *Riego*, 27–28.
327. Revzin, *Riego*, 381–83 (qu. 382).
328. Román Ojeda, *Riego*, 121–22; Méndez García, *Historia documental*, 82.
329. Gil Novales, *Trienio liberal*, 20.
330. Rafael del Riego, *Vindicación de los estravíos imputados al General D. Rafael del Riego el 7 de setiembre en las Cortes* (Oviedo, 1820), 4 and passim.
331. Vaudoncourt, *Letters*, 53–55 and 384 (Riego's August 12, 1821 letter of refusal to Vaudoncourt); Riego, *Revolución de 1820*, 119; Gil Novales, "Quién fue Riego?" in Román Ojeda, *Riego*, 232.
332. Riego, *Revolución de 1820*, 119, 124–27.
333. Ibid., 136–39, 142–45, 148–52; Gil Novales, *Trienio liberal*, 41–42.
334. Román Ojeda, *Riego*, 147–48; Fernández de Pinedo, *Centralismo*, 300; Gil Novales, *Trienio liberal*, 45 (qu.).
335. Esdaile, *Spain in the Liberal Age*, 57–58.

336. Gil Novales, *Sociedades patrióticas*, I:178.
337. Blaquiere, *Historical Review*, 576; Fernández de Pinedo, *Centralismo*, 301; Esdaile, *Spain in the Liberal Age*, 57–58.
338. Fernández de Pinedo, *Centralismo*, 299; Gil Novales, *Trienio liberal*, 27, 35–36; Carr, *Spain*, 142 n. 1.
339. Vaudoncourt, *Letters*, 32, 110–118, 243–44.
340. Payne, *History of Spain and Portugal*, II:432–33, 514–20; Gil Novales, *Trienio liberal*, 23; Herr, "Spanish Road," 380 n. 105.
341. Gil Novales, *Trienio liberal*, 23–25.
342. F. Rosen, *Bentham, Byron, and Greece: Constitutionalism, Nationalism, and Early Liberal Political Thought* (Oxford, 1992), 130; *VE* 2 (January 1821): 152.
343. Giorgio Spini, *Mito e realtà della Spagna nelle rivoluzioni italiane* (Rome, 1950), 52–57.
344. Guglielmo Pepe, *Guglielmo Pepe*, ed. Ruggero Moscati (Rome, 1938), I:222–27.
345. Spini, *Mito e realtà della Spagna*, 75–81 (qu. 80), 104; Dodolev, *Rossiia i Ispaniia*, 186. Not all radicals showed such sympathy. Months after the suppression of Neapolitan liberalism, *Eco de Padilla* in August 1821 ridiculed the Neapolitan kingdom as a land of miracles, Jesuits exiled from Spain, and superstitious believers in St. Gennaro's blood wonder: Moliner, "Opinión pública y anticlericalismo," 84.
346. Vaudoncourt, *Letters*, 8 (qu.), 9, 22 (qu.).
347. Spini, *Mito e realtà della Spagna*, 105.
348. Fernández de Pinedo, *Centralismo*, 302; Gil Novales, *Trienio liberal*, 48–49; Vaudoncourt, *Letters*, 126 (qu.).
349. Artola, *Partidos y programas políticos*, I:211 n. 19.
350. Riego, *Revolución de 1820*, 166.
351. *VE* 6 (March 1822): 146.
352. *VE* 5 (April 1822): 71. For judgment on his presidency, see Gil, *Trienio*, 48.
353. Vaudoncourt, *Letters*, 203.
354. Gil Novales, *Trienio liberal*, 51–52; Carr, *Spain*, 136. Events from *Gaceta de Madrid* in Hargreaves-Mawdsley, *Spain Under the Bourbons*, 254–56.
355. Revzin, *Riego*, 408–10.
356. Vaudoncourt, *Letters*, 201; Gil Novales, *Trienio liberal*, 50–53; Fernández de Pinedo, *Centralismo*, 304. The military phrase "They shall not pass" long predated Marshal Philippe Pétain and Dolores Ibárruri. Hargreaves-Mawdsley, *Spain Under the Bourbons*, 256; Bergamini, *Spanish Bourbons*, 177; *DBTL*, 233.
357. Gil Novales, "Quién fue Riego?" in Román Ojeda, *Riego*, 234.
358. Revzin, *Riego*, 410.
359. Riego, *Revolución de 1820*, 177 (July 6, 1822).
360. Román Ojeda, *Riego*, 168; Pecchio, *Journal*, 2.
361. Sarrailh, *Homme d'état espagnol*, 113–14, 121–23; Quin, *Visit to Spain*, 70–71.
362. General Ballesteros protested this idea since it served triumphalism rather than reconciliation. Pecchio, *Journal*, 42–43.
363. Carr, *Spain*, 137, 142, Ruíz, *El peso de la Iglesia*, 604–9.
364. Gil Novales, *Trienio liberal*, 11–14; Orlik, *Dekabristy i evropeiskoe osvoboditel'noe dvizhenie*, 58–59 (qu.).
365. Carr, *Spain*, 134.
366. Pecchio, *Journal*, 63.
367. Payne, *History of Spain and Portugal*, II, 433–34.
368. *British and Foreign State Papers*, IX:1006–1011 (the proclamation); Artola, *Partidos y programas políticos*, I:213–16.
369. *British and Foreign State Papers*, IX:963–66 (qu. 964).
370. Ibid., IX:815–16.
371. Vaudoncourt, *Letters*, 335.
372. Jean Sarrailh, *La Contre-révolution sous la Régence de Madrid* (Ligugé, 1930), 38, n 2.
373. A. Debidour, *Le Général Fabvier: sa vie militaire et politique* (Paris, 1904), 199–202 (some names from sources too numerous to cite).
374. Hoffman, *Peste à Barcelone*, 39 n. 1; Vaudoncourt, *Letters*, 120, 175.

375. José Luis Comellas García-Llera, *Los realistas en el Trienio constitucional, 1820–1823* (Pamplona, 1958), 52.
376. Dufour, *Sermones revolucionarios*, 40.
377. Gil Novales, *Trienio*, 131, citing General Sainte-Yon.
378. The French poet Alfred de Vigny in 1822 glorified the deeds of the Trappist Marañon for God and king. Portions of his epic poem were printed and sold for the benefit of the Trappist order in Spain: Alfred de Vigny, "Le Trappiste," in *Poésies complètes* (Paris, 1937), 97–104, 234–35. See contemporary caricatures of Marañon in Artola Gallego, *España de Fernando VII*, 784 (whip and crucifix), 793 (sword and crucifix). Hoffman, *Peste à Barcelone*, 39 n. 1; Ruíz, *El peso de la Iglesia*, 604–9.
379. Blaquiere, *Historical Review*, 611–12.
380. George Rudé, *The Crowd in the French Revolution* (Oxford, 1959).
381. Comellas, *Realistas*, 42–43 and n. 21; 46–56 and n. 43 (qu. 51).
382. Quin, *Visit to Spain*, 82.
383. Armand Carrel, *Oeuvres* (Paris, 1857–59), V:94–96.
384. Méndez García, *Historia documental*, 138. Gil Novales, *Trienio*, 130, citing a French general, gives a slightly different but no less sinister version of the Castelfullit inscription, written in blood.
385. Steele, *Notes on the War in Spain*, 326; Méndez García, *Historia documental*, 141–42.
386. Carr, *Spain*, 138.
387. Schop Soler, *Siglo de relaciones*, 280–81.
388. Artola Gallego, *España de Fernando VII*, 804.
389. Hoffman, *Peste à Barcelone*, 28.
390. Reproduction in Artola Gallego, *España de Fernando VII*, 637.
391. Carr, *Spain*, 137.
392. Pietro Colletta, *History of the Kingdom of Naples* (Edinburgh, 1858), II:462–63.
393. Sarrailh, *Homme d'état espagnol*, 111.
394. Spini, *Mito e realtà della Spagna*, 75.
395. *British and Foreign State Papers*, IX:895.
396. *VE* 17 (September 1822): 70; *VE* 21 (November-December 1822): 70.
397. Hargreaves-Mawdsley, *Spain Under the Bourbons*, 256–58 (qu. 256, 257).
398. Ibid., 258–59.
399. Quin, *Visit to Spain*, 144–47 (qu. 145, 147), 153–54.
400. Debidour, *Général Fabvier*, 199–202; Vaudoncourt, *Letters*, 275, 292; Quin, *Visit to Spain*, 151 and 152 (qu.), 215. See *Diplomatisches Archiv*, III:460–65 for the exchange.
401. I have misplaced the reference for the Carnival episode. Perhaps the reader will trust my memory?
402. Hoffman, *Peste à Barcelone*; C. Chastel, "La 'peste' de Barcelone: epidémie de fièvre jaune de 1821," *Bulletin de la Société de pathologie exotique*, 92 bis (1999): 405–7. Losses also reported in a Russian journal: *VE* 21 (November 1821), 71.
403. Hoffman, *Peste à Barcelone*, 35, 37 (quotes) and passim; Chastel, "La 'peste' de Barcelone."
404. Carrel, *Oeuvres*, V:90.
405. Hoffman, *La peste à Barcelone*, 22, 32, 34, 39 and passim.
406. Cited in *VE* 18 (September-October 1822): 226–31.
407. Carr, *Spain*, 139.
408. Isabelle Backouche, *La monarchie parlementaire, 1815–1848: de Louis XVIII à Louis-Philippe* (Paris, 2000), 102–4.
409. Quin, *Visit to Spain*, 165.
410. Chateaubriand, *Congrès de Vérone; Guerre d'Espagne* (Paris, 1838), 246–49 (qu. 246), 363–82 and passim; Maurice Paléologue, *Romantisme et diplomatie: Talleyrand, Metternich, Chateaubriand* (Paris, 1924), 115–17.
411. Backouche, *Monarchie parlementaire*, 102–4.
412. Revzin, *Riego*, 421.
413. Zamoyski, *Holy Madness*, 220.
414. Carrel, *Oeuvres*, V, 103, 109–11.
415. Hughes, *Goya*, 378; Zamoyski, *Holy Madness*, 220.

416. Beevor, *Spanish Civil War*, 335.
417. Carrel, *Oeuvres*, V:103–5.
418. *SO* 14 (1823): 91–93, tr. from the French press.
419. Pietro [Peter] Gamba, *A Narrative of Lord Byron's Last Journey to Greece* (Paris, 1825), 4.
420. Rosen, *Bentham, Byron, and Greece*, 134.
421. Schuster, *Die geheimen Gesellschaften*, II:381.
422. Debidour, *Général Fabvier*, 186–87 and passim; William St. Clair, *That Greece Might Still Be Free: The Philhellenes in the War of Independence* (London, 1972), 245–46.
423. Debidour, *Général Fabvier*, 186–213 (qu. 211).
424. Ibid., 213–52 (qu. 235–36).
425. Carrel, *Oeuvres*, V:87–131 (see esp. 124–29); Piero Pieri, *Storia militare del Risorgimento: guerre e insurrezioni* (Turin, 1962), 106–7.
426. Vaudoncourt, *Letters*, 21–23 (qu. 21), 40–42, 150, 242, passim.
427. Quin, *Visit to Spain*, 69.
428. Robert Harvey, *Liberators: South America's Savage Wars of Freedom, 1810–1830* (London, 2000), 130.
429. Carr, *Spain*, 139–40.
430. Quin, *Visit to Spain*, 307.
431. Gil Novales, *Trienio liberal*, 54; *DBTL*, 233.
432. Quin, *Visit to Spain*.
433. *VE* 18 (September-October 1822): 151.
434. Fernández de Pinedo, *Centralismo*, 305.
435. Fieffé, *Histoire des troupes étrangères*, II:388–90.
436. Lucas-Dubreton, *Madrid*, 184.
437. Carr, *Spain*, 141.
438. Quin, *Visit to Spain*, 333.
439. Lucas-Dubreton, *Madrid*, 183.
440. *Diplomatisches Archiv*, III:531–36.
441. Fieffé, *Histoire des troupes étrangères*, II:390.
442. Carrel, *Oeuvres*, V:119–21; Revzin, *Riego*, 424.
443. Artola Gallego, *España de Fernando VII*, 774.
444. Gil Novales, *Trienio liberal*, 57; Pecchio, *Journal*, 93.
445. Quin, *Visit to Spain*, 320–21.
446. Gil Novales, *Trienio liberal*, 57; Vaudoncourt, *Letters*, 349–54.
447. Quin, *Visit to Spain*, 327–28.
448. Gil Novales, *Trienio liberal*, 58.
449. Carr, *Spain*, 141; Pecchio, *Journal*, 118; Gil Novales, "¿Quién fue Riego?" in Román Ojeda, *Riego*, 171, 235; Carrel, *Oeuvres*, V:117–18.
450. Vaudoncourt, *Letters*, 336, 411–12.
451. *ODNB*, LIX:631–35; Steele, *Notes on the War in Spain*, 252–56; Vaudoncourt, *Letters*, 341–42.
452. Steele, *Notes on the War in Spain*, 1–104; *Diplomatisches Archiv*, III:531–36.
453. Fieffé, *Histoire des troupes étrangères*, II:391–93; Steele, *Notes on the War in Spain*, 88–89. Their figures diverge.
454. Jean-Louis Bory, *Eugène Sue: le roi du roman populaire* (Paris, 1962), 61–63.
455. *Diplomatisches Archiv*, III:531–36.
456. Riego, *Revolución de 1820*, 196–97.
457. Revzin, *Riego*, 427–29; Román Ojeda, *Riego*, 171–72; Méndez Garcia, *Historia documental*, 146–47. Some biographers, including the last one cited here, contest Riego's alleged crimes in Malaga.
458. Riego, *Revolución de 1820*, 199–200. Four native Spanish-speakers whom I consulted found this an exceptionally obscure passage.
459. George Matthewes, *The Last Military Operations of General Riego* (London, 1820), 1–36; Tarle, "Voennaia revoliutsiia," 17; Riego, *Revolución de 1820*, 201–2 (letter of thanks to John George Lambton, a British MP, September 3).
460. Matthewes, *Last Military Operations*, 36–41.

461. Núñez Muñoz, "Pronunciamiento de Riego," 109.
462. Matthewes, *The Last Military Operations*, 41–42 (qu.) and passim.
463. Lucas-Dubreton, *Madrid*, 185 (qu.).
464. Esteban, *Constitutiones españoles*, I:133–34 (qu. 133).
465. Edict in Hargreaves-Mawdsley, *Spain Under the Bourbons*, 259–60; Steele, *Notes on the War in Spain*, 178–79.
466. Lucas-Dubreton, *Madrid*, 185–86.
467. F. D. Klingender, *Goya in the Democratic Tradition* (1946; London, 1968), 203. See also Bergamini, *Spanish Bourbons*, 179 for the 112 figure.
468. Hughes, *Goya*, 378.
469. Revzin, *Riego*, 440.
470. Carr, *Spain*, 146–54.
471. Lucas-Dubreton, *Madrid*, 185; Álvarez Chillida, *Antisemitismo en España*, 114.
472. Gil Novales, "La fama de Riego," in Gil Novales, *Ejército, pueblo y Constitución*, 365. For other prison and capital sentences for gestures in favor of Riego, see Francisco Tuero Bertrand, *Riego: proceso a un liberal*, intro. Manuel Fernández Álvarez (Oviedo, 1995), 98.
473. Petrov, *Rossiia i Nikolai I*, 63 n. 1. The Inquisition was finally suppressed in 1834. For the zigzag policies of various regimes, 1808–1834, and legends surrounding the Inquisition, see Kamen, *Spanish Inquisition*, 304–20 and his *Imagining Spain*, 126–49.
474. Astolphe, Marquis de Custine, *L'Espagne sous Ferdinand VII* (Paris, 1838), II: passim, IV:222–26 (the widow) and passim.
475. Vaudoncourt, *Letters*, 344.
476. Carr, *Spain*, 143.
477. Sarrailh, *Contre-Révolution*, 86–87, 103, and passim.
478. *VE* 11 (June 1823): 311.
479. Vaudoncourt, *Letters*, 356.
480. Sarrailh, *Contre-Révolution*, 52–57, 66–72.
481. Astur, *Riego*, 500 n. 1; *DBTL*, 46.
482. Quin, *Visit to Spain*, 335.
483. Carr, *Spain*, 146 and n. 2; Lucas-Dubreton, *Madrid*, 184.
484. Hughes, *Goya*, 388; Sarrailh, *Contre-Révolution*, 80–85, 93–106, 140–43.
485. Harold Acton, *The Bourbons of Naples, 1734–1825* (London, 1956), 666–67, 689–94.
486. Steele, *Notes on the War in Spain*, 181–98, 214–17, 239. The British in Gibraltar were divided in their views of the defeated liberals, in marked contrast to the unrelieved hostility of the British navy and the Gibraltar authorities towards the Republic in the Spanish Civil War of 1936–39: Beevor, *Spanish Civil War*, passim.
487. *DBTL*, 233.
488. Riego, *Revolución de 1820*, 202.
489. Fehrenbach, "Moderados and Exaltados," 52–69.
490. Quin, *Visit to Spain*, 92–93, 95–96.
491. Blaquiere, *Historical Review*, 359–72.
492. Debidour, *Général Fabvier*, 201–2.
493. Sarrailh, *La Contre-Révolution*.
494. Ibid., 36 (qu.), 37, n.1.
495. *Circulares de la Junta Provisional del Gobierno de España y Indias* (Seville, 1823), 6.
496. Álvarez Chillida, *Antisemitismo en España*, 113.
497. Sarrailh, *La Contre-Révolution*, 36–39; 37 n.1.
498. Javier Herrero, *Los orígines del pensiamiento reaccionario español* (Madrid, 1988), 383–84, 386, 397 (qu.).
499. Quin, *Visit to Spain*, 204, 253 (qu.).
500. Sarrailh, *La Contre-Révolution*, 82.
501. Tarle cited in Dodolev, "Rossiia i ispanskaia revoliutsiia," 122 n. 66; Carr, *Spain*, 138.
502. Astur, *Riego*, 499.
503. Riego, *Revolución de 1820*, 203 n. 217.
504. Revzin, *Riego*, 442.
505. Astur, *Riego*, 527–30.

506. *Causa formada en octubre de 1823 a virtud de órden de la Regencia por el señor alcalde Don Alfonso de Cavía contra Don Rafael del Riego*, 2d ed. (Madrid, 1835), 100–102 (qu. 101 n. 1).
507. Román Ojeda, *Riego*, 165.
508. *Causa*. The original transcript of the trial has been lost or destroyed. This document was prepared from the papers of Riego's lawyer by the lawyer's son, Vicente de Santos. See also Tuero Bertrand, *Riego: proceso a un liberal*.
509. *Causa*, 49.
510. Lucas-Dubreton, *Madrid*, 185, one example of many erroneous reports. See Astur, *Riego*, 525 and n. 1, for the correction. An account of 1837 related that Riego's body was quartered while still quivering: Pedro Mata and R. Stirling, *Historia de General D. Rafael del Riego*, tr. from French (Barcelona, 1837), 110.
511. Riego, *Revolución de 1820*, 203–4.
512. Astur, *Riego*, 526 (qu.) and 527.
513. See Tuero Bertrand, *Riego*, 81, for a reasoned discussion.
514. De Burgos, *Gloriosa vida y desdichada muerte de Don Rafael del Riego*, 233; Revzin, *Riego*, 446–48.
515. Gil Novales, *Sociedades patrióticas*, I:349 and n. 69.
516. *Causa*, 101 and 103 and n. 1 (qu.). On facing death in Spain, see Bartolomé Benassar, "To Die Well," in *The Spanish Character* (Berkeley, 1979). For fuller discussion or the confession, see Astur, *Riego*, 541–50 and Riego, *Revolución de 1820*, 204–5 n. 220.
517. *Causa*, 94 (qu.), 104.
518. Tuero Bertrand, *Riego*, 81–84, specifies a white donkey. See also Hughes, *Goya*, 197–99.
519. Descriptions in Román Ojeda, *Riego*, 191; Astur, *Riego*, 537 (qu. eyewitness). Illustration: Carr, ed., *Spain: A History*, 146. Pérez Galdós in one of his novels described the condemned man as weeping: *El terror de 1824*, in *Obras completas*, 12th ed. (Madrid, 1970) I:1738–40.
520. *El terror de 1824*, in *Obras completas*, I:738–40.
521. *La ejecución de Riego* (Madrid, 1928), 56 and cover. The correct version: "Thus Arco-Agüero perished, dragged; so will Riego die of hanging—soon will follow López de Bañoz and then Quiroga." Astur, *Riego*, 500. It might be noted that another sensationalist account, José Montero Alonso, *Himno y marcha fúnebre de Riego* (Madrid, 1930), is largely a plagiarism of this book. Other accounts, including a contradictory one by de Santos—who spoke of both "ferocious jubilation" and the silence of the onlookers—report a mostly silent crowd along the route.
522. Both paintings hang in Madrid's Museo Municipal. See descriptions of Seville balconies in Quin, *Visit to Spain*, 319.
523. Pérez Galdós, *La segunda casaca*, 85.
524. Astur, *Riego*, 536–37.
525. Mata and Stirling, *Historia de General D. Rafael del Riego*, 109.
526. Astur, *Riego*, 537–38. The author's source was the decades-old memory of the daughter. During the Civil War of the 1930s, upper-class women in Nationalist Spain brought their children to executions for didactic purposes: Beevor, *Spanish Civil War*, 110.
527. Tuero Bertrand, *Riego*, 85. The garrote: Hughes, *Goya*, 97. An 1837 garroting in Madrid is described by George Borrow, *Bible in Spain*, 117–18.
528. Lucien Domergue, "Don Rafael del Riego ahorcado," in Gil Novales, *Ejército, pueblo y Constitución*, 115–24.
529. Astur, *Riego*, 531, 533 (qu.), 538–39; Mata and Stirling, *Historia de General D. Rafael del Riego*, 109. Gil Novales claimed that, except for the hangmen, all spectators remained silent and that contrary stories were false, including Pérez Galdós' treatment, which showed a "notable lack of historical understanding." Gil Novales, "¿Quién fue Riego?" in Román Ojeda, *Riego*, 235. Riego was "hanged before a silent and dumbfounded multitude." Gil Novales, *Trienio liberal*, 59.

Chapter 3

1. Guglielmo Pepe, *Guglielmo Pepe*, ed. Ruggero Moscati (Rome, 1938), I:59–61; *Diplomatisches Archiv für die Zeit-und Staatengeschichte* (Stuttgart, 1821–26), I:19–25 (texts in German and French).

2. The following sources and those noted below noted below show only minor discrepancies. *An Eye-Witness* [Richard Keppel Craven], *Sketch of the Late Revolution at Naples* (London, 1820), 32–33 (qu.); Giorgio Candeloro, *Storia dell'Italia moderna*, vol. II, *Dalla restaurazione alla rivoluzione nazionale*, 2d ed. (Milan, 1960), 78; Harold Acton, *The Bourbons of Naples, 1734–1825* (London, 1956), 676–77; Antonio Ghirelli, *Storia di Napoli*, new ed. (Turin, 1992), 195. French and other painters working in Italy often used brigands captured between Naples and Rome in 1819 as models for "peasant" revelers: Richard and Caroline Brettell, *Painters and Peasants in the Nineteenth Century* (Geneva, 1983), 17.

3. Craven, *Sketch*, 32–33 (qu.); Giuseppe Buttà, *I Borboni di Napoli* (Bologna, 1878), I:672.

4. Grégoire Orloff [Grigorii Vladimirovich Orlov], *Mémoires historiques, politiques et littéraires sur le Royaume de Naples*, ed. Amaury Duval (Paris, 1819–21), III:381–82 (qu.); Guglielmo Pepe, *Memorie del Generale Guglielmo Pepe intorno alla sua vita* (Paris, 1847), I:403.

5. Michael F. Robinson, *Naples and Neapolitan Opera* (Oxford, 1972), 9.

6. Marta Petrusewicz, "Before the Southern Question: 'Native' Ideas on Backwardness and Remedies in the Kingdom of the Two Sicilies, 1815–1849," in *Italy's "Southern Question": Orientalism in One Country*, ed. Jane Schneider (Oxford, 1998), 27–49. Spain and Naples, though no longer hitched to the same monarchical yoke, still shared a dynasty. The Borbone Ferdinando IV (originally) of Naples was the uncle of the Borbón Fernando VII of Spain. Ferdinando ruled as King of Naples (1759–1806), of Sicily (1759–1816), and of the Two Sicilies (1816–1825). For convenience I mostly refer to his realm as the Kingdom of Naples.

7. For the background, see Antonio de Francesco, "How Not to Finish a Revolution," in *Naples in the Eighteenth Century: The Birth and Death of a Nation State*, ed. Girolamo Imbruglia (Cambridge, 2000), 167–82.

8. Harry Hearder, *Italy in the Age of the Risorgimento, 1790–1870* (London, 1983), 127–28; John A. Davis, *Naples and Napoleon: Southern Italy and the European Revolutions, 1780–1860* (Oxford, 2006), 76.

9. Davis, *Naples and Napoleon*, 78–91; Robert Palmer, *The Age of the Democratic Revolution* (Princeton, 1959–64), II:382–91.

10. John Davis, "1799: The Santafede and the Crisis of the Ancien Régime in Southern Italy," in *Society and Politics in the Age of the Risorgimento*, ed. John Davis and Paul Ginsborg (Cambridge, 1991), 15–16. After the suppression of the regime, Neapolitan slum dwellers created an image showing Saint Gennaro being beaten by Saint Anthony, the patron saint of the anti-republican Holy Faith army: Tommaso Astarita, *Between Salt Water and Holy Water: A History of Southern Italy* (New York, 2005), 253–54.

11. Davis, "1799," 14.

12. Palmer, *Age of the Democratic Revolution*, II:386.

13. Raymond Grew, "The Paradoxes of Italy's Nineteenth-century Political Culture," in *Revolution and the Meanings of Freedom in the Nineteenth Century*, ed. Isser Woloch (Stanford, 1996), 405 n. 145.

14. Orloff, *Mémoires historiques*, II:193–97 (qu. 197). Volume III (1821) of Orlov's work appears to have been the first extended analytical history of the 1820 Neapolitan Revolution by a non-participant. It contains well-informed and detailed reports on contemporary events. The author (1777–1826), a wealthy Russian nobleman, served his country in various capacities, including senator. He lived in Naples in 1816–17 and spent much time there pursuing the arts. His sympathetic contacts with liberal elements and his views brought him scorn from European and Russian conservatives: *RBS*, X:347–49; M. I. Koval'skaia, *Dvizhenie karbonariev v Italii, 1808–1821 gg.* (Moscow, 1971), 195–96.

15. Hearder, *Italy*, 129. That Ruffo's name has given us the English word "ruffian" is a myth.

16. Davis, "1799," 7; Luisa Basile and Delia Morea, *I briganti napoletani* (Naples, 1996), 18–20. Eugène Scribe wrote the text of a comic opera set in Italy with brigand Fra Diavolo masquerading as a nobleman: "Fra Diavolo, ou l'hotellerie de Terracine" (1830), in Scribe, *Oeuvres complètes* (Paris, 1874–75), XXIX/4:1–83.

17. Benedetto Croce, *Storia del Regno di Napoli* (Bari, 1925), 223.

18. G. A. Sibireva, *Neapolitanskoe korolevstvo i Rossiia v poslednei chetverti XVIII v.* (Moscow, 1981), 99 n. 76; Palmer, *Age of the Democratic Revolution*, II:383.

19. Vincenzo Cuoco, *Saggio storico sulla rivoluzione napoletana del 1799*, 2d ed. (1806; Bari, 1929), 188.

20. Astarita, *Between Salt Water*, 103–5, 112–15.

21. Baron d'Haussez, *Voyage d'un exilé de Londres à Naples et en Sicilie* (Paris, 1835), II:165.

22. Nelson's role and that of his mistress Emma Hamilton in the vindictive cruelties applied to their Neapolitan foes are part of legend, fiction, and film. See Susan Sontag, *The Volcano Lover* (New York, 1992).

23. Astarita, *Between Salt Water*, 255.

24. Sibireva, *Neapolitanskoe korolevtsvo*, 120; N. Boretskii-Bergfel'd, "Imperator Pavel I i politicheskie sud'by Italii," *RS*, March 1912, 513.

25. Gino Doria, *Le strade di Napoli*, 2d ed. (1943; Milan, 1971), 500.

26. Orloff, *Mémoires historiques*, II:384 (qu.), 388.

27. Astarita, "Between Salt Water and Holy Water" (manuscript).

28. Doria, *Strade di Napoli*, 292–93.

29. Palmer, *Age of the Democratic Revolution*, II:386.

30. Doria, *Strade di Napoli*, 165–66.

31. Orloff, *Mémoires historiques*, II:195 (qu.), 214–16.

32. Cited in Astarita, *Between Salt Water*, 252.

33. In Davis, "1799," 3.

34. Palmer, *Age of the Democratic Revolution*, II:389–91.

35. De Francesco, "How Not to Finish a Revolution," 167. See also Sibireva, *Neapolitanskoe korolevtsvo*.

36. A. Manhès and R. McFarlan, *Il brigantaggio nell'Italia meridionale primo e dopo l'unità* (Bologna, 1991), 175.

37. Norman Douglas, *Old Calabria* (New York, 1928), 289.

38. Basile, *Briganti napoletani*, 21; Charles J. Esdaile, *The Wars of Napoleon* (London, 1995), 137 and passim—the Calabrian story is interwoven throughout the book; Manhès and R. McFarlan, *Il brigantaggio*, 197.

39. Franco Della Peruta, *Esercito e società nell'Italia napoleonica* (Milan, 1988), 345.

40. George Romani, *The Neapolitan Revolution of 1820–21* (Evanston, 1950), 10.

41. Astarita, *Between Salt Water*; Derek Beales and Eugenio Biagini, *The Risorgimento and the Unification of Italy* (London, 2002), 37.

42. Quoted in Gino Doria, *Storia di una capitale: Napoli dalle origini al 1860* (Naples, 1935), 266.

43. H. A. and J. Burford, *Description of the View of Naples and Surrounding Scenery* (London, 1821), 7; Cesare De Seta, *Napoli* (Naples, 1981), 225 and passim.

44. Burford, *Description*, 5.

45. Paolo Giovanni Maione, notes from the compact disc, *Salon napolitain: the Neapolitan Salon from the Revolution to the Restoration*.

46. Matilde Serao, *Il ventre di Napoli* (1884; Naples, 2002), 153. Other authors were not so kind about their own "lower depths." Cf. Eugène Sue, *Les mystères de Paris* (Paris, 1842–43); *Sinks of London Laid Open* (London, 1848); and V. V. Krestovskii, *Peterburgskie trushchoby* (St. Petersburg, 1864).

47. Margaret Blessington, *The Idler in Italy* (London, 1839–40), II:208.

48. Dieter Richter, *Napoli cosmopolita: viaggiatori e comunità straniere nell'Ottocento*, tr. M. L. Calfiero (Naples, 2002), 19–20; August Kotzebue, *Souvenirs d'un voyage en Livonie, à Rome et à Naples* (Paris, 1806), I:292–360; II:227–29.

49. Maione notes from *Salon napolitain*, 10–12.

50. Burford, *Description*, 5.

51. Antonio Ghirelli, *Storia di Napoli*, 189 (qu.); Herbert Weinstock, *Rossini: A Biography* (New York, 1968), 66; Acton, *Bourbons of Naples*, 656–59 and passim.

52. Acton, *Bourbons of Naples*, 644, 650 (qu.), 663, 665–66.

53. Gentz in John Santore, ed., *Modern Naples: A Documentary History, 1799–1999* (New York, 2001), 123; Blessington, *Idler in Italy*, II:234–35.

54. Massimo de Leonardis, "Gli stati dell' Italia preunitaria," in *La rivoluzione italiana: storia critica del Risorgimento*, ed. Massimo Viglione (Rome, 2001), 85.

55. Astarita, *Between Salt Water*, chap. 9.
56. David Laven, "The Age of Restoration" in John A. Davis, ed., *Italy in the Nineteenth Century, 1796–1900* (Oxford, 2000), 54–55.
57. Petrusewicz, "Before the Southern Question," 32.
58. Candeloro, *Storia dell'Italia moderna*, II:64. See also Acton, *Bourbons of Naples*, 672.
59. Silvio Vitale, "I controrivoluzionari," in *Rivoluzione italiana*, ed. Viglione, 200–1 and passim.
60. Owen Chadwick, *The Popes and European Revolution* (Oxford, 1981), 550–51; Acton, *Bourbons of Naples*, 647, 649.
61. Beniamino Costantini, *I moti d'Abruzzo da 1798 al 1860 e il clero* (Pescara, 1960), 40.
62. Romani, *Neapolitan Revolution*, 16–17.
63. Santore, ed., *Modern Naples*, 101–2.
64. Paolo Macry, "The Southern Metropolis: Redistributive Circuits in Nineteenth-Century Naples," in *The History of the New Italian South: The Mezzogiorno Revisited*, ed. Robert Lumley and Jonathan Morris (Exeter, 1997), 72–75.
65. Romano Bracalini, *L'Italia prima dell'unità, 1815–1860* (Milan, 2001), 262–63; Lacy Collison-Morley, *Naples Through the Centuries* (New York, 1925), 166–72.
66. Hearder, *Italy*, 134–35; Ghirelli, *Storia di Napoli*, 190; Candeloro, *Storia dell'Italia moderna*, II:65.
67. Pepe, *Memorie*, I:365; Giorgio Spini, *Mito e realtà della Spagna nelle rivoluzioni italiane* (Rome, 1950), 22–23.
68. Orloff, *Mémoires historiques*, II:274–95.
69. Cited in Bracalini, *Italia prima dell'unità*, 50.
70. Pepe, *Memorie*, I:390, citing Generals Carascosa and Colletta.
71. Ghirelli, *Storia di Napoli*, 191 (qu.); Bracalini, *Italia prima dell'unità*, 118–19; Astarita, *Between Salt Water*, 265.
72. Alfonso Scirocco, "La rivoluzione del 1820," in *Storia del Mezzogiorno* (Naples, 1991–), IV/ii:655; Hearder, *Italy*, 135.
73. Ghirelli, *Storia di Napoli*, 190; Acton, *Bourbons of Naples*, 643.
74. Beales, *Risorgimento*, 38; Scirocco, "Rivoluzione del 1820," 655; Davis, *Naples and Napoleon*, 298; Romani, *Neapolitan Revolution*, 8, 26.
75. Spini, *Mito e realtà della Spagna*, 17.
76. Nino Cortese, *Il Mezzogiorno ed il Risorgimento italiano* (Naples, 1965), 273–325; Scirocco, "Rivoluzione del 1820," 656.
77. Ol'ga Orlik, *Dekabristy i evropeiskoe osvoboditel'noe dvizhenie* (Moscow, 1975), 32; R. De Matei, "Società segrete," in *Rivoluzione italiana*, ed. Viglione, 131.
78. Eric Hobsbawm places the point of origin of the south Italian Carbonari sometime after 1806, with roots in the freemasonry of Eastern France and among anti-Bonapartist French officers serving in Italy: *The Age of Revolution, 1789–1848* (1962; London, 2003), 145.
79. Hearder, *Italy*, 178; R. John Rath, "The Carbonari: Their Origins, Initiation Rites, and Aims," AHR, lxix /2 (January 1964), 353–70.
80. Mario Themelly, introduction to Luigi Minichini, *Luglio 1820: cronaca di una rivoluzione*, ed. Themelly (Rome, 1979), xxi.
81. Costantini, *Moti d'Abruzzo*, 44.
82. Illust. in Orlik, *Dekabristy*, 64ff.
83. Acton, *Bourbons of Naples*, 671; A. Drago, *Donne e amori del Risorgimento* (Milan, 1960).
84. R. M. Johnston, *The Napoleonic Empire in Southern Italy and the Rise of the Secret Societies* (1904; New York, 1973), II:35–38; Rath, "Carbonari," 357–59.
85. Rath, "Carbonari," 364–65; Johnston, *Napoleonic Empire in Southern Italy*, 42. See also Théodore Saint-Edme, *Constitution et organisation des Carbonari, ou documens exacts*, 2d ed. (Paris, 1822), 52–80; *Memoirs of the Secret Societies of the South of Italy, Particularly the Carbonari*, tr. Anon. (London, 1821), 194–98.
86. Semevskii, "Dekabristy-masony," *Minuvshie gody* (May-June, 1906), 423.
87. Johnston, *Napoleonic Empire in Southern Italy*, II:39–43; Rath, "Carbonari."
88. Cited by Themelly in Minichini, *Luglio 1820*, xxi and xxii (qu.).
89. Giuseppe Gabrieli, *Massoneria e Carboneria nel Regno di Napoli* (Rome, 1981), 17–63: Costantini, *Moti d'Abruzzo*, 35–44.

90. Themelly, in Minichini, *Luglio 1820*, xx–xxvi and xxvii (qu.). See also Aurelio Lepre, *Storia del Mezzogiorno d'Italia* (Naples, 1986), II:232; Gabrieli, *Massoneria e Carboneria*, passim.

91. *Memoirs of the Secret Societies*, 56; Chadwick, *Popes and European Revolution*, 558–59.

92. Scirocco, "Rivoluzione del 1820," 655.

93. General Carascosa, cited in Michele Manfredini, *Luigi Minichini e la carboneria a Nola* (Florence, 1932), 31–32; Acton, *Bourbons of Naples*, 670; Piero Pieri, *Storia militare del Risorgimento: guerre e insurrezioni* (Turin, 1962), 57–58.

94. Craven, *Sketch*, 23–24.

95. Scirocco, "Rivoluzione del 1820," 655.

96. Pieri, *Storia militare del Risorgimento*, 59.

97. Semevskii, "Dekabristy-masony," 422–23; Hearder, *Italy*, 178.

98. De Matei, "Società segrete" in Viglione, *Rivoluzione italiana*, 130–31.

99. Costantini, *Moti d'Abruzzo*, 42.

100. *Memoirs of the Secret Societies*, 26–27; Johnston, *Napoleonic Empire in Southern Italy*, II: 41–44; Rath, "Carbonari."

101. Cited in Candeloro, *Storia dell'Italia moderna*, II:72 (qu.); Themelly, introduction to Minichini, *Luglio*, xvi–xvii.

102. Cited by Duval in Orloff, *Mémoires historiques*, II:421, 422 (qu.).

103. Constantini, *Moti d'Abruzzo*, 38.

104. Orlik, *Dekabristy i evropeiskoe osvoboditel'noe dvizhenie*, 60; Rath, "Carbonari," 366–67.

105. Themelly, in Minichini, *Luglio 1820*, xix–xx; *Memoirs of the Secret Societies*, 103.

106. Davis, *Naples and Napoleon*, 267. The text is in A. Aquarone et al., eds., *Le costituzioni italiane* (Milan, 1958), 382–97.

107. Romani, 94; Acton, *Bourbons of Naples*, 675.

108. Salvatore Candido, "La revolución de Cádiz de enero de 1820 y sus repercusiones en Italia, en los Reinos de Nápoles, y de Cerdeña (1820–1821)," in *La revolución liberal*, ed. Alberto Gil Novales (Madrid, 2001), 252; Vittorio Scotti Douglas, "La constitución de Cádiz y las revoluciones italianas en Turin y Nápoles de 1820 y 1821," in *Revolución liberal*, ed. Gil Novales, 258.

109. Pepe, *Memorie*, I:366.

110. Davis, *Naples and Napoleon*, 268.

111. Stendhal, *Rome, Naples, and Florence*, tr. R. Coe (London, 1960), 424.

112. Romani, *Neapolitan Revolution*, 17; Candeloro, *Storia dell'Italia moderna*, II:73.

113. Romani, *Neapolitan Revolution*, 21–23; Scirocco, "Rivoluzione del 1820," 655.

114. Pieri, *Storia militare del Risorgimento*, 59.

115. Alfonso Scirocco, *L'Italia del Risorgimento, 1800–1860* (Bologna, 1990), 83 (he mistakes the date of the Spanish revolt); Romani, *Neapolitan Revolution*, 23.

116. Davis, *Naples and Napoleon*, 297–98.

117. Pieri, *Storia militare del Risorgimento*, 57.

118. Pietro Colletta, *History of the Kingdom of Naples, 1734–1825*, tr. S. Horner (Edinburgh, 1858), II:323.

119. Scirocco, *Italia del Risorgimento*, 83–84.

120. Guglielmo Pepe [Guillaume Pépé], *Relation des événemens politiques et militaires qui ont eu lieu à Naples en 1820 et 1821* (Paris, 1822), 12–13; Candeloro, *Storia dell'Italia moderna*, II:75.

121. Johnston, *Napoleonic Empire in Southern Italy*, II:78.

122. Spini, *Mito e realtà della Spagna*, 6–14 (qu. 13).

123. Pepe, *Memorie*, II:263, I:365–66 (qu.). A few minor contacts existed between Spanish leftist masons and the Italian Carbonari. Spini, *Mito e realtà della Spagna*, 12–13; Koval'skaia, *Dvizhenie karbonariev*, 101 n. 2.

124. Cortese, *Mezzogiorno ed il Risorgimento*, 16.

125. Moscati, in Pepe, *Pepe*, I:lvii–lxi.

126. Guglielmo Pepe, *A Narrative of the Political and Military Events Which Took Place at Naples, in 1820 and 1821* (London, 1821), 73; Pepe, *Relation des événemens*, 84 (qu.); Pepe, *Memorie*, I:112–26. Quotations and translations vary among these accounts.

127. Moscati in Pepe, *Guglielmo Pepe*, I:lxiii–lxv, 8–12; Cortese, *Mezzogiorno ed il Risorgimento*, 254.

128. Quotations, respectively: Pieri, *Storia militare del Risorgimento*, 77; Doria, *Strade di Napoli*, 129; Romani, *Neapolitan Revolution*, 26, quoting Francesco Carrano, *Vita di Guglielmo Pepe* (Turin, 1857), 191.

129. Davis, *Naples and Napoleon*, 298–99 (qu. 299); Johnston, *Napoleonic Empire in Southern Italy*, I:303–4.

130. Romani, *Neapolitan Revolution*. 70.

131. Pepe, *Relation des événemens*; Pepe, *Memorie*, I:366–67.

132. Antonio Morelli, *Michele Morelli e la rivoluzione napoletana del 1820–1821*, 2d ed. (Rome, 1969), 75–76. See also Manfredini, *Minichini* 38, n. 1.

133. Pepe, *Relation des événemens*, 14; Moscati in Pepe, *Guglielmo Pepe*, I:lxix–lxxi.

134. Pieri, *Storia militare del Risorgimento*, 59; Johnston, *Napoleonic Empire in Southern Italy*, II:76; Moscati in Pepe, *Guglielmo Pepe*, I, lxxi.

135. Johnston, *Napoleonic Empire in Southern Italy*, II:71–72.

136. Romani, *Neapolitan Revolution*, 24–25.

137. Manfredini, *Minichini*, 32–39.

138. Romani, *Neapolitan Revolution*, 25.

139. Ghirelli, *Storia di Napoli*, 193; Pepe, *Narrative*, 19–20; Johnston, *Napoleonic Empire in Southern Italy*, II:72; Romani, *Neapolitan Revolution*, 30–31; Craven, *Sketch*, 25–26.

140. Pieri, *Storia militare del Risorgimento*, 61.

141. Santore, ed., *Modern Naples*, 107–8.

142. Manfredini, *Minichini*, 29–30, 84.

143. Morelli, *Morelli*, 130.

144. Doria, *Strade di Napoli*, 21.

145. Pieri, *Storia militare*, 63.

146. Paul Johnson, *The Birth of the Modern* (London, 1991), 639.

147. Constantini, *Moti d'Abruzzo*, 43, 72.

148. Romani, *Neapolitan Revolution*, 38–39.

149. Morelli, *Morelli*, 111–23, 299–301; Raffaele Scalamandrè, *Michele Morelli e la rivoluzione napoletana del 1820–1821*, 2d ed. (Rome, 1993), 23–50, 78; Doria, *Strade di Napoli*, 320; Manfredini, *Minichini* (illust. 48ff.). Silvati (1791–1822), a veteran of the war in Spain, has remained a secondary figure in the literature.

150. Morelli, *Morelli*, 132, 148–51; Scalamandrè, *Morelli*, 6, 83–87 (qu. 84). See Colletta, *History*, II:327 for alternative figures on the Morelli-Silvati squadron.

151. Morelli, *Morelli*, 132–33; Candeloro, *Storia dell'Italia moderna*, II:76 (qu.).

152. Romani, *Neapolitan Revolution*, 41 and n.16.

153. Morelli, *Morelli*, 132–33; Pieri, *Storia militare*, 63; Ghirelli, *Storia di Napoli*, 193–94.

154. Morelli, *Morelli*, 132–33; Johnston, *Napoleonic Empire in Southern Italy*, II:80; Candeloro, *Storia dell'Italia moderna*, II:76.

155. Pepe, *Memorie*, I:383; Romani, *Neapolitan Revolution*, 40–42; Morelli, *Morelli*, 76, 134–36.

156. Craven, *Sketch*, 2; Davis, *Naples and Napoleon*, 300; Candeloro, *Storia dell'Italia moderna*, II:76–77; Scalamandrè, *Morelli*, 109. Accounts differ on whether Morelli entered before permission was given and on the extent of De Concilj's wavering.

157. Candeloro, *Storia dell'Italia moderna*, II:77; Morelli, *Morelli*, 135–36; Scalamandrè, *Morelli*, 110–15.

158. Buttà, *Borboni di Napoli*, I:664.

159. Orloff, *Mémoires historiques*, III:377 (qu.), 380; Acton, *Bourbons of Naples*, 673–74.

160. Koval'skaia, *Dvizhenie karbonariev*, 103, 103 n. 9 (qu.), 104–5.

161. Craven, *Sketch*, 4–8.

162. Pepe cited in Santore, ed., *Modern Naples*, 108–10; Colletta, *History*, II:328–34.

163. Candeloro, *Storia dell'Italia moderna*, II:77; Davis, *Naples and Napoleon*, 300; Johnston, *Napoleonic Empire in Southern Italy*, II:82–83.

164. Vittorio Gleijeses, *La storia di Napoli dalle origini ai nostri giorni* (Naples, 1974), 728–29.

165. Pepe, *Memorie*, I:388–89; Craven, *Sketch*, 12–13; Candeloro, *Storia dell'Italia moderna*, II:77.

166. Pepe, *Memorie*, I:389–90.

167. Colletta, *History*, II:356.

168. Varying accounts in Colletta, *History*, II:328–36; Davis, *Naples and Napoleon*, 300; Ghirelli, *Storia di Napoli*, 194–95; Acton, *Bourbons of Naples*, 674; Hearder, *Italy*, 137; Romani, *Neapolitan Revolution*, 64.

169. Candeloro, *Storia dell'Italia moderna*, II:78 (qu.); Pepe, *Memorie*, I:393.

170. Morelli, *Morelli*, 154; Craven, *Sketch*, 16, 29.

171. Colletta claimed that the royal court opposed Pepe's decision to mount a triumphal parade; Pepe said that the king and vicar invited him to Naples in order to keep order: Colletta, *History*, II:344 n. 1, 345.

172. Craven, *Sketch*, 30–31.

173. Scalamandrè, *Morelli*, 139.

174. Laura Barletta, *Fra regola e licenze: chiesa e vita religiosa, feste e beneficenza a Napoli ed in Campania, secoli XVIII–XX* (Naples, 2003), 310.

175. Colletta, *History*, II:348; Koval'skaia, *Dvizhenie karbonariev*, 108.

176. Romani, *Neapolitan Revolution*, 80; Colletta, *History*, II:348–50.

177. Pepe, *Pepe*, I:64–65 (letter), 68 (proclamation).

178. Pepe, *Narrative*, 21–24, 30; Craven, *Sketch*, 37.

179. The oath is cited in Santore, ed., *Modern Naples*, 115–16.

180. Cited in Orlik, *Dekabristy i evropeiskoe osvoboditel'noe dvizhenie*, 61.

181. Pieri, *Storia militare*, 67.

182. Candeloro, *Storia dell'Italia moderna*, II:79.

183. Morelli, *Morelli*, 148–51.

184. Hostile writers have also singled him out as responsible for revolt: Gleijeses, *Storia di Napoli*, 729.

185. Romani, *Neapolitan Revolution*, 75–76; Koval'skaia, *Dvizhenie karbonariev*, 109.

186. Pepe, *Narrative*, 34.

187. Koval'skaia, *Dvizhenie karbonariev*, 107. The text: Aquarone, *Costituzioni italiane*, 465–505.

188. Davis, *Naples and Napoleon*, 306 and n. 32. Figures vary in Koval'skaia, *Dvizhenie karbonariev*, 121, and Romani, *Neapolitan Revolution*, 119 n. 44, 120 n. 46.

189. Romani, *Neapolitan Revolution*, 120–21.

190. *Atti del Parlamento delle Due Sicilie, 1820–1821*, ed. A. Alberti et al. (Bologna, 1926–31), I:157–66.

191. Sandro Castronuovo, *Via Toledo e dintorni: la strada dei napoletani dalle origini al Duemila* (Naples, 2006), 80–81.

192. Colletta, *History*, II:384–85.

193. Orloff, *Mémoires historiques*, III:403–4. The first Neapolitan parliament unfolded in various stages and components. First came the Ordinary Parliament, which sat from October 1, 1820, to January 31, 1821; after that was the Permanent Deputation, which sat February 1–12, 1821. An Extraordinary Parliament met from February 13 to February 28 in response to the menace of intervention by the Holy Alliance. The second Ordinary Parliament convened from March 1 to March 24, when it was scattered by the Austrians: *Atti del Parlamento*, I, xlvi.

194. Cited in Acton, *Bourbons of Naples*, 682–83.

195. Romani, *Neapolitan Revolution*, 131.

196. Ibid., 132.

197. Croce, *Storia del Regno di Napoli*, 237.

198. Colletta, *History*, II:372 (qu.), 384.

199. Johnston, *Napoleonic Empire in Southern Italy*, II:105–7.

200. Guido de Ruggiero, *Il pensiero politico meridionale nei secoli XVIII e XIX*, 2d ed. (Bari, 1946), 228–29.

201. Michele Romano, *Un grande del Risorgimento: Gabriele Pepe* (Modena, 1940); Doria, *Strade di Napoli*, 130 (qu).

202. Speech given in January 1821: *Atti del Parlamento*, III:15; Aurelio Lepre, *La rivoluzione napoletana del 1820–1821* (Rome, 1967), 135.

203. Romani, *Neapolitan Revolution*, 92, n. 72.

204. See Esther Taliento, *Appunti storico-bibliografici sulla stampa periodica napoletana durante le rivoluzioni del 1799 e 1820–21* (Bari, 1920) for a detailed treatment; Mario Sansone, "La

letteratura a Napoli dal 1800 al 1860," in *Storia di Napoli*, ed. Ernesto Pontieri et al. (Naples, 1975–81), X:26; Koval'skaia, *Dvizhenie karbonariev*, 112–13; *Atti del Parlamento*, I, xxxii–xxxvi.

205. Scirocco, "Rivoluzione del 1820," 658; Koval'skaia, *Dvizhenie karbonariev*, 113; Johnston, *Napoleonic Empire in Southern Italy*, II:97.

206. Colletta, *History*, II:355; Pepe, *Narrative*, 26.

207. Taliento, *Appunti storico-bibliografici sulla stampa*, 79.

208. Vittorio Scotti Douglas, "Constitución de Cádiz," 260–61.

209. *Costituzione politica della monarchia spagnola* (London, 1820); *Costituzioni politiche delle principali nazioni*, ed. Angelo Lanzellotti (Naples, 1820). See also a translation of the French liberal Dominique de Pradt's defense of the Spanish constitution: *Esame della costituzione spagnola* (Naples, 1820).

210. Fiorilli, *La miglior possibile costituzione politica per tutte le genti sul calcolo di razione* (Naples, 1821).

211. G. M. Olivier-Poli, *Cenno storico su la rigenerazione dell'Italia meridionale* (Naples, 1820), 7–8 (qu. 7).

212. *Osservazioni sopra alcuni articoli principali della costituzione spagnola* (Naples, 1820), 9–11.

213. *Catechismo costituzionale della monarchia spagnola* (Naples, 1820), 7.

214. Ibid. See also *Brevi riflessioni su' miglioramenti essenziali . . . allo sviluppo della nazione del Regno delle Due Sicilie* (Naples, 1820).

215. *Discorso di tre studenti sulle circonstanze attuali* (Naples, 1820), 6.

216. Colletta, *History*, II:343.

217. Apparently the Neapolitan right did not take up this means of reaching an audience with a quasi-religious medium until the next generation of Italian disturbances in 1848, in response to which a royalist author produced *A Political and Moral Catechism* (Catechismo politico-morale [Naples, 1850]).

218. Margaret Wicks, *The Italian Exiles in London, 1816–1848* (1937; Freeport, NY, 1968), 163–64. See also D. K. Petrov, *Rossiia i Nikolai I v stikhotvoreniiakh Espronsedy i Rossetti* (St. Petersburg, 1909).

219. Gabriele Rossetti, *A Versified Autobiography*, tr. Wm Rossetti (London, 1901), 10–48 (qu. 46).

220. Cited in Scalamandrè, *Morelli*, 85.

221. Rossetti, *Versified Autobiography*, 43.

222. Acton, *Bourbons of Naples*, 683.

223. Romani, *Neapolitan Revolution*, 93; *Memoirs of the Secret Societies*, 87.

224. Manfredini, *Minichini*, 88.

225. John A. Davis, "Opera and Absolutism in Restoration Italy, 1815–1860," *Journal of Interdisciplinary History* 36, no. 4 (Spring 2006): 569–71, 583.

226. Kotzebue, *Souvenirs d'un voyage*, II:303.

227. Louis Bignon, *Du congrès de Troppau, ou examen des prétensions des monarchies absolues à l'égard de la monarchie constitutionelle de Naples* (Paris, 1821), 3.

228. Weinstock, *Rossini*, 46–47.

229. Stendhal, *Life of Rossini*, tr. R. Coe (New York, 1970), 171 and passim; Stendhal, *Rome, Naples, and Florence*, tr. R. Coe (London, 1960), 354 (qu.).

230. Told to me by the curator of the San Carlo, November 2004; one such mirror is still in place. A French visitor to the San Carlo in the 1780s described the mirrors as amplifying the candlelight for brilliant illumination but did not mention the king. Jean Chenault Porter, ed., *Baroque Naples: A Documentary History, 1600–1800* (New York, 2000), 109. A British resident of the 1820s claimed that the king rarely occupied the royal box, but sat rather in a loge near the stage. Blessington, *Idler in Italy*, II:253. John Davis relates that patrons had mirrors on the back wall of their boxes for watching the stage: Davis, "Opera and Absolutism," 581.

231. Acton, *Bourbons of Naples*, 682–83.

232. Richard Stites, *Serfdom, Society, and the Arts in Imperial Russia* (New Haven, 2005), 141–43.

233. Bruno Cagli, "Al gran sole di Rossini," in *Il teatro di San Carlo, 1737–1987*, ed. Bruno Cagli et al. (Naples, 1987), II:158.

234. Craven, *Sketch*, 38–39.
235. Pepe, *Memorie*, I:429.
236. Davis, "Opera and Absolutism," 587; Stendhal, *Rome, Naples, and Florence.*
237. Cagli, "Al gran sole di Rossini," 158–59; Weinstock, *Rossini*, 103; Anthony Arblaster, *Viva la Libertà: Politics in Opera* (London, 1992), 66.
238. Weinstock, *Rossini*, 124–25, 178; Arblaster, *Viva la Libertà*, 66.
239. Davis, "Opera and Absolutism," 588; Davis, *Naples and Napoleon*, 313.
240. Koval'skaia, *Dvizhenie karbonariev*, 144.
241. Davis, "Opera and Absolutism," 587.
242. On the issue of public reception, urban folklore has it that a Neapolitan audience at the premiere of Rossini's *Otello* in 1816 tried to "save" Desdemona from Othello by shouting to her, "Watch out he has a knife!" Charles Rosen, *The Romantic Generation* (Cambridge, MA, 1995), 602.
243. Ghirelli, *Storia di Napoli*, 195.
244. Guido d'Agostino, *Per una storia di Napoli capitale* (Naples, 1988), 137.
245. Laven, "The Age of Restoration," 57; Davis, *Naples and Napoleon*, 308.
246. Scirocco, *Italia del Risorgimento*, 94–95.
247. Ibid., 95; Koval'skaia, *Dvizhenie karbonariev*, 122–23, 126–29.
248. Cited in Orlik, *Dekabristy i evropeiskoe osvoboditel'noe dvizhenie*, 62.
249. *Memoirs of the Secret Societies*, vi–vii.
250. Romani, *Neapolitan Revolution*, 90; Candeloro, *Storia dell'Italia moderna*, II:84.
251. Pieri, *Storia militare*, 68.
252. Johnston, *Napoleonic Empire in Southern Italy*, II:93; Romani, *Neapolitan Revolution*, 103, 104n.
253. Colletta, *History*, II:373; Romani, *Neapolitan Revolution*, 144; Davis, *Naples and Napoleon*, 305.
254. Candeloro, *Storia dell'Italia moderna*, II:84; Romani, *Neapolitan Revolution*, 131.
255. Koval'skaia, *Dvizhenie karbonariev*, 114–16, 118.
256. Davis, *Naples and Napoleon*, 305, 313.
257. Ricciardi in Santore, ed., *Modern Naples*, 119–22.
258. Pieri, *Storia militare*, 68.
259. Koval'skaia, *Dvizhenie karbonariev*, 117.
260. Astarita, *Between Salt Water*, 145–49; Paolo Macry, *I giochi dell'incertezza: Napoli nell' ottocento* (Naples, 2002), 27.
261. Porter, *Baroque Naples*, 169–72 (Kelly); Blessington, *Idler in Italy*, II:300.
262. Orloff, *Mémoires historiques*, III:426 (qu.).
263. Scirocco, "Rivoluzione del 1820," 667–68; Scirocco, *Italia del Risorgimento*, 95.
264. Romani, *Neapolitan Revolution*, 142, n. 3.
265. Davis, *Naples and Napoleon*, 313.
266. Ruggiero, *Pensiero politico meridionale*, 222; Pieri, *Storia militare*, 68.
267. Davis, *Naples and Napoleon*, 268–70; Beales, *Risorgimento*, 198–99. The document: Aquarone, *Costituzioni italiane*, 403–60. When someone suggested the Spanish constitution as a model, Francesco, the heir apparent, called that document "the precursor of democracy and revolution." John Rosselli, *Lord William Bentinck and the British Occupation of Sicily, 1811–1814* (Cambridge, 1956), 56.
268. Davis, *Naples and Napoleon*, 301; Orloff, *Mémoires historiques*, III:385–88.
269. Romani, *Neapolitan Revolution*, 136; Davis, *Naples and Napoleon*, 301–2; Colletta cited in Santore, ed., *Modern Naples*, 118.
270. Manfredini, *Minichini*, 213.
271. Colletta, *History*, II:395–96; Johnston, *Napoleonic Empire in Southern Italy*, II:128–29.
272. Pepe, *Narrative*, 39, 40.
273. Johnston, *Napoleonic Empire in Southern Italy*, II:99.
274. Cortese, *Mezzogiorno ed il Risorgimento*, 303–4.
275. Davis, *Naples and Napoleon*, 295–96.
276. D'Agostino, *Napoli capitale*, 144.
277. Craven, *Sketch*, 47–50 (qu. 49).

278. *Memoirs of Prince Metternich, 1815–1829,* ed. R. Metternich, tr. A. Napier (1881; New York, 1970), III:386.
279. The literature on Metternich is simply too huge to cite. But see Chapter 5 and the old but still useful W. Alison Phillips, *The Confederation of Europe,* 2d ed. (London, 1920).
280. Candeloro, *Storia dell'Italia moderna,* II:93.
281. Koval'skaia, *Dvizhenie karbonariev,* 136; Johnston, *Napoleonic Empire in Southern Italy,* II:110.
282. Giuseppe Berti, *Russia e stati italiani nel Risorgimento* (Turin, 1957), 453.
283. Candeloro, *Storia dell'Italia moderna,* II:79.
284. Romani, *Neapolitan Revolution,* 109–11 and n. 22.
285. Koval'skaia, *Dvizhenie karbonariev,* 233.
286. Phillips, *Confederation of Europe,* 208.
287. Orloff, *Mémoires historiques,* III:408–22; Santore, ed., *Modern Naples,* 122.
288. Romani, *Neapolitan Revolution,* 113 n. 25, 128.
289. Pepe, *Pepe,* I:247 (Lafayette to Pepe, 1822).
290. Koval'skaia, *Dvizhenie karbonariev,* 138.
291. Berti, *Russia e stati italiani,* 455–64 (qu. 456, 460).
292. Romani, *Neapolitan Revolution,* 60–61.
293. Koval'skaia, *Dvizhenie karbonariev,* 140 n. 130 (letter to Vienna, September 1820); 141 n. 132 (letter to the tsar of December 21, 1820); Candeloro, *Storia dell'Italia moderna,* II:80.
294. "Farò di tutto onde i miei popoli godano di una costituzione saggia e liberale." Candeloro, *Storia dell'Italia moderna,* II:95; Colletta, *History,* II:386.
295. Romani, *Neapolitan Revolution,* 148.
296. Candeloro, *Storia dell'Italia moderna,* II:96; Davis, *Naples and Napoleon,* 311; Colletta, *History,* II:388–90; Johnston, *Napoleonic Empire in Southern Italy,* II:116–19.
297. Spini, *Mito e realtà della Spagna,* 87.
298. Johnston, *Napoleonic Empire in Southern Italy,* II:127, 132; Colletta, *History,* II:400; Santore, ed., *Modern Naples,* 123.
299. Davis, *Naples and Napoleon,* 311; Orloff, *Mémoires historiques,* III:455 (qu.).
300. Romani, *Neapolitan Revolution,* 158 n. 75; Johnston, *Napoleonic Empire in Southern Italy,* II:125, 127–28; Candeloro, *Storia dell'Italia moderna,* II:97; Colletta, *History,* II:418.
301. Ghirelli, *Storia di Napoli,* 199; Colletta, *History,* II:400–11; Pepe, *Narrative,* 108–13.
302. Davis, *Naples and Napoleon,* 310.
303. Romani, *Neapolitan Revolution,* 146 (qu.); Ghirelli, *Storia di Napoli,* 199.
304. Johnston, *Napoleonic Empire in Southern Italy,* II:128.
305. Buttà, *Borboni de Napoli,* I:709.
306. Carlo de Nicola, *Diario napoletano, 1798–1825* (Naples, 1906), III:242.
307. M. I. Koval'skaia, "Italianskie karbonarii i peredovaia Rossiia," *VI,* xlii/8 (August 1967), 83.
308. Johnston, *Napoleonic Empire in Southern Italy,* II:129, 131.
309. Pieri, *Storia militare,* 78.
310. Koval'skaia, *Dvizhenie karbonariev,* 141–42.
311. Ibid., *Dvizhenie karbonariev,* 145–46; Pepe, *Narrative,* 41.
312. Spini, *Mito e realtà della Spagna,* 85, 127.
313. Ibid., 82–93, 138–39; Pepe, *Memorie,* II:102–3; Pepe, *Narrative,* 46, 104.
314. Pieri, *Storia militare,* 79; Candeloro, *Storia dell'Italia moderna,* II:97–98; Ghirelli, *Storia di Napoli,* 199.
315. Davis, *Naples and Napoleon,* 314; Colletta, *History,* II:406–10.
316. Pepe, *Relation des événemens,* 47.
317. Pepe, *Narrative,* 46; Pepe, *Memorie,* II:92. Pepe calls Persat "Cavalry Captain Persan." The name Marszewski is spelled variously in the sources.
318. For the tactical details, see Pieri, *Storia militare,* 79–86.
319. Pepe, *Memorie,* II:95. A slightly different version appears in his *Relation des événemens,* 124: "The enemy is advancing toward our frontiers. And what is their reason? Are we the first or the last to grant ourselves a constitution? Why do they not move against Spain or Portugal? Are we to be regarded as Helots by the Austrian minister, we who have taken the classical names of our forebears?"

320. Colletta, *History*, II:412–13; Candeloro, *Storia dell'Italia moderna*, II:98.
321. Pepe, *Narrative*, 50–56; Pepe, *Memorie*, II:264.
322. Koval'skaia, *Dvizhenie karbonariev*, 151; Colletta, *History*, II:411 n. 1, 419; Davis, *Naples and Napoleon*, 314.
323. Pieri, *Storia militare*, 86 (qu.); Ghirelli, *Storia di Napoli*, 200; Candeloro, *Storia dell'Italia moderna*, II:99; Orloff, *Mémoires historiques*, III:446. Orlov's tone toward the uprising was consistently positive. "The month of July 1820," he wrote, "will be celebrated in the annals of Naples." On the other hand, in a work originally dedicated to the tsar, he voiced no laments or condemnations of the intervention: *Mémoires historiques*, III:376.
324. *VE* 3 (February 1821), 227.
325. Augusto Placanica, "Calabria e calabresi come mito arcaico," in *La Calabria*, ed. Piero Bevilacqua and Augusto Placanica (Turin, 1985), 600–2.
326. Placanica, "Calabria e calabresi," 600–1. Carlo Bianco di Saint-Jorioz, *Ai militari italiani*, ed. Enrica Melossi (1833; Turin, 1975). Bianco (1795–1843), a rebel colleague of Santarosa in Piedmont, also fought in Spain and Greece. See also Tommaso Pedio, *Brigantaggio meridionale, 1806–1863* (Cavellino di Lecce, 1987); Della Peruta, *Esercito e società*, 350–51.
327. Hearder, *Italy*, 147.
328. "Della guerra di partigiani," cited in Franco Della Peruta, "La guerra di liberazione spagnola e la teoria della guerra per bande nel Risorgimento," in *L'Italia del Risorgimento* (Milan, 1997), 11–29.
329. *RA* (1865), 803–4.
330. Pepe, *Narrative*, 5–6, 44, 61–66; Pepe, *Relation des événemens*, 34, 70, 74–75.
331. Spini, *Mito e realtà della Spagna*, 92.
332. Candeloro, *Storia dell'Italia moderna*, II:97–98; Koval'skaia, *Dvizhenie karbonariev*, 150.
333. Santore, ed., *Modern Naples*, 124; Johnston, *Napoleonic Empire in Southern Italy*, II:133–34.
334. Colletta, *History*, II:438–39.
335. Koval'skaia, *Dvizhenie karbonariev*, 152–53; EI, XXX:113–14; LUI, XIX:379.
336. Constantini, *Moti d'Abruzzo*, 38.
337. Colletta, *Storia del Reame di Napoli* (Naples, 1992), 609; Colletta, *History*, II:419–20.
338. Pepe, *Relation des événemens*, 79–80.
339. Ibid., 21–22.
340. Colletta in Santore, ed., *Modern Naples*, 117.
341. Croce, *History of the Kingdom of Naples*, tr. of 6th ed. (1925; Chicago, 1965), 217.
342. Romani, *Neapolitan Revolution*, 172.
343. Ibid., 56 n. 60.
344. Croce, *Storia del Regno di Napoli*, 235.
345. Guido de Ruggiero, *The History of European Liberalism*, tr. R. G. Collingwood (Boston, 1959), 297.
346. Scirocco, *Italia del Risorgimento*, 86 (qu.); Davis, *Naples and Napoleon*, 312–13.
347. Saverio Cilibrizzi, *Il pensiero, l'azione, e il martirio della città di Napoli nel Risorgimento italiano e nelle due guerre mondiali* (Naples, 1961–68), I:338. See also Spini, *Mito e realtà della Spagna*.
348. Acton, *Bourbons of Naples*, 685.
349. Colletta, *History*, II:440.
350. Ghirelli, *Storia di Napoli*, 201; Davis, *Naples and Napoleon*, 314–15. Interpol was founded in Vienna 1923 as an international anti-crime cooperative board. Something like an international political police stalked occupied Europe during World War II in the form of the Gestapo.
351. Colletta, *Storia del Reame di Napoli* (Naples, 1992), 625–26; Colletta, *History*, II:441; Ghirelli, *Storia di Napoli*, 201.
352. *VE* 13 (July 1821), 71–72; Colletta, *History*, II:443.
353. John A. Davis, "Cultures of Interdiction: The Politics of Censorship in Italy from Napoleon to the Restoration," in *Napoleon's Legacy: Problems of Government in Restoration Europe*, ed. David Laven and Lucy Riall (Oxford, 2000), 246.
354. Cagli, "Al gran sole di Rossini," in Cagli, *Teatro di San Carlo*, II:138.

355. Théodore Saint-Edme, *Constitution et organisation de Carbonari, ou documens exacts*, 2d ed. (Paris, 1822), 33–36; Frederick Artz, *Reaction and Revolution, 1814–1832* (New York, 1934), 166.

356. Colletta, *Storia*, 625; Colletta, *History*, II:440.

357. Santore, ed., *Modern Naples*, 125. In the revolutions of 1848–49, the Austrian general Haynau and the Croat Jelačić commanded brutal counterrevolutionary suppressions.

358. Colletta, *History*, II:436–37; Santore, ed., *Modern Naples*, 128; Davis, *Naples and Napoleon*, 315.

359. Pepe, *Relation des événemens*, 77; Pepe, *Narrative*, 67–68; Acton, *Bourbons of Naples*, 687; Koval'skaia, *Dvizhenie karbonariev*, 231.

360. Morelli, *Morelli*, 167, 219, 234–41, 300–1.

361. Ibid.; Scalamandrè, *Morelli*, 193–202; and Atto Vanucci, *I martiri della libertà italiana dal 1794 al 1848* (1849; Florence, 1860), 150–53.

362. Scalamandrè, *Morelli*, 203–42 (qu. 242); Morelli, *Morelli*, 241–50.

363. Guido Panico, *Il carnefice e la piazza: crudeltà di stato e violenza popolare a Napoli in età moderna* (Naples, 1985).

364. Kotzebue, *Souvenirs d'un voyage*, III:71–81.

365. Macry, "The Southern Metropolis," 62; Giuseppe Galanti, *Nuova guida per Napoli e suoi contorni* (1829; Naples, 1845), 102–3.

366. Scalamandrè, *Morelli*, 243; Pepe, *Memorie*, II:167.

367. Scalamandrè, *Morelli*, 242–48 (qu. 243); de Nicola, *Diario napoletano*, III:286. One of Morelli's biographers maintained, against most written and iconographic evidence, that the two men were guillotined. His thesis is based on a single but crucial official document that mentions beheading (not by guillotine) and a reference to the guillotine later by Pepe: Scalamandrè, *Morelli*, 243 n. 30 and 244–45. Another biographer, Antonio Morelli, earlier challenged the beheading report as inexact, and argued that punishment for treason by law required hanging: Morelli, *Michele Morelli*, 258 n. 1.

368. Colletta, *History*, II:459.

369. Pepe, *Memorie*, II:167–68.

370. Tito Battaglini, *L'organizzazione militare del Regno delle Due Sicilie* (Modena, 1940), 61.

371. Candeloro, *Storia dell'Italia moderna*, II:131–32.

372. Colletta, *History*, II:440ff.

373. Gleijeses, *Storia di Napoli*, 732; Acton, *Bourbons of Naples*, 694.

374. Ghirelli, *Storia di Napoli*, 201.

375. Tarle, "Voennaia revoliutsiia."

376. Luisa Conti Camaiora, "Italy Real and Imagined in the Letters of John Keats," in *L'Italie dans l'Europe romantique*, ed. Annarosa Poli and Emmanuele Kanceff (Moncalieri, 1996), I:153; W. J. Bate, *John Keats* (Cambridge, 1963), 668–70.

377. Jacques Misan-Montefiore, "Une image de vérité et d'amour: l'Italie des doctrinaires," in *Italie dans l'Europe romantique*, ed. Poli and Kanceff, I:283, 302 n. 135.

378. Collison-Morley, *Naples Through the Centuries*, 156.

379. Leslie Marchand, *Byron: A Biography* (London, 1957), II:849.

380. Adolfo Colombo, *La vita di Santorre di Santarosa*, vol. I, *1783–1807* (Rome, 1938).

381. Santorre Santarosa, *On the Piedmontese Revolution* (London, 1821), 22–25 (qu. 22), 73.

382. Giuseppe Pecchio, *Semi-Serious Observations of an Italian Exile During His Residence in England* (London, 1833), 171–73 (qu. 172). The text of 1821 was a direct translation of the Spanish document, complete with Iberian and New World nomenclature: Aquarone, *Costituzioni italiane*, 512–52.

383. Beales, *Risorgimento*, 42–43; Hearder, *Italy*, 56.

384. Wicks, *Italian Exiles*, 91–92.

385. Colletta, *History*, II:441–42; Candeloro, *Storia dell'Italia moderna*, II:131; Vanucci, *Martiri della libertà*, 154–63.

386. Doria, *Storia di una capitale*, 267.

387. Giovanni Jannone, *I Poerio nel loro secondo esilio* (Rome, 1924); Sansone, "La letteratura a Napoli," 148, 189–98; Nino Cortese, *Il mezzogiorno*, 60 (qu.).

388. Romani, *Neapolitan Revolution*, 169. Gabriele Pepe, released in 1823, went to Florence and fought a duel there in 1826 with Alphonse de Lamartine, then secretary in the French legation, who had called Italy the "land of the dead." Lamartine, slightly wounded, apologized. *LUI*, xvi, 427; Romano, *Un grande del Risorgimento*.

389. Candeloro, *Storia dell'Italia moderna*, II:131. Rossaroll was also sentenced to capital punishment in absentia.

390. Pecchio, *Semi-Serious Observations*, 151–54, 168, and passim.

391. Wicks, *Italian Exiles*, 71 and passim; Johnston, *Napoleonic Empire in Southern Italy*, II:136 n. 1; Pepe, *Pepe*, I:294 and n. 1.

392. Petrov, *Rossiya i Nikolai I*, 159.

393. Rossetti, *Versified Autobiography*, 13, 47, 182–83; Johnston, *Napoleonic Empire in Southern Italy*, II:129; Wicks, *Italian Exiles*, 165.

394. Manfredini, *Minichini*, 206 and frontispiece.

395. Morelli, *Morelli*, 220.

396. Doria, *Strade di Napoli*, 21–22.

397. Manfredini, *Minichini*, 143.

398. Santorre di Santarosa, *Lettere dall'esilio (1821–1825)*, ed. A. Olmo (Rome, 1969) intro. 9–12 (qu. 9); 518–24 (French jail diary).

399. Wicks, *Italian Exiles*, 111.

400. Candeloro, *Storia dell'Italia moderna*, II:146.

401. Mikhail Dodolev, *Rossiia i Ispaniia, 1808–1823 gg.* (Moscow, 1984), 183 n. 55.

402. *Diplomatisches Archiv für die Zeit-und Staatengeschichte* (Stuttgart, 1821–26), III:406–7. The recipients included De Concilj though he was only a colonel: Spini, *Mito e realtà della Spagna*, 104.

403. Cited in Salvo Mastellone, "Santorre di Santarosa, combattente per la Grecia," *Indipendenza e unità nazionale in Italia ed in Grecia* (Florence, 1987), 36.

404. *VE* 11 (June 1821): 237; Léon-Francois Hoffman, *La peste à Barcelone* (Paris, 1964), 28.

405. Pepe, *Narrative*, 67–68, 123–24 (letter); Pepe, *Relation des événemens*, 76.

406. Pepe, *Memorie*, II:144–45; Pepe, *Pepe*, I:228. The signatories, mostly *exaltados*: Alvaro Flórez Estrada, Juan Romero Alpuente, José Moreno Guerra, Francisco Diaz de Morales, Lorenzo de Zavala, Manuel García, and Juan López Constante.

407. Pepe, *Pepe*, I:233–34 (qu. 234); Koval'skaia, *Dvizhenie karbonariev*, 233 n. 197.

408. Pepe, *Pepe*, I:229 n. 3; Pepe, *Memorie*, II:147.

409. Wicks, *Italian Exiles*, 67–70, 212.

410. Pepe, *Memorie*, II:169–70.

411. Wicks, *Italian Exiles*, 70–71 and 214 (police report).

412. Pepe, *Pepe*, I:248–49.

413. Pepe, *Memorie*, II:171–72.

414. Ibid., II:146, 183.

415. Vanucci, *Martiri della libertà*, 154–209; Battaglini, *Organizzazione militare*, 61; Colletta, *Storia del Reame di Napoli*, 625.

416. Pieri, *Storia militare*, 106–7.

417. Giuseppe Pecchio, *Journal of Military and Political Events in Spain During the Last Twelve Months*, tr. Edward Blaquiere (London, 1824), 13–15.

418. Pecchio, *Journal*, 18–19, 23–24, and passim.

419. Wicks, *Italian Exiles*, 78.

420. Santarosa, *Lettere dall'esilio*, 310 (qu. on Pepe), 314–315, 333, 382 (qu. on Riego).

421. Ibid., 15–16.

422. Mastellone, "Santorre di Santarosa," 36–37, 40 (qu. 37).

423. Santarosa, *Lettere dall'esilio*, 26, quoting (without an exact reference) Mastellone, "Un aristocratico in esilio: Santorre di Santarosa," *Rivista storica italiana* (1953).

424. Mastellone, "Santorre di Santarosa," 40.

425. Byron, *Childe Harold's Pilgrimage* (London, 1910), 159.

Chapter 4

1. Byron, "The Age of Bronze" (1823), in *Works* (London: Niccolls, n.d.), VII:283.

2. I. F. Iovva, *Bessarabiia i grecheskoe natsional'no-osvoboditel'noe dvizhenie* (Kishinev, 1974), 73. Maxime Raybaud exaggerated the number in the crossing: *Mémoires sur la Grèce* (Paris, 1824), I:190.

3. Thomas Gordon, *History of the Greek Revolution* (Edinburgh, 1832), I:95, 99. See also *VE* 7–8 (April 1821): 299–300.

4. Dated February 24 /March 8 in Richard Clogg, ed., *The Movement for Greek Independence, 1770–1821: A Collection of Documents* (London, 1976), 201–3 (qu. 201 and 202) citing L. I. Vranousis et al., *Athanasiou Xodilou* (Athens, 1964), 24–28. *Diplomatisches Archiv für die Zeit-und Staatengeschichte* (Stuttgart, 1821–26), II:524–25, offers a slightly different version in German and French of the second quotation: "Think of Spain, which, first and by itself, defeated the usurper and his Grande Armée."

5. *VE* 7–8 (April 1821): 299.

6. Clogg, ed., *Movement for Greek Independence*, 203; *Diplomatisches Archiv*, II:524–25.

7. "I. P. Liprandi," in Andrei Oţetea et al., eds., *Documente privind istoria Romaniei*, vol. 5, *Răscoala din 1821* (Bucharest, 1962), 184. On Ivan Liprandi, see the next chapter.

8. Anton von Prokesch-Osten, *Geschichte des Abfalls der Griechen* (Vienna, 1867), I:24.

9. For a brief survey, see Richard Clogg, "Aspects of the Movement for Greek Independence," in *The Struggle for Greek Independence*, ed. Richard Clogg (London, 1973), 1–40.

10. George Frangos, "The Philiki Etairia: A Premature National Coalition," in *Struggle for Greek Independence*, ed. Clogg, 90.

11. Nicholas Kaltchas, *Introduction to the Constitutional History of Modern Greece* (New York, 1940), 10, 14.

12. Clogg, "Aspects of the Movement."

13. Deno Geanakoplos, "The Diaspora Greeks: The Genesis of Modern Greek National Consciousness," in *Hellenism and the First Greek War of Liberation, 1821–1830* (Thessaloniki, 1976), 59–77.

14. Catherine Koumarianou, "The Contribution of the Intelligentsia Towards the Greek Independence Movement, 1798–1821," in *Struggle for Greek Independence*, ed. Clogg, 67–86.

15. Roderick Beaton, "Romanticism in Greece," in *Romanticism in a National Context*, ed. Roy Porter and Mikuláš Teich (Cambridge, 1988), 92–108; William St. Clair, *That Greece Might Still Be Free: The Philhellenes in the War of Independence* (London, 1972).

16. Frangos, "Philiki Etairia," 91–92 (qu. 92).

17. Kaltchas, *Constitutional History*, 19.

18. Rhigas Velestinlis, *Revolutionary Scripts: Revolutionary Proclamation, Human Rights, the Constitution, Thourios*, ed. D. Karaberopoulos, tr. V. Zervoulakos (Athens, 2002), 155–65 (qu. 158–59, 162–63—Greek and English facing pages). The translator mistranslates Arabia as Africa. See also Veselin Trajkov, "La coopération Bulgaro-grecque dans les luttes de libération nationale," in *Pneumatikes kai politistikes scheseis Hellenon kai Voulgaron apo ta mesa tou 15 eos ta mesa tou 19. aiona; Kulturni i literaturni otnošenija meždu Gărci i Bălgari ot sredata na XV do sredata na XIX vek* (Thessaloniki, 1980), 47.

19. Clogg, ed., *Movement for Greek Independence*, 149–50.

20. Ibid., 150–63; Kaltchas, *Constitutional History*, 21.

21. David Brewer, *The Flame of Freedom: The Greek War of Independence, 1821–1833* (London, 2001), 17–21.

22. All this advice came forth in an 1821 work on Aristotle's *Politics*: Stephen Chaconas, *Adamantios Korais: A Study in Greek Nationalism* (New York, 1942), 11–121. Kaltchas, *Constitutional History*, 11–18; Brewer, *Flame of Freedom*, 21–25.

23. C. M. Woodhouse, *Capodistria: The Founder of Greek Independence* (London, 1973), 27, 56, 152–53 (qu. 152), and passim.

24. Ibid., 13–46; Kaltchas, *Constitutional History*, 22–27.

25. St. Clair, *That Greece Might Still Be Free*, 20.

26. Brewer, *Flame of Freedom*, 13.

27. Patricia Herlihy, *Odessa: A History, 1794–1914* (Cambridge, MA, 1986), 92, 126.

28. Brewer, *Flame of Freedom*, 26–35 (qu. 27); V. I. Semevskii, *Politicheskie i obshchestvennye idei dekabristov* (St. Petersburg, 1909), 251; Douglas Dakin, *The Greek Struggle for Independence, 1821–1833* (London, 1973), 41–47; "The Memoirs of Emmanouil Xanthos," in *Movement for Greek Independence*, ed. Clogg, 182–200; Theophilus Prousis, *Russian Society and the Greek Revolution* (DeKalb, IL, 1994), 20.

29. Frangos, "Philiki Etairia," 87–103 (see table on 88); Brewer, *Flame of Freedom*, 34.

30. Cited in Olga Shparo, *Osvobozhedenie Gretsii i Rossiia, 1821–1829* (Moscow, 1965), 37.

31. George Waddington, *A Visit to Greece in 1823 and 1824* (London, 1825), xviii–xix; Semevskii, *Politicheskie i obshchestvennye idei*, 250; Brewer, *Flame of Freedom*, 27.

32. Dakin, *Greek Struggle*, 44.
33. George Waddington, *The Present Condition and Prospects of the Greek, or Oriental, Church* (London, 1829); Waddington, *Visit to Greece*, xxi (qu.); painting: War Museum, Athens.
34. Xanthos, "Memoirs," 185.
35. Ignatius Moschake, *The Catechism of the Orthodox Eastern Church* (London, 1894).
36. Waddington, *Present Condition*; Waddington, *Visit to Greece*, xxiii–xxx; Clogg, ed., *Movement for Greek Independence*, 175–82 (qu. 178); Shparo, *Osvobozhedenie Gretsii*, 37.
37. Clogg, ed., *Movement for Greek Independence*, 175–82.
38. Prousis, *Russian Society*, 13; M. Valsa, *Le théâtre grec moderne de 1453 à 1900* (Berlin, 1960), 192–96.
39. Valsa, *Théâtre grec*, 183–91. For theatrical activity throughout the diaspora, see Anna Tabaki, "La résonance des idées révolutionnaires dans le théâtre grec des lumières (1800–1821)," in *Révolution française et l'hellénisme moderne* (Athens, 1989), 478–85.
40. Valsa, *Théâtre grec*, 184–85 (qu. 185), 192 n. 3, 228–31.
41. Gordon, *History of the Greek Revolution*, I:136.
42. Shparo, *Osvobozhdenie Gretsii*, 37–40; Prousis, "The Greeks of Russia and the Greek Awakening, 1774–1821," *BS* XXVIII, no. 2 (1987): 274–75; Semevskii, *Politicheskie i obshchestvennye idei*, 251.
43. Charles Frazee, *The Orthodox Church and Independent Greece, 1821–1882* (Cambridge, 1969), 12.
44. Frangos, "Philiki Etairia," 95.
45. Prousis, *Russian Society*, 21.
46. Shparo, *Osvobozhedenie Gretsii*, 39.
47. Prousis, *Russian Society*, 5.
48. Dakin, *Greek Struggle*, 47–49. For the complex interaction between Capodistria and the Friendly Society, see Woodhouse, *Capodistria*, 218–37.
49. Grigorii Arsh, "On the Life in Russia of the Greek Patriotic Family of Ypsilanti," *BS* XXVI, no. 1 (1985): 73–90, a translation of his "Ipsilanti v Rossii," *BS* VI, no. 3 (March 1985), 88–101; James Farsolas, "Ypsilanti (Hypsilantis) Family," *Modern Encyclopedia of Russian and Soviet History*, XLV:35–44; Prousis, *Russian Society*, 8–9. Ypsilanti's brothers, Georgios (b. 1795), Nikolaos (b. 1794), and Demetrios (Dmitry, b. 1793), had all been serving officers in Russian Guards regiments. Demetrios served under General N. N. Raevskii, relative of several future Decembrists.
50. Arsh, "Life," 77 (qu.).
51. Dakin, *Greek Struggle*, 48–49; Woodhouse, *Capodistria*, 218–37.
52. Xantos, "Memoirs," 192–94.
53. Farsolas, "Ypsilanti (Hypsilantis) Family," 44–45; Herlihy, *Odessa*, 92; Arsh, "Life," 86.
54. Orlik, *Dekabristy i vneshniaia politika*, 100, and Grigorii Arsh, *Eteristskoe dvizhenie v Rossii* (Moscow, 1970), 273, with slightly different wording in the two translations.
55. Brewer, *Flame of Freedom*, 50; Orlik, *Dekabristy i vneshniaia politika*, 86.
56. Orlik, *Dekabristy i vneshniaia politika*, 86; Brewer, *Flame of Freedom*, 50; Konstantinos Hatzopoulos, "Was Alexander Ypsilantis Struck Off the List of Officers in the Russian Army?" *BS* XXVIII, no. 2 (1987): 281 n. 1. The hostile Russian Ivan Liprandi attributed Ypsilanti's choice of the Balkans to his cowardly need for a quick exit in case of defeat: E. D. Tappe, "The 1821 Revolution in the Rumanian Principalities," in *Struggle for Greek Independence*, ed. Clogg, 136.
57. Prousis, *Russian Society*, 23.
58. Arsh, *Eteristskoe dvizhenie*, 293 and n. 157.
59. Orlik, *Dekabristy i vneshniaia politika*, 86; Xantos, "Memoirs," 194–97; Arsh, "Life," 86–87.
60. Dakin, *Greek Struggle*, 54–55; Orlik, *Dekabristy i vneshniaia politika*, 85–86.
61. Dakin, *Greek Struggle*, 51–52.
62. Arsh, *Eteristskoe dvizhenie*, 295–96.
63. Grigorii Arsh and G. M. Pyatigorskii, "Nekotorye voprosy istorii Filiki Eterii v svete novykh sovetskikh arkhivov," in *Politicheskie, obshchestvennye, i kul'turnye sviazi narodov SSSR i Gretsii, XIX–XX vv.*, ed. Grigorii Arsh (Moscow, 1989), 24–42 (qu. 40).
64. Tappe, "The 1821 Revolution in the Rumanian Principalities," 135.
65. Arsh, *Eteristskoe dvizhenie*, 292–93 and n. 154. Gornovsky (also identified as an ethnic Pole, W. Garnowski) was a Vitebsk noble and local official. Xantos, "Memoirs," 200; Ivan

Iovva, *Iuzhnye dekabristy i grecheskoe natsional'no-osvoboditel'noe dvizhenie* (Kishinev, 1963), 12 n. 1.

66. Gordon, *History*, I:91; Charles Pertusier, *La Valachie, la Moldavie, et de l'influence politique des Grecs du Fanal* (Paris, 1822), 44.

67. Iovva, *Bessarabiia*, 93–94.

68. Liprandi in Oțetea, *Documente*, V:183.

69. Dated February 21/March 5. Prokesch-Osten, *Geschichte des Abfalls der Griechen*, III:54 (in German); a slightly different version, in French and German dated February 23, is in *Diplomatisches Archiv für die Zeit-und Staatengeschichte* (Stuttgart, 1821–26), II:516–19 (German and French texts); Gervinus, *Insurrection et régénération*, I:184. See Mladen Pantschoff on the Prokesch-Osten version: *Kaiser Alexander I und der Aufstand Ypsilantis 1821* (Leipzig, 1891), 57 n. 2.

70. *Diplomatisches Archiv*, II:528–31 (pp. 530 and 531 are misprinted in this text as 330 and 331).

71. Prokesch-Osten, *Geschichte des Abfalls der Griechen*, III:55.

72. Liprandi in Oțetea, *Documente*, V:184; Gordon, *History*, I:101.

73. *VE*, 7–8 (April 1821): 300.

74. *Diplomatisches Archiv*, II:526–29.

75. Liprandi in Oțetea, *Documente*, V:183 and n. 2.

76. Raybaud, *Mémoires sur la Grèce*, I:195–96. Various views in George Finlay, *History of the Greek Revolution* (Edinburgh, 1861), I:146–47; W. Alison Phillips, *The War of Greek Independence, 1821 to 1833* (London, 1897), 32–33; Gordon, *History of the Greek Revolution*, I:100.

77. Iovva, *Bessarabiia*, 94.

78. Phillips, *War of Greek Independence*, 33–34; Gordon, *History*, I:137 and n. 4; Liprandi in Oțetea, *Documente*, V:183–84.

79. Iovva, *Bessarabiia*, 94–95.

80. Hatzopoulos, "Was Alexander Ypsilantis Struck Off the List," 282.

81. Orlik, *Dekabristy i vneshniaia politika*, 88 (qu.); Dakin, *Greek Struggle*, 58.

82. Phillips, *War of Greek Independence*, 37. Soutsos also wrote to Laibach and had the boyars sign appeals to Tsar Alexander and various Russian officials: Tappe, "Revolution in the Rumanian Principalities," 141. One scholar floated the theory that the tsar actually authorized Ypsilanti's venture in order to stir up the Balkans and thus lead to a Russian invasion. He then disowned his general for the clumsiness of the revolt. This notion was convincingly refuted in Alexandre Despotopoulos, "La révolution grecque, Alexandre Ypsilantis et la politique de la Russie," *BS* VII, no. 2 (1966): 395–410. Ypsilanti was not cashiered, as is commonly thought, but resigned: Hatzopoulos, "Was Alexander Ypsilantis Struck Off the List."

83. Orlik, *Dekabristy i vneshniaia politika*, 86; Dakin, *Greek Struggle*, 57; Nikolai Todorov, "Quelques renseignements sur les insurgés grecs dans les Principautés danubiennes," in *Essays in Memory of Basil Laourdas* (Thessaloniki, 1975), 471.

84. V. Beševliev, "Die griechischen Einflüsse auf die bulgarische Wiedergeburt," in *Pneumatikes kai politistikes scheseis*, 31–38.

85. Trajkov, "La coopération Bulgaro-grecque," 48–49.

86. Maxime Raybaud, *Mémoires sur la Grèce* (Paris, 1824), I:192–93.

87. A. A. Skalkovskii, *Pervoe tridtsatiletie istorii goroda Odessy* (1837; Odessa, 1998), 249–51 (qu. 249). See also Theophilus Prousis, "The Greeks of Russia and the Greek Awakening, 1774–1821," *BS* XXVIII, no. 2 (1987), 259–89; Prousis, *Russian Society*, 55–83; Brewer, *Flame of Freedom*, 142–44; A. V. Fadeev, "Grecheskoe natsional'no-osvoboditel'noe dvizhenie i russkoe obshchestvo pervykh desiatiletii XIX veka," *Novaia i noveishaia istoriia* 3 (1964), 41–52.

88. The merchant, Iakov Bulgarin or Vulgaris. Semevskii, *Politicheskie i obshchestvennye idei*, 255; Prousis, *Russian Society*, 44.

89. Alexander Pushkin, *The Letters of Alexander Pushkin*, tr. J. Thomas Shaw (Madison, 1967), 80; Semevskii, *Politicheskie i obshchestvennye idei*, 253–54.

90. Xantos, "Memoirs," 199.

91. Liprandi in Oțetea, *Documente*, V:185.

92. Gordon, *History*, I:101; Raybaud, *Mémoires sur la Grèce*, I:193–94.

93. Liprandi in Oțetea, *Documente*, V:187; *VE* 15 (August 1821): 243.

94. Prousis, *Russian Society*, 13; Prousis, "Greeks of Russia," 271; Edward Blaquiere, *The Greek Revolution* (London, 1824), 73–74.

95. Georg Gervinus, *Insurrection et régénération de la Grèce*, tr. J.-F. Minssen and Leonidas Sgouta (Paris, 1863), I:190; Finlay, *History of the Greek Revolution*, I:153.

96. Liprandi in Oțetea, *Documente*, V:185; Gordon, *History*, I:101–2; Gervinus, *Insurrection et régénération*, I:187–88.

97. Frazee, *Orthodox Church*, 7 and passim.

98. Pertusier, *Valachie, la Moldavie*, 34–36.

99. The consul's account cited in *Movement for Greek Independence*, ed. Clogg, 47–52; Finlay, *History of the Greek Revolution*, I:139.

100. Phillips, *War of Greek Independence*, 31.

101. Tappe, "Revolution in the Rumanian Principalities," 141.

102. Liprandi in Oțetea, *Documente*, V:185–86; Raybaud, *Mémoires sur la Grèce*, I:228–29. Liprandi in 1821 was serving in the Russian Yakutiia Regiment of General Orlov's division. While in Kishinev, he socialized with Alexandros Ypsilanti (Ivan Liprandi, "Notele lui I. P. Liprandi," in Oțetea, *Documente*, V:460–61) and developed an intense animus toward him.

103. Gervinus, *Insurrection et régénération*, I:185; Raybaud, *Mémoires sur la Grèce*, I:227–28.

104. Phillips, *War of Greek Independence*, 36; Finlay, *History of the Greek Revolution*, I:152.

105. Gordon, *History*, I:104, 133–34.

106. François Recordon, *Lettres sur la Valachie* (Paris, 1821), 142–43.

107. Soutsos [Soutzo], *Mémoires du Prince Nicolas Soutzo, Grand-Logothète de Moldavie, 1798–1871*, ed. P. Rizos (Vienna, 1899), 38; Tappe, "Revolution in the Rumanian Principalities," 143.

108. Tappe, "Revolution in the Rumanian Principalities," 137–38, 145; Andrei Oțetea, *Tudor Vladimirescu* (Bucharest, 1971), 32–36; Prokesch-Osten, *Geschichte des Abfalls der Griechen*, I:25. A convincing case for Tudor's membership is made in Nestor Camariano, "Les relations de Tudor Vladimirescu avec l'Hétairie avant la Révolution de 1821," *BS* VI, no. 1 (1965): 139–64.

109. Finlay, *History of the Greek Revolution*, I:152.

110. Andrei Oțetea, *The History of the Romanian People* (New York, 1970), 316–23; Oțetea, *Tudor Vladimirescu*, 33.

111. Recordon, *Lettres sur la Valachie*, 138–39.

112. Tappe, "Revolution in the Rumanian Principalities," 139–40.

113. Raybaud, *Mémoires sur la Grèce*, I:230; Blaquiere, *The Greek Revolution*, 68–69.

114. Tappe, "Revolution in the Rumanian Principalities," 149–52; Liprandi in Oțetea, *Documente*, V:204; Gordon, *History*, I:113, 139–40.

115. Which would descend in fury in 1907.

116. Tappe, "Revolution in the Rumanian Principalities," 150–52; Brewer, *Flame of Freedom*, 58–59; Phillips, *War of Greek Independence*, 39–40.

117. Phillips, *War of Greek Independence*, 41; Finlay, *History of the Greek Revolution*, I:167–68.

118. Constantinos Vacalopoulos, "Probleme in Bezug auf das Leben und den Tod von Alexander Ypsilantis," *BS* XVI, no. 1 (1974): 61–79.

119. N. Corivan, "La captivité d'Alexandre Ypsilanti," *BS* 8, no. 1 (1969): 87–102; Polychronis Enepekides, *Die neugefundenen Akten des Wiener Kriegsarchivs zur siebenjahrigen Festungshaft Alexander Ypsilantis* (Sofia, 1969); Farsolas, "Ypsilanti Family," 46; Arsh, "Life," 89.

120. Vacalopoulos, "Probleme," 61–79.

121. Prousis, *Russian Society*, 122. See also Glynn Barratt, *Ivan Kozlov: A Study and a Setting* (Toronto, 1972), 128.

122. Finlay, *History of the Greek Revolution*, I:143–50.

123. Gervinus, *Insurrection et régénération*, I:194–95.

124. Raybaud, *Mémoires sur la Grèce*, I:190 n. 1; Tappe, "Revolution in the Rumanian Principalities," 136.

125. St. Clair, *That Greece Might Still Be Free*, 6; Dakin, *Greek Struggle*, 62.

126. Glynn Barratt, "Notice sur l'insurrection des Grecs contre l'empire Ottomane: A Russian View of the Greek War of Independence," *BS* 14, no. 1 (1973): 77.

127. Samuel G. Howe, *An Historical Sketch of the Greek Revolution* (New York, 1828), 50–51.
128. Phillips, *War of Greek Independence*, 30.
129. Finlay, *History of the Greek Revolution*, I:136–37, 166 (qu.).
130. Dennis Skiotis, "Mountain Warriors and the Greek Revolution," in V. J. Parry and M. E. Yapp, eds., *War, Technology and Society in the Middle East* (London, 1975), 309, 322–28.
131. Demetrios Vikelas [Bikelas], *Loukis Laras*, tr. J. Gennadios and D. Trollope (1879; London, 1972), 74. This is a novelized version of the recollections of a survivor, Loukis Tzifos, told to Vikelas long after the events.
132. Pantschoff, *Kaiser Alexander I*, 56, 62.
133. For early ties between Italy and Greece, see *Risorgimento greco e filellenismo italiano: lotte, cultura, arte* (Rome, 1986), 1–70 and passim (esp. 67).
134. Prokesch-Osten, *Geschichte des Abfalls der Griechen*, I:39.
135. Waddington, *Visit to Greece*, li (qu.). He also reported that "proofs" of Friendly Society-Carbonari ties were presented at Verona: xiii.
136. The word "primate" in this context came into the English language long before zoology gave it quite another meaning.
137. Phillips, *War of Greek Independence*, 45.
138. Dakin, *Greek Struggle*, 53–54, 56–57.
139. Ibid., 59; Brewer, *Flame of Freedom*, 70.
140. Phillips, *War of Greek Independence*, 47–48.
141. St. Clair, *That Greece Might Still Be Free*, 13 (qu.); Douglas Dakin, "The Formation of the Greek State, 1821–33," in *Struggle for Greek Independence*, ed. Clogg, 162.
142. Giuseppe Pecchio, *Relazione degli avvenimenti della Grecia nella primavera del 1825* (Lugano, 1826), 60, 124–25.
143. John Koliopoulos, *Brigands with a Cause: Brigandage and Irredentism in Modern Greece, 1821–1912* (Oxford, 1987); Clogg, "Aspects of the Movement," 9; Eric Hobsbawm, *Bandits* (London, 1967), 61–83.
144. Marion Sarafis, "Ejército, Constitución y Pueblo en Grecia," in *Ejército, pueblo y Constitución: homenaje al General Rafael del Riego*, ed. Alberto Gil Novales (Madrid, 1987), 558.
145. Mark Mazower, *Inside Hitler's Greece: The Experience of Occupation* (New Haven, 2001).
146. Koliopoulos, *Brigands with a Cause*, 39–66.
147. Skiotis, "Mountain Warriors," 313–15, 319.
148. Brewer, *Flame of Freedom*, 64–65; Theódoros Kolokotrónis, *Kolokotronès: The Klepht and the Warrior* (London, 1892). See also [Yannis] Makriyannis, *The Memoirs of General Makriyannis* (London, 1966), who recounted similar adventures but also deplored Greek atrocities upon innocent Turks.
149. Frazee, *Orthodox Church*, 27. The shaykh refused the request and was replaced.
150. Finlay, *History of the Greek Revolution*, I:184–85.
151. Pier Giorgio Camaiani, "La religiosità patriottica nel '21 greco e nel '48 italiano," in *Indipendenza e unità nazionale in Italia ed in Grecia* (Florence, 1987), 61.
152. St. Clair, *That Greece Might Still Be Free*, 2.
153. Frazee, *Orthodox Church*, 29; Brewer, *Flame of Freedom*, 104–6; K. Oekonomos, *Discours prononcé en Grec à Odessa, le 29 juin 1821* (Paris, 1821). All told, the Turks executed eighty bishops: John Petropoulos, *Politics and Statecraft in the Kingdom of Greece, 1833–1843* (Princeton, 1968), 41. For a restrained atrocity account, see Raybaud, *Mémoires sur la Grèce*, I:217–27.
154. St. Clair, *That Greece Might Still Be Free*, 80–81.
155. Ibid., 1.
156. Phillips, *War of Greek Independence*, 61; Gordon, *History*, I:244–45.
157. St. Clair, *That Greece Might Still Be Free*, 77. For similar hideous episodes, see the artillery officer L. De Bollmann's *Remarques sur l'état moral, politique et militaire de la Grèce* (Marseilles, 1822) and M. Lascaris, "La révolution grecque vue de Salonique," *Balcania* VI (1943): 145–68.
158. Arsh, *Eteristskoe dvizhenie*, 293; Frangos, "Philiki Etairia," 95; Kaltchas, *Constitutional History*, 41–42.
159. Dakin, "Formation of the Greek State, 1821–33," 160–61.

160. Spyros Loukatos (Loucatos), "Le philhellénisme balkanique pendant la lutte pour l'indépendance hellénique," *BS* XIX, no. 1 (1978): 249.

161. Kaltchas, *Constitutional History*, 3–7.

162. St. Clair, *That Greece Might Still Be Free*, 186; Alexis Dimaras, "The Other British Philhellenes," in *Struggle for Greek Independence*, ed. Clogg, 205–7.

163. Jeremy Bentham, *Collected Works* (Oxford, 1983–2000), XI:268, 363.

164. Bentham, *Security Against Misrule and Other Constitutional Writings for Tripoli and Greece*, ed. Ph. Schofield (Oxford, 1990), 195, 218.

165. Bentham, *Collected Works*, XI:320–21. See also Evaggelos Vallianatos, "Jeremy Bentham's Constitutional Reform Proposals to the Greek Provisional Government, 1823–1825," *BS* X, no. 2 (1969): 325–34.

166. St. Clair, *That Greece Might Still Be Free*, 191.

167. Dimaras, "Other British Philhellenes," 205–7; F. Rosen, *Bentham, Byron, and Greece: Constitutionalism, Nationalism, and Early Liberal Political Thought* (Oxford, 1992), 77–102; Bentham, *Security Against Misrule*, xli.

168. St. Clair, *That Greece Might Still Be Free*, 94; Dakin, *Greek Struggle*, 79–81.

169. St. Clair, *That Greece Might Still Be Free*, 25; Kaltchas, *Constitutional History*, 36.

170. Giorgio Spini, "Il significato storico dello Statuto di Epidauro," in *Risorgimento greco e filellenismo italiano: lotte, cultura, arte* (Rome, 1986), 136.

171. David Armitage, *The Declaration of Independence: A Global History* (Cambridge, 2007), 108.

172. *British and Foreign State Papers, 1821–1829*, IX (London, 1829), 620–21.

173. Ibid., IX:629–32.

174. *Constitutions, loix, ordonnances des Assemblées nationales, des Corps legislatif, et du Président de la Grèce* (Athens, 1835), 25; Gordon, *History*, I:323.

175. Sketchy biographical information in Carlo Francovich, "Il movimento filoellenico in Italia ed in Europa" in *Indipendenza e unità nazionale*, 7–8; Spyros Loukatos, *O Italikos filellenismos kata ton agona tes Ellenikes anexartesias, 1821–1831* (Athens, 1996), 26–27; and *LUI*, VIII:484.

176. Dakin, "The Formation of the Greek State," 166.

177. Kaltchas, *Constitutional History*, 36.

178. St. Clair, *That Greece Might Still Be Free*, 9.

179. Spini, "Significato storico dello Statuto di Epidauro," 135–36; Kaltchas, *Constitutional History*, 45–48; Gordon, *History*, I:323–24; Rosen, *Bentham, Byron, and Greece*, 84. See *British and Foreign State Papers*, IX:620–29 for the French text.

180. Frazee, *Orthodox Church*, 47; Prokesch-Osten, *Geschichte der Abfalls der Griechen*, III:249; Georges Vlachos, "L'idée constitutionelle et la conception révolutionnaire de Nation pendant la révolution hellénique de 1821," in *Révolution française et l'hellénisme moderne*, 337 n. 35.

181. Brewer, *Flame of Freedom*, 184.

182. Spini, "Significato storico dello Statuto di Epidauro," 135.

183. Chaconas, *Adamantios Korais*, 112–13, 123–27.

184. Kaltchas, *Constitutional History*, 47.

185. Rosen, *Bentham, Byron, and Greece*, 100.

186. Kaltchas, *Constitutional History*, 56.

187. For the deeper ideological roots of schism, see Koumarianou, "Contribution of the Intelligentsia," 72–73. For a brief treatment of the civil war chronology, see Brewer, *Flame of Freedom*, 226–33.

188. Dakin, *Greek Struggle*, 132–41.

189. Kaltchas, *Constitutional History*, 50–53.

190. John Kakridis, "The Ancient Greeks and the Greeks of the War of Independence," *BS* IV, no. 2 (1963): 251–64.

191. Paul Johnson, *The Birth of the Modern* (London, 1991), 695.

192. Valsa, *Théâtre grec*, 228–31. Athens got its first stage in 1835 and only in the 1830s, after independence, a steady outpouring of Greek drama.

193. F.-C.-H.-L. Pouqueville, *Histoire de la régénération de la Grèce* (Paris, 1824), II:497–98.

194. Romilly Jenkins, *Dionysius Solomós* (Cambridge, 1940), 68.

195. Dionísios Solomós, *O ymnos eis ten eleytherian . . . The Hymn to Liberty* (Athens, 1999), 85–109. See also M. Byron Raizis, *Dionysios Solomos* (New York, 1972), and Beaton, "Romanticism in Greece," 100–1.

196. Harold Parker, *The Cult of Antiquity and the French Revolutionaries* (1937; New York, 1965); Emmet Kennedy, *A Cultural History of the French Revolution* (New Haven, 1989); Mona Ozouf, *Festivals and the French Revolution* (Cambridge, MA, 1988).

197. Virginia Penn, "Philhellenism in Europe, 1821–1828," *Slavonic and East European Review* XVI, no. 48 (April 1938): 648.

198. Camaiani, "Religiosità patriottica," 78.

199. Peter [Pietro] Gamba, *A Narrative of Lord Byron's Last Journey to Greece* (London, 1825), 209–10.

200. Brewer, *Flame of Freedom*, 196, 204–19; St. Clair, *That Greece Might Still Be Free*, 66, passim.

201. Penn, "Philhellenism in Europe," 639.

202. Brewer, *Flame of Freedom*, 139.

203. J. D. Elster, *Das Battalion der Philhellenen* (Baden, 1828), 194–95; Wilhelm Barth and Max Kehrig-Korn, *Die Philhellenenzeit* (Munich, 1960), 196.

204. St. Clair, *That Greece Might Still Be Free*, 356. The four largest contingents came from Germany, France, Italy, and Britain.

205. Clogg, "Aspects of the Movement," 12.

206. Nils Aschling, *Försök till grekiska Revolutionens historia* (Stockholm, 1824), 73.

207. Elster, *Battalion der Philhellenen*, passim.

208. Spyros Loukatos, "Le Philhellénisme balkanique pendant la lutte pour l'indépendance hellénique," *BS* XIX, no. 1 (1978): 249–83 (see 249 n. 1 and 250); Loukatos, "Les relations des révolutionnaires grecs et des Bulgares volontaires à la lutte pour l'indépendance hellénique," 201, 201 n. 10, 202–3.

209. Nikolai Todorov, *Filiki eteriia i Bŭlgarite* (Sofia, 1965), 67–101; Nikolai Todorov and Veselin Traikov, *Bŭlgari uchastnitsi v borbite za osvobozhdenieto na Gŭrtsiia, 1821–1828* (Sofia, 1971), 5–47, 950–52. I use the standard Library of Congress transliteration from Bulgarian, which differs from the transliteration of the Bulgarian portion on the title page of *Pneumatikes kai politistikes scheseis*, which has both Greek and Bulgarian titles.

210. Irina Dostian (Dostyan), "L'attitude de la société russe face au mouvement de libération national grec," in *Les relations gréco-russes pendant la domination turque et la guerre d'indépendance grecque* (Thessaloniki, 1983), 75.

211. For example Brewer, *Flame of Freedom*, 144; St. Clair, *That Greece Might Still Be Free*, 356 (his list). No Russians or Balkan Slavs appear on the list.

212. Gamba, *Narrative*, 234–35.

213. Spyros Loukatos, "'Pamyatnik' russkim filellenam," in *Politicheskie, obshchestvennye, i kul'turnye sviazi narodov SSSR i Gretsii, XIX–XX vv.*, ed. G. L. Arsh (Moscow, 1989), 74–86; Todorov, "Quelques renseignements sur les insurgés grecs," 471–77. See also Prousis, *Russian Society*, 52, which lists Sultanov as a retired lieutenant.

214. Loukatos, "'Pamyatnik' russkim filellenam"; Prousis, *Russian Society*, 52.

215. Dostian, "L'attitude de la société russe," 75–76; B. Markevich, "N. A. Raiko: biograficheskii ocherk," *RA* 11 (1868): 297–302, 302 n. 2; Loukatos, "'Pamyatnik' russkim filellenam"; N. I. Lorer, "Iz zapisok dekabrista," *RB* 3 (1904): 68.

216. Solomós, *O ymnos eis ten eleutherian*, 87, 89. An alternative translation—"From his tower roars loudly / The strong Lion of Spain, / And to greet you he shakes proudly / His rich and royal mane"—is given in Dionysios Solomós, *Faith and Motherland: Collected Poems*, tr. M. B. Raizis (Minneapolis, 1998), 25.

217. Phanos Vagenas, "O ispanikos philellenismos kata ten Helleniken epanastasin," *Philellenika*, January-March 1955, 6–9.

218. Mikhail Dodolev, *Rossiia i Ispaniia, 1808–1823 gg.* (Moscow, 1984), 184.

219. Quoted in Brewer, *Flame of Freedom*, 107.

220. Quoted in Kaltchas, *Constitutional History*, 35.

221. Vagenas, "O ispanikos philellenismos," 30 and passim.

222. Kolokotrónis, *Kolokotronēs*, passim (qu. 127, 151, 252); Clogg, "Aspects of the Movement," 26; Kaltchas, *Constitutional History*, 44.

223. Rosen, *Bentham, Byron, and Greece*, 136, 148, 247–48, 168, 172, and passim.

224. A. Debidour, *Le Général Fabvier: sa vie militaire et politique* (Paris, 1904), 253–69.

225. St. Clair, *That Greece Might Still Be Free*, 125, 291.

226. I. K. Khasiotes, "O ispanikos philellenismos," *Makedonike zoe* 70 (March 1972): 10–11, 14 (poem in Spanish and Greek).

227. Sarafis, "Ejército, constitución y pueblo en Grecia," 558–59; Dodolev, *Rossiya i Ispaniia*, 187–88.

228. Bentham, *Security Against Misrule*, xxvi.

229. Brewer, *Flame of Freedom*, 220; Vagenas, "O ispanikos philellenismos," 10.

230. Vagenas, "O ispanikos philellenismos," 6–9; Khasiotes, "O ispanikos philellenismos," 12. I have not identified the signatories, though one might have been F. D. Morales, a deputy who had welcomed Pepe to Spain. The name Vurinos is given as Bornoz in Khasiotes.

231. Leicester Stanhope, *Greece During Lord Byron's Residence in That Country in 1823 and 1824* (Paris, 1825), I:37.

232. Khasiotes, "O ispanikos philellenismos," 13–14; Vagenas, "O ispanikos philellenismos," 13–34 (I have corrected the spelling of Spanish from these works). St. Clair, *That Greece Might Still Be Free*, 329–30 and 390 n. 11.

233. Vagenas, "O ispanikos philellenismos," 31–34 (qu. 31); Khasiotes, "O ispanikos philellenismos," 14.

234. Vagenas, "O ispanikos philellenismos," 21–24; Khasiotes, "O ispanikos philellenismos," 14.

235. Loukatos, *O italikos philellenismos*, 16–17.

236. Elena Persico, *Letteratura filellenica italiana, 1787–1870* (Rome, 1920), 15–28 and passim; St. Clair, *That Greece Might Still Be Free*, 257; Zeffiro Ciuffoletti and Luigi Mascilli Migliorini, "Il mito della Grecia tra politica e letteratura," *Indipendenza e unità nazionale*, 44, 50–59.

237. *Risorgimento greco*, 231–382, richly illustrated.

238. Tommaso Astarita, *Between Salt Water and Holy Water: A History of Southern Italy* (New York, 2005), 97.

239. Loukatos, *O italikos philellenismos*, 7–15.

240. Narciso Nada, "La partecipazione degli Italiani alla guerra di Indipendenza ellenica," in *Risorgimento greco*, 88.

241. St. Clair, *That Greece Might Still Be Free*, 215. This work provides the best available numerical count (see 356). See also Vassilis Sfyroeras, "Filelleni italiani in Grecia," in *Risorgimento greco*, 84–86.

242. For overview and some individual details: Francovich, "Movimento filoellenico," 1–23; Persico, *Letteratura filellenica italiana*, 55–56; Loukatos, *O italikos philellenismos*, 30–37.

243. St. Clair, *That Greece Might Still Be Free*, 257.

244. Giorgio Candeloro, *Storia dell'Italia moderna. II. Dalla restaurazione alla revoluzione nazionale*, 2d ed. (Milan, 1960), II:149.

245. Francovich, "Movimento filoellenico," 14.

246. Collegno, Rossaroll, Santarosa, Palma, Romei, Barberis, Barandier, Aimino, Morandi, Ritatori, Isaia, Gambini, and Ferero in the first category; Pisa, Porro, Pecorara, Pecchio, Andrietti, and Giacomuzzi in the second. St. Clair, *That Greece Might Still Be Free*, 385 n. 18.

247. Francovich, "Movimento filoellenico," 15.

248. Enrica Lucarelli, "L'emigrazione come problema politico," in *Risorgimento greco*, 144.

249. Guglielmo Pepe, *Guglielmo Pepe*, ed. Ruggero Moscati (Rome, 1938), I:229.

250. Pepe, *Pepe*, I:8 n. 1; Nino Cortese, *Il mezzogiorno ed il Risorgimento italiano* (Naples, 1965), 254.

251. Guglielmo Pepe, *Memorie del Generale Guglielmo Pepe intorno all sua vita* (Paris, 1847), II:172.

252. Pepe, *Pepe*, I:282 (qu.), 283–85.

253. Pepe, *Memorie*, II:173–74; Pepe, *Pepe*, I:295–96; Santorre di Santarosa, *Lettere dall'esilio (1821–1825)*, ed. A. Olmo (Rome, 1969), 389 n. 1.

254. See chapter 3 and Loukatos, *O italikos philellenismos*, 127–29; Tito Battaglini, *L'organizzazione militare del Regno delle Due Sicilie* (Modena, 1940), 61; Pietro Colletta, *Storia del Reame di Napoli* (Naples, 1992), 624–25; *EI*, XXX:113–14; *LUI*, XIX:379.

255. Francovich, "Movimento filoellenico," 15; St. Clair, *That Greece Might Still Be Free*, 253; *EI*, XXX:113–14; *LUI*, xix, 379; Gino Doria, *Le strade di Napoli*, 2d ed. (1943; Milan, 1971): 119 on the son; Barth, *Philhellenzeit*, 210–11. Sources differ on how he died.

256. Francovich, "Movimento filoellenico," 15, 22–23 and n. 47; Loukatos, *O italikos philellenismos*, 109–111; Nada, "Partecipazione degli Italiani," 88; St. Clair, *That Greece Might Still Be Free*, 257–58, 290.

257. St. Clair, *That Greece Might Still Be Free*, 319–322. For other Neapolitan philhellenes, see this work and Loukatos, *O italikos philellenismos*.

258. Biographical notes in Giorgio Marsengo and Giuseppe Parlato, *Dizionario dei Piemontesi compromessi nei moti de 1821* (Turin, 1982) and *Dizionario biografico degli Italiani* (Rome, 1960–). See also Loukatos, *O italikos philellenismos*, 27, and St. Clair, *That Greece Might Still Be Free*, 258.

259. Francovich, "Movimento filoellenico," 9–10; Loukatos, *O italikos philellenismos*, 28, 67–68, 144–45; Marsengo, *Dizionario dei Piemontesi*, II:243–44; Barth, *Philhellenzeit*, 240; Nada, "Partecipazione degli Italiani," 88.

260. Francovich, "Movimento filoellenico," 10–12 and n. 24; St. Clair, *That Greece Might Still Be Free*, 101.

261. St. Clair, *That Greece Might Still Be Free*, 101; Loukatos, *O italikos philellenismos*, 32–33.

262. Howe, *Historical Sketch*, 261.

263. Eugène Dalleggio, ed., *Les philhellènes et la guerre de l'indépendance: lettres inédits de J. Orlando et A. Louriotis* (Athens, 1949): 119–21.

264. D'Azeglio in Giacinto Collegno, *Diario dell'assedio di Navarino* (Turin, 1857), 3–22; Charles de Mazade, "Une vie d'émigré italien," *Revue des deux mondes*, March 15, 1859, 460–67.

265. St. Clair, *That Greece Might Still Be Free*, 256.

266. Collegno, *Diario dell'assedio di Navarino*, 23–128; Mazade, "Une vie d'émigré italien"; *Dizionario biografico degli Italiani*, XXVI:802–7; *EI*, X:743; *LUI*, V:152.

267. Santarosa, *Lettere dall'esilio*, 24–27; Margaret Wicks, *The Italian Exiles in London, 1816–1848* (1937; Freeport, NY, 1968), 120.

268. Loukatos, *O italikos philellenismos*, 16, quotes only the first three words of this passage, known to every Greek: "Deute paises Hellenon."

269. Wicks, *The Italian Exiles*, 257.

270. Pecchio, *Relazione*, 64.

271. Santarosa, *Lettere dall'esilio*, 482, letter of April 1825; Mastellone, "Santorre di Santarosa," *Indipendenza e unità nazionale*, 39.

272. Collegno, *Diario dell'assedio di Navarino*, 88; Mazade, "Une vie d'émigré italien."

273. Nada, "Partecipazione degli Italiani," 87; *EI*, XXX:777; *LUI*, xx, 54; Mastellone, "Santorre di Santarosa," 41 (qu.).

274. Collegno, *Diario*, 95–97, 123 (qu.); Mazade, "Une vie d'émigré italien."

275. Francovich, "Movimento filoellenico," 12, 13, n. 27 (qu.); Gamba, *Narrative*, 201.

276. Kaltchas, *Constitutional History*, 39.

277. Konstantin Khadzopoulos, "Obrashchenie vosstavshikh Grekov Peloponnesa k tsariu Aleksandru I," in *Politicheskie, obshchestvennye, i kulturnye sviazi*, ed. Arsh, 45–46.

278. Ol'ga Orlik, *Dekabristy i vneshniaia politika Rossii* (Moscow, 1984), 85.

279. Jean Dimakis, *La presse française face à la chute de Missolonghi et la bataille navale de Navarin* (Thessaloniki, 1976), 77–78, 138, 163, 363–64, and passim.

280. Dakin, "The Formation of the Greek State," 172–77.

281. St. Clair, *That Greece Might Still Be Free*, 57.

282. Gary Bass, *Freedom's Battle: The Origins of Humanitarian Intervention* (New York, 2008), 124–28 and passim.

Chapter 5

1. I have used Max Eastman's free but elegant translation from Marc Raeff, *The Decembrist Movement* (Englewood Cliffs, 1966), 178. For Pushkin's "sinewy political path" and his relations with the Decembrists, see Sergei Davydov's balanced essay in *The Pushkin Handbook*, ed. David Bethea (Madison, 2005), 283–320.

2. P. E. Shchegolev, "Katekhizis Sergeia Murav'eva-Apostola," in his *Istoricheskie etiudy* (St. Petersburg, 1913), 350. Original in *MG* 11 (November 1908): 50–80, and reprinted in his *Dekabristy* (Moscow, 1926), 229–60. Note the alternative spelling of the official word *katikhizis*.

3. A. K. Borozdin, ed., *Iz pisem i pokazanii dekabristov: kritika sovremennogo sostoianiia Rossii i plany budushchego ustroistva* (St. Petersburg, 1906), 85–87; *VD*, VI:128–29.

4. I. I. Gorbachevskii, *Zapiski dekabrista* (Moscow, 1916), 125. See notes below under "Catechism of Revolt" for documentation.

5. *VD*, VI:140 (Baron Soloviev's testimony).

6. D. K. Petrov, *Rossiia i Nikolai I v stikhotvoreniiakh Espronsedy i Rossetti* (St. Petersburg, 1909), 69.

7. Patricia Grimsted, *The Foreign Ministers of Alexander I: Political Attitudes and the Conduct of Russian Diplomacy, 1801–1825* (Berkeley, 1969), 32–65 (qu. 37).

8. Richard Wortman, *Scenarios of Power: Myth and Ceremony in Russian Monarchy* (Princeton, 2006), 79, 83 (qu.).

9. Anatole Mazour, *The First Russian Revolution, 1825: The Decembrist Movement, Its Origins, Developments, and Significance* (Stanford, 1961), 262.

10. Grimsted, *Foreign Ministers*, 50; Janet Hartley, *Alexander I* (London, 1994), 2 (qu.); C. M. Woodhouse, *Capodistria: The Founder of Greek Independence* (London, 1973), 80, 146.

11. Hartley, *Alexander I*, 130–33.

12. Ibid., 121, 126–27 (qu. 126).

13. Giuseppe Berti, *Russia e stati italiani nel Risorgimento* (Turin, 1957), 264.

14. Berti, *Russia e stati italiani*, 455.

15. Grimsted, *Foreign Ministers*, 62–63 n. 46.

16. Woodhouse, *Capodistria*, 137.

17. Hartley, *Alexander I*, 133–36.

18. Grimsted, *Foreign Ministers*, 61 and 246 (quotes), 245.

19. R. M. Johnston, *The Napoleonic Empire in Southern Italy and the Rise of the Secret Societies* (1904; New York, 1973), II:74; Mikhail Dodolev, "Zapiski russkogo diplomata ob Italii (1816–1822 gg.)," *ISSSR* 5 (September-October 1976): 157–64.

20. Ol'ga Orlik, *Dekabristy i evropeiskoe osvoboditel'noe dvizhenie* (Moscow, 1975), 50–51.

21. Harold Acton, *The Bourbons of Naples, 1734–1825* (London, 1956), 666–67; Woodhouse, *Capodistria*, 199.

22. M. I. Koval'skaia, "Ital'ianskie karbonarii i peredovaia Rossiia," *VI* XLII, no. 8 (August 1967): 83–84; S. S. Landa, *Dukh revoliutsionnykh preobrazovanii: iz istorii formirovaniia i politicheskoi organizatsii dekabristov, 1816–1825* (Moscow, 1975), 347 n. 6.

23. Koval'skaia, *Dvizhenie karbonariev*, 220.

24. V. I. Semevskii, "Dekabristy-masony," *MG* 5–6 (May-June 1908): 423.

25. M. Bignon, *Du congrès de Troppau, ou examen des prétensions des monarchies absolues à l'égard de la monarchie constitutionelle de Naples* (Paris, 1821), 68–72; Koval'skaia, *Dvizhenie karbonariev*, 205 n. 110.

26. *RA* 11 (1886): 405–7 (qu. 406, original italics).

27. I. V. Vasil'chikov, "Bumagi," *RA* 1 (1875): 350–51.

28. V. A. Fedorov, *Soldatskoe dvizhenie v gody dekabristov, 1816–1825* (Moscow, 1963), 72–204 (esp. 125–34); John L. H. Keep, *Soldiers of the Tsar: Army and Society in Russia, 1462–1874* (Oxford, 1985), 299.

29. Semevskii, "Volnenie v Semenovskom Polku v 1820 g.," *Byloe* 2 (February 1907): 83–86. See also Joseph Wieczynski, "The Mutiny of the Semenovsky Regiment in 1820," *RR*, 29, no. 2 (April 1970): 167–80.

30. *RA* 12 (1875): 432 (qu.); Orlik, *Dekabristy i evropeiskoe osvoboditel'noe dvizhenie*, 61.

31. *Nevskii zritel'* 5 (February 1821): 175; *VE*, January-March 1821.

32. Orlik, *Dekabristy i evropeiskoe osvoboditel'noe dvizhenie*, 82; M. V. Nechkina, *Dvizhenie dekabristov* (Moscow, 1955), I:306.

33. Koval'skaia, *Dvizhenie karbonariev*, 226.

34. Grimsted, *Foreign Ministers*, 53, 248 (qu.).

35. Semevskii, *Politicheskie i obshchestvennye idei dekabristov* (St. Petersburg, 1909), 248; Berti, *Russia e stati italiani*, 462.

36. Koval'skaia, *Dvizhenie karbonariev*, 241; Koval'skaia, "Ital'ianskie karbonarii," 90 n. 58.
37. Semevskii, "Dekabristy-masony," *MG* 2 (February 1908): 33.
38. *RA* 12 (1875): 401.
39. "Golos blagomysliashchago roialista," *VE* 7–8 (April 1821): 270–76.
40. E. A. Kushelev, "Unichtozhenie masonskikh lozh v Rossii, 1822," *RS*, March 1877, 465. See also G. A. Sibireva, *Neapolitanskoe korolevtsvo i Rossiia v poslednei chetverti XVIII v.* (Moscow, 1981), 126. A year earlier, Pope Pius VII, building on eighteenth-century precedent, condemned freemasonry and the Carbonari: Roberto de Matei, "Società segrete," in *La rivoluzione italiana: storia critica del Risorgimento*, ed. Massimo Viglione (Rome, 2001), 129.
41. Grigorii Arsh, *Eteristskoe dvizhenie v Rossii* (Moscow, 1970), 294–95.
42. Grand Duke Nikolai Mikhailovich, *L'Empereur Alexandre Ier* (St. Petersburg, 1912), II:415. For other negative reactions, see T. N. Zhukovskaia, "Tainye obshchestva pervoi treti XIX v. i organizatsionnye modeli dekabrizma," *14 Dekabria 1825 g. Istochniki, issledovaniia, istoriografiia, bibliografiia* (St. Petersburg, 2002), 5: 85.
43. Mladen Pantschoff, *Kaiser Alexander I und der Aufstand Ypsilantis, 1821* (Leipzig, 1891), 65.
44. Grimsted, *Foreign Ministers*, 263–68; Woodhouse, *Capodistria*, 283–305.
45. Irina Dostian, *Russkaia obshchestvennaia mysl' i balkanskie narody: ot Radishcheva do dekabristov* (Moscow, 1980), 227 (qu.); Dodolev, *Rossiia i Ispaniia, 1808–1823 gg.* (Moscow, 1984), 220.
46. David Brewer, *The Flame of Freedom: The Greek War of Independence, 1821–1833* (London, 2001), 107, 252–53.
47. M. P. Alekseev, "Etiudy iz istorii ispano-russkikh otnoshenii," in *Kultura Ispanii: sbornik* (Moscow, 1940), 392–93; Alekseev, *Ocherki istorii ispano-russikikh literaturnykh otnoshenii XVI-XIX vv.* (Leningrad, 1964), 97.
48. Dodolev, "Rossiia i voina ispanskogo naroda za nezavisimost' (1808–1814) gg.," *VI* 11 (November 1972): 34–38 (qu. 37).
49. Dodolev, "Rossiia i voina ispanskogo naroda," 37 and n. 25.
50. Davydov, *Sochineniia* (St. Petersburg, 1848): quotes: 508, 509, 510 (see also pp. 487–640). Not everyone praised the guerrillas. A. Voeikov in October 1812 wrote that "Moscow and Kaluga peasants were better at defending their homes than the Spanish." Alekseev, "Etiudy," 395 n. 2.
51. Dodolev, "Rossiia i voina ispanskogo naroda," 38.
52. Alekseev, "Etiudy," 394.
53. Dodolev, "O vliianii ispanskoi revoliutsii 1808–1814 godov na vneshniuiu politiku evropeiskikh gosudarstv," *Novaia i noveishaia istoriia* 2 (March-April 1968): 40.
54. A. G. Tartakovskii, *Voennaia publitsistika 1812 goda* (Moscow, 1967), 22–23.
55. *Listovki Otechestvennoi voiny 1812 goda: sbornik dokumentov*, ed. R. E. Alt'shuller and A. G. Tartakovskii (Moscow, 1962), 47–49 (qu. 48).
56. Robert Wilson, *Narrative of Events During the Invasion of Russia by Napoleon Bonaparte*, ed. H. Randolph (London, 1860), 254–61.
57. A. P. Vronchenko, *Kirilovtsy*, cited in Alekseev, *Ocherki*, 103–4.
58. Janet Hartley, "The Patriotism of the Russian Army in the 'Patriotic' or 'Fatherland' War of 1812" in *Popular Resistance in the French Wars: Patriots, Partisans, and Land Pirates*, ed. Charles Esdaile (London, 2005), 181–200 (esp. 181–94).
59. Paul Austin, *1812: The March on Moscow* (London, 1993), 231, 377 n. 1.
60. Dodolev, "Rossiia i voina ispanskogo naroda," 38–9.
61. In June the ceremonies were reenacted with minor variations. *SO* V, no. 19 (1813): 301–15 (qu. 310) and VII, no. 27 (1813): 120–23 and addendum XII, 1–3.
62. Dodolev, "Rossiia i ispanskaia revoliutsiia 1820–1823 gg.," *ISSSR* 1 (January-February 1969): 113–15.
63. See chapter 2. *Catecismo civil, y breve compendio de las obligaciones del Español* (Madrid, 1808) in *Catecismos políticos Españoles arreglados a las constituciones del siglo XIX*, ed. Ramón Espinar Gallego (Madrid, 1989), 16–20; its Seville version translated as "Grazhdanskii katikhizis, ili Kratkoe obozrenie dolzhnostei ispantsa," *SO* 1 (October 1812): 53–60 (and, confusingly, 50–57 in another version of the same issue).

64. Petrov, *Rossiia i Nikolai I*, 69 n. 1.
65. Dodolev, "Rossiia i voina ispanskogo naroda," 40–44, with positive and negative press reactions.
66. Enno Krahe, "Strange Bedfellows: Alexander I and Ferdinand VII, 1812–1823," in Ronald Caldwell, et al. eds., *The Consortium on Revolutionary Europe, 1750–1850* (Tallahassee, 1994), 3.
67. *Diplomatisches Archiv für die Zeit-und Staatengeschichte*, 6 vols. (Stuttgart, 1821–26), III:438–41.
68. Ana María Schop Soler, *Un siglo de relaciones diplomáticas y comerciales entre España y Rusia, 1733–1833* (Madrid, 1984), 276; Dodolev, *Rossiia i Ispaniia*, 171, 180 (qu.).
69. Dodolev, *Rossiia i Ispaniia*, 186, 188.
70. Ibid., 167 n. 4.
71. Schop Soler, *Siglo de relaciones*, 266 (qu.), 421.
72. Dodolev, *Rossiia i Ispaniia*, 171–77; Dodolev, "Rossiia i ispanskaia revoliutsiia," 117–18.
73. Frederick Artz, *Reaction and Revolution, 1814–1832* (New York, 1934), 167–68.
74. For one example: Schop Soler, *Siglo de relaciones*, 288–89.
75. Krahe, "Strange Bedfellows," 10.
76. *VE* 2 (January 1822): 239; *VE* 20 (October 1822): 316.
77. Dodolev, *Rossiia i Ispaniia*, 166–70.
78. Nikolai Mikhailovich, *L'Empereur Alexandre Ier*, II:415–16.
79. Schop Soler, *Siglo de relaciones*, 421.
80. Semevskii, "Volnenie v Semenovskom Polku," 94; Vasil'chikov, "Bumagi," *RA* 5 (1875): 57 (there are slight disparities between these two accounts). See also Fedorov, *Soldatskoe dvizhenie*, 118.
81. Schop Soler, *Siglo de relaciones*, 326–28 (a March 24 conversation with La Ferronais).
82. Dodolev, *Rossiia i Ispaniia*, 221–22 n. 40.
83. Alekseev, *Ocherki*, 111–14.
84. Petrov, *Rossiia i Nikolai I*, 45–46 n. 2.
85. Grimsted, *Foreign Ministers*, 48–49.
86. Hartley, *Alexander I*, 152.
87. Dodolev, *Rossiia i Ispaniia*, 215–16 and n. 19.
88. Natan Eidelman, *Conspiracy Against the Tsar: A Portrait of the Decembrists*, tr. C. Carlile (Moscow, 1985), 75.
89. Keep, *Soldiers of the Tsar*, 257–58, 260.
90. Schop Soler, *Siglo de relaciones*, 427.
91. Semevskii, *Obshchestvennye dvizheniia v Rossi v pervuiu polovinu XIX veka* (St. Petersburg, 1905), I:182–83.
92. Mikhail Lunin, *Sochineniia* (1923; New York, 1976), 75.
93. V. S. Ikonnikov, *Krest'ianskoe dvizhenie v Kievskoi gub. v 1826–27 gg. v sviazi s sobytiiami togo vremeni* (St. Petersburg, 1905), 5 n. 4.
94. Borozdin, *Iz pisem*, 25 (qu.), 40, 55–72, 75–81, and passim.
95. See Baron Rosen's comments in *Pisateli-dekabristy v vospominaniiakh sovremennikov* (Moscow, 1980), I:174.
96. Borozdin, *Iz pisem*, 12, 35–36.
97. *VD*, I:9.
98. Franco Venturi, "Italo-russkie otnosheniia s 1750 do 1825 g." in *Rossiia i Italiia: iz istorii russko-ital'ianskikh kul'turnykh i obshchestvennykh otnoshenii* (Moscow, 1968), 48–49.
99. Hartley, "The Patriotism of the Russian Army," 195–96; Keep, *Soldiers of the Tsar*, 257.
100. S. S. Volk, *Istoricheskie vzgliady dekabristov* (Moscow, 1958), 155–207.
101. N. V. Koroleva, *Dekabristy i teatr* (Leningrad, 1975).
102. *SO* 1 (large version, 1812): 164 (there are several versions of *SO* for no. 1 [1812], with varying pagination and some common contents. See also Stephen Norris, *A War of Images: Russian Popular Prints, Wartime Culture, and National Identity, 1812–1945* (DeKalb, 2006), 22.
103. Elise Wirtschafter, *The Play of Ideas in Russian Enlightenment Theater* (DeKalb, 1997), 166–71; Richard Stites, *Serfdom, Society, and the Arts in Imperial Russia* (New Haven, 2005), 181–89.

104. Koroleva, *Dekabristy i teatr*, 73–75, 78 (qu.). See also E. Grosheva, "Dekabristy (opera Yu. Shaporina)," *Sovetskaia muzyka* 8 (August 1953): 9–18.

105. K. F. Ryleev, "Grazhdanskoe muzhestvo," in *PSS*, ed. A. G. Tseitlin (Moscow, 1934), 233–36; Patrick O'Meara, *K. F. Ryleev: A Political Biography of the Decembrist Poet* (Princeton, 1984), 177–80 and passim.

106. Volk, *Istoricheskie vzglyady dekabristov*, 61.

107. Lunin, *Sochineniia*, 85 and passim; Eidelman, *Conspiracy Against the Tsar*, 22.

108. *VD*, I:343.

109. Susan Morrissey rightly stresses the cult of Cato among the Decembrists: *Suicide and the Body Politic in Imperial Russia* (Cambridge, 2006), 59. At least three of them committed suicide.

110. O'Meara, *Ryleev*, 180. See also Ryleev, *PSS*, 660 for classical models.

111. Mikhail Zetlin, *The Decembrists*, tr. G. Panin (New York, 1958), 118.

112. Cited in introduction to Lunin, *Sochineniia*, 7.

113. Wortman, *Scenarios of Power* (2006), 95. See also Hans Lemberg, *Die nationale Gedanken-welt der Dekabristen* (Graz, 1963), 99–102.

114. One of several notable exceptions, Alexander Ulybyshev, sketched out a utopian society three hundred years in the future where the faith of priests and monks was replaced by a deistic, civic religion: Marc Raeff, *The Decembrist Movement* (Englewood Cliffs, 1966), 60–66.

115. O'Meara, *Ryleev*.

116. Glynn Barratt, *The Rebel on the Bridge: A Life of the Decembrist Baron Andrey Rozen* (London, 1975).

117. Morrissey, *Suicide and the Body Politic*, 59.

118. F. Timiriazov, "Stranitsy proshlago," *RA* I (1882): 155–80 (qu. 172). Timiriazov heard this story after the 1825 uprising from his father who was allegedly present in Paris. See also O'Meara, *Ryleev*, 40 n. 56. Variants of the seer's name: Lenormand and Lenormanche.

119. "Bunt chernigovskago polka," *RA* 1 (1871): 262 n. His friend, for whom Le Normand also predicted a violent death, later shot himself over some unhappy affair.

120. Hippolyte Auger, "Iz zapisok Ippolita Ozhe," *RA* 4 (1877): 537.

121. *VD*, V:187.

122. Zetlin, *Decembrists*, 158.

123. *Pisateli-dekabristy*, I:21–22.

124. Raeff, *Decembrist Movement*, 69–99; Nechkina, *Dvizhenie dekabristov*, I:197–203.

125. N. N. Bolkhovitinov, "Dekabristy i Amerika," *VI* 4 (April 1974): 91–92; Koval'skaia, *Dvizhenie karbonariev*, 214–15.

126. Sibireva, *Neapolitanskoe korolevstvo*, 142; Isabel de Madariaga, "Spain and the Decembrists," *European Studies Review* 3, no. 2 (January-October 1973): 144 n. 9 and 145. The list can be found in N. M. Druzhinin, *Dekabrist Nikita Murav'ev* (Moscow, 1933), 297–302.

127. Druzhinin, *Dekabrist Nikita Murav'ev*, 303.

128. Raeff, *Decembrist Movement*, 103–18 (the text).

129. "Istochnik verkhovnoi vlasti est' narod, kotoromu prinadlezhit iskliuchitel'noe pravo delat' osnovnye postanovleniia dlia samogo sebia." Druzhinin, *Dekabrist Nikita Murav'ev*, 181.

130. "La soberanía reside esencialmente en la Nación, y por lo mismo pertenece a ésta exclusi-vamente el derecho de establecer sus leyes fundamentales." *Constitución de Cádiz de 1812*; N. V. Minaeva, "K voprosu ob ideinykh svyazyakh dvizheniia dekabristov i ispanskoi revoliutsii," *IZ* 96 (1975): 68–69.

131. Druzhinin, *Dekabrist Nikita Murav'ev*, 222–23.

132. "Russkii narod svobodnyi i nezavisimyi, ne est' i ne mozhet byt' prinadlezhnost'iu nikak-ogo litsa i nikakogo semeistva." Druzhinin, *Dekabrist Nikita Murav'ev*, 181. D. K. Petrov in 1909 was the first to decode the footnote: *Rossiia i Nikolai I*, 71–72 n. 4. Petrov also cites the Spanish text: "Nación española es libre e independiente sin ser ni poder ser patrimonio de ninguna familia o persone." The modern version uses slightly different wording: "La Nación española es libre e independiente, y no es ni puede ser patrimonio de ninguna familia ni persona": Constitución de Cádiz de 1812.

133. Second version, chapter II, article 42 cited in Raeff, *Decembrist Movement*, 107.

134. The best works on Pestel's life are Patrick O'Meara, *The Decembrist Pestel: Russia's First Republican* (Basingstoke, 2003) and Oksana Kiianskaia, *Pavel Pestel: offitser, razvedchik, zagovorshchik* (Moscow, 2002). See also N. P. Pavlov-Silvanskii's, the first good biography of Pestel in *RBS* (1902), 599–615.

135. I. V. Maiorov, "Krest'ianskie vospominaniia o P. I. i B. I. Pestele," *Byloe* 5 (May 1906): 271–72.

136. Ikonnikov, *Krest'ianskoe dvizhenie*, 10.

137. O'Meara, *Pestel*, 143. The Bolshevik Bronshtein recognized that he was still seen as a Jew even after taking the name Trotsky; and he hesitated accepting the post of Commissar for Foreign Affairs in the first Bolshevik government.

138. *Pushkin i ego vremia* (Leningrad, 1962), 130–31; O'Meara, *Pestel*, 52. For the evolution of his thinking, see pp. 72–88.

139. Franco Venturi, "Destutt de Tracy and the Liberal Revolutions," in Venturi, *Studies in Free Russia*, tr. F. S. Walsby and M. O'Dell (Chicago, 1982), 76–78; Bolkhovitinov, "Dekabristy i Amerika," 92.

140. Chapter III, article 11 of the first draft in *VD*, VII:173–744; Mazour, *First Russian Revolution*, 50–51; O'Meara, *Pestel*, 79–80.

141. Raeff, *Decembrist Movement*, 151 (qu.). Chapter III, article 6 of the second draft; Mazour, *First Russian Revolution*, 105.

142. Mazour, *First Russian Revolution*, 105–7.

143. Charles Esdaile, *Spain in the Liberal Age: From Constitution to Civil War, 1808–1939* (Oxford, 2000), 33–34.

144. *VD*, VII:129.

145. *VD*, VII:146–48.

146. O'Meara, *Pestel*, 82.

147. "Narod rossiiskii ne est' prinadlezhnost' kakogo-libo litsa ili semeistva. Naprotiv togo, pravitel'stvo est' prinadlezhnost' naroda, i ono uchrezhdeno dlia blaga narodnogo, a ne narod sushchestvuet dlia blaga pravitel'stva." *VD*, VII:69; Raeff, *Decembrist Movement*, 128.

148. *Constitución de Cádiz de 1812*, title I, chapter I, article 3; and title II, chapter III, article 13.

149. Minaeva, "K voprosu ob ideinykh sviaziakh," 70.

150. O'Meara, *Pestel*, 75–76.

151. *VD*, V:414.

152. *VD*, V:22 (qu.); Georges Luciani, *La Société des Slaves Unis, 1823–1825* (Bordeaux, 1963), 38–41.

153. Nechkina, *Dvizhenie dekabristov*, II:161; Koval'skaia, "Ital'ianskie karbonarii," 79–80.

154. *VD*, V:17–18; Luciani, *La Société des Slaves Unis*, 58–59.

155. Semevskii, *Politicheskie i obshchestvennye idei*, 311–12 and n. 2. Semevskii speculates about how the Italian oath might have reached the Slav founders.

156. Koval'skaia, "Ital'ianskie karbonarii," 80.

157. I. V. Porokh, "Vosstanie chernigovskogo polka," in *Ocherki iz istorii dvizheniia dekabristov: sbornik statei*, ed. N. M. Druzhinin et al. (Moscow, 1954), 140.

158. Porokh, "Vosstanie chernigovskogo polka," 141–49.

159. Nechkina, "Revoliutsiia napodobie ispanskoi," *KiS* 10 (1931): 18 (qu.); Koval'skaia, *Dvizhenie karbonariev*, 219.

160. Edward Blaquiere, *An Historical Review of the Spanish Revolution* (London, 1822), 274.

161. Landa, *Dukh revoliutsionnykh preobrazovanii*, 183.

162. V. F. Raevskii, *Materialy o zhizni i revoliutsionnoi deiatel'nosti* (Irkutsk, 1980–83), I:25, 169, 238–39, 257, 396 n. 113, and II:223.

163. Raevskii, *Materialy*, I:86–92 (qu. 88, 89; italics in original); Nechkina, "Revoliutsiia napodobie ispanskoi," 22.

164. *Pisateli-dekabristy*, I:22; Pierre Corneille, *The Cid, Cinna, The Theatrical Illusion*, ed. and tr. J. Cairncross (Harmondsworth, 1975), 130–31.

165. O'Meara, *Pestel*, 65.

166. O'Meara, *Ryleev*, 108–16, 209.

167. *VD*, I:189.

168. *VD*, III:339–40 (quot.), 346–47.

169. M. V. Dovnar-Zapol'skii, *Memuary dekabristov*, I:120.
170. Mazour, *First Russian Revolution*, 97.
171. O'Meara, *Pestel*, 141–47 and passim.
172. Mazour, *First Russian Revolution*, 95–96.
173. Orlik, *Dekabristy i evropeiskoe osvoboditel'noe dvizhenie*, 45.
174. Koval'skaia, *Dvizhenie karbonariev*, 202.
175. Orlik, *Dekabristy i evropeiskoe osvoboditel'noe dvizhenie*, 66.
176. *VD*, I:481–82.
177. A. P. Beliaev, "Vospominaniia o perezhitom i perechuvstvovannom," *RS*, March 1881, 487–88.
178. Semevskii, *Obshchestvennye dvizheniia*, 487.
179. Borozdin, *Iz pisem*, 11, 12–13, 25.
180. Ryleev, *PSS*, 417.
181. *Pisateli-dekabristy*, I:174; Barratt, *Rebel on the Bridge*.
182. N. V. Basargin, *Zapiski*, ed. P. E. Shchegolev (Petrograd, 1917), iv-xiii, 6–13.
183. M. F. Orlov, "Zapiski o tainom obshchestve generala-maiora Orlova," in Dovnar-Zapol'skii, *Memuary dekabristov*, I:10.
184. Nechkina, *Dvizhenie dekabristov*, II:25.
185. *VD*, IV:105.
186. Dovnar-Zapol'skii, *Memuary dekabristov*, I:191–92, 194.
187. A. V. Podzhio, "Zapiski," in *Vospominaniia i rasskazy deiatelei tainykh obshchestv 1820-kh godov* (Moscow, 1931), I:22–89, esp. 73–76 (qu. 76).
188. F. F. Vigel', *Zapiski* (Moscow, 2000), 413.
189. Koval'skaia, *Dvizhenie karbonariev*, 83, 202–4 (qu. 204).
190. Orlik, *Dekabristy i evropeiskoe osvoboditel'noe dvizhenie*, 28–29 (qu. 29); Koval'skaia, "Ital'ianskie karbonarii," 81; *RA* 6 (1886): 206. For other Russo-Italian connections, see Koval'skaya, "Revolutsionnoe dvizhenie i oppozitsionnye krugi russkogo dvorianstva (1818–1821 gg.)," in *Rossiia i Italiia*, 133–37.
191. Koval'skaia, *Dvizhenie karbonariev*, 214, 216.
192. S. G. Volkonskii, *Zapiski* (Irkutsk, 1991), 297–99, 458 n. 418, 459 n. 423. See also Volkonskii, *Zapiski* (St. Petersburg, 1903), 317–18; Semevskii, *Politicheskie i obshchestvennye idei*, 248. Liprandi later abandoned whatever radicalism he had in 1820 when he infiltrated the Petrashevsky circle as a tsarist spy in 1848–49. *VD*, VIII:343.
193. Druzhinin, *Dekabrist Nikita Murav'ev*, 113.
194. [M. A. Fonvizin], "Zapiski dekabrista, 1823 g," *GM* 10 (1916): 144.
195. Koval'skaia, "Ital'ianskie karbonarii," 86.
196. Ibid., 90.
197. *RA* 12 (1875): 401.
198. L. A. Medvedskaia, *Sergei Ivanovich Murav'ev-Apostol* (Moscow, 1970), 45–46 (ellipses hers).
199. Theophilus Prousis, *Russian Society and the Greek Revolution* (DeKalb, 1994), 26–54. (Khomyiakov, 53; Bulgarin, 36); Koval'skaia, *Dvizhenie karbonariev*, 205.
200. Dostian, *Russkaia obshchestvennaia mysl'*, 232–33.
201. Prousis, *Russian Society*, 41, 45 and passim; I. F. Iovva, *Iuzhnye dekabristy i grecheskoe natsional'no-osvoboditel'noe dvizhenie* (Kishinev, 1963), 18–41; Janusz Strasburger, "Le Philhellénisme en Pologne aux années de l'insurrection grecque, 1821–1828," *BS* XII, no. 1 (1974): 107.
202. Wortman, *Scenarios of Power* (2006), 119.
203. Prousis, *Russian Society*, 98–101 and 103–34; Irina Dostian, "L'attitude de la société russe face au mouvement de libération national grec," in *Les relations gréco-russes pendant la domination turque et la guerre d'indépendance grecque* (Thessaloniki, 1983), 77.
204. Demetrios Farsolas, "Alexander Pushkin: His Attitude toward the Greek Revolution, 1821–1829," *BS* XII, no. 1 (1971): 62–77; Prousis, *Russian Society*, 135–58. See also Dostian, "L'attitude de la société russe," 67, for other philhellene voices.
205. Vil'gel'm Kiukhel'beker, *Stikhotvoreniia* (Leningrad, 1952), 106; Prousis, *Russian Society*, 112–13.

206. Ryleev, *PSS*, 240–41.
207. Semevskii, *Politicheskie i obshchestvennye idei*, 254.
208. Dostian, "L'attitude de la société russe," 67 (Basargin); Prousis, *Russian Society*, 115, 109 (Küchelbecker and Glinka); Ol'ga Orlik, *Dekabristy i vneshniaia politika Rossii* (Moscow, 1984), 92 (Turgenev). See also S. I. Kolmykov, "Deiateli russkoi kultury o natsional'no-osvoboditel'noi bor'be grecheskogo naroda," in Arsh, *Politicheskie sviazi*.
209. Dostian, *Russkaia obshchestvennaia mysl'*, 228.
210. B. E. Syroechkovskii, "Balkanskaia problema v politicheskikh planakh dekabristov," in his *Iz istorii dvizheniia dekabristov* (Moscow, 1969), 274.
211. Dostian, *Russkaia obshchestvennaia mysl*, 224, 231 (qu.).
212. Syroechkovskii, "Balkanskaia problema," 223.
213. M. F. Orlov, *Kapituliatsiia Parizha*, ed. S. Ya. Borovoi and M. I. Gillel'son (Moscow, 1963), 232.
214. N. I. Lorer [Lohrer], "Iz zapisok dekabrista," *RB* 3 (1904): 68.
215. Ryleev, *PSS*, 118.
216. Borozdin, *Iz pisem*, 15, 67.
217. Lunin, *Sochineniia*, 63 (qu.), 75; Dostian, *Russkaia obshchestvennaia mysl'*, 230.
218. Medvedskaia, *Murav'ev-Apostol*, 46–49 (all quotes, ellipses hers), 50. See also Syroechkovskii, "Balkanskaia problema," 240n. and 274.
219. Orlik, *Dekabristy i vneshniaia politika*, 98–101.
220. Semevskii, *Politicheskie i obshchestvennye idei*, 251–53.
221. Dostian, *Russkaia obshchestvennaia mysl'*, 233–52; Orlik, *Dekabristy i vneshniaia politika*, 98–101; O'Meara, *Pestel*, 22–25
222. Orlik, *Dekabristy i vneshniaia politika*, 91–92; Syroechkovskii, "Balkanskaia problema," 186–275 (qu. 273–74, his ellipses).
223. Syroechkovskii, "Balkanskaia problema," 281 (qu.), 282; Varban Todorov, *Greek Federalism During the Nineteenth Century* (Boulder, 1995), 17–18.
224. Dostian, *Russkaia obshchestvennaia mysl'*, 235–36.
225. Syroechkovskii, "Balkanskaia problema."
226. Dostian (Dostian), "L'attitude de la société russe," 70–71.
227. Dodolev, *Rossiia i Ispaniia*, 225.
228. Orlik, *Dekabristy i vneshniaia politika Rossii*, 85.
229. Semevskii, *Politicheskie i obshchestvennye idei*, 255; Iovva, *Iuzhnye dekabristy*, 60–103.
230. Volk, *Istoricheskie vzgliady dekabristov*, 277.
231. Orlik, *Dekabristy i vneshniaia politika*, 94–95. See also Dostian (Dostian), "L'attitude de la société russe," 72–73.
232. Alekseev, "Etiudy," 401.
233. Borozdin, *Iz pisem*, 153.
234. Alekseev, "Etiudy," 405.
235. Orlik, *Dekabristy i evropeiskoe osvoboditel'noe dvizhenie*, 54–57; Dodolev, *Rossiia i Ispaniia*, 194; Schop Soler, *Siglo de relaciones*, 417 and n. 41.
236. Dodolev, *Rossiia i Ispaniia*, 206.
237. Nechkina, *Dvizhenie dekabristov*, I:305–6.
238. Landa, *Dukh revoliutsionnykh preobrazovanii*, 225.
239. Alekseev, "Etiudy," 403; Alekseev, *Ocherki*, 119.
240. Landa, *Dukh revoliutsionnykh preobrazovanii*, 225. See also the brief comments in Alexandre Zviguilsky, "Riego y los masones rusos," in *Ejército, pueblo y Constitución: homenaje al General Rafael del Riego*, ed. Alberto Gil Novales (Madrid, 1987), 272–75.
241. *Pisateli-dekabristy*, II:350–51 n. 5; Dodolev, *Rossiia i Ispaniia*, 210–11.
242. *Nevskii zritel'* I, no. 5 (January 1821): 70–74 (qu. 70).
243. Dodolev, *Rossiia i Ispaniia*, 202.
244. Nechkina, "Dekabristy vo vsemirno-istoricheskom protsesse," *VI* 12 (December 1975): 10.
245. Alekseev, *Ocherki*, 125–26.
246. Dodolev, *Rossiia i Ispaniia*, 200–1 (qu. 200).
247. Juan Van Halen, *Narrative of Don Juan Van Halen's Imprisonment in the Dungeons of the Inquisition at Madrid* (New York, 1828), 299 (qu.), 364.

248. Nechkina, *A. S. Griboedov i dekabristy*, 2d ed. (Moscow, 1951), 208–9; Dodolev, *Rossiia i Ispaniia*, 201–2.
249. Semevskii, "Dekabristy-masony" (May-June 1908), 418–19.
250. Dodolev, *Rossiia i Ispaniia*, 181–82; Nechkina, *Griboedov i dekabristy*, 582 n. 324. See also Dodolev, "Van-Galen v Rossii (1818–1820 gg.)," *ISSSR* 2 (March-April 1980): 145–57; N. Belozerskaia, "Zapiski Van-Galena," *IV* (June 1884), 651–78.
251. Orlik, *Dekabristy i evropeiskoe osvoboditel'noe dvizhenie*, 74.
252. Alekseev, "Etiudy," 403–4.
253. *Pisateli-dekabristy*, II:350 n. 5.
254. Borozdin, *Iz pisem*, 13.
255. Cited in Dodolev, *Rossiia i Ispaniia*, 226.
256. Volk, *Istoricheskie vzgliady dekabristov*, 275.
257. Basargin, *Zapiski*, 25 n. 1, 28 n. 1.
258. *PSS*, 245.
259. Orlov, "Zapiski o tainom obshchestve," in Dovnar-Zapol'skii, *Memuary dekabristov*, I:10.
260. A. S. Gangeblov, "Vospominaniia," *RA* 6 (1886): 181–268.
261. Borozdin, *Iz pisem*, 13.
262. Dovnar-Zapol'skii, *Memuary dekabristov*, I:245.
263. Beliaev, "Vospominaniia o perezhitom i perechuvstvovannom," *RS*, January 1881, 8–10 (qu. 10).
264. Nikolai Grech, *Zapiski moei zhizni* (Moscow, 2002), 330–31 (he has the year wrong); Petrov, *Rossiia i Nikolai I*, 58 n. 1; *Vospominaniia Bestuzhevykh*, ed. M. K. Azadovskii (Moscow, 1951), 597.
265. Poggio in Dovnar-Zapol'skii, *Memuary dekabristov*, I:202–3.
266. De Madariaga, "Spain and the Decembrists," 144–6.
267. Syroechkovskii, "Balkanskaia problema," 292, 293 (qu.).
268. Ibid., 292.
269. Nechkina, *Dvizhenie dekabristov*, I:276–77.
270. *Vospominaniia Bestuzhevykh*, 605–6; O'Meara, *Ryleev*, 111, 137–42; *VD*, II:73. General Batenkov contested Ryleev's Kronstadt plan, preferring an island on the Volkov River or on Lake Ilmen in order to strike at Gruzino, the estate of Count Arakcheev. Petrov, *Rossiia i Nikolai I*, 68 and n. 4.
271. O'Meara, *Ryleev*, 229–36.
272. Keep, *Soldiers of the Tsar*, 268.
273. *New York Review of Books* (June 26, 2008), 44.
274. Raeff, *Decembrist Movement*, 101–3.
275. *Pisateli-dekabristy*, II:103.
276. Semevskii, *Obshchestvennye dvizheniia*, I:488.
277. A. M. Bulatov in Dovnar-Zapol'skii, *Memuary dekabristov*, I:238.
278. O'Meara, *Ryleev*, 195. Though not published or so titled until 1856, the poem circulated among friends. It also headed the proclamation of the radical Nikolai Shelgunov et al., "To the Younger Generation," in 1861: Ryleev, *Stikhotvoreniia, stat'i, ocherki, dokladnye zapiski, pis'ma* (Moscow, 1956), 62, 360–61. The claim made by Alexandre Zviguilsky, "Riego y los masones rusos," in Gil Novales, *Ejército, pueblo, y Constitución*, 273, that Ryleev read out "The Citizen" on Senate Square that day has no basis in fact.
279. Natan Eidel'man, *Apostol Sergei* (Moscow, 1975).
280. Luciani, *La Société des Slaves Unis*, 161–62 and n.
281. Medvedskaia, *Murav'ev-Apostol*, 7–12; M. I. Murav'ev-Apostol, *Vospominaniia i pis'ma*, ed. S. Ya. Shtraikh (Petrograd, 1922), 26. This corrects the errors in Mikhail Balas, "S. Murav'ev-Apostol," *RS* 5 (1873): 653–76, but has its own fraternal bias and errors. On the father, see also Andreas Schönle, *Authenticity and Fiction in the Russian Literary Journey, 1790–1840* (Cambridge, Mass., 2000), 144–57.
282. P. E. Shchegolev, "Katekhizis Sergeia Murav'eva-Apostola," in his *Istoricheskie etiudy* (St. Petersburg, 1913), 337.
283. A. I. Mikhailovskii-Danilevskii, "Vstuplenie na prestol Imperatora Nikolaia I," *RS*, November 1890, 496.

284. Medvedskaia, *Murav'ev-Apostol*, 13–14.
285. Ibid., 15–20.
286. Shchegolev, "Katekhizis," 332.
287. "Bunt chernigovskogo polka," *RA* 1 (1871): 259, 261, 283.
288. Medvedskaia, *Murav'ev-Apostol*, 21–24; L. N. Tolstoi, "Stydno," in *PSS* (Moscow, 1928–58), XXXI:72–77, 277–78.
289. Eidel'man, "K biografii Sergeia Ivanovicha Murav'eva-Apostola," in *Iz potaennoi istorii Rossii XVIII-XIX vekov* (Moscow, 1993), 363.
290. Vigel', *Zapiski*, 421.
291. Medvedskaia, *Murav'ev-Apostol*, 26–38.
292. E. P. Machul'skii, "Novye dannye o biografii dekabrista M. P. Bestuzheva-Riumina," *IZ* 96 (1975): 347–58 (qu. 349).
293. *VD*, IX:44; Porokh, "Vosstanie chernigovskogo polka," 128–29.
294. Medvedskaia, *Murav'ev-Apostol*, 86–87.
295. Ibid., 110; O'Meara, *Pestel*, 147–48.
296. Nechkina, *Dvizhenie dekabristov*, II:25.
297. Medvedskaia, *Murav'ev-Apostol*, 88.
298. *VD*, IV:349–51.
299. Medvedskaia, *Murav'ev-Apostol*, 88.
300. Borisov in *VD*, V:62.
301. Gorbachevskii, *Zapiski* (1916), 39 (qu.), 40. The "Gorbachevskii" memoirs probably were written or written down by Peter Borisov, though there have other candidates. This does not change their value as a source for some events, though they must be treated gingerly. The work is partly memoir and partly, including on the January events, based on accounts of other participants, with elements of literary license. Nechkina, *Dvizhenie dekabristov*, II:135–40 and 467 n.7; Gorbachevskii, *Zapiski, pis'ma*, ed. B. E. Syroechkovskii (Moscow, 1963), 257–58. I shall cite him as the author in order to avoid recurrent confusion.
302. Gorbachevskii, *Zapiski* (1916), 40; Gorbachevskii, *Zapiski*, 2d ed., ed. B. E. Syroechkovskii (Moscow, 1925), 789 and n. 1.
303. Gorbachevskii, *Zapiski, pis'ma* (1963), 26, 312 n. 14; and Nechkina, *Dvizhenie dekabristov*, II:161–62, 470 nn. 58 and 59.
304. Gorbachevskii, *Zapiski* (1925), 59 (qu.). See also Porokh, "Vosstanie Chernigovskogo polka," 141–49.
305. Nechkina, "Revoliutsiia napodobie ispanskoi," 24.
306. *VD*, V:63.
307. Porokh, "Vosstanie Chernigovskogo polka," 141–9.
308. Luciani, *La Société des Slaves Unis*, 46–49.
309. Gorbachevskii, *Zapiski* (1916), 45–46.
310. Nechkina, "Revoliutsiia napodobie ispanskoi," *KiS* 10 (1931): 3.
311. Gorbachevskii, *Zapiski dekabrista* (1916), 53 n. 1.
312. Gorbachevskii, *Zapiski* (1916), 46 (see also 1963 ed., 313 n. 16).
313. Nechkina, "Revoliutsiia napodobie ispanskoi," 19.
314. Comment by Syroechkovskii, partly based on the testimony of the police spy Maiboroda, in Gorbachevskii, *Zapiski i pis'ma* (1963), 312–13 n. 16.
315. Kiianskaia, *Iuzhnyi bunt: vosstanie Chernigovskogo pekhotnogo polka* (Moscow, 1997), 56, 59.
316. Medvedskaia, *Murav'ev-Apostol*, 85, 110.
317. Semevskii, "Volnenie v Semenovskom Polku," 92.
318. *VD*, VII:153–56 (qu. 153).
319. Nechkina, "Revoliutsiia napodobie ispanskoi," 26.
320. Gorbachevskii, *Zapiski* (1916), 45–48 (qu. 46, 47).
321. As on many issues, the Biblical references to monarchy contain conflicting views: see Baruch Halpern, "Kingship and Monarchy," in Bruce Metzger and Michael Coogan, eds., *The Oxford Companion to the Bible* (New York, 1993), 413–16.
322. Gorbachevskii, *Zapiski* (1916), 46–48.
323. Shchegolev, "Katekhizis," 335 (qu.), 336.

324. Gorbachevskii, *Zapiski* (1916), 42–44 (qu. 43); see also Luciani, *Société des Slaves Unis*, 182–94 for the Leshchin meetings.

325. *Khristianskii Katikhizis: pravoslavnyia kafolicheskiia vostochnyia greko-rossiiskiia tserkvi*, 3d ed. (Moscow, 1824), 1–8 and passim.

326. *The Doctrine of the Russian Church*, tr. R. W. Blackmore. (Aberdeen, 1845), 15–27 (p. 26 qu.).

327. *VD*, I:176.

328. O'Meara, *Ryleev*, 201; Borozdin, *Iz pisem*, 175. The Spanish *Civil Catechism, or a Brief Summary of the Duties of the Spaniard* inspired the fifteen-year-old Wilhelm Küchelbecker's *Symbol of a Russian's Political Faith* (Simvol politicheskoi very russkogo). Orlik, *Dekabristy i evropeiskoe osvoboditel'noe dvizhenie*, 20.

329. Shchegolev, "Katekhizis," 324–27. See commentary in Dovnar-Zapol'skii, *Idealy dekabristov*, 303–6 (qu. 304, 305).

330. *Catecismo político para instrucción del pueblo español* (Cadiz, 1810), in Alfonso Capitán Díaz, *Los catecismos políticos en España, 1808–1822* (Granada, 1978), 114, 127 (qu.), 129.

331. Minaeva, "K voprosu ob ideinykh sviaziakh," 72. I. V. Karatsuba highlights the parallels between "Curious Conversation" and the Orthodox Catechism: "Pravoslavnyi katekhizis S. I. Murav'eva-Apostola: kommentarii," in *Dekabristy: aktual'nye problemy i novye podkhody*, ed. Oksana Kiianskaia (Moscow, 2008), 460–76.

332. A. Trachevskii, *Ispaniia deviatnadtsatago veka* (Moscow, 1872), 152.

333. See chapter 2 for documentation.

334. G. I. Revzin, *Riego* (Moscow, 1939), 189–90.

335. Testimony in *VD*, IX:60.

336. Petrov, *Rossiia i Nikolai I*, 69 n. 1. For variants and the Russo-German context of Ernst Moritz Arndt's *Short Catechism for German Soldiers* published in St. Petersburg in 1812, see Emilie Delivré, "The Pen and the Sword: Political Catechisms and the Resistance to Napoleon," in *Popular Resistance in the French Wars: Patriots, Partisans, and Land Pirates*, ed. Charles Esdaile (London, 2005), 167–69.

337. *VD*, IX:60; Shchegolev "Katekhizis," 347; Medvedskaia, *Murav'ev-Apostol*, 160.

338. Shchegolev "Katekhizis," 353–56.

339. *Khristianskii Katikhizis*, 6.

340. Philip Pomper, *Sergei Nechaev* (New Brunswick, 1979), 87–93.

341. B. B. Glinskii, *Borba za konstitutsiiu, 1612–1861 gg.* (St. Petersburg, 1908), 191–94.

342. Mazour, *First Russian Revolution*, 186 n. 29.

343. *VD*, IX:202, 229; Shchegolev "Katekhizis," 338–42. Shchegolev singled out the novel as the model and quoted several pages from it. But he wrongly quoted Trachevskii's potpourri as a genuine Spanish catechism.

344. Nechkina, *Dvizhenie dekabristov*, II:367. This did not contradict her original 1931 formulation of a Russian revolt "in the Spanish manner"–i. e., a bloodless military operation: "Revoliutsiia napodobie ispanskoi."

345. Yu. G. Oksman, "Vosstanie Chernigovskogo polka," *VD*, VI:lii–liii n. 1. Some of the teaching materials he cites appeared after the Decembrist revolt.

346. Medvedskaia, *Murav'ev-Apostol*, 148–56; Nechkina, *Dvizhenie dekabristov*, II:352. For the chronology of late December, early January, I have relied on the treatment in Nechkina, *Dvizhenie dekabristov*, II:345–78 and cited her only for particular arguments or emphases.

347. Kiianskaia, "K istorii vosstaniia Chernigovskogo polka," *OI* 6 (1995): 21–33. M. I. Murav'ev-Apostol, though not present, denies that this happened and also claimed that Goebel was hated by the soldiers, a disputed claim: *Vospominaniia*, 52.

348. Lieutenant I. I. Sukhinov acted the tough cop to the more lenient Murav'ev. When after Goebel was recaptured, some unruly men in the ranks attempted to kill him and his wife and children, Sukhinov promised death to any who violated discipline—including deserters: Gorbachevskii, *Zapiski i pis'ma* (1963), 67; Nechkina, *Dvizhenie dekabristov*, II:362–65.

349. Medvedskaia, *Murav'ev-Apostol*, 35–36, 69.

350. *VD*, VI:140.

351. Shchegolev, "Katekhizis," 346–47; *VD*, IV:310–311; and *VD*, VI:278–89.

352. Eidel'man, *Apostol Sergei*, 250.
353. Gorbachevskii, *Zapiski* (1916), 123 (qu.); *VD*, VI:298–300 (Keizer's version); Shchegolev "Katekhizis," 348. Nechkina, *Dvizhenie dekabristov*, II:371, argued that the money was for a cart to take the priest along on the march.
354. *Sokrashchennyi Katikhizis dlia obucheniia iunoshestva Pravoslavnomu zakonu Khristianskomu* (St. Petersburg, 1818).
355. *VD*, VI:298–99; Shchegolev "Katekhizis," 349–50.
356. Gorbachevskii, *Zapiski* (1916), 124.
357. *VD*, VI:299 (Keizer); Shchegolev "Katekhizis," 350–51; Balas, "Murav'ev-Apostol," 671. Details vary. Keizer, for his participation in these events, was later stripped of his status as a noble, defrocked, and sentenced to various terms of hard labor and detention. Shchegolev, "Katekhizis," 360–63.
358. Shchegolev, "Katekhizis," 351.
359. Gorbachevskii, *Zapiski* (1916), 124–25. Nor was Borisov, the probable author or compiler.
360. Testimony in *RA* 6 (1902): 296.
361. See Appendix below for the document; also Porokh, "Vosstanie Chernigovskogo polka," 170–71 n. 4.
362. *VD*, VI:295; Shchegolev, "Katekhizis," 352.
363. *VD*, VI:296; Shchegolev "Katekhizis," 351.
364. Gorbachevskii, *Zapiski* (1916), 125. The veteran recalled that a drunken soldier asked him who was being sworn to. When the lieutenant moved on, the soldier shouted "now [we have] freedom [*vol'nost'*]." Shchegolev "Katekhizis," 352. *Vol'nost'*, a kind of personal freedom, stands somewhere between *svoboda*, often implying political liberty, and *volia*—a popular term for untrammeled license.
365. "Bunt chernigovskogo polka," 282.
366. Shchegolev, "Katekhizis," 345 and note 1; Gorbachevskii, *Zapiski* (1916), 124–26.
367. Eidel'man, *Apostol Sergei*, 253; Nechkina, *Dvizhenie dekabristov*, II:371.
368. "Bunt chernigovskogo polka," 264.
369. Porokh, "Vosstanie Chernigovskogo polka," 170.
370. Nechkina, *Dvizhenie dekabristov*, II:371–72.
371. Nechkina, *Dvizhenie dekabristov*, II:372; Shchegolev, "Katekhizis," 359.
372. *VD*, VI:146.
373. Gorbachevskii, *Zapiski* (1916), 125; "Bunt chernigovskogo polka," 271.
374. Medvedskaia, *Murav'ev-Apostol*, 163.
375. Gorbachevskii, *Zapiski i pis'ma* (1963), 319 n. 42.
376. Gorbachevskii, *Zapiski* (1916), 138–39. Another version: "God help him who does his best for us." Nechkina, *Dvizhenie dekabristov*, II:373.
377. Medvedskaia, *Murav'ev-Apostol*, 162–63.
378. "Bunt chernigovskogo polka," 286–87.
379. Nechkina, *Dvizhenie dekabristov*, II:373; *VD*, VI:339.
380. A. I. Mikhailovskii-Danilevskii, "Vstuplenie na prestol Imperatora Nikolaia I," 495–96; Ikonnikov, *Krest'ianskoe dvizhenie*, 31.
381. Kiianskaia, *Iuzhnyi bunt*, 98–112; Kiianskaia, "K istorii vosstaniia Chernigovskogo polka," 24–28.
382. For just two examples from the rosier side: "Bunt chernigovskogo polka," 261; Porokh, "Vosstanie Chernigovskogo polka," 174. For the corrective: see Kiianskaia, "K istorii vosstaniia Chernigovskogo polka," and her *Iuzhnyi bunt*.
383. Nechkina, *Dvizhenie dekabristov*, II:377.
384. "Bunt chernigovskogo polka," 275, 286.
385. Eidel'man, *Apostol Sergei*, 252.
386. Eidelman, *Conspiracy Against the Tsar*, 63.
387. Ikonnikov, *Krest'ianskoe dvizhenie*, 30–31.
388. "Bunt chernigovskogo polka," 287.
389. Mazour, *First Russian Revolution*, 199; Nechkina, *Dvizhenie dekabristov*, II:369–70.
390. Medvedskaia, *Murav'ev-Apostol*, 159.
391. S. Bersenev [Mariya Yakhontova], *Sergei Ivanovich Murav'ev-Apostol* (Moscow, 1920), 5.

392. Medvedskaia, *Murav'ev-Apostol*, 49–50.

393. I. I. Fomin, ed., *Sobranie stikhotvorenii dekabristov* (Moscow, 1906–7), II:177 and n. 1.

394. Second draft, chapter II, article 37 in Druzhinin, *Dekabrist Nikita Murav'ev*, 325.

395. Raeff, *Decembrist Movement*, 163.

396. Patrick O'Meara, "*Vreden sever*: The Decembrists' Memories of the Peter-Paul Fortress," in *St. Petersburg, 1703–1825*, ed. Anthony Cross (London, 2003), 186 n.15.

397. O'Meara, "*Vreden sever*," 168.

398. Beliaev, "Vospominaniia o perezhitom i perechuvstvovannom," *RS*, March 1881, 488.

399. Lorer, "Iz zapisok dekabrista," 92.

400. *Pisateli-dekabristy*, I:92–111 and passim.

401. *Vospominaniia Bestuzhevykh*, 113, 430, 451, 651, 659, 664, 712–13 n. 113, and "My Prisons" (Moi tiurmy): 51–124.

402. *Pisateli-dekabristy*, I:93.

403. Kjeld Winding, *Danmarks Historie* (Copenhagen, 1967), 141–43; Eidelman, *Conspiracy Against the Tsar*, 18–19; Lunin, *Sochineniia*.

404. Lunin, *Pis'ma iz Siberi*, ed. I. A. Zhelvakova and N. Ya. Eidel'man (Moscow, 1967), 257; Ann Radcliffe, *The Mysteries of Udolpho: A Romance* (1794; London, 2001).

405. Semevskii, *Obshchestvennye dvizheniia*, 460.

406. Nechkina, *Dvizhenie dekabristov*, II:285.

407. Dovnar-Zapol'skii, *Memuary dekabristov*, I:245. On the concept of honor and suicide, see Morrissey, *Suicide*, 60. Ivan Bogdanovich shot himself on December 15 for not having done enough for the rebels on Senate Square the day before: Morrissey, *Suicide*, 59; Nechkina, *Dvizhenie dekabristov*, II:266.

408. Eidelman, *Conspiracy Against the Tsar*, 78.

409. O'Meara, *Ryleev*, 249; Beliaev, "Vospominaniia o perezhitom i perechuvstvovannom," *RS*, March 1881, 507.

410. O'Meara, *Pestel*, 40, 172–73, 175–76.

411. N. M. Lebedev, *Pestel': ideolog i rukovoditel' dekabristov* (Moscow, 1972), 156–57.

412. P. N. Myslovskii, "Iz zapisnoi knizhki," *RA*, IX (1905), 132–33.

413. O'Meara, *Pestel*, 176.

414. Myslovskii, "Iz zapisnoi knizhki," 133. If the story is true, did the Orthodox priest bless Pestel and thus win another soul for his branch of Christianity?

415. A. I. Gertsen, *Sobranie sochinenii* (Moscow, 1954–65), XVI:282. This dubious story originated with an officer who had convoyed Murav'ev-Apostol to Petersburg. Commentary: Eidel'man, "K biografii Sergeia Ivanovicha Murav'eva-Apostola," 366; S. E. Erlikh, *Istoriia mifa: "Dekabristkaia legenda" Gertsena* (St. Petersburg, 2006), 211.

416. Eidel'man, "K biografii Sergeia Ivanovicha Murav'eva-Apostola," 367–68.

417. Kiianskaia, "K istorii vosstaniia Chernigovskogo polka," 31.

418. Medvedskaia, *Murav'ev-Apostol*, 170–71.

419. I. M. Murav'ev-Apostol, *Pis'ma iz Moskvy v Nizhnii Novgorod*, ed. V. A. Koshelev (St. Petersburg, 2002), 228.

420. Balas, "Murav'ev-Apostol," 675.

421. I. M. Murav'ev-Apostol, *Pis'ma iz Moskvy*, 228–30.

422. O'Meara, *Pestel*, 6.

423. Keep, *Soldiers of the Tsar*, 260–61.

424. For the tsar's penchant for weeping, see Wortman, *Scenarios of Power*.

425. Raeff, *Decembrist Movement*, 167–68.

426. Zetlin, *Decembrists*, 259.

427. Petrov, *Rossiia i Nikolai I*, 75–76 n. 1; N. K. Shil'der, *Imperator Nikolia Pervyi, ego zhizn' i tsarstvovanie* (St. Petersburg, 1903), I:340–43 (qu. 341).

428. Zetlin, *Decembrists*, 231.

429. Mikhailovskii-Danilevskii, "Vstuplenie na prestol Imperatora Nikolaia I," 498.

430. Grech, *Zapiski*, 331, 34–35.

431. Fomin, *Sobranie stikhotvorenii dekabristov*, II:10–11.

432. O'Meara, *Pestel*, 210 n. 31.

433. Ibid., 179; Semevskii, *Obshchestvennye dvizheniia*, 460.

434. Gorbachevskii, *Zapiski* (1916), 44 n.1.
435. Myslovskii, "Iz zapisnoi knizhki," 133.
436. Balas, "Murav'ev-Apostol," 676.
437. The report of Sand's beheading had appeared in *VE*, II (1820), cited in Orlik, *Dekabristy i evropeiskoe osvoboditel'noe dvizhenie*, 51.
438. Erlikh, *Istoriia mifa*, 214; O'Meara, *Pestel*, 180; O'Meara, *Ryleev*, 304–6.
439. Zetlin, *Decembrists*, 277.
440. Borozdin, *Iz pisem*, 87–88. The word *vozzvanie*, though literally meaning "appeal" or "calling forth," has the same force as "pronunciamento" or "proclamation."

Chapter 6

1. Cited in Thomas Steele, *Notes on the War in Spain* (London, 1824), 252–55.
2. Zefirro Ciuffoletti and Luigi Mascilli Migliorini, "Il mito della Grecia tra politica e letteratura" in *Indipendenza e unità nazionale in Italia ed in Grecia* (Florence, 1987), 50.
3. Evgenii Tarle cited in K. F. Miziano [C. F. Misiano], "Ital'ianskoe Risordzhimento i peredovoe obshchestvennoe dvizhenie v Rossii XIX veka," in *Rossiia i Italiia: iz istorii russko-ital'ianskikh kul'turnykh i obshchestvennykh otnoshenii* (Moscow, 1968), 97.
4. Ol'ga Orlik, *Dekabristy i evropeiskoe osvoboditel'noe dvizhenie* (Moscow, 1975), 74.
5. Report of March 1826 by a Russian diplomat, in V. I. Semevskii, "Dekabristy-masony," *Minuvshie gody* (May-June, 1906), 424.
6. Frédéric François Guillaume Vaudoncourt, *Letters on the Internal Political State of Spain During the Years 1821, 22, & 23*, 2d ed. (London, 1824), 241.
7. Margaret Macmillan, *Paris 1919* (New York, 2003), 348, 352.
8. Marion Sarafis, "Ejército, Constitución y Pueblo en Grecia," in *Ejército, pueblo y Constitución: homenaje al General Rafael del Riego*, ed. Alberto Gil Novales (Madrid, 1987), 560–70.
9. Basil Laourdas, "Modern Greek Historical Novels," *BS* VI, no. 1 (1965): 55–66.
10. Georges Margaritis, "La présence de la Révolution française dans la Grèce occupée, 1941–44: images, symboles et fonctions," in *Révolution française et l'hellénisme moderne* (Athens, 1989), 587–93.
11. Mark Mazower, *Inside Hitler's Greece: the Experience of Occupation, 1941–44* (New Haven, 1995), 93–94 (qu.), 277, 310–31.
12. Grigorii Arsh, "On the Life in Russia of the Greek Patriotic Family of Ypsilanti," *BS* XXVI, no. 1 (1985)" 90.
13. My thanks to Onur İşçi of Georgetown University for researching Turkish sources.
14. Luigi Salvatorelli, *The Risorgimento: Thought and Action*, tr. M. Domandi (1943; New York, 1970), 80.
15. Aurelio Lepre, *La rivoluzione napoletana del 1820–1821* (Rome, 1967), 307.
16. Alberto Banti, *La nazione del Risorgimento: parentela, santità e onore alle origini dell'Italia unita* (Turin, 2000); see also Lucy Riall, *Garibaldi: Invention of a Hero* (New Haven: 2007), 137.
17. *La lunga vita de Marianna Ucrìa* (Milan, 1990), tr. as *The Silent Duchess* by D. Kitto and E. Spottiswood (New York, 1998).
18. *Vanina Vanini* (Stendhal; Roberto Rosselini, 1961, Balzac Video).
19. Antonio Morelli, *Michele Morelli e la rivoluzione napoletana del 1820–1821*, 2d ed. (Rome, 1969), 97, 171–74, 241, 256.
20. Margaret Wicks, *The Italian Exiles in London, 1816–1848* (1937; Freeport, New York, 1968), 72.
21. *LUI*, XVI:427–28; Nino Cortese, *Il mezzogiorno ed il Risorgimento italiano* (Naples, 1965), 70.
22. Cortese, *Mezzogiorno ed il Risorgimento*, 276–77.
23. Vittorio Scotti Douglas, "La constitución de Cádiz y las revoluciones italianas en Turin y Nápoles de 1820 y 1821," in *La revolución liberal*, ed. Alberto Gil Novales (Madrid, 2001), 260.
24. Cited in Miziano, "Ital'ianskoe Risordzhimento," 106.
25. Adam Zamoyski, *Holy Madness: Romantics, Patriots, and Revolutionaries, 1776–1871* (New York, 2001), 320 and passim.

26. Peter Christoff, *I. V. Kireevskij* (The Hague, 1961); and his *A. S. Khomjakov* (The Hague, 1961), 28 and n. 12; Abbott Gleason, *European and Muscovite: Ivan Kireevsky and the Origins of Slavophilism* (Cambridge, Mass., 1972), 41–42.

27. Anatole Mazour, *Women in Exile: Wives of the Decembrists* (Tallahassee, 1975).

28. I. I. Fomin, ed. *Sobranie stikhotvorenii dekabristov* (Moscow, 1906–1907), I:211–12. Tr. Valentine Snow in Marc Raeff, *The Decembrist Movement* (Englewood Cliffs, 1966), 179.

29. S. E. Erlikh, *Istoriia mifa: "Dekabristkaia legenda Gertsena"* (St. Petersburg, 2006).

30. Kathryn Feuer, *Tolstoy and the Genesis of War and Peace*, ed. Robin Feuer Miller and Donna Orwin (Ithaca, 1996).

31. K. S. Gorbachevich and E. P. Khablo, *Pochemu tak nazvany?* (Leningrad, 1967), 89–90, 254, 261, 403.

32. Franco Venturi, "The Army and Freedom: Alexander Poggio and the Decembrists," in *Studies in Free Russia*, tr. F. S. Walsby and M. O'Dell (Chicago, 1982), 133, n. 11.

33. Sandra Pujals, "When Giants Walked the Earth: The Society of Former Political Prisoners and Exiles of the Soviet Union, 1921–1935," Ph.D. dissertation, Georgetown University, 1999.

34. L. F. Katsis, "Dekabrist v kino i v povsedenevnoi zhizni," in *Dekabristy: aktual'nye problemy i novye podkhody*, ed. Oksana Kiianskaia (Moscow, 2008), 620–36. The film title is *SVD (Soyuz Velikogo Dela)*.

35. Cited in Antony Beevor, *Berlin: The Downfall* (London, 2004), 422. See also Catherine Merridale, *Ivan's War: Life and Death in the Red Army, 1939–1945* (New York, 2006).

36. Vladislav Zubok, *Zhivago's Children: The Last Russian Intelligentsia* (Cambridge, Mass., 2009), 30, 287–88, 293, 327.

37. Neil Edmunds, "Classical Music" (ms.).

38. Yuri Shaporin, *The Decembrists* (CD, Freiser Records, Mono 90574). First performance reviewed by E. Grosheva, "Dekabristy (opera Iu. Shaporina)," *Sovetskaia muzyka* 8 (August 1953): 9–18.

39. M. V. Nechkina, *Dvizhenie dekabristov: ukazatel' literatury, 1928–1959* (Moscow, 1960) and *Dvizhenie dekabristov: ukazatel' literatury, 1960–1976* (Moscow, 1983).

40. B. N. Mironov, in a review of Erlikh, *Istoriia mifa* in *VI* 6 (June 2006): 170. For a compact and informative treatment of Soviet historiography, see Kiianskaia, *Iuzhnyi bunt: vosstanie Chernigovskogo pekhotnogo polka* (Moscow, 1997), 7–25.

41. Patrick O'Meara in *Kritika* 7, no. 3 (2006): 619–32.

42. Kiianskaia, "K istorii vosstaniia Chernigovskogo polka," *OI* 6 (1995): 21 (qu.) and her *Iuzhnyi bunt*, 118. See her edited book *Dekabristy*. Additional current scholarship is in the periodical *14 Dekabria* (1997–).

43. Erlikh, *Istoriia mifa*; see esp. 131–35. See also Patrick O'Meara's review of another Erlikh book on the same subject, *Rossiia koldunov*, in *SEER* 84, no. 4 (2006): 764–65.

44. Mironov, review of Erlikh in *VI* 6 (2006): 170–72 (qu. 172).

45. Erlikh, "Dekabristy.ru: istoriia v kiberprostranstve," in Kiianskaia, *Dekabristy*, 550–619.

46. A. P. Kovaleva, "Soslagatel'noe naklonenie v 'dele dekabristov': obzor sovremennykh po alternativnoi istorii sobytii 1825–1826 gg.," in *14 Dekabria* VII (2005): 553–72.

47. "Fantasticheskii 1826–oi," in *Apostol Sergei* (Moscow), 255–64.

48. *1825: Zagovor* (Moscow, 1990); Robert Fassier, *Les Décémbristes: les sociétés secrètes militaires et la naissance du mouvement révolutionnaire russe*, 2 vols. (Poisy, 2006).

49. V. S. Ikonnikov, *Krest'ianskoe dvizhenie v Kievskoi gub. v 1826–27 gg. v sviazi s sobytiiami togo vremeni* (St. Petersburg, 1905), 54–78 (qu. 61).

50. "Pamiat' v narode o dekabristkikh sobytiiakh 1825 g. v Vasil'kove," *Ukrainskaia zhizn'* 1 (1914): 90.

51. M. P. Alekseev, *Ocherki istorii ispano-russikikh literaturnykh otnoshenii XVI–XIX vv.* (Leningrad, 1964), 127, 137–38.

52. N. Nevedomskii, "Tri poslednie glavy iz istorii gveril'iasov," *Sovremennik*, XXVII (1842): 47.

53. E. V. Tarle, "Voennaia revoliutsiia na zapade Evropy i dekabristy," in *Sochineniia* (Moscow, 1957–62), V:9–20 and passim.

54. Blaquiere, introduction to Giuseppe Pecchio, *Journal of Military and Political Events in Spain During the Last Twelve Months*, tr. Edward Blaquiere (London, 1824), iii–xii (qu. viii).

55. Robert Hughes, *Goya* (London, 2003), 379.

56. Francisco Tuero Bertrand, *Riego: proceso a un liberal* (Oviedo, 1995), 101–3; Alberto Gil Novales, "Fama," in *Ejército, pueblo, y Constitución*, ed. Gil Novales 365–72; Alberto Gil Novales, *El trienio liberal* (Madrid, 1980), 128–29.

57. Raymond Carr, *Spain, 1808–1975*, 2d ed. (Oxford, 1982), 185.

58. *Causa formada en octubre de 1823 a virtud de órden de la Regencia por el señor alcalde Don Alfonso de Cavía contra Don Rafael del Riego*, 2d ed. (Madrid, 1835), 107–9.

59. Eugenia Astur, *Riego: estudio istórico-político de la Revolución del año veinte* (Oviedo, 1984), 525.

60. Gonzalo Butrón Prida, "Fiesta y revolución: las celebraciones políticas en el Cádiz liberal, 1812–1837," in *Revolución liberal*, ed. Gil Novales, 159, 167–68.

61. Antonio Benigno de Cabrera and Romualdo de Lafuente, *El triunfo del Pueblo libre en 1820* (Madrid, 1856), 8–9 (qu.), 15, and passim. The play premiered at the Teatro de Variedades in Madrid on January 5, 1856. Tuero Bertrand, *Riego*, 109.

62. Benigno de Cabrera, *Triunfo del Pueblo*, 88 and passim.

63. Riall, *Garibaldi*, 26–27.

64. Joaquin Costa, *Historia crítica de la revolución española*, ed. A. Gil Novales (Madrid, 1992), 36–37, 193 (qu.), 201–5.

65. Gil Novales, "Fama," 365–72.

66. Francisco Domingo Román Ojeda, *Riego: "Héroe de Las Cabezas"* (Las Cabezas de San Juan, 1985), 203.

67. Fernán Caballero, *Un servilón y un liberalito* (1855; Puerto de Santa María, 1976), 33. See also Lawrence Kibbe, *Fernán Caballero* (New York, 1973).

68. Pío Baroja, *Los caminos del mundo: novela* (1914; Barcelona, 1967), 25–26.

69. Tuero Bertrand, *Riego*, 44; see pp. 89–107 for a review of the legends and debates. See also Ojeda, *Riego*, 218–24 and passim; Ginés Alberola, *Don Rafael del Riego, 1820–1823: centenario glorioso* (n.p., 1927), 6.

70. S. Cánovas Cervantes, *El pronunciamiento de Riego: otra vez la constitución de 1812* (Madrid, 1930).

71. Gil Novales, "Fama," 374–83 (qu. 382 n. 62).

72. Diego San José, *Martirologio fernandino: victimas y verdugos del absolutismo, 1814–1833* (Madrid, 1931).

73. *Gloriosa vida y desdichada muerte de Don Rafael del Riego: un crimen de los Borbones* (Madrid, 1931); Maryellen Bieder, "Carmen de Burgos: Modern Spanish Woman," in *Recovering Spain's Feminist Tradition*, ed. Lisa Vollendorf (New York, 1001), 241–59.

74. Astur, *Riego*.

75. Ojeda, *Riego*, 218–24, passim.

76. José Antonio Balbontín, *La Canción de Riego* (Barcelona, 1936), 47. Tuero Bertrand says that it was also performed at the Teatro Chueca in Madrid: *Riego*, 109.

77. Gregorio Marañon, *Españoles fuera de España* (Buenos Aires, 1947), 46–47.

78. Charles Foltz, *The Masquerade in Spain* (Boston, 1948), 164.

79. Paul Preston, *Franco* (London, 1995), 787; Ojeda, *Riego*, 218–24 and passim.

80. *El Trienio liberal* (Madrid, 1980), 3.

81. Gil Novales, "Fama," 365.

82. "Quién fue Riego," in Ojeda, *Riego*, 235–36.

BIBLIOGRAPHY

Abbreviations

ANSSSR Academy of Sciences of the USSR
APS *Atti del Parlamento delle due Sicilie, 1820–1821*
AUC *Anales de la Universidad de Cádiz*
BS *Balkan Studies*
CDF Colección documental del Fraile, Archivo General Militar, Madrid (titles marked *
below come from the Fraile microfilm collection). The indispensable tool for using
this enormous archive is Ana María Freire López, *Índice bibliográfico de la colección
documental del Fraile* (Madrid, 1983)
CDO *Colección de decretos y ordenes de las Cortes de Cádiz.* 4 vols. in 2. Madrid, 1987
CNC Collection of Napoleonic Catechisms at the Bibliothèque des Fontaines
DBTL *Diccionario biográfico de Trienio liberal.* Ed. A. Gil Novales. Madrid: Museo Universal,
1991
EI *Enciclopedia italiana.* 35 vols. Rome, 1929–37
GM *Golos minuvshego*
GDU *Grand dictionnnaire universel*
HAHR *Hispanic American Historical Review*
HDMS *Historical Dictionary of Modern Spain, 1700–1988.* Ed. Robert Kern and Meredith D.
Dodge. Westport, 1990
ISSSR *Istoriia SSSR*
IV *Istoricheskii vestnik*
IZ *Istoricheskie zapiski*
Izd. *Izdatel'stvo*
JMH *Journal of Modern History*
KiS *Katorga i ssylka*
LUI *Lessico universale italiano.* 24 vols. (Rome, 1968–81)
MG *Minuvshie gody*
NYRB *New York Review of Books*
ODNB *The Oxford Dictionary of National Biography.* 60 vols. Oxford: Oxford University
Press, 2004
OI *Otechestvennaia istoriia*
OZ *Otechestvennye zapiski*
PSC *Preliminary Discourse read in the Cortes at the Presentation of the Constitution by the
Committee of the Constitution, to which is added the Present Spanish Constitution.*
London: Pamphleteer, 1823
PSS Pushkin, *Polnoe sobranie sochinenii*

    RA   *Russkii arkhiv*
    RB   *Russkoe bogatsvo*
    RBS   *Russkii biograficheskii slovar'*. 19 vols. St. Petersburg, 1896–1913.
    RGGU   Rossiiskii Gosudarstvennyi Gumanitarnyi Universitet
    RS   *Russkaia starina*
    SO   *Syn otechestva*
    VD   *Vosstanie dekabristov: materialy*. 18 vols. 1925–86.
    VE   *Vestnik Evropy*
    VI   *Voprosy istorii*
    ZhMNP   *Zhurnal Ministerstva Narodnago Prosveshcheniia*

General: Primary Sources

Beethoven, Ludwig van, and Joseph Sonnleithner. *Fidelio*. New York: G. Schirmer, 1935.

Bentham, Jeremy. *Collected Works*. 11 vols. Oxford: Clarendon Press, 1983–2000.

———. *On the Liberty of the Press and Public Discussion*. London: W. Hone, 1821.

Bianchi, Nicomede. *Storia documentata della diplomazia europea in Italia dall'anno 1814 all'anno 1861*. 8 vols. Turin: Unione tipografico, 1865–72.

Blaustein, Alfred, and Jay Sigler, eds. *Constitutions That Made History*. New York: Paragon, 1988.

British and Foreign State Papers, 1821–1822. Vol. IX. London: Harrison, 1829.

British and Foreign State Papers, 1821–1829. Vol. IX. London: Ridgway, 1851.

Byron, Lord. *Childe Harold's Pilgrimage*. Boston: Houghton Mifflin, 1894.

———. *The Complete Poetical and Dramatic Works*. Philadelphia: Claxton, 1883.

Canning, George. *Select Speeches of the Right Honourable George Canning*. Ed. Robert Walsh. Philadelphia: Crissy, 1848.

Carrel, Armand. *Oeuvres politiques et littéraires d'Armand Carrel*. 5 vols. Paris: Chamerot, 1857–59.

Catéchisme à l'usage de toutes les églises de l'Empire français. Paris: Veuve Nyon, 1807, in CNC, 484.

Catéchisme de toutes les eglises de l'Empire français. Clermont: Jacques Veysset, 1806.

Chateaubriand, François Auguste. *Congrès de Vérone. Guerre d'Espagne. Négociations. Colonies espagnoles*. Paris: Delloye, 1838.

Collection of Napoleonic Catechisms at the Bibliothèque des Fontaines on Microfiche, Nos. 471–523.

Constant, Benjamin. *Principles of Politics Applicable to All Governments*. Ed. E. Hoffman. Tr. D. O'Keeffe. Indianapolis: Liberty Fund, 2003.

Diplomatisches Archiv für die Zeit-und Staatengeschichte. 6 vols. Stuttgart, 1821–26.

Lusi, Comte de. *Réflexions sur l'ouvrage de M. de Pradt intitulé: De la révolution actuelle de l'Espagne et de ses suites*. Berlin: Nicolai, 1820.

Memoirs of Prince Metternich, 1815–1829, 3 vols. Ed. R. Metternich. Tr. A. Napier. New York: Fertig, 1970 [1881].

Pellico, Silvio. *Le mie prigioni*. Milan: Lucchi, 1957 [1832].

———. *Moi temnitsy*. St. Petersburg: M. M. Lederle i K, 1894.

———. *My Imprisonments: Memoirs of Silvio Pellico da Saluzzo*. Tr. T. Roscoe. New York: J. & J. Harper, 1833.

Pradt, Dominique de. *Sur l'ouvrage de Mr. De Pradt: L'Europe après le congrès d'Aix-la-Chapelle*. Paris: Béchet, 1819.

———. *Récit historique sur la restauration de la royauté en France: le 31 Mars 1814*. London: J. Booth, 1816.

Pushkin, Alexander. *Eugene Onegin: A Novel in Verse*. Tr. Babette Deutsch. Harmondsworth: Penguin, 1964.

———. *The Letters of Alexander Pushkin*. Tr. J. Thomas Shaw. Madison: University of Wisconsin Press, 1967.

———. *Polnoe sobranie sochinenii*. 10 vols. Moscow: ANSSSR, 1956–58.

Radcliffe, Ann Ward. *The Mysteries of Udolpho: A Romance*. Intro. Jacqueline Howard. London: Penguin, 2001 [1794].

Shelley, Percy. *Essays, Letters from Abroad, Translations and Fragments*. Ed. M. Shelley. 2 vols. London: Moxon, 1852.

Stendhal. *The Charterhouse of Parma*. Tr. Richard Howard. New York: Modern Library, 2000 [1839].

General: Secondary Works

Abensour, Liliane. *Romantisme noir*. Ed. Françoise Charras. Paris: L'Herne, 1978.

Armitage, David. *The Declaration of Independence: A Global History*. Cambridge, MA: Harvard University Press, 2007.

Artz, Frederick. *Reaction and Revolution, 1814–1832*. New York: Harper and Row, 1934.

Backouche, Isabelle. *La monarchie parlementaire, 1815–1848: de Louis XVIII à Louis-Philippe*. Paris: Pygmalion, 2000.

Billington, James. *Fire in the Minds of Men: Origins of the Revolutionary Faith*. New York: Basic Books, 1980.

Brombert, Victor. *The Romantic Prison: The French Tradition*. Princeton: Princeton University Press, 1978.

Caldwell, Ronald, et al., eds. *The Consortium on Revolutionary Europe, 1750–1850*. Tallahassee: Florida State University, Institute on Napoleon and the French Revolution, 1994.

Carnochan, W. B. "The Literature of Confinement." In Norval Morris and D. J. Rothman, eds., *The Oxford History of the Prison*, 427–55. New York: Oxford University Press, 1995.

Carter, Karen. "Creating Catholics: Catechism and Primary Education in Early Modern France." Ph.D. dissertation, Georgetown University, 2006.

Chadwick, Owen. *The Popes and European Revolution*. Oxford: Clarendon Press, 1981.

Cohen, Deborah, and Maura O'Connor, eds. *Comparison and History: Europe in Cross-National Perspective*. New York: Routledge, 2004.

Collins, James. *The State in Early Modern Europe*. 2nd ed. Cambridge: Cambridge University Press, 2009.

Debidour, A. *Le général Fabvier: sa vie militaire et politique*. Paris: Plon-Nourrit, 1904.

Delivré, Emilie. "The Pen and the Sword." In Charles Esdaile, ed., *Popular Resistance in the French Wars: Patriots, Partisans and Land Pirates*, 161–79. Basingstoke: Palgrave Macmillan, 2005.

Esdaile, Charles, ed. *Popular Resistance in the French Wars: Patriots, Partisans, and Land Pirates*. Basingstoke: Palgrave Macmillan, 2005.

———. *The Wars of Napoleon*. London: Longman, 1995.

Fieffé, Eugène. *Histoire des troupes étrangères au service de France*. 2 vols. Paris: Librairie Militaire, 1854.

Furet, François, and Mona Ozouf, eds. *Dictionnaire critique de la Révolution française*. Paris: Flammarion, 1988.

Gaunt, William. *Bandits in a Landscape: A Study of Romantic Painting from Caravaggio to Delacroix*. London: Studio Limited, 1937.

Head, Brian. *Politics and Philosophy in the Thought of Destutt de Tracy*. New York: Garland, 1987.

Herlihy, Patricia. *Odessa: A History, 1794–1914*. Cambridge, MA: Harvard University Press, 1986.

Hobsbawm, Eric. *The Age of Revolution, 1789–1848*. London: Abacus, 2003 [1962].

———. *Bandits*. London: Weidenfeld and Nicolson, 1969.

———. *Primitive Rebels: Studies in Archaic Forms of Social Movement in the 19th and 20th Century*. Manchester: Manchester University Press, 1959.

Holtman, Robert. *The Napoleonic Revolution*. Philadelphia: Lippincott, 1967.

Johnson, Paul. *The Birth of the Modern: World Society, 1815–1830*. London: HarperCollins, 1991.

Kennedy, Emmet. *A Philosophe in the Age of Revolution: Destutt de Tracy and the Origins of "Ideology."* Philadelphia: American Philosophical Society, 1978.

Lauris, George de. *Benjamin Constant et les idées libérales*. Paris: Plon-Nourrit, 1904.

Laven, David, and Lucy Riall, eds. *Napoleon's Legacy: Problems of Government in Restoration Europe*. Oxford: Berg, 2000.

Lévy, Maurice. *Images du roman noir*. Paris: Losfeld, 1973.

Libéralisme chrétien et Catholicisme libéral en Espagne, France, et Italie dans la première moitié du XIXe siècle. Aix-en-Provence: Université de Provence, 1989.

MacKenzie, Norman, ed. *Secret Societies*. London: Aldus, 1967.

Marchand, Leslie. *Byron: A Biography*. 3 vols. London: John Murray, 1957.

Marx, Karl. *On Revolution*. Ed. Saul Padover. New York: McGraw-Hill, 1971.

Mason, H. T., and William Doyle, eds. *The Impact of the French Revolution on European Consciousness*. Gloucester: Sutton, 1989.

May, Arthur. *The Age of Metternich, 1814–1848*. 2nd ed. New York: Holt, Rinehart, and Winston, 1963.

Ozouf, Mona. *Festivals and the French Revolution*. Tr. Alan Sheridan. Cambridge, MA: Harvard University Press, 1988.

Paléologue, Maurice. *Romantisme et diplomatie: Talleyrand, Metternich, Chateaubriand*. Paris: Hachette, 1924.

Palmer, Robert. *The Age of the Democratic Revolution: A Political History of Europe and America, 1760–1800*. 2 vols. Princeton: Princeton University Press, 1959–64.

Parker, Harold. *The Cult of Antiquity and the French Revolutionaries: A Study in the Development of the Revolutionary Spirit*. New York: Octagon Books, 1965 [1937].

Phillips, W. Alison. *The Confederation of Europe*. 2nd ed. London: Longmans, Green, 1920.

Rudé, George. *The Crowd in the French Revolution*. Oxford: Clarendon Press, 1959.

Ruggiero, Guido de. *The History of European Liberalism*. Tr. R. G. Collingwood. Boston: Beacon, 1959.

Schofield, Philip. *Utility and Democracy: The Political Thought of Jeremy Bentham*. Oxford: Oxford University Press, 2006.

Scott, Geoffrey. *The Architecture of Humanism: A Study in the History of Taste*. 2nd ed. New York: Doubleday, 1954 [1924].

Scott, H. M., ed. *The European Nobilities in the Seventeenth and Eighteenth Centuries*. 2 vols. Basingstoke: Palgrave Macmillan, 2007.

Spitzer, Alan. *Old Hatreds and Young Hopes: The French Carbonari Against the Bourbon Restoration*. Cambridge, MA: Harvard University Press, 1971.

Stanley, John. "The Polish Military in the Napoleonic Era." In David Stefancic, ed., *Armies in Exile*, 3–51. Boulder, CO: East European Monographs, 2005.

Stefancic, David, ed. *Armies in Exile*. Boulder, CO: East European Monographs, 2005.

Stephen, Leslie. *The English Utilitarians*. 3 vols. London: Duckworth, 1900.

Tolczyk, Dariusz. "The Politics of Resurrection: Evgeniia Ginzburg, the Romantic Prison, and the Soviet Rhetoric of the Gulag." *Canadian-American Slavic Studies* 39/1 (Spring 2005): 53–70.

Venturi, Franco. "Destutt de Tracy and the Liberal Revolutions." In F. Venturi, *Studies in Free Russia*, 59–93. Chicago: University of Chicago Press, 1982.

Vovelle, Michel, ed. *L'image de la Révolution française*. 4 vols. Paris: Pergamon Press, 1990.

Webster, Charles. *The Foreign Policy of Castlereagh, 1812–1815, Britain and the Reconstruction of Europe*. London: G. Bell and Sons, 1950.

Woloch, Isser, ed. *Revolution and the Meanings of Freedom in the Nineteenth Century*. Stanford: Stanford University Press, 1996.

Wolfe, Alan. *The Future of Liberalism*. New York: Alfred A. Knopf, 2009.

Zamoyski, Adam. *Holy Madness: Romantics, Patriots, and Revolutionaries, 1776–1871*. New York: Penguin, 2001.

Spain: Primary Sources

Arcas, Matías Jorge de. *Memoria sobre la alianza de España con Rusia, y la gratitud que los españoles deben al Emperador Alexandro*. Madrid: F. de la Parte, 1814.

Aviso al verdadero y legítimo pueblo español sobre la conducta de los españoles falsos bastardos ó sea aviso a los blancos sobre el proceder de los negros. Madrid: Martinez Dávila, 1823.

*Balbontin, José Antonio. *La canción de Riego: biografía dramática con un prólogo y tres actos; cada uno de estos dividido en tres cuadros.* Barcelona: Ediciones Borea, 1936.

Baroja, Pío. *Los caminos del mundo: novela.* Barcelona: Planeta, 1967 [1914].

Benigno de Cabrera, Antonio, and Romualdo de Lafuente. *El triunfo del Pueblo libre en 1820.* Madrid: González, 1856.

Bentham, Jeremy. *Declaracion ó protesta de todo individuo del cuerpo legislativo al tomar posesion de su destino.* London: R. Taylor, 1825.

———. *Letters to Count Toreno on the Proposed Penal Code.* London: R. and A. Taylor, 1822.

———. *Plan de provisión de empleos que es el cap. IX del código constitucional.* London: T. C. Hansard, 1825.

———. *Principios que deben servir de guía en la formación de un código constitucional para un estado.* London: R. Taylor, 1824.

———. *Propuesta de código dirigida por Jeremias Bentham a todas las naciones que profesan opiniones liberales.* London: R. and A. Taylor, 1822.

* *La bestia de siete cabezas y diez cuernos, o Napoleon Emperador de los Franceses: exposicion literal del capitulo XIII del apocalipsis.* Málaga: Martìnez, 1808.

Blaquiere, Edward. *An Historical Review of the Spanish Revolution, Including Some Account of Religion, Manners, and Literature, in Spain.* London: Whittaker, 1822.

Borrow, George. *The Bible in Spain.* London: Dent, 1924 [1842].

Caballero, Fernán. *Un servilón y un liberalito.* Puerto de Santa Maria: Casa de la Cultura, 1976 [1855].

Castillo, Ignacio María del. *Exhortación que en la Santa Iglesia Patriarcal de Sevilla hizo a los cuerpos de infanteria y caballeria de la milicia voluntaria local al tiempo de prestar el juramento solemne de defender la constitución.* Seville: Mayor de la Ciudad, 1820.

Catecismo para el uso de todas las iglesias del Imperio Frances. Madrid: Villalpando, 1807.

Circulares de la Junta Provisional de Gobierno de España y Indias. Seville, 1823.

*El C.N.S. y V. *Catecismo liberal y servil.* Segovia, 1814.

Colección de decretos y ordenes de las Cortes de Cádiz. 4 vols. in 2. Madrid: Cortes Generales, 1987. [Includes the constitution of 1812: vol. I/2:104–71.]

Constitución política de la monarquia española promulgada en Cadiz á 19. de Marzo de 1812. Cadiz: Imprenta Real, 1812.

Constitution politique de la monarchie espagnole: publiée à Cadix le 19 mars 1812. Tr. Abbé Vialar. St. Petersburg: Pluchart, 1812.

Custine, Astolphe Marquis de. *L'Espagne sous Ferdinand VII.* 4 vols. Paris: Ladvocat, 1838.

Dufour, Gérard, ed. *Sermones revolucionarios del Trienio liberal, 1820–1823.* Alicante: Instituto de Cultura, 1991.

Españoles. *La Regencia, al encargarse del gobierno de la Monarquía Española.* Cadiz, 1812.

Esteban, Jorge de, ed. *Constituciones españolas y extranjeras.* 2 vols. Madrid: Taurus, 1977.

Ford, Richard. *Gatherings from Spain.* London: Dent, 1906 [1846].

Gallego, Ramón Espinar. *Catecismos politicos Españoles arreglados a las constituciones del siglo XIX.* Madrid: Consejeria de Cultura, 1989.

"Grazhdanskii katekhizis, ili Kratkoe obozrenie dolzhnostei ispantsa." *SO* 2 (October 1812): 53–60.

Haller, Ludwig. *Della costituzione delle cortes di Spagna.* Naples: Porcelli, 1822. [Tr. from a Bern ed. of 1820, written in 1814.]

Hargreaves-Mawdsley, W. N., ed. *Spain Under the Bourbons. 1700–1833: A Collection of Documents.* Columbia: University of South Carolina Press, 1973.

Laumier, Charles. *Histoire de la Révolution d'Espagne en 1820: précédée d'un aperçu du règne de Ferdinand VII, depuis 1814, et d'un précis de la Révolution de l'Amérique du Sud.* Paris: Chaignieau, 1820.

*Lema y Rull, Hugo de. *Advertencias al catecismo civil de D. Andres de Moya y Luzuriaga por D. Hugo de Lema y Rull.* Cadiz: Junta Superior de Gobierno, 1811.

Martinez de Aguilar, Francisco. *Melo-Drama en un acto, que en celebridad de la victoria conseguida por las armas españoles en la Andalucia.* Cadiz: Don Nicolas Gomez de Requena, 1808.

Martínez de la Rosa, Francisco. *Obras completas.* 5 vols. Paris: Baudry, 1844–45.

———. *Obras dramáticas.* 2nd ed. Madrid: Espasa-Calpe, 1947.

Mases, José Antonia, ed. *Asturias vista por viajeros románticos extranjeros y otros visitantes y cronistas famosos. Siglo XV al XX.* 3 vols. Gijón: Ediciones Trea, 2001.

Mata, Pedro, and R. Stirling. *Historia de General D. Rafael del Riego.* Tr. from French. Barcelona, 1837.

Mateo, Archbishop of Badajoz. *Carta pastoral que dirige el ilustrísimo señor D. Mateo Delgado y Moreno, arzobispo de Badajoz.* Badajoz, 1822.

Matthewes, George. *The Last Military Operations of General Riego.* London: Valpy, 1820.

Mora, José Joaquín de. *Mémoires historiques sur Ferdinand VII, roi des Espagnes, et sur les événements de son règne.* Tr. M.G.H. Paris: P. Mongie aîné, 1824.

Niegolewski, Andrzej. *Les Polonais à Somo-Sierra en 1808 en Espagne.* Paris: Martinet, 1854.

Noticias sobre el exercito de los rusos y el de Napeoleon en la Polonia. Seville, 1812.

Osservazioni sopra' alcuni articoli principali della costituzione spagnola. Naples, 1820.

Pecchio, Giuseppe. *Journal of Military and Political Events in Spain During the Last Twelve Months.* Tr. Edward Blaquiere. London: Whittaker, 1824.

Preliminary Discourse read in the Cortes at the Presentation of the Constitution by the Committee of the Constitution, to which is added the Present Spanish Constitution. London: Pamphleteer, 1823.

Un Presbytero. Instruccion popular en forma de catecismo sobre la presente guerra: la consagra al exército y al pueblo de España. Seville, Imprenta Real, 1809.

Proyecto al catecismo universal y su compendio, intitulada: El Niño instruido por la Divina Palabra. Madrid, 1807.

Quin, Michael J. *A Visit to Spain: Detailing the Transactions Which Occurred During a Residence in That Country, in the Latter Part of 1822, and the First Four Months of 1823.* 2nd ed. London: Hurst, 1824.

Riego, Rafael del. *Causa formada en octubre de 1823 a virtud de órden de la Regencia por el señor alcalde don Alfonso de Cavía contra Don Rafael del Riego.* 2nd ed. Madrid: D.M. de Burgos, 1835.

———. *La revolución de 1820, día a día—cartas, escritos, y discursos.* Ed. Alberto Gil Novales. Madrid: Tecnos, 1976.

———. *Vindicación de los extravíos imputados al general D. Rafael del Riego el 7 de setiembre en las Cortes.* Oviedo: D. Francisco Perez Prieto, 1820.

———, et al. *Representación hecha al Rey y a las Cortes por los generales del Ejército de observación D. Rafael del Riego.* Cadiz: Benavente, 1820.

Salvandy, Narcisse-Achille de. *Don Alonso, ou l'Espagne: histoire contemporaine.* 6th ed. 2 vols. Paris: Dedier, 1857.

———. *Don Alonzo, ou l'Espagne: histoire contemporaine.* 4 vols. Paris: Baudouin, 1824.

———. *Du parti a prendre envers l'Espagne.* Paris: Baudouin, 1824.

San Miguel, Evaristo. *Memoria sucinta sobre lo acaecido en la columna movíl de las tropas nacionales al mando del comandante general de la primera division, D. Rafael del Riego.* Oviedo: D. Francisco Perez Prieto, 1820.

Steele, Thomas. *Notes of the War in Spain; Detailing Occurences Military and Political, in Galicia, and at Gibraltar and Cadiz, from the Fall of Corunna to the Occupation of Cadiz by the French.* London: Sherwood, Jones, 1824.

Van Halen, Juan. *Narrative of Don Juan Van Halen's Imprisonment in the Dungeons of the Inquisition at Madrid.* New York: Harper, 1828.

Vaudoncourt, Frédéric. *Letters on the Internal Political State of Spain.* 2nd ed. London: Lupton Relfe, 1825.

Vidal, Josef. *Idea ortodoxa de la divina institución del estado religioso contra los errores de los liberales y pistoyanos monacómacos.* Valencia: Benito Monfort, 1823.

Vigny, Alfred de. *Poésies complètes.* Paris: Cluny, 1937.

Ysidoro, Bishop of Segovia. *Pastoral del obispo de Segovia.* Segovia: Espinosa Biblioteca Digital de Castilla y León, 1822.

Spain: Secondary Works

Alberola, Ginés. *Don Rafael del Riego, 1820–1823 (centenario glorioso)*. Alicante, 1927.

Álvarez Chillida, Gonzalo. *El antisemitismo en España: la imagen del Judio, 1812–2000*. Madrid: Pons, 2002.

Annino, Antonio, and François-Xavier Guerra, eds. *Inventando la nación: Iberoamérica, siglo XIX*. Mexico City: Fondo de Cultura Económica, 2003.

Artola, Miguel. *Partidos y programas políticos, 1808–1936*. 2 vols. Madrid: Aguilar, 1974–75.

———. *La España de Fernando VII*. 3rd ed. Madrid: Espasa-Calpe, 1983.

Astur, Eugenia. *Riego: estudio histórico-político de la Revolución del año veinte*. Oviedo: Consejería de Educación, Cultura y Deportes, 1984 [1933].

Atkinson, William. *A History of Spain and Portugal*. Harmondsworth: Penguin, 1960.

Ávila, Alfredo. *En nombre de la Nación: la formación del gobierno representativo en México (1808–1824)*. Mexico City: Taurus, 2002.

Aymes, Jean-René. *Los españoles en Francia (1808–1814): la deportación bajo el Primer Imperio*. Madrid: Siglo Veintiuno, 1987.

Bartley, Russell. *Imperial Russia and the Struggle for Latin American Independence, 1808–1828*. Austin: University of Texas Press, 1978.

Beevor, Antony. *The Spanish Civil War*. London: Cassell, 2004 [1982].

Bergamini, John. *The Spanish Bourbons: The History of a Tenacious Dynasty*. New York: Putnam, 1974.

Boppe, Paul. *Los españoles en el ejército napoleónico*. Tr. A. Salafranca Vázquez. Málaga: Algazara, 1995 [1899].

Bory, Jean-Louis. *Eugène Süe: le roi du roman populaire*. Paris: Hachette, 1962.

Bulgin, Kathleen. *The Making of an Artist: Gautier's Voyage en Espagne*. Birmingham, AL: Summa, 1988.

Burgos, Carmen de (Colombine). *Gloriosa vida y desdichada muerte de Don Rafael del Riego: un crimen de los Borbones*. Madrid: Biblioteca Nueva, 1931.

Butrón Prida, Gonzalo. "Fiesta y revolución: las celebraciones políticas en el Cádiz liberal, 1812–1837." In Gil Novales, ed., *Revolución liberal*, 159–77.

Callahan, William. *Church, Politics, and Society in Spain, 1750–1874*. Cambridge, MA: Harvard University Press, 1984.

———. "The Origins of the Conservative Church in Spain, 1793–1823." *European Studies Review* 10/2 (April 1979): 199–223.

Candido, Salvatore. "La revolución de Cádiz de enero de 1820 y sus repercusiones en Italia, en los Reinos de Nápoles, y de Cerdeña." In Gil Novales, ed., *Revolución liberal*, 251–55.

Cánovas Cervantes, S. *El pronunciamiento de Riego (otra vez la constitución de 1812)*. Madrid: Editorial del Norte, 1930.

Capitán Díaz, Alfonso. "Los catecismos políticos en España (1808–1822)." Ph.D. dissertation, University of Granada, 1978.

Carr, Raymond. *Spain, 1808–1975*. Oxford: Clarendon Press, 1982.

———, ed. *Spain: A History*. Oxford: Oxford University Press, 2000.

Casado Burbano, Pablo. "El pensamiento politico-militar de Riego." In Gil Novales, ed., *Ejército, pueblo, y Constitución*, 186–95.

Chastel, C. "La 'peste' de Barcelone: epidémie de fièvre jaune de 1821." *Bulletin de la Société de pathologie exotique* 92, 5 (1999): 405 8.

Christiansen, E. *The Origins of Military Power in Spain, 1800–1854*. London: Oxford University Press, 1967.

Comellas Garcia-Llera, José Luís. *Los realistas en el Trienio constitucional (1820–1823)*. Pamplona: Gómez, 1958.

Corbière, Emilio. *Los catecismos que leyeron nuestros padres: ideología e imaginario popular en el siglo XX*. Buenos Aires: Sudamericana, 2000.

Costa, Joaquín. *Historia crítica de la revolución española*. Ed. A. Gil Novales. Madrid: Centro de Estudios Constitucionales, 1992 [1874].

Costeloe, Michael. *Response to Revolution: Imperial Spain and the Spanish American Revolutions, 1810–1840.* Cambridge: Cambridge University Press, 1986.

Crawley, C. W. "French and English Influences in the Cortes of Cadiz, 1810–1814." *Cambridge Historical Journal* vi/2 (1939): 176–208.

Dérozier, Albert. *Manuel Josef Quintana et la naissance du libéralisme en Espagne.* Paris: Les Belles Lettres, 1968.

Douglas, Carrie. *Bulls, Bullfighting, and Spanish Identities.* Tuscon: University of Arizona Press, 1997.

Douglas, Vittorio Scotti. "La constitución de Cádiz y las revoluciones italianas en Turin y Nápoles de 1820 y 1821." In Gil Novales, ed., *Revolución liberal,* 257–62.

Dowling, John. *Leandro Fernández de Moratín.* New York: Twayne, 1971.

La ejecución de Riego. Madrid: Prensa Moderna, 1928.

Elliott, John H. *Empires of the Atlantic World: Britain and Spain in America, 1492–1830.* New Haven: Yale University Press, 2006.

Esdaile, Charles. *Fighting Napoleon: Guerrillas, Bandits, and Adventurers in Spain, 1808–1814.* New Haven: Yale University Press, 2004.

——. *Spain in the Liberal Age: From Constitution to Civil War, 1808–1939.* Oxford: Blackwell, 2000.

——. *The Spanish Army in the Peninsular War.* Manchester: Manchester University Press, 1988.

Esteban, Jorge de, ed. *Constituciones españolas y extranjeras.* 2 vols. Madrid: Taurus, 1977.

Esteban, José. *El himno de Riego.* Barcelona: Argos Vergara, 1984.

Fernández de Pinedo, Emiliano, Alberto Gil Novales, and Albert Dérozier. *Centralismo, ilustración, y agonía del Antiguo Régimen, 1715–1833.* 2nd ed. Barcelona: Labor, 1982.

Ferrer Benimeli, José A. "Masonería e iglesia en España." In *Libéralisme chrétien,* 63–94.

Fuentes, Juan Francisco. "De la sociabilidad censitaria a la sociabilidad popular en la España liberal." In Fuentes and Roura i Aulinas, eds., *Sociabilidad y liberalismo,* 207–24.

Fuentes, Juan Francisco, and Lluís Roura i Aulinas, eds. *Sociabilidad y liberalismo en la España del siglo XIX: homenaje al profesor Alberto Gil Novales.* Lleida: Milenio, 2001.

Gil Novales, Alberto, ed. *Ejército, pueblo y Constitución: homenaje al General Rafael del Riego.* Madrid: Trienio, 1987.

——. *El Trienio liberal.* Madrid: Siglo veintiuno de España, 1980.

——. "Iglesia nacional y constitución, 1820–1823." In *Libéralisme chrétien,* 109–25.

——. "La fama de Riego." In Gil Novales, *Ejército, pueblo, y Constitución,* 365–83.

——. "La independencia de América en la conciencia española, 1820–1823." *Revista de Indias,* January–December 1979, 235–65.

——, ed. *La revolución burguesa en España: Actas del coloquio hispano-alemán, celebrado en Leipzig los días 17 y 18 de noviembre de 1983.* Madrid: Universidad Complutense, 1985.

——, ed. *La revolución liberal.* Madrid: Orto, 2001.

——. *Las sociedades patrióticas (1820–1823): las libertades de expresión y de reunión en el origen de los partidos políticos.* 2 vols. Madrid: Tecnos, 1975.

——. "Quién fue Riego." In Román Ojeda, *Riego,* 227–36.

——. "Una interminable guerra civil." In Gil Novales, ed., *La revolución liberal,* 1–12.

Guerra, Francois-Xavier, ed. *Las revoluciones hispánicas independencias americanas y liberalismo español.* Madrid: Complutense, 1995.

Gutiérrez Nogales, Mercedes. *Rafael del Riego: datos biográficas, romancero, y documentos.* Seville: M. Gutiérrez, 1988.

Haliczer, Stephen. *The Comuneros of Castile: The Forging of a Revolution, 1475–1521.* Madison: University of Wisconsin Press, 1981.

Hamnett, Brian. "Constitutional Theory and Political Reality: Liberalism, Traditionalism, and the Spanish Cortes, 1810–1814." *JMH* 49/1 suppl. (March 1977): D1071–D1110.

Hanisch Espíndola, Walter. *El catecismo político-cristiano: las ideas y la época: 1810.* Santiago de Chile: Bello, 1970.

Harvey, Robert. *Liberators: South America's Savage Wars of Freedom, 1810–1830.* London: Robinson, 2000.

Herr, Richard. *The Eighteenth-Century Revolution in Spain*. Princeton: Princeton University Press, 1958.

Herrero, Javier. *Los orígenes del pensamiento reaccionario español*. Madrid: Alianza Editorial, 1988.

Hocquellet, Richard. *Résistance et révolution durant l'occupation napoléonienne en Espagne, 1808–1812*. Paris: Boutique de l'histoire, 2001.

Hoffmann, Léon-François. *La peste à Barcelone*. Paris: Presses Universitaires de France, 1964.

Hughes, Robert. *Goya*. London: Harvill Press, 2003.

Kamen, Henry. *The Spanish Inquisition: A Historical Revision*. New Haven: Yale University Press, 1998.

Klibbe, Lawrence. *Fernán Caballero*. New York: Twayne, 1973.

Klingender, F. D. *Goya in the Democratic Tradition*. London: Sidgwick and Jackson, 1968 [1946].

Lamanskii, Vladimir. *O slavianakh v Maloi Azii, v Afrike, i v Ispanii*. St. Petersburg, 1859.

Lucas-Dubreton, J. *Madrid*. Paris: Fayard, 1962.

Lynch, John. *The Spanish-American Revolutions, 1808–1826*. New York: Norton, 1973.

MacKay, Ruth. *"Lazy, Improvident People": Myth and Reality in the Writing of Spanish History*. Ithaca: Cornell University Press, 2006.

Madariaga, Isabel de. "Spain and the Decembrists." *European History Quarterly* 3/2 (January-October 1973): 141–56.

Marañón, Gregorio. *Españoles fuera de España*. Buenos Aires: Espasa-Calpe Argentina, 1947.

Martínez Gallego, Francesc-Andreu. "El rescate del Héroe: el pantéon sincopado del liberalismo español (1808–1836)." In Manuel Chust and Víctor Mínguez, eds., *La construcción del héroe en España y México (1789–1847)*, 253–79. Valencia: Universitat de Valencia, 2003.

Martínez Ruíz, Enrique, ed. *El peso de la Iglesia: cuatro siglos de órdenes religiosas en España*. Madrid: Actas Editorial, 2004.

Martínez Torrón, Diego. *Los liberales románticos españoles ante la descolonización americana (1808–1833)*. Madrid: Mapfre, 1992.

McNeill, John. "Yellow Fever, Empire, and Revolution." Paper given at the conference "When Disease Makes History," Helsinki University Collegium for Advanced Studies, October 15, 2004.

Méndez García, Zoilo. *Historia documental de Riego; su ascendencia paterna y materna, su vida, persecución, muerte y actuales parientes*. Luarca: Heredera, 1932.

Millán-Chivite, José Luís. "La segunda crisis del antiguo régimen en el estado de Medinasidonia: el trienio constitucional (1820–1823)." *AUC* I (1984): 149–68.

Moliner, Antonio. "Opinión pública y anticlericalismo en la prensa exaltada del Trienio liberal." In Fuentes and Roura i Aulinas, eds., *Sociabilidad y liberalismo*, 73–101.

Montero Alonso, José. *Himno y marcha fúnebre de Riego*. Madrid, 1930.

Moore, John. *Ramón de la Cruz*. New York: Twayne, 1972.

Morán Orti, Manuel. "La 'Miscelánea' de Javier de Burgos: la prensa en el debate ideológico del Trienio Liberal." *Hispania sacra* 41/83 (January-June 1989): 237–44.

Moreno Alonso, Manuel. *Blanco White: la obsesión de España*. Seville: Alfar, 1998.

Mosquera, Alejandro. *Rafael del Riego*. Coruna: Ateneo Republicano de Galicia, 2003.

Museo Municipal de Madrid et al. *Guía de Museo Municipal de Madrid: la historia de Madrid en sus colecciones*. Madrid: Ayuntamiento de Madrid, 1995.

Núñez Díaz-Balart, Mirta. "El enemigo desaparecido: el combate ideológico contra el liberalismo en la propaganda carcelaria franquista." In Gil Novales, ed., *Revolución liberal*, 697–707.

Nuñez Muñoz, María. "El pronunciamiento de Riego en las Actas Capitulares Jerezanas." In Gil Novales, ed., *Ejército, pueblo y Constitución*, 96–110.

Payne, Stanley. *A History of Spain and Portugal*. 2 vols. Madison: University of Wisconsin Press, 1973.

Pérez Galdós, Benito. *Cádiz*. Madrid: Alianza Editorial, 2001 [1874].

———. *Obras completas*. 12th ed. 6 vols. Madrid: Aguilar, 1970.

———. *La segunda casaca*. Madrid: Alianza Editorial, 2003 [1876].

Pérez González, Fernando Tomás, and Asunción Fernández Blasco. "Reivindicaciones políticas de la mujer en los orígenes de la revolución liberal española." In Gil Novales, ed., *Revolución liberal*, 433–41.

Pérez López-Portillo, Raúl. *La España de Riego.* Madrid: Sílex, 2005.

Priego Fernández del Campo, Carmen and José María Álvarez del Manzano y López del Hierro, Eduardo Alaminos López, et al. *Abanicos: la colección del Museo Municipal de Madrid.* Madrid: Ayuntamiento de Madrid, 1995.

Ramos Oliveira, A. *Politics, Economics and Men of Modern Spain, 1808–1946.* Tr. Teener Hall. London: Gollancz, 1946.

Revzin, G. I. *Riego.* Moscow: Zhizn' zamechatelnykh liudei, 1939.

———. *Riego.* Moscow: Molodaia Gvardiia, 1958.

———. *Riego: héroe de España.* Montevideo: Pueblos unidos, 1946.

Ribbans, Geoffrey. *History and Fiction in Galdós's Narratives.* Oxford: Clarendon Press, 1993.

Román Ojeda, Francisco Domingo. *Riego: Héroe de las Cabezas.* Ed. Gil Novales. Las Cabezas de San Juan: Los Palacios, 1988.

Russell, Peter, ed. *Introducción a la cultura hispánica.* 2 vols. Barcelona: Crítica, 1982.

Sánchez Agesta, Luis. *Historia del constitucionalismo español.* Madrid: Instituto de Estudios Políticos, 1955.

Sarrailh, Jean. *La contre-révolution sous la régence de Madrid (mai-octobre, 1923).* Ligugé: Aubin, 1930.

———. *Un homme d'état espagnol: Martínez de la Rosa (1787–1862).* Bordeaux: Feret, 1930.

Schop Soler, Ana María. *Las relaciones entre España y Rusia en la época de Fernando VII.* Barcelona: Universidad de Barcelona, 1975.

———. *Die spanisch-russischen Beziehungen im 18. Jahrhundert.* Wiesbaden: Harrassowitz, 1970.

———. *Un siglo de relaciones diplomáticas y comerciales entre España y Rusia, 1733–1833.* Madrid: Condór, 1984.

Sisinio Pérez Garzón, Juan. "Ejército nacional y Milicia Nacional." In Gil Novales, ed., *Revolución burguesa,* 181–84.

Solis, Ramón. *El Cádiz de las Cortes: la vida en la ciudad en los años 1810 a 1813.* Madrid: Alianza Editorial, 1969.

Tartakovskii, A. G. *Voennaia publitsistika 1812 goda.* Moscow: Mysl', 1967.

Tomás y Valiente, Francisco. *La tortura en España.* 2nd ed. Barcelona: Ariel, 1994.

Trachevskii, A. *Ispaniia deviatnadtsatogo veka.* Moscow: Grachev, 1872.

Troyano, Alberto González. "Libelos ilustrados en el Cádiz romántico: los panfletos liberales de Bartolomé José Gallardo." *AUC* II (1985): 367–74.

Tuero Bertrand, Francísco. *Riego: proceso a un liberal.* Oviedo: Ediciones Nobel, 1995.

Vicens Vives, Jaime. *An Economic History of Spain.* Princeton: Princeton University Press, 1969 [1955].

Williams, Gwyn. *Goya and the Impossible Revolution.* London: Allen Lane, 1976.

Zimmerman, A. F. "Spain and its Colonies, 1808–1820." *HAHR* 11/4 (November 1931): 437–63.

Zviguilsky, Alexandre. "El concepto de revolución frustrada en El Grande Oriente de Pérez Galdós, y en Tierras Virgenes, de Ivan Turgueniev." In Gil Novales, ed., *Revolución liberal,* 677–82.

———. "Riego y los masones rusos." In Gil Novales, ed., *Ejército, pueblo, y Constitución,* 272–75.

Naples: Primary Sources

Alberti, A., ed. *Atti del Parlamento delle Due Sicilie, 1820–1821.* 6 vols. Bologna: Zanichelli, 1926–31.

Aquarone, A., et al. *Le costituzioni italiane.* Milan: Comunità, 1958.

Barker, H. A., and J. Burford. *Description of the View of Naples and Surrounding Scenery.* London: Adlard, 1821.

Beccaria, Cesare. *On Crimes and Punishments and Other Writings.* Ed. R. Bellamy. Tr. R. Davies et al. Cambridge: Cambridge University Press, 1995.

Bertoldi. *Memoirs of the Secret Societies of the South of Italy, Particularly the Carbonari,* London: Murray, 1821.

Bianco di Saint-Jorioz, Carlo. *Ai militari italiani.* Ed. Enrica Melossi. Turin: Istituto per la Storia del Risorgimento italiano, 1975 [1833].

Bignon, Louis. *Du congrès de Troppau, ou examen des prétentions des monarquies absolues à l'égard de la monarchie constitutionelle de Naples.* Paris: Didot, 1821.

Blessington, Margaret. *The Idler in Italy.* 3 vols. London: Colburn, 1839–40.

Brevi riflessioni su' miglioramenti essenziali . . . allo sviluppo della nazione del Regno delle Due Sicilie. Naples, 1820.

Catechismo costituzionale. Naples, 1820.

Catechismo costituzionale della monarchia spagnola. Naples, 1820.

Catechismo politico-morale. Naples: Reale Tipografia, 1850.

Colletta, Pietro. *History of the Kingdom of Naples, 1734–1825.* 2 vols. Tr. S. Horner. Edinburgh: Constable, 1858.

———. *Storia del Reame di Napoli dal 1754 sino al 1825.* 4 vols. Capolago: Helvetica, 1837.

———. *Storia del Reame di Napoli.* Naples: SARA, 1992.

Costituzione politica della monarchia spagnola. London, 1820.

Costituzioni politiche delle principali nazioni. Comp. Angelo Lanzellotti. Naples, 1820.

Craven, Richard Keppel. *See* Eye-Witness.

Cuoco, Vincenzo. *Saggio storico sulla rivoluzione napoletana del 1799.* Bari: Laterza, 1929 [1806].

Discorso di tre studenti sulle circonstanze attuali. Naples, 1820.

An Eye-Witness [Richard Keppel Craven]. *Sketch of the Late Revolution at Naples.* London: Carpenter, 1820.

Fiorilli, B. *La miglior possibile costituzione politica per tutti le genti sul calcolo di razione.* Naples, 1821.

Galanti, Giuseppe. *Nuova guida per Napoli e suoi contorni.* Naples: Presso i Principali Librai, 1845 [1829].

Galanti, Luigi. *Catechismo costituzionale.* Naples: Sangiacomo, 1820

Haussez, Baron d'. *Voyage d'un exilé de Londres à Naples et en Sicile, en passant par la Hollande, la Confédération germanique, le Tyrol et l'Italie.* 2 vols. Paris: Allardin, 1835.

Kotzebue, August. *Souvenirs d'un voyage en Livonie, à Rome et à Naples.* 4 vols. Paris: Barba, 1806.

Lyman, Theodore. *The Political State of Italy.* Boston: Wells and Lilly, 1820.

Minichini, Luigi. *Luglio 1820: cronaca di una rivoluzione.* Ed. Mario Themelly. Rome: Bulzoni, 1979 [1838].

Nicola, Carlo de. *Diario napoletano, 1798–1825.* 3 vols. Naples: Società napoletana di storia patria, 1906.

Olivier-Poli, G. M. *Cenno istorico su la rigenerazione dell'Italia meridionale.* Naples, 1820.

Orlov, Grigorii. *Mémoires historiques, politiques et littéraires sur le Royaume de Naples.* Ed. Amaury Duval. 5 vols. Paris: Chasseriau et Hécart, 1819–21.

Pecchio, Giuseppe. *Semi-Serious Observations of an Italian Exile During His Residence in England.* London: Wilson, 1833.

Pepe, Guglielmo. *Guglielmo Pepe.* Ed. Ruggero Moscati. 2 vols. Rome: Vittoriano, 1938.

———. *Memorie del generale Guglielmo Pepe intorno alla sua vita e ai recenti casi d'Italia.* 2 vols. Paris: Baudry, 1847.

———. *Narrative of the Political and Military Events, Which Took Place at Naples, in 1820 and 1821.* London: Treuttel and Würtz, 1821.

———. *Relation des événemens politiques et militaires qui ont eu lieu à Naples en 1820 et 1821.* Paris: Crapelet, 1822.

Porter, Jeanne Chenault, ed. *Baroque Naples: A Documentary History, 1600–1800.* New York: Italica Press, 2000.

Regolamento del governo interno delle Corti. Naples, 1820.

Rossetti, Gabriele. *A Versified Autobiography.* Tr. W. M. Rossetti. London: Sands, 1901.

Saint-Edme, Théodore, ed. *Constitution et organisation de Carbonari, ou documens exacts.* 2nd ed. Paris: Brissot-Thivers, 1822.

Saint-Non, Jean Claude Richard de. *Voyage pittoresque à Naples et en Sicile.* 2 vols. Paris: Dufour, 1829.

Sansone, Gregorio. *Ricordo ai rappresentanti della nazione napoletana.* Naples, 1820.

Santarosa, Santorre di. *Lettere dall'esilio (1821–1825).* Ed. A. Olmo. Rome: Istituto per la Storia del Risorgimento italiano, 1969.

———. *On the Piedmontese Revolution*. London: Pamphleteer, 1821.

Santore, John, ed. *Modern Naples: A Documentary History, 1799–1999*. New York: Italica Press, 2001.

Scribe, Eugène. *Oeuvres complètes*. 46 vols. Paris: E. Dentu, 1874–75.

Stendhal. *Life of Rossini*. Tr. R. Coe. New York: Orion Press, 1970.

———. *Rome, Naples, and Florence*. Tr. R. Coe. New York: Braziller, 1960.

Naples: Secondary Works

Acton, Harold. *The Bourbons of Naples (1734–1825)*. London: Methuen, 1956.

Arblaster, Anthony. *Viva la libertà!: Politics in Opera*. London: Verso, 1992.

Astarita, Tommaso. *Between Salt Water and Holy Water: A History of Southern Italy*. New York: Norton, 2005.

Banti, Alberto. *La nazione del Risorgimento: parentela, santità e onore alle origini dell'Italia unita*. Turin: Einaudi, 2000.

Barletta, Laura. *Fra regola e licenza: chiesa e vita religiosa, feste e beneficenza a Napoli e in Campania, secoli XVIII–XX*. Naples: Edizioni Scientifiche Italiane, 2003.

Basile, Luisa, and Delia Morea. *I briganti napoletani*. Naples: Newton, 1996.

Battaglini, Tito. *L'organizzazione militare del Regno delle Due Sicilie*. Modena: Società Tipografica Modenese, 1940.

Beales, Derek, and Eugenio Biagini. *The Risorgimento and the Unification of Italy*. London: Longman, 2002.

Berti, Giuseppe. *Russia e stati italiani nel Risorgimento*. Turin: Einaudi, 1957.

Bevilacqua, Piero, and Augusto Placanica, eds. *La Calabria*. Turin: Einaudi, 1985.

Bracalini, Romano. *L'Italia prima dell'unità (1815–1860)*. Milan: Rizzoli, 2001.

Brettell, Richard and Caroline. *Painters and Peasants in the Nineteenth Century*. Geneva: Skira, 1983.

Buttà, Giuseppe. *I Borboni di Napoli*. 2 vols. Bologna, 1878.

Cagli, Bruno. "Al gran sole di Rossini." In Bruno Cagli et al., eds., *Il teatro di San Carlo, 1737–1987*, II:133–70. Naples: Electa, 1987.

Candeloro, Giorgio. *Storia dell'Italia moderna. II, Dalla restaurazione alla rivoluzione nazionale*. 2nd ed. Milan: Feltrinelli, 1960.

Castronuovo, Sandro. *Via Toledo e dintorni: la strada dei napoletani dalle origini al Duemila*. Naples: Valentino, 2006.

Cilibrizzi, Saverio. *Il pensiero, l'azione, e il martirio della città di Napoli nel Risorgimento italiano e nelle due guerre mondiali*. 3 vols. Naples: Conte, 1961–68.

Collison-Morley, Lacy. *Naples Through the Centuries*. New York: Stokes, 1924.

Colombo, Adolfo. *La vita di Santorre di Santarosa, vol. I, 1783–1807*. Rome: Vittoriano, 1938.

Cortese, Nino, ed. *La condanna e l'esilio di Pietro Colletta*. Rome: Vittoriano, 1938.

———. *Il Mezzogiorno ed il Risorgimento italiano*. Naples: Libreria Scientifica 1965.

Costantino, Beniamino. *I moti d'Abruzzo dal 1798 al 1860 e il clero*. Pescara: Amoroso, 1960.

Croce, Benedetto. *History of the Kingdom of Naples*. Tr. of 6th ed. Chicago: University of Chicago Press, 1965 [1925].

———. *La rivoluzione napoletana del 1799*. Bari: Laterza, 1912.

———. *Storia del Regno di Napoli*. Bari: Laterza, 1925.

D'Agostino, Guido. *Per una storia di Napoli capitale*. Naples: Liguori, 1988.

Davis, John A. *Naples and Napoleon: Southern Italy and the European Revolutions, 1780–1860*. Oxford: Oxford University Press, 2006.

———. "Opera and Absolutism in Restoration Italy, 1815–1860." *Journal of Interdisciplinary History* 36/4 (Spring 2006): 569–94.

———. "1799: The Santafede and the Crisis of the Ancien Régime in Southern Italy." In Davis and Ginsborg, eds., *Society and Politics in the Age of the Risorgimento*, 1–25. Cambridge: Cambridge University Press, 1991.

Davis, John A., and Paul Ginsborg, eds. *Society and Politics in the Age of the Risorgimento*. Cambridge: Cambridge University Press, 1991.

De Francesco, Antonino. "How Not to Finish a Revolution." In Girolamo Imbruglia, ed., *Naples in the Eighteenth Century: The Birth and Death of a Nation-State*, 167–82. Cambridge: Cambridge University Press, 2000.

Della Peruta, Franco. *Esercito e società nell'Italia napoleonica*. Milan: F. Angeli, 1988.

———. "La guerra di liberazione spagnola e la teoria della guerra per bande nel Risorgimento." In *L'Italia del Risorgimento*, 11–29. Milan: Angeli, 1997.

———. "War and Society in Napoleonic Italy: The Armies of the Kingdom of Italy at Home and Abroad." In Davis and Ginsborg, eds., *Society and Politics in the Age of the Risorgimento*, 26–48. Cambridge: Cambridge University Press, 1991.

De Seta, Cesare. *Napoli*. Naples: Laterza, 1981.

Dizionario biografico degli Italiani. Rome: Istituto della enciclopedia italiana, 1960–

Doria, Gino. *Le strade di Napoli: saggio di toponomastica storica*. Naples: Ricciardi, 1943.

Doria, Gino. *Le strade di Napoli*. 2nd ed. Milan: Ricciardi, 1971.

———. *Storia di una capitale: Napoli dalle origini al 1860*. Naples: Guida, 1935.

Douglas, Norman. *Old Calabria*. New York: Modern Library, 1928.

Francovich, Carlo. "Il movimento filoellenico in Italia e in Europa." In Spadolini, ed., *Indipendenza e unità nazionale*, 1–23. Florence: Olschki, 1987.

Gabrieli, Giuseppe. *Massoneria e Carboneria nel Regno di Napoli*. Rome: Atanòr, 1981.

Galasso, Giuseppe, et al. *Storia del mezzogiorno*. 7 vols. Naples: Edizione del Sole, 1991–.

Gamboa, Biagio. *Storia della rivoluzione di Napoli*. Naples: Il Trani, 1820.

Ghirelli, Antonio. *Storia di Napoli*. New ed. Turin: Einaudi, 1992.

Gleijeses, Vittorio. *La storia di Napoli dalle origini ai nostri giorni*. Naples: Società Editrice Napoletana, 1974.

Gregory, Desmond. *Napoleon's Italy*. Madison, NJ: Fairleigh Dickinson University Press, 2001.

Hearder, Harry. *Italy in the Age of the Risorgimento, 1790–1870*. London: Longman, 1983.

Jannone, Giovanni. *I Poerio nel loro secondo esilio*. Rome: Rassegna Nazionale, 1924.

Johnston, R. M. *The Napoleonic Empire in Southern Italy and the Rise of the Secret Societies*. 2 vols. New York: Da Capo, 1973 [1904].

Kauchtschischwili, Nina. *Silvio Pellico e la Russia*. Milan: Vita e Pensiero, 1963.

King, Bolton. *The Life of Mazzini*. London: Dent 1912.

Koval'skaia, M. I. *Dvizhenie karbonariev v Italii, 1808–1821 gg*. Moscow: Nauka, 1971.

Laven, David. "The Age of Restoration." In John A. Davis, ed., *Italy in the Nineteenth Century, 1796–1900*, 51–73. Oxford: Oxford University Press, 2000.

Lepre, Aurelio. *La rivoluzione napoletana del 1820–1821*. Rome: Riuniti, 1967.

———. *Storia del Mezzogiorno d'Italia*. 2 vols. Naples: Liguori, 1986.

Lucarelli, Enrica. "L'emigrazione come problema politico." In *Risorgimento Greco*, 144–47. Rome: Edizioni del Sole, 1986.

Macry, Paolo. *I giochi dell'incertezza: Napoli nell'ottocento*. Naples: L'Ancora del Mediterraneo, 2002.

———. "The Southern Metropolis: Redistributive Circuits in Nineteenth-Century Naples." In Robert Lumley and Jonathan Morris, eds., *The History of the New Italian South: The Mezzogiorno Revisited*, 59–82. Exeter: University of Exeter Press, 1997.

Manfredi, Michele. *Luigi Minichini e la carboneria a Nola*. Florence: F. de Monnier, 1932.

Manhès, A., and R. McFarlan. *Il brigantaggio nell'Italia meridionale prima e dopo l'unità*. Tr. F. Stochetti. Bologna: Forni, 1991.

Marsengo, Giorgio, and Giuseppe Parlato. *Dizionario dei Piemontesi compromessi nei moti del 1821*. 2 vols. Turin: Istituto per la Storia del Risorgimento Italiano, 1982.

Mastellone, Salvo. "Santorre di Santarosa, combattente per la Grecia." In Spadolini, ed., *Indipendenza e unità nazionale*, 35–41. Florence: Olschki, 1987.

Mazade, Charles de. "Une vie d'émigré italien." *Revue des deux mondes*, March 15, 1859, 460–76.

Morelli, Antonio. *Michele Morelli e la rivoluzione napoletana del 1820–1821*. 2nd ed. Rome: Capelli, 1969.

Moscati, Ruggero. Introduction to Pepe, *Guglielmo Pepe*, lvii–cvii. Rome: Vittoriano, 1938.

Panico, Guido. *Il carnefice e la piazza: crudeltà di stato e violenza popolare a Napoli in età moderna.* Naples: Edizioni scientifiche italiane, 1985.

Pedio, Tommaso. *Brigantaggio meridionale (1806–1863).* Cavallino di Lecce: Capone, 1987.

Petrusewicz, Marta. "Before the Southern Question: 'Native' Ideas on Backwardness and Remedies in the Kingdom of the Two Sicilies, 1815–1849." In Jane Schneider, ed., *Italy's "Southern Question": Orientalism in One Country,* 27–49. Oxford: Berg, 1998.

Pieri, Piero. *Le società segrete ed i moti degli anni 1820–21 e 1830–31.* Milan: Vallardi, 1931.

———. *Storia militare del Risorgimento: guerre e insurrezioni.* Turin: Einaudi, 1962.

Poli, Annarosa, and E. Kanceff, eds. *L'Italie dans l'Europe romantique.* 2 vols. Moncalieri: CIRVI, 1996.

Pontieri, Ernesto, et al., eds. *Storia di Napoli.* 10 vols. Naples: Società Editrice Storia di Napoli, 1975–81.

Rath, R. John. "The Carbonari: Their Origins, Initiation Rites, and Aims." *American Historical Review* 64/2 (January 1964): 353–70.

Riall, Lucy. *Garibaldi: Invention of a Hero.* New Haven: Yale University Press, 2007.

Richter, Dieter. *Napoli cosmopolita: viaggiatori e comunità straniere nell'Ottocento.* Tr. M. L. Calfiero. Naples: Electa Napoli, 2002.

Robinson, Michael F. *Naples and Neapolitan Opera.* Oxford: Clarendon Press, 1972.

Romani, George. *The Neapolitan Revolution of 1820–21.* Evanston, IL: Northwestern University Press, 1950.

Romano, Michele. *Un grande del Risorgimento: Gabriele Pepe.* Modena: Società tipografica modenese, 1940.

Rosselli, John. *Lord William Bentinck and the British Occupation of Sicily, 1811–1814.* Cambridge: Cambridge University Press, 1956.

Rossiia i Italiia: iz istorii russko-ital'ianskikh kul'turnykh i obshchestvennykh otnoshenii. Moscow: Nauka, 1968.

Ruggiero, Guido de. *Il pensiero politico meridionale nei secoli XVIII e XIX.* 2nd ed. Bari: Laterza, 1946.

Salvatorelli, Luigi. *The Risorgimento: Thought and Action.* Tr. M. Domandi. New York: Harper, 1970.

Scalamandrè, Raffaele. Michele Morelli e la rivoluzione napoletana del 1820–1821. Rome: Gangemi, 1993.

Scirocco, Alfonso. *L'Italia del Risorgimento, 1800–1860.* Bologna: Il Mulino, 1990.

———. "La rivoluzione del 1820." In Galasso et al., *Storia del mezzogiorno,* IV/ii:655–72.

Serao, Matilde. *Il ventre di Napoli.* Naples: Avagliano, 2002 [1884].

Sontag, Susan. *The Volcano Lover.* New York: Farrar, Straus, and Giroux, 1992.

Spadolini, Giovanni. *Indipendenza e unità nazionale in Italia ed in Grecia.* Florence: Olschki, 1987.

Spetsieri Beschi, Caterina. *Risorgimento greco e filellenismo italiano: lotte, cultura, arte.* Rome: Sole, 1986.

Spini, Giorgio. *Mito e realtà della Spagna nelle rivoluzioni italiane.* Rome: Perrella, 1950.

Stendhal. "Vanina Vanini." In *The Abbess of Castro and Other Tales.* Tr. C. K. Scott Moncrief. New York: Boni and Liveright, 1926.

Taliento, Esther. *Appunti storico-bibliografici sulla stampa periodica napoletana durante le rivoluzioni del 1799 e 1820–21.* Bari: STEB, 1920.

Vanucci, Atto. *I martiri della libertà italiana dal 1794 al 1848.* Florence: F. de Monnier, 1860 [1849].

Venturi, Franco. *Studies in Free Russia.* Tr. F. Segre Walsby and M. O'Dell. Chicago: University of Chicago Press, 1982.

Viglione, Massimo, ed. *La rivoluzione italiana: storia critica del Risorgimento.* Rome: Minotauro, 2001.

Weinstock, Herbert. *Rossini: A Biography.* New York: Knopf, 1968.

Wicks, Margaret. *The Italian Exiles in London, 1816–1848.* Freeport, NY: Books for Libraries, 1968 [1937].

Greece: Primary Sources

Aschling, Nils. *Försök till grekiska Revolutionens historia.* Stockholm: Rumstedt, 1824.

Barratt, Glynn. "Notice sur l'insurrection des Grecs contre l'empire Ottoman: A Russian View of the Greek War of Independence." *BS* 14/1 (1973): 47–115.

Bentham, Jeremy. *Security Against Misrule and Other Constitutional Writings for Tripoli and Greece.* Ed. P. Schofield. Oxford: Clarendon Press, 1990.

Blaquiere, Edward. *The Greek Revolution.* London: Whittaker, 1824.

Bollmann, Louis de. *Remarques sur l'état moral, politique, et militaire de la Grèce.* Marseilles: Carnaud et Simonin, 1823.

Clogg, Richard, ed. *The Movement for Greek Independence, 1770–1821: A Collection of Documents.* London: Macmillan, 1976.

Collegno, Giacinto. *Diario dell'assedio di Navarino.* Turin: Pelazza, 1857.

Constitutions, loix, ordonnances des assemblées nationales, des corps législatif, et du President de la Grèce. Athens: Imprimerie Royale, 1835.

Dalleggio, Eugène, ed. *Les Philhellènes et la guerre de l'Indépendance: lettres inédites de J. Orlando et A. Louriotis.* Athens: Institut Français d'Athènes, 1949.

Elster, J. D. *Das Battaillon der Philhellenen.* Baden: Diebold, 1828.

Emerson, James, Count Pecchio, and W. H. Humphrey. *A Picture of Greece in 1825.* 2 vols. London, 1826.

Enepekides, Polychronis. *Die neugefundenen Akten des wiener Kriegsarchivs zur siebenjährigen Festungshaft Alexander Ypsilantis.* Sofia: Académie Bulgare des Sciences, 1969.

Gamba, Pietro. *A Narrative of Lord Byron's Last Journey to Greece.* Paris: Galignani, 1825.

———. *A Narrative of Lord Byron's Last Journey to Greece.* London: Murray, 1825.

Gordon, Thomas. *History of the Greek Revolution.* 2 vols. Edinburgh: Blackwood, 1832.

Howe, Samuel. *An Historical Sketch of the Greek Revolution.* New York: White, Gallaher, and White, 1828.

Humphrey, W. H. *W. H. Humphrey's First "Journal of the Greek War of Independence" (July 1821– February 1822).* Ed. Sture Linnér. Stockholm: Almqvist and Wiksell, 1967.

Jourdain, Jean P. *Mémoires historiques et militaires sur les événements de la Grèce depuis 1822 jusqu'au combat de Navarin.* 2 vols. Paris: Brissot-Thivars, 1828.

Kolokotrones, Theodoros. *Kolokotrones: The Klepht and the Warrior.* Tr. E. Edmonds. London: Fisher Unwin, 1892.

Lascaris, M. "La révolution grecque vue de Salonique." *Balcania* VI (1943): 145–68.

Liprandi, Ivan. "Notele lui I. P. Liprandi" In Oțetea et al., eds., *Documente,* V.

Makryannis. *The Memoirs of General Makriyannis 1797–1864.* Tr. H. A. Lidderdale. London: Oxford University Press, 1966.

Mengous, Petros. *Narrative of a Greek Soldier.* New York: Elliot and Palmer, 1836.

Moschake, Ignatius. *The Catechism of the Orthodox Eastern Church.* London: Society for Promoting Christian Knowledge, 1894.

Oekonomos, K. *Discours prononcé en Grec à Odessa, le 29 juin 1821.* Paris: Bobée, 1821.

Oțetea, Andrei, et al., eds. *Documente privind istoria României, vol. V. Răscoală din 1821.* 5 vols. Bucharest: Acad. Rep. Pop. Romîne, 1959–1962).

Pecchio, Giuseppe. *Relazione degli avvenimenti della Grecia nella primavera del 1825.* Lugano: Vanelli, 1826.

Pertusier, Charles. *La Valachie, la Moldavie, et de l'influence politique des Grecs du Fanal.* Paris: De Fain, 1822.

Pouqueville, F.-C.-H.-L. *Histoire de la régénération de la Grèce.* 4 vols. Paris: Didot, 1824.

Prokesch von Osten, Anton. *Geschichte der Abfalls der Griechen.* 6 vols. Vienna: Gerold in Komm, 1867.

Raffenel, C. D. *Histoire des événemens de la Grèce.* 2 vols. Paris: Dondey-Dupré, 1822–24.

Raybaud, Maxime. *Mémoires sur la Grèce: pour servir à l'histoire de la guerre de l'indépendance.* 2 vols. Paris: Tournachon-Molin, 1824–25.

Recordon, François. *Lettres sur la Valachie.* Paris: Lecointe et Durey, 1821.

Rhigas Velestinlis. *Revolutionary Scripts: Revolution, Proclamation, Human Rights, the Constitution, Thourios.* Ed. D. Karamperopoulas. Tr. V. Zervoulakas. Athens: Scientific Society of Studies, 2002.

Solomós, Dionysios. *Faith and Motherland: Collected Poems.* Tr. M. B. Raizis. Minneapolis: Nostos, 1998.

———. *O ymnos eis tin eleytherian/The Hymn to Liberty.* Athens: Greek Parliament, 1999.

Soutsos, N. *Mémoires du Prince Nicolas Soutzo, Grand-Logothète de Moldavie, 1798–1871*. Ed. Panaïoti Rizos. Vienna: Gerold, 1899.

Stanhope, Leicester. *Greece During Lord Byron's Residence in That Country in 1823 and 1824*. 2 vols. Paris: Galignani, 1825.

Vikelas, Demetrios. *Loukis Laras*. Tr. J. Gennadios and D. Trollope. London: Doric, 1972 [1879].

Waddington, George. *The Present Condition and Prospects of the Greek, or Oriental, Church*. London: Murray, 1829.

———. *A Visit to Greece in 1823 and 1824*. London: Murray, 1825.

Greece: Secondary Works

Arsh, Grigorii. *Eteristskoe dvizhenie v Rossii*. Moscow: Nauka, 1970.

———. "Ipsilanti v Rossii." *VI* 3 (March 1985): 88–101.

———. "On the Life in Russia of the Greek Patriotic Family of Ypsilanti." *BS* xxvi/1 (1985): 73–90. [A translation of his "Ipsilanti v Rossii."]

———, ed. *Politicheskie, obshchestvennye i kul'turnye sviazi narodov SSSR i Gretsii, XIX-XX vv*. Moscow: Nauka, 1989.

———. *Tainoe obshchestvo "Filiki Eteriia": iz istorii bor'by Gretsii za sverzhenie Osmanskogo iga*. Moscow: Nauka, 1965.

Athanassoglu-Kallmyer, Nina. *French Images from the Greek War of Independence, 1821–1830*. New Haven: Yale University Press, 1989.

Barth, Wilhelm, and Max Kehrig-Korn. *Die Philhellenzeit*. Munich: Huber, 1960.

Bass, Gary. *Freedom's Battle: The Origins of Humanitarian Intervention*. New York: Knopf, 2008.

Beaton, Roderick. "Romanticism in Greece." In Roy Porter and M. Teich, eds., *Romanticism in a National Context*, 93–107. Cambridge: Cambridge University Press, 1988.

Beševliev, V. "Die griechischen Einflüsse auf die bulgarische Wiedergeburt." In *Pneumatikes kai politistikes scheseis*, 31–38. Thessaloniki: Institute for Balkan Studies, 1980.

Brewer, David. *The Flame of Freedom: The Greek War of Independence, 1821–1833*. London: Murray, 2001.

Camaiani, Pier Giorgio. "La religiosità patriottica nel '21 greco e nel '48 italiano." In Spadolini, ed., *Indipendenza e unità nazionale*, 61–78. Florence: Olschki, 1987.

Camariano, Nestor. "Les relations de Tudor Vladimirescu avec l'Hétairie avant la Révolution de 1821." *BS* VI/1 (1965): 139–64.

Chaconas, Stephen. *Adamantios Korais: A Study in Greek Nationalism*. New York: Columbia University Press, 1942.

Ciuffoletti, Zeffiro, and Luigi Mascilli Migliorini. "Il mito della Grecia in Italia tra politica e letteratura." In Spadolini, ed., *Indipendenza e unità nazionale*, 43–59. Florence: Olschki, 1987.

Clogg, Richard. "Aspects of the Movement for Greek Independence." In Clogg, ed., *The Struggle for Greek Independence*, 1–40. London: Macmillan, 1973.

———, ed., *The Struggle for Greek Independence*. London: Macmillan, 1973.

Corivan, N. "La captivité d'Alexandre Ypsilanti." *BS* viii/1 (1967): 87–102.

Dakin, Douglas. "The Formation of the Greek State, 1821–33." In Clogg, ed., The Struggle for Greek Independence, 156–81. London: Macmillan, 1973.

———. *The Greek Struggle for Independence, 1821–1833*. London: Batsford, 1973.

Despotopoulos, Alexandros. "La révolution grecque, Alexandre Ypsilantis et la politique de la Russie." *BS* vii/2 (1966): 395–410.

Dimakis, Jean. *La presse française face à la chute de Missolonghi et la bataille navale de Navarin*. Thessaloniki: Institute for Balkan Studies, 1976.

Dimaras, Alexis. "The Other British Philhellenes." In Clogg, ed., *The Struggle for Greek Independence*, 200–223. London: Macmillan, 1973.

Dostian, Irina. "L'attitude de la société russe face au mouvement de libération nationale grec." In *Les relations gréco-russes pendant la domination turque et la guerre d'indépendance grecque*, 63–86. Thessaloniki: Institute for Balkan Studies, 1983.

Droulia, Loukia. "La Révolution française et l'Hellénisme moderne." In Michel Vovelle, ed., *L'image de la Révolution française*, II:1437–45. Paris: Pergamon, 1990.

Fadeev, A. V. "Grecheskoe natsional'no-osvoboditel'noe dvizhenie i russkoe obshchestvo pervykh desiatiletii XIX veka." *Novaia i noveishaia istoriia* 3 (1964): 41–52.

Farsolas, Demetrios. "Alexander Pushkin: His Attitude Toward the Greek Revolution, 1821–1829." *BS* xii/1 (1971): 57–80.

———. "Ypsilanti (Hypsilantis) Family." *Modern Encyclopedia of Russian and Soviet History*, XLV:35–46.

Finlay, George. *A History of Greece*. 6 vols. Oxford: Clarendon Press, 1877.

———. *History of the Greek Revolution*. 2 vols. Edinburgh: Blackwood, 1861.

Frangos, George. "The Philiki Etairia: A Premature National Coalition." In Clogg, ed., *The Struggle for Greek Independence*, 87–103. London: Macmillan, 1973.

Frazee, Charles. *The Orthodox Church and Independent Greece, 1821–1852*. Cambridge: Cambridge University Press, 1969.

Geanakoplos, Deno. "The Diaspora Greeks: The Genesis of Modern Greek National Consciousness." In *Hellenism and the First Greek War of Liberation (1821–1830)*. Thessaloniki: Institute for Balkan Studies, 1976.

Gervinus, Georg. *Insurrection et régénération de la Grèce*. Tr. J.-F. Minssen and Leonidas Sgouta. 2 vols. Paris: Durand, 1863.

Hatzopoulos, Konstantinos. "Was Alexander Ypsilantis Struck Off the List of Officers in the Russian Army?" *BS* xxviii/2 (1987): 281–95.

Hidryma Meletōn Chersonēsou tou Haimou. *Pneumatikes kai politistikes scheseis Hellenon kai Voulgaron apo ta mesa tou 15 eos ta mesa tou 19. aiona; Kulturni i literaturni otnošenija meždu Gărci i Bălgari ot sredata na XV do sredata na XIX vek*. Thessaloniki: Institute for Balkan Studies, 1980.

Iovva, I. F. *Bessarabiia i grecheskoe natsional'no-osvoboditel'noe dvizhenie*. Kishinev: Shtiintsa, 1974.

Jenkins, Romilly. *Dionysius Solomós*. Cambridge: Cambridge University Press, 1940.

Kakridis, John. "The Ancient Greeks and the Greeks of the War of Independence." *BS* iv/2 (1963): 251–64.

Kaltchas, Nicholas. *Introduction to the Constitutional History of Modern Greece*. New York: Columbia University Press, 1940.

Khasiotes, I. K. "O ispanikos philellenismos." *Makedonike zoe* 70 (March 1972): 10–16.

Knežević, Djordje. "Meternih i grčki ustanak 1821–1829 godine." In *Synergasia Hellenon kai Servon kata tou Apeleutherotikous agones, 1804–1830/Saradnja izmedju Srba i Grka za vreme svoih oslobodilačkih pokreta, 1804–1830*, 37–42. Thessaloniki: Institute for Balkan Studies, 1979.

Koliopoulos, John. *Brigands with a Cause: Brigandage and Irredentism in Modern Greece, 1821–1912*. Oxford: Clarendon Press, 1987.

Koumarianou, Catherine. "The Contribution of the Intelligentsia Towards the Greek Independence Movement, 1798–1821." In Clogg, ed., *The Struggle for Greek Independence*, 67–86. London: Macmillan, 1973.

Laourdas, Vasileios. "Modern Greek Historical Novels." *BS* vi/1 (1965): 55–66.

Loukatos (Loucatos), Spyros. "Le Philhellénisme balkanique pendant la lutte pour l'indépendance hellénique." *BS* xix/1 (1978): 249–83.

———. "Les relations des révolutionnaires grecs et des Bulgares volontaires à la lutte pour l'indépendance hellénique." In *Pneumatikes kai politistikes scheseis*, 199–209. Thessaloniki: Institute for Balkan Studies, 1980.

———. *O Italikos filellenismos kata ton agona tes Hellenikes anexartesias, 1821–1831*. Athens: Graphikes Technes, 1996.

Lucarelli, Enrica, et al. *Risorgimento greco e filellenismo italiano: lotte, cultura, arte*. Rome: Sole, 1986.

Margaritis, Georges. "La présence de la Révolution française dans la Grèce occupée, 1941–44: images, symboles et fonctions." In *Révolution française et l'hellénisme moderne*, 587–93.

Mazower, Mark. *Inside Hitler's Greece: The Experience of Occupation*. New Haven: Yale University Press, 2001.

Nada, Narciso. "La partecipazione degli Italiani alla guerra di Indipendenza ellenica." In *Risorgimento Greco*, 87–89. Rome: Edizioni del Sole, 1986.

Oțetea, Andrei, ed. *The History of the Romanian People*. Tr. E. Farca. New York: Twayne, 1970.

———. *Tudor Vladimirescu*. Bucharest: Inst. de Stud. Ist., 1971.

Pantschoff, Mladen. *Kaiser Alexander I und der Aufstand Ypsilantis, 1821*. Leipzig: Schmidt, 1891.

Penn, Virginia. "Philhellenism in Europe, 1821–1828." *Slavonic and East European Review* 16/48 (April, 1938): 638–53.

Persico, Elena. *Letteratura filellenica italiana, 1787–1870*. Rome: Bondi, 1920.

Petropoulos, John. *Politics and Statecraft in the Kingdom of Greece, 1833–1843*. Princeton: Princeton University Press, 1968.

Phillips, W. Alison. *The War of Greek Independence, 1821 to 1833*. London: Smith, Elder, 1897.

Prousis, Theophilus. "The Greeks of Russia and the Greek Awakening, 1774–1821." *BS* 28/2 (1987): 259–89.

———. *Russian Society and the Greek Revolution*. DeKalb: Northern Illinois University Press, 1994.

Raizis, M. Byron. *Dionysios Solomos*. New York: Twayne, 1972.

Les relations gréco-russes pendant la domination turque et la guerre d'indépendance grecque. Thessaloniki: Institute for Balkan Studies, 1983.

Révolution française et l'hellénisme moderne. Athens: Centre de Recherches Néohelléniques, 1989.

Rosen, F. *Bentham. Byron, and Greece: Constitutionalism, Nationalism, and Early Liberal Political Thought*. Oxford: Clarendon Press, 1992.

Sarafis, Marion. "Ejército, Constitución y pueblo en Grecia." In Gil Novales, ed., *Ejército, pueblo, y Constitución*, 558–72.

Sfyroeras, Vassilis. "Filelleni italiani in Grecia." In *Risorgimento greco*, 84–86.

Shparo, Olga. *Osvobozhedenie Gretsii I Rossiya, 1821–1829*. Moscow: Mysl, 1965.

Skalkovskii, A. A. *Pervoe tridtsatiletie istorii goroda Odessy, 1793–1823*. Odessa: OKFA, 1998 [1837].

Skiotis, Dennis. "Mountain Warriors and the Greek Revolution." In V. J. Parry and M. E. Yapp, eds., *War, Technology and Society in the Middle East*, 308–29. London: Oxford University Press, 1975.

Spadolini, Giovanni. *Indipendenza e unità nazionale in Italia ed in Grecia*. Florence: Olshki, 1987.

Spini, Giorgio. "Il significato storico dello Statuto di Epidauro." In *Risorgimento greco*, 135–36.

St. Clair, William. *That Greece Might Still Be Free: The Philhellenes in the War of Independence*. London: Oxford University Press, 1972.

Strasburger, Janusz. "Le Philhellénisme en Pologne aux années de l'insurrection grècque, 1821–1828." *BS* xii/1 (1974): 103–16.

Tachiaos, A.-E. N. "The National Regeneration of the Greeks as Seen by the Russian Intelligentsia." *BS* xxx/2 (1989): 291–310.

Tappe, E. D. "The 1821 Revolution in the Rumanian Principalities." In Clogg, ed., *The Struggle for Greek Independence*, 135–55. London: Macmillan, 1973.

Todorov, Nikolai. *Filiki eteriia i Bulgarite*. Sofia: Bulg. Akad. Na Naukite, 1965.

———. "Quelques renseignements sur les insurgés grecs dans les Principautés danubiennes." In *Essays in Memory of Basil Laourdas*, 471–77. Thessaloniki: Gregoris, 1975.

Todorov, Nikolai, and Veselin Traikov. *Bŭlgari-uchastnitsi v borbite za osvobozhdenieto na Gŭrtsiia, 1821–1828*. Sofia: Bŭlg. Akad. Na Naukite, 1971.

Todorov, Varban. *Greek Federalism During the Nineteenth Century: Ideas and Projects*. Boulder: East European Quarterly, 1995.

Trajkov, Veselin. "La coopération Bulgaro-grecque dans les luttes de liberation nationale." In *Pneumatikes kai politistikes scheseis*, 47–53.

Vacalopoulos, Constantinos. "Probleme in Bezug auf das Leben und den Tod von Alexander Ypsilantis." *BS* xvi/1 (1974): 61–79.

Vagenas, Phanos. "O ispanikos philellenismos kata ten Elleniken epanastasin." In *Philellenika*, January-March 1955, 5–34.

Vallianatos, Evaggelos. "Jeremy Bentham's Constitutional Reform Proposals to the Greek Provisional Government, 1823–1825." *BS* x/2 (1969): 325–34.

Valsa, M. *Le théâtre grec moderne de 1453 à 1900*. Berlin: Akademie Verlag, 1960.

Woodhouse, C. M. *Capodistria: The Founder of Greek Independence*. London: Oxford University Press, 1973.

Woodhouse, C. M. *The Philhellenes*. Rutherford, NJ: Fairleigh Dickinson University Press, 1969.

Russia: Primary Sources

An indispensable though dated tool is the alphabetical directory of Decembrists in vol. VIII of *VD* (Leningrad, 1925).

Al'tshuller, R. E., and Tartakovskii, A. G., eds. *Listovki Otechestvennoi voiny 1812 goda: sbornik dokumentov*. Moscow: ANSSSR, 1962.

Auger, Hippolyte. "Iz zapisok Ippolita Ozhe." *RA*, 1 (1877): 257–87.

Azadovskii, M. K., ed. *Vospominaniia Bestuzhevykh*. Moscow: ANSSSR, 1951.

Basargin, N. V. *Zapiski*. Ed. P. E. Shchegolev. Petrograd: Ogni, 1917.

Beliaev, A. P. "Vospominaniia o perezhitom i perechuvstvovannom." *RS*, September 1880, 1–42; December 1880, 823–58; January 1881, 1–26; March 1881, 487–518; April 1881, 799–838; September 1881, 1–46; October 1881, 251–86; December 1881, 679–704.

Borozdin, A. K., ed. *Iz pisem i pokazanii dekabristov: kritika sovremennogo sostoianiia Rossii i plany budushchego ustroistva*. St. Petersburg: Pirozhkov, 1906.

Bulgarin, Faddei. *Sochineniia*. 12 vols. St. Petersburg, 1830.

———. *Vospominaniia*. 6 vols. St. Petersburg, 1846–49.

"Bunt chernigovskogo polka." Ed. M. Shugurov. *RA* 1 (1871): 257–87.

Davydov, Denis. *Sochineniia*. St. Petersburg: Smirdin, 1848.

The Doctrine of the Russian Church. Tr. R. W. Blackmore. Aberdeen: Brown, 1845.

Dovnar-Zapol'skii, M. V., ed. *Memuary dekabristov*. Kiev: Ivanov, 1906.

Fomin, I. I., ed. *Sobranie stikhotvorenii dekabristov*. 2 vols. Moscow: Mamontov, 1906–7.

Fonvizin, M. A. "Zapiski dekabrista, 1823 g." *GM* 10 (1910): 135–54.

Gangeblov, A. S. "Vospominaniia." *RA* (1886): 181–268.

Gertsen, A. I. *Sobranie sochinenii*. 30 vols. Moscow: ANSSSR, 1954–65.

Gorbachevskii, I. I. *Zapiski dekabrista*. Moscow: Zadruga, 1916.

———. *Zapiski i pis'ma dekabrista*. 2nd ed. Ed. B. E. Syroechkovskii. Moscow: Stoliar, 1925.

———. *Zapiski, pis'ma*. Ed. B. E. Syroechkovskii et al. Moscow: ANSSSR, 1963.

"Grazhdanskii katekhizis, ili Kratkoe obozrenie dolzhnostei ispantsa." *SO* 2 (October 1812): 53–60.

Grech, Nikolai. *Zapiski moei zhizni*. Moscow: Zakharov, 2002.

Herzen, A. I. *See* Gertsen.

Khristianskii Katikhizis: Pravoslavnyia kafolicheskiia vostochnyia greko-rossiiskiia Tserkvi. 3rd ed. Moscow: Sinodal'naia Tipografiia, 1824.

Kiukhel'beker, Vil'gel'm [Wilhelm Küchelbecker]. *Stikhotvoreniia*. Leningrad: Sovetskii Pisatel', 1952.

Kushelev, E. A. "Unichtozhenie masonskikh lozh v Rossii, 1822." *RS*, March 1877, 455–79; April 1877, 641–64.

Lorer [Lohrer], N. I. "Iz zapisok dekabrista." *RB* 3 (1904): 51–92.

Lunin, Mikhail. *Pis'ma iz Sibiri*. Ed. I. A. Zhelvakova and N. Ya. Eidel'man. Moscow, 1967.

———. *Sochineniia*. New York: Khronika, 1976 [1923].

Maiorov, I. V. "Krest'ianskie vospominaniia o P. I. i B. I. Pestel." *Byloe* 5 (May, 1906): 271–72.

Mikhailovskii-Danilevskii, A. I. "Vstuplenie na prestol Imperatora Nikolaia I." Ed. N. K. Schilder [Shil'der]. *RS*, November 1890, 489–523.

Modzalevskii, V. A., and Oksman, Yu. G., eds. *Dekabristy: neizdannye materialy i stat'i*. Moscow: Pushkinskii Dom, 1925.

Murav'ev-Apostol, I. M. *Pis'ma iz Moskvy v Nizhnii Novgorod*. Ed. V. A. Koshelev. St. Petersburg: Nauka, 2002.

Murav'ev-Apostol, M. I. *Vospominaniia i pis'ma*. Ed. S. Ya. Shtraikh. Petrograd: Byloe, 1922.

Myslovskii, P. N. "Iz zapisnoi knizhki." *RA* ix (1905): 132–33.

Nevskii zritel'. [Journal.] St. Petersburg, 1821.

Orlov, M. F. *Kapituliatsiia Parizha*. Ed. S. Ya. Borovoi and M. I. Gillel'son. Moscow: ANSSSR: 1963.

"Pamiat' v narode o deakabristkikh sobytiiakh 1825 g. v Vasil'kove." *Ukrainskaia zhizn'* 1 (1914): 90.

Pisateli-dekabristy v vospominaniiakh sovremennikov. 2 vols. Moscow: Khudozhestvennaia Literatura, 1980.

Pushkin, A. S. *Polnoe sobranie sochinenii*. 10 vols. Moscow, 1956–58.

Raeff, Marc. *The Decembrist Movement*. Englewood Cliffs: Prentice-Hall, 1966.

Raevskii, V. F. *Materialy o zhizni i revoliutsionnoi deiatel'nosti*. 2 vols. Irkutsk: Vostochno-Sibirskoe Izd., 1980–83.

Romanov, Vladimir. "Otryvok iz pokhodnykh zapisok v Ispaniiu." *OZ* ii/3 (1820): 27–41.

Ryleev, K. F. *Polnoe sobranie sochinenii*. Ed. A. G. Tseitlin. Moscow: Academia, 1934.

———. *Polnoe sobranie sochinenii*. Ed. A. V. Arkhipov, Leningrad: Pisatel', 1971.

———. *Stikhotvoreniia, stat'i, ocherki, dokladnye zapiski, pis'ma*. Moscow: Gos. Izd. Khudozh. Lit., 1956.

Sokrashchennyi Katikhizis dlia obucheniia iunoshestva o Pravoslavnom zakone Khristianskom. St. Petersburg, 1818.

Timiriazev, F. "Stranitsy proshlogo." *RA* 1(1882): 155–80.

Trubetskoi, S. P. *Materialy o zhizni i revoliutsionnoi deiatelnosti*. 2 vols. Irkutsk: Vostochno-Sibirskoe Knizh. Izd., 1983–87.

Vasil'chikov, I. V. "Bumagi." *RA* 1 (1875): 339–59; 5 (1875): 44–98.

Vigel', F. F. *Zapiski*. Moscow: Zakharov, 2000.

Volkonskii, S. G. *Zapiski*. Irkutsk: Vostochno-Sibirskoe Knizh. Izd., 1991.

———. *Zapiski*. St. Petersburg: Sinod. Tip., 1902.

Vospominaniia i rasskazy deiatelei tainykh obshchestv 1820-x godov. Moscow: Vsesoiuznoe Obshchestvo Politkatorzhan i Ssyl'no-Poselentsev, 1931.

Vosstanie dekabristov: materialy. Moscow: Gos. Izd., 1925–.

Wilson, Robert. *Narrative of Events During the Invasion of Russia by Napoleon Bonaparte*. Ed. H. Randolph. London: Murray, 1860.

Russia: Secondary Works

14 Dekabria 1825 goda. [Journal.] St. Petersburg, 1997–.

Alekseev, M. P. "Etiudy iz istorii ispano-russkikh otnoshenii." In *Kul'tura ispanii: sbornik*, 353–427. Moscow: ANSSSR, 1940.

Alekseev, M. P. *Ocherki istorii ispano-russikikh literaturnykh otnoshenii XVI–XIX vv*. Leningrad: Leningradskii Universitet, 1964.

Austin, Paul. *1812: Napoleon in Moscow*. London: Greenhill, 1995.

———. *1812: The Great Retreat*. London: Greenhill, 1996.

———. *1812: The March to Moscow*. London: Greenhill, 1993.

Balas, Mikhail. "S. Murav'ev-Apostol." *RS* 5 (1873): 653–76.

Barratt, Glynn. *Ivan Kozlov: A Study and a Setting*. Toronto: Hakkert, 1972.

———. *The Rebel on the Bridge: A Life of the Decembrist Baron Andrey Rozen (1800–84)*. London: Elek, 1975.

Bazanov, V. G. *Dekabristy v Kishineve: M. F. Orlov I V. F. Raevskii*. Kishinev: Izd. Moldavii, 1951.

Belozerskaia, N. "Zapiski Van-Galena." *IV*, May 1884, 402–19, and June 1884, 651–78.

Bersenev, S. [Mariia Yakhontova]. *Sergei Ivanovich Murav'ev-Apostol*. Moscow: Altsiona, 1920.

Bolkhovitinov, N. N. "Dekabristy i Amerika." *VI* 4 (April 1974): 91–104.

Boretskii-Bergfel'd, N. "Imperator Pavel I i politicheskie sud'by Italii." *RS*, March 1912, 509–22.

Christoff, Peter. *An Introduction to Nineteenth-Century Russian Slavophilism: A Study in Ideas*, vol. I, *A. S. Xomjakov* (The Hague, 1961) and vol. II, *I. V. Kireevskij* (The Hague, 1961).

Dodolev, M. A. "O vliianii ispanskoi revoliutsii 1808–1814 godov na vneshniuiu politiku evropeiskikh gosudarstv." *Novaia i noveishaia istoriia* 2 (March-April 1968): 30–40.

———. Rossiia i Ispaniia 1808–1823 gg.: voina i revoliutsiia v ispanii i russko-ispanskie otnosheniia. Moscow: Nauka, 1984.

———. "Rossiia i ispanskaia revoliutsiia 1820–1823 gg." *ISSSR* 1 (January-February 1969): 113–22.

———. "Rossiia i voina ispanskogo naroda za nezavisimost' (1808–1814) gg." *VI* 11(November 1972): 33–44.

———. "Van-Galen v Rossii (1818–1820 gg.)." *ISSSR* 2 (March-April 1980): 145–57.

———. "Zapiski russkogo diplomata ob Italii (1816–1822 gg.)." *ISSSR* 5 (September-October 1976): 157–64.

Dostian, Irina. *Russkaia obshchestvennaia mysl' i balkanskie narody: ot Radishcheva do dekabristov*. Moscow: Nauka, 1980.

Dovnar-Zapol'skii, M. V. *Idealy dekabristov*. Moscow: Sytin, 1907.

Druzhinin, N. M. *Dekabrist Nikita Murav'ev*. Moscow: Obshchestvo Politkatorzhan i Ssyl'no-Poselentsev, 1933.

Druzhinin, N. M., et al., eds. *Ocherki iz istorii dvizheniia dekabristov: sbornik statei*. Moscow: Gos. Izd. Polit. Lit., 1954.

Edmunds, Neil. "Classical Music." Ms.

Eidelman (Eidel'man), Natan. *Apostol Sergei: povest' o Sergee Murav'eve-Apostole*. Moscow: Politizdat, 1975.

———. *Conspiracy Against the Tsar*. Moscow: Progress, 1985.

———. "K biografii Sergeia Ivanovicha Murav'eva-Apostola" (1975). In *Iz potaennoi istorii Rossii XVIII–XIX vekov*, 349–71. Moscow: Vysshaia Shkola, 1993.

Eimontova, R. G., et al. *Dvizhenie dekabristov: ukazatel' literatury, 1928–1959*. Moscow: Vsesoiuz. Knizh. Palata, 1960.

———. *Dvizhenie dekabristov: ukazatel' literatury, 1960–1976*. Moscow: Vsesoiuz. Knizh. Palata, 1983.

Erlikh [Erlich], S. E. *Istoriia mifa: "Dekabristkaia legenda" Gertsena*. St. Petersburg: Aleteiia, 2006.

Fassier, Robert. *Les Décémbristes: les sociétés secrètes militaires et la naissance du mouvement révolutionnaire russe*. 2 vols. Poisy: Le Main Multiple, 2006.

Fedorov, V. A. *Soldatskoe dvizhenie v gody dekabristov*. Moscow: Moskovskii Universitet, 1963.

Feuer, Kathryn. *Tolstoy and the Genesis of War and Peace*. Ed. Robin Feuer and Donna Orwin. Ithaca: Cornell University Press, 1996.

Frank, Joseph. *Dostoevsky*. 5 vols. Princeton: Princeton University Press, 1976–2002.

Glinskii, B. B. *Bor'ba za konstitutsiiu, 1612–1861*. St. Petersburg: Karbasnikov, 1908.

Grimsted, Patricia. *The Foreign Ministers of Alexander I: Political Attitudes and the Conduct of Russian Diplomacy, 1801–1825*. Berkeley: University of California Press, 1969.

Grosheva, E. "Dekabristy (opera Yu. Shaporina)." *Sovetskaia muzyka* 8 (August 1953): 9–18.

Hartley, Janet. *Alexander I*. London: Longman, 1994.

Ikonnikov, V. S. *Krest'ianskoe dvizhenie v Kievskoi gub. v. 1826–27 gg. v sviazi s sobytiiami togo vremeni*. St. Petersburg: Imp. Akad. Nauk, 1905.

Il'in, P. V. *Novoe o dekabristakh*. St. Petersburg, Nestor-Istoriia, 2004.

Iovva, I. F. *Iuzhnye dekabristy i grecheskoe natsional'no-osvoboditel'noe dvizhenie*. Kishinev: Kartya Moldovenyaske, 1963.

Karatsuba, I. V. "Pravoslavnyi katekhizis S.I. Murav'eva-Apostola: kommentarii." In Kiianskaia, ed., *Dekabristy*, 460–76.

Keep, John L. H. *Soldiers of the Tsar: Army and Society in Russia, 1462–1874*. Oxford: Clarendon Press, 1985.

Kiianskaia, Oksana, ed. *Dekabristy: aktual'nye problemy i novye podkhody*. Moscow: RGGU, 2008.

———. "K istorii vosstaniia Chernigovskogo polka." *OI* 6 (1995): 21–33.

———. *Pavel Pestel: ofitser, razvedchik, zagovorshchik*. Moscow: Paralleli, 2002.

———. *Iuzhnyi bunt: vosstanie Chernigovskogo pekhotnogo polka*. Moscow: RGGU, 1997.

Kolesnikova, Anna. *Bal v Rossii: XVIII–nachalo XX veka*. St. Petersburg: Azbuka-Klassika, 2005.

Koroleva, N. V. *Dekabristy i teatr*. Leningrad: Iskusstvo, 1975.

Koval'skaia, M. I. "Ital'ianskie karbonarii i peredovaia Rossiia." *VI* xlii/8 (August 1967): 78–90.

Kraehe, Enno. "Strange Bedfellows: Alexander I and Ferdinand VII, 1812–1823." In Ronald Caldwell et al., eds., *The Consortium on Revolutionary Europe, 1750–1850*, 1–12. Tallahassee: Florida State University, 1994.

Kulman, N. "K istorii masonstva v Rossii." *ZhMNP* 10 (October 1907): 343–73.

Landa, S. S. *Dukh revoliutsionnykh preobrazovanii: iz istorii formirovaniia i politicheskoi organizatsii dekabristov, 1816–1825*. Moscow: Mysl', 1975.

Lebedev, N. M. *Pestel': ideolog i rukovoditel' dekabristov*. Moscow: Mysl', 1972.

Lemberg, Hans. *Die nationale Gedankenwelt der Dekabristen*. Graz: Böhlau, 1963.

Luciani, Georges. *La Société des slaves unis (1823–1825)*. Bordeaux: Université de Bordeaux, 1963.

Machul'skii, E. P. "Novye dannye o biografii dekabrista M. P. Bestuzheva-Riumina." *IZ* 96 (1975): 347–58.

Madariaga, Isabel de. "The Russian Nobility in the Seventeenth and Eighteenth Centuries." In Scott, ed., *European Nobilities*, II:311–76. London: Longman, 1995.

———. "Spain and the Decembrists." *European Studies Review* 3/2 (January-October 1973): 141–56.

Mazour, Anatole. *The First Russian Revolution, 1825: The Decembrist Movement, its Origins, Developments, and Significance*. Stanford: Stanford University Press, 1961 [1937].

Medvedskaia, L. A. *Sergei Ivanovich Murav'ev-Apostol*. Moscow: Prosveshchenie, 1970.

Minaeva, N. V. "K voprosu ob ideinykh sviaziakh dvizheniia dekabristov i ispanskoi revoliutsii." *IZ* 96 (1975): 60–78.

Mironov, B. N. Review of Erlikh, *Istoriia mifa*. *VI* 6 (2006): 170–72.

Morrissey, Susan. *Suicide and the Body Politic in Imperial Russia*. Cambridge: Cambridge University Press, 2006.

Nechkina, M. V. *A. S. Griboedov i dekabristy*. 2nd ed. Moscow: ANSSSR, 1951.

———. "Dekabristy vo vsemirno-istoricheskom protsesse." *VI* 12 (December 1975): 3–18.

———. *Dvizhenie dekabristov*. 2 vols. Moscow, 1955.

———. "Krizis Iuzhnogo Obshchestva dekabristov." *Istorik marksist* VII (1930): 30–47.

———. "Revoliutsiia napodobie ispanskoi." *KiS* 10 (1931): 3–40.

Nevedomskii, N. "Ocherk Ispanii." *Sovremennik* xxvii (1841): 35–74.

———. "Tri poslednie glavy iz istorii gveril'iasov." *Sovremennik* xxvii (1842): 1–55.

Nikolai Mikhailovich, Grand Duke. *L'Empereur Alexandre Ier*. 2 vols. St. Petersburg: Manufacture des papiers de l'état, 1912.

Norris, Stephen. *A War of Images: Russian Popular Prints, Wartime Culture, and National Identity, 1812–1945*. DeKalb: Northern Illinois University Press, 2006.

Oksman, Yu. G. "Vosstanie Chernigovskogo polka." In *VD*, VI:ix–lxvii.

O'Meara, Patrick. *The Decembrist Pavel Pestel: Russia's First Republican*. Basingstoke: Palgrave Macmillan, 2003.

———. *K. F. Ryleev: A Political Biography of the Decembrist Poet*. Princeton: Princeton University Press, 1984.

———. "Vreden Sever: The Decembrists' Memories of the Peter-Paul Fortress." In Anthony Cross, ed., *St Petersburg, 1703–1825*, 165–89. London: Palgrave Macmillan, 2003.

Orlik, Ol'ga. *Dekabristy i evropeiskoe osvoboditel'noe dvizhenie*. Moscow: Mysl, 1975.

———. *Dekabristy i vneshniaia politika Rossii*. Moscow: Nauka, 1984.

Petrov, D. K. *Rossiia i Nikolai I v stikhotvoreniiakh Espronsedy i Rossetti*. St. Petersburg: Vineke, 1909.

Pomper, Philip. *Sergei Nechaev*. New Brunswick, NJ: Rutgers University Press, 1979.

Porokh, I. V. "Vosstanie chernigovskogo polka." In Druzhinin, *Ocherki*, 121–85.

Pushkin i ego vremia. 2 vols. Leningrad: Gos. Ermitazh, 1962.

Schiemann, Theodore. *Zur Geschichte der Regierung Paul I. und Nikolaus I: neue Materialien*. 2nd ed. Berlin: G. Reimer, 1906.

Schuster, Georg. *Die geheimen Gesellschaften, Verbindungen, und Orden.* 2 vols. Leipzig: Leibing, 1906.

Schuster [Shuster], Georg. *Tainye obshchestva, soiuzy, i ordena.* Tr. O. A. Volkenstein. 2 vols. St. Petersburg, 1905–7.

Semevskii, V. I. "Dekabristy-masony." *MG*, February 1906, 1–50, March 1906, 127–70, May-June1906, 379–433.

———. *Obshchestvennye dvizheniia v Rossi v pervuiu polovinu XIX veka.* 2 vols. St. Petersburg: Gerold, 1905.

———. *Politicheskie i obshchestvennye idei dekabristov.* St. Petersburg: Pervaia Spb. Trudovaia Artel, 1909.

———. "Volnenie v Semenovskom polku v 1820 godu." *Byloe*, January 1907, 1–35, and February 1907, 83–118.

Shchegolev, P. E. "Katekhizis Sergeia Murav'eva-Apostola." In *Istoricheskie etiudy*, 317–63 (St. Petersburg, 1913).

Sibireva, G. A. *Neapolitanskoe korolevtsvo i Rossiia v poslednei chetverti XVIII v.* Moscow: Nauka, 1981.

Syroechkovskii, B. E. "Balkanskaia problema v politicheskakh planakh dekabristov." In *Iz istorii dvizheniia dekabristov*, 186–275.

———. *Iz istorii dvizheniia dekabristov.* Moscow: Moskovskii Universitet, 1969.

Tarle, E. V. "Voennaia revoliutsiia na zapade Evropy i dekabristy." In *Sochineniia*, V:9–20. Moscow: ANSSSR, 1957–62.

Volk, S. S. *Istoricheskie vzgliady dekabristov.* Moscow: ANSSSR, 1958.

Wieczynski, Joseph. "The Mutiny of the Semenovsky Regiment in 1820." *Russian Review* 29/2 (April 1970): 167–80.

Wirtschafter, Elise. *The Play of Ideas in Russian Enlightenment Theater.* DeKalb: Northern Illinois University Press, 1997.

Wortman, Richard. *Scenarios of Power: Myth and Ceremony in Russian Monarchy from Peter the Great to the Abdication of Nicholas II.* Princeton: Princeton University Press, 2006.

Zetlin, Mikhail. *The Decembrists.* New York: International Universities Press, 1958.

Zhukovskaia, T. N. "Tainye obshchestva pervoi treti XIX v. i organizatsionnye modeli dekabrizma." *14 Dekabria 1825 g.* 5 (2002): 63–94.

Zviguilsky. Alexandre. "Riego y los masones rusos." In Gil Novales, ed., *Ejército, pueblo, y Constitución*, 272–75.

Audio/Video/Web

For 1,500 titles on the Spanish War of Independence that have appeared since 1950, see www.unav.es/historia/congreso.

Shaporin, Yuri. *The Decembrists.* 1953. [Opera.] CD. Freiser Records. Mono 90574.

Salon napolitain: The Neapolitan Salon from the Revolution to the Restoration. CD. OPS 30-255. Notes by Paolo Giovanni Maione.

SVD [Soiuz velikogo dela]. Film. Trauberg and Kozintsev, 1927.

Rossellini, Roberto. *Vanina Vanini.* Film. 1961. Dalzac Video.

INDEX

Note: Page numbers in *italics* indicate illustrations.

"A Mighty Fortress Is Our God" (Bach), 331
About the Soldier (Raevskii), 270
Achilles Disciples, 136
Acton, Harold, 18, 131, 178
Adriatic Sea, 7
Aegean Sea, 7, 19
Aeschylus, 236
Afanasiev, Ivan, 226
afrancesados, 33, 37, 57, 75, 78, 113, 115, 132
agrarian reforms, 158
Aguilar, Martínez de, 49
Aimino, Vincenzo, 234
Aix-la-Chappelle congress, 255
Alberola, Ginés, 336
Alcalá Galiano, Antonio, 64–65, 71, 77, 107–8,
    113, 180, 183
Alcalá Zamora, Niceto, 336–37
Alejandro Regiment, 56, 57–58, 69–70, 252
Alexander I of Russia
    and authoritarianism, 8
    and Capodistria, 192
    and coups, 268
    death of, 289–90, 321
    and the Decembrist movement, 242–56, 271,
        272, 274, 277, 286, 288
    early liberalism, 243–45
    and the Greek revolt, 202, 226, 228, 238
    and the Holy Alliance, 14, 245, 263
    liberalism of, 260
    and the Naples revolt, 155, 164–66, 182, 248
    orientalist view of, 242–43
    and revolutionary Cadiz, 55, 56
    and revolutionary theater, 258
    and the Spanish revolution, 100, 102,
        253–54
    and the Treaty of Tilsit, 197
    tyrannical image of, 327
    and Wilson, 108
    and Ypsilanti's plans, 200–201
Alexander II of Russia, 320
Alfieri, Vittorio, 49, 81
Algeciras, Spain, 67
Ali, Mehmet, 222
Ali Pasha, 199–200, 206, 210, 212, 324
Allegory of the Constitution of 1812, 50
Álvarez y Mendizábal, Juan, 64, 65, 113, 335
American Revolution, 216
Amerindians, 32
Anatomy of Revolution (Brinton), xi–xii
Andalusia, 31, 40, 68
Andersen, Hans Christian, 6
Androutsos, Odysseas, 217
Androvich, Foma, 226
Anglo-Russian Protocol, 238
Angoulême, Louis Bourbon, Duc d', 102–3, 109,
    112, 254, 334
Añilleros (Ring Wearers), 91
Annibale Santorre di Rossi de Pomarolo, 184,
    232
Antequera, Spain, 68
anticlericalism, 74
Antigone (Sophocles), 14
Anti-Journal, 154
anti-Semitism, 43–44, 80, 114, 333
Antonino, Duke of Serracapriola, 166
Apennine peninsula, 9
Apostle Sergei (Eidelman), 332
Apostol, Danilo, 294
Apostolic Junta, 80, 96
Apostólicos, 333–34
Appeal to the French People, 239
Arakcheev, Aleksei, 248, 257

Arco-Agüero, Felipe de
  and the Army of the South, 88–89
  and British public opinion, 98
  and counterrevolutionary sentiment,
    112, 118
  and martyrdom, 94
  and restoration of Fernando, 64
  and snuffbox designs, 85
  and theatrical productions, 81
Argüelles, Augustín, 40, 44, 79, 89, 90, 113, 180
Aris (guerrilla leader), 324
aristocracy, 219
armatoles, 211, 213–14
Army of La Isla. *See also* Army of the South
Army of Liberals, 225, 234
Army of Spain, 103
Army of the South (Army of La Isla), 88–89
Arnauts, 186–87, 202, 204, 205
Arndt, Ernst Moritz, 22
Ashkenazic Jewish community, 266
assassination
  Capodistria, 239
  and *Cinna*, 270
  and cult of revolutionary martyrdom, 27
  and the Decembrist movement, 292
  Duc de Berry, 160, 246
  of informers, 291
  Kotzebue, 14, 164, 272
  plots against Alexander I, 271, 291, 298–99
  and restoration of Fernando, 61
  and revolutionary Cadiz, 41, 48
  and Senate Square rebellion, 291–92
  Tsar Paul, 243
assembly rights, 190, 263
Athénée Royale, 12
Austerlitz, Battle of, 197
Austria
  and the Decembrist movement, 255
  and the Greek revolt, 208
  and the Holy Alliance, 99
  and influence of Alexander I, 253
  intervention in Naples, 92–93, 158, 164–75,
    246, 248
  and prisons, 26
  and the Restoration, 4
  and revolutions of the 1820s, 4
  and Russia relations, 250
Avellino, Naples, 3, 121–22, *122*, 129, 141,
  143–44, 145–49, 291, 326, 338

Bailén, Battle of, 34
Bakunin, Mikhail, 301, 304–5, 323
Balbontin, José Antonio, 337
Balearic Sea, 7
Balkans, 6, 9, 19, 188, 203, 225, 238
Ballesteros, Francisco, 78, 108, 110, 183, 255

banditry and brigandage
  in the Balkans, 186
  braceros, 31
  and Carbonari, 138
  causes of, 8
  and civil violence, 125–26
  and the Greek revolt, 211–14, 234
  and guerrilla warfare, 34–35, 133
  and the Naples revolt, 128, 138, 143, 158
  and the Spanish revolt, 97–98
  ubiquity of, 8
Banti, Alberto, 325
Barbaja, Domenico, 129, 157
Barcelona, Spain, 19, 100–101, 182
Bardaxi, Eusebio, 252
Baroja, Pío, 336
"barricade revolutions," 4
barrios bajos, 31
Barron, Augustín, 82
Basargin, Nikolai, 274, 279
Batenkov, Gavriil, 279
Battalion of Lala, 230
Battalion of Philhellenes, 225
Bautista, Iglesia de San Juan, 28
Bavaria, 239
Bayonne constitution, 33–34, 63, 128, 139
The Beast with Seven Heads and Ten Horns, 51
Beccaria, Cesare, 45, 72, 177, 262, 267
Belaia Tserkov', 296
Beliaev, Aleksandr, 273, 287, 315, 316
Belinskii, Vissarion, 301
Bellini, Giuseppe, 125
Bellini, Vincenzo, 157–58
Bentham, Jeremy, 12–14, 45–46, 73, 216–17, 219,
  262, 267
Bentinck, William, 162
Beresford, William, 92
Berezanskii, Iosif, 226–27
Bermúdez, Zea, 55, 252–53, 285
Berry, Charles-Ferdinand de Bourbon, duc de,
  14, 164, 246, 272
Berti, Giuseppe, 245
Bessarabia, 186, 202
*The Best Possible Political Constitution for All
  Peoples from a Rational Viewpoint*, 154
Bestuzhev, Aleksandr, 257–59, 287, 291, 331
Bestuzhev, Mikhail, 265, 273, 291, 315
Bestuzhev, Nikolai, 320
Bestuzhev-Riumin, Mikhail, 268, 288, 295–300,
  302, 303–8, 318, 320, 331–32
Bianco de Saint-Jorioz, Carlo, 171
bicameral legislatures
  and the Decembrist movement, 244, 262, 264
  and the French Charte, 11
  and the Greek revolt, 190
  and the Naples revolt, 142, 179
  and the Spanish revolt, 33, 46, 91, 124–25

Bidasoa, Battle of, 237
Bignon, Baron Louis, 13, 157, 262, 267
Bishop Ysidoro of Segovia, 83
Black Sea, 19
Blanch, Luigi, 135, 138
Blaquiere, Edward, 57–58, 73, 93, 103, 113, 207, 217, 224, 228–29, 334
Blessington, Marguerite, Countess of, 131, 161
Blue Division, 55
Böhl de Faber, Cecilia, 336
Bolívar, Simón, 25, 75, 87, 106
Bolshevik Revolution, 14, 323, 329, 331
Bonald, Louis Gabriel Ambroise de, 21
Bonapartism, 9
Borbón dynasty, 32. *See also* Bourbons
Borelli, Pasquale, 173
Borgo, Pozzo di, 18
Borisov, Andrei, 267, 297–98
Borisov, Petr, 267, 298
Bornholm Island, 315
Borodino, Battle of, 264
Borrow, George, 61
Bourbons, 8, 9, 32, 104–5, 124, 132. *See also specific rulers*
Bowring, 228
braceros, 31
The Brave Youth (anonymous), 324
Brenet, Nicolas-Guy, 70
Brengeri (colonel), 237
Brewer, David, 193, 224–25
brigands. *See* banditry and brigandage
Brinton, Crane, xi–xii, 85
Britain
    and Austrian intervention in Naples, 167
    and Bentham, 13
    and exile of revolutionaries, 180, 185, 334
    and Fernando's restoration, 59
    and the Greek revolt, 237, 238
    and influence of constitutional systems, 121
    influence on constitutional systems, 162
    occupation of Sicily, 162
    and philhellenism, 224–25
    response to Spanish constitution, 98
    and the Restoration, 4
    and revolutions of the 1820s, 4–5
Brothers of Peace and Charity, 117
Browning, Robert, 24
Brutus, 27
Brutus (Voltaire), 259, 260
Bucharest, 205
Bulatov, Aleksandr, 293, 316
Bulgakov, A. Ia., 250
Bulgari, M. N., 253–54
Bulgaria, 188, 203, 225–26
Bulgarin, Faddei, 252, 254, 278
Buonarotti, Philippe, 21, 323
Burgos, 32

Burgos, Carmen de (Columbine), 337
Burke, Edmund, 21, 49
Byron, George Gordon, Lord
    and Austrian intervention in Naples, 169
    Childe Harold's Pilgrimage, 322
    and the Greek revolt, 224, 229, 235, 237, 239, 279
    in Pushkin's work, 20
    on revolutionary sentiment, 185
    and romanticized bandits, 8
    and the Spanish revolt, 31, 179
    and Zhukovskii, 315
Byron Brigade, 224, 225
Byzantine Christianity, 223

Cabezas de San Juan, 3
Cadiz, Spain
    and anti-liberalism, 80–81
    Cadiz Cortes, 11, 45, 55–56, 59, 63, 76–77, 139
    celebration of the constitution in, 70, 83–85, 87
    and counterrevolutionary invasion, 107–10, 112–13
    and cultural expression, 20–21
    and the Inquisition, 74
    and Latin American patriots, 20–21
    liberalism in, 37, 63–64
    prisons in, 25
    and reformism, 72
    and revolutionary catechisms, 54
    and Riego's trial, 115–16
    role in revolution, 39–56, 65–66
    and violence against civilians, 98–99
cafés, 39–40, 58, 77–78
Cagli, Bruno, 157
cahiers, 37
Calabrian insurgency, 171, 182–83
Calderari (Braziers), 15, 132–33, 138
Calle Concepción Jerónimo, 118
Camorra, 133
Campana (general), 147–48
Candeloro, Giorgio, 170
Canning, George, 219, 238
Canosa, Prince of, 133, 139–40, 175
Canova (sculptor), 131
Cánovas y Cervantes, 336
capital punishment, 30, 115–20, 177, 260, 320–21
capo bianco, 137
Capodistria, Ioannis
    and Alexander I, 246, 248
    background, 191–92
    and the Decembrist movement, 249
    Greek presidency, 208, 222
    and international liberalism, 18
    and Kolokotrónis, 214
    and liberalism of Alexander I, 243–44

Capodistria, Ioannis (*continued*)
  and the Naples revolt, 166
  and Pepe, 182
  and Raiko, 227
  on reform, 17
  on the Spanish constitution, 253
  and Turkish wars, 196–97, 238–39
  and Ypsilanti's background, 198
  on Ypsilanti's revolt, 202
Caracca Arsenal Fortress of the Four Towers, 25
Caracciolo, Francesco, 125
Carascosa, Michele, 134, 147–49, 151, 168–70,
  180, 184
Carbonari
  and Alexander I, 246–47, 249
  and Austrian intervention in Naples, 167–68,
    168–71
  and Carrel, 105
  and the Catholic Church, 133, 161–62
  Chateaubriand on, 102
  and class divisions, 163–64
  and the *Commentary*, 13
  and Comuneros, 78
  and counterrevolutionaries, 15, 133, 154, 165,
    168, 175–76
  and the Decembrist movement, 246–49, 258,
    261–62, 267–69, 273, 276, 278, 281, 302
  and exile of revolutionaries, 182
  and failure of constitutional regimes, 159–60,
    173–74
  in film, 326
  and Giampietro's murder, 163, 178
  and the Greek revolt, 188, 210–11, 218–21,
    224, 227–28, 232, 234–35, 237
  and the Naples revolt, 148–50
  origin of, 128–29, 135
  and parades, 123
  and Pepe's revolt, 142–44, 144–50
  politics of, 138–39
  and provincial governance, 160
  and recruitment, 137–38
  repression of, 176
  and revolutionary catechisms, 302
  and Rossetti, 156
  and Sardinia-Piedmont revolt, 179
  and schisms among revolutionaries, 19
  secrecy and symbols of, 135–37, 153
  and Spanish liberalism, 92, 103, 139–41, 162,
    167
  Stendhal on, 24
  structure of, 78, 135–37
  and theater, 158, 326
Carbonari Assembly, 159
Carceri (Piranesi), 23
Carlo Alberto of Sardinia, 179
Carlo Felice of Sardinia, 179
Carlos III of Spain, 32, 33

Carlos IV of Spain, 8, 32, 33, 47
Carnival, 100
Carr, Raymond, 71, 98, 115
Carrel, Armand, 24, 101, 103, 105
Cartwright, John, 334
Castelfullit, 98
Castillo, Ignacio María del, 83
The Castle of Otranto (Walpole), 24
Castlereagh, Robert Stewart, Viscount, 40, 165,
  192, 228
Catalonia, 7, 34
"Catechism of a Free Person," 302–3
Catechism of a German, 54
Catechism of Christian Learning and Civic Duties,
  175–76
catechisms
  and the Decembrist movement, 240–42, 252,
    302–14
  and the Greek revolt, 193–94
  and the Naples revolt, 125, 154–55, 159, 175–76
  and the Spanish revolt, 21–22, 27, 50–55,
    53–54, 79, 83–84
Catherine II, 196, 243, 258, 268
Catherine the Great, 227, 243, 264, 281
Catholic Church
  and Carbonari, 136–37
  and catechisms, 21
  and international liberalism, 21
  and the Naples revolt, 132–33, 134
  and the Parthenopean Republic, 125
  and political polarization in Spain, 38–39
  power in Spain, 264
  and Riego's execution, 116–20
  and the Spanish Civil War, 36
  and Spanish constitutional liberalism, 41
  and Spanish constitutionalism, 42–43
Cato, 27, 50, 259
Cato the Younger, 27
censorship, 19, 134, 175, 277–78
centralization, 76
Cepero, Manuel López, 83
Cervantes, Miguel de, 81
Chaadaev, Petr, 259–60, 284
Chabrier, Emmanuel, 6
Charles I of England, 95, 298
Charles V, 50
Charles X of France, 102–3, 132
Charter of 1815 (France)
  and Alexander I, 248
  and the Decembrist movement, 244, 258, 275
  and the Greek revolt, 191, 192
  and the Holy Alliance, 14
  and the Naples revolt, 134, 142, 163
  Russian sponsorship of, 11
  and Spanish constitution of 1837, 335
The Charterhouse of Parma (Stendhal), 24, 115,
  164–65

Chateaubriand, François de, 101–2, 112, 114, 141, 224, 286
Chernigov Regiment, 305, 307, 312, 319
"The Child Instructed in the Divine Word," 51
Childe Harold's Pilgrimage (Byron), 31, 235, 322
Children of Jesus Christ, 97
China, 15
Chłopicki, Józef, 36
Choza, Manuel de, 119
Christian Political Catechism for the Youth of the Free People of South America, 53
Christianity, xi, 214, 316. *See also* Catholic Church; clergy; Orthodox Christianity; religion
Church, Richard, 222, 234
Church of the Spirito Santo, 152
Church of the Virgin of Aragon, 72
Ciappe, Guiseppe, 234
Cinna (Corneille), 270
Cirillo, Domenico, 127
Cisalpine Republic, 124
Citadel of Parma, 25–26
"The Citizen" (Ryleev), 259, 293
citizenship rights, 11, 45, 76, 201, 220, 263
Civic Catechism (Salvandy), 303–4
Civic Catechism and Brief Summary of the Obligations of the Spaniard, 53–54
civil war, 16, 34, 215–16, 221
class divisions, 42, 76, 80–81, 163–64, 219, 266
clergy
   and the Decembrist movement, 251
   and failures of liberalism, 113–14
   and French antiliberal resistance, 107
   and the Greek revolt, 191, 194–95, 203, 214, 220
   and guerrilla warfare, 145
   and "mushroom despots," 97
   and revolutionary catechisms, 52
   role in revolutionary movements, 21, 23
   and the Spanish revolt, 32, 38, 42–43, 80, 109, 110
Club Lomo, 124
Club Romo, 124
Cochrane, Thomas, 222
Codrington, Edward, 223
Colbran, Isabella, 131, 157
Collegno, Giacinto, 235–37
Colletis, Ioannis, 324
Colletta, Pietro
   and Austrian intervention in Naples, 167–68, 170
   on banditry, 133
   conflict with other liberal leaders, 134–35
   and constitutional sentiment, 142
   on exile of constitutionalists, 180
   memoirs, 173, 178, 326
   and the Naples parliament, 153, 163

on Pepe's proclamations, 148
and political catechisms, 176
and political journals, 154
and Spanish revolt, 140
unpopularity of, 158
colonialism, 6–7, 18, 39, 45, 64, 318. *See also* Latin America
Comellas, 97
Commentary on Montesquieu's Spirit of the Laws (Destutt), 12–13, 265
Company of Philhellenes, 225
Compostela, Santiago de, 61
Comuneros, 50, 73, 78, 91, 95, 98, 137
Concert of Europe, 99, 247
Condorcet, Jean-Antoine-Nicolas de Caritat, marquis de, 191
Congress of Laibach, 165
Congress of Troppau, 165
Congress of Vienna, 4, 5, 58, 197
Congress System, 99
Constant, Benjamin, 12, 45, 65, 262
Constantine I of Russia, 16, 201, 271, 289–91, 309–12, 314, 333
The Constitution Vindicated, 81
Constitutional Brotherhood of Europe, 182
Constitutional Catechism of the Spanish Monarchy, 83, 84, 154
constitutional liberalism, xi, 9, 10, 16
constitutional monarchies, 12, 44, 142, 311
constitutional sermons, 82. *See also* catechisms
Contract Fair (Kiev), 296
A Conversation Among Three Students on the Present Situation, 155
Cordoba, Spain, 69
corporal punishment, 175, 295. *See also* torture
Corpus Christi processions, 85
Cortés, Hernando, 81
Cossacks, 204, 226, 248, 251, 269, 282
coups d'état, 275
Cousin, Victor, 236
Cózar, Juan, 97
Craven, Richard Keppel, 149, 164
Cris de Pétersbourg, 130
Croce, Benedetto, 126, 127–28, 153, 173–74
cross-national analysis, xi–xii
Cruz y Cano, Manuel de la, 119
Cuoco, Vincenzo, 126, 127, 326
"A Curious Conversation," 302–3
Custine, Marquis de, 111

Dacia, 201
Dakin, Douglas, 209
d'Alembert, Jean le Rond, 175
Dania, Andrea, 234–35
David, Jacques-Louis, 27, 223
Davydov, Denis, 250, 314

Davydov, Vasili, 296
d'Azeglio, Massimo, 235
De Concilj, Lorenzo, 134–35, 146–47, 150–51, 180–82
de Vigny, Alfred, 224
The Death of Caesar, 195
The Death of Demosthenes (Pikkolos), 195
The Death of Marat (David), 27
death penalty, 73, 176. *See also* executions
Decemberists (band), 332–33
Decembrists and Decembrist uprising, 161, 188, *241*
  and constitutionalism, 11
  and cultural expression, 20
  cultural legacy, 330–31, 332–33
  and Destutt de Tracy, 13
  failures of, 9, 16
  and the Greek revolt, 199
  and international liberalism, 19
  legacy of, 327–28
  and martyrdom, 27
  origins of, 197, 260–61
  and patriotic rhetoric, 106
  and Pepe's influence, 121
  and political schisms, 19
  Pushkin on, 3
  and religion, 15–16
  and restoration of Fernando, 62
  and revolutionary catechisms, 22, 53, 54, 302–14
  and secret societies, 198
  trial of leaders, 12
Declaration of Rights (Parthenopean Republic), 125
Delacroix, Eugène, 224, 231
Delfico, Melchiorre, 13, 151
Dembowski, Ludwik Mateusz, 36
democracy
  and the 1812 constitution, 45–46
  and the Decembrist movement, 267–68, 284, 299
  and free press, 50
  and the Greek revolt, 219
  and the *inmovilistas*, 338
  and the Naples revolt, 134, 136, 163, 174
  and religion, 21
  and the Spanish revolt, 76–78
desertions, 109, 169, 173, 177, 311
Destutt de Tracy, A. L. C., 12–13, 65, 262, 265, 267
diaspora populations, 189–90, 193
Dick, Thomas, 24
Díez, Juan Martín ("El Empecinado"), 49, 60, 98, 106, 108, 111, 250–51, 287, 337
Dikaios, Grigórios ("Papaphlessas"), 212
The Disasters of War (Goya), 36
diseases and epidemics, 63
divine authority, 8, 10–11, 22, 53

Divov, Vasilii, 319
Dmitriev-Mamonov, M. A., 283
doceañistas, 76
Doktorov, Mikhail, 226
Dominicans, 117
Don Alonzo (Salvandy), 54–55, 240, 303, 305
Donizetti, Gaetano, 28
Dos de Mayo, 34, 95–96
Dostoevsky, Fyodor, 332
Drogonşani, Battle of, 195
Druzhinin, Nikolai, 276
due process, 190
duels, 180
Duma, 265
Dumas, Alexandre, 5, 6, 224

EAM movement, 324
"Eastern Question," 199
Ecclesiastical Affairs ministry, 161
Eco de Padilla (Alcalá), 78, 81
education and literacy, 76–77, 82, 190
Eguía, Francisco, 57, 99
Egypt, 9
Eidelman, Natan, 330, 332
1825: The Conspiracy (comic book), 332
El Empecinado. *See* Díez, Juan Martín ("El Empecinado")
"El General Riego" (portrait), 87
El Pardo Palace, 94
El Restaurador, 115
"El Trájala" (song), 89–90, 95
El Trapense en los Campos de Ayerve (play), 82
elections, 30, 40, 45–48, 75, 94, 151, 190, 217, 221, 245, 300
Elío, Francisco Javier, 57, 62, 92
Elixir of Love (Donizetti), 28
Elizabeth of Russia, 268
England, 18
Enlightenment
  and constitutionalism, 10, 11–12
  and the Greek revolt, 189–90, 216
  ilustrados, 31
  and Muraviev's ideology, 262
  and the Naples revolt, 124
  and reformism, 37
  and revolutionary Cadiz, 41
  and Riego's revolt, 65
  and the Spanish Inquisition, 32
  and the Trienio, 72
  and U.S. national anthem, 17
Enlightenment as the Handmaid of Irreligion, 192
Ental'tsev, Colonel, 299
Epidaurus assembly, 218–19, 220–21
Epidaurus Provisional Constitution of 1822, 219
episcopal courts, 43
Erlikh, S. E., 331–32

Ermolov, Aleksey, 248, 278, 280, 285
Eroles, Joaquin Ibañez, Baron de, 96
Esdaile, Charles, 36
Espinosa (guerrilla commander), 106, 287
Espinoza de los Monteros, Battle of, 65
Espoz y Mina, Francisco, 38, 49, 60–61, 69, 78, 98, 105–8, 220, 250–52, 334
ethnic conflicts, 206–7
ethnika ktímata (national property), 220
Evgenii Onegin (Pushkin), 3, 20
exaltados
    and the Army of the South, 89
    and Austrian intervention in Naples, 172
    and Cortes leadership, 89–95, 100–101
    and political schisms, 19, 76–78, 93–95, 134
executions, 97, 115–20, 127, 177, 320–21

Fabvier, Charles, 103–5, 113, 183, 227, 229–30, 235–37, 290
"The Factious," 97
Falangists, 337
famines, 101
fans, 85–86
Farnese Tower, 25–26
Fascism, 5
fashion, 85–86
fatwas, 214
Fedeloni (loyalists), 134
Federal Republic of Daunia, 147
Ferdinando I of Naples
    Alexander I contrasted with, 243
    and Austrian intervention in Naples, 165–67, 172, 174, 248
    and Bourbon lineage, 8
    and British occupation of Sicily, 162
    and Carlo Felice, 179
    and constitutional rule, 151–52
    and court culture, 9
    death of, 178
    depictions of, 131–32
    and the Greek revolt, 234
    and the Holy Alliance, 13
    and the Kingdom of the Two Sicilies, 129
    and Pepe's march, 123–24, 148–50
    restoration of, 126, 128, 132, 134, 142–43, 175
    and Rossetti, 156–57
    Rossetti on, 180
    and the Spanish constitution, 140
    and Verona conference, 99
Fernando VII of Spain
    and the 1812 constitution, 57
    Alexander I contrasted with, 243
    and anti-Bonaparte sentiment, 37
    and anti-Godoy sentiment, 33
    and Austrian intervention in Naples, 165, 166–67

and Bourbon lineage, 8
conflicts with Riego, 95
and constitutional restrictions, 96
dealings with Riego, 94
and the Decembrist movement, 243, 254–55, 274, 283, 286–87, 296, 298, 303
efforts to undermine liberalism, 98–99
and executions, 119, 333, 334
and exile of revolutionaries, 57
and fan designs, 86
and Ferdinando, 132, 140
final years of, 110–11
and French antiliberal resistance, 107
and the Greek revolt, 230
and guerrilla warfare, 61
and "Hymn of Riego," 336–37
last years on throne, 333–34
and the Naples revolt, 149–50, 185
restoration of, 58–60, 110–13, 114, 175–78
return from exile, 252–53
and revolutionary Cadiz, 40, 41, 47, 55–56
and revolutionary catechisms, 54
and Riego's march, 30, 69–70
and Rossini, 158
and Russian assistance, 253
and the Trienio, 72
and Van Halen, 284–85
Fidelio (Beethoven), 24, 335
Filangieri, Gaetano, 158, 177, 262, 267
Filippov, Ivan, 226
Finland, 291
Finlay, George, 210, 214
The First Brutus, 49
First Year of the Republic (Vershinin), 332
Flórez Estrada, Alvaro, 77, 183
folk tales, 333
Fonseca, Eleonora Pimentel, 127
Fontana de Oro club, 89, 91
Fonvizin, Mikhail, 256, 277, 294–95
Forzano, Antonio, 234
Four Sergeants, 104
France
    and Austrian intervention in Naples, 167
    and Bourbon rule, 7
    and catechisms, 22
    and the Decembrist movement, 255
    Foreign Legion, 237
    French Enlightenment, 45
    and influence of constitutional systems, 121
    intervention in Spain, 98–100, 100–107, 112–13, 115
    and the Restoration, 4
    and revolutions of the 1820s, 4–5
    and Russia relations, 250
    and the Verona Congress, 99–100
    See also French Revolution; Napoleon I, Emperor of the French

Francesco II of the Two Sicilies, 151, 163, 167, 176, 178
Franco, Francisco, 73, 94, 337
Free Pythagoreans, 136, 268
Free Rome, 49
free speech, 190
Freemasonry
and Alexander I, 249
and Carbonari, 153
and the Decembrist movement, 260–61, 285
and the Greek revolt, 193, 220
and the Liberal Triennium, 73
and the Naples revolt, 133, 136, 138–39
and restoration of Fernando, 60, 62, 64–65
and revolutionary Cadiz, 40, 43–44
and state repression, 19
and the Trienio, 77–78
Freikorps, 4
French Charte. *See* Charter of 1815 (France)
French Revolution
and the 1812 constitution, 57
and constitution of 1791, 44
and constitutionalism, 12
and the Decembrist movement, 323
and the Greek revolt, 190, 216, 223, 228
influence throughout Europe, 14
monarchs' fear of, 9
and the Naples revolt, 124
and revolutionary Cadiz, 48
and use of public spaces, 84
Freyre, Manuel, 70
friars, 137, 144
Friend of the Constitution, 154, 171
Friend of the Law, 234
Friendly Society
and anticlericalism, 220
and the Decembrist movement, 267
and the Greek revolt, 205–7, 211–14, 216–18, 220
and Kolokotrónis, 214
origin and structure of, 192–97
and Pestel, 280–82
and revolutionary catechisms, 302
and state repression, 19
and Vladimirescu, 199
and Ypsilanti, 198–203, 221
Friends of the Fatherland, 154
Frimont, Johann, 176
frusta, 175–76
Füssli, Johann Heinrich, 22

Galați, 201–2, 207
Galdi, Matteo, 152
Galich, Alexander, 330
Galicia, 34, 69
Gallina, Vincenzo, 218–19

Gamba, Pietro, 103, 224, 237
Gangeblov, Kakhovski, 287
García, Atanasio, 97
Garcia de Villalta, José, 230–31
Garibaldi, Giuseppe, 67, 292, 325–26, 334
garroting, 119
Gautier, Théophile, 5, 6
Gay, Delphine, 101
Genoa, 19
genocide, 238
Gentz, Friedrich, 131
George III, 9
Germanos III of Old Patras, 212
Germany, 5, 225, 237
Gerusalemme liberata, 130
Giampietro, Francesco, 163, 168, 178
Gigli, Mariano, 276
Gil Novales, Alberto, 71–72, 77, 79, 338
glasnost, 331, 332
Gleijeses, Vittorio, 178
Glinka, Fedor, 276, 279, 283
Glinka, Mikhail, 6
Glorious Life and Unhappy Death of Don Rafael del Riego (Burgos), 337
Gnedich, N. I., 278
Godoy, Manuel, 32–33, 53, 294
Goebel, Gustav, 305–6, 312
Gogol, Nikolai, 332
Gorbachev, Mikhail, 332
Gorbachevskii, Ivan, 267, 297–301, 308–10, 313
Gornovskii, Vencheslav, 200
Goya, Francisco, 8, 20, 31–32, 34, 36, 110–11
Goya Caprichos, 118
Gran Sasso d'Italia, 169
Gran Turco (ship), 99–100, 100–101
Grand Duchy of Finland, 244
Grand Tour, 6
Grande Armée, 9, 18, 56, 93, 197, 244
Greece
and anti-Turkish sentiment, 15
and autocracy, 9
and Bentham's influence, 13
and civil conflict, 16
and constitutionalism, 11, 219
and cultural expression, 20
and European philhellenism, 5–6
and exile of revolutionaries, 184, 185
and maritime activity, 19
and patriotic rhetoric, 106
and Pepe's influence, 121
and political schisms, 19
and revolutionary catechisms, 22
and the Spanish revolt, 104–5
and Ypsilanti's march, *187*, 188
Greek Chronicle, 217
Greek Committee (London), 217, 224, 229
Greek Committee (Madrid), 229

Greek Corps, 238
"Greek Song" (Küchelbecker), 278
Greek War of Independence, 202, 211–22
Green Lamp Society, 283
Gribovskii, M. K., 272
Grida de' venditori di Napoli, 130
Grigórios V, Patriarch of Constantinople, 192, 203, 215
grito, 78
Guerra, José Moreno, 77, 93
Guerra, Moreno, 253
guerrilla warfare and fighters
    and Austrian intervention in Naples, 171–72
    and Calderari, 133
    and clergy, 31–32, 144–45
    and the Decembrist movement, 250–51, 254, 269, 303
    El Trapense, 82, 97, 337
    and French invasion of Spain, 106–8
    and the Greek revolt, 203, 207, 210, 213–14, 217, 219
    and Murat, 15, 129
    and the Naples revolt, 126, 129, 133, 169, 177, 181, 183
    at Puerta del Sol, 95
    and restoration of Fernando, 60–61
    and revolutionary catechisms, 52
    and the Spanish revolt, 34–39, 56, 91, 95, 97, 111
    and "The Factious," 97
    and theatrical productions, 82
    and World War II, 324
Guizot, François, 224
Gushchevarov, Stepan, 254

habeas corpus, 42, 219, 244, 263
Habsburgs, 81, 164, 172
Halévy, Léon, 101
Haller, Karl Ludwig, 45
Hammershus, 315
Hartley, Janet, xii
Haskalah, 266
Haussez, Charles Le Mercher de Longpre, baron d', 126
Heismar (general), 312
Henry III of Castile, 89–90
heretics and heresy, 43–44, 111. *See also* Inquisition
Heroine of the Greek Revolution (Xenos), 324
Herzen, Alexander, 317–18, 329, 331–32
High General Vendita, 140
Historical Gallery and Images of National Heroes, 81
History of a Myth: Herzen's Decembrist Legend (Erlikh), 332
Hobsbawm, Eric, 14

Holland, Henry Richard Vassall, baron, 46, 182
Holy Alliance
    and Alexander I, 245, 246
    and Austrian intervention in Naples, 92–93, 167, 169
    Bignon on, 13–14
    and the Decembrist movement, 253, 276, 279, 281–82, 284, 286
    and failure of the Naples revolt, 173
    and the French Charte, 11
    and the Greek revolt, 216, 220, 227, 229–30, 232, 239
    and international impact of uprisings, 323
    and the Naples revolt, 134, 181
    and philhellenism, 224–25
    and religion, 22
    and restoration of Fernando, 58
    and revolutions of the 1820s, 4
    and Riego's death, 334
    Rossetti on, 180
    and the Spanish revolt, 104, 105–6
    and Troppau conference, 99
    and the Verona conference, 99–100
Horthy, Miklós, 4
hospodar system, 207
House of Savoy, 179
Household Cavalry Regiment, 197
Howe, Samuel, 235
Huerta, A. T., 68–69
Hugo, Victor, 20, 101
Hundred Days (1815), 12
Hundred Thousand Sons of Negrín, 103
Hundred Thousand Sons of St. Louis, 103, 106–7
Hydra, 211, 212
"Hymn of Riego," 68–69, 336, 337

Iakubovich, A. I., 257
Iakushkin, I. D., 279, 295
Iaşy, Moldavia, 3, 187–88, 195–96, 200–202, 208–9
Ibañez, Juan Toribio, 230
Iberian peninsula, 9, 32
Ibrahim Pasha of Egypt, 215, 222
Ikonnikov, V. S., 333
The Iliad, 278
illiteracy, 31, 82
Ilya Dissident (pseud), 332
Imbriani, Matteo, 153–54
impalement, 235
Impartial, 154
imprisonment, 23–26
The Incompatibility of Spanish Liberty with the Reestablishment of the Inquisition, 43
industrialization, 23
informers, 291
Inglesi, Dimitrios, 193

Inquiry Boards, 176
Inquisition
  abolition of, 70
  and Alpuente, 77
  and catechisms, 51
  and class divisions, 81
  and the Decembrist movement, 286
  and the Liberal Triennium, 74
  and *limpieza* doctrine, 111
  and the Naples revolt, 132
  and origin of Spanish revolt, 30
  political impact of, 32
  and political polarization in Spain, 37–38
  and popular literature, 24–25
  and restoration of Fernando, 57, 62–63
  and revolutionary Cadiz, 43
  and the Spanish revolt, 102, 118
  and theatrical productions, 81
  and Van Halen, 284–85
The Inquisition (ballet), 82
internationalism, xi, 19, 187, 258, 323, 327, 337
Investigating Commission, 319
Ioannovna, Anna, 268
Ionian Islands, 7, 9, 192, 234, 244
"The Iron Shroud" (Mudford), 24
irregular fighters, 213. *See also* guerrilla warfare
  and fighters
Irving, Washington, 6
Isabella II of Spain, 334–35
Islam, 220
Istanbul, 188
Istúriz, Francisco Xavier, 64, 77, 183

Jacobins and Jacobinism
  and Alexander I, 247
  and Austrian intervention in Naples, 166
  contrasted with revolutions of 1820s, 18
  and counterrevolutionary sentiment, 15, 110
  and the Decembrist movement, 247, 266
  and European absolutism, 8–9
  and guerrilla warfare, 36
  and *liberal* term, 40
  and the Liberal Triennium, 77, 79
  and the Naples revolt, 124, 130, 138
  and religion, 21–23
  and revolutionary Cadiz, 47, 50
  and the Spanish revolt, 112
  and the Trienio, 79
"Jailbird Government," 72
James II, 298
Jerez, Spain, 66
Jesuits, 58, 74, 102, 132, 176
Jesus, 21, 22
Jews and Judaism, 32, 64, 220, 266
João VI of Portugal, 92
José Napoléon Regiment, 55

Joseph Bonaparte, King
  abolition of monastic orders, 128
  and the Bayonne constitution, 33–34
  and execution methods, 119
  and international liberalism, 18
  as king of Spain, 128
  and political polarization in Spain, 37
  and restoration of Fernando, 62
  and revolutionary Cadiz, 40, 43, 47, 56
Journal des Débats, 102
Journal of the Two Sicilies, 149
Jovellanos, Gaspar Melchior de, 40, 46
Julius Caesar, 195
justice and judicial systems, 10, 71, 72, 263

Kaisarov, P. S., 250
Kakhovskii, Peter, 257, 259, 273, 279–80, 286,
  291–92, 320, 331–32
Kalamos, Georgy, 227
Kantakouzinos, Georgeos, 198
Kantemir, Antiokh, 253
Kapp putsch, 4
Karamzin, Nikolai, 284
Karavia, Vasilios, 202, 207
Katechismus der Deutschen, 22
Katenin, Pavel, 270
Katevskii, Ivan, 227
Keats, John, 178–79
Keizer, Daniil, 307–9
Kelly, Michael, 161
Key, Francis Scott, 17
Khomiakov, Aleksei, 278, 284, 328
Kiianskaia, Oksana, 311–12, 331
Kingdom of Naples, 6, 15, 35, 121, *122*
Kingdom of Piedmont, 176
Kingdom of the Two Sicilies, 129, 162
Kireevskii, Ivan, 328
The Kirilovites, or Enemy Invasion, 251
Kleist, Heinrich von, 22, 54
klephtopólemos, 213
klephts, 211–14
Kochubei, Viktor, 247–48, 276
Kologrivov, M. A., 334
Kolokotrónis, Theódoros, 189, 214, 221–22,
  228
Koraïs, Adamántios, 20, 191, 196, 220, 228
Kornilov, Lavr, 4
Kotzebue, August von, 14, 130, 157, 177, 246
Koval'skaia, M. I., 159
Kozintsev, Grigory, 330
Kozlov, Ivan, 208
Kronstadt, 290, 320
Krüdener, Julie de, 245
Küchelbecker, Wilhelm, 278–79, 284, 320
Kulikovskii, Arkhip, 226
Kulikovskii, Silvester, 226

Kurzer Katechismus für deutsche Soldaten, 22
Kushelev, E. A., 249

La Ferronais (French ambassador), 249, 254–55, 319
La Harpe, Frédéric-César de, 243, 251
"La Santa Alleanza," 157
Labrador, Pedro, 133
Lacy, Don Luis, 37, 61, 117, 208
Lafayette, Gilbert du Motier, Marquis de, 26, 102, 166, 183, 255, 334
Laguna (marshal), 42
Laibach conference, 253
Lalo, Édouard, 6
Lamartine, Alphonse de, 224
L'amico della costituzione, 150
Lampedusa, Giuseppe di, 326
land reforms, 7–8, 128, 158
Landaburian Society, 78–79, 95, 106
Landáburo, Mamerto, 94–95
Lanuza, 100
Lanzana, Serafim de, 230
Las Cabezas de San Juan, Spain, 28, 94, 116, 335–36
Las Platerías, 91
Lasalle, Antoine Charles Louis de, 24
Lascaris, Victorio, 230
The Last Days of Odysseas Androutsou (1928), 324
Latin America
    Blaquiere on, 113
    cultural influence of, 49
    and European liberal activists, 289
    and Fabvier, 105
    and the Greek revolt, 224, 232
    and guerrilla monks, 144–45
    independence movements in, 63
    influence on European revolts, 28–30, 32, 39, 71, 322
    and liberation theology, 21
    and maritime activity, 19
    Pepe on, 183
    and revolutionary catechisms, 52–53, 52–54
    and Riego's march, 66
    and Russia/Spain relations, 59–60
    Spanish colonies in, 13, 16
    and the Trienio, 75
Lazuna, Juan de, 78
lazzaroni, 126
Le Normand, Marie Anne, 260
The League of the Great Cause (1927), 330
League of Virtue, 261
Lefebvre, Henri, 250
Legislative Science (Filangieri), 158
legislatures. *See* bicameral legislatures; unicameral legislatures
León (La Isla), Spain, 39, 40–41

Leonidas, 27, 169, 188, 280
The Leopard (Lampedusa), 326
Leopardi, Giacomo, 179, 231
Lepre, Aurelio, 325
Les Huguenots (Meyerbeer), 331
Lhufrior, Juan Maria, 231
Liberal Foreign Legion, 105, 108, 184
Liberal Triennium. *See* Trienio
liberation theology, 21
Ligurian Republic, 154
Ligurian Sea, 7
limpieza (cleansing) doctrine, 111
Liprandi, Ivan, 276
Lishin, Lieutenant, 310–11, 313
literacy, 23–24
Little Sally (ship), 235, 236
Llorente, Juan Antonio, 74
Lochos, Hieros, 203–4
Lohrer, Nikolai, 227, 280, 315
Lombardy, 164–65
London Spanish Committee, 108, 334
The Long Life of Marianna Ucría (Maraini), 326
looting, 205, 311
López, Simón, 48
López de Baños, Miguel
    and the Army of the South, 88–89
    and Beliaev, 287
    and British public opinion, 98
    and cultural artifacts, 85
    and restoration of Fernando, 64
    and the restoration of Fernando VII, 113
    and San Miguel, 106
    and the Spanish revolt, 95
Louis IX of France, 103
Louis XIV of France, 8, 44
Louis XVI of France, 32, 70, 95, 166, 298
Louis XVIII of France, 11, 90, 102, 132, 183, 199
Loukis Laras (Vikelas), 210
Louriótis, Andreás, 217, 228, 230
Louvel *vendite*, 159
Love of Country (play), 157, 163
Lubliński, Julian, 267
Lunin, Mikhail, 24, 257, 280, 315–16

Macchiaroli, Rosario, 140
Macedonia, 188
Madariaga, Isabel de, xii
Madrid, Spain, 16, 20, 39
Madrid Municipal Museum, 86
Mafia, 133
magic lantern shows, 81
Magna Carta, 154
Magnitskii, M. L., 257
Mahmud II, 8
mail service, 272–89
Maistre, Joseph de, 10

majos and *majas*, 31
Malaga, Spain, 67–68
Maltese Cross, 79
Manhès, A., 128
Manicheanism, 51, 80
Maniots, 211
Mannerheim (general), 4
Maometto II, 157
Maraini, Dacia, 326
Marañon, Antonio ("El Trapense"), 82, 97, 337
Marañon, Gregorio, 337
Marat, Jean-Paul, 27
Marathon, Battle of, 69, 106
Marcus Junius Brutus, 259
Marie Antoinette, 166
Markevich, Petr, 226
Marquis de Mataflorida, 96
Marseilles, France, 19, 185
Martínez de la Rosa, Francisco
    and the Greek revolt, 229
    and the Liberal Triennium, 76–77, 78
    and mistrust of the masses, 16
    and public culture, 20
    and religious conflict, 81
    and restoration of Fernando, 57
    and revolutionary Cadiz, 40, 49, 56
    tensions with Riego, 94
    tensions with the Cortes, 95
    on Vinuesa murder, 91–92
Martinovics, Ignac, 22
Martyrology of the Reign of Fernando: Victims and Executioners of Absolutism (San José), 337
martyrs and martyrdom, 26–27, 84–85, 117, 190, 328–29, 334
Marx, Karl, 21, 33, 45
Marxism, 282
Masaniello, 125, 126
Masons. *See* Freemasonry
Massacre on Chios (Delacroix), 231
massacres, 214–15
Matthewes, George, 109, 113
Mavrokordatos, Alexandros, 216–19, 222, 233
Mavromikhalis, Petrobey, 212, 219, 221, 238
Mavrophorites, 203–4
Mayer, Enrico, 231
Mazzini, Giuseppe, 182, 237, 288–89, 327–28, 334
Mazzini, Silvio Pellico, 326
Medici, Luigi de, 133, 144, 147
Mediterranean Sea, 7, 322
Mejía, Félix, 334
Meloy, Colin, 332
Méndez García, Zoilo, 337
mercenaries, 18, 186–87, 202. *See also* guerrilla warfare and fighters
meridionalism, 5–6, 164
Merimée, Prosper, 6

Merino, Jerónimo ("El Cura"), 38
"Message to Siberia" (Pushkin), 240, 328–29
Messenger of Europe, 187–88, 248, 249, 253, 278
Metternich, Klemens Wenzel Fürst von
    and abduction plots, 143
    and Alexander I, 245, 246, 247, 248
    and Austrian intervention in Naples, 164, 166–67
    and Capodistria, 192
    on Ferdinando, 131–32
    and the Greek revolt, 210, 228
    and the Holy Alliance, 14
    on impact of Spanish revolt, 100
    and international liberalism, 18
    on Neapolitans, 6
    and Rossini, 158
    and the Spanish revolt, 254
    and the Spielberg Fortress, 26
Meyerbeer, Giacomo, 331
Mikhail Alexandrovich of Russia, 165
Mikhailovskii-Danilevskii, A. I., 311, 313
military academies, 42
Military Settlements, 257
militias, 83, 138, 251. *See also* guerrilla warfare and fighters; mercenaries
Mill, James, 262
Milner, H. M., 334
Miloradovich, Mikhail, 292
Miloš Obrenovic I, Prince of Serbia, 199
Milossevitz, 36
Miltiades, 188, 223, 280
Minichini, Luigi
    and Austrian intervention in Naples, 168
    and exile of revolutionaries, 180–82
    and failure of Naples revolt, 174
    and the Greek revolt, 203, 210, 212
    and legacy of political martyrs, 174, 326
    and Pepe's march, 123, 144–47, 149–51
    popularity of, 156, 163
    on the Spanish constitution, 140–41
Miranda, Francisco de, 25, 39
Mironov, Boris, 332
Missolonghi, 238
moderados
    and the Army of the South, 89
    and Cortes leadership, 89–91, 93, 95
    and failure of Naples revolt, 172
    and the Liberal Triennium, 76–77, 79
    and political schisms, 19, 76–78, 93–95, 134
    reconciliation with *exaltados*, 100
    and state repression, 19
Moldavia, 186, 189, 198, 200–201, 204–5, 207, 249
Montesquieu, 191
Moors, 7, 32, 52, 97, 283
Morales, Domingo, 97, 230
Moratín, Leandro, 81

Moravia, 26
More del Ebro, 112
Morea, 189, 211, 212, 216, 221
Morelli, Michele, 122, 141, 145–47, 149–51, 176–78
Morelos, José María, 145
Morillo, Pablo, 59, 63, 108
mortmain, 73
Most Christian Armada of the Holy Faith, 125–26
Motovilovka, 310–11
Mucius Scaevola (Carbonari chapter), 144, 258
Mudford, William, 24
mummery, 100, 123
Murat, Joachim
    and Austrian intervention in Naples, 171
    and the Bayonne constitution, 139
    and Bonapartism, 9
    and the Greek revolt, 233
    and guerrilla warfare, 15
    as king of Naples, 128–29
    and Morelli, 145
    occupation of Madrid, 33
    and Pepe, 142
    reforms of, 132–34
    and revolutionary catechisms, 53
    and Rossetti, 156
    and Rossini, 158
Muraviev, Alexander, 295, 315, 319
Muraviev, M. N., 293–94
Muraviev, N. N., 256, 288, 293
Muraviev, Nikita
    and constitutional monarchy plans, 271
    education, 259
    on European intervention, 282
    mistrust of the masses, 16
    and nationality issues, 265–66
    and the Northern Society, 262–63
    and revolutionary catechisms, 302
    trial of, 319
    and the Union of Salvation, 295
Muraviev-Apostol, Ippolit, 294, 295, 313
Muraviev-Apostol, Ivan, 294, 318
Muraviev-Apostol, Matvei, 294, 295, 305, 318, 320
Muraviev-Apostol, Sergei
    and Constantine, 15–16
    cultural legacy of, 330–33
    education, 294
    execution of, 3, 320
    on failure of Naples revolt, 277
    family background, 256–57, 293–95
    imprisonment, 25, 317–18
    launch of revolt, 305–13
    martyrdom, 26
    and the Napoleonic wars, 3, 18
    and nationalism, 265–66

and Pestel, 264
    preparations for revolt, 295–98, 299–302
    and religion, 260, 301–2
    and revolutionary catechisms, 55, 240–42, 303–5
    revolutionary influences, 16, 240
    and the Southern Society, 274, 280
    tactical errors, 313–14
Muslim invaders, 7
Mussolini, Benito, 4, 169, 178
My Prisons (Pellico), 26
Myslovskii, Petr, 317
The Mysteries of Paris (Sue), 109
The Mysteries of Udolpho (Radcliffe), 24, 315

Naples
    and absolutism, 8
    and Alexander I, 155, 164–66, 182, 248
    and anticlericalism, 220
    Austrian intervention in, 92–93, 158, 164–75, 246, 248
    and Bentham's influence, 13
    and Bourbon rule, 7
    and cultural expression, 20
    and the Greek revolt, 189
    and the Holy Alliance, 99
    and maritime activity, 19
    and patriotic rhetoric, 106
    and political schisms, 19
    and populist sentiment, 15–16
    and prisons, 26
    and reactions to liberalism, 10
    and revolutionary catechisms, 22
    and Riego's revolt, 70–71
    and Spanish constitution of 12, 17
    and the Spanish constitution of 1812, 11
Napoleon I, Emperor of the French
    and Alexander I, 254, 286
    and catechisms, 21–22
    and the Decembrist movement, 251–52
    and the Greek revolt, 233
    and incitement of revolts, 17–18
    and the Naples revolt, 124
    on necessity of religion, 21
    occupation of Iberian Peninsula, 250
    and political polarization in Spain, 37
    and Portugal conquest, 33
    and religious mobilization, 21, 32, 301
    and revolutionary Cadiz, 43, 55
    and revolutionary catechisms, 50–51, 53
    and Riego's revolt, 68
    Russian defeat of, 6, 289
    and the Treaty of Tilsit, 197
Napoleonic Wars, 3–4, 17–18, 100, 303, 322–23
Narodnoe Veche (National Council), 262–63, 265

National Assembly (Greece), 218, 220–21
National War Museum (Athens), 186, 194, 325
nationalism
  and the Decembrist movement, 246, 258, 265–67
  and the Greek revolt, 189, 200, 225–26, 237, 239
  "peasant nationalism," 14–15
  and Polish soldiers, 18–19
  and religion, 21
  and restoration of Fernando, 60
  and revolutionary Cadiz, 54
  and war atrocities, 36
  See also internationalism
Nauplion, 223, 231, 234, 236
Navarino, Battle of, 222, 234, 238
Neapolitan Minerva, 154, 172
Neapolitan Monitor, 127
Nechkina, M. V., 289, 300, 305, 310, 316
Nechkina, Sergei, 304–5
Negrín, Juan, 103
Negris, Teódoros, 216, 218–19
negros (liberals), 61, 107, 110, 114
Nelson, Horatio, 126
Nepos, Cornelius, 267
Nesselrode, Karl, 176, 197, 200, 228, 252–53
Netherlands, 121, 165
Neva Observer, 248, 284
New Testament, 261
newspapers, 48, 87, 150
Nicholas I of Russia
  and arrest of Decembrists, 319
  and assassination plans, 317
  and constitutional monarchy plans, 271, 272
  depicted on stage, 331
  and the Greek revolt, 226, 238
  and peasant folk tales, 333
  and Steinhel, 273
  and succession issues, 289–90, 291, 292
  and suppression of revolts, 255–56
  and the Third Section, 266
  tyrannical image of, 327
  and Ypsilanti's release, 208
Niegolewski, Andrzej, 36
Nola, Naples, *122*
  and Carbonari chapters, 258
  and constitutional rule, 155–56
  and legacy of political martyrs, 326
  and Pepe's march, 129, 144–45, 147
  and Riego's march, 141
  Sacred Squadron, 122–23
Northern Society
  and Alexander's death, 290
  and Batenkov, 279
  and Bulatov, 293
  and constitutional monarchy plans, 271, 272
  cultural legacy of, 333
  and Fonvizin, 277

  and Nikita Muraviev, 262
  and Pestel, 265, 267, 305
  and revolutionary catechisms, 311
  and Senate Square debacle, 305
  and state repression, 19
  and Steinhel, 273
  and Trubetskoi, 292
Novel of the Five Who Were Pardoned (Ilya Dissident), 332
Novikov, Mikhail, 265
Nugent von Westmeath, Laval, 18, 147–48
Nunziante, Vito, 147–48

oaths to constitutions, 70, 83, 146–47, 151–52, 194
"Ode to Naples" (Shelley), 121
Odessa, 19, 192–93, 203
Odoevskii, Aleksandr, 260, 265, 328–29
O'Donnell, Enrique, 64, 69–70, 108, 147
Oksman, Yuri, 320
Okudzhava, Bulat, 330
Olenin, Aleksei, 295
Olmütz, 26
Olympios, Georgakis, 206–9
On the National War of Insurrection by Bands, 171
"On the Occasion of Byron's Death" (Ryleev), 279
Onís y González-Vara, Luís de, 133, 169, 182
oral culture, 82
organized crime, 31
orientalism, 5, 164
Orlandos, Ioannis, 217
Orlov, Grigory, 125, 127, 170, 171, 227, 282
Orlov, Mikhail, 13, 199, 256, 270, 274–75, 282, 287
"Orthodox Catechism," 303–5, 307–8
Orthodox Christianity, 188–89, 191–92, 194, 220, 223, 238, 240, 317
Otho, King of Greece, 239
Ottoman Empire, *187*
  and Austrian intervention in Naples, 169
  and autocracy, 9
  and autocratic rule, 8
  and Egypt, 9
  and the Greek revolt, 229
  and Italian revolutionary exiles, 185
  and orientalism, 5
  and Russia relations, 250, 278
  and World War I, 324

Pacchiarotti, Giuseppe, 184
Padilla, Juan, 50, 85, 120
Pagano, Mario, 125
Pahlen, N., 246
Paisiello, Giovanni, 157

Palace of the Inquisition, 24
Palacio de Santa Cruz, 115
Palafox, José de, 250
Palermo, 16
Palma, Alerio, 228, 232
Palmar plot, 64
Palmas, 230
Pamplona, 60
pan-European liberalism, 187, 258, 323
Pantschoff, Mladen, 210
Papal Index, 175
parades, 123, 149
Paris Commune, 19
Parisi, Giuseppe, 151
parliamentary systems, 173, 247
Parthenopean Republic, 124–29, 141, 161, 166, 173, 325
partisan war, 251. *See also* guerrilla warfare and fighters
Parvus, Alexander, 282
Passek, Tatiana, 272
pastoral letters, 82, 83
Paternal Exhortation, 192
patriotic societies. *See* Carbonari; Comuneros; Freemasonry; secret societies
Patriotism, or January 1, 1820, 81
Paul I of Russia, 100, 127, 243, 298
Paulucci, Filippo, 248
Pavlovich, Konstantin, 309
Pavlovich, Mikhail, 316
Pecchio, Giuseppe
    exile of, 181–82
    and exile of revolutionaries, 182
    and the Greek revolt, 212–13, 228, 232–33
    and the Liberal Triennium, 74, 78
    memoirs, 184, 262
    and religious conflict, 81
    on Riego's cultural impact, 87
    and Santarosa, 179
    on Spanish revolt, 6
    on theatrical productions, 81
Pellico, Silvio, 26, 315
Peloponnese, 189. *See also* Morea
penal codes, 72
Peninsular War, 108, 139, 213
Pepe, Florestano, 151, 163, 168, 180, 218, 290
Pepe, Gabriele, 153, 180
Pepe, Guglielmo
    and Austrian intervention in Naples, 93, 165, 168–71, 173–74
    background, 141–42
    and Carbonari soldiers, 138, 143–44
    and conflicts among revolutionaries, 134–35
    and constitutional rule, 139, 141, 142–43, 151–64
    death sentence, 174
    and the Decembrist movement, 262, 294, 312

and execution of revolutionaries, 177
and exile of revolutionaries, 3, 173, 180, 182–84, 183
and the Greek revolt, 233
imprisonment, 25
legacy of, 323
and martyrdom, 26
memoir, 326
and the Napoleonic wars, 3, 18
places named for, 325
and prison imagery, 24
and revolutionary sentiment, 16
ride to Naples, 121–23, 144–51
and Riego's legacy, 336
Peretz, Grigorii, 276
Pérez Galdós, Benito, 16, 118, 119, 329
Persat, Maurice, 169
Persians, 57, 76–77, 84, 96
The Persians (Aeschylus), 236
Pestel, Pavel
    arrest of, 305
    and constitutional monarchy plans, 271–72
    cultural legacy of, 331–32
    death sentence, 320
    and the Friendly Society, 198, 280–82
    and influence of 1820s revolts, 275
    and international liberalism, 288, 323
    interrogation of, 18
    legacy of, 323
    and propaganda, 300
    and regicide plans, 297–98
    and religion, 260
    Southern Society, 264–67
    and the Southern Society, 296, 314
Pestel, Vladimir, 328
Peta, Battle of, 225, 234–35
Peter and Paul Fortress, 279, 290–91, 315, 317, 320
Peter the Great, 244, 290
Petrograd Soviet, 159
Petrov, D. K., 242, 314
Pezza, Michele (Fra Diavolo), 126
Phanariots, 189, 197, 204, 207, 209, 211, 324
Pharmakidis, Theoklitos, 208
Philellene Committee, 229–30
philhellenism, 5, 6, 218–19, 222–31, 278, 324
Philip II, 78, 118
Philip II (Alfieri), 81
Philip of Macedon, 135
Phillips, W. Alison, 209
Philosophy of Religion (Dick), 24
Photius, Archimandrite, 257
Piazza Del Mercato, 127, 177
Piedmont, 92, 99, 179
Pieri, Piero, 150
Pikkolos, Nikolaos, 195
Piranesi, Giovanni Battista, 23

Pisa, Vincenzo, 169–70, 182, 183, 234
"The Pit and the Pendulum" (Poe), 24, 335
Pius VII, pope, 161
Plaza de la Cebada, 115–20, 119, 338
Plutarch, 267
Poe, Edgar Allan, 24
Poerio, Alessandro, 326
Poerio, Guiseppe, 153–54, 168, 180, 233
poetry, 227, 231, 239, 255, 324–25
Poggio, Aleksandr, 269, 272, 275–76, 279, 288, 323
Poggio, Vittorio, 275
Poland, 18, 36, 154, 245–46
The Polar Star, 329
*Political Catechism for the Instruction of the
    Spanish People*, 52
political catechisms, 83
political parties, 153
Polotsk, Battle of, 197
populacho, 31
*Popular Instruction in the Form of a Catechism on
    the Current War*, 51
populism, 15, 77
Porlier, Juan Díaz, 37, 60–61, 71, 117, 208
Porro, Count, 181
portraiture, 87
Portugal, 11, 92, 104
poverty, 31, 216
Pradt, M. de (Dominique Georges Frédéric),
    5–6, 45, 262
Praed, W. M., 334
"Praetorian option," 3
Prati, Gioacchino, 234
press and publishing
    and Austrian intervention in Naples, 168
    danger to autocrats, 10
    and the Decembrist movement, 244, 263, 283
    and failure of Naples revolt, 173
    Ferdinando's opposition to, 99
    and the Greek revolt, 190, 199, 211, 217, 219
    and international liberalism, 19
    and the Liberal Triennium, 75, 80
    and the Naples revolt, 150, 153–54, 164
    and prison imagery, 23
    and restoration of Fernando, 58
    and revolutionary Cadiz, 40, 42–43, 48–50
    and the Spanish constitutional regime, 80–81
priests. *See* clergy
Prince of Canosa, 132
Prisoner of Chillon (Byron), 315
Procession of the Virgin (Choza), 119
pronunciamentos, 17, 28, 61, 69, 71, 143, 149, 175,
    188, 323
propaganda, 22–23, 26, 51, 80–88, 156, 300–301,
    338. *See also* catechisms; press and publishing
property rights, 76
Protestants, 32
Provisional Giunta, 151, 152

provisional regencies, 107–8
Prussia, 4–5, 99, 248, 253
Psara, 211, 212
public speech, 80
Puerta del Sol, 34, 94–95
Pugachev, Emel'ian, 269, 284
Pugachev Rebellion, 15
Pushkin, Alexander
    on Chaadaev, 259–60
    on Decembrist uprising, 3, 328–29
    and the Greek revolt, 203
    on international impact of uprisings, 322
    "Message to Siberia," 240
    and public culture, 20
    on Pugachev rebellion, 15, 269
    on Riego's arrest, 286–87
    and Stalinist culture, 330
    on Ypsilanti's revolt, 278

quartering, 116, 177, 319–20
Quin, Michael, 79, 100, 107, 113, 114
Quintana, Manuel José, 20, 37, 40, 46, 48, 58
Quiroga, Antonio
    and the Army of the South, 88
    and British public opinion, 98
    and the Decembrist movement, 270, 296
    and exile of revolutionaries, 183
    and fan designs, 86
    honors bestowed upon, 87–88
    and the Inquisition, 74–75
    and origin of Spanish revolt, 30
    and the Palmar plot, 64–65
    and restoration of Fernando, 63, 67, 113
    and Riego's march, 70–71
    and snuffbox designs, 85
    and theatrical productions, 81

Racine, Jean, 259
Radcliffe, Ann, 24, 315
radicalism, 10, 14, 21
Rados, Konstantinos, 210
Raevskii, N. N., 256, 270
Raevskii, Vladimir, 270, 276
Raiko, Nikolai, 227
Rakuza, Ignatii, 308
Ramo, Mosen, 97
Ravelin, Alekseevskii, 317
Raybaud, Louis-Maxime, 207
Red Army, 330
Red Shirts, 292
regicide, 297–98
religion
    and Alexander I, 244
    and the Decembrist movement, 270, 300–301,
        316–17

and failure of Naples revolt, 173
and the Greek revolt, 201, 220
and international impact of uprisings, 323
and liberalism, 21
and Muraviev-Apostol, 260, 301–2
and the Parthenopean Republic, 161
and persecution, 12
and political propaganda, 21
and reformism, 73
religious freedom and tolerance, 45, 161, 190,
  220, 244, 263, 266
and Riego's execution, 116–20
and secret societies, 261
and Spanish liberalism, 80–88
See also catechisms; clergy; *specific religions*
Religious, Moral, and Political Catechism (Cepero),
  83
René (Chateaubriand), 102
The Republic Justified by the Holy Gospel, 125
Republic of Eastern Lucania, 147
Republic of the Seven Islands, 192
Restoration governments, xi, 4, 12, 18, 23
"Revolutionary Catechism," 304
Revzin, Grigorii, 303
Rheinboth (pastor), 317
Rhigas Pheraios, 190–91, 196, 198, 218, 278
Ricardo, David, 262
Ricci, Federico, 130
Ricciardi, Francesco, 151, 159, 168
Richart, Vicente, 61
Riego, Miguel, 65, 335
Riego, Rafael del
  and the Army of the South, 88–98
  birthplace, 338
  and British public opinion, 98
  and the constitution of 1812, 11
  and counterrevolutionary sentiment, 110–15
  and the Decembrist movement, 271, 277, 279,
    284, 286–87, 292–93, 294, 296, 306
  execution of, 3, 287–88
  and exile of revolutionaries, 183
  and French intervention, 107–9
  and the Greek revolt, 218
  honors bestowed upon, 87–88, 94
  imprisonment, 25
  legacy of, 334–38
  and the Liberal Triennium, 72–80
  and martyrdom, 26
  and military order, 146
  and Muraviev-Apostol, 240, 242, 314
  and the Naples revolt, 140, 156, 253
  and the Napoleonic wars, 3, 18
  and origin of Spanish revolt, 28–31, 31–39
  and the Palmar plot, 64–65
  and Pepe, 150
  pronunciamiento and march, 65–72
  at Puerta del Sol, 95

and religious conflict, 81
and restoration of Fernando, 57–65
and revolutionary Cadiz, 39–56
and revolutionary catechisms, 303, 312
and revolutionary sentiment, 16
and secret societies, 78
and sermons, 82–83
and snuffbox designs, 85
and storming of the Trocadero, 98–110
and theatrical productions, 81
trial and execution, 115–20
and Vaudoncourt, 106
Riego's Shout (newspaper), 87
Rieti, Battle of, 172, 277
"Rights of Man," 190
Rimsky-Korsakov, Nikolai, 6
Risorgimento, 5, 67, 142, 182–83, 245, 323,
  325–26
Rivero, Miguel Fernando, 230
Robertson, Etienne, 81
Robespierre, 253, 324
Romagoso (bandit leader), 97
Roman Catholic Church, 154, 161
Romani, George, 173–74
Romania, 9, 199, 205, 209
Romanov dynasty, 8, 297. *See also specific rulers*
Romanticism, 20, 27, 190, 214, 224–25, 315, 322
  and Riego's legacy, 335
Romero Alpuente, Juan, 74, 77–79, 95, 113, 183
Rosen, Andrei, 260, 274
Rossaroll, Cesare, 234
Rossaroll, Giuseppe, 163, 172, 183–84, 233–34
Rossellini, Roberto, 326
Rossetti, Gabriele, 20, 131, 155–56, 168, 180,
  208, 231, 326
Rossini, Gioacchino, 86, 129, 131, 158
Rostopchin, Fedor, 246, 251
Roth, L. O., 309
Rousseau, Jean-Jacques, 9, 48, 175, 191–92, 261
Royal Army of the Kingdom of the Two Sicilies,
  121
Ruffo, Fabrizio, 125, 132
Ruffo, Luigi, 161
Ruggiero, Guido de, 162, 174
Rulikowski, Józef, 311
Rumelia, 189
Rumiantsev, N. P., 55
Russian Invalid, 283
Russian Justice, 265, 266–67, 300–301
Russian Orthodox Church, 264, 302, 304
Russkaia Pravda, 265
Russo, Vincenzo, 125, 127
Russo-Turkish wars, 196–97, 206, 209
Ryleev, Kondratii
  cultural legacy, 331–32
  death sentence, 320
  and the Decembrist movement, 284–85

Ryleev, Kondratii (*continued*)
  and Greek culture, 279–80
  and Herzen, 329
  imprisonment, 316
  influence on revolutionaries, 273–74
  and martyrdom theme, 259
  "On the Occasion of Byron's Death," 279
  political legacy, 20
  and radical republicanism, 271–72, 288–93
  and religious faith, 260
  and revolutionary catechisms, 302

The Saber, 126
Sacred Battalion, 176, 203–4, 205, 207, 287
Sacred Company, 225
Sacred Squadron, 122, 149
Sagrado Código (Sacred Codex), 46–47
Said, Edward, 5
sainete, 31, 49
Salmon, M. G., 181
salotto (salons), 131
Salvandy, Narcisse-Achille de, 54–55, 240,
  303–4, 305
Salvatorelli, Luigi, 325
San Carlo Theater, 129, 147, 157–58, 179
San Fernando Day, 41
San José, Diego, 337
San Miguel, Evaristo, 64, 68, 90, 95, 98–99, 104,
  106
Sand, Karl, 246, 292, 320
Sanfedisti, 132–33
Sanfelice, Luigia (or Luisa), 127
Santarosa, Annibale Santorre di Rossi, 179, 181,
  235–36
Santiago de Compostela, 69
Santos, Faustino Julián de, 115–17
Sarafis, Marion, 213
Sardinia, 92, 179, 244
Sardou, Victorien, 24
Sarrailh, Jean, 113–14
Sarsfield, Pedro, 64
Say, Jean-Baptiste, 262
Scaevola lodge, 123
schisms, 19
Schwartz, F. E. (colonel), 247
Scirocco, Alfonso, 158, 174
Scott, Walter, 24
Scottish Enlightenment, 12
secret societies
  and Alexander I, 246–48
  Añilleros (Ring Wearers), 91
  and Austrian intervention in Naples, 168
  Camorra, 133
  and catechisms, 22
  and the Decembrist movement, 249, 260–61
  and failure of Naples revolt, 175

  and the Greek revolt, 190, 193
  and international impact of uprisings, 323
  and international liberalism, 19
  and martyrdom, 26, 27
  and religious radicalism, 21
  and the Spanish revolt, 112
  and the Trienio, 77–78, 78–80
  See also Carbonari; Comuneros; Freemasonry
Semenovskii Regiment, 247–48, 257, 291,
  294–95
Seminario patriótico, 48
Senate (Spanish), 33
Senate Square uprising, 291, 293, 331, 333
Sephardic Jewish Greeks, 211
Serbia, 199
serfs, 285, 299, 310
sermons, 21, 82
A Servile and a Liberal (Fernán Caballero), 336
Serviles, 41, 43, 45, 57, 60, 73, 90, 107–8
The Seventh of July, 95–96
Seville, Spain, 40
Shaporin, Yuri, 331
Shchedrin, Silvester, 168
Shelley, Percy Bysshe, 121, 218
Sheremet, Pandelie, 226
"shirtless ones," 102
Shishkov, Alexander, 251
Short Catechism, 307
Shouts of London, 130
Siberian penal settlements, 320
Sikelianos, Angelos, 324–25
Silvati, Giuseppe, 122, 141, 145, 149, 151, 176–78,
  181, 326
Skiotis, Dennis, 210
Skouphas, Nikolas, 193, 195, 216
slavery, 215
smugglers, 31, 34, 128
snuffboxes, 85
Sobolev, Cuirassier, 127
Society for the Regeneration of Europe, 103
Society of United Slavs, 259, 267–68, 288, 299,
  305–7, 312–13
Solomós, Dionísios, 20, 223, 227
Soloviev, Ven'iamin, 306, 313
Son of the Fatherland, 54, 55, 252, 276, 303
Song of Riego (play), 337
Sophocles, 14
South America, 16. *See also* Latin America
Southern Army, 295, 296
Southern Society
  and arrest of Pestel, 305
  and Basargin, 274
  and the Chernigov Regiment, 296
  and constitutional monarchy plans, 271
  contrasted with Northern Society, 262
  film based on, 330
  and Greek revolt, 280

and informers, 314
and Muraviev-Apostol's leadership, 257
and peasant folk tales, 333
and Pestel, 264–67, 281
and regicide plans, 298
and revolutionary catechisms, 305
schisms in, 19
and the Society of United Slavs, 288
and the United Slavs, 268
Soutsos, Mikhail, 187, 199–202, 205
Soviet Society of Political Exiles and Prisoners, 330
The Spanish Bee, 56
Spanish Civil War, 36, 69, 225
Spanish Committee, 230
Spanish Constitution of 1812
    and Alexander I, 244
    celebrations of, 84–86
    and cultural artifacts, 86–87
    and the Decembrist movement, 244, 252–53, 258, 263, 283–84, 286
    and the Greek revolt, 220
    influence of, 11
    and the Liberal Triennium, 80
    and the Naples revolt, 121, 123, 134–35, 138–41, 148–49, 150, 152, 154, 160, 162, 165, 175, 179
    and origin of Spanish revolt, 28–30
    and the Parthenopean Republic, 124
    Pepe's opinion of, 141
    and restoration of Fernando, 57, 58, 61
    and revolutionary Cadiz, 44–45, 47
    and revolutionary catechisms, 50, 54–56
    and Riego's revolt, 69–71
    and Romanticism, 20
Spanish Enlightenment, 40, 43
Spanish Greek Committee, 105
Spanish Martyrs, or the Death of Riego (Milner), 334
Spanish Revolt of 1820, 29
Spanish War of Independence, 34
Spartans, 223
Speranskii, Mikhail, 243, 318
Spetsas, 211, 212
Spielberg Fortress, 26
Spini, Giorgio, 141
Spyromelios, Michael, 210
St. Clair, William, 209
St. Gennaro, 125, 129, 161
St. Petersburg, 290, 313–14
St. Theobaldo, 136–37, 145
Stackelberg, Gustav Ernst von, 165, 166–67
Stanhope, Leicester, 217
state building, 216
State Council, 44, 152
Steele, Thomas, 58, 108
Steinhel, Vladimir, 257, 273, 280, 292–93

Stendhal (Marie-Henri Beyle)
    and Austrian intervention in Naples, 164–65
    on Calabria, 139
    and Colbran, 157
    and court culture, 9
    and the Naples revolt, 131, 179
    and prison depictions, 24–26
    on Riego's death, 115
    and Rossini, 158
    on The Toledo, 129
    and *Vanina Vanini*, 326
Stourdza, Alexandre, 245, 249
street storytellers, 82
Stroganov, Sergei Grigoriyevich, 200
succession issues, 289–90
Sue, Eugène, 109
suffrage, 46–47, 151. *See also* voting rights
suicide, 27, 316, 318
Sukhinov, I. I., 310
Sultanov, Vasilii, 226
Sunlight of Justice, 50
Supreme Central Junta, 34, 37
Supreme Criminal Tribunal, 318
Supreme Executive Magistracy, 140
Supreme Vendita, 137
Sweden, 165
Sweden-Norway constitution, 154
Swift (ship), 287
Switzerland, 165

Talleyrand, Charles Maurice de, 9
Tarella, Pietro, 234–35
Tarle, Evgenii, 115
Tasso, Torquato, 130
Tatars, 6–7, 281, 283
Tatishchev, Dmitry, 59
Tavassi, Pasquale, 136
taxation and tax reforms
    and the Decembrist movement, 262
    and the Greek revolt, 189, 206, 213, 219
    and the Naples revolt, 125, 128, 133, 148, 159, 163
    and the Spanish revolt, 29, 71, 77
Tblisi, 285
tertulias, 40, 58, 60, 77–78, 131
theater
    and the Decembrist movement, 251, 330
    and the Greek revolt, 195–96
    and the Naples revolt, 156–58
    and religious conflict, 81
    and revolutionary Cadiz, 48–49, 50
    and the Spanish revolt, 31, 81–82, 89
Themistocles, 223
There Can Be No Union with Tyrants . . . or Riego and Spain in Shackles (Mejía), 334

Thermopylae, Battle of, 27, 223
Thiesenhausen (colonel), 299
Third National Assembly (Greece), 222
"Thourios," 190
Tideev, Nikolai, 226
Tilsit treaty, 250
Times, 334
Tipaldos, Georgeos, 199
Tocqueville, Alexis de, 21
Toledo, Pedro de, 129
Toledo Inquisition, 24
Tolstoy, Leo, 295, 329
Tombasis, Yakovos, 223
Toreno, Count of, 37
Toreno, José María Queipo de Llano, Count of,
    40
Torre Alta, Conte de, 115
Torrero, Diego Múñoz, 41, 44, 57
Torrijos, José María, 334, 337
Torson, Konstantin, 290
torture
    abolition of, 42, 125, 219, 288, 315
    and the Greek revolt, 194, 202, 207–8, 215
    and the Inquisition, 6, 24
    Llorente on, 74–75
    and Mucius Scaevola, 144
    and Napoleonic armies, 35–36
    and quartering, 116, 177, 319–20
    Riego on, 109
    and Van Halen, 24, 62–63
Tosca (Sardou), 24
tourkokratia, 189, 279
Trafalgar, Battle of, 32, 62, 64
Transylvania, 205, 208
Trauberg, Leonid, 330
Treaty of Akkerman, 238
Treaty of London, 238
Treaty of Tilsit, 192, 197
Treaty of Velikie Luki, 252–53
Triangulo conspiracy, 61
Trienio, 44, 46, 72–80, 81, 94, 113, 229, 336
Tripolitsa, 215
The Triumph of a Free People in 1820, 335–36
The Trocadero, 98–115
Troppau Protocol, 93
Trotsky, Leon, 264, 282
Troysi, Vincenzo, 125
Trubetskoi, Sergei, 258, 263, 282, 292–93, 295
Trukhin, S. S., 306
Tsakalov, Athanasios, 193, 195, 216
Tsoukas, Theophilas, 186
Tugendbund, 261
Turgenev, Nikolai, 279, 285
Turgenev, Sergei, 209, 272, 277
Türkenfurcht, 224–25
Turkey, 18
Tyrrhenian Sea, 7

Ukraine, 9, 202, 226, 296, 333
Ulybyshev, Alexander, 283
unicameral legislatures
    and the Greek revolt, 219, 220
    and the Naples revolt, 139, 152, 184
    and the Spanish revolt, 37, 44–46, 50, 76, 79,
        263
Union of Salvation, 256, 261, 265, 270, 295
Union of Welfare, 261–62, 264, 274–75, 276, 283
United States
    American Revolution, 216
    Constitution as model, 44, 138, 154
    and the Decembrist movement, 298–99
    and Fernando's restoration, 59
    and the Greek revolt, 198–99, 224
    and influence of constitutional systems, 121
    and the Spanish constitution, 98
Urgel Regency, 96–97, 99
utilitarianism, 13

Vadim of Novgorod, 259
Valdés, Catayano, 106, 287
Van Halen, Juan, 24–25, 62–63, 283–85, 334,
    337
Vandals, 68
Vanina Vanini (1961), 326
Vardarelli, Gaetano, 128
Vasil'chikov, I. V., 247, 248–49, 277, 307, 310
Vatican, 80
Vaudoncourt, Frédéric François Guillaume, 90,
    93–95, 97, 105–6, 112, 183
veinteañistas, 77
Vejer, Spain, 67
Veleiras (colonel), 230
vendita, 136, 137, 144, 145, 160, 168
Venetia, 164–65
Vengeur (ship), 167
Venice, Italy, 189
Venizelos, Eleutherios, 324
Venturi, Franco, 13
Verona Congress, 99–100, 102–3, 106, 158, 254
Vershinin, L. P., 332
Vesuvius eruption, 161
Viazemskii, Alexander, 166
Vidal, Josef, 62, 80, 92
Vietnam, 15
Vigel, Filipp, 276
Villa Campa (captain general), 182
Villèle, Jean-Baptiste, 101–2
Vinuesa, Augustín, 91
Visigoths, 46
Vistula Legion, 36
Vitebsk, Battle of, 294
Vitoria, Battle of, 56
Vittorio Emanuele I of Sardinia, 179, 292
Vladimirescu, Tudor, 199, 205–7, 209, 281

Voice of the Century, 154
Voice of the People, 154
Volkonskii, Sergei, 256, 257, 282, 296–97
Voltaire, 5, 9, 175, 259, 260, 295
Vorontsov, S. R., 6
voting rights, 45, 219, 244, 263
"Vozzvanie K Narodu" (Appeal to the People), 321
Vulidzevich, Mark, 226
Vurinos, 230

Waddington, George, 194
Wallachia, 189, 201, 204–7, 249
Walpole, Horace, 23–24
War and Peace (Tolstoy), 329
war atrocities, 214–15, 279
"War Cry of the Neapolitan Nation," 171
"War Hymn" (Rhigas Pheraios), 278
"War Hymn to the Constitutionalists," 157
warship deals, 59
Washington, George, 75, 270
Waterloo, Battle of, 129
Wellesley, Henry, 58
Wellington, Arthur Wellesley, Duke of, 45, 58, 86, 213, 238
"What!" (Byron), 322
When a Girl Says Yes (Moratín), 81
White Eagle, 276
The White Terror, 57
"Whites," 4
The Widow of Padilla, 50, 78, 81
William à Court, First Baron Heytesbury, 112, 152, 157, 165, 176
Wilson, Robert, 108–9, 169, 182, 322
Winter Palace, 290
Wolfe, Alan, 12
Workshop of Monumental Theater, 331
World War I, 4, 324
World War II, 324, 327

Xanthos, Emmanouil, 193, 198, 216
Xenos, Stephanos, 324

yellow fever, 63, 100–101
Young Italy, 327
Ypsilanti, Alexandros
    background, 197–98
    and the Decembrist movement, 249, 294
    described, 209
    and failure of Naples revolt, 173
    impact on Friendly Society, 221
    imprisonment, 3, 25
    legacy of, 9, 323–25
    and martyrdom, 26
    and the Napoleonic wars, 3, 18
    press accounts of, 229
    and revolutionary catechisms, 310
    and revolutionary sentiment, 16–17
    and Riego's legacy, 336
    size of force, 202–3
    war wounds, 186
Ypsilanti, Demetrios, 203, 208, 216–18, 238–39, 325
Ypsilanti, Georgeos, 208
Ypsilanti, Konstantinos, 197
Ypsilanti (Michigan), 325
Ypsilanti, Nikolas, 193, 208
Yugoslavia, 15

Zante, 189
zarzuela, 49
Zavashilin, Dmitrii, 271
Zhukovskii, Vasilii, 315–16
Zionism, 266
Živkovič, Stefan, 199
Zolotarev, Vasilii, 331
Zudáñez, Jaime de, 53
Zurlo, Giuseppe, 151, 154, 156–57, 159, 168